Teaching & Learning
in the
ELEMENTARY SCHOOL

Teaching & Learning in the

DOROTHY G. PETERSEN
Chairman, Education Department
and *Chairman, Graduate Studies*

AND

VELMA D. HAYDEN
Dean of the College
Both of Trenton State College

ELEMENTARY SCHOOL

APPLETON-CENTURY-CROFTS, Inc.
New York

To
BERTRAM S. PETERSEN
and
BEULAH D. HAYDEN

PREFACE

HISTORIANS OF THE FUTURE might well refer to the present educational era as the "age of contradiction." We have, on the one hand, a growing mound of reputable theory and valid research which points the way to effective teaching in the elementary school. On the other hand, we have a substantial amount of classroom practice which is rooted in tradition, habit, lack of experience, or lack of knowledge which is not supportive of the high quality of education demanded by our modern democratic culture. This book attempts to close the gap between these two extremes by surveying current theories and principles of elementary education and by offering specific suggestions for their implementation in classroom practice. The illustrative lessons, descriptions of procedures and techniques, suggestions for student projects, carefully selected bibliographies, and illustrations have been included to help the reader relate the theory of modern elementary education to his particular classroom situation.

The book is written in practical, "down-to-earth" language but avoids the dangers of oversimplification. It recognizes that teaching is a complex, difficult, and creative endeavor which calls for great skill and much knowledge. It is, therefore, more than a "how-to-do" book which encourages mechanical and imitative teaching. It is hoped that its depth and comprehensiveness will make it a valuable text for all students of elementary education, either on the undergraduate or graduate level. It may also be used in workshops or courses designed to "upgrade" teachers with provisional or emergency certificates, *or* as an inservice text to help teachers check their practices and methods against accepted theory and research.

The scope of the book extends from the past to the probable future of the elementary school. It has been said that he who views things in their beginnings will have the clearest understanding of them. Part I, therefore, includes a brief historical background of elementary education in this country, identifying the influences of the early colonists and of the outstanding educators from abroad and indicating the contributions of the nineteenth and twentieth centuries. The purpose of the first part of the book is to bring into proper focus and perspective the issues now facing elementary school education.

In Part II, the authors have emphasized emerging goals and concepts. This section serves as a backdrop to the detailed discussion of the specific curricular areas found in the elementary school of today. Goals and objectives are discussed; a synopsis of past and present theories of child growth and development is presented; and types of curricular patterns and concepts regarding curricular study are indicated.

Part III is devoted to a detailed analysis of practices and evolving trends in each of the following curricular areas: the language arts, foreign languages, the social studies, science, arithmetic, the visual arts and music, and health, safety, and physical education. Because of the tremendous wealth of research in the language arts area, the authors have divided their discussion into three separate chapters, arranged in the sequence of how language is learned: listening and speaking, reading, and writing. The discussion of each curricular area in Part III contains an examination of research and suggestions for materials, activities, resources, and procedures. Included also are several illustrative lessons.

Research in child growth and development during the past twenty years has emphasized the importance to classroom teachers and to all other elementary school educators of becoming increasingly aware of individual differences in their teaching and in their working relationships with boys and girls. The authors, therefore, believe that no elementary education text is complete without a survey of the guidance services increasing rapidly in the elementary schools of this country. The addition of pupil personnel functionaries and the increasing importance of the classroom teacher as the focal point of the guidance program are viewed by the authors as one of the forward-looking movements in present-day elementary education. Also in Part IV, which emphasizes this need for an increasing awareness of individual differences, is a discussion of pupil progress, involving evaluation, reporting, and classification.

Without claiming any particular aptitude for clairvoyance, the authors have identified in the last Part pertinent developments and experiments of today which will undoubtedly merit the attention of future educators. The dimensions and outline of the elementary school of 1975 are nebulous and indistinct, but one thing is certain: The school of the future will be molded by many forces and influences, among which will be the results of current research and experimentation, societal changes, scientific and technological advances, and international developments. The book closes with a discussion of these forces and their implications on the education of future citizens.

It would be impossible to name the many colleagues, students, and friends whom the authors consulted in the preparation of this book. To all these individuals, the authors are deeply grateful for their constructive ideas and helpful suggestions. They are especially indebted to Miss Marie Blessing, formerly of the Lanning Demonstration School Staff of the Trenton State College for the outline of the social studies unit contained in Chapter 9; to Mr. James Silver, Assistant Professor of Education, Trenton State College for his advice on the preparation of the skills section of Chapter 9; and to Miss Dean Andrews, Assistant Professor of Physical Education, Trenton State College, for her advice on the physical education section of Chapter 13. The entire library staff of the Trenton State College has been most helpful, and the authors wish to acknowledge especially the co-operation and assistance of Miss Joyce Brodowski, Dr. Felix Hirsch, Mr. Charles Packard, Miss Doris Perry, Mrs. Helen Sixta, and Mr. Parker Worley. The illustrations were secured through the courtesy of Miss F. Myrtle Goetz and the faculty of the Joseph Stokes Memorial School, Trenton, New Jersey and Mr. Roland Glenn and the faculty of the William L. Antheil School, Ewing Township, New Jersey.

A special debt of gratitude is owed to Dr. William H. Burton, Consulting Editor of textbooks in Education for our publishers, for his constructive criticisms and helpful editing of the entire manuscript. Last, but not least, the authors are grateful for the interest, encouragement, patience, and understanding of the members of their families, without which the book would not have been written.

DOROTHY G. PETERSEN
VELMA D. HAYDEN

CONTENTS

Part III: EVOLVING EMPHASES IN CONTENT AND METHOD

Part IV: INCREASING AWARENESS OF INDIVIDUAL DIFFERENCES

Part V: PROJECTING TRENDS OF THE FUTURE

PART I

Developing Issues

CHAPTER I

Elementary Education:
Past and Present

TODAY IN THE UNITED STATES we face considerable unfinished business in public education, for the complexities of modern society have left their impact on current educational issues. Populations are increasing rapidly. The world is shrinking steadily as a result of the rapid progress made in transportation and communication. Many differing ethnic groups—some unable to speak English, some bilingual or even multilingual—are appearing in our elementary school classrooms. Children are moving frequently, many of them changing schools five or six times in fewer than four years— children completely without the security of firmly established roots. Space travel, rockets, jets, comic books, radio and television vie for the interests of each child, creating for him images of an exciting world. An exciting world, but also a confusing one. Broken homes and juvenile delinquency are not uncommon; and the child of today, as the adult of today, can scarcely be expected to remain unaware of the tensions and upheavals in the modern world. Already he senses that if the promise of the future is immense, so is the danger.

With conditions as unsettled as these and with the realization that the schools of any nation reflect significantly the attitudes, beliefs, frustrations, and feelings of the society in which they are located, are the reasons not *very* clear why the schools of this country face many phases of unfinished business at this time?

But it is impossible to understand a society or its schools through comprehension of the practices and philosophies of only the present. Past, present (and future) are intertwined. The educator in the elementary school, whether teacher or administrator, must not only have a knowledge of the elementary school curriculum, but must also have some grasp of how this curriculum developed. The elementary school educator must not only be aware of issues that are controversial in today's schools, but must also understand these issues in their historical context.

During the past decade, elementary education has without question gained a new importance in the eyes of both American educators and the lay public. The present, therefore, seems most propitious for one to pause for a detailed consideration of both the past and the present as well as a projected view of the future of elementary education.

EDUCATION IN EARLY AMERICA

The development of elementary education in this country has been influenced by marked differences among the early colonists. The United States of America is a relatively young nation; yet it has passed through decades of struggle, strife, and uncertainty as well as patriotic enthusiasm. Each of these feelings has influenced the development of our elementary schools as well as have the changing periods in the socio-economic and political history of the American people.

The elementary school in the United States has always been considered "the school of the people" . . . All the way from its origins in the seventeenth century to the middle of the twentieth, it has been a constituent part of American culture; and its history is one of the most fascinating and hopeful chapters in the whole story of the growth of American democracy.[1]

The first colonists to set foot on American soil were groups of people who sought religious freedom, freedom of speech, and freedom in their economic pursuits. Some came as a result of adventurous curiosity, some to make money. These people were different, and so were the beginnings of education in this country. It was only natural, however, that each of these colonies should bring to this country its own values, its own beliefs, its own attitudes, its own religious concepts, and its own educational patterns.

New England Colonies. For the colonists who arrived in New England, a singleness of religious purpose was a determining influence in the development of their early educational programs. They believed in a close unity between the church and the state. To them it was the responsibility of the government to "govern," to support the Calvinistic theology, and to foster the intellectual growth of their boys and girls.

This was made clear as early as 1642, when the governmental leaders in Massachusetts were empowered to require parents and masters to educate their children. While this law did not require the establishment of schools, it did require compulsory instruction for youth. It even set up the minimum

[1] E. W. Knight, *Fifty Years of American Education, 1900–1950* (New York, The Ronald Press Company, 1952), p. 31.

essentials: the reading of English, knowledge of the capital laws, the catechism, and apprenticeship in a trade.[2]

In 1647 in Massachusetts "the Old Deluder Satan Act" decreed that every community of fifty house-holders or more should select someone to teach children to read and write. Its claim to delusion was that Satan, "the old deluder," was believed to have encouraged illiteracy so that no man, woman, or child would be able to read the Scriptures.

During these early days also the dame schools developed in New England communities. In these schools, housewives baked, sewed, and did their kitchen chores while teaching the neighborhood children to read.

Middle Colonies. The settlers in the middle colonies (New York, Pennsylvania and Delaware) represented different nationalities—such as Dutch, English, Scotch-Irish, German and Swedish—and consequently they had differing religious faiths. Education in these colonies became, in general, the responsibility of the different churches, which conducted programs in their native languages. With parochial schools as their form of education, the Middle Colonists naturally came to oppose any interference from the state or any suggested form of uniform taxation for the schools.

Here we find a different type of educational organization from that of colonial New England, but the same early concern for the education of youth. There was, nevertheless, a lack of equality of educational opportunity in these colonies, for apprentices and orphans either received no education or were compelled to carry the stigma of attending the so-called "pauper schools."

Southern Colonies. Inequalities of educational opportunity between social classes were found in the South from the beginning. Colonial leaders in the South looked upon education as did English noblemen: ". . . the laborers should be kept ignorant as well as poor; the business of the poor was to work, not to think." [3]

Here again education reflected the attitudes, beliefs and values of the people. These well-to-do colonists, essentially English "gentlemen," brought tutors from England to instruct their children; and later these youth were sent abroad for further educational experiences. As Meyer writes, "[Education] was a privilege which marched with wealth and blood." [4]

In summary, the early educational developments in this country clearly reflected the religious beliefs, the political ideas, the values, the attitudes, the cultural heritage, and the socio-economic strata of the people. Each of the groups of colonists represented a different group of people. Each

[2] R. F. Butts, *A Cultural History of Western Education,* 2nd ed. (New York, McGraw-Hill Book Company, Inc., 1955), p. 250.

[3] G. W. Frasier, *An Introduction to the Study of Education,* rev. ed. (New York, Harper and Brothers, 1956), p. 109.

[4] A. E. Meyer, *An Educational History of the American People* (New York, McGraw-Hill Book Company, 1957), p. 48.

had to develop its own form of government. Each had its own issues to resolve. Education became as it is today a relatively local prerogative.

During the nineteenth century seven historical battles were waged on behalf of public education. With the adoption of the Constitution of the United States public education that was truly free, non-sectarian, and tax-supported was by no means guaranteed. No specific reference to "education" appears on the pages of our Constitution. The responsibility for the education of the boys and girls of this country was left by implication to the states in the Tenth Amendment: "the powers not delegated to the United States by the Constitution, or prohibited by it to the States are reserved to the States respectively or to the people."

The educational system as we know it today had a very meager and unpretentious beginning. As the decades passed, men with vision and fortitude fought steadily for the continually growing recognition of the importance of education. Elementary education from 1776 to 1900 passed through two primary stages: (1) an awakening of educational consciousness and a struggle for free schools; and (2) reorganization within the system as the result of new theories from abroad.[5] Cubberley[6] originally identified seven battles, all but two of which were in direct relation to elementary education. Let us review each of them.

1. *Battle to Effect Support of the Schools through Taxation.* A major effort was made to develop a systematic support of our schools, rather than to continue indefinite support through tuition, gifts, lotteries, or land grants. The bases that were utilized for taxation varied. Connecticut attempted to finance its educational program by earmarking all taxes on liquor for schools. Louisiana, particularly New Orleans, raised money by licensing theaters which were to turn over a set sum of money to education. In other states lotteries were held. Even though there was a sincere interest in education, the early American educators began to realize that there had to be a more systematic approach to the financing of the total educational program.

By 1825, the educational leaders had agreed that the "wealth of the State must educate the children of the State."[7] This marked the beginning of a long, hard-fought battle to secure direct and effective local, county, district, and state taxation for educational purposes. The most satisfactory basis of taxation for school purposes is even today still not fully determined in many communities.

2. *Battle Against Pauper Education.* Another issue facing some of the early educators was the stigma attached to boys and girls who found them-

---

[5] E. Reinhardt, *American Education* (New York, Harper and Brothers, 1954), p. 142.

[6] E. P. Cubberley, *A Brief History of Education* (Boston, Houghton Mifflin Co., 1922), pp. 370–393.

[7] *Ibid.*, p. 371.

selves compelled to attend pauper schools. These were schools for the poor. Children attended whose parents were unable to finance educational opportunities—children who had to be educated at public expense. Many youths refused to attend these pauper schools because of this stigma of poverty.

This type of education seemed unfitting for a democracy built on the equality of all people. Those who desired to eliminate the pauper school, however, were confronted by many obstacles. They had to overcome the determined opposition of the taxpayer and of established church-supported and privately-operated schools; then too they were up against the always powerful example of England, which still maintained its system of pauper schools.

The Free School Act of 1834 in Pennsylvania finally dealt a crushing blow to pauper school education. The proposal to extend free public education to the entire state of Pennsylvania, rather than only within the limits of Philadelphia, became the basic issue during the campaign of 1834 in Pennsylvania. It was the result of the untiring effort and brilliant oratory of Thaddeus Stevens (1792–1868) that the abolition of the pauper school finally occurred in Pennsylvania, although it was not until 1873 that the last district concurred.

3. *Battle to Expand Free Public Education.* The pressure of church and private school interests continued to be difficult to combat as our forefathers struggled to make American schools entirely free. In addition to these interests, the opposition consisted of citizens of two groups: those who had no school-age children of their own and could see no personal advantage to help finance an education for others, and those who believed that education was a commodity for which individuals must pay, not an item provided for all.

A popular practice that was in direct opposition to the establishment of completely free public schools was the "rate bill," a practice brought over from England. It was a fee levied on parents, based on the number of their school-age children enrolled in the school and the length of time each child attended the school. The rate was fixed to cover the total expenses of the school.[8] Although the fee was never very large, it was frequently large enough to deprive some children of educational opportunity.

Where Pennsylvania had led in the passing of the School Act of 1834, New York took the initiative in the attack against the rate bills. There were two referenda, one in 1849 and one in 1850, before the question was resolved in New York. Even then a compromise was in operation for some time.

In the South, it was not until the educational reorganization following the Civil War that there was a free, public school system.

[8] R. F. Butts, *op. cit.,* p. 317.

4. *Battle to Eliminate Sectarianism.* Another issue faced by the early American educators (and which is still not completely resolved today) was the position of public and private schools in regard to state support. From the days of the early colonists, the church was highly involved in the education of the young. The first school curriculum dealt almost entirely with morals and the Scriptures. The clergy in many places was responsible for the employment of suitable teachers.

As the state assumed more responsibility for a free, public educational system of schools, a conflict naturally ensued. Horace Mann (1796–1859) led an attack against the Scriptures as a basis for public school education—although he did not question the educational values that might be gained from religion.

Finally, a rather severe blow was dealt to private and parochial schools when the states decided to appropriate funds only to public education units. "No state admitted to the Union after 1858, except West Virginia, failed to insert such a provision in its first state constitution." [9] Even today the most effective and most satisfactory division of funds between public and private schools is still a debatable issue.

5. *Battle for State Supervision.* During the first half of the nineteenth century, men like Mann, Henry Barnard (1811–1900), and others saw the need for strong state supervision of educational opportunities within each state. In 1812 New York became the first state to identify a state officer whose responsibility it was to provide leadership, vision, enforcement of school laws, statistical studies, and assistance to communities. Mann became the first state executive of the first state board of education (in Massachusetts) and Barnard held a comparable position in Connecticut and Rhode Island. Mann also became the first United States Commissioner of Education.

Barnard fought hard for the belief that

> The common school should not be regarded as *common* because it is cheap, inferior, and attended only by the poor and those who are indifferent to the education of their children, but *common* as the light and air because its blessings are open to all and enjoyed by all.[10]

The other two battles, identified by Cubberley, to establish the American high school and to crown our educational pattern with a state university, are not directly related to elementary school education.

The development of elementary education was affected by political and socio-economic forces. As the development of elementary education was paralleling a growth of nationalism in this country, many political and socio-economic events occurred that affected educational growth and expansion. During the nineteenth century universal suffrage was gradually

[9] E. P. Cubberley, *op. cit.*, p. 384.
[10] E. Reinhardt, *op. cit.*, p. 146.

accepted. With the trend toward universal suffrage, the importance of the educated vote was impressed on the minds of many Americans. At the same time there occurred significant increases in population and an expansion of industry and commerce. The Western movement was leveling off, and people were flocking to industrial centers.

The Industrial Revolution made a significant impact on the development of a national educational consciousness. Populations continued to grow rapidly; the number of laborers with hopes for the education of their children increased; the relationship between apprentices and masters became more impersonal; and children flocked to factories and worked long hours.

The curriculum also was influenced by the Industrial Revolution, marked by an increasing emphasis on science. Darwin's *The Origin of Species*, Huxley's *Science and Education*, and the writings of Spencer were representative of this feeling. As Eby writes, "Greek began to disappear; Latin became an elective; both were to be subordinated to science and other subjects." [11]

CONTRIBUTIONS FROM ABROAD

Educators in this country during the nineteenth century also became concerned regarding instructional methods and the education of teachers. For ideas they turned to outstanding educators abroad, the most influential of whom are discussed briefly in this section.

John Amos Comenius. Educational leaders looked with favor on John Amos Comenius (1592–1671), who devoted his life to religion and education. Comenius, in his *The Great Didactic*, not only emphasized the importance of sense perception in learning experiences and the unique needs of boys and girls at varying age levels, but also advocated the education of the rich and the poor in the same schools and equal educational opportunities for girls and boys. [12]

Comenius recommended the division of the educational program into four basic parts:

a mother's school at home for children . . . from birth to age six; . . . a vernacular school in every village for children from 6–12; a gymnasium in every city for children from 12–16; . . . and a six year program at the University. [13]

In *The School of Infancy*, which he wrote to help mothers, he set forth some modern-sounding ideas and insights. Parents and teachers today would find this rewarding reading.

[11] F. Eby, *The Development of Modern Education* (Englewood Cliffs, N.J., Prentice-Hall, Inc., 1952), p. 586.

[12] J. A. Comenius, *The Great Didactic*, Part Two, translated by M. W. Keatinge (London, A. and C. Black, 1923), pp. 66–75.

[13] *Ibid.*, pp. 255–286.

Jean Jacques Rousseau. During the eighteenth century in France, Jean Jacques Rousseau (1712–1778) emphasized the importance of the "child;" believed that children were inherently good; and taught that formal education was harmful.[14] Rousseau was a reactionist against the formalism of the eighteenth century, and, as many reactionists, he may have become an extremist to the degree to which he advocated freedom in each child's development. He wrote,

God makes all things good; man meddles with them, and they become evil. He forces one soil to yield the products of another, one tree to bear another's fruit. He confuses and confounds time, place, and natural conditions. He mutilates his dog, his horse, and his slave. He destroys and defaces all things; he loves all that is deformed and monstrous; he will have nothing as nature made it, not even man himself. . . .[15]

Rousseau believed in the "noble savage" approach to learning—that a child is better educated during the first twelve years of his life if he is not contaminated by society and civilization. Rousseau wrote,

I do not like verbal explanations. Young people pay little heed to them, nor do they remember them. Things! Things! I cannot repeat it too often. We lay too much stress upon words. We teachers babble. . . .[16]

Although Rousseau tended to belittle the role of classroom education, he set forth many truths in his writings and many surprisingly current ideas—ideas that influenced the development of elementary education in this country. He emphasized: (1) the importance of the child as an individual; (2) the need for each child to learn through a variety of experiences; (3) the realization that some things are better taught in the classroom or laboratory, others through direct contact with nature; (4) the importance for the child to have his unique needs met and to be aware of the usefulness of each learning experience; (5) the need for each child to develop according to his age and not be trained as a miniature adult; and (6) the prime importance of health and physical exercise.

Johann H. Pestalozzi. A third European educator who influenced American education in the nineteenth century was Johann H. Pestalozzi (1746–1827). He was influenced by Rousseau and attempted to test some of Rousseau's educational theories. To check their practicality, Pestalozzi surrounded himself with fifty abandoned children and spent many hours teaching them basic skills and gardening.

Pestalozzi wrote a story of Swiss peasant life titled *Leonard and Gertrude*, in which he set forth many of his educational theories as he described how Gertrude cared for her children. Pestalozzi exerted his influence most significantly in his position as director of the institute founded in Yverdon.

---

[14] J. J. Rousseau, *Émile*, translated by Barbara Foxley, Everyman's Library (London, J. M. Dent & Sons, Ltd., 1911 and New York, E. P. Dutton & Co., Inc., 1911).
[15] *Ibid.*, p. 5
[16] *Ibid.*, p. 143.

For twenty years educational leaders from all over Europe came there to observe his methods. Pestalozzi wrote, "Sense impression of Nature is the only true foundation of human instruction, because it is the only true foundation of human knowledge." [17]

The first educational program in this country which was directly influenced by Pestalozzi's educational theories was in Oswego, New York, under the direction of Superintendent E. A. Sheldon. The program emphasized the importance of the child, the importance of relating learning experiences to the needs of children, the need for a kinder, more humane treatment of children, the importance of sense impressions, the importance of industry, the use of basic instincts and capacities, and the need for continual study and utilization of the unfolding potentialities of the child.[18] This program gained so much publicity that Superintendent Sheldon started the Oswego Normal School in 1865 to demonstrate the Pestalozzian philosophy and methods.

Frasier writes, "[Pestalozzi] took the torch from Rousseau and carried it far in his lifetime; with it he kindled torches for Herbart, Froebel, and a host of other educators to carry forward." [19]

Freidrich Froebel. Freidrich Froebel (1782–1852) in Germany was a student of Pestalozzi and is best known for the founding of the first kindergarten. In his *The Education of Man,* Froebel set forth some educational principles that we today would consider sound, such as:

that the vigorous and complete development and cultivation of each successive stage (of life) depends on the vigorous, complete and characteristic development of each and all preceding stages of life.[20]

that the young, growing human being should be trained early . . . for creative and productive activity.[21]

that play is the highest phase of child development, for it is self-active representation of the inner [self] . . . .[22]

While Froebel believed in the unfolding of a child's life through an appeal to his interests, his senses, and his wishes and desires, he did not, like Rousseau, believe in isolated meditation with nature, for Froebel placed considerable importance on the value of socialization, and the importance of playing, working, and living together.

It is of interest to note that the idea of the kindergarten has received more acceptance and popularity in the United States than it ever did abroad.

[17] J. H. Pestalozzi, *How Gertrude Teaches Her Children* (Syracuse, New York, C. W. Bardeen, 1898), p. 316.

[18] J. H. Pestalozzi, *Leonard and Gertrude,* translated by Eva Channing (Boston, D. C. Heath and Company, 1910).

[19] G. W. Frasier, *op. cit.,* p. 105.

[20] F. Froebel, *The Education of Man,* translated by W. N. Hailmann (New York, D. Appleton and Company, 1900), p. 28.

[21] *Ibid.,* p. 34.

[22] *Ibid.,* pp. 54–55.

Johann F. Herbart. Johann F. Herbart (1776–1841), influenced modern elementary education in a slightly different fashion. Herbart was a scholar, a man who approached education in a systematic manner, with the emphasis on *system*. He rejected many earlier and then current philosophies of education, such as those expounded by Locke, Rousseau, and Pestalozzi. He was interested in educational methods, goals, objectives, and the essential content of *true* education.[23]

Herbart stressed a format for methods of teaching. He believed that: "Pedagogy is the science which the teacher needs for himself, but he must also be master of the science of imparting his knowledge." [24]

He believed that "instruction must universally point out, connect, teach, and philosophize." [25] Today whenever one finds a teacher using the inductive approach to learning, one usually can identify, to some degree at least, Herbart's steps of preparation, presentation, comparison, and conclusion. As a result of the current pragmatic emphasis, we have added "application" to the four basic steps outlined by Herbart.

The Herbartian influence was brought to this country by American educators who studied at Jena, for Herbart's followers carried on his ideas in many German universities long after his death. The American supporters were so enthusiastic that on their return to this country, they organized the National Herbartian Society (1895) which later became the National Society for the Study of Education.

In summary, elementary education in this country evolved slowly during the eighteenth and nineteenth centuries. Victories were won by our early educators, and ideas were introduced from abroad. These laid the foundation for significant educational advances during the twentieth century.

THE TWENTIETH CENTURY

John Dewey's influence was far-reaching. One of the chief educators in the first half of the twentieth century was John Dewey (1859–1952) who was interested in making learning experiences more functional and in helping teachers meet the pressures of the crowded curriculum. In approximately 1896 Dewey established a laboratory school at the University of Chicago where teachers were encouraged to experiment in methods of teaching. Dewey emphasized that teachers should provide all kinds of experiences to help pupils develop their inner resources. His teachings were frequently referred to as "learning by doing." Dewey believed that the school should be a miniature society if teachers were to prepare youth to live in a complex society as adults.

Dewey wrote,

[23] J. F. Herbart, *The Science of Education,* translated by Henry M. and Emmie Felkin (Boston, D. C. Heath and Company, 1900), pp. 78–93.
[24] *Ibid.*, p. 84.
[25] *Ibid.*, p. 147.

The teachers started with question marks, rather than with fixed rules. We started on the whole with four such questions or problems as:

1. What can be done and how can it be done, to bring the school in closer relation with the home and the neighborhood life . . . instead of having the school a place where the child comes solely to learn certain lessons? . . .

2. What can be done in the way of introducing subject matter in history and science and art that shall have a positive value and real significance to the child's own life? . . .

3. How can instruction in these formal, symbolic branches—the mastering of the ability to read, write, and use figures intelligently—be carried on with every day experiences and occupations as their background and in definite relations to other studies of more inherent content, and be carried on in such a way that the child shall feel their necessity through their connection with subjects which appeal to him on their own acocunt? . . .

4. How can individual attention be assured? [26]

Dewey's educational philosophy has had a tremendous influence abroad as well as in this country. Among Dewey's disciples are Bode, Kilpatrick, Rugg, Counts, and numerous other well-known educators.

The Progressive Education Association left its impact on the elementary school. The Progressive Education Association was initiated about 1919 as a reform movement against the formalism in education and continued until 1955 when it voted itself out of existence. Although this association had great impact on elementary education, its actual membership was never very large.

The leaders of the progressive education movement emphasized the importance of individualized education, the need for a child-centered school, the necessity for direct relation of learning experiences to the interests and current needs of each child, and the relationship of the child to his cultural and social environment. Unfortunately this movement became popularly identified with the concept that teaching and learning require a "laissez-faire" approach and should be dependent solely on the interests and desires of the boys and girls.

The "Scientific Movement" became an important emphasis in elementary education during the first half of the twentieth century. The scientific movement, of which testing and evaluation was an important part, contributed greatly to the progress of elementary education during the early decades of the present century. The outstanding leaders in testing and evaluation procedures during this period were Binet (1857–1911) in France and Thorndike (1871–1933) in the United States. Under their influence standardized tests were developed to measure the abilities and limitations of boys and girls.[27]

[26] J. Dewey, *The School and Society*, 3rd ed. (Chicago, University of Chicago, 1900), pp. 116–119.
[27] Standardized tests will be discussed further in Chapter Fifteen.

Related to this development was the formation of child study groups and the beginnings of child guidance. Here began the team and inter-disciplinary approach in elementary education: the teacher, psychiatrist, social worker, counselor and psychologist began to work together. Today in the public school one finds an increasing acceptance of the team ap-proach, which often utilizes such personnel as a school physician, a school nurse, a school dentist, a dental hygienist, a school psychologist, a guidance counselor, a social worker, and a community social service representative.

There have been many changes in elementary education in the United States since 1900. Some of the changes which the authors believe to be most significant are the following:

1. A more dynamic and creative elementary school curriculum has been developed.

2. Many disciplines, such as psychology and sociology, have contributed facts and concepts that have led to improved educational practices.

3. Extensive research in the field of education has increased our under-standing of the child and has improved the methods of teaching in the elementary school.

4. More attractive and more functional school plants have been designed and constructed.

5. Teaching materials and teaching aids have improved in quality and increased in quantity.

6. The staff of the elementary school is more competent today and has been strengthened by the employment of specialized personnel.

7. There has been a growing interest on the part of the school staff and the lay public in curriculum study and development.

8. The elementary school educator has gained a better understanding of the relationship between in-class and out-of-class activities.

9. There has been a growing sensitivity in the education of boys and girls to the importance of understanding other nations and other regions of our own nation.

CURRENT ISSUES

One can scarcely pick up an evening paper or a popular periodical with-out seeing such glaring titles as, "Why Can't Johnny Read?" "What Are We Teaching in Our Schools?" "Elementary Education—Fads and Frills," "Let's Clean House in Our Schools," "Where Have the Three R's Gone?", and other similarly critical titles. Most educators realize that while some of these criticisms are justified, most of them result from a lack of knowledge of what is being accomplished.

The critical attitude taken by so many citizens during the past decade, however, has not been completely unfortunate. In fact, it has been fortu-nate for at least three reasons: (1) it has reflected an interest of the lay public in the educational program; (2) it has aroused additional interest on the part of some who have been almost completely complacent; and (3) it has caused professional educators to take a second look at what they believed they were accomplishing.

Cressman and Benda attempt to explain the increase of attacks on education as follows:

(1) merely an indication of an increased interest in education; ... (2) increased cost of education has brought the work of the school sharply to public attention; ... (3) small but rather active groups that feel that public schools as we now have them are wrong; ... (4) criticism of established institutions that always occurs during times of insecurity and fear.[28]

One important current issue is the people's concern that the schools are neglecting the teaching of the basic skills of reading, writing, spelling, and arithmetic. This, of course, is not a new issue, for during the eighteenth century, William Cowper wrote,

> To them the sounding jargon of the schools
> Seems what it is ... a cap and bells for fools.

Also, Charles Dickens wrote that education was "a smattering of everything, and a knowledge of nothing."

Many citizens today look askance at the "enriched" elementary school curriculum which appears to be taking time away from the learning of fundamental concepts. Teachers in junior and senior high schools and colleges have reported that many of their students seem limited in their knowledge of basic skills; employers in many communities have reported a lack of skill in spelling, communication, and basic arithmetic.

Yet reliable data generally report the opposite. A well-known business magazine has compared the quality of the student of today with his counterpart of yesterday as follows:

Test data seem to indicate nationally that on the whole we are doing better than we did during past years.

The College Entrance Examination Board indicates no decline in the quality of the entering college freshman, when he is compared with the college freshman of a quarter of a century ago. . . .

The 1947 youngsters heavily outscored those of 1848 in definition [of words], beat them in mental arithmetic, and nosed them out in written arithmetic . . . over-all, the 1947 boys and girls outscored those of a century before by compiling a total of 955 correct answers to 924. It was a clear-cut victory for the modern-day student." [29]

A study made in a relatively stable community with excellent educational records reported that "pupils attending Evanston schools at the primary,

[28] G. R. Cressman and H. W. Benda, *Public Education in America* (New York, Appleton-Century-Crofts, Inc. © 1956), p. 443.
[29] "The Truth About Our Schools," *Changing Times, The Kiplinger Magazine* (June, 1954), pp. 7–11.

intermediate, and junior high school levels read with more comprehension and understand the meaning of words better than did children who were enrolled in the same grades and schools more than two decades ago." [30]

Facts tend to indicate, therefore, that there has been no backward trend in the preparation of the elementary school child in the areas of reading, writing, spelling, and arithmetic in spite of the changes in elementary school methods.

A second current issue is the complete separation of church and school. We accept without question today the wisdom of the separation of the church and the state; yet we debate whether religion should be taught in our public schools, whether released time should be available for religious instruction, and what services should be provided for the parochial schools.

The Supreme Court has had to deal with this issue several times. In 1922 an appeal resulting from a previous Oregon ruling forbade any state from requiring all pupils to attend public schools. In 1946 a Supreme Court decision (5–4) permitted a state to provide transportation to parochial schools as well as to public schools. In 1948, the McCollum Case (8–1) established the ruling that sectarian religious teachings could not be taught on public school premises. In 1951 the Court ruled (6–3) that public schools may allow "released time" for religious instruction, provided such instruction is voluntary and not supported by public tax money.

The issue of separation of church and school still has many unresolved problems. One finds a wide variety of practices involving the type and number of services provided parochial schools. Some parochial schools, for example, profit from the transportation and health services of the public schools; some do not. There is also a variety of practices regarding the amount of "released time" provided and in the procedures for administering this "time." Also in some schools one hears the Bible read each morning; in others the teachers never refer to it.

Without any question, the relationship of public to private parochial education is as basic an issue today as it was back in the nineteenth century. The importance of religion in American life is little questioned; yet its rightful place in the public educational program is still undetermined.

A third current issue today is whether the public schools are effectively teaching moral and ethical values. At least three inevitable questions are raised in the consideration of this issue: (1) Is this the responsibility of the school? (2) If so, can the school achieve success in this area without the support of other institutions, such as the home and church? (3) What are the most effective methods of instruction?

When one considers the violence and crime on our streets and the questionable moral standards of elements within our society, one is forced to the conclusion that the public schools should emphasize the development

---

[30] V. V. Miller and W. C. Lanton, "Reading Achievement of School Children—Then and Now," *Elementary English,* Vol. 33 (February, 1956), p. 96.

of moral attitudes among pupils and should help them identify moral values.

While the schools alone undoubtedly cannot do as effective a job in this as they could do with the assistance of the home and the church, in some cases they are the only agency that seriously considers the need. In 1951, the Educational Policies Commission reported its belief that the schools should emphasize the following values: (1) supremacy of the human personality; (2) moral responsibility; (3) institutions as the servants of man; (4) common consent; (5) devotion to truth; (6) respect for excellence; (7) moral equality; (8) brotherhood; (9) pursuit of happiness; and (10) spiritual enrichment.[31]

How this should be done is still a moot question. Hook writes,

> I do not believe that the intellectual and moral virtues . . . whether a love of truth, a sense of chivalry and fair play, a feeling of outrage before cruelty, sympathy for the underdog, or a passion for freedom . . . can be instilled by didactic instruction.[32]

It is the authors' opinion that values, beliefs, and attitudes may be learned in a variety of ways, such as by: (1) imitation; (2) identification; and (3) identifying goals and objectives, planning procedures, and evaluating the results. These values, beliefs, and attitudes must be directly related to other types of learning in the classroom.

A fourth current issue in education today is the battle to provide equal educational opportunities for all boys and girls. Separate but equal facilities are not the answer. One merely has to visit many of the schools for Negro youth in our Southern states to note that these schools do not have the best-educated teachers, the most recent and helpful teaching materials and teaching aids, and many of the enriching experiences enjoyed by the white boys and girls. Also, to separate boys and girls according to race is not only harmful to those in the minority, but is in discord with the democratic principles by which we live in America.

In May, 1954, the Supreme Court took a significant step forward in outlawing segregation in our schools and in requiring that equal educational opportunities be provided "with all deliberate speed" for all youth. In that year, seventeen states and the District of Columbia had mandatory segregation. Southerners believed that their problem was unique because of the large numbers of Negroes in their states. (According to the 1950 census there were approximately 10,500,000 Negroes in eleven Southern states.) Southerners also felt that the relatively poor health of Negroes would harm white children if both were integrated in the same schools and that Negroes' lack of cultural enrichment would lower the standards for the white children.

[31] Educational Policies Commission, *Moral and Spiritual Values in the Public Schools* (Washington, D.C., National Education Association, 1951).

[32] S. Hook, "What is Education?" in B. Blanshard, ed., *Education in the Age of Science* (New York, Basic Books, Inc., 1959), p. 9.

Many believed that the Supreme Court had overstepped its power. The administration of the schools was a state prerogative, and this was a sociological and psychological problem rather than a legalistic one. What happened? There were examples of opposition and examples of compliance. Ever since the Supreme Court decision there has been a continuous filing and passing of legislation in Southern states in an attempt to delay or to prevent integration and, if necessary, to provide for a private school system.

There has been a growing compliance, however, particularly among the border states. Methods used to desegregate the schools have varied.

Robinson identified various procedures as:

(1) *from the top down* as practiced in St. Louis; (2) *from the bottom up,* initiating integration in the primary grades, as practiced in parts of Kentucky and Maryland; (3) *all grades at once,* an approach used in Baltimore, Louisville, and the District of Columbia; and (4) *selective integration,* a plan transferring a certain number of Negro students to formerly all-white schools, where space and program would permit.[33]

While progress is being made, it is slow. The zero hour, however, is approaching when some type of integration must occur in all Southern school districts.

This is not just a Southern problem, however, for in all parts of the country one may find many segregated schools resulting from zoning laws or the fact that parents have withdrawn their sons or daughters from integrated schools and sent them to private schools. We must not forget that this problem is country wide; in fact it is world wide. Another seriously complicating factor is that the

reciprocal attitudes of the Negro groups to ethnic groups, the Puerto Rican, Jewish, or Asian, for instance, are such as to indicate that the desegregation in schools may not solve, but, instead, often may heighten the racial and ethnic tensions.[34]

A fifth current issue is Federal support for education. While Federal aid to education has been with us since the middle of the nineteenth century, beginning with the Federal grants of land, there still is a wariness on the part of American educators to encourage Federal assistance. Even though many school districts are profiting today from such bills as the Smith-Hughes Act, the George-Barden Act, and many others, and even though many individuals benefitted from the G. I. Bill, there are still many misgivings about Federal support.

[33] G. Robinson, "Man in No Man's Land," in D. Shoemaker, ed., *With All Deliberate Speed* (New York, Harper and Brothers, 1957), p. 191.
[34] G. Bereday, "The Race Problems in America," in G. Bereday and L. Volpicelli, eds., *Public Education in America* (New York, Harper and Brothers, 1958), p. 107.

The dread that Federal largess is but the first stage of Federal control and that on some not too remote tomorrow national agents will come swooping down on the state to oversee its schools and teachers is a real one—so real, indeed, as to be a decided obstacle.[35]

Let us briefly review the pros and cons of Federal support:

The supporters of Federal assistance point to the inequalities of educational opportunities in this country, inequalities resulting not only from race discrimination, but also from a lack of equality of funds in each of the states. Approximately one-third of American boys were rejected for military service in World War I, World War II, and the Korean conflict because of educational, mental, or physical handicaps. In states where the educational opportunities are particularly limited, the rejection rate was much higher than this average. No state, rich or poor, is free from the responsibility of educating all of its youth. For some, Federal aid seems the only answer.

Those opposing Federal aid base their arguments on the fact that it is unconstitutional; that there is a justified fear of interference from the Federal government; and that state, county, district, and local communities might tend to shift their responsibilities to the Federal Government. While this is still an unresolved issue, it is of concern to every school system in this country.

A sixth current issue involves the relationship in our schools between loyalty and conformity and creative thinking and learning. Loyalty may be defined as one's identification with a cause in which he strongly believes. To be loyal to the American tradition and our cultural heritage must not rule out our right and responsibility to be objective, to raise questions, to evaluate, to follow data wherever they may lead us, and to arrive at scientific, objective conclusions—conclusions that may later be verified or rejected in light of additional data. Merely to accept the past because it is the past minimizes the importance of critical and creative thinking. A subversive teacher should not be teaching in our schools, but teachers and pupils must have sufficient academic freedom to explore the pros and cons of philosophies that are contrary to ours.

Teachers and pupils must be encouraged to think critically, to question, to be creative. Conformity often leads to mediocrity. We are seeking a "freedom of education" that refers to an atmosphere or climate where true learning takes place. We need classroom environments that will not cause parents to ask such questions as: How freely can my children learn? How inhibited is the education of our children? How restricted is their access to enlightenment? [36]

Care should be taken that fewer and fewer pupils become parrots of teachers' words and of ideas as they are found in textbooks. Elementary

[35] A. Meyer, op. cit., p. 401.

[36] H. Ehlers and G. C. Lee, eds. Adapted from Crucial Issues in Education (New York, Holt, Rinehart, and Winston, Inc., 1959), p. 77.

school youth are by no means too young to explore relationships, to go beyond the boundaries of their classrooms, to question, to think critically, and to be both intellectually curious and creative.

Questions that should be continually discussed by teachers and administrators are such as these: How do we free the pupils and the teachers in our public schools for creative thinking and action? How do we help teachers establish a balance between radicalism or a laissez-faire philosophy on one hand and overconformity on the other?

If democratic education can encourage each oncoming generation to be fearless and imaginative in its thinking, to express differences of opinion in an atmosphere of mutual respect, to strive for rational and humane values by means of open-confrontation and free discussion, and to avoid totalitarian methods of fear and repression,—then perhaps our multigroup society may provide a pattern and an inspiration from which a new world order may emerge.[37]

A seventh current issue deals with the role of discipline in the modern elementary school. The formal discipline of the ruler and the hickory stick has been replaced by an attempt to develop self-discipline in each boy and girl. Self-discipline does not mean no discipline. It is not a laissez-faire policy, for no one today will question the need for limits to be set within which boys and girls are able to operate with freedom. In the nineteen thirties and forties some believed that youth should not be criticized or disciplined in any way, for it would hinder their normal growth and development. Children themselves were not happy under this policy. Many a counselor has heard these boys and girls pitifully state that they felt that their parents just were not interested.

The problem today revolves about such questions as: (1) What limits of freedom should be set? (2) What is the best way of identifying these limits? (3) What are the best methods for developing self-discipline?

Recently there have been several articles supporting the belief that school authorities should be given the right to administer corporal punishment when necessary. Most educators would agree, however, that self-discipline developed through an understanding and acceptance of standards and values, interests carefully motivated, an acceptance of one's strengths and limitations, and a climate motivating each student to do his best is preferable to coercion through force and fear.

These are only a few of the many issues facing the American educators and the lay public at the beginning of the seventh decade of this century. Educators are also seeking answers to such questions as: (1) How may we meet most effectively the needs of the so-called gifted youth, youth gifted in both academic and/or other areas? (2) How may the schools more effectively promote international understanding and communication? (3) How may the schools utilize more effectively national, international, scientific, and technological developments? (4) How may teachers and

[37] *Ibid.*, p. 79.

pupils develop a more balanced curriculum—balanced between general and specialized education? (5) How can we organize grades 1–6 more functionally? (6) How may the teachers and pupils make more effective utilization of audio-visual aids, closed-circuit television, and other types of teaching aids needed if the increased enrollments necessitate larger classes? (7) How may we meet the teacher shortage, yet also promote better preparation of teachers? (8) How may the school staffs help boys and girls satisfy more effectively their individual needs? (9) How may we define more effectively the role of the classroom teacher? (10) How might we redefine the goals and objectives of elementary education?

If one were to list in parallel columns the issues that faced our forefathers and those still unresolved today, one would be impressed with their similarity. The forward movement of education is not rapid. The thinking is often far ahead of practice. As one reviews current educational issues today, it is obvious that a great deal of research is needed, that the elementary schools of this country must resist pressure groups which wish to add continually to the present educational offerings without re-evaluating the entire curricular pattern, that a continual appraisal must be made, that school authorities must keep in mind constantly that the school cannot be all things to all people. To help resolve these issues, elementary school staffs must have a clear understanding of the essential goals and objectives of elementary education so that they may be used as a sound basis for study and evaluation. These are discussed in the following chapter.

Summary

This chapter discusses past and present elementary education in this country in four topic-areas: (1) The development of education in colonial America; (2) the contributions made by outstanding educators from abroad; (3) the educational strides that occurred during the first part of the twentieth century; and (4) current issues that elementary education is facing today.

Five "battles" were fought by our forefathers in the development of the elementary school program as we know it today: (1) attempts to effect the support of the schools through taxation rather than to continue the indefinite support through tuition, gifts, lotteries, or land grants; (2) the battle to eliminate the pauper school; (3) the battle to expand free public education; (4) the battle to eliminate sectarianism; and (5) the need for state supervision of educational opportunities within state borders.

As early educators began to focus their attention on ways to improve the education of teachers and the teaching methods, they turned to the influence of the works and thinking of such men as: John Amos Comenius, Jean Jacques Rousseau, Johann H. Pestalozzi, Freidrich Froebel, and Johann F. Herbart.

At about the turn of the century and during the succeeding decades, a great deal of activity occurred in this country in the field of education: the contributions of John Dewey; the influence of the progressive education movement; increasing emphasis on testing, evaluation, and research; development of new methods of instruction; the development of the child-study movement and child-guidance centers; and the addition of new school functionaries.

The last section dealt with the identification of current issues that are facing the American educators and the lay public today. It is of interest to note the close similarity between the problems that confronted our forefathers and the issues that are facing us today.

STUDENT PROJECTS

1. In this chapter we have discussed the early history of elementary education in this country. We have learned that several battles were fought by our forefathers in an attempt to develop a free, universal, public educational system. What was the role of your state in the waging of these battles? Who were the outstanding leaders in the development of elementary education in your state?

2. Viewing the development of elementary education as a continuous process, what would you identify as the chief battle that we who are interested in elementary education are engaged in today? What is the goal of this battle? In what ways do you feel that its victory would contribute to a more effective educational program?

3. One of the most difficult issues facing the elementary school staff is to identify the best procedures for helping boys and girls develop sound moral and ethical values. Visit several elementary school classrooms and record as many experiences as possible that you observed which helped the boys and girls in the classes develop moral and ethical values. Evaluate these procedures in terms of your own thinking and reading.

4. The elementary school staff attempts to help each pupil develop self-discipline. Visit elementary school classrooms and record incidents that, in your opinion, contributed to the development of self-discipline. Add to the list ways that you believe self-discipline could have been developed. Discuss your listings with teachers, parents, and pupils.

5. It is always difficult to appraise objectively the contributions of any present-day leader. Whom would you identify as the leaders of elementary education at this time? How would you justify your answer?

6. In this chapter the authors identified some of the current issues of elementary education facing the American people. Select one of these, or an issue that you believe is equally important, and prepare a plan for a panel discussion examining both sides of the issue. Outline your discussion to present to the members of a lay committee who are interested in hearing objective evidence about an educational issue in which they are interested.

7. The organizational pattern varies from one school system to another. There are the 8-4 plan, the 6-3-3 plan, the 6-6 plan, the 6-4-4 plan, and the 3-3-3-3 plan. Try to find examples of at least two of these patterns in nearby communities. Interview the superintendent of each of these systems regarding what

he believes are the advantages and disadvantages of the plan or plans he directs. You may find examples of one or more organizational plans in a given school system. Discuss plans other than these with the superintendent. Report to your class.

8. Federal aid to education is one of the most frequently discussed issues of the present day. List in detail as many pros and cons of Federal aid to education as you can find. Survey the literature and talk to educators and lay people whom you know. Prepare a speech that could be given to a board of education that would give them an objective, unbiased presentation of facts. This talk should help the members of the board answer questions raised by the members of the community.

9. Talk to six parents and six teachers regarding the question of effective discipline. List the ways in which they agreed and differed. Try to explain the reasons for their differences. Try to find documentary evidence to support or to refute their opinions. If they were to question you, what would your answer be? How would you document your answers?

10. Read extensively in current periodicals that reflect the thinking of professional educators and the lay public regarding the current issues in education. Compare, in your opinion, the effectiveness of each of these publications in terms of its comprehensive covering, its objectivity, its scholarship, and in as many other ways as you can.

11. If you accept the belief that problems should be tackled at the grass roots and if you are really interested in facing facts and feelings of those interested in elementary education in this country, plan to interview six elementary school teachers and six laymen regarding what to you is probably the most significant current issue at this time.

BIBLIOGRAPHY

ADAMS, F. G., *Educating America's Children* (New York. The Ronald Press Company, 1954).

BEREDAY, George and VOLPICELLI, Luigi, Eds., *Public Education in America* (New York, Harper and Brothers, 1958).

BRUBACHER, John S., *A History of the Problems of Education* (New York, McGraw-Hill Book Company, 1947).

BUTTS, R. Freeman, *A Cultural History of Western Education*, 2nd ed. (New York, McGraw-Hill Book Company, 1955).

BUTTS, R. Freeman and CREMIN, Lawrence A., *A History of Education in American Culture* (New York, Holt, Rinehart and Winston, Inc., 1953).

CRAMER, John Francis and BROWNE, George S., *Contemporary Education* (New York, Harcourt, Brace and Company, 1956).

CRESSMAN, G. R., and BENDA, H. W., *Public Education in America*, 2nd ed. (New York, Appleton-Century-Crofts, Inc., 1961).

CUBBERLEY, E. P., *A Brief History of Education* (Boston, Houghton Mifflin Co., 1922).

CUBBERLEY, E. P., *Public Education in the United States*, rev. ed. (Boston, Houghton Mifflin Co., 1934).

EBY, Frederick, *The Development of Modern Education*, 2nd ed. (Englewood Cliffs, N. J., Prentice-Hall, Inc., 1952).

EDWARDS, Newton and RICHEY, Herman G., *The School in the American Social Order* (Boston, Houghton Mifflin Co., 1947).

EHLERS, Henry and LEE, Gordon C., Eds., *Crucial Issues in Education* (New York, Holt, Rinehart and Winston, Inc., 1959).

FRASIER, G. W., *An Introduction to the Study of Education,* rev. ed. (New York, Harper and Brothers, 1956).

GOOD, H. G., *A History of Western Education* (New York, The Macmillan Company, 1947).

HANSEN, Kenneth H., *Public Education in American Society* (Englewood Cliffs, N. J., Prentice-Hall, Inc., 1956).

KANDEL, I. L., *American Education in the Twentieth Century* (Cambridge, Mass., Harvard University Press, 1957).

LEE, Gordon C., *Education in Modern America,* rev. ed. (New York, Holt, Rinehart and Winston, Inc., 1957).

MACLEAN, Malcolm S., and LEE, Edwin A., *Change and Process in Education,* (New York, Holt, Rinehart and Winston, Inc., 1956).

MEYER, Adolphe E., *An Educational History of the American People* (New York, McGraw-Hill Book Company, 1957).

MULHERN, James, *A History of Education,* 2nd ed. (New York, The Ronald Press Company, 1959).

REINHARDT, Emma, *American Education* (New York, Harper and Brothers, 1954).

SCOTT, C. Winfield and HILL, Clyde M., *Public Education Under Criticism* (Englewood Cliffs, N. J., Prentice-Hall, Inc., 1954).

PART II

Emerging Goals and Concepts

CHAPTER 2

Identification of Objectives in Elementary Education

THE YOUNG PEOPLE OF THE 1960s find excitement and challenge in the fact that their lives as Americans during the next fifteen, twenty or fifty years will be filled with uncertainty. Children of today—to the amazement and wonder of teachers and parents—casually accept jet travel and the exploration of outer space. These children expect that a visit to the moon, for example, will be a natural experience of their adult lives.

The uncertainty and potentialities of the future, however, raise many problems for the elementary school educator in regard to the appropriateness of the learning experiences in today's elementary school. The teacher or administrator needs to be able to identify goals and objectives for elementary education in order to prepare the children adequately for the Space Age. What might the appropriate objectives of elementary education be? How should the elementary school staff proceed to formulate these objectives?

Objectives may be stated in a general way, or they may be extremely specific in terms of specific knowledges, skills, attitudes, values, and beliefs. Herrick [1] and others identify the functions of objectives as follows:

FUNCTIONS OF OBJECTIVES

Objectives define the direction of educational development. They serve as guide posts rather than ends in themselves, guides both to the instructional staff and to the learners. They point the direction toward which an elementary school program is heading in its selection of learning experiences.

[1] V. E. Herrick and others, *The Elementary School* (Englewood Cliffs, N.J., Prentice-Hall, Inc., 1956), pp. 83–85.

Learning which results in development related to, or moving toward, educational objectives constitutes education. Learning which results in development opposed to, or moving away from, educational objectives constitutes mis-education.[2]

Objectives are not the specific learning experiences, but many times are by-products of the total learning activities.

Objectives help select desirable learning experiences. From the multi-complex array of possible learning activities, teachers and other elementary school functionaries must have some assistance in the selection of the most appropriate and most satisfying experiences. While each individual activity frequently contributes to many objectives (some previously identified by the group, others developed during the learning experience), teachers and pupils have found learning more fun and more effective if at least to some degree they know what they are trying to achieve and are able later to evaluate these accomplishments. With an eye to objectives teachers and learners can check regularly on whether the desirable aims and goals are being achieved or whether one or more are being overlooked.

Objectives help define the emphasis to be made in an educational program. How do we know what emphases to make? To determine effectively what emphasis each of the component parts of our educational program should take, we must be familiar with research in the areas of child psychology and child development and be sensitive to the needs and expectations of the flesh-and-blood boys and girls in our classrooms. Objectives must also be re-evaluated regularly in terms of changing times, changing school populations, resources, and needs.

Objectives form one of the major bases for evaluation. Objectives carefully thought through by a staff not only help teachers and learners to identify desirable outcomes, but they also help to define changes in behavior that can be measured or evaluated both objectively and subjectively. Without carefully defined objectives, teaching and learning become like traveling without knowing *where* you are heading and hence not knowing *when* you have arrived and whether you have gone the most direct way. Objectives also help us to answer the very important question of *why* we are teaching what we are and *why* we have selected the learning experiences that we have.

PREVIOUS STATEMENTS OF OBJECTIVES

Six of the seven Cardinal Principles, formulated by the Commission on the Reorganization of Secondary Education, are applicable to elementary education. In 1918, this Commission was one of the first to outline educational objectives of depth and breadth. The six Principles which are pertinent and significant to elementary education include: health, command

2 *Ibid.,* p. 83.

of the fundamental processes, worthy home membership, civic education, worthy use of leisure time, and the development of ethical character.[3] The only other one identified was vocational education, and even that has importance to us in the increasing emphasis in many elementary grades on attitudes toward work and on specific occupations.

Health was defined by the commission as,

[To] provide health instruction, inculcate health habits, organize an effective program of physical activities, regard health needs in planning work and play, and cooperate with home and community in safeguarding and promoting health interests.[4]

Command of the fundamental processes included (as one might expect) "reading, writing, arithmetical computations and the elements of oral and written expression." [5]

Worthy home membership involved the use of all classes, such as social studies, literature, music and art, to help boys and girls develop "those qualities that make the individual a worthy member of a family, both contributing to and deriving benefit from that membership." [6]

Civic education included such essentials as,

a many-sided interest in the welfare of the communities to which one belongs; loyalty to ideals of civic righteousness; practical knowledge of social agencies and institutions; good judgment as to means and methods that will promote one social end without defeating others; and as putting all these into effect, habits and cordial cooperation in social undertakings.[7]

Worthy use of leisure time was defined as,

education to "equip the individual to secure from his leisure the recreation of body, mind, and spirit, and the enrichment and enlargement of his personality." [8]

Ethical character included,

the development on the part of pupils of the sense of personal responsibility and initiative, and, above all, the spirit of service and the principles of true democracy . . .[9]

Warning must be given, however, that this list (or any other) should be used wisely by any school staff. It should be used only as a guide by a staff that is in the process of developing its own dynamic list of objectives for its *own* boys and girls in its *own* school in its *own* community.

[3] National Education Association, Commission on the Reorganization of Secondary Education, *Cardinal Principles of Secondary Education*, Bulletin 1918, Number 35 (Washington, D.C., Government Printing Office, 1918).
[4] *Ibid.*, p. 11.
[5] *Ibid.*
[6] *Ibid.*, p. 12.
[7] *Ibid.*, p. 13.
[8] *Ibid.*, p. 15.
[9] *Ibid.*

Cardinal objectives in elementary education were identified during the late twenties and early thirties by those interested in elementary education in New York state.[10] They emphasized the need for every child: (1) to understand and practice desirable social relationships; (2) to discover and develop his own desirable individual aptitudes; (3) to cultivate the habit of critical thinking; (4) to appreciate and desire worthwhile activities; (5) to gain command of the common integrating knowledge and skills; and (6) to develop a sound body and normal mental attitudes. The key words in this listing are: social relationships, self-expression, critical thinking, worthwhile activities, knowledge and skills, and health.[11]

During the days of the depression in the 1930s the Educational Policies Commission identified four major objectives of education. The commission attempted to spell out the most essential components of each objective in a publication titled *The Purposes of Education in American Democracy*.[12] The objectives included: (1) self-realization; (2) human relationships; (3) economic efficiency; and (4) civic responsibility.

The Commission listed the objectives of *self-realization* to include,

the inquiring mind, speech, reading, writing, counting and calculating, sight and hearing, health knowledge, health habits, public health, recreation, intellectual interests, esthetic interests, and character.[13]

Human relations included,

respect for humanity, friendships, co-operation, courtesy, appreciation of the home, conservation of the home, homemaking, and democracy in the home.[14]

Economic efficiency included,

attitude toward work, occupational information, occupational choice, occupational efficiency, occupational adjustment, occupational appreciation, personal economics, consumer judgment, efficiency in buying, and consumer protection.[15]

Civic responsibility included,

social justice, social activity, social understandings, critical judgment, tolerance, conservation, social applications of science, world citizenship, law observances, economic literacy, political citizenship, and devotion to democracy.[16]

Kearney, at mid-century, identified a detailed, comprehensive, and specific listing of elementary school objectives. His headings, carefully

10 Committee for Elementary Education, Council of New York Superintendents, *Cardinal Objectives in Elementary Education*, 3rd Report (Albany, N.Y., University of the State of New York, 1932).
11 *Ibid.*, p. 13.
12 Educational Policies Commission, *The Purposes of Education in American Democracy* (Washington, D.C., National Education Association, 1938).
13 *Ibid.*, p. 50.
14 *Ibid.*, p. 72.
15 *Ibid.*, p. 90.
16 *Ibid.*, p. 108.

delineated in his mid-century report, include: (1) physical development, health, and body care; (2) individual social and emotional development; (3) ethical behavior, standards, and values; (4) social relations; (5) the social world; (6) the physical world; (7) esthetic development; (8) communication; and (9) quantitative relationships.[17]

The Yale-Fairfield Study, in 1956, defined the following objectives: (1) physical health; (2) mental and emotional health; (3) communication; (4) quantitative understanding; (5) social relationships; (6) understanding the social environment; (7) moral and spiritual values; (8) understanding the physical world; (9) critical thinking; and (10) aesthetic and creative development.[18]

Obviously each of these lists of objectives is similar. Since objectives guide teachers in their selection of learning experiences, they should always be paramount in a teacher's thinking and planning, not as restrictions but as motivating sign posts that guide the learning experiences and the evaluations. With this in mind the authors believe that the following objectives are worthy of consideration:

NINE BASIC OBJECTIVES OF ELEMENTARY EDUCATION

1. The importance of the individual is a basic goal or objective. Every teacher must be sincerely interested in the importance and in the value of each individual child. Boys and girls, likewise, should be taught to develop a sensitivity to individual differences, individual rights, and individual responsibilities.

Each teacher must train himself to see the individual child as a person. Each boy and girl must be helped to develop a positive self-concept and must be given an opportunity to expand his or her potentialities to the maximum. One of the most important principles in a successful teacher's life is his sincere belief in this importance of the individual and in his ability to motivate his pupils to feel the same way. The personality of the teacher, the classroom climate, the classroom management, and the individual and group learning experiences contribute to the attainment of this objective.

2. Provision for individual differences is a major goal for elementary school teachers. Each boy and girl brings to the classroom situation different experiences, different attitudes, different values, different interests, as well as different degrees of intellectual, physical, social, and emotional maturity. No two children are identical; no two children react alike; no two children, therefore, should be treated alike.

Because children are in many respects alike is a justification for group

[17] N. C. Kearney, *Elementary School Objectives* (New York, Russell Sage Foundation, 1953), pp. 52–120.

[18] C. M. Hill and others, *Yale-Fairfield Study of Elementary Teaching* (New Haven, Connecticut, Yale University, 1956), Chapter Six.

experiences in a classroom; because individuals also differ is the justification for the truth that no effective teaching occurs without opportunity for individual experiences.

Teachers must realize that pupils differ, for example, in the degree of sound physical and mental health; in the areas of visual and auditory acuity, verbal fluency and ability, number facility, reasoning, and memory skills; in the roles that heredity and environment have played; in motivation; in interests; in emotional security; and in social maturity.

In any average sixth-grade class, one may find a spread of eight years in child development: from characteristics that one might perceive in the second grade to those one might find in a tenth grade. Those who believe in homogeneous grouping may try hard to group a given class homogeneously, but complete homogeneous grouping in any given classroom is impossible.

A teacher, therefore, who respects the individual and who recognizes the individual differences within his class will consider and utilize these differences as he plans his learning experiences.

3. The elementary school must provide a type of continuous guidance for all children. By "continuous," the authors mean that a person's adjustment is not a state; it is a process. It never stays static; it never stays put. What a person is today depends on his previous experiences. What he will be tomorrow depends upon his past plus his present experiences.

Whenever a teacher studies and guides Jimmy, he is concerned with the child's present development, how he compares with the average boy of his chronological age, and with the previous experiences that have contributed to Jimmy's current development.

No longer are we *primarily* concerned with helping a child develop for *future* life adjustment. Rather we know that every boy and girl passes through periods of development during which time there are "typical tasks" to be performed.[19] If each child is provided the needed experiences and if he satisfactorily performs these tasks at each age level, his future adjustment will take care of itself. Teachers must be aware of these tasks, must study to see the degree of success with which each child experiences each one, and must determine in many cases *why* the optimum development has not occurred. These tasks serve as guides to the types of learning experiences that should be provided.

Havighurst outlines the following developmental tasks experienced during *middle childhood* (ages six to twelve), the years when most boys and girls are attending the elementary grades:

Learning physical skills necessary for ordinary games (throwing, catching, kicking, tumbling, swimming, and handling simple tools). The successful achievement of this task is more significant for boys than for girls, for it seems to in-

[19] R. Havighurst, *Human Development and Education* (New York, Longmans, Green & Co., Inc., 1953).

fluence more directly their self-concepts. However, the development of effective co-ordination by girls contributes to needed grace.[20]

Building wholesome attitudes toward oneself as a growing organism. Teachers must continually be sensitive to the self-concept of each boy and girl and to the experiences that will contribute positively to the development of a favorable self-concept.[21]

Havighurst notes that youth should develop

a sense of physical normality and adequacy, ability to enjoy using the body, and a wholesome attitude toward sex.[22]

Learning to get along with age mates. One of the basic goals of our schools is to help each boy and girl to mature socially and to develop interpersonal skills. During these early years, youth move out of their home environment socially; so acceptance among their peers gains significant importance.[23]

Learning appropriate masculine and feminine social roles. During this period young boys should learn how to act as boys, that is, the types of behavior that are acceptable for boys and the types that are unacceptable. Young girls should become acquainted with acceptable feminine behavior. Girls who tend to be tomboys and boys who tend to practice feminine activities should be helped, never ridiculed.[24]

Developing skills in reading, writing, and calculating. Reading, writing, and arithmetic are basic skills that should be developed during these six or seven years of a child's life. Because children do vary in the time of their readiness for learning these basic skills, there is an increased interest in experimenting with ungraded primary groupings (as discussed in Chapter Fifteen). Mental, emotional, social, and physical development plus an opportunity for enriching experiences contribute significantly to the child's readiness to learn these basic skills.[25]

Developing concepts necessary for everyday living. During the years of six to twelve, the youth in our schools formulate several thousand concepts including those of time, space, number, hot or cold, high or low, and fast or slow. It is one of the basic responsibilities of each teacher to help each boy and girl to develop as many meaningful concepts as possible.[26]

Developing conscience, morality, and a scale of values. While this developmental task is extremely important, it is probably one of the most difficult to achieve in the elementary schools. In Havighurst's opinion the school probably affects the child's conscience and morality through such things as teachings about morality, through the teacher's punishments and rewards, through the example of the teacher, and through the child's experiences in his peer groups.[27]

Achieving personal independence. Gradually during this period the child begins to realize that Daddy, Mommy, and teacher *could* be wrong. He finds himself relatively independent at times and then becomes extremely dependent at other times. He wants to be independent, and yet he covets the protection of

[20] *Ibid.*, pp. 28–29.
[21] *Ibid.*, pp. 29–30.
[22] *Ibid.*, p. 29.
[23] *Ibid.*, pp. 30–31.
[24] *Ibid.*, p. 32.
[25] *Ibid.*, pp. 33–34.
[26] *Ibid.*, pp. 34–35.
[27] *Ibid.*, pp. 36–37.

depending. Experiences must be provided for boys and girls to make appropriate decisions, to evaluate their decisions, and to accept the consequences. Youth should be helped to achieve independence without feeling rejected and without developing unnecessary feelings of insecurity.[28]

Developing attitudes toward social groups and institutions. Between the ages of six and twelve, boys and girls develop attitudes toward religious, social, and political groups.

Havighurst believes that by the time a child leaves the elementary school,

he has a full complement of social attitudes, picked up or absorbed from his family, his teachers, his peer group, and his contact with the community and the wide world through movies, radio, television, books, and lectures.[29]

Obviously, some boys and girls will need more guidance than others, but we must not operate under the assumption that only boys and girls with serious maladjustments need help. A bright, alert, popular young lady may be secretly concerned about something and want very much to share her concern.

Roeber, Smith, and Erickson identified four parts of a Bill of Rights that should be provided for all children:

Each pupil has the right to use accurate information about himself and his environment: his strengths, his weaknesses, and his interests . . .

Each pupil has the right to plan his activities in a non-authoritarian atmosphere . . .

Each pupil has the right to individual attention in planning his goals . . .

Each pupil has the right to organized assistance in following through his plans.[30]

4. Teachers and administrators must recognize the importance of considering all phases of the pupil's development. The chief responsibility of any teacher is to help each boy and girl enjoy a productive and satisfying life. We know that to do this we must be concerned with the total individual. We must be concerned with the physical health of boys and girls, with their social skills and social attitudes, with their degree of emotional security, and with their degree of intellectual development. We cannot, however, expect the most brilliant boy or girl to be receptive to the learning of the basic skills if he is hungry; if he cannot see the chalk board; if he is emotionally disturbed because possibly he has quarreled with his mother or dad that morning; or even more serious, if he is emotionally disturbed because his parents are getting a divorce, and he has developed guilt feelings, feeling a little unsure about his role in the breaking up of his once happy home.

[28] *Ibid.*, pp. 38–40.
[29] *Ibid.*, p. 40.
[30] E. C. Roeber, G. E. Smith, and C. E. Erickson, *Organization and Administration of Guidance Services* (New York, McGraw-Hill Book Company, 1955), pp. 1–4.

The medical profession has also seen the need for considering the total man. In such medical centers as the Mayo Clinic, the Leahy Clinic, or others in our country, an individual who goes for observation and study is examined and is given all kinds of tests by medical specialists, but never is any diagnosis made or any recommendation suggested or any interpretation given until all these data are related to the individual. It is the *whole* individual in whom they are interested, and it is the *whole* individual who should be the concern of every teacher.

5. Each child's intellectual development is a paramount goal of the elementary school staff. It is the responsibility of every teacher to help each boy and girl in his class identify his or her intellectual potentialities and to help him or her realize these potentialities. Each student must be taught basic facts and basic understandings; skills and competencies must be developed; opportunities to develop interests, attitudes, values, and appreciations must be provided; and each boy and girl must be taught to think critically, to communicate clearly, and to be creative.

A child should understand that intellectual development is not synonymous with the amassing of facts. No elementary school teacher should ever encourage even the brightest pupil to become a walking encyclopaedia who can produce at a moment's notice—like a magician's rabbit—an isolated fact that might be interesting but not very significant. A modern teacher's goal, on the contrary, is to help each pupil to develop a sound intellectual curiosity, to be interested in following data wherever they may lead, and to be concerned with the interrelatedness of facts and understandings and their utilization.

In the development of intellectual competency each pupil should see the need for identifying goals and objectives and for using them as guides and as a basis for necessary evaluation. Students must be taught to broaden their horizons, to be interested in the humanities, in the social sciences, in mathematics, science, and other technological developments, in other cultures of the world, and in all other phases of current knowledge.

Students should be encouraged to challenge ideas, not merely for the sake of challenging, but for an opportunity to do some creative, bold thinking on their own. With challenging and questioning comes the responsibility to do careful thinking.

A basic goal for teachers in all grades is to help each child develop sound attitudes, beliefs, and values. This is not an easy responsibility. Experiences should be provided where pupils may identify values, attitudes, and beliefs and be given ample opportunity to test each one. The elementary grades are not, by any means, too early to help boys and girls to begin to develop a philosophy of life.

To help boys and girls enjoy intellectual curiosity and intellectual integrity, to help each of them understand, appreciate, evaluate, create, think critically, and communicate clearly is a major task for any teacher in today's elementary school.

6. Every teacher must emphasize the importance of the physical development of each boy and girl. To attain this goal the teacher must play several roles. He must provide a healthful climate in the classroom, proper ventilation, correct heating, and effective lighting. He must be sensitive to the effect of lighting, color, illustrations, and general over-all atmosphere on both the physical and mental health of his pupils. He must make every effort to remove unnecessary tension and conflict. A consistency in reacting to boys and girls contributes more than one realizes to the mental health and ultimately to the physical health of many a boy or girl. A calm voice and manner, a sense of humor, and a positive attitude are only a few of the personal qualities an elementary school teacher must have to attain these desirable goals.

In addition to providing a healthful atmosphere in the classroom, the elementary school teacher teaches health education daily and often many times a day. Working closely with the nurse, he stresses the basic fundamentals for good health, the importance of medical care and first aid, and the development of a knowledge of medical resources both in the school and in the community.

It is the responsibility of every elementary school teacher to know the health status of each of his pupils, to observe carefully the daily health of his group, to report changes in behavior to the school nurse, to provide health education, to help boys and girls understand the importance of physical examinations, to help those with physical disabilities adjust to them, to provide health guidance in many ways, and to provide at all times in the classroom a healthful atmosphere. A teacher must never lose sight of the close interrelationship between physical and mental health.

7. The development of social intelligence is an important goal of elementary education. Social intelligence may be defined as the ability to evaluate experiences in terms of satisfactory individual and group living and is, therefore, the ability to act effectively in social situations.

The role of the elementary school teacher in developing social intelligence in each of his boys and girls involves many types of activities. One of the most important responsibilities is to help each boy and girl develop a sound self-concept. Unless one has a feeling of security in his relationship with others, he is unable to operate effectively in many situations. Unfortunately the elementary school inherits many bad social patterns. As Pressey and Robinson write,

A child who has lived in a quarrelsome home or has been constantly shouted at or yanked about for the first six years of his life is likely to be callous, noisy, and self-assertive.[31]

[31] S. L. Pressey and F. P. Robinson, *Psychology and the New Education,* rev. ed. (New York, Harper and Brothers, 1944), p. 200.

The development of social intelligence is an important goal.

Children, like adults, need recognition and opportunities for success. Therefore, one must help the child develop a self-concept that helps him to evaluate his strengths and his limitations and to live with them effectively. The school as well as the home plays an important role in this.

Teachers must also help youth to learn and practice effective social usage, including the ability to accept and adjust to certain social amenities. All types of experiences must be provided to help each child become sensitive to the needs of others; to provide ways of meeting these needs; and to develop a feeling of security as he relates to his peers, to those older than he is, and to those younger.

Simpson outlined a possible program to effect this:

1. Congenial atmosphere in the classroom where children assemble in small groups for study . . .

2. Need for a thorough study of the children's social adjustment in and out of group work and elsewhere in the school and community . . .

3. Need for knowledge of children's social assets and liabilities . . .

4. Need to develop socially useful skills with children who do not seem to possess talent for getting along with others . . .

5. Schools must provide ways for children to learn how to live with others by having actual experiences in a wide variety of situations . . .[32]

This goal and the following one, the emotional development of boys and girls, are very closely related, for emotional problems make social development extremely difficult.

8. The effective emotional development of each boy and girl is also an important goal for every elementary school staff. Some people believe that one of the most traumatic experiences in a child's life is his first day of school:

A day away from the security of his home, a day spent in a classroom with twenty-five to thirty-five other youngsters whose interests and needs may be quite different from his own, a day spent under the direction of a total stranger—in reality, a captive experience. Nursery school, kindergarten, and first grade teachers, as well as parents, must be sensitive to the conflicts experienced by the child as he faces for the first time these new kinds of limitations. He may not go home when he pleases; he may not go out to play when he pleases; he may not even play when he pleases. It may be the first time he comes to recognize the authority of people outside his immediate family.[33]

This entrance into school can be a pleasant, satisfying experience, or it can be extremely traumatic and may provide a feeling of emotional insecurity that might ultimately lead to a basic dislike for school.

Periods of transition, such as from home to school, from grade to grade, and from the security felt by boys and girls in the elementary school to the larger and more complex junior high school are specific periods when the goal to establish emotional security must not be overlooked.

A close relationship between the home and the school may often contribute to the emotional security of children. Though it is true that the school staffs cannot be expected to assume a major responsibility for the guidance of youth before their arrival, the school has a real "stake" in this question, for they find themselves dealing with the results of what has happened during the first six years of the child's life. Teachers should seek answers early in the year to such questions as:

Were Mary's parents sensitive to her needs as she passed through those "terrible twos," "trusting threes," "frustrating fours," and "fascinating fives"? [34] Was she criticized so frequently that she became a youngster who thought of herself as one very different from other youngsters—one disliked, a bother to all? Was she rejected to the extent that to gain any recognition by any means became very important to her? Was she so over-protected that she had no part in making child decisions? [35]

[32] R. G. Simpson, *Fundamentals of Educational Psychology* (Philadelphia, J. B. Lippincott Company, 1949), pp. 111–112.
[33] F. C. Rosecrance and V. D. Hayden, *School Guidance and Personnel Services* (Boston, Allyn and Bacon, Inc., 1960), p. 28.
[34] These are film titles. See F. A. Kraher, ed., *Educational Film Guide*, 11th Ed. (New York, Crawley Films, Wilson Company, 1955).
[35] F. C. Rosecrance and V. D. Hayden, *op. cit.*, p. 29.

Some boys and girls come to school happy; some come unhappy; some are seriously disturbed before they reach the portals of the elementary schools. To help each boy and girl develop a satisfactory emotional adjustment is a most challenging goal for the elementary school staff today.

No boy or girl wants to be troublesome. There must be a reason if he is. Each elementary school staff member must be concerned with "why" Jimmy and Mary act as they do. Attempts must be made to help each child meet his needs satisfactorily. Much can be accomplished through creative learning experiences provided by the classroom teacher. A teacher must also establish a sound balance between reaching out to each child to offer support and yet not being overly protective.

As has been indicated earlier, emotional adjustment is closely allied with intellectual, physical, and social development, for often a lack of sound emotional development results from a lack of success in one or more of the other areas. The development of emotional security is an important aspect of the child's total development and must not be overlooked or minimized.

9. The previously discussed objectives, if effectively achieved, result in the realization of the most fundamental objective: that the elementary schools produce effective citizens in our democracy. To define the term "effective citizen" is not easy. It is very true, however, that the ultimate goal of the elementary school staff should be to provide experiences that will help boys and girls become happy and productive democratic citizens in our society. The authors believe that Heffernan summarizes this goal as effectively as possible when she writes,

A democratic person has self-respect, self-reliance, and self-regard; a democratic person must have status himself to be willing to accord status to others.

A democratic person has respect for others, as shown by his:
Respect for human personality,
Appreciation for other cultures than his own,
Respect for public and private property,
Acceptance of properly constituted authority.

A democratic person is able to maintain democratic relations by:
Co-operating in a friendly and willing spirit,
Feeling and expressing appreciation for others,
Adjusting to situations and people.

A democratic person acts responsibly and courageously in accordance with accepted personal and social ideals . . . has moral integrity.[36]

As suggested earlier, these aims and objectives for elementary education should be used merely as guides for individual elementary school staffs to consider as each staff develops its own specific aims and goals. Objectives are very necessary, however, if careful planning and meaningful evaluation are to take place.

[36] H. Heffernan, "The Teacher Helps Children to Build Values," *California Journal of Elementary Education*, Vol. 23 (May, 1955), p. 252.

This brings us to another important question: Whose responsibility is it to help attain these goals? Much is being written during the twentieth century regarding the importance of the team approach. In this situation, the team approach is a "must."

Elementary school teachers and the principal in each school are working at the grass roots. To them goes the primary responsibility for developing specific goals or objectives for any given school. To do this, they must make a study of the community in terms of its assets, its liabilities, and its specific characteristics. Lay committees working with the teachers and the principal can be very helpful in this study of the community by identifying the type of citizen the school would like to help develop and by interpreting the school to the community.

Goals and objectives, however, are tentative; they are not static. They must be continually evaluated and re-evaluated. After an elementary school staff develops a tentative set of aims and goals, the next responsibility falls to the classroom teacher. It is his responsibility to develop a series of learning experiences that will help provide many opportunities for each boy and each girl to achieve the desired objectives. Here it would be extremely helpful if the school and the home could work together.

Superintendents and boards of education should give wholehearted support and leadership to any school staff that conscientiously tries to identify goals and to provide opportunities for their attainment. The contributions of such disciplines as psychology, sociology, guidance, child study, medicine, and economics should be carefully explored and utilized.

Summary

This chapter dealt with the basic aims and objectives for elementary education. The authors emphasized the importance of every elementary school staff studying and developing its own aims and goals rather than accepting some vague, impressive-looking listing. These goals must be translated into meaningful learning experiences by classroom teachers working with their pupils. The team approach is a "must." The classroom teacher, the principal, the supervisor, the superintendent, and the board of education each has a very important role to play.

Aims and objectives of elementary education may be presented in a general form or may be very specific. Those outlined by such groups as the National Association for Secondary Education and the Educational Policies Commission tend to be general in nature. Those outlined by Kearney are more specific.

The authors identified the following objectives as ones that they suggest to elementary school staffs to use as guides: (1) the importance of the individual is a basic goal; (2) every teacher must be constantly aware of the individual differences within his classroom; (3) the elementary school must provide a type of continuous guidance for all children; (4) teachers and administrators must recognize the importance of considering all phases of each pupil's development; (5) each child's intellectual development is a paramount goal of the elementary school staff; (6) every teacher must emphasize the importance of the physical development of each boy and girl; (7) the development of social intelligence is an important goal of elementary education; (8) the effective emotional development of each boy and girl is also an important goal for every elementary school staff; and the sum total of these objectives add up to the final objective: (9) that elementary schools should help boys and girls to become effective citizens in our democracy.

While the authors realize that there are hundreds of specific goals and objectives that can be identified as part of the elementary school plan, it is hoped that these broader categories may be used to help teachers and principals to identify the more specific ones that are appropriate in the individual schools.

STUDENT PROJECTS

1. Since you plan to enter the teaching profession or since you plan to re-evaluate your current practices, you should be identifying some goals and objectives for yourself as an elementary school teacher. Identify and discuss five important goals that you wish to achieve. Be specific.

2. Goals and objectives are of very little value unless they are put into action. Visit an elementary school classroom and see whether you can identify experiences which the teacher provided for the children that would help you, if you were the teacher, to achieve your goals. Visit several classes if necessary. Discuss these experiences with other members of your class to see whether these same experiences would have helped them to achieve their goals.

3. Goals and objectives are an important part of an evaluation program. How would you set up a program to evaluate (in terms of your goals and objectives) experiences that you observed in your visit to the elementary school? Ask other members of your class to react to your evaluation procedures.

4. You may be applying for a position during the coming months or next year. If so, how will you be able to apprise yourself of the goals and objectives that have been identified in the school whose staff you are thinking of joining? Indicate questions that you would ask the principal and the superintendent and things that you would look for as you visited the classrooms.

5. Write an editorial for the local paper in defense of one of the goals or objectives identified in this chapter or a goal that you believe to be important. Indicate what effect the achievement of this goal might have on the future well-being of the community.

6. Select one of Havighurst's developmental tasks to keep in mind when you visit an elementary school. Indicate what learning experiences you saw in Grade Two and Grade Four that would help boys and girls to achieve this task. How did these experiences differ at the different grade levels?

7. Goals and objectives should reflect the contributions of related disciplines. Talk to a psychologist, a sociologist, and a school nurse. Ask each to identify as many ways as possible that his discipline has contributed to the achieving of an objective that you believe important for the elementary school.

8. Select one of the objectives listed in this chapter or one that you believe to be important and list as many meaningful learning experiences as possible that you believe would translate this goal into action.

9. Visit an elementary school principal, a school superintendent, and a member of a board of education and ask each one to define his or her role in helping elementary school staffs identify goals and objectives for a particular school.

10. Talk with ten elementary school parents and ask them to identify one or two things that they would like to have the elementary school staff do for their youngsters. Compare their listings with the lists of objectives and goals in this chapter. How would you translate their desires into meaningful learning experiences?

11. Suppose you were the teacher of a fifth-grade class in an elementary school, what kinds of goals and objectives would you ask the pupils in the class to identify for themselves? How would you help them translate these goals into action? What procedures would you use to help these boys and girls evaluate these experiences in terms of the goals? Be specific.

12. Review carefully some of the literature in the field of elementary education and try to identify trends that appear to be developing in the kinds of objectives or goals selected for elementary education. In what ways is curriculum development tending to reflect these goals in the elementary school you visited or in any of the reading that you have done?

BIBLIOGRAPHY

ADAMS, F. G., *Educating America's Children* (New York, The Ronald Press Company, 1954).

ARCHER, C. P., *Elementary Education in Rural Areas* (New York, The Ronald Press Company, 1958).

BAXTER, B. and others, *Role of Elementary Education* (Boston, D. C. Heath and Company, 1952).

BEAUCHAMP, G. A., *Basic Dimensions of Elementary Method* (Boston, Allyn and Bacon, Inc., 1959).

BLOOM, B. S., ed., *Taxonomy of Educational Objectives* (New York, Longmans, Green & Co., Inc., 1954).

BROGAN, P. D., and FOX, L. K., *Helping Children Learn* (New York, Harcourt, Brace & World, Inc, 1955).

CASWELL, H. and FOSHAY, A., *Education in the Elementary School*, 3rd ed. (New York, American Book Company, 1957).

Committee on Elementary Education, New York Council of Superintendents, *Cardinal Objectives in Elementary Education* (Albany, University of the State of New York, 1929).

CRONBACH, L. J., *Educational Psychology* (New York, Harcourt, Brace & World, Inc., 1954).

Department of Elementary School Principals, *Bases for Effective Learning*, 31st Yearbook (Washington, D.C., National Education Association, 1952).

Educational Policies Commission, *The Purposes of Education in American Democracy* (Washington, D.C., National Education Association, 1938).

FRANDSEN, A. N., *How Children Learn* (New York, McGraw-Hill Book Company, 1957).

HAVIGHURST, R., *Human Development and Education,* (New York, Longmans, Green, & Co., Inc., 1953).

HEFFERNAN, H. W., "The Teacher Helps Children to Build Values," *California Journal of Elementary Education,* Vol. 23 (May, 1955), pp. 243–253.

HERRICK, V. E., and others, *The Elementary School* (Englewood Cliffs, N.J., Prentice-Hall, Inc., 1956).

JORDAN, W. C., *Elementary School Leadership* (New York, McGraw-Hill Book Company, 1959).

KALLEN, H. M., "Aims and Content of a Philosophy of Education," *Harvard Educational Review,* Vol. 26 (Spring, 1956), pp. 175–179.

KEARNEY, N. C., *Elementary School Objectives: A Report Prepared for the Mid-Century Committee on Outcomes in Elementary Education* (New York, Russell Sage Foundation, 1953).

KYTE, G. C., *Elementary School Teacher at Work* (New York, Holt, Rinehart and Winston, Inc., 1957).

MITCHELL, L. S., *Our Children and Our Schools* (New York, Simon and Schuster, Inc., 1950).

National Education Association, Commission on the Reorganization of Secondary Education, *Cardinal Principles of Secondary Education,* Bulletin 1918, Number 35 (Washington, D.C., Government Printing Office, 1918).

OHLSEN, M. M., ed., *Modern Methods in Elementary Education* (New York, Holt, Rinehart and Winston, Inc., 1959).

SHANE, R. G., "Aims of Elementary Education," *Review of Educational Research,* Vol. 29 (April, 1959), pp. 137–145.

STRATEMEYER, F. B. and others, *Developing a Curriculum for Modern Living,* 2nd ed. (New York, Teachers College, Columbia University, 1957).

WARNER, R. H., *The Child and His Elementary School World* (Englewood Cliffs, N.J., Prentice-Hall, Inc., 1957).

CHAPTER 3

The Teacher and The Child

To be able to teach children, teachers must understand children. This is the basic justification for requiring study of child growth and development in almost every teacher education program in this country. Parents and teachers alike are frequently disturbed or at least confused by the actions and reactions of boys and girls. The quiet child needs our help as much as does the obstreperous youth; yet it is the latter that more frequently absorbs our attention. We know that we should not focus on whether Mary is noisy or quiet or whether we approve or disapprove; we should be concerned with the "why" of her reactions and of every other child's reactions. *Why* is Jimmy so quiet? *Why* is Jackie so noisy? *Why* is Veronica hostile to any suggestions? *Why* does Joe meet all tension with giggles? *Why* does Susie react with tears? *Why* is it easier to teach certain skills in certain grades? *Why* did Miss Brown find it difficult to teach Mike to read in the first grade, but Miss Jackson finds relatively little difficulty in teaching Mike to read in grade two?

Each child is different. One merely has to walk through an elementary school to note some of these differences: differences in stature, in complexion, in facial expressions, in physical well being, in alertness and general personality, in co-ordination, and in many other ways. Boys and girls arrive in our classrooms each September with different experiences, different attitudes, different values, different interests and appreciations, and with differing degrees of physical, intellectual, social, and emotional maturity.

Teachers should be able to answer at least *three* basic questions regarding children: (1) What are the theories regarding society's concept of a child? (2) What is the current thinking regarding child growth and de-

44

velopment? (3) How may a teacher gain as much information as possible about each child?

SOCIETY'S CONCEPT OF THE CHILD

To know a society's attitude toward its children and youth gives one a fairly good indication of the development and characteristics of the society itself.

One of the earliest concepts was to train children for the state. This concept was advanced by the Spartans and the Athenians. It is widely known that a baby in Sparta not found to be physically able was left to perish in the wilderness. To the Spartans the primary objective was not to develop individuals, but rather to train boys to be brave and hardy warriors. At the age of seven, a Spartan youth was taken away from his family, was admitted into a military company, and was subjected to rigorous discipline. He was trained to develop his body and to protect himself at all times. A girl's only mission was to rear strong, healthy boys, future soldiers for the state.

In more recent years an attitude similar to that found in Sparta has existed in the more authoritarian countries, such as Germany, Italy, and Russia. Under any authoritarian government, standardized patterns of behavior are in vogue, and the superiority of the state over the individual is emphasized.

In Athens during the early days, the attitude toward youth was somewhat different. Only the intellectually elite enjoyed educational opportunities, and the emphasis was to educate youth to be effective citizens. Both Sparta and Athens were interested more in the state than in the individual, but their approaches were different, for the Athenians believed that only through effective education of individuals could the superiority of the state be maintained.

A second concept emphasized the innate depravity of the child. All youth were evil as a result of the fall of Adam and Eve, and it was the responsibility of education to remove this evil. Standards were identified; children were made to conform; discipline was rigorous. Such a phrase as "spare the rod and spoil the child" became a by-word. Teachers were employed on the basis of the strictness of their discipline, and situations in many classrooms have been described as being more cruel and inhuman than conditions existing in many penal institutions today.

Another historical concept, also with an emphasis on conformity, was the concept of the child as a miniature adult. Many a child was not only considered a miniature adult physically, intellectually, emotionally, and socially, but he was also dressed as an adult. Naturally childish pranks were not tolerated. Free, harmless play activities were frowned upon. Boys and girls were "little men" and "little women," different from adults only in size. They were expected to conform to adult beliefs, conventions, social customs, values, attitudes, and interests. Naturally they did not; hence harsh discipline resulted. Children were to be seen, but not heard.

In this country, in England, and in many other countries, there was also the attitude that the role of many children should be that of an apprentice, that education should be through work. Little thought was given to the resultant effect on a child's development if he were a "chimney sweep," as described by Charles Dickens in his novels, or if he were an apprentice assigned to a master. As was indicated earlier, attitudes toward children reflect a country's political, social, and economic philosophies. In a primarily mechanistic country, children tend to become the pawns of labor.

Fortunately the reforms during the nineteenth century and the passing of the labor laws during the first part of the twentieth century reflected a much-needed change in our attitude toward children and youth. The extensive research performed at New Haven, Connecticut, under the direction of Gesell and Senn; research studies conducted at other educational centers; the proposing of the developmental tasks theory by Havighurst; and the contributions of anthropologists, sociologists, biologists, psychologists, medical teams, and child guidance centers have contributed significantly to our present attitude toward boys and girls. Freud's emphasis that emotional and social difficulties found in disturbed adults are the result of childhood experiences was an impetus to the development of the child-study movement and the child guidance centers.

Child psychologists have discarded arm-chair musings for a more direct method of studying children. Present-day research emphasizes the importance of both longitudinal and latitudinal studies, the importance of studying the interrelationships of growth patterns, and the need for direct observation. Boys and girls of all ages, not merely the younger ones, are now studied to help psychologists identify basic laws of behavior related to each boy and girl as a developing organism. Careful observations, accurate and objective recordings of each of the observations, and a merging of many kinds of knowledge have produced the bulwark of what we know today about child growth and development.

There are still many questions that are unanswered. Teachers must be sensitive to the fact, however, that while they themselves may and should be well informed regarding the *current* theories and beliefs about the growth and development of boys and girls, there are many parents who believe and who practice one or more of the theories that we have discussed earlier in this chapter. It is very important for today's teacher: (1) to have an understanding of the boys and girls who come from these homes; (2) to attempt continually to apprise these parents regarding the current findings; and (3) to keep currently informed regarding the latest data in the area of child growth and development. Continued study and changing concepts in developmental psychology are occurring every year.

GROWTH AND DEVELOPMENT OF THE CHILD

Some of the questions raised can be at least partially answered by what we know today about child growth and development. There is still, however, considerable unfinished business. Much research is still needed in this area. A complete discussion of this topic cannot be presented on as few pages as can be assigned in this volume. For this reason the authors have included an extensive bibliography at the close of this chapter.

Growth is a continuous, but uneven process. Before our eyes we see children grow, but we sometimes lose sight of the fact that the child not only increases in physical size, but also his mental and emotional processes become more complex. As Gesell and Ilg indicated, the basic growth of each boy and girl follows a fairly fixed pattern:

He sits before he stands; he babbles before he talks; he says "no" before he says "yes"; he fabricates before he tells the truth; he draws a circle before he draws a square; he is selfish before he is altruistic; he is dependent on others before he achieves dependence on self. All his abilities, including his morals, are subject to laws of growth.[1]

Although growth is continuous and will continue almost regardless of what we do, we must realize that growth does not proceed at a regular and steady pace. Parents are most aware of the rapid growth that takes place during the first few years of an infant's life. There is a tendency for the rate to lessen. During later years the rate of increase of height, for example, is much more accelerated prior to age seven than it is between the ages of seven and ten. At certain times a child learns many words, and then he fails to increase his vocabulary as rapidly during the next two or three months. At other times, intellectual growth seems to lag, to be replaced by physical growth.

Authorities in child growth and development are in considerable agreement, however, that apparently decreased activity does not mean, in reality, a period of stagnancy. Rather it may better be viewed as a time of integration and adjustment and a period of gathering force for future periods of more rapid growth.

Each child follows a unique, individual pattern of growth. The fluctuating peaks and plateaus of growth may follow a general, over-all pattern, but each child also follows his own individual growth pattern.

As has been indicated earlier, a teacher merely has to observe his class during a short period of time to become aware of some of the differences in the growth and development of his twenty to thirty boys and girls. Some are tall, while others are short; some are underweight, while others are stocky; some seem full of energy, while others appear weak and lackadaisical; some are gracefully well co-ordinated, while others are pathetically

[1] A. L. Gesell and F. Ilg, *The Child from Five to Ten* (New York, Harper and Brothers, 1946), pp. 35–36.

Boys surpass girls in muscular
strength.

Girls excel in manual dexterity.

awkward. Prescott believes that four factors contribute to the uniqueness of each individual's growth pattern.

(1) physical processes that affect the body and its operation; (2) love relationships and the emotional climate in which the child lives; (3) the various cultural elements that the child internalizes from the family, neighborhood, and social groups of which he is a part; and (4) the peer-group processes to which the child is exposed as he seeks to win belonging among the children with whom he goes to school.[2]

Since this uniqueness of growth pattern is found in all classrooms, teaching must be flexible and creative. "The teacher must not operate as though the groups were homogeneous or as though the learners could and should be poured into a mold." [3]

Physical growth has been more adequately studied and described than has any other phase in the development of the child between the ages of six and twelve. Current research has emphasized the importance of longitudinal studies that point up the variations in growth patterns of youth at any one age-level. These variations in growth patterns increase significantly with the increase of chronological age.

During the years boys and girls are in the elementary grades, the rate of increase of height tends to decelerate. It follows a period of acceleration and then hesitates and seems to anticipate a further increase in height with the onset of puberty. This increase comes approximately between the ages of nine and twelve for girls and eleven and fourteen for boys. During childhood, "the rate of weight gain is nearly twice the rate of height gain." [4]

At this time muscles are developing slowly, both the large and the smaller muscles, and the child's arms, trunk and legs are gaining in thickness and in breadth. As the child proceeds through the elementary school, he begins to look less and less fragile as compared with his general appearance the day he entered kindergarten or grade one.

These are the years when both boys and girls are interested in developing their motor skills. For one thing, as Watson indicated, boys and girls become "aware of what others think of them, including their status in motor skills. A high premium is placed upon motor skills by older children." [5] Related to the development of these skills also is increasing effectiveness of the child in co-ordination. During the latter part of childhood, boys seem to surpass girls in muscular strength, in speed, and

[2] D. A. Prescott, *The Child in the Educative Process* (New York, McGraw-Hill Book Company, 1957), p. 377.

[3] Association for Supervision and Curriculum Development, *Learning and the Teacher*, 1959 Yearbook (Washington, D.C., National Education Association, 1959), p. 35.

[4] H. Thompson, "Physical Growth," in L. Carmichael, ed., *Manual of Child Psychology*, 2nd ed. (New York, John Wiley and Sons, Inc., 1954), p. 307.

[5] R. I. Watson, *Psychology of the Child* (New York, John Wiley and Sons, Inc., 1959), p. 474.

in co-ordination of gross body movement. Girls, on the other hand, generally excel in manual dexterity.[6] This contributes to the fact that boys turn to sports, and girls to sewing, embroidery, and knitting.

Blair and Burton describe the years from nine to twelve as a period when most children have "increased manual dexterity, increased strength, and increased resistance to fatigue." [7]

Although teachers in the elementary school are unable to observe skeletal development as easily or as accurately as they can height and weight, recent research supports the fact that it is the best indicator of the child's physical maturity. It has been used in determining the anatomical age, which is "the degree of physical development in terms of the eruption of the permanent teeth or the hardening of the bones." [8] Psychologists, school physicians, and nurses, working with classroom teachers in many school systems, study X-ray charts to furnish more information about the growth and development of the individual child.

It has been found that the many bones in a child's hand continue to increase in size and to alter in shape. The final wrist bone generally forms in girls when they are about nine and in boys when they are about ten. Such a fact can be used to appraise and to predict a child's physical development. Also, during this period the bones in a child's face grow and give the effect of growing maturity. Deciduous teeth are replaced by permanent ones.

Teachers must be sensitive to the fact that children's eyes are not fully developed when boys and girls enter the elementary school. Some children are eight or nine before complete development occurs. Prior to this time, children tend to be far-sighted.

The authors wish to emphasize the need for placing more emphasis on physical inspections or examinations for boys and girls who are having academic difficulties. Inattention, forgetfulness, irritability, or academic difficulty in general frequently results from lack of adequate nourishment or some physical disability that may not be easily observed.

In studying the physical development of boys and girls in the elementary school, emphasis must be placed on the *individual* growth patterns of *individual* boys and girls. Averages are dangerous, and must be used only as guides. As Gallagher wrote, "There is no average boy. . . . It is better to upset the scales than to upset the home." [9]

The study of intellectual growth cannot be separated from that of

[6] A. Anastasi and J. P. Foley, *Differential Psychology* (New York, The Macmillan Company, 1949), p. 648.

[7] A. W. Blair and W. H. Burton, *Growth and Development of the Preadolescent* (New York, Appleton-Century-Crofts, Inc., 1951), p. 139.

[8] K. C. Garrison, *Growth and Development* (New York, Longmans, Green & Co., Inc., 1952), p. 86.

[9] R. V. Gallagher, "There Is No Average Boy," *Atlantic Monthly*, Vol. 183 (March, 1949), p. 43.

physical growth. During the same years that a child is developing physically, his mental concepts and skills are taking form. Studies have indicated a positive correlation between physical maturity and intellectual ability although, of course, caution should be exercised in making sweeping generalizations from this coincidence. Studies of Stanford-Binet scales correlated with indices of physical maturity have borne out this statement.

While considerable research has been focused on the mental growth and development of boys and girls, the results of these studies have tended to be less conclusive than one would hope. This inconclusiveness results primarily from difficulty in defining intelligence and in measuring it effectively. There have been many definitions of intelligence, such as: (1) ability to adjust to one's environment; (2) ability to cope with material found on an academic aptitude test; and (3) "the degree of availability of one's experiences for the solution of immediate problems and the anticipation of future ones." [10]

Most intelligence tests today furnish more than one score because of the difficulty in defining what this thing is that we call "intelligence." Data seem to indicate that academic aptitude results have more predictive value for elementary school-age boys and girls than they do for preschool children. Watson pointed out that the score made by a child of eight years of age correlates about .72 with his score at the age of eighteen. [11] For very young children, Gesell has developed a DQ (development quotient) showing the percentage of so-called normal development identifiable at a given age.[12]

In studying the progress of the mental growth of boys and girls in an elementary school, one must never lose sight of two basic principles: (1) that the range in mental abilities found in a first-grade classroom is broad and that this range continues to widen during each succeeding grade; and (2) that children grow mentally according to their own individual pace. Teachers must be basically interested in *individual* mental growth patterns of *individual* boys and girls. The curve of intellectual ability tends to increase with chronological age, but the shape of the curve of growth is a basis of considerable disagreement. Mental growth curves for individual children based on academic measurement may vary from one test to another.[13]

Considerable study has been given to the identification of the thought processes of children in the elementary grades. Piaget, who used the clinical approach to study children in Switzerland and who contributed significantly to the thinking in child growth and development in this

[10] H. H. Goddard, "What is Intelligence?" *Journal of Social Psychology*, Vol. 24 August, 1946), p. 68.
[11] R. I. Watson, *op. cit.*, p. 494.
[12] A. Gesell and C. S. Amatruda, *Developmental Diagnosis*, 2nd ed. (New York, Paul B. Hoeber, Inc., 1947), p. 111.
[13] Academic aptitude testing will be discussed in Chapter Fifteen.

country, identified the following stages: (1) sensory-motor activities; (2) egocentric thought; and (3) rational thought. He believed that youth did not develop rational, logical thought until between the ages of seven and eleven—when they develop an understanding of the concept of relationship.[14]

Teachers must be sensitive to the fact that when children enter the first grade, they are more ready to move ahead in developing additional concepts and understandings than were children a quarter century ago. Today children develop early many concepts of time, of place, and of things from television and other experiences. Teachers must learn to utilize these experiences in providing meaningful learning activities.

Current research upholds the belief that children in the elementary grades are able to identify objectives, to solve problems, to think critically, and to be creative as long as learning experiences are appropriate to the children's stages of development. Individualized, yet interrelated, physical and mental growth patterns for each boy and girl must guide teachers and pupils in planning activities.

Emotional development in each child is also interrelated with his physical and mental growth. Emotion is derived from the Latin word *emovere*, which means "to move out." Emotions are sometimes described as reactions or responses to external happenings. Garrison defines emotions as "responses developing through the continuous interaction of the child's innate constitution and environmental forces and conditions." [15]

Children tend to display different emotional characteristics at different age levels. Anger in small children is expressed frequently through tantrums or crying, but in older children, partly as the result of social pressures, anger is expressed through fussiness, sulking, or just being generally disagreeable. Watson in describing the increase in the deviousness with which older children express their anger wrote,

> Just as in adults a whisper may take the place of a blow, an upraised eyebrow the place of a scream, a joke in the place of name-calling, so too, in later childhood, these and other subtle forms of anger may appear.[16]

There seems to be a tendency among older children toward more verbalism to express anger, rather than overt physical violence.

Fear is a dominant emotion in young children. A. O. England studied one hundred children whose average age was about eleven years and eight months. He asked these youngsters to draw illustrations of the most important events in their lives. Not a mention was made or implied in the instructions that fear should appear in the pictures; yet "27.4% of the most

---

[14] J. Piaget, *Factors Determining Human Behavior* (Cambridge, Mass., Harvard University, 1937); and J. Piaget, *The Origins of Intelligence in Children* (New York, International Universities Press, 1952).

[15] K. C. Garrison, *op. cit.*, p. 157.

[16] R. I. Watson, *op. cit.*, p. 477.

important events of their lives were composed of fear experiences or representations." [17] Pratt reported a study that showed that children in the
upper grades (grade five through grade eight) reported both more fears
and different fears than did the children in the first four grades.[18] As
children grow older, they tend to be more apprehensive regarding ordinary
daily occurrences and less reactive to imaginary fears. As Almy writes:
"It appears that around the age of eight or nine shifts in differentiation
and integration occur, which tend to alter the child's emotional and social
outlook." [19]

There is always the danger that children, as they grow older, tend to
repress their emotional responses abnormally. Children naturally encounter
many situations that cause them to be frightened, angry, and jealous. "If
a teacher is sensitive both to [a child's] continuing baby needs and his wish
to be worthy of his new status, school comes to be a very positive force in
his life." [20]

There is a very high correlation between one's increasing emotional
maturity and the healthfulness of his social environment. Children must be
helped to control their emotions normally and to channel them into constructive activities. Children need help during their years of emotional
growing-up. They tend to reject adult standards and turn to their peers
for emotional empathy. One cannot, however, minimize the value of a
child's feeling of security in his home life and the importance of his developing a positive and realistic self-concept. A child who feels secure at home;
is protected from unnecessary and excessive emotional situations; enjoys
a satisfying relationship with his peers; and develops a positive self-concept,
is likely to be the child who achieves positive emotional growth. The
importance of such sound emotional growth can be seen from the fact
that,

Of every one hundred school students in the United States, four will end in a
mental hospital; one will turn to crime; eight will be shattered by emotional
breakdowns.[21]

**Whenever a child does not experience satisfying physical, mental, and
emotional growth, his social maturity may well be in jeopardy.** The roles
of the home, the community, the teacher, and the child's peers are extremely
important in helping any child to develop social maturity. His own self-
concept, however, is probably the most important. A child who learns to

[17] A. O. England, "Non-structured Approach to the Study of Children's Fears,"
Journal of Clinical Psychology, Vol. 2 (October, 1946), p. 366.
[18] K. C. Pratt, "A Study of Fears of Rural Children," *Journal of Genetic Psychology*,
Vol. 67 (December, 1945), pp. 179–194.
[19] M. Almy, *Child Development* (N.Y., Holt, Rinehart, and Winston, Inc., c. 1955),
p. 347.
[20] *Ibid.*, p. 349.
[21] H. E. Bullis and E. E. O'Malley, *Human Relations in the Classroom* (Wilmington,
Del., Delaware Society for Mental Hygiene, 1948), p. 2.

know his strengths and his weaknesses, who learns to develop these strengths and to live with his limitations, who is made to feel that he is loved and valued, and that he has a significant contribution to make is usually the child who grows socially. Such a child experiences little difficulty in moving from egocentricity to socialization.

The years a child spends in the elementary grades are frequently referred to as the peer-group age. The importance of a child's socialization with his peers must not be minimized. Here he tests his horizons. He learns how to get along with others, how to meet frustrations, how to develop leadership traits, and how to feel and express empathy with others. These are the years of a child's life when he is seeking independence—an opportunity to try his wings. Peer groups furnish him this opportunity.

Children tend to choose friends similar to themselves or at least similar to their concepts of what they would like to be. Davitz, in a study of the sociometric choices of a group of eleven-year-old boys, found a tendency of children to identify with those characteristics that they would like to possess.[22]

One of the most important phases in the development of social maturity in a child is the growth of his values and attitudes. During the ages from eight to twelve, value judgments in boys and girls tend to develop rapidly. MacRae discusses research data from American children concerning Piaget's earlier observation that,

a child's morality changes as he grows older, from strict and specific moral rules deriving force from parental authority to more general principles supported by groups of equals.[23]

There is a need for both peer groups and a healthful parent-child relationship in helping children develop sound values and attitudes. Both overly strict and overly indulgent parents are detrimental to a child in his growth toward co-operation and social empathy.

A child's growth must be viewed as a whole—as an integrated unit. One must never minimize the total interrelationships that occur within the individual child in his physical, mental, emotional, and social growth and development. These areas are so closely interrelated that a barrier in one is likely to hinder the normal development of another. A cardinal principle for effective teaching is that every teacher must be sensitive to the total growth and development of each boy and girl in his classroom— physical growth and mental, emotional, and social development.

Both heredity and environment are important factors in the individual's development. The relative importance of these factors has been the basis for considerable research involving twins and adopted children. There

    [22] J. R. Davitz, "Social Perception and Sociometric Choice of Children," *Journal of Abnormal and Social Psychology*, Vol. 50 (March, 1955), pp. 173–176.
    [23] D. MacRae, Jr., "A Test of Piaget's Theories of Moral Development," *Journal of Abnormal and Social Psychology*, Vol. 49 (January, 1954), p. 14.

seems currently to be no doubt in the minds of the researchers that both heredity and environment play significant roles in the total development of boys and girls. Through the process of heredity, each child acquires specific traits and potentialities. The degree to which these potentialities are realized is directly related to the child's experiences and environment. As Gesell observed,

> Growth is a unifying concept which resolves the dualism of heredity and environment. Environmental factors support, inflect, and modify, but they do not generate the progressions of development.[24]

Variation in tested intelligence among school children has been accounted for (according to one set of data) as follows, "seventy-five percent by heredity; twenty-one percent by environment; and four percent by accidental factors." [25]

The concept of readiness is very important. From studies of our cultural processes and of child growth and development, we know that there are certain periods in a child's life when he probably is best able to experience new learning situations. These studies have led to the development of a concept of *readiness:* the sum total of a child's patterns and abilities at any given time. A child's readiness involves his intellectual, physical, emotional, and social development, his needs and his goals, and his learned concepts and skills. Readiness tends to change from day to day as the child passes through new experiences.

If one were to be so absurd as to try to teach a five-year-old child to drive the family car, he would find the child not ready physically or intellectually. On the other hand it might be equally unwise to teach a seventy-five-year-old person to drive a car. "Too soon" and "too late" are equally ineffectual. Teachers are constantly looking for "teaching moments"—moments when the child's receptiveness is at its optimum peak. As William James aptly phrased it, "the teacher must strike while the iron is hot." Cronbach points to the learning of French as an example:

> A child can learn the French language early and naturally at the age of two, if he hears his parents speak it daily. Another child, not exposed to French until high school, finds the learning difficult and may never twist his tongue into the proper pronunciation of "u" and "r". Long disuse of the muscular combinations for these sounds (which he was making, once, in his infantile babbling) has deprived him of some readiness.[26]

During the discussion of child growth and development in this chapter, we have emphasized the importance of individual growth patterns; however, one must not minimize the need for studying the child latitudinally

[24] A. Gesell, "The Octogenesis of Infant Behavior" in L. Carmichael, ed., *Manual of Child Psychology*, 1st ed. (New York, John Wiley & Sons, 1946), p. 316.
[25] L. J. Cronbach, *Educational Psychology* (New York, Harcourt, Brace, & World, Inc., 1954), p. 210.
[26] *Ibid.*, p. 221.

as well as longitudinally. While there is no such thing as an "average" child, there are "average" growth patterns for each age level. A child psychologist or a teacher studying an eight-year-old boy or girl should be interested in studying, not only the past experiences of the child, but also his degree of development as compared with the average characteristics of eight-year-old children in general. Anderson reported that

one job for the future is to view systematically what we know about age changes and then fill in the gaps, both by cross-section and by longitudinal techniques in order to obtain a complete picture of what happens with time.[27]

Teachers in viewing the child as he compares with average patterns of behavior for a particular chronological age *must* constantly heed the warning that children *cannot* be categorized, that there is no "average" boy or girl, that these characteristic patterns must be used only as guides, and that each of the characteristics described can probably be found at any age in any classoom in any typical elementary school in this country.

Age six has been described by many authorities as the age of change, the age of transition.

At five he was such a well-organized child, at home with himself and at home with the world. But as early as the age of five-and-a-half, be began to be brash and combative in some of his behavior, as though he were at war with himself and with the world. At other times he was hesitant, dawdling, indecisive, and then again overdemanding and explosive, with strangely contradictory spurts of affection and antagonism . . . The six-year-old proves to be not a bigger and better five-year-old. He is a different child because he is a changing child.[28]

At the age of seven, much to the joy of parents and teachers, there is a kind of quieting down.

The seven-year-old goes into lengthening periods of calmness and of self-absorption, during which he works his impressions over and over, oblivious to the outer world. It is the assimilative age, a time for salting down accumulative experiences and for relating new experiences to the old. The seven-year-old is a good listener. He likes to read and likes to hear a twice-told tale . . . He resents intrusions . . . [He experiences] occasional brooding, heedlessness, minor strains of sadness and complainingness, sulks, mutterings, shynesses, and a certain pensiveness. . . . He is increasingly sensitive to the attitude of others. . . . He shows a new interest in his father and in playmates of an older age. . . . Tantrums are vanishing. Instead he removes himself from the scene through fits of sullenness, or through a hasty retreat with a slam of the door. . . . He is susceptible to praise. He is sensitive to the point of tears to disapproval.[29]

An eight-year-old seems more grown up according to adult standards. Individual differences are great among the eight-year-olds, for each child

---

[27] J. E. Anderson, "Child Development Research: The Next Twenty-five Years," Society for Research in Child Development, *Child Development,* Vol. 31 (March, 1960), p. 193.

[28] A. Gesell and F. L. Ilg, *op. cit.,* pp. 88–89.

[29] *Ibid.,* pp. 131–138.

burgeons in so many different directions. The child is growing up rapidly. Teachers in the third and fourth grades become well aware of the fact that they have extremely heterogeneous groups and that they must be sensitive to the differences among the children and to the many differences often occurring in the same child daily. As Gesell and Ilg write,

> He is less brooding, . . . more centrifugal, . . . more rapid in his responses. He may be characterized by speediness, expansiveness, and evaluativeness. He is in general healthier and less fatiguable. . . . Boys and girls are beginning to move apart. . . . The eight-year-old listens closely when adults talk among themselves. He watches their facial expressions; he keeps looking and listening for cues and indicators in the social environment. . . . He is naively docile and compliant. . . . He is a little sensitive about being told too directly what to do. He prefers a cue or hint. He expects and asks for praise. . . . But he does not want to be joked about his shortcomings. His sense of self is becoming a sense of status.[30]

The nine-year-old is in-between.

> He is no longer a mere child; nor is he yet a youth. . . . Self-motivation is the cardinal characteristic of the nine-year-old. . . . The [nine-year-old] is able to summon reserves of energy and renews his attack for repeated trials. This is due to the greater maturity of his whole behavior equipment. No wonder that he is such an excellent pupil, ready to tackle anything that lies reasonably within his powers.[31]

To a teacher who understands the characteristics of nine-year-old youth, a nine-year-old child is a joy to teach. Generally he is skilled in self-criticism and in the criticism of others. He is honest, insists on fair play, and enjoys assuming a feeling of responsibility.

At ten sex differences are becoming clearly evident. A ten-year-old girl tends to have many characteristics quite different from a ten-year-old boy. The girl is becoming interested in the opposite sex and is beginning to think of her future marriage and family. She appears much more matured. Gesell and Ilg describe the ten-year-old child as,

> relaxed and casual, yet alert. He has himself and his skills in hand; he takes things in his stride; he works with executive speed and likes the challenge of mental arithmetic. He often shows a genuine capacity to budget his time and his energy. His general behavior and his demeanors are more modulated . . . The ten-year-old is peculiarly receptive to social information, to broadening ideas, and to prejudice, good and bad. It is relatively easy to appeal to his reason. He is ready to participate in elementary discussions of social problems.[32]

The eleven- and twelve-year-olds continue to take on adult characteristics, although the unpredictableness of the true adolescent is becoming evident and is most confusing to teachers and parents. During these later elementary school years, more and more "a full grown body is entrusted

[30] *Ibid.*, pp. 160–168.
[31] *Ibid.*, pp. 188–189.
[32] *Ibid.*, pp. 213–214.

to an unexperienced mind." [33] This inevitably helps to make adolescence a difficult period for both young people and adults.

Additional research on how the child grows and develops is needed. At the Twenty-fifth Anniversary Meeting of the Society for Research in Child Development, Anderson reported,

> As one views the mass of data as a whole, one is struck by the incompleteness of the data horizontally in relation to function and process and vertically in relation to time.[34]

The following specific areas were mentioned at this meeting as areas where research will be concentrated during the next twenty-five years: (1) changes which take place with age or time in the growing organism of the child; (2) "types and amounts of stimulation needed by the growing child at various periods of his development in order to make the most effective use of his resources and to develop a good personality"; (3) procedures for helping children who have experienced poor environments and what the "end" or "long-term" effects are of both negatively and positively introduced conditions; (4) analysis of "stimulation in reference to the 'flow concept' of human behavior, or the effect of iteration and continuity of stimulation upon the organism"; (5) study in "moving away from the specific patterns, skills and activities, with which we have so far been concerned, to an examination of the way in which the different patterns, activities, and attitudes are fitted together into a total system of behavior or are integrated within the time schedule into a pattern of living"; and (6) a re-evaluation of the role creativity plays in child development.[35]

Stuart at this meeting, emphasized one further need for research during the next twenty-five years:

> to promote comparable studies of different groups of children racially, nationally, and geographically with full consideration of the differences between them in environmental factors, including cultures and socio-economic circumstances and in knowing the adaptations made by these children to these different circumstances.[36]

LEARNING ABOUT THE CHILD

The job of the teacher to meet the needs of his boys and girls and to provide individualized, meaningful experiences is not an easy one. The job of the child is not an easy one either, for a child passing through the first six grades of any elementary school has much to learn. Teachers are eager

[33] G. G. Jenkins, H. Shacter, and W. W. Bauer, *These Are Your Children* (Chicago, Scott, Foresman and Company, 1953), p. 211.
[34] J. E. Anderson, *op. cit.*, p. 193.
[35] *Ibid.*, pp. 193–198.
[36] H. C. Stuart, "Child Development Research: The Next Twenty-Five Years," *Child Development* (March, 1960), p. 207.

to have each child achieve these learnings; every parent wants his or her son or daughter to do so; and every child basically wants to learn. Teaching, therefore, must be varied, flexible, and creative. To do this every teacher must secure as much information as possible regarding each boy and each girl in his classroom.

Many sources of information are available to the classroom teacher, for no functionary in the school spends more time with each youngster. No one else is in a position to observe each child in situations as varied. The authors would therefore like to think through with teachers the varied procedures for collecting, for recording, and for utilizing the data available. Each teacher should learn about the past, the present, and the potential future of each of his pupils. Some of the most commonly used procedures are identified on the following pages.

Study of Records. Early in the fall of each year, a conscientious teacher will study whatever cumulative records are available regarding his boys and girls. A teacher must be cautious at all times to use records positively, not negatively—not as a means to identify the boy or the girl who has been troublesome the year before so that the teacher is "ready" to outsmart him —but rather to find answers to the child's apparent pattern of behavior, to identify information that will help the child. The comprehensiveness of the records will naturally vary according to the degree to which the records have been developed within the school system and according to the educational placement of the child. Some of the pertinent questions to which teachers might find answers that can be translated into meaningful experiences are: (1) What range do I appear to have in general academic ability among my pupils? (2) How many appear to be retarded in any way? (3) What are the chief areas of academic difficulty found among this group? (4) What range is there in socio-economic strata? (5) What health problems are apparent? (6) What kinds of information do I have regarding the needs, the interests, and the social adjustment of each of my pupils? (7) Who are the pupils who seem to be the ones who will need the most help immediately? (8) What are the apparent strengths of each child? (9) What previous experiences have these boys and girls had that will serve as motivating factors in planning future school activities? [37]

Initial Talks. After a classroom teacher has reviewed carefully the records for each of his pupils, he should next devote considerable time to becoming acquainted with each boy and girl in his class. Informal talks with each child as frequently as possible and early in the fall will help the pupil feel that the teacher is interested in him, will establish a needed rapport between the teacher and the child, and will gain helpful information to assist the teacher in understanding the youngster and in planning

[37] F. C. Rosecrance and V. D. Hayden, *School Guidance and Personnel Services* (Boston, Allyn and Bacon, Inc., 1960), p. 54.

meaningful activities. Time spent in getting acquainted with boys and girls, in the opinion of creative teachers, is never time wasted.

These talks can be held in the classroom before or after school, in the cafeteria during lunch duty, in the halls, on the playground, or at any time an opportunity presents itself. They need not be long, nor are they usually clinical in nature. Often during a casual conversation with a child, however, a strong feeling may be made quite clear. One day a third-grade boy brought to class a small kitten. The teacher, in talking to the youngster about the kitten, suggested that it might be wise for Jimmy to leave the kitten at home so that it would not be harmed. The expression on the child's face suddenly changed from one of excitement to one of concern. He looked up at the teacher and said, "If I don't bring my kitten, who will be my friend?" As was indicated here, many clues for teachers develop unexpectedly during these informal chats. Teachers must be constantly aware, however, that there is no one procedure for collecting data and that we are constantly looking for ways to collect more data to support or to refute what we already know.

Observation. Rousseau wrote, "Watch nature long, and observe your pupil carefully before you say a word to him." [38] Observation is probably one of the most valuable procedures a teacher can use. A young doctor once commented to one of the authors that among the most valuable courses he had while he was in medical school was a course essentially in observation. Medical students sat around a table with a professor; people suffering from various ailments were asked to come into the room, to walk around the table, and to go out a farther door. Each student was directed to observe the symptoms, to record them, and to indicate what additional data he would need before he could diagnose the illness.

For years teachers in elementary schools have observed their pupils conscientiously. They have watched for paleness, rashes, flushed faces, cold hands, and bruises. These are very important, but they are not enough. The teacher should note significant changes that may occur in the behavior pattern of any child and should help determine the reasons for the changes. He must not overlook Debbie, who sits quietly by herself most of the time, not entering into the gaiety of others in her class. Her withdrawn characteristics need investigating. Jimmy, who had been the class clown for weeks, suddenly becomes sullen and surly. Martha is quick to anger; Jane cries easily. Jo fell asleep in the middle of the morning and again right after lunch. Behavior patterns that are not typical of an average child of a given age or patterns that change abruptly in any child and without apparent cause are worthy of observation and recording.

Anecdotal Records. As was just mentioned, a teacher must observe, but he must also carefully record his observations. These recordings are identi-

[38] J. J. Rousseau, *Émile* (New York, D. Appleton and Company, 1898), p. 58.

fied as anecdotal records. They are word pictures of samples of behavior that may or may not have significance. They are snapshots of boys or girls in action. An occasional temper tantrum, an occasional tear, or an occasional pout means very little, but a recurring pattern warrants study.

There is a "right" and a "wrong" way to record observations to make them the most meaningful. Let us consider a few of the "Do's" a teacher might follow.

1. A teacher should carefully separate the recording of his observations from his interpretations and suggested action. Notice the following example in which the three headings are used. An *interpretation* often is not recorded until several observations have been made. A *suggested action* is frequently withheld until considerable data can be checked.

2. Recorded observations should be objective. Loaded words, such as "lazy," "silly," "fickle," "childish," or "difficult," mean different things to different people and are meaningless unless one knows well the observer and recorder. Direct conversation plus an exact description of what happened are much more meaningful.

3. Boys and girls should be observed in a variety of situations, such as in the classroom, on the playground, before and after school in group situations, in individual study and play. The more varied a picture a teacher can gain, the more information he will have to compare with other data secured.

4. Teachers should observe and record descriptions of favorable as well as unfavorable behavior. Too frequently the emphasis in anecdotal records is on unacceptable behavior. This tends to distort the teacher's perspective and fails to give a fair picture of the child. In New York City, studies showed that,

entries of incidents showing desirable, passive, inconspicuous behavior are just as important in giving a true picture of the child as incidents of undesirable or dramatic behavior.[39]

5. There should be observation and recording of behavior of all types of pupils: the academically skillful and the retarded, the socially aggressive and the socially withdrawn, the emotionally disturbed and the well adjusted, the physically handicapped and the physically well co-ordinated.

6. All anecdotal records must be dated, should give the time of day and the description of the situation, and should include the name of the recorder.

Teachers should be encouraged to write as many anecdotal records as seems possible and helpful. An administrative edict, however, may defeat the program. If a teacher is shown the value of making these recordings, his willingness and co-operation are readily secured.

[39] Board of Education of the City of New York. *A Guide to the Use of Anecdotal Records*, Educational Research Bulletin, Evaluation Series Number 1 (New York, Board of Education of the City of New York, 1955), p. 9.

The following is an excerpt from an anecdotal record for Timothy D., a student in the fifth grade.

ANECDOTAL RECORD

NAME: Timothy D.   AGE: 11   GRADE: Fifth   TEACHER: Miss J_____

Date	Record of Observation	Interpretation	Action Suggested
10/20/60	Timothy arrived ten minutes late. He sat down in a chair at the table. No other pupil was near him. He sat and stared out the window. He made no effort to join his reading group until the teacher asked him to do so. He read well when invited to read.		
10/24/60	Timothy asked to stay inside when the others went out to play. He complained of a headache, but the nurse after examining him, could find no indication of illness. Timothy later said, "I feel O.K. now. I just didn't want to go out with the others."		
10/27/60	When the pupils discussed the trip to the new industrial plant in town, Timothy refused to participate. He said, "I don't want to go on a silly old trip. My dad works at the plant. I've been there."	The teacher studied a sociogram of the group. No one selected Timothy to be on his committee. Timothy's test scores were also reviewed. He shows above average potentialities. The teacher is interested in learning whether Timothy is shy, is on the defensive because the other pupils reject him, or whether he is disinterested because of his home situation.	

ANECDOTAL RECORD (Cont.)

NAME: Timothy D.   AGE: 11   GRADE: Fifth   TEACHER: Miss J_____

Date	Record of Observation	Interpretation	Action Suggested
11/1/60	Timothy was reported to the principal by the school patrol captain who saw him throw his report card in the rubbish container.		The teacher plans to continue to observe Timmie. He will also capitalize on Timothy's competencies and interests. He will try to visit the home and talk with the parents. He will attempt to improve Timmie's self-concept by involving him in a self-evaluation of his behavior.

Autobiographies. When boys and girls reach the age when they are able to write about themselves, they should be encouraged to do so. Before they are able to write, they can talk about themselves. The introspective approach to understanding children is gaining in favor as one more means of securing data. As Mortensen and Schmuller conclude, "It is not behavior, as commonly interpreted, which is revealed in the autobiography, but what is, perhaps, even more important, the attitudes behind the behavior." [40]

Pupils should be encouraged to write freely about pleasant and unpleasant experiences in their lives. Autobiographies vary in form, for they may be structured or unstructured. While the age of the boys and girls helps the teacher to determine which is the preferable procedure, probably both methods should be used as the child progresses through the elementary grades. In unstructured autobiographies, the child is given more freedom in deciding what he is going to write and what emphases he will place on the incidents presented.

Structured autobiographies include a series of questions to which pupils are asked to react. (The following questions should be rephrased depending on the age level of the child.) (1) Where were you born? (2) Do you

[40] D. G. Mortensen and A. M. Schmuller, *Guidance in Today's Schools* (New York, John Wiley and Sons, Inc., 1959), p. 170.

think the location of your birth influenced in any way your life? If so, how? (3) What information have you learned about your grandparents and others of your ancestors that interested you particularly? (4) Did this information about your ancestors and the lives they lived influence your life in any way? If so, how? (5) What early experiences in school do you recall? Why? (6) What memories of your early life at home do you have? Why? (7) What are some of your most pleasant experiences? (8) What are some of your most unpleasant experiences? (9) What friends have made the most lasting impressions on you? Why? (10) What are your hobbies and interests? (11) What are your future goals and plans? Have they changed any from a year ago? If so, how and why? (12) How do you hope to achieve these plans? (13) What in your life do you value most? (14) If you could do anything you wanted to, what would you do? (15) What else would you like to write about? [41]

In the elementary grades boys and girls, in addition to writing and telling about themselves, may also be asked to finish such sentences as, My favorite person is ——————. My most exciting experience was ——————. The saddest thing that has ever happened to me is ——————.

Children should be encouraged to write freely, and their confidences must be completely respected. If your goal is to know about the child, this is not the time to insist upon perfect grammar, punctuation, and handwriting.

Sharing Periods. Considerable information regarding boys and girls may be gained through effective use of sharing periods. Interests, values, biases, and attitudes are frequently identified as youngsters in the early grades talk about things of interest to them.

Diaries and Daily Logs. Pupils should also be encouraged occasionally to record their daily activities for a period of time. Many times the information reflected in these records is as revealing to the child as it is to the parents and teachers.

Standardized Tests.[42] Another procedure which is used extensively in the elementary schools is the use of standardized tests. These furnish more objective data and can be helpful in supporting or refuting the more subjective data collected. Teachers must always be cautious of the fact, however, that test results alone do *not* give us the answers. They merely contribute additional facets to the total picture of the child. Tests must be carefully selected and must be employed in relation to specific purposes.

Sociometry. One of the most effective pupil-centered instruments is sociometry or the use of sociograms. While it is true that teachers through careful observations of the behavior of boys and girls in a given classroom can often gain a relatively accurate picture of the degree to which pupils

[41] F. C. Rosecrance and V. D. Hayden, *op. cit.*, pp. 70–71.
[42] Standardized tests will be discussed in more detail in Chapter fifteen.

are accepted or rejected by their peers, an additional dimension is added by a sociogram—the way a pupil would like to see himself accepted. Sociometry is a study of group relationships, and a sociogram is a pictorial diagram of social interrelationships.

The current relatively wide use of sociograms in the elementary school resulted from a series of experimental studies in group relationships and inter-group education, sponsored by the American Council on Education.[43] These studies reinforced the beliefs of Moreno [44] and Jennings [45] of the importance of groups in promoting emotional and social maturity in the individual.

If a teacher wishes to use this procedure, he may request each of his boys and girls to list on a slip of paper (in order of preference) the names of three classmates with whom the boy or girl would enjoy working on a committee or with whom he would like to plan a class project. From studying the data collected, the teacher can see clearly who chooses whom; who are the so-called "stars," the most popular students in the class; who comprise the "triangles" or cliques; who are the "pairs;" and who are the "isolates." He can identify those boys and girls who are seldom if ever chosen and therefore, perhaps, whose personal desires are frustrated daily.

To secure the most helpful data, rapport must have been established between the class and the teacher; the pupils of the group must have known one another for some time; the situation must be a real one; and the teacher must carry through on his announced plans to use the student choices just as soon as possible. Research has indicated that pupils of all ages will respond more honestly to questions related to real situations rather than to hypothetical ones, such as, "With whom would you like to travel to the moon?"

Rating Scales. Since the days of World War I when rating scales gained their initial importance, rating scales of many types have been widely used in the schools of this country. The three most common forms are: (1) graphic scales; (2) the common check list; and (3) descriptions of behavior. While it is possible to purchase copies of professionally structured scales, the authors believe that more effective and more functional utilization of these scales would occur if elementary school staffs were to develop their own in terms of: (1) types of information desired; (2) a careful defining of terms used to identify the traits observed; and (3) the identification of overt behavior representative of certain traits.

One merely needs to ask a group of teachers about the "co-operation" or "dependability" of a certain child to find a variety of reactions, for each

[43] H. Jennings, *Sociometry in Group Relations* (Washington, D.C., American Council on Education, 1948).

[44] J. L. Moreno, *Who Shall Survive?* (New York, Beacon House, 1953).

[45] H. Jennings, "Sociometry Groupings in Relation to Child Development," in Association for Supervision and Curriculum Development, *Fostering Mental Health in Our Schools* (Washington, D.C., National Education Association, 1950).

teacher is possibly defining the terms differently and is seeing Jimmy or Mary in different situations and acting under different conditions. Rating scales, therefore, must be used cautiously and in reference to specific situations. To minimize subjective judgment many schools average the ratings of several staff members in reference to any one child, such as, the rating of the previous teacher the child has had; the rating of the current teacher; that of the art, music, and/or health and physical education supervisors; and that of the principal.

In the opinion of the authors, however, the most effective use of rating scales in the upper grades includes the involvement of the boys and girls in the discussion of the traits identified by the school staff as desirable and in requesting each of them to rate himself on each trait. At times the discrepancies between the teachers' rating and the students' self-rating may be used as a basis for individual conferences. Such self-evaluation and subsequent discussion many times will help the boys and girls develop more realistic self-concepts and will help the teacher plan improved learning activities.

Road blocks or danger signals that teachers must heed in the rating of boys and girls are tendencies toward personal bias, toward a "halo effect," and toward a central or average tendency. We like a boy or a girl; so we rate him high on all traits. On the contrary, we are not equally fond of another child; so we tend to rate him low on all traits. Some teachers have a tendency to avoid extremes and to rate everybody near the average. In some schools, manuals for teachers have been developed to help new teachers orient themselves to the thinking of the school staff in the use of rating scales.

Home Visitations. The importance of the home is not minimized by most educators today. Each child is a product of his home. To understand the child, teachers need to understand the home from which the child comes and to know how the child himself sees his home situation. Although home visitations from some member of the school staff are helpful, elementary school staffs must not lose sight of the fact that careful planning of these visitations is necessary. It seems wise to designate one or two people to visit the home and for the other staff members to work closely with the person or persons designated so as to profit from the information secured.

Whoever visits the home needs to do everything possible to establish rapport with the parents. Appointments must be carefully made; a detailed knowledge of the child must be gained by the visitor prior to his visit; visits should be made not only when the child is in some difficulty; the visitor must be sufficiently well informed regarding the school program so that he is able to interpret the school to the parent as well as the home to the school staff; and the visitor must be constantly sensitive to the needs and the feelings of the parents.

Much can be gained from these visits that will be of help to a con-scientious, creative teacher: (1) the establishment of a healthful rapport between the parents and the school staff; (2) an increasing interest on the part of parents in the school; (3) an opportunity for both the parents and the teacher to become more sensitive to the needs of the child through a sharing of information and feelings; and (4) an opportunity for both parents and the staff to plan co-operatively to help the child make wise decisions and to enjoy more satisfying self-development.[46]

Other Procedures. There are other procedures that can be used by elementary school teachers to gather additional information, such as a personal data sheet to be filled out by parents of young children or by the children themselves in the upper grades, careful examination of each pupil's written and art work, and data secured from health inspections. A teacher should work in close co-operation with the school nurse, the school physi-cian, the school dentist, and the dental hygienist to learn as much as possible about the health of each boy and girl in his class.

Case History, Case Study, and Case Conference. After a classroom teacher has employed as many of the previously listed procedures as possi-ble to secure information about his students, there comes a need to assimi-late the data and to take an over-all view. Remember that we are looking for recurring patterns and for facts that will support or refute our hypotheses. Care must be taken that we do not get so bogged down by the collected data that we cannot see the forest for the trees.

A case history is the picture of the student that is found in a well-organ-ized cumulative record. It includes data about the child's family history, his early experiences, his educational experiences, test data, his health history, facts showing his emotional and social development, his interests, values, hobbies, goals, and any other data that would be helpful in understand-ing the child.

A case study includes the examination of the interrelationship of the data collected with the hope of identifying recurring patterns of behavior or projecting possible trends. Additional data can frequently be secured through a case conference which is the sharing and the studying of in-formation by those people who have worked with the child, such as, the classroom teacher; the principal; the school social worker or attendance worker; the members of the medical team (including the school psy-chologist); any other member of the pupil personnel staff; and at times representatives from referral agencies.

These are the chief procedures that may be used to secure additional data regarding each pupil in a given classroom. A conscientious, creative teacher will use as many of these techniques as possible, for he will con-stantly seek ways of resolving the many enigmas in the behavior

---

[46] F. C. Rosecrance and V. D. Hayden, *op. cit.,* p. 65.

patterns of his boys and girls. A teacher must know the basic principles of
growth and development, must keep continually apprised of current research, and must use every method possible to learn about each of his
pupils if he is to do an effective job of teaching and if the children are to
enjoy an effective and a satisfying job of learning.

Summary

The child is the focal point of the school's program; hence teachers and
other personnel are interested in securing as much information as possible
about every boy and every girl. The authors considered in this chapter the
following basic questions: (1) What are the theories regarding society's
concept of a child? (2) What is the current thinking regarding child growth
and development? (3) How may a teacher gain as much information as
possible about each child?

A society's concept of its children generally reflects its attitudes and its
values. Attitudes considered in this chapter included the concept of (1)
the child trained to serve the state, (2) the child as a creature of evil,
(3) the child as a miniature adult, (4) the child as a pawn of labor, and
(5) the child as an active, developing organism, the center of both longitudinal and latitudinal studies.

The basic principles of the physical, intellectual, emotional, and social
growth of the child were considered separately, but with an emphasis upon
the important interrelationship of these growth patterns in each child. Also
discussed were procedures for developing readiness, the role of heredity
and environment, and specific characteristics of children in the primary
grades and those in the upper elementary grades.

The child was shown to be a complex, developing organism, and therefore every teacher must have as much information as possible about each
boy and girl in his class. Procedures for securing such data include: (1)
study of records; (2) initial talks; (3) observation; (4) anecdotal records;
(5) autobiographies; (6) sharing periods; (7) diaries and daily logs; (8)
standardized tests; (9) sociometry; (10) rating scales; (11) home visitations; (12) personal data sheet; (13) examination of a pupil's written and
art work; (14) health inspections; and (15) case histories, case studies,
and case conferences. No one procedure is sufficient, for each contributes
additional data needed to complete the essential understanding of each
boy and girl by each teacher.

STUDENT PROJECTS

1. Describe as completely as you can *your* concept of a "child." Visit an elementary school and see whether you can identify the concept of a child accepted
generally by the school staff. Show how various teachers in the school seem to
reflect differing concepts of children in the classrooms of your chosen school.

2. Through newspaper accounts and through interviews try to document the attitude of the schools and the lay public in your community toward *all* children: the intellectually gifted; those talented in art, music, dramatics, or athletics; the mentally retarded; the physically handicapped; and the juvenile delinquent. Indicate ways in which the attitude toward and opportunity for the growth and development of these boys and girls might be improved.

3. Select a child whom you know, but preferably not a member of your immediate family. See how much information you can collect regarding the child. Summarize the data as carefully and as meaningfully as you can. Indicate recurring patterns of behavior. What are the implications for teaching this child?

4. Visit an elementary school. On the basis of your observations and as a result of your reading prepare a talk for a PTA meeting documenting the statement, "To be able to teach children, teachers must understand children." Be as specific as you can, giving reasons and examples.

5. Select three different grades in an elementary school. Visit each of these grades at least three times. During your visits list as many as possible of the characteristics of physical, intellectual, emotional, and social development exhibited by the boys and girls in each classroom. Compare your listing with those found in your reading. Indicate what implications for teaching resulted from your observations

6. Select a fourth-grade class in an elementary school. Observe characteristics in the physical, intellectual, emotional, and social development of specific boys and girls who do not exhibit "average" patterns of behavior for their chronological age. Explain why children differ in their stages of development and why it is possible for a child to be matured physically and intellectually, but retarded emotionally and socially. Indicate procedures that the teacher used to meet these individual differences.

7. Visit several classes in an elementary school and note the experiences provided by the teachers to help each child develop emotionally and socially at different age levels. Try to identify ways that the teacher used to learn the current stage of development of each child. Compare the different types of experiences presented, showing the relation of each to the theories of growth and development.

8. Prepare an editorial for the local newspaper clearly showing the roles of the home, the church, and the community as well as the school in helping each youth to develop physically, intellectually, emotionally and socially. Prepare a talk also for a service club dealing with the same subject.

9. Select three boys or girls in an elementary school class and arrange to talk with them several times. Indicate the kinds of information you can learn about them merely from talking with them. What procedures would you use to supplement these facts? What implications for teaching are there in the information you gained?

10. Visit an elementary school and select a boy or a girl in an elementary school class. Try to visit the school at least three times. Write an anecdotal record based on the child's actions and reactions. Indicate clearly what you would suggest doing on the basis of the facts you recorded and why you would make such suggestions.

11. Select a class in an elementary school. Ask the teacher to identify several boys and girls who are academically alert. Study these children carefully and list behavior characteristics that they seem to exhibit. After studying them, try to formulate a working definition of "intelligence."

12. Write an autobiography. See how much information you can furnish regarding your own experiences and the reasons for your physical, intellectual, emotional, and social development. Identify your values, your attitudes, your prejudices, your strengths, and your limitations. As you review your stages of development are there any implications for effective teaching?

13. Visit an elementary school and see how many of the facts of growth you can observe by merely staying an hour. Summarize clearly your examples and indicate what implications for teaching you feel may be indicated in what you observed.

14. Visit three homes and talk to parents. List the types of information that these parents would like to know about the school program and about their children's participation in the school activities. Talk to three teachers and list the types of information they would like to have about the home. Show how each type of information desired would be helpful in the total understanding of each child.

15. Assume that you are talking to another beginning teacher and that you both are interested in visiting an elementary school classroom. You have not been in one since you left the elementary grades many years ago. You ask the classroom teacher what to look for. Summarize in detail what he might suggest you observe regarding the room, the boys and girls, and the classroom management and climate.

16. Review the literature carefully and enumerate twelve basic principles of growth and development that seem to be currently accepted. Document each of your statements with as many references as possible.

BIBLIOGRAPHY

ALMY, M., *Child Development* (New York, Holt, Rinehart and Winston, Inc., 1955).

American Association for Health, Physical Education, and Recreation, *Children in Focus*, 1954 Yearbook (Washington, D.C., National Education Association, 1954).

ANDERSON, J. E., *The Psychology of Development and Personal Adjustment* (New York, Holt, Rinehart and Winston, Inc., 1949).

Association for Supervision and Curriculum Development. *Growing Up in an Anxious Age*, 1952 Yearbook (Washington, D.C., Association for Supervision and Curriculum Development, 1952).

AUSUBEL, David P., *Theory and Problems of Child Development* (New York, Grune and Stratton, Inc., 1958).

BALDWIN, Alfred L., *Behavior and Development in Childhood* (New York, Holt, Rinehart and Winston, Inc., 1955).

BLAIR, A. W. and BURTON, W. H., *Growth and Development of the Preadolescent* (New York, Appleton-Century-Crofts, Inc., 1951).

BLUM, Henrik L. and others, *Vision Screening for Elementary Schools: The Orinda Study* (Berkeley, Calif., University of California Press, 1959).

BOSSARD, J. S., *The Sociology of Child Development*, rev. ed. (New York, Harper and Brothers, 1954).

BRECKENRIDGE, M. E. and VINCENT, E. L., *Child Development*, 3rd ed. (Philadelphia, W. B. Saunders Company, 1955).

BUHLER, Karl, *Mental Development of the Child* (New York, Humanities Press, 1954).

CARMICHAEL, L., ed., *Manual of Child Psychology*, 2nd ed. (New York, John Wiley and Sons, Inc., 1954).

CATTELL, Raymond B., *Personality and Motivation Structure and Measurement* (Yonkers, N.Y., World Book Company, 1957).

CRONBACH, L. J., *Educational Psychology* (New York, Harcourt, Brace and World, Inc., 1954).

CROW, Lester and CROW, Alice, *Human Development and Learning* (New York, American Book Company, 1956).

D'EVELYN, Katherine, *Meeting Children's Emotional Needs* (Englewood Cliffs, N.J., Prentice-Hall, Inc., 1957).

DREIKURS, Rudolf, *Psychology in the Classroom* (New York, Harper and Brothers, 1957).

EELLS, Kenneth and others, *Intelligence and Cultural Differences* (Chicago, University of Chicago Press, 1951).

FOREST, Ilse, *Child Development* (New York, McGraw-Hill Book Company, 1954).

FOSHAY, Arthur W. and WANN, Kenneth B., *Children's Social Values* (New York, Teachers College, Columbia University, 1954).

FOSTER, C. R., *Guidance for Today's Schools* (Boston, Ginn and Company, 1957).

FRANDSEN, Arden N., *How Children Learn* (New York, McGraw-Hill Book Company, 1957).

GARRISON, Karl C., *Growth and Development*, 2nd ed. (New York, Longmans, Green and Company, Inc., 1959).

GESELL, A. L. and ILG, F., *The Child From Five to Ten* (New York, Harper and Brothers, 1946).

HAVIGHURST, R. J., *Human Development and Education* (New York, Longmans, Green and Company, Inc., 1953).

HURLOCK, Elizabeth B., *Child Development*, 3rd ed. (New York, McGraw-Hill Book Company, 1956).

HYMES, J., *A Child Development Point of View* (Englewood Cliffs, N.J., Prentice-Hall, Inc., 1955).

JERSILD, Arthur T., *Child Psychology*, 4th ed. (Englewood Cliffs, N.J., Prentice-Hall, Inc., 1954).

KAPLAN, Louis, *Mental Health and Human Relations in Education* (New York, Harper and Brothers, 1959).

LANE, Howard and BEAUCHAMP, Mary, *Understanding Human Development* (Englewood Cliffs, N.J., Prentice-Hall, Inc., 1959).

LEE, J. Murray and LEE, Dorris M., *The Child and His Development* (New York, Appleton-Century-Crofts, Inc., 1958).

LINDGREN, H. C., *Educational Psychology in the Classroom* (New York, John Wiley and Sons, Inc., 1956).

LOOMIS, M. J., *Pre-Adolescent: Three Major Concerns* (New York, Appleton-Century-Crofts, Inc., 1959).

MARTIN, William E. and STENDLER, Celia B., *Child Behavior and Development*, rev. ed. (New York, Harcourt, Brace and Company, 1959).

MILLARD, C. V., *Child Growth and Development in the Elementary School Years* (Boston, D. C. Heath and Company, 1951).

MORTENSEN, Donald G. and SCHMULLER, Allen M., *Guidance in Today's Schools* (New York, John Wiley and Sons, Inc., 1959).

MOUSTAKAS, Clark E., *The Teacher and The Child* (New York, McGraw-Hill Book Company, 1956).

Mussen, P. H. and Conger, J. J., *Child Development and Personality* (New York, Harper and Brothers, 1956).

Olson, Willard C., *Child Development,* 2nd ed. (Boston, D. C. Heath and Company, 1959).

Peters, Herman J. and Farwell, Gail F., *Guidance: A Developmental Approach* (Chicago, Rand McNally and Company, 1959).

Prescott, Daniel, *The Child in the Educative Process* (New York, McGraw-Hill Book Company, 1957).

Rosecrance, F. C. and Hayden, V. D., *School Guidance and Personnel Services* (Boston, Allyn and Bacon, Inc., 1960).

Stone, Alan A. and Onque, Gloria C., *Longitudinal Studies of Child Personality* (Cambridge, Mass., Harvard University Press, 1959).

Stretch, L. B., *Guiding Child Development in the Elementary School* (Minneapolis, Minn., Education Test Bureau, 1959).

Tanner, James M. and Inhilder, Barbel, eds., *Discussions on Child Development* Vol. III (New York, International Universities Press, 1958).

Thompson, George G., *Child Psychology: Growth Trends in Psychological Adjustment* (Boston, Houghton Mifflin Co., 1952).

Thorpe, L. P. and Cruze, W. W., *Developmental Psychology* (New York, The Ronald Press Company, 1956).

Traxler, Arthur E., *Techniques of Guidance* (New York, Harper and Brothers, 1957).

Tyler, Leona E., *The Psychology of Human Differences,* 2nd ed. (New York, Appleton-Century-Crofts, Inc., 1956).

Warters, Jane, *Techniques of Counseling* (New York, McGraw-Hill Book Company, 1954).

Watson, Robert I., *Psychology of the Child* (New York, John Wiley and Sons, Inc., 1959).

White, Verna, *Studying the Individual Pupil* (New York, Harper and Brothers, 1958).

Zirbes, Laura, *Focus on Values in Elementary Education* (New York, G. P. Putnam's Sons, 1960).

CHAPTER 4

Designing the Curriculum

To PROVIDE CHILDREN with the most meaningful learning experiences is not a simple task. The function of the curriculum of the elementary school is to accomplish this task: (1) by giving general direction to specific learning experiences, and (2) by integrating them into a plan acceptable to the school and the community. Over the years, the objectives of the curriculum have varied and the philosophies implicit in the curriculum have changed. Curricular patterns have reflected these variations and, recently, have been increasingly influenced by the findings of educational, psychological, and sociological research.

This chapter focuses on the general problems of designing a curriculum in order to provide a backdrop for the more detailed discussion of specific curricular areas that appears in the next Part of this book. In this chapter, the authors will discuss the following questions: (1) What is an operational definition of curriculum? (2) What are the principal types of curricular patterns? (3) What are some guiding principles that elementary school staffs should consider in designing or revising a curriculum? (4) What are some common procedures that may be used in the continual evaluation of a curriculum in an elementary school?

DEFINITION OF CURRICULUM

The term, "curriculum," in reference to the elementary school, has been defined in many ways in American educational thought. For many years, the "curriculum" of a school and its "course of study" were synonymous terms. They were defined as "a body of specified subject matter . . . to be learned by the child." [1]

[1] H. L. Caswell and A. W. Foshay, *Education in the Elementary School*, 3rd ed. (New York, American Book Company, 1957), p. 248.

The term, "curriculum," was later broadened to include all the varied experiences enjoyed by the child within the four walls of the classroom. Experiences outside the classroom were still, however, specifically "extra-curricular."

Today "curriculum" is an even more inclusive term, being practically synonymous with the term, "education." As Jameson and Hicks write,

> The curriculum is viewed . . . as the experiences for which the school accepts responsibility . . . organized and guided in order that acceptable objectives and needs of children may be met . . . and sequentially planned so that pupil needs . . . will be satisfied.[2]

Beauchamp emphasizes the more socialized concept of the curriculum. He proposes that "the curriculum for the elementary school be conceived as the design of a social group for the educational experiences of their children in school."[3]

For the purposes of discussion, however, the authors of this book wish to define "curriculum" as *the sum total of all experiences which the child has within the classroom or during out-of-class activities that contribute to the total development of the child and which are directed or sponsored by a member of the school staff.* Curricular offerings are designed for the group and for the development of each child as an individual and as a member of the group.

Without question, however, curricula vary from school to school. In some elementary schools today the curriculum is cramped within the classroom. In other schools the curricular offerings are flexible, varied, and creative, encompassing the child's out-of-school activities, field trips, audio-visual aids, and community activities.

As Herrick and others write,

> Good curriculum planning helps bring breadth and significance to the experiences children have in school; it realizes the intelligence and imagination of teachers; and it helps marshal the resources of the school and community for effective learning. It is one sure way of insuring good education for all America's children.[4]

TYPES OF CURRICULAR PATTERNS

There are several types of curricular patterns found in the elementary schools of this country. Let us review the most common ones on the following pages.

[2] M. C. Jameson and W. V. Hicks, *Elementary School Curriculum* (New York, American Book Company, 1960), p. 39.

[3] G. Beauchamp, *Planning the Elementary School Curriculum* (Boston, Allyn and Bacon, Inc., 1956), p. 1.

[4] V. E. Herrick, J. I. Goodlad, F. J. Estvan, and P. W. Eberman, *The Elementary School* (Englewood Cliffs, N.J., Prentice-Hall, Inc., 1956), p. 151.

The earliest type of curriculum was the separate-subjects curriculum. During the early days of education in this country, one subject after the other was added to public school offerings. A specific amount of time was assigned to each subject, and the teachers attempted to emphasize the logical content of arithmetic, history, geography, or reading. The subject matter of each was presented completely unrelated to that of the others. Generally speaking, those who advocated this type of curricular pattern believed: (1) that it permitted more readily a planned development of each subject area; and (2) that it helped to give a more adequate balance to the entire curricular offering by preserving the integrity of each academic area. The following diagram represents a cross section of subjects studied as part of a sixth-grade program using this type of curricular pattern. Notice that each of the sample subjects is completely unrelated to every other subject.

Example of a Separate-Subjects Curriculum

AREAS OF STUDY   SUBJECTS WHICH MIGHT BE
                                  STUDIED ON ANY GIVEN DAY

HISTORY	Colonization of New England
GEOGRAPHY	Geography of Switzerland
ARITHMETIC	Multiplication of Decimals
MUSIC	Songs about Autumn
ART	Figure Drawing
SCIENCE	Magnetism
PHYSICAL EDUCATION	Rhythmic Drills

There have been and are many critics of the separate-subjects curriculum. They assert that the children are not assisted in perceiving the relationships among the subjects that they study daily and that such a pattern focuses too much attention on content and too little on child growth and development. The separate-subjects curriculum tends to compartmentalize what the child studies.

Although elementary schools throughout the country tend generally to use the subject-centered approach, programs vary as a result of the roles played by classroom teachers. The fact that a teacher finds himself working within the rigid framework of a curricular pattern does not free him from the responsibility to vitalize the curricular offerings in his classroom. A truly creative teacher will provide a dynamic program, offering opportunities for all children to have meaningful learning experiences.

Dissatisfaction felt by many creative teachers, however, in the relatively disjointed approach to learning in the subject-centered curricular pattern led during the early decades of the twentieth century to experimentation which resulted in the correlated curriculum.

In the correlated curriculum the separate identity of each subject is retained, but there is some attempt to relate them through content. During a six-week program, for example, the relationship of art, history, geography, and science is focused on a special topic, such as early New England. The following diagram illustrates the role played by each of several subjects in a correlated curriculum. Notice the sample subjects are correlated because they are concentrating upon one topic.

Although the correlated approach may offer some advantages as compared with the separate-subjects pattern, occasionally it is carried to such a point that the correlation results in a forced relationship and in extreme artificiality. This overemphasis on a single theme caused considerable dissatisfaction and paved the way toward a fusion or "broad fields" curricular pattern.

The broad fields curriculum fuses several subjects into a broad area. Smith, Stanley, and Shores write:

> This curriculum varies from the conventional subjects by dissolving certain subject-matter boundaries, by creating a few comprehensive categories to take the place of the multiplicity of specialized subjects, and by adding new content to the broad categories.[5]

In this type of curricular pattern, a subject loses its identity as it is fused with other subjects into larger blocks of content. Social studies led the way in this type of organization. History and geography became the social studies, with an emphasis on the identification of social concepts, understandings, and processes. Other experimentation included the language arts

---

[5] B. O. Smith, W. O. Stanley, and J. H. Shores, *Fundamentals of Curriculum Development* (New York, Harcourt, Brace & World, Inc., 1950), p. 409.

Example of a Correlated Curriculum

AREAS OF STUDY   SUBJECTS WHICH MIGHT BE STUDIED
                                        ON ANY GIVEN DAY

| HISTORY | History of New England Colonies |

| GEOGRAPHY | Geography of New England States |

| ARITHMETIC | Problems involving the Population and Area of New England |

| MUSIC | Songs of Early Colonists |

| ART | New England Scenes |

| SCIENCE | Study of Navigation Instruments used by Early Explorers and Colonists |

| PHYSICAL EDUCATION | Early American Dances |

(or the "communication" arts)—listening, writing, speaking, and reading. Music and art became the creative arts. Each area would have a planned sequence. In the broad fields curriculum, there may or may not be a relationship between the larger curricular blocks. In other words, the social studies, language arts, and the creative arts are curricular areas containing related subjects, but they are not necessarily related to one another.

Saylor and Alexander have identified the following strengths and limitations of the broad fields curriculum.[6] On the favorable side, they list: (1) better integration of subject matter; (2) provision for a more functional organization of knowledge; (3) opportunity to encompass more subject matter and to provide a broader understanding of modern affairs; and (4) emphasis on basic principles and generalizations, rather than on information and facts. As limitations, they list: (1) dangers of providing only a

---

[6] J. G. Saylor and W. M. Alexander, *Curriculum Planning* (New York, Holt, Rinehart and Winston, Inc., 1954), pp. 270–273.

sketchy knowledge of a subject area; (2) possibility of ending with an abstract, academic type of course that is beyond the grasp of many students; and (3) danger of pupils' not grasping the inherent logic of subject matter.

Other Curricular Patterns. There can be found many additional descriptive terms that identify attempts of elementary school educators to find the best procedures for organizing and presenting subject matter. Examples would include: the "activities of daily living" curriculum,[7] which emphasizes the developmental needs of the learner and the societal factors of the communities in which the child operates; the "experience" curricular pattern; [8] and the so-called "emerging" curricular pattern.[9] In each of the last two the developing needs of the child are the center of emphasis and firsthand experiences are emphasized in lieu of an overemphasis on textbooks and vicarious experiences. Jameson and Hicks in referring to the emerging curriculum write,

> From the point of view of human growth, the last type mentioned, [emerging curriculum], is perhaps the most acceptable, because it is based largely on readiness, motivation, individual differences, and the realistic needs of children. It is the least common, however, because it is difficult to organize and because it represents the farthest extreme from the traditional separate-subjects curriculum.[10]

Variations of these and other curricular patterns are found in many elementary schools in this country. There is no blueprint that answers the problem for all schools. Rather, there is a need for continual experimentation, research, and evaluation. There is certainly an opportunity here for creative, critical, and bold thinking.

It is hoped that the following guides may be helpful in assisting staffs to evaluate their own offerings and to do some critical and creative thinking in the area of curriculum revision.

GUIDES FOR CURRICULAR STUDY

1. Curricular study and reorganization in an elementary school should involve the entire staff. With the addition of other functionaries to our school staffs, we must not minimize the contributions that they can make. While the medical staff (including the school psychologist), the school social worker, the teachers, the principal, and lay committees view the curriculum in a slightly different manner and represent a different discipline, each has the same objectives and goals—the desire to provide

---

[7] H. J. Klausmeier and others, *Teaching in the Elementary School* (New York, Harper and Brothers, 1956), pp. 115–120.

[8] G. A. Beauchamp, *op. cit.*, p. 31.

[9] H. L. Caswell and A. W. Foshay, *op. cit.*, pp. 265–268

[10] M. C. Jameson and M. V. Hicks, *op. cit.*, p. 40.

as meaningful learning experiences as possible for each boy and girl. As Pritzkau writes,

Since the development of the conditions for learning experiences is the responsibility of every individual in the school, it follows that curriculum improvement is everyone's responsibility. It is necessary, however, for someone to provide the impetus for these initial attempts.[11]

The initial motivation may result from the action of a teacher, a coordinator of curriculum, an administrator, or any other functionary of the school. Suggestions and questions voiced by lay committees sometimes provoke curricular study.

Caswell and Foshay aptly summarize the role of the school staff as follows:

The development of a general curriculum plan by a school staff not only provides a basis for a unified curriculum, avoiding a situation in which the idiosyncracies of individual teachers dominate unduly various aspects of the program, but also affords a means whereby teachers may exchange experiences.[12]

2. The elementary school curriculum should reflect research in the area of effective learning. Teachers and other school personnel working in the area of curricular revision should be familiar with the definition of learning and the changes that have occurred in the learning theories with the passing of time. Such knowledge serves to highlight the complexities of the learning process and to provide a caution that the learning theories advanced today in education may not be the ultimate answer.

Learning has been defined in many ways by many different people. Currently we define learning as *the process of changing behavior, either through direct or through vicarious experiences.* As definitions of learning have changed with the passing of time, so have theories of learning.

Early Theories of Learning. We are able to trace theories of learning from the early days of the Oriental philosophers, who believed that the most effective learning resulted from the memorization of moral axioms; and from Plato, who basically regarded the human mind as a kind of storehouse, and learning as a process of recalling and identifying things forgotten. In contrast, John Locke viewed the child's mind at birth as completely blank and described it as a *tabula rasa* or "blank tablet."

Formal Discipline. The theory of formal discipline entertains the belief that the child's mind can and should be trained via certain processes. It is closely associated with faculty psychology, which conceives of the mind as composed of a number of faculties, such as judgment, memory, reasoning, and imagination. The teaching-learning process includes the providing of "exercise" for these faculties. It is of interest to note that many of the

[11] P. T. Pritzkau, *Dynamics of Curriculum Improvement* (Englewood Cliffs, N.J., Prentice-Hall, Inc., 1959), p. 8.
[12] H. L. Caswell and A. W. Foshay, *op. cit.,* p. 270.

subjects found in the current elementary curricula, such as arithmetic and
English grammar, were included because they were believed to furnish
exercise to these faculties. The assumption was that if one's memory
were exercised sufficiently, improvement in the ability to memorize would
be carried over to other fields of subject matter.

Although this theory seemed extremely plausible and influenced the
early development of the elementary school curriculum in this country,
it was later replaced by newer, and apparently more efficient concepts.[13]

Stimulus-Response Bond Theory. A theory in vogue for many years and
still with some value is the *S-R Bond Theory.* This theory teaches that learning results from repeated stimulus-response situations, which establish con-
nections or bonds in the human nervous system. If the connection is well
established, a specific stimulus will provoke a specific response. Thus, according to this theory, the teacher should concentrate upon repetition of
the material to be learned. The repetition should occur under the most
favorable circumstances. For instance, the teacher might provide a reward
for a child who successfully learns some fact or piece of knowledge.

Akin to this concept of a functional basis for learning is *behaviorism,*
initiated by Max Meier and popularized by John B. Watson.

Acceptance of these theories of learning was advanced by the many
experiments involving Ivan Pavlov and his dogs. One of the best known of
these experiments was as follows: If one rings a bell each time a dog is
fed, the mere ringing of the bell in time causes saliva to form in the dog's
mouth. It was believed that in a child learning could also occur from a
similarly well-established stimulus-response situation.

This emphasis on the stimulus-response reaction raised questions in the
minds of many educational psychologists regarding the practicality of setting up *all* the necessary stimulus-response situations that a child would
need to have as he grew older—as the knowledge and skills which he needed
to learn increased in complexity.

Thorndike's Laws of Learning. Stimulus-response theory was developed
in this country by E. L. Thorndike and became known as *connectionism.*
For over fifty years, Thorndike was the most influential American educator
in the development of testing procedures and of theories of learning. He
was one of the first educators in the United States to emphasize the importance of the association of ideas in learning. Further, through his studies
of thousands of high school students, he did much to minimize the acceptance of the then current theory of formal discipline. The practical
result of this latter work was a re-evaluation of which subject-matter areas
should be included in the elementary school curriculum.

Thorndike is well known for his laws of learning, including the *law of effect,* the *law of use,* and the *law of disuse.* Most teachers today would agree

[13] L. P. Thorpe and A. M. Schmuller, *Contemporary Theories of Learning* (New
York, The Ronald Press Company, 1954).

with Thorndike that effectual learning occurs when boys and girls experience some kind of effect from a learning experience and that better learning occurs if the effect is positive and pleasant. As Frandsen reports, "rewarding desired behavior has been found much more effective than punishing undesired behavior." [14] In a classroom the teacher should accept the responsibility, according to Thorndike, of being certain that children receive pleasant feelings of satisfaction from the provided learning experiences.

Thorndike also advanced the theory that knowledge, skills, and ideas not used for a period of time would be learned less permanently— the *law of use* and the *law of disuse*. Thorndike described this when he wrote,

> The connections formed between situation and response are represented by connections between the neurones . . . The strength or weakness of a connection means the greater or less likelihood that the same current will be conducted from the former to the latter than to some other place.[15]

By 1929, Thorndike was emphasizing the fact that use alone is not sufficient. Useless repetition without meaning and satisfaction will not result in permanent learning.

Gestalt Theory of Learning. Today the attention of educators is being focused on the Gestalt theory of learning. "Gestalt" is a German word for which there never has been found a satisfactory American equivalent. For want of a better interpretation it has been defined as "configuration."

Those supporting the Gestalt theory of learning tend to reject the mechanical explanation of learning in the stimulus-response theories and to emphasize the need of viewing learning as an integrating process. With the emphasis on the *whole,* the learner gains insight. This insight enables the learner to see the relation of the parts to the whole, but with the realization that the whole is greater than its parts. He sees arithmetic as a logical system, not just as a series of isolated exercises of addition, subtraction, multiplication, and division. He views geographical places, historical events, and important dates, not as isolated items, but with the proper perspective of time, location, and importance.

As Burton emphasizes,

> A natural corollary is the increasing emphasis in teaching upon the *wholes,* that is, upon unitary organizations of subject matter and learning experiences, with decreasing emphasis upon fragmentary assign-study-recite sequences.[16]

In the elementary schools of this country the Gestalt concept is gaining in importance as a basis for curriculum planning and revision.

[14] A. N. Frandsen, *How Children Learn* (New York, McGraw-Hill Book Company, 1957), p. 39.

[15] E. L. Thorndike, *Educational Psychology,* Vol. 1, *The Original Nature of Man* (New York, Teachers College, Columbia University, 1913), p. 227.

[16] W. H. Burton, *The Guidance of Learning Activities* (New York, Appleton-Century-Crofts, Inc., 1952), p. 186.

John Dewey reflected this integrative approach to learning by his emphasis on problem solving. Each child, he believed, learns as a result of thinking and acting in reference to one or more of life's problems.

The Field Theory. In close relationship to the Gestalt theory is the "field" theory, developed pre-eminently by Kurt Lewin. This theory also rejects the connectionist view that there is a pattern of specific stimulus and response in behavior, and conceives of the individual as being in a "field" or "life space," which consists of him and his entire environment. The behavior of the individual is determined by the dynamic interpendence of events—whether physical, social, or psychological—that occur within his field at a specific time. For instance, whether a pupil learns the lesson that is being taught within the classroom is affected by all the factors within himself and his environment—by his physical health, by his hopes and wishes, by the teacher's manner of presenting the lesson, by what his neighbor in the next seat is doing, by what he can see out of the window. The major positive and negative factors conducive to whether the pupil learns or does not learn this lesson might be summed up in a diagram in which such factors are denoted by means of arrows (similar to force-diagrams in physics).

Since each learning experience is unique, one should be cautious about presuming that any general laws of learning exist. The most we can do is to distinguish general types of learning. Lewin writes,

> The term *learning* is a popular one which refers in a more or less vague way to some kind of betterment. Around 1910, students of psychology were taught to explain any change in behavior by learning (which meant improvement in speed or quality), by fatigue (which meant decrease in speed or quality), or by a combination of the two. Actually, the term *learning* refers to a multitude of different phenomena. The statement, "Democracy, one has to learn; autocracy is imposed upon the person," refers to one type of learning. If one says that the "spastic child has to learn to relax," one is speaking of a different type of learning. Both types have probably very little to do with "learning French vocabulary," and this type again has little to do with learning to like spinach . . .
>
> Within what is called learning, we have to distinguish the following types of changes: (1) learning as a change in cognitive structure (knowledge), (2) learning as a change in motivation (learning to like or to dislike), (3) learning as a change in group belongingness or ideology (this is an important aspect of growing into a culture), (4) learning in the meaning of bodily control of the body musculature (this is one important aspect of acquiring skills, such as speech or self-control).[17]

A practical result of the work of Lewin and his associates has been the re-thinking of many of the concepts of the past. For instance, in the above case of learning, Lewin goes on to say that after we have reduced the vague concept of "learning" into concrete types, we should then attempt to

---

[17] K. Lewin, "Field Theory and Learning" in *Field Theory in Social Science* (New York, Harper, 1951), pp. 65–66.

discover laws governing each type, rather than to pursue a general law that would circumscribe all types of what is known by the popular term, "learning."

The field theory, in concentrating on the specific situation of the individual and on the problem of translating phenomena into proper concepts, has given researchers a tool by which they can produce more efficient knowledge from experimentation. A result will be the increasing effectiveness of elementary school education based upon this research.

3. The importance of effective motivation is of primary concern in curricular planning. Motivation involves a two-pronged responsibility which rests both with the teacher and the child. The child must want to learn and the teacher must provide motivating experiences. Elementary school staffs must be constantly sensitive to the various facets of motivation as they face the study, planning, and revision of their curricular offerings. They must be concerned with short-term and long-term motivation, intrinsic and extrinsic motivation, natural and contrived motivation, a child's level of aspiration, and the ultimate goal of self-motivation.

Short-term and Long-term Motivation. Teachers must provide experiences of both short-term and long-term motivation. For many months adults who are planning a trip to Europe read and study travel folders. They plan what to look for in each country and in each community. Should not pupils also be given the opportunity in their learning experiences to identify specific, immediate goals as well as to have the opportunity to see the relationship of these immediate goals to the total larger teaching-learning experience? As Burton states, "too frequently the teacher sets (assigns) the purpose and demands that the pupils fulfill it." [18] Boys and girls must be given the opportunity to understand clearly the purpose of each learning experience. As Seagoe states,

> Essentially, a purpose narrows the field of attention and focuses it on smaller and smaller areas with greater and greater intensity. When we are in a state of relaxation, we are open to widely diverse stimuli and energy in diverse kinds of action. When a purpose that functions for us is introduced, we drop out the peripheral activities and disregard the extraneous stimuli; we give attention to resolving the tension or fulfilling the purpose.[19]

It is the responsibility of the elementary school staff to help boys and girls see the relationship of learning experiences to their already on-going experiences and to help them identify immediate goals and purposes as well as long-termed objectives. To do this effectively teachers must know their pupils well.

Intrinsic and Extrinsic Motivation. As Emerson stated, "The reward of a thing well done is to have done it." While experiences in an elementary

[18] W. H. Burton, *op. cit.*, p. 68.
[19] M. V. Seagoe, *A Teacher's Guide To the Learning Process* (Dubuque, Iowa, William C. Brown Company, 1956), p. 16.

school program tend to be on a continuum of motivation from extrinsic at one end to intrinsic at the other, studies indicate that the latter forms a stronger base for permanent and effective learning. Extrinsic motivation in a school usually includes the awarding of gold stars, prizes, medals, or pins. Boys and girls enjoy receiving these awards, but if a child works for the award, his focus of attention will be divided, and less permanent learning is likely to result.

Learning that results from the meeting of a basic need, from a natural curiosity, from a desire to do a job well, or from a personal desire to continue to improve one's record results in a stronger feeling of satisfaction. Learning should be a joy in itself and should not require extrinsic rewards. Whenever new learning activities are related to some previous experience that the child has enjoyed, they are more likely to result in a more spontaneous, enthusiastic, and personally satisfying experience.

Seagoe summarizes procedures for promoting intrinsic motivation in an elementary school classroom. A teacher should provide,

(1) the opportunity for overt bodily activity, for manipulation, for construction, even for observing the movement of animals and vehicles of various sorts; (2) the opportunity for investigation, for using mental ingenuity in solving puzzles, for working through problems, for creating designs and the like; (3) the opportunity for adventure, for vicarious experiences in make-believe, in books, and in mass media; (4) the opportunity for social assimilation, for contacts with others suitable to the maturity level . . . of the child, for social events and for working together for human interest and humanitarianism and for conformity and display; and (5) the opportunity for use in real life, making the new continuous with past experience and projecting it in terms of future action.[20]

Effective intrinsic motivation is closely related to a satisfying self-realization. Maslow places self-actualization at the top of his hierarchy of motives.[21]

Natural and Contrived Motivation. Unfortunately the teacher who introduces his next topic by announcing, "Tomorrow we will begin our study of Holland," has not yet recognized the value of genuine motivation. In sharp contrast, effective teaching attempts to build a readiness for learning by arousing the interest and curiosity of the pupil toward a problem to which he desires an answer. The problem may be presented either through natural or through contrived motivation. Natural motivation is derived from the natural interests of the children. For instance, when a class discovers that its newest member cannot speak English, that he has just arrived from Argentina, and that his clothes and mannerisms are slightly different, their curiosity and interest may make them want to learn something about the stranger's homeland. This study would probably have a great deal of

---

[20] *Ibid.*, p. 28.
[21] A. H. Maslow, "A Theory of Human Motivation," *Psychological Review*, Vol. 50 (July, 1943), pp. 382–383.

value for this particular class because it is related to an area of immediate interest to them.

Many illustrations of natural motivation could be cited. As a matter of fact, almost any incident or item, such as reports, current happenings, television programs, hobbies, everyday occurrences about the school, letters, stories, or personal experiences, may be used to motivate effective learning experiences.

Obviously this type of motivation has some advantages, chief of which is its vitalization of content through the natural interests and needs of the learners. Today, however, many authorities feel that its advantages are outnumbered by its disadvantages. These disadvantages are grouped into four major categories:

1. It is difficult to determine the valid interest of the majority of the pupils. Often a teacher may mistake the enthusiasm of one or two vocal members of the class for a widespread interest of the entire group. As Shane writes,

> The patterns of interest in a group of children do not coalesce at the same time, and it is unlikely that a teacher can find a group interest which is appealing to all the thirty or so children in his room.[22]

2. It prohibits previous planning and preparation by the teacher. The teacher whose newest pupil generated a general interest in Argentina may have had to do some hurried planning and reading in order "to keep ahead of his pupils."

3. It is limited by the number of available reading materials. A fifth-grade class recently was charmed by an exchange student teacher from India. They loved her warm personality, pleasant manner, pretty face, and exquisite sari, and they were eager to learn more about her country. But all kinds of problems faced the classroom teacher as he tried to provide the pupils at short notice with materials about India written on a fifth-grade reading level.

4. Most serious of all, it may result in a haphazard, hit-or-miss type of educational program. The gaps and overlapping of content in this type of curricular planning and teaching has elicited strong protest and criticisms from teachers. As Preston writes,

> It would be hazardous . . . to let a major proportion of school experience be charted by the ebb and flow of chance experience. . . . Intelligent living in society today places many demands upon the individual and requires a greater volume of systematic knowledge than would be required through allegedly "natural" motivation.[23]

[22] H. G. Shane, "Children's Interests: How Do They Affect the Elementary School Program?" *NEA Journal,* Vol. 46 (April, 1957), p. 238.

[23] R. Preston, *Teaching Social Studies in the Elementary School,* rev. ed. (New York, Holt, Rinehart and Winston, Inc., 1958), p. 43.

It seems wise, therefore, for elementary school classroom teachers in planning learning experiences in the curriculum to be familiar with procedures of contrived motivation. Some common devices are: (1) a news item of current history; (2) a display or exhibit; (3) a visual aid; (4) stories, songs, and games; and (5) personal experiences. Examples of contrived motivation are referred to in many chapters in this book.

In general, most educators agree upon the validity of contrived motivation which is, after all, only putting the law of readiness into operation. It is most unfortunate that, although contrived motivation has been accepted in theory, artificiality and pseudo-democratic procedures have invited serious criticism from some sources. This has occurred when contrived motivation has been misused. The need for adequate time, a variety of devices, and flexibility must be understood and practiced.

Level of aspiration. Every child and adult must enjoy some degree of success, for continual failure has an inhibiting effect on his motivation toward future learning experiences. Children must be taught to identify realistic levels of aspiration for themselves and must be helped to achieve these levels. This is a major facet in developing sound self-concepts in elementary school youth. As Frandsen writes,

> The "moral" to draw from the studies on success and failure is, of course, that every child needs, from the points of view of both efficient learning and healthy development of personality, a curriculum in which he can succeed.[24]

Children must be challenged, but effective motivation cannot be achieved if this challenge is unrealistic in terms of their physical, intellectual, emotional, and social development. Sears, in her study of the effect of levels of aspiration on children, clearly indicates that a child who continually experiences failure will either place his level of aspiration too high, thinking he will win social approval by doing so, and will subsequently continue to fail, or he will identify a low level of aspiration as his only means of enjoying any degree of personal satisfaction.[25] In either case the motivation does not lean toward helping him to understand himself or to develop a sound self-concept.

Self-motivation. The ultimate goal of all these facets of motivation, whether the identification of short-termed and long-termed goals; the emphasis on intrinsic motivation; the effectual use of both natural and contrived motivation; or the identification of realistic levels of aspirations, is to help each boy and each girl develop self-motivation, an intellectual curiosity, and a creative desire to learn.

This discussion of motivation leads us to the next "guide," for matura-

[24] A. N. Frandsen, *op. cit.*, p. 226.
[25] P. S. Sears, "Levels of Aspiration in Academically Successful and Unsuccessful Children," *Journal of Abnormal and Social Psychology,* Vol. 35 (October, 1940), pp. 498–536.

tion is closely identified with the providing of motivating experiences in our schools.

4. The maturation and readiness of boys and girls influence directly the thinking of educators who are planning curricular experiences for an elementary school. Maturation and readiness will not be discussed at length in this chapter, for they are intrinsic to the discussions in many chapters of this book. This testifies to their importance in curricular planning. Maturation in educational literature has been used to refer to *potentials of physical growth,* while readiness refers to the *process of total development,* involving not only physical development but also intellectual, emotional, and social development. Maturation results from internal natural growth, including physical, motor, and sensory structures. As Burton tersely states, "The individual possesses a growth potential; he will mature willy-nilly. This process is called maturation." [26]

It was indicated in Chapter Three, that a child's maturation and development involve contributions from both heredity and environment. Here we are concerned with the role of maturation and readiness in curricular planning. Educators and lay committees working on curricular planning must be very sensitive to the fact that there are stages of development in a child's growth and that certain knowledges and skills are better taught at one time than at another. However, this is not enough. Teachers must always be sensitive to the fact that children in the same classroom at the same chronological age differ in their maturation and readiness and that curricular offerings and experiences must be sufficiently flexible to meet these needs. As Cronbach writes,

> The pupil's readiness for any situation is the sum of all his characteristics which make him more likely to respond in one way than another . . . Readiness involves the pupil's equipment, his needs and goals, and his learned ideas and skills. [27]

Cronbach also summarizes four principles regarding readiness in curricular planning: (1) all aspects of development interact; (2) physiological maturing prepares one to profit from experience; (3) experiences have a cumulative effect; and (4) certain times in one's life are formative periods when a basic readiness for a particular activity is established. [28]

The student should note as he studies the remaining chapters in this book that curricular planning is affected by: (1) the general stage of development of boys and girls at varying age levels; (2) the uniqueness of individual children; (3) the relationship of the philosophy of the school, the instructional methods, and cultural influences to the readiness of children

[26] W. H. Burton, *op. cit.,* p. 171.
[27] L. J. Cronbach, *Educational Psychology* (New York, Harcourt, Brace & World, Inc., 1954), p. 74.
[28] *Ibid.,* p. 75.

for different curricular experiences; and (4) the uniqueness of procedures for determining readiness in each of the subject areas.

Motivation, maturation, and readiness are directly related to the consideration of direct and vicarious experiences in curricular planning.

5. Curricular planning must provide for appropriate direct and vicarious learning experiences. In studying and in revising the curricular offerings in any elementary school, the staff must be sensitive to the importance of both direct and vicarious experiences. Both are important. In the lower grades the more direct experiences that can be provided the better, for small children are less able to deal with abstractions. The dangers, however, of personal experience being fragmentary and biased must not be overlooked even with children in the lower grades. They too must be taught to evaluate what they see, hear, and do. While there is little question regarding the effectiveness of direct experiences, there is also a need for vicarious experiences in curricular offerings. Otherwise much of our cultural heritage would be lost. Children cannot experience all history directly, nor can they all be fortunate enough to travel to far corners of the earth.

One of the chief advantages of direct experience is its vividness to the learner. A truly creative teacher, however, can make vicarious experiences vivid too. There are many levels of vicarious experiences, and a truly effective curricular plan will include opportunities for the appropriate use of each of these in relation to the subject-matter areas and the degree of maturity of the child. Burton lists the following levels:

I. DIRECT EXPERIENCE—actual participation, doing, undergoing (including dramatizing).

II. VICARIOUS EXPERIENCE

    A. *Through direct observation.*
        1. Seeing actual events take place; handling concrete objects and materials.
        2. Seeing the events acted out as in drama or pantomiming by persons who represent the original characters and who use authentic costumes and settings.

    B. *Through pictorial means.*
        1. Seeing motion picture portrayal of events, of persons, of processes.
        2. Seeing photographs of persons, places, and objects.

    C. *Through graphic means.*
        1. Using maps, diagrams, graphs, blueprints, and similar representations of objects, facts, and relationships.

    D. *Through verbal means.*
        1. Reading narrations and descriptions of persons, places, events, and things.
        2. Listening to narrations, descriptions of persons, places, events, and things.

E. *Through symbolic representation.*
  1. Use of technical symbols, terminology, formulae, indices, coeffi-
     cients, or other special recondite signs.[29]

The use of both direct and vicarious experiences should be found in
the elementary school classroom. Those who believe that a boy or girl
learns only from direct experiences limit the child's horizons. Educators
who believe that children learn only from books and other publications
are equally wrong. Wherever possible, direct experiences are preferable,
and they will probably result in more permanent learning, but there are
understandings and concepts that must be experienced only vicariously.

**6. The curricular offerings in an elementary school should help boys and
girls develop motor and intellectual skills.** These are commonly accepted
goals for education at any level, for without them boys and girls would be
unable to live satisfying and productive lives.

Motor Skills. The development of motor skills is a part of any functional
curriculum. While every boy and girl develops motor skills as a natural
process of growing up, some skills require a special program of development. As Crow and Crow indicate,

The value to the individual of motor learning comes in the success with which
he can develop to automatic habit level the motor responses or skills that will
make him proficient in any learning area.[30]

Procedures for this have been discussed in many chapters of this book.
The development of motor skills involves such steps as: (1) an understanding on the part of the child regarding what he is to learn; (2) instruction and demonstration regarding the skill to accompany the developing understanding; (3) a provision of time and activities for meaningful
practice; and (4) an opportunity and procedure necessary for helping
the child evaluate his own development.

Effectual practice is directly related to its meaningfulness. As Kingsley
writes,

Practice should be conducted under conditions similar to those which will
attend the use of the skill, and the procedures practiced should be those in which
the skill is desired.[31]

Repetition of a skill may not necessarily be meaningful practice. Studies
have shown that practice with a definite purpose, scheduled at frequent
intervals, and under constructive guidance produces the best results.

Experiences in an elementary school curriculum should be provided for
the meeting of individual differences. As Crow and Crow write, "The rate

[29] W. H. Burton, *op. cit.*, p. 44.
[30] L. D. Crow and A. Crow, *Human Development and Learning* (New York, American Book Company, 1956), pp. 272–273.
[31] H. L. Kingsley, *The Nature and Conditions of Learning* (Englewood Cliffs, N.J.,
Prentice-Hall, Inc., 1946), p. 241.

of learning and the degree of skill to be attained should be adjusted to the abilities and interests of the learners." [32]

Intellectual Skills. Pritzkau has described this challenge in curricular planning as a need for "developing an environment for ideas." [33] The environment in schools much be rich with resources for the development of ideas. Boys and girls must be taught to observe, to hypothesize, to secure data, to evaluate data, to develop conclusions, and to evaluate these conclusions. They must learn to follow data wherever these data may guide them—always with critical, creative minds. This necessitates that those planning meaningful curricular experiences should provide many enriching opportunities for children to see, touch, hear, smell, and taste—as well as reading materials and other sources of knowledge to check and to supplement direct learning experiences. Human resources as well as audio-visual aids should be utilized as part of the curricular pattern. Creative thinking must always be encouraged. As Gould writes,

> The curriculum should be a vast reservoir of unanswered and unanswerable questions—all answers and all solutions are only partial, leaving open doors through which the student must go, driven by curiosity or patient conscientiousness or pride or ambition or even infuriation. The curriculum is thus no more than a threshold, nor should it be represented to be anything more.[34]

Boys and girls differ in their levels of comprehension as they do in the development of motor skills. These individual differences must be provided for. Opportunities must exist for each child to develop meaningful concepts in relation to his age, his previous experience, and his ability. These are important facets of curricular planning. As Russell writes,

> The clarity and completeness of a child's concepts are the best measure of his probable success in school learning because meaning is fundamental to such learning. The adult's concepts determine pretty well what he knows, what he believes, and thus in a large part what he does.[35]

With the popularity of television and radio, with the opportunities for children to travel and to see new things, with periodicals filled with illustrative material, and with the wealth of reading materials at varying levels, boys and girls today come to the elementary school classrooms with many well-formed concepts. Elementary school staffs must have a curricular plan that enables teachers to help youth utilize and expand these concepts. Russell outlines eight basic categories of concepts that youth

[32] L. D. Crow and A. Crow, *op. cit.*, p. 290.
[33] P. T. Pritzkau, *op. cit.*, pp. 210–248.
[34] S. B. Gould, "The Teacher's Impact on the Curriculum," *School and Society,* Vol. 88 (April 9, 1960), p. 177.
[35] D. H. Russell, *Children's Thinking* (Boston, Ginn and Company, 1956), p. 120.

must be helped to develop: (1) mathematical concepts; (2) concepts of time; (3) scientific concepts; (4) concepts of the self; (5) social concepts; (6) aesthetic concepts; (7) concepts of humor; and (8) miscellaneous concepts.[36] The curricular pattern in a school must provide the broad background that makes it possible to help each child develop these concepts, think critically, and develop creativity. Sound attitudes and values must also be developed through curricular experiences. Attitudes and values should be an integral part of the curricular offerings.

7. Integrative experiences must be a focal part of curricular planning. With the emphasis on the Gestalt theory of learning, effective curricular patterns today do not compartmentalize subjects studied, but attempt to provide opportunities for the unitary, integrative presentation of subject matter. The "unit" is the basis for much of this integration in the elementary school program. Otto endorses this pattern of curricular offerings when he writes,

> Unit method (sometimes called the unit organization of teaching-learning situations) was evolved and is today the best known vehicle for combining appropriate pupil motivation, learning outcomes, learning activities, and an effective utilization of content. Unit method holds the best promise of enabling the pupil to acquire meaningful insights, problem solving skills, and the translation of knowledge and attitude into behavior.[37]

The historical development of unit teaching reflects various interpretations and terminology during the past several decades. It was first used by Morrison in 1926 to refer to a type of independent work assignment. Since then the literature has been filled with such terms as: "subject-matter units," "experience units," "process units," "resource units," "teaching units," "problem units," and with untold other names. Fortunately, most educators today have stopped trying to draw fine distinctions and recognize only two categories—*resource units and teaching units.* Curricular offerings in today's elementary schools provide for the utilization of resource units or "source volumes," as Burton describes them. These are usually compiled by committees of teachers, and are sources of motivating devices, materials, references, and learning experiences which are used by the individual teacher. The teaching unit can be defined as the actual experiences that the teacher develops in his classroom.

What is a unit? It is a teaching-learning organization which calls for the integration of curricular areas, which has certain distinctive characteristics of teaching, and which usually extends over a period of several weeks.

In viewing unit teaching as a basic curricular pattern for a school, one must note that all subjects need not and probably should not be related to a given unit. To insist that they be related will result in the same artificial

[36] *Ibid.*, p. 125.
[37] H. J. Otto, *Social Education in Elementary Schools* (New York, Holt, Rinehart and Winston, Inc., 1956), p. 412.

teaching which led to the unpopularity of the correlated curricular pattern. Today's educators frown on complete integration because it may result in: (1) a disproportionate emphasis upon the core areas; (2) a surfeit of one topic (children get bored with reading, writing, singing, talking, and drawing Mexico); and (3) a neglect of the basic skills in other areas.

In practice, the core of the unit may be related to other subjects in at least two ways. First the discussion in the unit may reveal a need for drill in another subject. For instance, in a unit on *The Earth as a Whole,* a fourth grade teacher tried to have his pupils compare the sizes of the continents. He quickly discovered that his pupils could not read nor write large numbers, and consequently, he spent the next few arithmetic lessons on this skill. In this case, the relationship was an out-going one from the core to another subject.

In an opposite case, a fifth grade class which had studied fractions as part of its sequential arithmetic program, found many opportunities for using this skill as they built a scaled model colonial kitchen as part of their unit study. In this case, the relationship was an in-going one, developed separately but eventually applied in the unit.

The use of unit teaching as part of over-all curricular planning provides an opportunity for the teacher and the pupils to plan co-operatively the scope, the direction, the procedures, and the activities to be included. A further discussion of unit planning and a sample unit plan included in Chapter Nine contain suggestions as to how this may be accomplished.

8. A sound balance must be maintained in the curricular offerings of the elementary school program. Many pressures are exerted by lay and professional groups on elementary school staffs in reference to their curricular planning. Each group believes its area to be of utmost importance. Each probably has a justifiable reason for thinking so, but the school cannot be all things to all people. As Boodish writes,

> Schools should not undertake every educational job that some person or group recommends. One of the ways to strengthen the curriculum is to select the most important educational tasks which the school is best able to achieve and to focus the curriculum on these tasks.[38]

Breslow and others list some of the pressures that are influencing curricular development in our public schools.[39] They include: power politics, foreign educational practices, scientific development and research, shifts in values, changes in family life, mass media and automatic teaching, and influences of small special interest groups.

Educators and representatives of the lay public who are studying and

[38] H. M. Boodish, "Strengthening the Curriculum of the American Public Schools," *The Social Studies,* Vol. 50 (October, 1959), p. 189.
[39] A. Breslow and others, "Forces Influencing Curriculum," *Review of Educational Research,* Vol. 30 (June, 1960), pp. 199–214.

revising the curricula of our elementary schools today must resist undue pressures. They must be cautious of the "activity of pseudo-experts in education, armed with the results of some measure of inquiry and adroit in techniques of publicity and persuasion, ready to prescribe specific modifications in school curriculums." [40]

Educators must be creative and must think critically. It is not an easy responsibility for them to preserve the integrity of the American heritage, to maintain a balance among curricular offerings, to evaluate and to utilize the contributions of the many disciplines, and to keep an eye on the ever-changing future. As Gould writes, "The curriculum . . . deserves the most meticulous treatment, a treatment which guarantees its breadth, adaptability, and relevance." [41]

9. Curricular experiences that will promote a transfer of learning are an important facet of curricular planning and revision. The need to teach for transfer of learnings is the focal point of this guide for curricular development. For many years, educators have been concerned with identifying procedures for a general application of knowledges and skills learned. Teachers are constantly sensitive to the need for providing learning experiences which boys and girls may transfer effectively to life situations outside the school environment, as well as to subsequent learning situations.

In an attempt to arrive at a helpful solution to this problem, we have passed through the vogue of formal discipline, discussed earlier in this chapter, where attempts were made to "train" the faculties of one's mind. The belief was that the stronger the "exercise," the more successful would be the transfer in use of each faculty to other learning situations. Judd, James, and other educational psychologists questioned this theory. Thorndike subsequently developed his "identical element" theory, which is still accepted to some degree today.[42] It stated that the more direct the relationship between what one learns and what one does with the training, the more successful the transfer will be. If a classroom teacher wishes a child to *speak* correctly, he must provide frequent opportunities for the child to develop his language patterns through oral usage. Other things being equal, to request the child to write correct language forms will not result in as effective transfer as will oral practice on specific errors.

Educators have a specific responsibility to provide learning experiences that facilitate *positive* transfer. Negative transfer sometimes exists and is best explained by examples of the idiosyncracies of spelling in the English language. A child, for example, who learns carefully the generalization of "i" before "e" will write "hieght" for "height." If the teacher, therefore, had emphasized the general rule, negative transfer might occur.

[40] *Ibid.*, p. 199.
[41] S. B. Gould, *op. cit.*, p. 178.
[42] E. L. Thorndike, *Educational Psychology* (New York, Teachers College, Columbia University, 1914), pp. 267–282.

Curricular offerings must provide opportunities for boys and girls to identify and to achieve the specific objectives of modern elementary education, to develop the habit of identifying functional generalizations for themselves from meaningful learning experiences, and to experience the general application of the knowledges and skills that they learn. Teachers must teach for transfer.

Two very important factors must be emphasized in conclusion: (1) the importance of the teacher in making a curriculum operational and effective; and (2) the need for careful and continual evaluation. (As the authors discuss the curricular areas in the following chapters, the importance of the role of the classroom teacher will be emphasized.) Let us now briefly identify some suggestions for curricular evaluation.

EVALUATION OF THE CURRICULUM

In order to promote curricular improvement, the machinery for careful evaluation must be set up. The evaluation program must not be haphazard. It must be carefully planned. Objectives and goals should be carefully identified; individual and group experiences must be appraised in terms of their meaningfulness to the child in his total development; and each staff member must be encouraged to have an open mind, a critical attitude, and a desire for creativity.

The most fruitful evaluations are made by those who use the curriculum. Pritzkau believes that the focus of all curricular improvement is in the classroom. He emphasizes that "each classroom would become an 'idea' room for the purpose of promoting quality with respect to the learning experiences of children." [43] Action research involving classroom teachers working together for curricular improvement is probably one of the most fruitful approaches and one of the most beneficial forms of in-service education. Action research is the application of scientific methods to the solution of social problems. The emphasis is on discovering means to help solve the problem, rather than upon discovering the causes of the problem. There is no blueprint for all school systems to use. Standardized testing, teacher-made tests, and all other measures or indications of child growth and development must be employed. Caswell and others identify the ultimate criterion as "an improvement in the experience of all pupils." [44]

Questions designed by the staff as a basis for their evaluations are often helpful. The more detailed these questions are, the more successful the evaluation and curricular improvement will be. Sample questions regarding scope, purpose, and procedures would include these:

[43] P. T. Pritzkau, *op. cit.*, p. 32.
[44] H. L. Caswell and others, *Curriculum Improvement in Public School Systems* (New York, Teachers College, Columbia University, 1950), p. 98.

Scope and Purpose

1. Is the experience conception of the curriculum employed as a guide in developing all phases of the program?

2. Is the program comprehensive in scope—dealing with all aspects of the educational needs of the community served by the school system?

3. Is a unified educational program fostered, with various parts interrelated so as to supplement one another?

4. Is there a common direction and purpose so that the various activities in the program possess consistency?

5. Does the program provide for the definition and continuous refinement of the conception of democratic goals held by the staff of the school system?

Procedures

1. Is teacher growth considered the primary avenue of curriculum improvement?

2. Are means employed to stimulate leadership in curriculum work on a wide basis?

3. Is a variety of activities provided in order that each member of the instructional staff may participate in the program in a way recognized by him as being of value?

4. Is provision made for those who have to carry out plans to participate in making them?

5. Is provision made for work on both individual school and system-wide problems?

6. Is provision made for the practical testing on a limited basis of ideas for curriculum improvement and for the dissemination of good results? [45]

Additional questions may be found in Caswell's book; additional questions should be developed by the local staff.

The curriculum of a school is the sum total of all experiences which the child has within the classroom or during out-of-class activities that contribute to the total development of the child and that are directed or sponsored by the school staff. Other experiences enjoyed by the child frequently will need to be related to the purely curricular offering. Designing such a curriculum is a large responsibility. Without any question, it is not a one-man job.

Summary

In an attempt to provide a backdrop for the more detailed discussion of each curricular area in Part Three of this book, the authors have discussed the following four questions in this chapter: (1) What is an operational definition of the curriculum? (2) What are the principal types of curricular patterns? (3) What are some guiding principles that ele-

[45] *Ibid.,* pp. 99–100.

mentary school staffs should consider in designing or in revising a curriculum? (4) What are some common procedures that may be used in the continual evaluation of a curriculum in an elementary school?

The authors emphasized the fact that the elementary school curriculum is broader today than it was during the days when curriculum and course of study were synonymous or when every experience outside the classroom was referred to as being "strictly extra-curricular." Today the curricular offerings in a school are more synonymous with the term "education." The authors defined the curriculum as *the sum total of all experiences which the child has within the classroom or during out-of-class activities that contribute to the total development of the child and that are directed or sponsored by a member of the staff.* They also emphasized the fact that experiences that the child has out-of-class should be utilized in the process of his growth and development during school hours.

The types of curricular patterns discussed included: (1) the separate-subjects curriculum; (2) the correlated curriculum; and (3) the broad fields curriculum. Examples of each were given and the advantages and disadvantages of each type were discussed. Other curricular patterns include: the daily living curriculum, which emphasizes the developmental needs of the learner and the societal factors of the communities in which the children operate; the experience curriculum; and the emerging curriculum. Both of the latter emphasize experiences.

Nine guides were listed that elementary school staff members should consider as they design or revise an elementary school curriculum. They include: (1) the involvement of the entire school staff; (2) the reflection of research in the area of effective learning; (3) the importance of effective motivation; (4) consideration of maturation and readiness; (5) the effective use of both direct and vicarious experiences; (6) the need for opportunities for youth to develop motor skills and to explore meaningful ideas; (7) the importance of integrative experience; (8) the maintaining of a sound balance in curricular offerings; and (9) opportunities for teachers to teach for transfer and for pupils to learn for transfer.

Everyone agrees that curricular offerings in a school should be continually evaluated. This evaluation must not be haphazard or left to chance. Objectives and goals must be carefully identified; individual and group experiences must be appraised in terms of their meaningfulness to the child in his total development; and each staff member must be objective, must be open-minded, must have a critical attitude, and must show a desire for creativity.

Curricular evaluation in the school itself is extremely valuable. Action research projects developed by groups of elementary school staff members to evaluate the curriculum have proved to be very fruitful during the past few years.

STUDENT PROJECTS

1. Read extensively in the literature and prepare a detailed definition of a functional curriculum for an elementary school. Describe carefully the role of the classroom teacher, the administrator, and the community in designing the curriculum for an elementary school.

2. Visit two elementary schools in two different communities. Identify the kind of curricular pattern or patterns that you found in each school. Describe the procedures that helped you to identify the type of pattern.

3. Form a panel in your class. Ask each member of the panel to select one of the types of curricular patterns. Each member will then present as many advantages and as many disadvantages as possible of his pattern. Follow the presentation with a discussion of the possible use of each pattern.

4. Prepare a talk to be given to new teachers in a community stressing the important role played by the truly creative classroom teacher in providing meaningful learning experiences regardless of the type of curricular pattern.

5. Read extensively regarding the Gestalt theory of learning. Describe to your classmates three elementary school experiences that would be examples of the Gestalt theory. See how many other examples can be described in the subsequent class discussion.

6. Talk with three elementary school teachers and question them regarding specific examples of the use of short-term and long-term goals and objectives as a means of motivating their pupils. Share your findings with other members of your class.

7. Visit several classes in a nearby elementary school and identify examples of intrinsic, extrinsic, natural, and contrived motivation that you observe. If you are taking college courses, try to identify examples of motivation that are used by your instructors. What other examples can you mention?

8. Write an autobiography identifying levels of aspiration that you have had at different times in your life. Explain clearly how you identified these levels and discuss any changes that might have occured. List as many procedures as you can that will help teachers to help boys and girls to identify realistic levels of aspiration.

9. Visit four classes in a nearby elementary school. List as many examples of direct and vicarious experiences as you can observe. Describe any differences between the classes that you visited. Visit at least two classes at the primary level and two at the upper level.

10. Prepare a talk for a community group to answer a question that they have raised. The question is: What is being done in the elementary school to help boys and girls "think big"—to be critical, to be creative? How are they helped to explore new ideas?

11. Observe an elementary school teacher teaching a unit. Visit his class regularly so that you can observe the specific steps. Describe to your class this unit, explaining the reasons for each of the procedures followed by the teacher. If the teacher could meet with your class for the discussion, he could provide helpful information.

12. Write an editorial for a local newspaper in which you carefully discuss the role of the community and of society in general in defining the curricular plan for

an elementary school. By what processes does the community indicate the type of curriculum that it would like to have in the school? Indicate procedures for evaluating the "suggestions" of the community.

13. Identify four topics for action research by a local elementary school curriculum committee. Describe the steps that this group would follow in its study. The study may be either evaluative of present conditions or forward-looking.

14. Interview a superintendent of schools and ask him to discuss with you the kinds of pressures that are made on him frequently and that have a definite relationship to the elementary school curriculum. How does he evaluate these pressures?

BIBLIOGRAPHY

Association for Supervision and Curriculum Development, *Creating a Good Environment for Learning*, 1954 Yearbook (Washington, D.C., 1954).

Association for Supervision and Curriculum Development, *Learning and the Teacher*, 1959 Yearbook (Washington, D.C., 1959).

BEAUCHAMP, George, *Planning the Elementary School Curriculum* (Boston, Allyn and Bacon, Inc., 1956).

BECK, R. H., COOK, W. W., and KEARNEY, N. C., *Curriculum in the Modern Elementary School* (Englewood Cliffs, N.J., Prentice-Hall, Inc., 1953).

BLAIR, G. M., JONES, R. S., and SIMPSON, R. H., *Educational Psychology* (New York, The Macmillan Company, 1954).

BURTON, William H., *The Guidance of Learning Activities* (New York, Appleton-Century-Crofts, Inc., 1952).

BURTON, W. H., KIMBALL, R. B., and WING, R. L., *Education for Effective Thinking* (New York, Appleton-Century-Crofts, Inc., 1960).

CASWELL, H. L. and others, *Curriculum Improvement in Public School Systems* (New York, Teachers College, Columbia University, 1950).

CASWELL, H. L. and FOSHAY, Arthur W., *Education in the Elementary School*, 3rd ed. (New York, American Book Company, 1957).

COLADARCI, Arthur P. ed., *Educational Psychology* (New York, Holt, Rinehart and Winston, Inc., 1955).

CRAIG, Robert C., *The Transfer Value of Guided Learning* (New York, Teachers College, Columbia University, 1953).

CRONBACH, Lee J., *Educational Psychology* (New York, Harcourt, Brace & World, Inc., 1954).

CROW, Lester D. and CROW, Alice, *Human Development and Learning* (New York, American Book Company, 1956).

FRANDSEN, Arden N., *How Children Learn* (New York, McGraw-Hill Book Company, 1957).

GAGNE, Robert M. and FLEISHMAN, Edwin A., *Psychology and Human Performance* (New York, Holt, Rinehart and Winston, Inc., 1959).

GUTHRIE, E. R., *The Psychology of Learning*, rev. ed. (New York, Harper and Brothers, 1952).

HILGARD, E. R., *Theories of Learning*, 2nd ed. (New York, Appleton-Century-Crofts, Inc., 1956).

JAMESON, M. C. and HICKS, W. V., *Elementary School Curriculum* (New York, American Book Company, 1960).

KLAUSMEIER, H. J. and others, *Teaching in the Elementary School* (New York, Harper and Brothers, 1956).

DESIGNING THE CURRICULUM 99

LINDGREN, Henry C., *Educational Psychology in the Classroom* (New York, John Wiley and Sons, Inc., 1956).

MOWRER, O. H., *Learning Theory and Personality Dynamics* (New York, The Ronald Press Company, 1950).

National Society for the Study of Education, *The Psychology of Learning*, 41st Yearbook (Bloomington, Ill., Public School Publishing Co., 1942).

PRITZKAU, P. T., *Dynamics of Curriculum Improvement* (Englewood Cliffs, N.J., Prentice-Hall, Inc., 1959).

RUSSELL, David H., *Children's Thinking* (Boston, Ginn and Company, 1956).

SAYLOR, J. G. and ALEXANDER, W. M., *Curriculum Planning* (New York, Holt, Rinehart and Winston, Inc., 1954).

SEAGOE, M. V., *A Teacher's Guide to the Learning Process* (Dubuque, Iowa, William C. Brown Company, 1956).

SMITH, B. Othanel, STANLEY, William O., and SHORES, J. Harlan, *Fundamentals of Curriculum Development* (Harcourt, Brace & World, Inc., 1950).

STRATEMEYER, F. B., and others, *Developing a Curriculum for Modern Living*, 2nd ed. (New York, Teachers College, Columbia University, 1957).

THORPE, L. P. and SCHMULLER, A. M., *Contemporary Theories of Learning* (New York, The Ronald Press Company, 1954).

WARNER, Ruby, *The Child and His Elementary World* (Englewood Cliffs, N.J., Prentice-Hall, Inc., 1957).

PART III

Evolving Emphases in Content and Method

CHAPTER 5

Listening and Speaking

Section 1: THE TOTALITY OF LANGUAGE

LISTENING, SPEAKING, READING, WRITING—these are the four constellations in the firmament of language skills, the attempted mastery of which begins at the moment of birth and is never completely realized during a lifetime. Each constellation is a distinct and separate facet of language, and yet all are irrevocably intertwined and interdependent. Before examining each separately, it seems desirable first to consider the totality of the language experience as it affects the curriculum and instructional program of the modern elementary school. The next few pages, therefore, are devoted to a brief discussion of the functions, developmental phases, and interrelatedness of the language skills.

FUNCTIONS OF LANGUAGE

Language is a tool of communication. Early students of language frequently considered its main function to be the "expression" of thoughts and emotions. Today, this concept has been replaced by one which places primary emphasis upon language as a tool of communication. Without it, one is locked in a prison of loneliness and ignorance; with it one is able to enjoy the social relationships which are his birthright. Such a concept of language, of course, has important implications for the elementary school teacher.

In the first place, as the world grows smaller, the need for adequate communication grows greater. If it were true in the seventeenth century that "No man is an Iland, intire of it selfe," how much more applicable it is today with our rapid technological progress, improved transportation, and powerful media of mass communication. The increasing need for close communication, therefore, demands a broader and more vital language program in our schools than ever before in our history.

Secondly, the emphasis on language as communication demands that we teach a *functional* language in our schools. In days gone by, language teaching frequently concentrated upon "correct" standards of oral and written expression, but their relationship to the language of daily, natural, and informal communication was completely ignored. The newer communicative emphasis on language derives its content from the life experiences and needs of boys and girls and is a far cry from the dry, sterile, and artificial subject taught in yesterday's schools.

Thirdly, language as communication has resulted in a greater awareness of its importance in *all curriculum areas.* One must listen to, speak, read, and write *something*—and frequently that "something" is derived from the content of other curriculum fields. All subjects and all experiences provide opportunities for language development and the competent teacher capitalizes upon these in a deliberate attempt to strengthen the language skills. To illustrate, in a social studies lesson devoted to committee reports there is as much or more opportunity and need to teach the skills of oral expression as there is to teach the content of the social studies. Similarly, in an arithmetic lesson involving problem solving, the teacher should be just as aware of teaching reading as he is of teaching computation. Likewise, a research science lesson will involve the skills of locating, evaluating, and summarizing information as much as it will scientific knowledge. It is unnecessary to cite illustrations in other curriculum areas, for the point is simply that effective teaching of language cannot be confined to a single curriculum area nor to a specified time of the school day. Growth in language is attained only when it is consciously emphasized by the teacher in every subject and during almost every moment of the daily program.

Language is a vehicle of thought. The idea that language is used only to put thoughts into words is considered invalid today by most educators. The consistently high correlation between language facility and intelligence has led to the acceptance of the theory that the use of language is an intrinsic part of the thought process. The important educational implications of this viewpoint are expressed by one author as follows:

Language, although perhaps not essential for all thinking, is so frequently involved in thought, and especially in making abstractions and fine distinctions and shades of meaning, as well as in communicating to others the results of one's thought processes, that a certain basic level of attainment in linguistic skills is practically an essential prerequisite to the child's formal education.[1]

DEVELOPMENTAL PHASES OF LANGUAGE GROWTH

Numerous studies have been made of the child's linguistic development. Many longitudinal studies of individual children as well as cross-sectional

[1] D. McCarthy, "Language Development in Children," in L. Carmichael, ed., *Manual of Child Psychology,* 2nd ed. (New York, John Wiley & Sons, Inc., 1954), pp. 493–494.

studies of large groups of children have contributed to our present knowledge of the developmental phases of language growth. In most studies a division is made between the early and later stages of language development, somewhat as follows:

EARLY STAGES OF LANGUAGE GROWTH

1. *The first few months*—the stage of first vocalizations—crying, cooing, and miscellaneous sounds.[2]

2. *The "babbling" stage*—the appearance of a ". . . much more phonetically diversified type of random vocalization . . . employing both vowels and consonants." [2]

3. *The beginnings of language comprehension*—latter part of the babbling stage—"first evidences of understanding and recognition of certain symbolic gestures, intonations, words, and phrase-structures." [2]

4. *The beginnings of symbolic communication*—approximately toward the end of the first year—" . . . first active, meaningful, 'voluntary' use of vocal language approximating words in adult language." [2]

5. *The beginnings of differentiated speech communication*—end of second year—period of "linguistic experimentation"—use of "first phrases, sentences, pronouns, and prepositions." [3]

LATER STAGES OF LANGUAGE GROWTH

1. *The rapid growth of aural-oral communication*—rapid but erratic growth from approximately ages two to six—at approximately age six the child has acquired a vocabulary of several thousand words and "uses every part of speech and every form of sentence." [4]

2. *The reading stage*—at approximate age six—"comprehension of numerous types of visual symbols, eventually of visual-verbal symbols, written or printed words attached to meanings." [5]

3. *The writing stage*—at approximately age six—begins with "copying" and graduates to "independent writing" (see Chapter Seven).

4. *The continuing improvement and refinement of all language skills.*

It should be kept in mind that no hard and fast divisions can be made between any levels of language growth. Development in this area, as in all other aspects of human growth, is a fluid process. The individual makes the transition from one phase to another, not by ladder-like steps, but by an "inclined plane" of continuous, on-going development.

[2] J. B. Carroll, "Language Development," in C. W. Harris, ed., *Encyclopaedia of Educational Research, 3rd ed.* (New York, The Macmillan Company, 1960), pp. 744–750.

[3] D. McCarthy, *op. cit.,* p. 504.

[4] W. J. Lodge, "Developmental Characteristics of Childhood Related to the Language Arts Curriculum," in *Child Development and The Language Arts,* Research Bulletin of the National Conference on Research in English (Champaign, Ill., National Council of Teachers of English, 1953), p. 18.

[5] From *Reading in Child Development,* by W. H. Burton, copyright (c), 1956, by The Bobbs Merrill Company, used by special permission of the publishers.

Several factors affect language growth. Although some of the literature is contradictory, the following factors appear to be most closely related to general language development:

Personal equipment. Numerous studies have been made of the various aspects of the child's personal equipment which may be related to his language growth. In general, these are considered to be intelligence, adequate hearing, physical structure for speech, and muscular co-ordination.[6] Deficiency in any one of them may prove to be a serious handicap in total language development although, of course, this depends upon the effectiveness of compensatory factors employed.

Home influences. McCarthy discusses such factors as mother-child relationships, sibling status, general home atmosphere, and bilingualism as important home factors which influence language growth. The amount of time the mother spends with the young child, the type of relationship present, (for instance, overprotectiveness) the type of discipline enforced, and the general emotional environment of the home all have been found to have definite implications for language development. Then too, studies agree on the fact that multiple-birth children are frequently retarded in language while single children may be accelerated, thus pointing up the importance of adult-child contacts in furthering language growth. Studies of bilingualism offer contradictory evidence, but there is little doubt that it is a factor which should be considered by every teacher in appraising the language ability of any pupil in the classroom.[7]

Sociological influences. In general, it has been found that the children of higher socio-economic status are superior to those of lower groups in several aspects of language. In addition, the possible influences of motion pictures, radio, television and comic books upon language growth have been investigated, but frequently with inconclusive results.[8] Templin's study discovered that children of today talk more and with more mature language than those of twenty-five years ago, a fact which she attributes to certain sociological influences. She states that,

> The increased talkativeness found in the present study would seem to reflect an increased amount of adult language in the child's environment whether as a result of increased viewing of TV, more inclusion in family activities, general permissiveness toward the child's behavior, or other factors.[9]

[6] C. Wells, "The Child's Equipment for Language Growth," in *Factors that Influence Language Growth*, Research Bulletin of the National Conference on Research in English (Champaign, Ill., National Council of Teachers of English, 1953), pp. 1–8.

[7] D. McCarthy, "Home Influences," *Ibid.*, pp. 8–17.

[8] J. J. DeBoer, "Some Sociological Factors in Language Development," in *Child Development and the Language Arts*, Research Bulletin of the National Conference on Research in English (Champaign, Ill., National Council of Teachers of English, 1953), pp. 6–16.

[9] M. C. Templin, *Certain Language Skills in Children: Their Development and Interrelationships* (Minneapolis, Minn., University of Minnesota Press, 1957), p. 151.

INTERRELATIONSHIPS AMONG LANGUAGE SKILLS

Considerable thought and study are presently directed toward the inter-relationships which exist among the four major groups of language skills. For instance, the extent of the relationship between listening and reading—the two receptive channels of language—is not yet fully determined. In some ways they are very similar. Their purposes, some of their skills (for instance, determining central ideas, using contextual clues) and, to some extent, their language patterns are related. In other respects they are completely dissimilar, as discussed later in this section.

By the same token, speaking and writing—the out-going channels of language—have some common aspects and also some dissimilar features. Also, speaking and listening—as opposite sides of the same coin—are related in many ways, the most obvious of which is the extent to which one's speech patterns are determined by the language he listens to. Similar relationships appear to exist between reading and writing, for one reads only what another has written and one's written efforts are usually read by others. Then too, speaking and reading have many common relationships, a fact to which the modern reading readiness program with its emphasis on oral language readily subscribes.

Obviously, the intricacies of the various interrelationships among all the language areas are many and varied. Generally speaking, however, they rest upon a broad foundation of common elements which have been identified by one writer as follows:

It is apparent that much of the interrelationship among the language arts is due to such common elements as vocabulary and the concepts the words express, the structure of our language, the fact that meaningful experiences strengthen each facet of the language arts, and the carryover of problems from one aspect of the language arts to another.[10]

What implications does the interrelationship of the language skills hold for teaching? In the first place, it demands that the teacher broaden his horizons and appraise *all* phases of the child's language ability in relation to any specific learning task. In trying to help the child who has difficulty in reading, for instance, the teacher should carefully appraise his listening and speaking abilities. In these fields, he may find the clue to the child's reading problem. Similarly, the teacher should be able to anticipate that the child with immature speech patterns may have considerable trouble in expressing himself fluently in writing. On the other hand, the pupil's high level of listening comprehension may indicate that the time is near to introduce him to reading. In these and in many other ways, the teacher

[10] M. A. Dawson, "Interrelationships between Speech and Other Language Arts Areas," in *Interrelationships Among the Language Arts,* Research Bulletin of the National Conference on Research in English (Champaign, Ill., National Council of Teachers of English, 1954), p. 29.

should realize that the child's language skills are interrelated and that they simply *cannot* be considered as distinctly separate areas of achievement.

Secondly, for most language lessons, teachers will realize the importance of dual or triple objectives extending into various areas. For instance, in a lesson aimed at developing fluency in oral reading, the teacher will attempt to improve standards of speech as well. Similarly, a lesson on letter writing will be strengthened by attention to the supplementary objectives of spelling, handwriting, and related skills.

Before leaving this point, it is important to stress that the interrelationships among the language skills do not prohibit the teacher from treating them separately *when the occasion demands*. Certainly, the individuality of each area will require frequent and concentrated periods of instruction. This is as it should be. We may summarize, therefore, by concluding that the interrelationships existing among the language skills imply that teachers should relate them when it is functionally desirable to do so, but should continue to teach them as separate subjects when concentrated drill on specific masteries is demanded. With this in mind, let us turn our attention to a closer examination of each of the four major language areas.

Section 2: LISTENING

IMPORTANCE OF LISTENING

No channel of communication is more important than listening. It represents the young child's sole contact with language for approximately the first year of his life and remains consistently important throughout childhood and adulthood. As a matter of fact, the universal popularity of our newer media of mass communication testifies to the fact that we, as a general rule, rely more heavily upon listening today than we have since we first became literate. On an average day, we probably spend more time in *listening* than we do on *any other single activity*. Nowhere, of course, is this more true than in the classroom—Wilt reported that 57.5 per cent of the school day is spent in listening (most of which is spent in listening to the teacher).[11]

It is ironic that the activity in which we engage the most is the one which we know the least about and which we teach the least in our classrooms. But this happens to be the case at the present time. Although increasing attention is being directed toward this language area, the number of studies concerning listening is considerably less than one finds in many other fields. There is much we have learned about listening in recent years; there is much more which we do not know.

As far as the elementary curriculum goes, also, listening is a "Johnny-

[11] M. Wilt, "A Study of Teacher Awareness of Listening as a Factor in Elementary Education," *Journal of Educational Research*, Vol. 43 (April, 1950), pp. 626-636.

come-lately" to the language program. As a matter of fact, in some schools it is still not part of the daily program, for teachers assume that growth in listening is a natural process of maturation and that children will automatically develop the necessary skills, attitudes and habits. Exactly the opposite is true, for there is some evidence which indicates that listening becomes a *less* effective method of learning as one grows older.[12] This does not seem to be surprising when one considers the number of adults who freely admit that their listening powers are limited and insist that they must "see" the page in order to grasp the meaning. Consider how much these individuals are missing when they cannot achieve full understanding through listening or when they are limited in their appreciation of oral reading and, in some cases, even music.

To repeat, we know today that: (1) listening is a major channel of communication; (2) many individuals are seriously incapacitated in their listening ability; (3) growth in listening is not a natural accompaniment of maturation; and (4) listening *can* be improved through proper teaching. Several studies report an increase in listening comprehension after a period of concentrated teaching. Those by Hollow [13] and Pratt [14] are especially interesting for the elementary teacher. In view of these four significant facts, it would seem imperative that we examine carefully an effective program for the teaching of listening at the elementary school level. Before turning our attention to the procedures for teaching, however, it might be well to examine briefly the exact definition of the term "listening." This is done in the following section.

LISTENING AND HEARING

There is considerable difference between "hearing" and "listening." Occasionally these two terms are used interchangeably, but there is a world of difference between them. For instance, the child who answers his irate mother who ordered him to bed ten minutes ago with, "I didn't hear you," really means, "I was not listening to you." Hearing refers to the perception of sound; listening involves this but includes other factors as well. Furthermore, each can be divided into various levels according to the skills they demand. Distinction between levels of each have been made as follows:

LEVELS OF HEARING

1. *Acuity:* ability of the ear to collect sounds from the environment and transmit them to nervous system.

[12] P. A. Witty and R. A. Sizemore, "Studies in Listening: I," *Elementary English,* Vol. 35 (December, 1958), pp. 538–552.

[13] Sr. M. K. Hollow, "Listening Comprehension at the Intermediate Grade Level," *Elementary School Journal,* Vol. 56 (December, 1955), pp. 158–161.

[14] E. Pratt, "Experimental Evaluation of a Program for the Improvement of Listening," *Elementary School Journal,* Vol. 56 (March, 1956), pp. 315–320.

2. *Understanding:* ability of the central nervous system to extract and interpret meaning from the patterns transmitted to it.

3. *Discrimination and retention:* abilities that permit the individual to differentiate each sound from every other sound and to hold each in mind well enough and long enough for the individual to moderate his speech or to make accurate phonic comparisons.[15]

LEVELS OF LISTENING

1. *Little conscious listening and then only when interest is closely related to the self:* easily distracted by people and things in the environment.

2. *Half listening:* holding fast to own ideas and waiting to insert them at the first opportunity.

3. *Listening passively:* apparent absorption but little or no reaction.

4. *Off again–on again listening:* mentally entering into what is said if and when it is closely related to own experience.

5. *Listening:* responding with items from own experience as result of associations brought to mind.

6. *Listening:* some reactions through questions or comments.

7. *Listening:* some genuine emotional and mental participation.

8. *Listening:* a meeting of minds.[16]

Many writers have substituted a new term for listening: "auding." The term "auding" first appeared in the literature approximately ten years ago and was used to designate *auditory comprehension.* **It has been accepted by some as a much more comprehensive term than "listening." Furness claims that auding is the more adequate term and defines it as consisting of at least six processes: (1) hearing, (2) listening, (3) recognizing spoken language, (4) interpreting oral symbols, (5) supplementing meaning and knowledge of the symbols, and (6) being aware of facts or assumptions not uttered.[17] It will be noted that, in general, these factors are somewhat similar to the levels of listening noted above. For purposes of the following discussion, therefore, the terms "auding" and "listening" have been used synonymously.**

THE INSTRUCTIONAL PROGRAM

The objectives of the program are determined by the needs and abilities of the pupils. It is impractical to attempt to list specific objectives of teaching listening, for these will vary considerably according to the particular situation. The objectives of teaching listening, for instance, in the sixth

[15] J. Wepman, "Auditory Discrimination, Speech, and Reading," *Elementary School Journal,* Vol. 60 (March, 1960), p. 327.

[16] R. Strickland, *The Language Arts in the Elementary School,* rev. ed. (Boston, D. C. Heath and Company, 1957), p. 119.

[17] E. L. Furness, "Listening: A Case of Terminological Confusion," *Journal of Educational Psychology,* Vol. 48 (December, 1957), p. 481.

grade will be quite different from those in the first grade. Similarly, one fourth grade teacher may direct his program toward the attainment of certain specific objectives which may not be needed by the fourth grade class across the hall. Each teacher must, therefore, diagnose the specific auding abilities and needs of his group and plan a program to meet them. The few general objectives listed below are intended only as guides to help each teacher formulate specific objectives to meet the needs of his group.

GENERAL OBJECTIVES OF LISTENING

To help children realize the importance of listening as a major channel of communication.

To develop such skills of critical listening as: (1) ability to determine sequence of ideas; (2) ability to derive meaning from context clues; (3) ability to follow oral directions; (4) ability to relate main and subordinate ideas; and others determined by the age, grade, and competencies of the pupils.

To help children attain habits of courteous and considerate listening.

To increase pupils' appreciation of poetry, drama, and other forms of aural-oral communication.

To help children diagnose their listening needs.

To help children evaluate their growth in listening power.

The teacher's personality and behavior greatly influence the teaching of listening. The teacher's personality and behavior are of primary importance in achieving the desirable instructional goals of listening. First, and most important, in all his relationships with pupils, the teacher must establish himself as an example of an attentive listener. Unfortunately, this is not as simple as it sounds, for teachers are notoriously in love with the sound of their own voices! All too often, teachers are avid talkers, enthusiastic lecturers, but, alas, very poor listeners. The teacher who is so engrossed with his own delivery that he only half-listens to a pupil's contribution or question before again launching into a monologue is a familiar figure in many schools. It is always this same teacher who is too "busy" with his own plans to listen completely to a child during any informal part of the day and thus leaves behind him a trail of frustrations as children eventually realize that he never really listens to them. The situation in which a teacher attempts to teach his pupils to be good listeners, while he, himself, represents the opposite extreme is too ironic to warrant further comment. "Teaching by example" is probably never more necessary than in the development of high-level listening skills.

Secondly, the teacher's role in developing positive listening habits depends to a considerable extent upon his wise and discriminating use of language. It was mentioned earlier, that children spend a considerable portion of the school day listening to the teacher.[18] Undoubtedly, much of

[18] M. Wilt, *op. cit.*

this time is wasted in listening to voluble teachers who have fallen into a trap of unnecessarily rephrasing or repeating all questions, directions, or incidental remarks. Not only is this monotonous and boring for children, but it is antithetical to the development of a sound listening program. Infinitely more desirable is the situation in which the teacher disciplines himself to: (1) secure the attention of all pupils first; (2) state directions simply and clearly; and (3) refuse to repeat directions for the benefit of those who were not listening. If such a pattern is consistently maintained, children will be encouraged to listen attentively, for they will know that there is little possibility of the material being repeated. It is assumed, of course, that in all situations the teacher will use common sense and good judgment, for no one would advocate a rigidity that permitted one set of standards for all occasions. With reasonable exceptions, however, the teacher should keep in mind that avoidance of verbosity and unnecessary repetition will help children develop good habits of listening.

The physical environment plays an important role in the listening program. To a considerable extent, effective listening depends upon an environment free from extraneous noises and distractions. Outside playground noises or heavy traffic sounds can be serious hindrances to the development of effective listening habits. Some of these, of course, may be beyond the control of the teacher. Others, however, may be minimized by a wise scheduling of classroom activities. Take, for example, the situation in which a teacher has another class of children on the playground outside his windows between ten and ten-thirty each morning. Obviously, it is inadvisable for him to plan his program so that group discussions, committee reports, or other activities which require concentrated listening are held during this time. On the contrary, small group or individual activities such as reading groups, art work, individual study, construction activities and numerous others may be carried on at this time with a minimum of distraction. In all such similar cases, it is strongly urged that teachers study the exterior environment of their classrooms very carefully before scheduling lessons which demand a high level of listening.

The physical environment within the classroom should also merit the attention of the teacher. Nothing was less conducive to the development of listening skills than the physical setting of the old-fashioned, traditional classroom with its regimented rows of desks all facing the front of the room. With no opportunity for face-to-face communication, it is impossible to understand how children could ever be expected to become attentive listeners. How much better is the classroom of today with its movable furniture arranged in such a manner that speaker and listeners may face each other in an informal life-like manner! Conversational discussions in informal groups which encourage an easy and natural flow of language will develop good listeners to a far greater extent than the rigid recitation period can ever achieve.

Standards of good listening should be formulated co-operatively between teacher and pupils. Equally important to the physical setting of the classroom is the social climate. Children who have poor social habits, who are discourteous and impatient while another is speaking, need to develop an awareness of and adherence to standards of good listening. Although these may be developed in a variety of ways, many teachers find effective the use of classroom charts containing rules or standards of listening. It is true that some educators have recently attacked these and similar charts because of their artificiality, but this does not need to be the case. Such charts can be extremely helpful if certain general guiding principles are followed concerning their construction and use.

In the first place, it is extremely important that standards are developed co-operatively by the teacher and pupils. A set of rules formulated by the teacher and imposed upon the children is, for all practical purposes, worthless in developing any type of lasting social habits. Secondly, all such charts should be "open-ended" so that teachers and pupils may record additional standards as the need arises. To prepare a hard and fast set of "rules" which will suffice for all time and all occasions is as artificial as it is impractical. For instance, a situation involving poor listening habits may arise during the first week of school. The teacher may evaluate this with his class and from the group discussion there may evolve one agreed-upon standard such as, "We should try not to interrupt the person who is speaking." The teacher may transfer this statement to a chart which will be placed somewhere in the room and to which other standards may be added when the occasion arises. In this way, standards for listening are constantly being consulted, evaluated, and reinforced. Thirdly, no chart should continue to occupy a prominent place in the classroom after its period of usefulness has expired. If the "standards" chart has become inoperative or impractical or if children give only lip-service to it, it should be replaced by a more meaningful teaching device. Lastly, the standards themselves should be attainable and should not demand such ridiculous behavior as, "We should always sit straight and tall when someone is speaking!"

The development of listening standards is, of course, only one method of promoting a social climate conducive to listening. Incidental but consistent emphasis upon good listening, frequent evaluations in which children analyze the attentiveness of the class in any audience situation, and individual attention to the consistently poor listener should be constantly employed by all teachers, regardless of the grade level.

Establishing a purpose for listening is important. All activities regardless of grade level should contain a *purpose* for listening. Stated simply, a child should always listen for *something*. Depending upon the type of activity, he may listen to answer a question, to find the "rhyming" words, to form an opinion on a controversial subject, or to follow directions. In all oral language activities, however, the wise teacher will develop the habit of providing a purpose for children's listening. If he is reading a story, he will preface it by encouraging children to "listen to see why Johnny wanted to visit grandmother" or if children are giving reports, he will encourage the class to "listen to John's report to find out why the prime minister is visiting this country." Regardless of the grade level, however, it is important that the teacher provide a listening purpose for any oral language activity which demands a high level of listening performance.

A listening program should provide many informal opportunities for listening in all the elementary grades. The following are examples of opportunities which may be utilized for the teaching of listening:

1. *Informal conversations* among pupils or between teacher and pupil will present many excellent opportunities to appraise and strengthen listening skills.

2. *Socialized group procedures* such as committee or individual reports, news reports, book reviews, panel discussions, debates, forums, and many others constitute potential sources for the teaching of listening.

3. *Audio-visual aids,* such as sound films, narrated filmstrips and slides, television and radio programs, tape recordings, and records should occupy a prominent place in the listening program.

4. *Oral readings of prose and poetry*—by teacher or pupils—should be utilized to the fullest advantage.

5. *Dramatizations, story-telling,* and other types of programs are helpful.

6. *Games* such as the following may be helpful in providing practice in auditory discrimination, which is needed for critical listening:
   a. "Today we have a new game. It's a listening game to see who has sharp ears. Close your eyes and tell me what sound I am making." (*Teacher claps hands, stamps foot, beats tom-tom, plays a note on piano or autoharp, closes desk drawer, or taps on window pane.*)
   b. "Are we ready to go home? Listen carefully to see who should get his wraps. All boys and girls whose names *begin* like Mary (*stressing the initial consonant*) may get their things. Now, all whose names *begin* like Timmie." (*Continue with other initial consonant sounds.*)
   c. Ask children to close their eyes while one child reads or speaks a few sentences. See who can guess who spoke.
   d. "Listen carefully as I say some words. (*fan-man, lock-dock, etc.*) If the words rhyme, clap your hands twice. If the words do not rhyme, clap once."

7. *"Sharing" periods* in which children share an experience with the group should have as a *primary* objective the developing of listening skills and habits.

8. *Oral directions and announcements* provide valuable opportunities to diagnose listening needs.

9 *Telephoning* skills are usually taught in the primary grades and may be used for developing listening abilities.

A direct program for teaching listening is also needed in the elementary school. The many informal activities cited previously provide splendid opportunities to teach listening, but they must be reinforced by a direct teaching program. Some teachers devote a regular lesson (twenty to

Informal conversational opportunities are important.

Telephoning skills are taught in the primary grades.

thirty minutes) once or twice a week to the teaching of specific listening skills. For instance, a specific lesson may be aimed at developing the skill of *distinguishing the main ideas of a selection.* The teacher would probably introduce this lesson by drawing attention to the ways a main idea may be recognized in an oral situation. Such expressions as "the most important thing," "the main point," "to summarize," and others should be discussed as language guideposts which will help the listener look for the speaker's main points of emphasis. Following this introduction, a selection may be read or a talk presented, which provides opportunity to practice the skill being taught. The remainder of the lesson is devoted to a discussion of the selection—the main ideas presented—how they were recognized—and an evaluation of the pupils' skill in separating them from the subordinate points. Similar lessons should be planned to develop other skills through-out the year, for only through such direct teaching will listening abilities be strengthened.

While on this point, one should mention that many of the skills required for critical listening are identical to those required for critical reading. (See Chapter Six.) The teacher should not assume, however, that there is a natural carry-over from one area to another. Actually, as has been previously stated, in many ways the reading and listening acts are entirely dissimilar. Reading, for instance, permits one to progress at his own rate, to read and re-read, and to reflect as long as necessary on any idea presented. The pace of listening, on the other hand, is set by the speaker, not the listener, and the listener has no opportunity to pause for reflection or to return for the clarification of a point. It should be reiterated, therefore, that the area of listening contains certain unique skills and features which cannot be developed solely through informal activities or other curricular areas, but must be attacked through a well-planned, consistent, and directed teaching program.

Section 3: SPEAKING

What adult cannot recall an incident in his elementary school days when he was severely punished for the cardinal crime of "talking" in school? In the days of formal rows of furniture and rigid standards of silence, one of the worst offenses a pupil could commit was to attempt to communicate with his neighbor, and even to whisper was to invite serious consequences if caught by the ever-watchful eye of the teacher. Children were permitted to recite when they were called upon by the teacher, and other than this, the traditional school of the past practically prohibited spoken communication during school hours.

Obviously, in such a climate, the skills of oral expression were neither recognized nor encouraged. Obviously, also, this is not true in the modern elementary school where the importance of oral language is generally recognized by every teacher on every grade level. The prominent place which speech occupies in today's curriculum is evidenced by the following quote:

> It seems evident, therefore, that every teacher, no matter what her background or training, is a teacher of speech and language. She is responsible for providing the child with every possible opportunity for his development. *A good classroom is not a silent classroom.* (Italics not in original.)[19]

"Speech" was introduced into the elementary schools during the latter part of the nineteenth century. As was stated earlier, listening is a fairly recent addition to the curriculum. The same might be said of speech, although not to the same extent, for the inclusion of oral language in the curriculum preceded that of listening by more than a half-century. It was approximately during the latter part of the nineteenth century that oral language became a recognized subject, and Cubberley includes it as a subject of "major importance" in the curriculum of 1900.[20] Actually, however, there is very little resemblance between this early subject and that of the present day, for, in its beginning stages, the teaching of oral language concentrated solely upon the skills of rhetoric, declamation, debating, or public speaking. Today, the subject, as it is taught in the elementary school, concentrates entirely upon the function of language as communication. In line with this concept, the following goals have been established:

The modern oral language program is based upon four fundamental goals. In attempting to identify the goals of a modern oral language program, it may be wise to ask simply, "What does an individual need to communicate orally with his neighbors?" The answer might be somewhat as follows. He needs to have: (1) an adequate experiential background which will give meaning to his oral expression, as well as an adequate vocabulary and the mental ability to organize and present his thoughts clearly; (2) emotional security and poise; (3) a mastery of acceptable speech patterns; and (4) the knowledge and habits of acceptable oral usage. Each of these is discussed on the following pages.

THE "CONTENT" OF THE ORAL LANGUAGE PROGRAM

In order to speak well, one must have something to say. Unfortunately, this is not as obvious as it sounds, for, in some classrooms, teachers are working vigorously to develop fluent and proficient skills of oral expression, with no regard to what the pupil has to say or how interested he is in saying it. The child, for instance, who has to give a ten-minute book report may

[19] The Commission on the English Curriculum of the National Council of Teachers of English, *Language Arts for Today's Children* (New York, Appleton-Century-Crofts, Inc., 1954), p. 107.

[20] E. Cubberley, *Public Education in the United States* (Boston, Houghton Mifflin Company, 1934), p. 327.

appear to be almost inarticulate as he pauses, fumbles, and gropes for words. Ten minutes later, however, the same boy may be seen on the playground describing with enthusiasm and perfect ease the world series game he saw, play by play, to his attentive audience. In order to have a functional and effective oral language program, therefore, the teacher must gear it to the interests of his pupils. Forcing the children to give talks on assigned topics is rarely going to do anything but hinder their oral language development. By the same token, also, most children will talk fluently and easily if they have something to talk about. A rich, exciting, classroom environment and a full and varied daily program should provide a never-ending succession of opportunities for the development of oral language. Following this, attention must be directed toward developing the pupil's ability to express his thoughts clearly and interestingly.

Oral language is closely related to mental development. As was stated earlier, language is recognized today as a vehicle of thought. Before one becomes adept at expressive language, therefore, he must have developed a "mental" language which he uses to formulate concepts and organize thoughts. In other words, the individual who says, "I know it but I just can't say it" is probably in error, *unless he suffers from a language disorder.* In "knowing" it, however, and therefore being able to say it, several factors are involved, among which the following are very important.

Formation of concepts. A concept is a "mental picture" which, if seen clearly, can be described vocally. The child, for instance, who says that, "a jungle is like—uh—like some trees, but—uh—more," has no real concept of a jungle and cannot, therefore, describe it intelligently. Instead of merely telling him to omit the "uhs" when he is talking, the teacher might better attempt to help him formulate a concept of what a jungle is. This can be done through experience; the more direct the experience—the clearer the concept. Also, concepts may be clarified by pointing out relationships—that, "three acres is a little more than our schoolyard." In these, and many similar ways, the elementary school teacher must add continually to the child's storehouse of concepts, which in turn will have a direct relationship to his growth in oral language.

Organization of thoughts. Oral language demands the ability to organize one's thoughts according to main and subordinate points as well as to sequence. In the primary grades, a major organizational task is to develop the use of the sentence as an expression of thought. In this connection, it is interesting to note that the average length of the sentence is still considered to be the most "reliable, easily determined, objective, quantitative, and easily understood measure of linguistic maturity." [21] The five-year-old child, therefore, who explains his picture to the group by pointing to each

---

[21] D. McCarthy, "Language Development in Children," in L. Carmichael, ed., *Manual of Child Psychology,* 2nd ed. (New York, John Wiley and Sons, Inc., 1954), pp. 550–551.

object and saying "cow," "truck," and "grass" is seriously retarded linguistically and must be encouraged to express himself more completely. The teacher may ask, "where is the truck going," or say, "tell us something about the cow," in order to develop gradually the ability of fuller expression.

Major organizational difficulties which confront teachers in the intermediate and upper grades are: (1) failure to show relationships between isolated thoughts; (2) rambling and digression from the central idea; (3) failure to group ideas according to main points; (4) failure to relate ideas in sequence; and (5) inclusion of irrelevancies and unrelated facts. All of these should constitute a major emphasis of the oral language program, for it is important to remember that they will all reappear later in the pupils' written expression unless they have been eliminated by successful teaching.

Adequate vocabulary. As has been stated previously, by the time the child enters school he has a vocabulary of several thousand words. Studies disagree on the number, chiefly because of the difficulties of obtaining exact measurements. Regardless of the absolute number, however, most authorities agree that the vocabulary of elementary school children is probably a good deal larger than most people realize. Smith's study, for instance, reported that "for grade one the average number of words in the total vocabulary (basic plus derivative words) was 23,700 with a range from 6,000 to 48,800." [22] It becomes the task of the teacher, therefore, to build upon the substantial vocabulary which many children bring to school with them. There are several guideposts for doing this.

In all the elementary grades, *nothing* is more important to vocabulary building than the example set by the teacher. The authors have found, over the years, that some primary grade teachers have a tendency to avoid "big" words in the fear that they will be "over the heads" of their pupils. Nothing could be more detrimental to a program of vocabulary development. Teachers who have this worry should be reminded that they are "over children's heads" only when they are outside their experiences and not when they are using multisyllable words! "Evaporate," "hibernate," "temperature," "experiment," and thousands of others are words which primary grade children may add easily to their speaking vocabularies if they are introduced to them through direct experience and at proper intervals.

Here again, it should be mentioned that a rich, experiential program is a "must" in an effective oral language program. If pupils are introduced to many different, vital, and fascinating experiences, their vocabularies can hardly keep from expanding. A trip to a modern dairy, for instance, may be followed by a discussion utilizing such words as *homogenization, separa-*

[22] M. K. Smith, "Measurement of the Size of General English Vocabulary Through the Elementary Grades and High School," *Genetic Psychology Monographs,* Vol. 24 (November, 1941), pp. 343–344.

tion, rotolactor, production, and *pasteurization.* Nothing will grow without food and no vocabulary will grow unless it is fed a rich diet of fascinating and meaningful experiences.

Another tremendously important factor in building vocabularies is the reading program. Encouraging children to read and then read some more, reading to them daily, providing them with new and exciting reading materials, and encouraging them to share with others what they have read simply cannot be overemphasized. In addition, various devices for calling children's attention to new words in speech and reading will, of course, strengthen vocabulary. Children love to "play" with words, and they should be encouraged to explore them, experiment with them, illustrate them, demonstrate them, and finally adopt them! Charts of *Our New Words,* group or individual card catalogues of recently learned words, commercial or pupil-made picture dictionaries, and vocabulary notebooks are among those which modern teachers find successful in their attempts to expand pupil vocabularies.

OPPORTUNITIES FOR ORAL EXPRESSION

Effective speaking is dependent upon emotional security. The extreme case of the child or adult who has withdrawn into a world of silence because of an emotional block is, unfortunately, not as uncommon as it should be. Many others find it extremely difficult to express themselves with any degree of articulateness because of tensions and insecurities. It would appear to be obvious, therefore, that unless the classroom is free from fears, tensions, humiliations, ridicule, sarcasm, and retaliation, it is impossible to develop an oral language program compatible with modern-day philosophy.

The daily schedule should provide numerous opportunities to develop informal conversational skills. The five- or ten-minute period prior to the actual start of the school day is a time when children may be permitted an informal conversational period. As the teacher circulates around the room, greets children, and visits with small groups, he is creating an opportunity to develop and evaluate conversational skills. Occasionally he may follow this session by a group discussion in which children are encouraged to analyze the characteristics of a successful conversationalist. Such skills and courtesies as keeping to the subject, not interrupting, not monopolizing, listening attentively, or speaking so that all may hear are conversational assets which may be stressed with all children. As pupils progress through the grades, the teaching of conversational skills may become somewhat more directed. In the intermediate and upper grades the teacher may divide his class into small groups and assign topics for informal discussion and conversation. These may be followed by a group evaluation session in which specific conversational skills are emphasized. In these grades, also, the teacher will want to spend considerable time on more formal skills, such as making or acknowledging introductions, acting as guest or host, or telephoning. Practicing these before the group, role-playing, and group evaluations are valuable in teaching these skills, although the maximum benefit probably comes from providing situations for their actual use. "Real" experiences, for instance, in acting as hosts for the class party will reinforce these skills a great deal more than if the children pretend to put these into practice.

Just as there should be numerous opportunities to use conversational skills so should there be an equal number and variety of opportunities utilizing discussion techniques. All children should be encouraged to enter freely into a discussion period, to contribute a thought, to ask or answer a question, to disagree or agree, or in any other way to be an active participant in the group. Many a teacher, unfortunately, may permit a few talkative children to dominate an entire discussion. This was illustrated in a recent incident in which an observer spent a day in a third-grade classroom. Early in the day she noticed that one little girl, sitting on the fringes of the group, did not make a single contribution to the morning conference period. She continued to observe the child and noted that she did not once contribute to a group discussion in science, social studies, or arithmetic. Moreover, the only time that the child spoke before the group at all was when she answered a question directed to her in a small reading group. Here, apparently, was a child who was perfectly capable but who, because of shyness, timidity, or insecurity, did not feel confident to volunteer a contribution to any major group discussion. Furthermore, as far as the observer could determine, the teacher was either unaware of, or indifferent to, the situation and made no attempt to build confidence and ability in this area. Obviously, with such a child, the teacher could do a great deal by reacting to her smallest contribution with praise and encouragement and working with her individually until she began to develop some of the confidence necessary for expressing herself orally.

A "participation index" will indicate the distribution of active participation in a discussion lesson. It is not unusual that the teacher, busy with other activities of the day, may be unaware that he allows most of his daily discussions to be dominated by only a small portion of the class. In order to avoid this pitfall, many teachers have found it profitable periodically to take a "participation index" of any discussion lesson. This is simply a tabulation of the number of times each member of the group contributes to the general discussion in any respect. In the upper grades a dependable pupil, unobserved by the group, may be asked to tabulate beside each child's name the number of times he participates orally in the discussion. At the close of the period the teacher may discover perhaps that six children have carried the bulk of the entire discussion while three have not uttered a word. Or, he may find, as a teacher recently did, that he is unconsciously directing the discussion around the contributions of the more advanced children while the average and slower pupils are almost ignored. Using this device from time to time will keep the teacher apprised of the balance he maintains in his discussion lessons and will enable him to evaluate whether or not he is succeeding in strengthening oral expression in all children. Obviously, progress in this direction will be slow and tedious, but much success can be realized by a teacher who is cognizant of this goal.

Specific discussion skills should be stressed in the language program. In addition to providing equal opportunities for discussion for all children, certain specific skills must be developed through direct teaching and continual group evaluations. Pronovost lists the following discussion skills to which specific lessons should be devoted.

1. *a.* Desire to contribute to the discussion.
   b. Willingness to listen to the other points of view.
2. *a.* Ability to stick to the topic of discussion while giving evidence to support one's point of view.
   b. Ability to listen for supporting evidence related to the main topic of discussion.
3. Ability to organize one's thoughts in speaking and listening according to a problem-solving pattern of definition, analysis, exploration, evaluation, and decision.
4. Ability to serve as leader or follow leadership in a discussion.
5. Ability to participate in meetings conducted according to parliamentary procedure.[23]

In addition to class discussions, children may be encouraged to contribute to the group in a variety of situations. Giving reports, telling original stories, dramatizing, oral reading, and other types of activities should have a prominent place in the daily program. Indeed, the writers know of one school which attempts to have *every child in the school* speak from the school stage at least once a year. Participating in programs and plays, conducting morning exercises, and making or reading announcements provide numerous opportunities to reach this goal. If all schools (1) provided some opportunities for free conversational periods; (2) encouraged all children to contribute freely to class discussions; (3) created an emotional climate conducive to free oral expression; and (4) gave each child opportunity to appear before a class or school group, children would develop a positive emotional attitude toward speaking.

COMMON TYPES OF SPEECH PROBLEMS

". . . generally speaking, impaired speech tends to make for a decrease in . . . (1) Confidence, (2) Self-esteem, (3) Enthusiasm, (4) Happiness, (5) Acceptance and understanding of others, (6) Friendliness toward others, (7) Cooperativeness, (8) Responsiveness toward others, feelings of belongingness. It

[23] W. Pronovost, *The Teaching of Speaking and Listening in the Elementary School* (New York, Longmans, Green & Company, Inc., 1959), p. 75.

tends to increase . . . (1) Feelings of inferiority, (2) Unworthiness, (3) Apathy, (4) Disappointment, discouragement, (5) Awe, contempt, or rejection of others, (6) Antagonism toward others, (7) Competitiveness, (8) Withdrawing tendencies, loneliness." [24]

When one relates this statement to the approximately two-and-a-half million speech defective school-age children, it becomes apparent that the need for a vital speech improvement program is a very real one. Fortunately, only about one-fourth of these children may be classified as involved or complicated problems who need treatment from a speech specialist. With such cases, "a little knowledge is a dangerous thing," and the classroom teacher should be extremely wary about diagnosing or prescribing for a pronounced speech problem. Referral to the speech specialist should be made immediately. He, in turn, should diagnose, prescribe treatment, and provide guidance for the classroom teacher for working with these children during the school day.

By far the larger group of speech problems are those which can be helped by an adequate program of speech instruction provided in the regular elementary classroom. As a general rule, these can be classified as follows:

Vocal Disorders

1. Disorders of voice quality, including:
   a. Nasal quality (with nasal resonance).
   b. Denasal quality (without nasal resonance).
   c. Breathy quality (with too much breath).
   d. Hoarse-husky quality (sounds are "low-pitched" and "throaty").
   e. Harsh quality (sounds are "high-pitched" and "shrill").
   f. Monotonous quality (a monotone).

2. Disorders of pitch, including a voice that is:
   a. Of unpleasant high-pitched level.
   b. Of unpleasant low-pitched level.
   c. Without adequate pitch variations (monopitch).

3. Disorders of intensity, including a voice that is:
   a. Too weak.
   b. Too loud.
   c. Lacking in variation in intensity (monoforce).

4. Disorders in time (or rhythm), including speech that is:
   a. Too fast.
   b. Too slow.
   c. Monotonous in time (monorate).
   d. Abnormal in sound duration or rhythm patterns.[25]

Common articulatory disorders. Into this classification fall by far the majority of speech disorders which the elementary teacher may expect to find in his classroom. Some authorities estimate that approximately three

[24] W. Johnson and others, *Speech Handicapped School Children,* rev. ed. (New York, Harper and Brothers, 1956), pp. 66–67.
[25] L. Cypreansen, J. Wiley, and L. Laase, *Speech Development, Improvement, and Correction* (New York, The Ronald Press Company, 1959), p. 56.

out of every four speech problems belong in this group. In its broadest sense this classification includes lisping, indistinct enunciation, incorrect pronunciation, and all other errors made by substitution, omission, or distortion. Some of these, of course, are caused by severe physical impairments, such as cleft palate, cerebral palsy, or deficient hearing. Others are caused by more minor physical abnormalities, as dental or subsidiary oral defects. Still others are caused by no organic factor but are simply the result of imitation, habit, or incorrect learning and teaching. If the classroom teacher seeks help from the speech therapist in diagnosing the cause of the articulatory defect, he may be able to develop a suitable speech program adapted to the individual needs of his pupils.

Infantile Speech. Strictly speaking, this may be classified under the broader heading of articulatory disorders, although it is so common in some primary classrooms that certain authorities choose to discuss it separately. Many children enter the kindergarten talking "baby talk" because they have never been corrected at home and some have even been encouraged to continue it because parents have thought it "cute." The child, for instance, who says *fink* for *think* and *tandy* instead of *candy* probably has no structural impairment but may simply need a consistent program of speech improvement under the wise guidance of a conscientious primary grade teacher.

Foreign Speech. This, again, may be classified as a type of articulatory disorder, but it is mentioned separately here because it may constitute a major problem for teachers in certain schools. As was mentioned earlier, it is extremely difficult to determine the exact relationship between bilingualism and language facility. Carrow, for instance, discovered that the bilingual group, in her study made "more and different types of articulatory and grammatical errors than the monolingual group," [26] although she suggests the possibility that this may have been due to the bilingual child's type of environment rather than to bilingualism, *per se.* Regardless of the cause, however, there is little doubt that many children who come from non-English homes will present specialized needs as far as the ordinary classroom speech improvement program is concerned.

Not only must the elementary oral language program be directed toward the improvement of these common speech disorders, but it must be equally concerned with the elimination of glaring errors of usage. These are considered in the following section.

COMMON ERRORS OF ORAL USAGE

Today, there is widespread, if not unanimous agreement, that the elementary oral language program should be more concerned with the production of clear, natural, and socially acceptable usage than with the teaching

[26] Sr. M. A. Carrow, "Linguistic Functioning of Bilingual and Monolingual Children," *Journal of Speech and Hearing Disorders,* Vol. 22 (September, 1957), p. 379.

of formal grammar. This viewpoint has been substantiated repeatedly by research studies which have consistently revealed the lack of relationship between oral (or written) expression and the teaching of formal grammar. Summarizing the major studies in this area, DeBoer says,

> The impressive fact is . . . that in all these studies, carried out in places and at times far removed from each other, often by highly experienced and disinterested investigators, the results have been constantly negative so far as the value of grammar in the improvement of language expression is concerned.[27]

With this in mind, the wise elementary teacher will devote his time and energy more to the correction of the glaring errors of usage prevalent in the informal speech of his pupils than to the formal teaching of the parts of speech or the rules of grammar. Pooley lists the following prevalent errors, the elimination of which should be a major goal of the elementary school language program:

ain't or hain't	he give	he run
hair are	I got for I've got	have saw
a orange	my brother, he (and	I says
have ate	other double subjects)	he seen
he begun	her, him, and me went	them books
was broke	hisself	theirselves
he brung	there is, was	this here
climb (short i)	four	that there
clumb	knowed, growed, etc.	us boys went
he come	learn me a song	we, you, they was
have did	leave me go	with we girls
he, she, it don't	me and Mary went	have went
I drunk	haven't no,	have wrote
didn't, hadn't	haven't nothing	it is yourn, hern,
ought		ourn, thern ([28])
was froze		

Forms of errors upon which instruction should be postponed until the secondary school are, according to Pooley:

None of us are, were there.	Do it like I do.
Can I go?	He acts like he is cold.
Do the work good.	It is me, him, her, them.
I haven't got a pencil.	Everybody, everyone said
I couldn't hardly do the	that they . . .
work.	Who did you choose?
I haven't hardly any.	If I was you, I'd play ball.
She gave it to John and I.	I wish I was you.
He lays down every day,	Who are you waiting for?
is laying down, laid	I will probably be late.
down, has laid down, etc.	One of my brothers were here. ([29])

[27] J. J. DeBoer, "Grammar in Language Teaching," *Elementary English,* Vol. 36 (October, 1959), p. 417.

[28] R. C. Pooley, *Teaching English Usage,* The National Council of Teachers of English (Appleton-Century-Crofts, Inc., 1946. By permission), p. 180.

[29] *Ibid.,* p. 181.

In summary, the elimination of the more common errors of speech and English usage is a major instructional goal of the elementary school teacher. To accomplish this goal, a functional program of informal activities as well as direct teaching is needed. The following section contains a description of this program.

THE ORAL LANGUAGE PROGRAM

Appraisal of children's errors in usage and speech constitutes the first step in a developmental program. In order to determine where to begin his double-edged program of speech and language correction, the teacher must be guided by the needs of the pupils. In plain words, he should *teach what the children need to learn.* How may these needs be determined? Probably the most satisfactory device is the *language inventory* used by many teachers. This may vary in purpose and appearance from the one suggested by Dawson and Zollinger [30] to a simplified version which consists only of a piece of blank paper divided into two vertical columns. Errors of speech (*din't* for *didn't,* or *punkin* for *pumpkin*) may be noted in one column and errors of usage (*done* for *did, me and John*) in the other. Through this type of accumulative record the teacher can easily tabulate the most prevalent errors, and these will become the focal point of a correctional program which will consist of an indirect as well as a direct approach.

A considerable proportion of language teaching should be done indirectly and incidentally. The indirect approach may be called the *Three I* program, for it is characterized by *imitation, individual needs, and incidental teaching.* Consider the importance of each of these for a few minutes.

It is probably not possible to overemphasize the importance of *imitation* as a factor in learning language. Obviously many *incorrect* forms have been learned solely through this channel, and it should be reasonable to suppose that *correct* forms could be learned just as easily. Unfortunately, this is not always true, particularly with younger children whose incorrect speech may be caused by immaturity or inability to make the required sounds. This becomes less true, however, as children mature, and in the intermediate grades their incorrect speech may be solely a matter of habit or imitation of their parents, peers, or TV personalities. Because of these and other considerations, it is imperative that the teacher, regardless of grade level, serve as an example of correct speech to his class. The extent, of course, to which children will desire to imitate their teacher will depend largely upon their relationship with him. All children (and adults) tend to imitate those whom they admire. If the teacher is a figure of respect and admiration for the children, it is probable that they will imitate his speech. If not, the reverse will be true. The important thing to remember is that, other things being

[30] M. Dawson and M. Zollinger, *Guiding Language Learning* (New York, Harcourt, Brace & World, Inc., 1957), p. 491.

equal, the teacher can do a great deal to strengthen his classroom oral language program simply by *setting the children a good example* of correct speech and usage.

The second *I*, *individuality*, indicates the stress which is placed today on correcting children individually and not before the entire group. The traditional and, in some places, still common practice of asking for a group evaluation of a child's oral report has questionable value in the eyes of many teachers. Even though most teachers accent the positive instead of the negative aspects, the fact that each report is inevitably followed by, "What did you think of John's report? What did you like? How do you think he can improve?" is considered by many to be extremely detrimental to the development of the language goals of a modern program.

In place of this procedure, some teachers have adopted a policy of correcting children privately and individually on their oral reports or contributions. After a lesson devoted to book talks, for instance, the teacher may choose, during the next four or five days, to discuss with certain individuals the strengths and limitations of their deliveries. These may be reinforced by a group discussion *prior* to the next book talk lesson. Such questions as, "What are some things we need to work on in giving our book talks?" or "How can we make our books sound exciting to the audience?" will help children evaluate themselves, without directing attention to any specific child. Group evaluations on generalities and individual conferences on specifics seem to be procedures which many teachers have found to be most successful.

The third *I* indicates the emphasis which the teacher places upon language learnings through numerous *incidental* activities in the daily program. In every subject, activity, and situation there is an opportunity to teach language. A teacher who casually asks a child to repeat the correct form immediately after he has used the incorrect one is developing better usage, provided he does not do it with such persistence that the pupil becomes annoyed or apprehensive. In the lower grades teachers may correct a child and urge him to use a better form merely upon the basis that "it sounds better." For instance, a second grade dramatized a story they had read concerning the animals' Christmas. In one corner of the room were the squirrels, in another the rabbits, and in another the deer. Sturdy, red-cheeked, bright-eyed Chuck was chosen to be Santa Claus. As he visited each group of animals, he was asked, "What do you have for us, Santa Claus?" and he replied with gusto, "I ain't got nothing for you," and proceeded to the next corner. At the close, the teacher made a few helpful comments and suggested that the group do it a second time, "to see if we can do it even better." Just before they started she suggested, "Chuck, most people think it sounds better to say, 'I have nothing for you' when you answer the animals. Shall we try it that way this time?" Sure enough, each time Chuck gave the correct reply and never slipped back to his incorrect form. Obviously, no one would claim that this error was permanently eliminated through this one incident, but similar occurrences throughout the year should result eventually in improved language patterns.

The success of directed teaching of oral language in the intermediate and upper grades depends, to a great extent, upon motivation. Although the indirect approach is used in all grades, it is fortified in the upper grades by the direct teaching of acceptable language and speech patterns. Probably no other factor is more important in determining the success of the direct approach than that of motivation. With the child who really does not "hear" that he is using incorrect language, or the child who knows but doesn't care, motivation is the teacher's major problem.

A direct attack upon the elimination of common faults of speech is largely futile unless the child understands that he is saying the incorrect form. Because none of us can really hear ourselves accurately, it may be extremely difficult to convince a child that he is not saying what he hears others say. This is, of course, particularly true of children with a foreign speech problem. The case of the teacher working with a child who says, "John, listen carefully to me. Say *look at them*," and John replying in exasperation, "That's what I am saying—*look at dem*," is a common one. Obviously, John does not hear that his speech is different from the teacher's. In such a situation, the first step of a direct attack is to provide opportunities, through the use of a tape or disk recorder, for the pupil to hear himself. Taping oral readings, dramatizations, reports, book talks, panel discussions, and similar activities will enable the pupil to hear his own speech—perhaps for the first time. Following this, the teacher may help him with specific difficulties and supplement this with functional oral language and reading opportunities until the use of the correct form becomes habitual.

The task of motivating correct language usage presents an entirely different problem, for here the trouble is, not that the child cannot hear himself, but that he sees no reason for change. Before he is introduced to the formal study of grammar in the later elementary or junior high school grades, he cannot comprehend why one form is correct and the other incorrect, nor can he understand why he should change from a pattern which is obviously satisfactory to him. It is very difficult to motivate a child to say "have gone" instead of "have went" when the latter expresses what he wishes to communicate. Nor, with intermediate grade children is it sufficient to say "it sounds better" as it usually is with primary children. With older children, therefore, two motivating approaches are suggested. The teacher might convince his pupils that, just as appearance and behavior create a favorable or unfavorable impression, so also does speech. Also, occasionally the teacher can demonstrate that incorrect usage hinders communication, for people cannot understand what is meant. The glaring error, "I stood home" for "I stayed home," for instance, may be explained so that children realize they are actually saying something other than what they mean. The

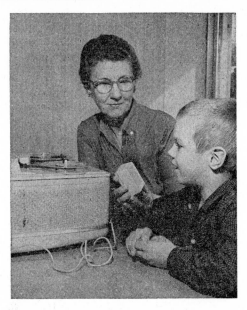

A valuable aid in the speech
program is the tape recorder.

teacher may stress that, since language is an instrument of communication,
if it does not serve this goal it is useless and must be changed.

**The direct language program emphasizes developmental lessons utiliz-
ing inductive reasoning.** In the intermediate and upper grades children
should be acquainted with the generalizations governing correct usage. In
most instances a teacher should lead children to understand the generalizations through a process of inductive reasoning. Presenting children in these
grades with several specific examples and then encouraging them to formulate the rule which has been demonstrated is a generally commendable
procedure. The following is a brief account of a developmental lesson in
which, from comparing specifics, children were led to the understanding
and formulation of the generalization:

DEVELOPMENTAL LESSON ON CORRECT USAGE
(Grade 4)

OBJECTIVE

To help children to understand the generalization which governs the correct
use of *saw* and *seen*.

PROCEDURE

Teacher: Boys and girls, I have noticed lately that many of us are confused
about two very common words which we use many times a day in
our speech and writing. Since we do use these words so often it might

be a good idea to talk about them and see if we can learn when to use them properly. Will you look at the board while I write these two words? (*Writes* saw *at top of one chalkboard and* seen *at top of another.*) Who will read each of these words for us? Let's take the first one and see if we can think of a good sentence using *saw* which sounds correct. Who will try?

Child: I saw a good movie on TV last night.

Teacher: Listen while I repeat John's sentence. (*Repeat*) Does that sound right to you? (*Discussion*) If we agree that it sounds right, watch while I write it on the *saw* board. (*Writes sentence on this board.*) Who can think of another sentence with this word in it?

Child: I saw the Michigan-Minnesota game Saturday.

Teacher: Does that sentence sound correct to you? Say it to yourselves. Do we agree? Then I'll write it on this board with our first sentence. Who can think of another? (*Repeat this procedure until satisfactory number of sentences have been contributed and listed on board. The number will depend upon the difficulty children have in formulating them. If many incorrect statements are offered, the teacher should persist until he has a considerable number of correct ones on the board.*)

Now, let's look at our other word. Can we do the same thing for this word? Who can think of a sentence in which he can use this word correctly?

Child: Charles has seen my electric train.

Teacher: Does this sound right? Say the sentence to yourself. Does it sound correct? If we agree, I'll write it on the board. (*Writes sentence on the second board.*) Who can give us another?

Child: Who has seen my soccer ball?

Teacher: Is this correct? Does it sound right? (*Writes it on the board and continues same procedure until reasonable number of correct sentences have been listed.*)

Now, let's look at our two boards and read all of the sentences very carefully. What do you notice about their use of our two special words? Look at the ones which use *seen*. Do all of these sentences contain certain other special words? What are words which are used in all these sentences?

Children: *Have, has,* or *had.*

Teacher: Now let's look at the sentences which use *saw.* Are these words also used in these sentences or are they left out? Now, who can make up a rule which will help us to remember an important thing about *saw* and *seen?*

Children: *Saw* stands alone in a sentence but *seen* needs the helping words of *have, has* or *had.*

Teacher: I will write this rule on the board and you may copy it in your notebooks. Now will you close your notebooks and look again at the board?

Who can repeat for us once again the rule we formulated to help us remember the correct use of these two words? Now that we have our rule, how can we test it to see if it always works?

Children: See if other people always follow this rule.

Teacher: Why don't we do this? Let's open reading (*or other*) books. On page 72, one of these words is used in a sentence. Who can read us the sentence? Does it follow the rule? On the next page one of them is used again. Who will read that sentence? Does it follow the rule? (*Continue until children have had thorough opportunity to test application of the generalization.*)

EVALUATION

Teacher: Who can tell us again the rule we formulated about the correct use of these two words? What are the helping words which must be used with *seen?* Did the rule seem to work when we tested it in our reading books? Now that we have formulated the rule, copied it in our notebooks, and tested it to see if it works, what's the most important thing we should do?

Child: Try to remember to use it ourselves.

Teacher: Let's see if we can do that.

Throughout the year many lessons similar to this can be used to strengthen children's knowledge of correct usage. They can, of course, be presented and reinforced in a variety of ways, but most people agree that frequent developmental lessons are necessary in an intermediate or upper grade program of systematic instruction.

Repetitive practice is needed to develop correct oral language. The emphasis upon practice exercises in teaching language has, like many other educational procedures, gone from one extreme to the other. From the traditional overemphasis upon isolated drill work, the pendulum swung to the other extreme in which any type of practice was completely omitted from the program. Today, most language authorities subscribe to the importance of practice, provided: (1) it does not dominate the entire program; (2) exercises are short, intensive, and varied; and (3) it is preceded always by understanding and rationalization. Concerning drill on correct oral language, Dawson and Zollinger state that, "The errors in using word forms first appear in speech and are commonest in speaking; therefore, the drill should be oral." [31] Greene and Petty support this point of view and urge the teacher to "use as much oral drill as possible." [32] Numerous games and other devices can be used on any grade level to achieve this goal and will have considerable value in reinforcing the developmental lessons which they follow.

Certain visual aids and supplementary materials may have value in reinforcing language learnings. In addition to drill exercises, certain other aids may have value in reinforcing a program of systematic language instruction. As is true in all cases, the value of these will depend upon how they are used, when they are used, and the needs and abilities of the pupils. Some may be valuable only for average or below-average children while others may be of equal benefit to all pupils. Those which are frequently recommended by teachers include:

1. *Notebooks.* Many authorities advocate the use of notebooks for older children in which they may record rules and generalizations of usage as well as their own individual errors. Examples of correct forms, rules, drill exercises, or specific difficulties may be accumulated in a notebook which may be used by the pupil throughout the school year.

2. *Charts and Posters.* Many teachers use large teacher-made or pupil-made charts which are displayed prominently in the classroom and which contain rules and examples of correct usage.

3. *Films and Filmstrips.* These are becoming increasingly available and may be used to give variety and interest to the language program.

4. *Diagrams and Cartoons.* Again, the value of these will depend largely upon the intellectual maturity and needs of certain classes. The following stick-figure illustrations were drawn by fourth-grade children who were asked to illustrate the generalization they had learned about *saw-seen.*

In summary, the oral language program, directed toward the attainment of natural, functional, and socially acceptable speech and usage, consists of a variety of informal procedures as well as "direct" teaching. Practice has a place in this program if used correctly, as do many visual aids and other teaching devices.

The remainder of the chapter is devoted to a brief discussion of the creative aspects of the oral language program.

Choral Speaking

Choral speaking is a twentieth-century addition to the elementary school. Choral speaking, although an ancient art, was introduced into the elementary schools of this country only two or three decades ago. Since its

[31] *Ibid.,* p. 497.
[32] H. Greene and W. Petty, *Developing Language Skills in the Elementary School* (Boston, Allyn and Bacon, Inc., 1959), p. 302.

introduction, its value in the elementary program has been proportionate to the way it has been used or misused by teachers. For a while, it was exploited as an "entertainment" device, and children were drilled and rehearsed for endless hours by teachers who struggled to achieve perfection for the approval of an audience. Fortunately, this distortion of the original values has generally disappeared, and today most teachers are returning to choral speech for its original purpose—as an enriching and creative experience for all children. Used with this purpose in mind, the activity has several values, the following of which are most often cited:

Choral speaking, when used correctly, offers many values to the elementary school language program. In the first place, choral speaking provides opportunity for the creative expression of poetry or prose. Gullan points out that many children (and adults) are sensitive to the appeal of poetry or prose but are too reserved or self-conscious to speak or read it aloud except in the company of a group.[33] To these individuals, choral speaking offers the satisfaction of participating in a rich and creative experience without fear of ridicule or criticism.

[33] M. Gullan, *Choral Speaking* (Boston, Expression Company, 1931), p. 1.

Secondly, choral speaking provides excellent opportunities for the improvement of speech errors, again without calling attention to a particular individual. As children read or recite together—the teacher can point out, for instance, that the word is *just* which rhymes with *must*—it is not *jist*, and would not sound right if pronounced this way in the poem. In addition, all of the common faults of speech production (for instance, disorders of voice quality, pitch, and intensity) can be attacked through choral speaking, often with results far surpassing those attained by any other method of speech improvement.

The social values of choral speaking should not be overlooked. It provides numerous opportunities for group co-operation, group planning, and group evaluation which will widen the horizons of social understanding.

Lastly, choral speaking will help to increase pupils' appreciation of poetry or prose, and many, for the first time, will be able to experience the rhythm, beauty, and imagery which can be expressed through the medium of language.

Various types of choral speaking or reading may be used. The pattern of choral speaking will depend solely upon the objectives of the teacher and pupils, the suitability of material, and the maturity of the pupils. In general, the following three arrangements can be used appropriately with elementary school children:

1. *Unison speaking.* This is usually considered the simplest arrangement and the one, therefore, most appropriate for young children. Pupils in the primary grades may enjoy speaking nursery rhymes, jingles, and some of the lovely poems for children which lend themselves to group expression.

2. *Refrain.* This is a combination of solo and unison speaking. It is more difficult than unison speaking and lends itself to selections which call for contrasts and variations in intensity, mood, and tempo.

3. *Part arrangements.* Numerous variations can be made with part arrangements, using soloists and groups. Generally speaking, this is the most difficult arrangement and is usually reserved for intermediate and upper grades. In this arrangement, as in all others, the teacher should keep in mind the values of choral speaking as they contribute to the broad objectives of elementary education. With some of the more difficult arrangements, the teacher may tend to become overly ambitious and emphasize the perfection of the final performance instead of the value of the experience. If this misplaced emphasis can be avoided, there is no doubt that choral speaking can be a deeply satisfying, creative, and socially constructive experience for elementary school children.

Dramatization

"Playmaking" should occupy an important place in the elementary school curriculum. Creative expression through the dramatic arts may take several forms in the elementary school. Today, there is considerable interest in "creative dramatics" or "playmaking" which capitalizes upon the free, natural, and spontaneous play of childhood. The value of this activity lies solely in its contribution to the participant. It has been defined as "a group activity in which meaningful experience is acted out by the participants as they create their own dialogue and action." [34] Accepting this definition, it is obvious that creative dramatics is a free and extemporaneous interpretative action; it does not depend on prepared scripts, rehearsals, or memorized lines. Usually the audience, if present at all, is a secondary consideration and may consist solely of the children who happen to be nonparticipants at that particular moment. Occasionally, hints of costumes and improvised props and scenery may be desired by the group, although often they are entirely unnecessary.

Creative dramatics derives its inspiration from numerous sources. It can be the re-creating of the ordinary experiences of childhood—playing store, playing house, going to the park, and others. *Housekeeping corners* in the primary room together with other miscellaneous equipment will help to satisfy the child's need for this type of dramatic play.

In addition to ordinary experiences, the young child uses his play to create the world of fantasy and make-believe. For this he uses the materials of stories—stories which have been read to him or which he has read or seen on TV or in the movies. He becomes a "gun-totin' " cowboy, a brave Indian chief, or a space pilot through the medium of his play. But he doesn't have to be just "people"—he can be the leaves on the trees, the gentle rain, the blustery wind, or the big red fire engine with the loud siren. Through all kinds and types of creative dramatics the child experiences the satisfaction of creating and expressing—and the sole goal is always the involvement of the child. To use a popular cliché—it is not what the child does in the play—but what the play does in the child—which is important. Ward summarizes the purposes of playmaking as:

1. To provide for a controlled emotional outlet.

2. To provide each child with an avenue of self-expression in one of the arts.

3. To encourage and guide the child's creative imagination.

4. To give young people opportunities to grow in social understanding and co-operation.

5. To give children experience in thinking on their feet and expressing ideas fearlessly.[35]

Creative drama also offers values. As children become older, their "playmaking" may merge gradually into an activity frequently called

[34] R. Lease and G. B. Siks, *Creative Dramatics in Home, School, and Community* (New York, Harper and Brothers, 1952), p. 3.

[35] W. Ward, *Playmaking with Children*, 2nd ed. (New York, Appleton-Century-Crofts, Inc., © 1957), pp. 3–8.

creative drama which may range from simple dramatic play to elaborate dramatization. In general, this is the natural result of playmaking. A reading group in the second grade, for instance, decides to act out the story they have just read. After the first time, they decide that it wasn't quite right —the giant should have spoken in a louder voice, or the father should have been braver, and they try it again—changing characters and parts—extemporizing freely as they go along. After several tries, they may be pleased enough with their actions to suggest that they act out the story for another group or even another class.

Now, for the first time, the audience becomes important—and the players are eager that their performance please someone other than themselves. The speech and action are still extemporaneous and improvisation is frequent, but the pure spontaneity of the original production has been lessened. In its place, however, have been substituted other values—for no one would deny that this type of creative activity has a definite place in the total development of children.

From this point on, the production can become more and more elaborate or involved—*still* contributing to the children's growth if the teacher keeps this in mind as the main purpose. Dialogue can finally be put into finished form in an original script prepared by children; scenery can be constructed, costumes designed and made, and all of these can be truly creative experiences if, again, the emphasis is on the "doing" and "creating" rather than on the "reception" it will receive from an audience.

Dramatizations which are not "creative" are not part of the educational program of the elementary school. Teachers are, unfortunately, all too familiar with the elaborate all-school "production" which leaves behind it a trail of tattered nerves among exhausted children and teachers. Whatever the values of these productions may be (and the authors realize that in some communities they are a strong link in the "public relations" program) they should *not* be considered as part of the educational program of the school, for this they definitely are not. There is nothing educational about children competing or "trying out" for parts; memorizing lines written by someone else; wearing costumes designed and made by another; and speaking lines according to another's feeling. If, for one reason or another, these performances are expected of the elementary school, neither teachers nor administrators should attempt to defend them on the grounds that they are "creative" or "educational." They are neither for ninety-nine per cent of the children involved.

To repeat: dramatic art can be a rich, vital, creative, and expressive experience which should play a major role in the entire elementary school program. From the simplest form of "playmaking" to the most elaborate "creative drama," innumerable opportunities can be offered which will contribute to the social, physical, emotional, and creative growth of the child. These should not be confused, however, with another type of dramatic performance—the values of which should be seriously questioned by educators interested solely in the constructive development of the individual child.

Puppets or marionettes are enjoyed by children in all grades in the elementary school. Puppet and marionette shows are other forms of dramatic activity which have a wide appeal for children. In addition to the opportunities for manipulation which these offer, they also constitute a wonderful dramatic medium for children who may, for some reason or another, be too inhibited to engage in creative drama, especially if an audience is present. Dulcie was such a child—shy, timid, soft-voiced. She preferred to sit on the fringes and watch others rather than participate actively in any kind of dramatic activity. But puppets were a different matter—behind the screen she could project herself completely and wholeheartedly into the fierce lion or gentle doe which her hands had become. This is true with children of all ages; and puppets can be used effectively in any grade from the kindergarten through the sixth grade. Marionettes are more involved since they are manipulated by strings and are usually only suitable for upper elementary grade children. But puppets can be very uncomplicated—and require only the simplest costuming and staging to create the situation so thoroughly enjoyed by young children. The type of puppet varies considerably, of course, and depends upon the purpose and maturity of the puppeteers. Mitchell lists seven types of puppets which may be used to advantage in the elementary school.

1. *Paper bag puppets.* Made by filling paper bags with crumpled paper—and tied over an inserted cylinder for the finger of the puppeteer—very easy to make.

2. *Potato puppets.* Made from round potatoes used for heads and bodies—features painted or made from thumb tacks—pipe stem cleaners for hair, etc.

3. *Mitten puppets.* Children can draw around own hands—three middle fingers serve for head—little finger and thumb drawn separately for arms—can be cut from cloth and stitched.

4. *Sock puppets.* Heel of sock makes upper jaw—half of the foot of the sock is pushed back in between the fingers and thumb to make throat—red felt tongue—button eyes and ears.

5. *Papier-maché puppets.* Appropriate for upper grades.

6. *String marionettes.*

7. *Bean bag puppets.* Made by attaching strings to bean bag dolls.[36]

In addition, there are, of course, several other media for dramatic expression which may be used by elementary school teachers. Shadow plays, pantomime, mime and others have been used often in a dramatic program designed by creative teachers for creative children.

[36] J. O. Mitchell, "Seven Kinds of Puppets," *School Arts,* Vol. 57 (March, 1958), pp. 15–18.

Puppets have a universal appeal for children.

Summary

The first section in the present chapter was devoted to an examination of the total language experience. The two functions of language were recognized to be: (1) a tool of communication, and (2) a vehicle of thought. The individual's continuous mastery of language was considered in its early and later stages of development. The first of these was subdivided into five phases and the latter into four. It was stressed that no hard and fast divisions could be made between the various phases, for the development of language facility occurs according to a fluid and continuous pattern rather than according to rigid "stages" of growth. The factors affecting the growth of language were considered according to: (1) personal equipment of the individual, (2) home influences, and (3) sociological influences. The interrelationships among the language skills were stressed as well as their implications for the elementary school program. Such interrelationships as are known to exist imply that the various language areas should be integrated when possible but that they should be taught separately when mastery of specific skills is demanded.

Section two was devoted to "listening," the major channel of human communication, but the one about which we know the least and which we teach the least in the elementary school. A distinction was made between hearing and listening, the latter denoting a much broader concept.

The instructional program stressed the importance of objectives determined by pupil needs, the influence of the teacher's personality and behavior, and the physical and social environment of the classroom. Informal opportunities as well as direct lessons for teaching specific skills were suggested as part of an effective listening program in all the elementary grades.

Section three was concerned with the "other side of the listening coin"—speaking. It was stressed that an adequate oral language program must give primary consideration to the *content* of the pupil's oral language expression as well as to his ability to organize his thoughts and the vocabulary he needs to express them clearly.

Opportunities for the development of oral language included mention of procedures for developing conversational and discussion skills. The common types of speech problems as well as the errors of usage were presented briefly. The correction of both of these was considered in an oral language program which stressed the importance of: (1) diagnosis of children's errors, (2) an informal attack on these deficiencies, (3) the direct teaching of certain forms, (4) the place of practice in the over-all program, and (5) the value of visual aids or other materials.

The more creative aspects of oral language—choral speaking and dramatizations—were each considered briefly at the close of the chapter.

STUDENT PROJECTS

1. Try to secure permission to observe a discussion lesson in a nearby elementary school. Take a participation index. Try to give specific reasons why certain children did not participate in the discussion. Do the same thing for one of your own college classes. What are your conclusions?

2. You are a "new" third-grade teacher. You discover that your class, as a whole, has very poor listening skills and habits. Outline a tentative program you would use to teach listening. Include specific objectives in terms of skills needed, teaching procedures, and activities. How would you evaluate the success of your program?

3. You have several children in your kindergarten who are "baby-talkers." How would you work with these children and their parents to remedy the situation?

4. Choose a grade level and list as many devices as you can think of to expand the listening and speaking vocabularies of your pupils. Are there certain cautions and safeguards you should observe in using these devices?

5. Take an oral language inventory of an elementary school class over a period of at least two weeks. What are the most glaring errors you have discovered? Give several suggestions for an "indirect attack" on these errors. Write a sample lesson plan of a practice or "drill" lesson you would use to attack these errors.

6. The newest arrival in your fifth-grade class is Manuel D. from Puerto Rico. Manuel can neither understand nor speak English. Outline a procedural plan you would use to help him. How would you involve the other pupils in the class?

7. Make a "picture book" of stick figures you could use to clarify certain correct usage forms for slow-learning children in the intermediate or upper grades.

8. Interview an experienced elementary teacher. Find out how he uses creative dramatics as part of his language program. What values does he think it has for his boys and girls? What limitations?

9. Your principal has just bought two tape recorders for the school. What use will you make of them in your fourth-grade class?

10. Make a concentrated study of one child over a period of several months. Accumulate evidence which will help you to appraise his growth in the four major areas of language skills. What interrelationships do you observe among his language competencies? What independencies? Some of the techniques for studying children suggested in Chapter Three should help you in your study.

11. Write a self-evaluation of your listening skills and habits. Do the same thing for your speaking competencies, using a tape recorder to appraise your own speech. In what respects should you improve your skills in these two fields in order to be a superior elementary school teacher?

12. Question a group of children, teachers, and administrators as to what qualities they think are necessary for successful teaching. How often is "quality and use of teacher's voice" mentioned? By what groups? What are the implications of your findings?

13. During an informal conversation with Charles, one of your fifth-grade "leaders," he mentioned that, "me and him went camping overnight." When you reminded him to say, "He and I went . . ." he replied in disgust, "Do you want me to talk like a sissy?" What type of oral language program will be most effective for Charles and his friends? What motivations will you use?

14. Bertram's investigation of the present use of creative dramatics in the elementary school quotes the following reply:

Creative dramatics is integrated with many areas of instruction as arithmetic; art education; music; language arts; social studies; health and safety education; and reading. In fact we are increasingly encouraging greater horizontal integration and the use of more diversified media for enriching instruction and improving teaching methods, creative dramatics being one of the media which is encouraged.[37]

Explain how this integration is possible. Offer several possibilities for integrating creative dramatics with each of the curricular areas mentioned above. Define the values these integrative experiences would have for elementary school children.

15. Define the role of the speech specialist in the elementary school program. What should be his responsibilities? His training and background? What certification does your state require for this position? Discuss the relationship of the classroom teacher to the speech specialist. How should the work of each supplement that of the other?

BIBLIOGRAPHY

ANDERSON, Virgil A., *Improving the Child's Speech* (New York, Oxford University Press, 1953).

BERRY, Mildred F. and EISENSON, Jon., *Speech Disorders: Principles and Practices of Therapy* (New York, Appleton-Century-Crofts, Inc., 1956).

[37] J. Bertram, "Creative Dramatics in the School," *Elementary English,* Vol. 35 (December, 1958), p. 517.

Commission on the English Curriculum of the National Council of Teachers of English, *Language Arts for Today's Children* (New York, Appleton-Century-Crofts, Inc., 1954).

Commission on the English Curriculum of the National Council of Teachers of English, *The English Language Arts* (New York, Appleton-Century-Crofts, Inc., 1952).

Committee of the National Conference on Research in English, *Interrelationships Among the Language Arts* (Champaign, Ill., National Council of Teachers of English, 1954).

Committee of the National Conference on Research in English, *Factors that Influence Language Growth* (Champaign, Ill., National Council of Teachers of English, 1953).

CYPREANSEN, L. and others, *Speech Development, Improvement, and Correction* (New York, The Ronald Press Company, 1959).

DAWSON, Mildred and ZOLLINGER, Marion, *Guiding Language Learning* (New York, Harcourt, Brace & World, Inc., 1957).

DAWSON, Mildred A., *Language Teaching in Grades 1 and 2*, rev. ed. (New York, Harcourt, Brace & World, Inc., 1957).

DURLAND, Frances C., *Creative Dramatics for Children* (Yellow Springs, Ohio, Antioch Press, 1952).

GREENE, Harry and PETTY, Walter, *Developing Language Skills in the Elementary School* (Boston, Allyn and Bacon, Inc., 1959).

HATCHETT, Ethel and HUGHES, Donald, *Teaching Language Arts in Elementary Schools* (New York, The Ronald Press Company, 1956).

HATFIELD, W. Wilbur, chairman, *An Experience Curriculum in English*, A Report of the Curriculum Commission of the National Council of Teachers of English (New York, Appleton-Century-Crofts, Inc., 1935).

JOHNSON, W. and others, *Speech Handicapped School Children*, 2nd ed. (New York, Harper and Brothers, 1956).

JOHNSON, Wendell, ed., *Speech Problems of Children* (New York, Grune and Stratton, 1950).

LEASE, Ruth G. and SIKS, Geraldine, *Creative Dramatics in Home, School and Community* (New York, Harper and Brothers, 1952).

McCARTHY, Dorothea, "Language Development in Children," L. CARMICHAEL, ed., *Manual of Child Psychology*, in 2nd ed., (New York, John Wiley and Sons, Inc., 1954).

National Elementary Principals Association, *Language Arts in the Elementary School*, 20th Yearbook (Washington, D.C., National Education Association, 1941).

National Society for the Study of Education. *Teaching Language in the Elementary School*, 43rd Yearbook, Part II (Chicago, University of Chicago Press, 1944).

PIAGET, Jean, *The Language and Thought of the Child*, 3rd ed. (New York, Humanities Press, 1959).

POOLEY, Robert C., *Teaching English Grammar* (New York, Appleton-Century-Crofts, Inc., 1957).

POOLEY, Robert C., *Teaching English Usage* (New York, Appleton-Century-Crofts, Inc., 1946).

PRONOVOST, Wilbert, *The Teaching of Speaking and Listening in the Elementary School* (New York, Longmans, Green, and Company, 1959).

SHANE, Harold G. *Research Helps in Teaching the Language Arts* (Washington, D.C., Association for Supervision and Curriculum Development, 1955).

STRICKLAND, Ruth, *The Language Arts in the Elementary School*, 2nd ed. (Boston, D. C. Heath and Company, 1957).

TEMPLIN, Mildred C., *Certain Language Skills in Children: Their Development and Interrelationships* (Minneapolis, Minn., University of Minnesota Press, 1957).

TIDYMAN, W. and BUTTERFIELD, M., *Teaching the Language Arts*, 2nd ed. (New York, McGraw-Hill Book Company, 1959).

VANRIPER, Charles and BUTLER, Katherine G., *Speech in the Elementary Classroom* (New York, Harper and Brothers, 1955).

WARD, Winifred, *Playmaking with Children*, 2nd ed. (New York, Appleton-Century-Crofts, Inc., 1957).

WERNER, Lorna S., *Speech in the Elementary School* (Evanston, Ill., Row, Peterson, and Company, 1947).

WOOD, Nancy E., *Language Development and Language Disorders: A Compendium of Lectures*, Monographs of the Society for Research in Child Development, Vol. 25, No. 3, Serial No. 77 (Yellow Springs, Ohio, Antioch Press, 1960).

CHAPTER 6

Reading

A DANGEROUS MYTH, to which a gullible public has been exposed in recent years, claims that the telephone, radio, motion pictures, and television have greatly diminished the importance and popularity of reading. It is true that these have increased the importance of aural-oral communication, a fact which was stressed in the preceding chapter. This does not mean, however, that the importance of reading has been lessened. In reality, exactly the opposite is true. Never has there been a more concerted interest in eliminating illiteracy in the most backward countries, and never, in this country, has more printed matter rolled off the presses.

Consider the following facts for the year 1959: It was a boom year for book publication, with the record-breaking number of 14,425 *new* books and new editions put into circulation. A total of 19,458 newspapers and magazines were published. The daily newspaper circulation reached a new level of over 58,000,000 and the circulation of Sunday papers reached an all time high of 47,848,477. Add to these figures the number of brochures, bulletins, pamphlets, advertisements, circulars, letters and other miscellaneous items distributed daily, and one has a fairly good idea of the amount of reading material consumed by the public. This does not mean, of course, that all adults are skilled, critical, and avid readers. Unfortunately this is not the case, and no argument is made here that people read as much or as well as they should. But this does not alter the fact that, since Mr. Gutenberg's famous invention, reading has been, is, and from all indications, will continue to be a most vital artery of communication.

PURPOSES OF READING

Reading is many things to many people. To some it is a necessity in pursuing their employment or education. To others it may be a satisfying

Reading is a major source of
pleasure.

Reading is a major source of information.

social experience, a spiritual solace, or a refuge from reality. In extreme cases, it may even be a matter of life and death to which signs such as *High Tension Wire*, *Strong Undertow*, and *Do Not Pass While Loading or Unloading* will readily testify. Gray and Rogers report that specific purposes for reading mentioned most frequently by adults are:

To keep informed concerning current events; to secure specific information of value in making plans; to learn more about events or problems of special interest; to secure the opinions of others concerning civic, social, or economic problems and the best means of solving them; to keep in touch with business or social developments; to advance in one's field of work; to broaden one's range of information; to keep one's mind stimulated with important things to think about; to develop a broad outlook on life; to satisfy interest and curiosity; to secure pleasure; to become acquainted with our literary heritage; and for spiritual guidance.[1]

In general, these specifics may be classified into two major purposes of equal importance: (1) to secure information, and (2) to derive pleasure.

Reading is a major source of information. Regardless of the popularity of other media of mass communication, reading is still the main source of information for a considerable number of adults. Even those who confess, "I never read a thing," probably do not realize how often they turn to the printed page for information. Obviously, this type of reading may be on many levels, depending upon the individual's interests and abilities. One may read to find out who won the ball game, when to seed a lawn, or how much air he should put in his tires. On the other hand, he may read to keep informed of domestic and international affairs, as well as daily developments in other fields, in order to function as an intelligent and contributory citizen in a democratic society. Regardless of the type of material or the level of his intellectual pursuits, however, the literate person turns repeatedly to the printed page for the information he needs or desires.

Reading is a major source of pleasure. From Seuss to Shakespeare may represent the gamut of reading maturity, but their primary purpose is the same—to please and delight the reader. When young children are introduced early to these pleasures, there is little doubt that their lives will be fuller and richer as the result. On this point, it is worth noting that there is *some* evidence today that children and youth are turning to books for pleasure to a greater degree than has been true in the past. The rising number of book clubs for children and teen-agers give some indication of this as do also the following statements:

From a number of sources, it seems evident that children today are reading a little more than they did a decade ago.[2]

[1] W. S. Gray and B. Rogers, *Maturity in Reading: Its Nature and Appraisal* (Chicago, University of Chicago Press, Copyright, 1956, by the University of Chicago), p. 3.
[2] P. Witty and P. Kinsella, "Children and TV—A Ninth Report," *Elementary English*, Vol. 35 (November, 1958), p. 455.

American teen-agers are reading abundantly, probably more than their parents.[3]

Again this is not to say that *all* children are reading the most desirable literature, but this is another problem. It is, however, somewhat encouraging that young people, whatever the stimulus may be, are turning toward books for pleasure and recreation. Furthermore, this divertive purpose of reading may become increasingly important to all ages in view of the increasing amounts of leisure time, earlier retirement, and longer life span. The act of reading, by serving two major purposes, plays a crucial role in our complex modern society. Therefore, a major responsibility of every elementary school is to initiate and develop a reading program which will equip all pupils with the skills and attitudes of reading commensurate with their abilities. The major instructional aims of this program are discussed in the following section.

INSTRUCTIONAL AIMS OF READING

The broad concept of "reading as thinking" is commonly accepted by most educators today. It has developed gradually over past years, and is considerably expanded over earlier ideas that reading was "calling words" or, later, "understanding the meaning." Both of these are, of course, still *parts* of reading, but the total process goes beyond them to include the more complex elements of creative thought. The instructional aims implied in this modern, broad concept of reading are summarized by Burton as:

1. To extend *experience.*
2. To provide *recreation.*
3. To form *favorable attitudes* toward reading and to develop *permanent interests* in reading.
4. To stimulate good *methods of thinking.*
5. To develop *moral and spiritual values.*
6. To develop *standards of appreciation and taste* in the selection of materials.
7. To develop the necessary *habits, abilities, and skills* for reading, which must be taught on a functional basis rather than in isolation.[4]

The various facets of an elementary school reading program geared to the broader concept of reading and the comprehensive instructional aims listed above are discussed in the remainder of the chapter.

READING READINESS

There are many types of reading readiness. That a state of readiness must be present prior to systematic instruction in reading meets with

[3] W. Gray, "What's Happening in Reading?" *The Reading Teacher,* Vol. 11 (October, 1957), p. 8.

[4] From *Reading in Child Development,* by W. H. Burton, Copyright ©, 1956, by The Bobbs-Merrill Company, used by special permission of the publishers.

almost unanimous agreement among modern educators. Most primary grade teachers would no more plunge their pupils into reading with no thought of readiness than they would throw them off a diving board before they had ever been near the water. In spite of this almost universal agreement on the importance of readiness, however, there are many questions yet to be answered and much research yet to be done on the *exact* relationship of readiness to reading success. At the present time, the types of readiness thought to have most bearing upon initial instruction in reading are: (1) physical; (2) social and emotional; (3) verbal; (4) mental; (5) experiential; and (6) attitudinal.

Physical Readiness. Reading is an exceedingly complex and difficult task, and the minimal equipment which a child should bring to it is a general state of physical well-being. Children who suffer from persistent toothaches or headaches, malnourishment, or fatigue are exceedingly handicapped when they try to apply themselves to the strenuous job of learning to read. In addition to satisfactory general health, the physical specifics of vision and hearing bear most significance to the reading act.

Research has not yet determined conclusively the relationships between visual factors and reading abilities. In mature readers, the relationship is particularly undetermined, for often the body compensates for the deficiency and reading ability does not suffer. Visual defects in young children, however, may lead to discomfort, fatigue, and in some cases, disinterest in reading. In general, the visual irregularities of young children which have greatest interest for the classroom teacher may be classified into two large categories. The first of these pertains to the structural eye defects such as astigmatism, poor fusion, and others. The teacher should be alert to such symptoms as rubbing the eyes, blinking, squinting, and frequent headaches. He should refer such symptoms immediately to the nurse, school doctor, or parent. Far more common visual irregularities among primary children, however, are those caused by immaturity of the eyes. Of these, lack of co-ordination and far-sightedness are of major interest to the primary grade teacher.

Some children of preschool or early school age have not achieved full, binocular co-ordination of their eyes. This simply means that, although both eyes are good, occasionally they fail to work together. As Brock points out, these children never know when their eyes "will misbehave." [5] It appears to be fairly obvious that physical immaturity of this type may be related to the youngster's interest and ability in beginning reading.

The second physical immaturity which has implications for reading readiness is far-sightedness. The majority of children are born far-sighted and remain so until their eyes are fully mature at the approximate age of

[5] F. W. Brock, "Two Eyes Can Be Worse Than One," *Education,* Vol. 77 (April, 1957), pp. 501–515.

eight years. In some cases this means that it is very difficult for certain children to focus their eyes on reading material which requires near-point vision. Several authorities recommend that the classroom teacher should be alert to signs of far-sightedness and adjust his reading program accordingly. This would mean increasing the number of far-point reading activities and decreasing the near-point activities. Schubert summarized the responsibility of the elementary school in this respect as follows:

> It is time that elementary schools realize the extreme importance of visual maturity and the role it plays in initial reading experience. It is time that they employ the proper near-point tests or seek the cooperation of visual specialists who can do a competent job of detecting visually immature children for them. And, finally, it is time that elementary schools make necessary provisions for children who they know are visually immature.[6]

In at least one school system at the present time, far-point reading activities are utilized by projecting all primary reading lessons on a screen with letters one inch high.[7] Whether this is the best solution to the problem is controversial, but the fact remains that eye immaturity must be taken into account in the early stages of reading.

More important to reading success than visual factors are auditory factors, which may be roughly classified into three main categories. The first of these is concerned with auditory *acuity*, or the extent to which the child can hear sounds. Frequently hearing losses will go undiscovered for several years and cases of hard-of-hearing children who were classified as stupid, lazy, or inattentive are too numerous to count. Part of the reason for this may be because, for some inexplicable reason, many children (and adults) are extremely sensitive about a hearing loss and go to great pains to conceal it. The alert teacher, therefore, must watch for signs of poor hearing and refer these children to the proper authority as well as make adjustments for them within the classroom.

A second hearing loss which is closely related to reading readiness is the inability to *discriminate* between sounds. Again, growth in discriminatory power is related to maturity and, according to one writer, "some children do not develop the ability to make fine aural distinctions until they reach the age of seven or eight."[8]

A third auditory factor which is receiving attention from educators is the relationship of listening *comprehension* and reading ability. The problems involved in measuring listening comprehension have been discussed by

[6] D. G. Schubert, "Visual Immaturity and Reading Difficulty," *Elementary English,* Vol. 34 (May, 1957), p. 325.

[7] G. McCracken, "Reading Instruction for the Space Age," *Education,* Vol. 80 (May, 1960), pp. 545–548.

[8] J. M. Wepman, "Auditory Discrimination, Speech, and Reading," *Elementary School Journal,* Vol. 60 (March, 1960), p. 328.

Barbe and others,[9] but there appears to be fairly widespread agreement that the level of listening comprehension may be used as a predictor of reading success.

Social and Emotional Readiness. As was noted previously, learning to read is a difficult task which requires a high level of social and emotional security. The timid child, for instance, who immediately reacts with "I can't" may have difficulty in persevering with reading. So also, will the one with the low frustrational level who goes into a temper tantrum when faced with a difficult task. This is true, also, of the socially immature youngster who lacks identity with the group or who is unwilling to "share" and take his turn in the group reading situation. All of these children will need help and understanding from the classroom teacher before they can be expected to realize much success in reading.

Verbal Readiness. As was noted in Chapter Five, the majority of evidence points toward a high correlation between oral language development and success in reading. Children whose normal speech consists of isolated words or fragmentary phrases will not be ready to read sentences. Similarly, those with faulty or immature speech must be helped to improve, if they are going to profit from reading experiences. The close interrelationship of reading with oral language is emphasized by Hildreth who says, "The richer the child's language associations and the better his command of the spoken language, the more rapid his progress in reading, as a general rule." [10] Artley expresses the same viewpoint with the statement,

Language development, particularly in the oral area, is related to reading, not only in the early stages, but throughout the entire period of reading growth. . . . Language skills and abilities show a considerable degree of "going-together-ness" as far along as the fifth-grade level. Oral language facilitates reading, and reading, in turn, facilitates oral language.[11]

Mental Readiness. There is no doubt that ability in reading is closely correlated with general intelligence, although there is considerable difference of opinion as to the mental age necessary for beginning reading. Most teachers still subscribe to an M.A. of 6.6 for beginning reading, and this is probably as defensible in a group situation as any other. The important considerations concerning mental age to which teachers should give attention are, not the precise age when instruction should begin, as much as: (1) there is a definite correlation between reading and intelligence; (2) intelligence is only one factor to be considered in appraising

[9] W. B. Barbe et al., "Research Report: Listening Comprehension as a Measure of Potential Reading Ability," in N. Larrick, ed., *Reading in Action,* International Reading Association Conference Proceedings, Vol. 2 (1957), pp. 120–124.

[10] G. Hildreth, "Reading and the Language Arts," *Education,* Vol. 79 (May, 1959), p. 566.

[11] A. S. Artley, "Oral Language Growth and Reading Ability," *Elementary School Journal,* Vol. 53 (February, 1953, Copyright 1953, by the University of Chicago), p. 327.

readiness; and (3) the intelligence test is not an infallible measure of native mental ability.

Experiential Readiness. If a child is to derive meaning from his reading, he must have an experiential backlog which will help him to interpret the printed material. Without this, reading at any level is completely sterile and useless. To realize fully the importance of many and varied experiences for the pre-reading youngster, consider an extreme but true example. A four-year-old child lives with his parents and young sister in one room on the sixth floor of an apartment house in New York City. To the authors' knowledge, the child has rarely, if ever, been on the street below. His only contact with the world outside the apartment house is through the window as he watches the world go by six stories beneath him. There is a good chance that he has never touched or seen at close range a dog, a cat, a tree, a house, a duck, a car, or any of the other most commonplace items he will meet in his earliest reading experiences. Imagine the meager and deprived background that he will bring to his early reading. What can he possibly receive from reading? The answer is obvious. What is the responsibility of his teacher? The answer is equally obvious.

Attitudinal Readiness. The last to be mentioned but certainly not the least in importance is the child's attitude toward reading and the total school experience. If a youngster comes from an average home where reading is a part of normal living, the chances are fairly good that he will be eager to read. He sees his mother reading a book, his father enjoying the newspaper, his older brother studying the directions for assembling his model airplane, and he is forced to conclude, "Here is something everyone can do but me." With this attitude, he is more than willing to be initiated into the reading fraternity when the time comes. But a word of caution, this is true of many children but not *all* children. Some may be completely indifferent to reading and reluctant to participate in reading experiences. The primary grade teacher, therefore, should be alert to her pupils' *attitudes* toward reading and should attempt to develop a genuine interest in, and desire for, learning to read.

There is no single instrument for appraising all types of reading readiness. It would seem to be quite obvious that, if readiness for reading is as inclusive as indicated here, that no single procedure or instrument for measuring it would be entirely valid. There are, of course, many excellent standardized readiness tests available which are helpful in *diagnosing* individual strengths and limitations as they relate to specific educational factors. Research has indicated, however, that these tests are not very accurate in predicting success in beginning reading as measured on a standardized achievement test.[12] To appraise accurately a pupil's total readiness and to predict his success in reading, there is probably nothing

[12] R. Karlin, "Research in Reading," *Elementary English*, Vol. 37 (March, 1960), pp. 177–183.

better than the careful judgment of a competent teacher. In order to make this judgment, however, the primary teacher must *observe* her pupils very carefully, keep accurate *records* of their progress, and use as many informal and standardized tests as are needed.

Readiness programs are of two general types. Some teachers prefer a "formal" or "directed" readiness program in which workbooks are used to develop discriminatory powers and other pre-reading skills. Such books accompany all the basal reading series and are closely related to the pre-primers which follow. Other teachers prefer an "informal" readiness program which substitutes direct experiences and varied activities for the workbook exercises. Numerous studies have been made to compare both methods, and there is little evidence of the superiority of one over the other *in terms of demonstrated reading achievement.* Haynes reported no significant difference among those who had or had not used a readiness workbook.[13] Ploghoft also concluded that workbooks did not contribute to the child's reading readiness, as measured on a standardized test.[14] It would seem, therefore, that the decision concerning the use or nonuse of readiness workbooks should be made by each individual school system in terms of its broad aims for the total reading program.

An effective readiness program provides an environment conducive to natural growth. Since many types of reading readiness are the natural accompaniments of maturation, the teacher cannot "force" their development. She can, however, provide an environment which will: (1) remove hindrances to growth and (2) provide experiences and activities to foster growth. The first implies a careful and consistent program of appraisal, observation, and diagnosis. Visual irregularities, hearing losses, physical illnesses, emotional instabilities, and social maladjustments should be carefully noted and constructively attacked in order to pave the road toward reading. The second major feature of an informal program is the creating of a rich, full, and exciting classroom environment. The world is a wonderfully exciting place when seen through five-year-old eyes, and the teacher has endless opportunities to capitalize upon this natural enthusiasm. Trips to the police station, fire house, flower nursery, dairy, grocery store, park, zoo, circus, farm, or museum can open young eyes and broaden horizons. These, in turn, can lead to many, many language experiences which will enlarge vocabularies and stimulate abilities to speak and understand language. Building, drawing, and painting activities will help to develop those immature eyes and eliminate emotional and social deficiencies. And, above all else, a luxurious environment of books will create that all-important love

[13] M. L. Haynes, *The Effect of Omitting Workbook-Type Reading Readiness Exercises on Reading Achievement in First Grade,* Unpublished Doctor of Education Thesis (George Peabody College for Teachers, 1959).
[14] M. H. Ploghoft, "Do Reading Readiness Workbooks Promote Readiness?" *Elementary English,* Vol. 36 (October, 1959), pp. 424–426.

and desire for reading. A library table is an absolute "must" in every kinder-garten and first grade room. So is a daily story hour. So, also, are as many rich book experiences as the creative teacher can provide, including periodic trips to the school and town library, and "guest" story hours from visiting librarians or upper-grade children who welcome the opportunity to read or tell a story to the younger ones.

A key-word in this type of environment is *individuality*. The statement that no two children are alike is trite but true. The primary grade teacher must realize that not all children will need the same amount or type of activity. *Some* children may possibly be at the pencil-and-paper stage. *Some* may be indifferent to even the most exciting story. Others may hypno-tize their classmates daily with stories of their own invention. Their needs are completely different. The teacher's main job is to provide a climate in which they all can grow—each in his own way.

In summary, the practice of putting a reading book in a child's hands because it is a certain day of the year or because he has reached a certain age or grade is as outdated as the hornbook and hickory stick. When he is ready to read he *will* read and the teacher must then turn to the next major task of the reading program: that of teaching him to recognize and to identify the printed word.

TEACHING WORD RECOGNITION AND IDENTIFICATION

In the first stages of reading, the child learns to recognize words by sight. When the pre-reading child is confronted by a group of strange printed symbols, he knows *only one thing* about them—they say something! After repeated exposures, he will be able to recognize a familiar group through *visual perception* and to attach a meaning to it. Hence he learns to recognize immediately that the group of symbols which looks like "Billy" stands for his name. Exactly what visual clues he uses to recognize this word by sight is not known, for he probably uses different ones for different words. Some words he may recognize by their total shape and others by certain dis-tinguishing features within the word.[15] However, when he can respond immediately to the printed form of the word, he has added that word to his *sight vocabulary.* A very common error of primary grade teachers is to assume that pupils enter school with *no* sight vocabularly. This is not true. Many children who enter school have acquired a sizable sight vocabulary of words which they have seen repeatedly on TV commercials, billboards, and cereal boxes or food cans. The first-grade teacher should continue to extend this sight vocabulary, not to any magic number, but to the point where success in pre-primer reading seems assured. How does he do this?

The sight vocabulary is expanded through informal reading experiences.

15 M. D. Vernon, "The Perceptual Process in Reading," *The Reading Teacher,* Vol. 13, (October, 1959), pp. 2–8.

The first reading materials which the child usually encounters are *experience charts* which pertain to any item of group interest. Their content can be dictated by the group, by an individual pupil, or occasionally composed by the teacher. After listening to the teacher read the material, children are encouraged to read it by sentences or in its entirety. Identicalities and similarities of words are discovered through "matching" and other devices and, step by step, children enlarge their vocabularies of sight words. In the following chart an attempt was made to emphasize the sight words *kitten, black, white,* and *like.*

OUR KITTEN

We have a kitten.
His name is Tommy.
He is black and white.
His head is black.
His paws are white.
We like our kitten.
Do you like him?

Another early reading experience aimed at enlarging sight vocabularies is the practice of using functional labels around the room. This does *not* mean tacking a sign on the desk saying *desk* and on the door saying *door.* What child needs to read *desk* when he knows perfectly well what object of furniture it is? But directional labels (*in, out, stop, go*) or designatory (*scissors, paste, paper*) are functional and will help to build sight vocabularies.

Use of the picture and context is a valuable aid to word recognition. There comes a day when the child, reading an experience chart or pre-primer, meets a strange word and looks to the teacher for help. Instead of merely telling him the word (as she has done in the past) she suggests that he look at the picture for help. Thus, the first step on the road to independence in word recognition is taken. Obviously, the help which the pupil receives from pictures is limited and becomes more so as he meets harder reading material, but it is helpful in building independence in word identification, if only to an imperceptible degree.

The use of the context is another early aid to word identification but its use becomes increasingly prevalent throughout all stages of reading. In the earliest type of reading, when the child reads the sentence, "Mary had a birthday party," he may not recognize the word *birthday*. The teacher can utilize the context by asking him to complete the sentence and then "guess" at the unknown word. "On what special day do you think Mary had her party?" Reliance on the context for identifying words is an extremely

The experience chart is an
important part of the primary
reading program.

important and frequently-used aid at all levels and should be given consistent attention by all teachers. Thus, the adult who has early learned to use the context may be able at once to identify the strange-to-him word, *predilection*, in the following sentence, "Pocket gophers eat underground tubers and have a special predilection for potato crops."

The configuration of the word is a clue to its identity. Learning to identify a word by its appearance or configuration is an extension of the process used by the child to build his initial sight vocabulary. The distinctive visual pattern of some words makes them easily recognizable and should be pointed out to the child. Words of unusual length (*grandmother*), of height (*little*) or depth (*puppy*) are usually easier to recognize than those of a more common pattern. Words whose configuration makes recognition difficult are: (1) those which have the same general pattern *and* initial letter (*than—there*), (2) those which have the same general pattern *and* same final letter (*what—that*), and, most of all, (3) those having the same general pattern *and* the same initial *and* final letter (*then—than*).[16]

The structure of a word is a clue to its identity. Often a word can be identified by recognizing its separate parts. A recognition of the root word plus knowledge of the common prefixes and suffixes will facilitate reading

16 *Ibid.*

at any level. Similarly, recognition of the components of a compound word will enable the reader to identify many strange words with little difficulty.

Phonetic analysis is an important aid to word identification. The "phonics controversy" has long been a topic of discussion in elementary education, and authorities differ on the role phonetic analysis should play in the modern reading program. However, careful analysis of the literature reveals that the differences of opinion are really not as great as one is frequently led to believe. In general, there are few people at either extreme of this topic, and most authorities are clustered in the middle of the continuum from "no phonics" to "all phonics."

Phonetic analysis was used in the elementary schools of the seventeenth and eighteenth centuries as the sole method of teaching reading. It superseded the "alphabet method" and differed from it in that it required children to analyze words by memorizing the *sounds* of their letters and syllables as well as their names. In the mid-nineteenth century, the method was challenged by the discovery of the "word method" which demonstrated that pupils could learn to read words without knowing the names or sounds of their individual letters. Still later, this idea was expanded to the "sentence method" and the "story method" which were used widely through the early years of the twentieth century. Emphasis on teaching reading solely through words and larger thought units continued approximately through the 1930's. The problems caused by an overreliance upon this method, however, were felt in many areas and gradually led educators to a re-examination of the place which phonetic analysis has in the reading program. It should be made clear, however, that this was, in no way, a process of "going back to the good old days." The main differences between today's treatment of phonics and that of more than a century ago are evident in the following statements:

1. *Phonetic analysis is used in conjunction with other methods of word analysis.* There seems to be very little disagreement on the basic point that phonetic analysis has value as *one* method of independent word attack. Russell's summary of the viewpoints of 220 teachers concerning the place of phonics is probably fairly representative of the opinions held by most teachers and educators today.

> Phonics is seen as only one method of word-attack, and word-attack skills in turn are viewed as only one goal in the total program of developing understanding and thoughtful readers in our schools and communities.[17]

2. *Formal instruction in phonetic analysis is not advocated for initial reading experiences.* Again, the majority of opinion favors beginning formal reading by emphasizing whole words and gradually encouraging the child to analyze the word according to its sound. This does not mean, however, that the informal activities of the kindergarten and first grade do not

---

[17] D. H. Russell, "Teachers' Views on Phonics," *Elementary English,* Vol. 32 (October, 1955), p. 375.

provide some phonetic training. Much of the readiness program is designed to refine auditory discrimination which will, in turn, lead to a knowledge of phonetics. Typical of such incidental training occurred in a kindergarten class recently while the teacher was collecting milk money. She asked the group, "Do you have your *milk money*? Does anyone notice anything about those words, *milk* and *money*?" One alert little fellow answered immediately, "They both begin the same! And so does my last name—*Morrow*." The group went on to think of other words which began in the same fashion. In such a manner children in the earliest grades are encouraged to listen and compare the sounds of words.

Systematic and more intensive instruction, however, is usually delayed until approximately the second grade or until children are about seven or eight years old. Witty and Sizemore concluded from their analysis of research that many phonic systems are too difficult for most five and six year olds,[18] as did Smith, who concluded that "it is advisable to delay intensive phonics instruction until a child has attained a mental age of seven years."[19] It seems fairly safe to generalize, therefore, that the majority of opinion today supports the practice of including some informal phonic work in the latter stages of readiness but delaying intensive instruction in it until the approximate age of seven for most children.

3. *The phonics program is integrated with all other phases of the reading program.* Today, all basal reading series make provision for work in phonics as part of their developmental programs. Reading texts, manuals, and accompanying workbooks are designed to provide adequate training in phonetic analysis. On the other hand, there are several other workbooks on the market which provide intensive phonic work unrelated to the basal reading program. The extent to which these phonic workbooks aid in total reading growth has been the subject of much study in recent years. Findings disagree, but the majority seem to indicate the negligible value of intensive supplementary phonics workbooks. Sparks and Fay concluded, for example, that the practice of using certain supplementary phonics materials "for a separate phonics period or to supplement another basal reading series should be seriously questioned."[20] Two recent doctoral studies arrived at essentially the same conclusion, namely:

The data secured at the end of the study . . . did not show that special phonetic training produced statistically significant improvement in reading achievement.[21]

[18] P. A. Witty and R. A. Sizemore, "Phonics in the Reading Program: A Review and an Evaluation," *Elementary English*, Vol. 32 (October, 1955), pp. 355–371.

[19] N. B. Smith, "What Research Tells Us About Word Recognition," *Elementary School Journal*, Vol. 55 (April, 1955), p. 445.

[20] P. E. Sparks and L. C. Fay, "An Evaluation of Two Methods of Teaching Reading," *Elementary School Journal*, Vol. 57 (April, 1957), p. 390.

[21] G. F. Nicholas, *The Relative Effectiveness of Two Types of Phonetic Materials on the Reading Achievement of Second Grade Pupils*, Unpublished Doctor of Education Thesis (University of Virginia, 1957).

The results of this experiment indicate that the use of phonics workbooks add little to the effectiveness of reading instruction when teachers make good use of the workbooks and teachers' guides of a good basic reading series.[22]

In general, the emphasis today is on teaching phonics as a functional part of the entire reading program rather than in isolation. Unless daily provision is made for the application of phonetic analysis to reading, the entire program becomes artificial and useless. Skill in phonetic analysis per se is no goal of modern education; skill in phonetic analysis as an aid to better reading is a worthy goal which should be sought on every grade level.

4. *A sequential program of phonetic analysis is advocated.* Most authorities are opposed to the mere incidental or haphazard development of phonetic analysis skills and advocate instead a systematic attack on elements graduated in difficulty. Several writers have prepared organizational tables of these elements for the teacher's guidance. However, as McKim points out, these recommendations presuppose that the teacher is using either a single basal system or a supplementary phonics workbook series.[23] She suggests that the most effective reading program utilize many experiences and varied materials. This would make it impossible to teach phonics in any predetermined order. The authors agree with this viewpoint and with McKim's recommendation that the sequential program of phonics learning be determined by the frequency with which children at various stages of reading growth meet specific difficulties. There is a difference between a planned program and a predetermined program. The former implies good teaching; the latter a certain rigidity or restriction, perhaps helpful to certain teachers, but not needed by the teacher who plans his program according to the needs of his particular group.

In summary, the question of phonetic analysis probably meets with more general agreement than disagreement among reputable authorities and experienced teachers today. A final word of advice. It is a means—not an end; it is a road—not a destination; it is a prescription—not a panacea!

The dictionary is an aid to word identification. The dictionary is the final aid to which people turn when the other clues have failed to unlock the identity of the word. Children are introduced to picture dictionaries as early as the first grade, and instruction in dictionary use is continued through all succeeding grades. The habit of consulting the dictionary for the identity and meaning of a word is stressed in all reading programs and, fortunately, is aided today by the availability of several good dictionaries written for children.

[22] F. W. Ibeling, *The Effect of Supplementary Phonics Activities on the Reading and Spelling Ability of Second-, Fourth-, and Sixth-Graders,* Unpublished Doctor of Philosophy Thesis (University of Minnesota, 1959).

[23] M. G. McKim, *Guiding Growth in Reading* (New York, The Macmillan Company, 1955), pp. 293–294.

Clues to word recognition and identification are usually used in conjunction with each other. For purposes of clarity, the aids to word recognition and identification have been discussed separately in this section. The reader should not conclude, however, that they are used separately, for this is rarely true. Most children and adults use a combination of methods in attacking new words. The adult, for instance, who sees the word *vicissitudes* for the first time will probably be able to identify and understand it through the use of phonetic analysis and the context. Similarly, a teacher who helps a child with the word *street* in the sentence, "Tim ran down the street," by asking, "What word would make sense?" is using context clues. If the child replies *road* she then turns to another clue with, "Look at the beginning sound of the word. What will tell you that it couldn't be *road?* What word would begin with this sound and make sense in this sentence?" Thus, the child has been encouraged to use the context *and* phonetic analysis. All clues are usually used in similar combinations, for the English language is too complex to permit overreliance upon a single aid to word identification.

It has been stressed several times that word recognition is not an entity in the reading program but is always closely allied with comprehension. It should be understood, also, that there are many levels or degrees of comprehension. For purposes of discussion, however, these are frequently grouped into two major classifications: (1) the level of factual or literal comprehension, and (2) the level of interpretative or critical comprehension. It is important, also, to keep in mind that no hard and fast distinction can be made between these two. It would be extremely difficult, for instance, to decide where factual comprehension stops and interpretation or critical analysis begins. One's reading does not progress methodically from word recognition to comprehension to interpretation. Rather, there is a fluidity among all factors, and the extent to which each is used depends upon the individual's reading maturity as well as the type and difficulty of material. In spite of their close interrelationships, however, each level of comprehension presents some rather specific implications for the elementary teacher. For purposes of clarification, therefore, they are discussed separately on the following pages.

UNDERSTANDING THE MEANING

Lack of experience is a major handicap to understanding meaning. It was pointed out previously that a dearth of experiences will delay the child's readiness for reading. It is equally true *on all levels* that lack of experience will incapacitate the individual for reading. Today, there is general agreement that there is really no such thing as "*getting* meaning *from* the printed page." It has no meaning. It is only a mass of symbols. The reader doesn't "get" meaning from the print; he *puts* meaning *into* it. The fact that two individuals can read the same article and arrive at opposite meanings is positive proof that the selection contains no intrinsic meaning. Rather it contains two different meanings for two different people who bring to it the sum of their own experiences. The implications of this for teaching are obvious. If a child is to bring meaning to his reading, he must do so from a wide background of experience. Such words, for instance, as *jungle, pyramid, toga, tepee, latitude, zone, vineyard,* and *cacao* form an endless list which will mean nothing to elementary school pupils unless they have the experience necessary to convert them to concepts. This is true on all grade levels but becomes increasingly more so as the child reaches the intermediate and upper grades and his reading materials recede further and further from his direct experiences. Unfortunately, on these grade levels, it is often impossible to provide the child with the *direct* experiences he will need to read meaningfully. One can, however, substitute vicarious experiences which will do the job efficiently. Films, film-strips, pictures, realia, models, and various other aids must be used *in abundance* in these grades to build an experiential background from which the child can "put" meanings into his reading.

Not only does lack of experience handicap the pupil in understanding *strange* words, but it frequently prevents him from understanding familiar words. This is because words have multiple meanings dependent upon the tone and related context of the selection. Care should be taken, therefore, to be sure that the child not only knows *a* meaning of the word, but that he knows the particular meaning demanded in the particular context. Recently, for instance, a child in the third grade complained that the sentence, "The princess had a delightful air," did not make sense. In this case, the commonplace word *air* caused the difficulty. He knew its meaning as something he breathed and also as a melody or tune, but he did *not* know its meaning in the context in which it was then used.

A fourth-grade group read about the Mayflower Compact and gave no indication that they did not understand what they read. When the teacher queried them about the meaning of the word *compact,* however, most of them knew only *one* meaning—the container for face powder which their mothers carried in their purses. If the teacher had not stopped to check the meaning of this familiar word, imagine what a peculiar concept these children would have had of the Mayflower Compact!

One could, of course, continue at length with similar examples. As someone has said, ask one man for a screwdriver and he will give you a metal tool. Ask another and he will give you a drink of vodka and orange juice!

In addition, children's limited experiences with language handicap comprehension of material containing ordinary figures of speech. These do not usually occur in the earliest reading materials, but are frequently met in second-grade books and stories. Again, it becomes a prime responsibility of the classroom teacher to be alert to these difficulties which are not always apparent on the surface. A second-grade group recently read a story which concluded with the moral, "John discovered that the longest way to grand-mother's was really the shortest way." The children discussed the story animatedly and the lesson was almost concluded when the teacher asked, "What does that mean? How can the longest way really be the shortest way?" Not a child in the group could answer! They had read the story—had enjoyed it—but would have completely "missed the point" unless the teacher had not been thorough in determining their comprehension.

Elementary comprehension depends upon a knowledge of punctuation and sentence structure. Very often failure to understand or regard punctuation and other elements of structure will retard meaningful reading. As soon as children are introduced to reading, their attention should be called to the use of the period and question mark as aids to understanding. Later, when other punctuation marks appear, their uses should be carefully taught as aids to understanding. Similarly, sentence and paragraph structure must be emphasized so that children can identify the main thoughts expressed. Teaching of these elements should be done solely in connection with reading in the earliest grades, but in the intermediate and upper grades this instruction should be supplemented by additional attention in the other language arts.

Pupils should be encouraged to make an aggressive attack upon meaning at all levels of reading. There is no more important point which the authors can stress than that teachers should encourage *all* pupils to make a consistently aggressive attack upon the meaning of their reading matter. As McKee points out, many students are not at all disturbed by their inability to understand what they read, and this complacency increases as they progress through high school and college.[24] Primary grade teachers know that this is not true of their pupils, for young children insist on knowing the meaning. They will usually ask, "What does that mean?" or complain, "I don't get it," when they fail to comprehend. However, as the difficulties and complexities begin rapidly to multiply, and the content becomes further removed from their experiences and interests, older children decide they are fighting a losing battle for comprehension. At this point, many of them discover substitutes for comprehension, such as memorization and verbalism which may, ironically, take them with little difficulty through high school and college.

To combat this complacency, therefore, is a major responsibility of all teachers and should be begun in dead earnest in the intermediate grades of the elementary school. Pupils should learn that comprehension *is* important, and teachers should learn not to be fooled by one of its substitutes. A sure-fire method for preventing this is asking the pupil to *demonstrate* his comprehension of the material.

[24] P. McKee, *The Teaching of Reading in the Elementary School* (New York, Houghton-Mifflin Company, 1948), pp. 45–46.

The extent of comprehension can best be determined by requiring the pupil to demonstrate his understanding. The most commonly used technique for determining comprehension is questioning. Certain types of thorough, probing thought questions *will* enable the teacher to determine the extent of pupils' comprehension. Many factual questions *will not*. Questions such as, "In what year was the peace treaty signed?" and "Who was the president of the United States?" can usually be answered correctly by a pupil *without* indicating his degree of understanding of the entire selection. The most effective technique to determine comprehension, however, is asking the pupil to *demonstrate* or *use* his understanding. "Tell us this in your own words"; "Write a story about it"; "Draw a picture of it"; "Draw a diagram for us"; and similar requests will demand a *use* of comprehension and will reveal quickly the degree to which it has been attained.

INTERPRETING THE MEANING

Developing skills of critical reading is a major emphasis in the modern reading program. As was mentioned earlier in the chapter, the present concept of reading is considerably expanded over earlier concepts. At one time reading was thought to be simply the act of *recognizing and identifying the printed word*. This accounted for the excessive emphasis upon phonetic analysis and oral reading which were designed to develop what was then considered reading. Later, reading came to be recognized as the *dual* process of recognizing printed symbols and understanding their meanings. Emphasis upon the sight method of reading and the importance of silent reading accompanied this concept. Today, the concept of reading has been expanded to include the higher thought processes of interpretation, evaluation, appraisal, selection, and comparison—commonly labeled the skills of critical reading. There are many different terms used to connote this newer concept. Some writers make no distinction between critical reading and critical thinking since the former is simply "reading with thinking." Other terms such as "creative reading," "inferential reading," and "analytical reading" are frequently encountered. Although authorities may differ on shades of meaning and precise definitions, they do not differ on the comprehensiveness of the modern concept of reading. A very simple and clear definition of this newer concept is offered by Sochor who says, "Reading is thinking with experiences and concepts in relation to printed language." [25]

The development of critical reading should be a major instructional task at all levels. This becomes increasingly important in the light of what is known today about child development. Children are not naturally

[25] E. E. Sochor, "The Nature of Critical Reading," *Elementary English*, Vol. 36 (January, 1959), p. 54.

"critical thinkers." Their immaturity and lack of experience prevent their attacking a problem critically and logically. Burton, Kimball and Wing list the general characteristics of young children which handicap them in thinking critically.

1. *Absolutistic tendency dominates.* Relativity has not yet been sensed; differences and degrees within a total event are not recognized.
2. *Egocentricity dominates.*
3. *The real is not yet distinguished from the non-real,* the objective from the subjective, what happens in their minds from what happens in the world.
4. *Ability to abstract* and generalize, though present from an early age, *develops very slowly.*
5. *Abstract relationships are not well understood,* particularly cause-and-effect relationships.[26]

In view of this, it becomes vital that the development of critical reading skills and attitudes is not postponed until the child reaches high school and college. Teachers have learned the hard way that this is often too late. Rather, the development of these should begin at the time the child enters school. As Artley says, "The teaching of critical reading begins when the child begins to read." [27] Lorge also stressed the importance of developing critical thinking on all grade levels in the following:

The development of thinking in pupils is a responsibility of all the teachers who meet the pupils. The emphasis should be upon developing in the child the ability for critical thinking. . . . The child should be made aware that critical thinking is an active process in which he can participate by collecting data, or suggesting examples of a principle, or demonstrating equivalencies or similarities. He should be encouraged to see that one of the first steps in critical thinking is to organize information and experiences about problems by recognizing similarities or differences.[28]

Today, not only is critical reading stressed on all grade levels, but in all types of reading experiences as well, with a major emphasis placed upon it in the basal reading program.

The basal reading program should provide numerous opportunities for the development of critical reading. The authors of most basal reading series have recognized the importance of critical reading and have tried to provide for it in textbooks, workbooks and teachers' manuals. Williams categorized the thinking abilities stressed in ten basic reading series into thirty-three critical reading skills, twenty-one of which were developed on

---

[26] W. H. Burton, R. B. Kimball, and R. L. Wing, *Education for Effective Thinking* (New York, Appleton-Century-Crofts, Inc., © 1960), p. 336.

[27] A. S. Artley, "Critical Reading in the Content Areas," *Elementary English*, Vol. 36 (February, 1959), p. 128.

[28] I. Lorge, "The Teacher's Task in the Development of Thinking," *The Reading Teacher*, Vol. 13 (February, 1960), p. 174.

all reading levels from preprimer through grade six.[29] There seems to be some indication, therefore, that basic reading materials have been designed to make some provision for critical reading although, according to Williams, this could be expanded and improved in several instances.

A second aspect of the basal reading program, which is vital to the development of critical reading, is the skillful questioning and directing of the teacher. In several series, the teacher's manual will help to formulate questions designed to stimulate these skills. However, the teacher should add to these as he helps the group interpret and analyze a selection. The following questions were accumulated from actual reading lessons conducted in various grades in the elementary school. They are illustrative of the type of questions and directions used constantly by teachers in their attempt to strengthen some of the more common skills and habits usually associated with critical reading.

ESTABLISHING AND RETAINING A PURPOSE FOR READING

1. Why do you think this story is called "John's Happiest Birthday"? What could have happened to make it such a happy day? Let's read to find out what it was. To be sure we don't forget what we want to find out, will Susan write the question on the board before we begin? Now, let's read to find the answer.

2. How does Jane look in the picture? Does she look happy or sad? What will we find out if we read the page? Let's read, then, to find out why Jane is happy.

PREDICTING OUTCOMES OR ESTABLISHING HYPOTHESES.

1. From what the title tells us, what do you think will happen in this story? What else could happen? Could the title mean anything else? Let's read to find out which of our guesses is correct.

2. Why do you think she was called "Lady with a Lamp"? Let's read to find out if we're right.

INTERPRETING EMOTIVE TONE OF THE CONTENT.

1. How did this story make you feel? How did the author write it to make you feel that way? Let's look for some of the words or sentences which made you feel this way.

2. Let's try to read the parts exactly the way we think the characters said them.

CHECKING DATA.

1. Let's look at our question again. Have we answered it completely? Do we have all the facts?

2. Apparently we do not agree on this point. Let's go back to the story to see exactly what it says on this topic.

RELATING READING TO DIRECT EXPERIENCES.

1. Have you ever felt the way John did? Tell us about it.

2. Did anything like this ever happen to you?

[29] G. Williams, "Provisions for Critical Reading in Basic Readers," *Elementary English,* Vol. 36 (May, 1959), pp. 323–331.

3. Do we have chocolate figurines in our stores like the ones which were in the Swiss chocolate shop described in our story? At what time of the year do we usually see them?

BUILDING READING PREFERENCES.

1. Did you like the story? Can you tell us what parts you particularly enjoyed? (Never ask—*why* did you like the story!!)

2. Would you like to read other stories by the same author?

A third major aspect related to the basal program which can be used to develop critical reading is the provision for many purposeful related activities. Some of these may be found in the workbook exercises which accompany the reading selection. The exact value of workbooks in the over-all reading program has yet to be determined, but it would seem that, *if used correctly,* they may have some value in developing or checking literal and critical reading. Other follow-up activities, which have far greater value, are those which relate the reading selection to various other purposeful experiences. For instance, a fourth-grade class decided to dramatize a story from their basal reader with a puppet show. They were faced with such questions as, "Should we make a moat around the castle?", "How shall we dress the old woman?", "What should the king look like?", and "How shall we make the queen show the way she felt when she heard the news?" These and other questions led pupils to seek answers from a variety of sources. Books illustrating historical costumes, books on medieval castles, encyclopedias, and numerous other references were read carefully and the children grew steadily in their abilities and awarenesses of the importance of reading critically.

Critical reading in the content areas receives considerable emphasis in the modern program. In addition to developing these skills in the basal reading program, considerable attention should be given them in other content fields. This is particularly true, of course, in the intermediate and upper grades. Although all curriculum areas probably lend themselves somewhat to this purpose, it is in social studies, science, arithmetic, and health that it can be developed to the fullest. As Artley stated, "Psychology of learning has long pointed out that what is taught is most effectively learned when it is presented within the context in which it is used." [30]

Obviously, therefore, if children are to read arithmetic problems critically, critical reading should be taught in arithmetic class. If they are to employ problem-solving procedures in science, critical reading must be taught during the science period. If they are to withhold judgment concerning an historical event or person until they consult numerous references, critical reading must be taught in the social studies. The following brief lesson illustrates how critical reading can be taught in connection with discussions of current news reports.

[30] A. S. Artley, *op. cit.,* p. 128.

LESSON ON CRITICAL READING
(Grade 6)

OBJECTIVE

To strengthen critical reading ability as applied to reportorial writing.

PROCEDURE

Teacher: Boys and girls, during the last few days we have been talking about the present crisis in the UN. What are some sources of information we use to learn about this important current happening?

Child: Newspapers, radio, television, magazines, and sometimes we hear other people talk about it.

Teacher: Good. Today, I thought it might be interesting to compare some of these sources. Let's take a closer look at the printed sources you mentioned. I have here several copies of *different* newspapers and magazines. Will you share them so that we can all see one?
Will you please *skim* through your paper or magazine until you find the article about the UN. Please don't read it until I ask you a question about it.
Now that you have located the article, I would like to ask you a question. How many of you think that, since we are reading about the same event, we will find the same information in all our articles? How many do not? Some think we will and some that we won't. Let's read the article *very carefully* now and then we can find out if we all receive information that is exactly alike.
(*Children read articles silently.*)
Now, I am going to write *one* word at the top of this chalkboard. The word is *agree*. Over here, I will write *disagree*. Now, who can tell us one item of information he learned through reading his article?

Child: I learned the names of the two countries disagreeing.

Teacher: Did every one read this same fact in his article? Do we all agree? Then, I'll list this fact *on the agree* board. Now, will someone tell us another?

Child: I read that the delegates were so mad at each other, they almost had a fight.

Teacher: Did we all read this?

Child: No, my article doesn't say anything about that.

Child: My article says a "sharp exchange of words occurred," but that's not the same as saying they almost had a fight.

Teacher: I'm so glad you're reading so carefully. I'll put this statement about almost having a fight on the *disagree* board.
(*Continues this procedure through remainder of the article*)
Now, let's look at our two chalkboards. Notice the things listed on the *agree* board. What do you see?

Child: They are statements *mostly* about *facts*—who was there—when it happened—and things like that.

Teacher: Good. This appears to be generally true. Now, look at the *disagree* board. What do you notice?

Child: Some of these are just opinions.

Child: Some are exaggerations compared to other articles.

Child: Some are just different ways of saying the same thing but they seem to change the meaning.

Child: Some were left out of some of the articles.

Teacher: Good, these are the chief differences we found as we compared articles. Now, what would explain these differences? After all, all the articles are about the *same* event. Shouldn't we expect them to be exactly the *same*? Why should there be any statements which disagree?

Child: Some reporters may have actually been there and others may not.

Teacher: That might be one reason. Another?

Child: Even though they were *all* present, they wouldn't necessarily all see the same thing.

Teacher: Good. That happens to us, doesn't it? We may all be in the room at the same time but some of us may notice things that others don't. What other reasons?

Child: Some reporters are better at describing things than others.

Child: Some reporters may not like a person or country and they might write so as to make them look bad in print.

Teacher: Good. Does anyone know what we call this? Yes, some reporters, like anyone else, may have certain *prejudices*. Any other reason?

Child: Some may try to make it sound more exciting than it actually was in order to sell more newspapers.

Teacher: That's a good point. Let's try to summarize all that we have been discussing today.
What have we learned about reading a newspaper or magazine today? Why should we expect some agreement among these sources of information? Why should we expect *some* disagreement?
Who can summarize what we have learned?

Child: Newspapers and magazines are good sources of information but you shouldn't think that everything you read in them is the absolute truth, because you may read different versions of the same thing in different newspapers.

Teacher: That's a very good summary. Perhaps soon we can spend another day examining newspapers and magazines to learn other things about them which will help us to get accurate information about what is happening in the world today.

READING-STUDY-SKILLS

The "study-skills" are emphasized in today's broadened reading program. Here again there are differences of terminology among educators who refer to these skills as "work-study jobs," "work-type reading," or "reading-study-skills." In general, these terms designate the skills which enable a reader to locate and organize his reading materials as well as to adjust his rate of reading to a specific purpose. These are discussed accordingly.

The ability to locate information is a necessary study-skill. McKim identifies the problems of locating information as centering around,

the use of such aids as tables of contents and indexes; knowledge of such standard reference books as encyclopedias, atlases, and the *World Almanac;* and ability to use the library.[31]

The first of these is introduced early in initial book reading experiences when the first-grade child is introduced to the *Table of Contents.* From then, throughout all more difficult reading, a steady attempt is made by all teachers to develop other locational skills, particularly the use of the index. In general, this can best be done through definite and specific lessons, supplemented, of course, with numerous incidental experiences. Children should be taught how to determine key words as well as a knowledge of main and subheadings. In addition, the page notations (*14, 15, 19–22*) and the use of italics are taught as early as the third grade. It has been the experience of the authors that these skills do not develop overnight and that pupils in all grades (even beyond the elementary school) need occasional lessons and exercises to reinforce their use of the index.

The use of standard reference sources is also usually begun in the third grade, and expanded in all succeeding grades. The development of this skill is greatly facilitated if a classroom library contains such standard aids as a good set of dictionaries, an encyclopedia, an atlas, and an almanac. If not, children should have ready and daily access to the school library.

There are, at present, several sets of encyclopedias recommended for elementary school libraries. In general, these are written on reading levels which make them suitable for pre-high school children. Edgerton reports two studies, made ten years apart, concerning the readability of certain sets of encyclopedias.[32] He concludes that the present vocabulary load and sentence length of these encyclopedias make them suitable for use in the elementary school.

As important as it is to teach pupils the use of these standard references, it is equally important to stress the limitations of such references. Very often children (and adults) who have learned the value of the encyclopedia are inclined to use it as their sole source of information. It is, therefore, a major responsibility of upper-grade teachers to develop the awareness that these reference books have a decided, but limited, value.

The ability to organize information is an important study-skill. Organizational abilities are generally begun in the primary grades with the analysis of the meaning of a sentence, as was discussed in the preceding chapter. In approximately the fourth grade, the ability to organize material

---

[31] M. McKim, *op. cit.,* p. 442.

[32] R. B. Edgerton, "How Difficult are Children's Encyclopedias?" *Elementary School Journal,* Vol. 55 (December, 1954), pp. 219–225.

The ability to locate information is a necessary study-skill.

is sharpened through an understanding of the main and secondary thoughts of a paragraph. Extensive practice in determining the main idea of a paragraph, and grouping related sub-ideas to it, is found in all areas of the upper-grade program. Such organizational skills as outlining and summarizing, which accompany understanding of main and secondary ideas, are discussed in the following chapter on writing.

Adjusting the rate of reading is an important skill. In the elementary school, little emphasis should be placed solely upon *increasing the speed of reading*, for accelerated speed usually accompanies greater facility in word recognition and increased comprehension. Furthermore, there is some danger in specifying the number of words per minute which a pupil of any age should read. Obviously, the rate of reading should be determined by the reader's purpose as well as the difficulty and type of material. Carrillo and Sheldon summarize this point of view as follows:

> The mature reader is the adaptable, versatile reader; he should be able to adapt his rate of reading to the purpose with which he approaches the printed page, and to the difficulty level of the material. The goal is understanding at an adequate level.[33]

[33] L. W. Carrillo and W. D. Sheldon, "The Flexibility of Reading Rate," *Journal of Educational Psychology*, Vol. 43 (May, 1952), p. 300.

It is, therefore, not rate—but *flexibility* of rate—which is important. Emphasis upon the importance of flexibility can be begun in the intermediate grades and continued thereafter. Children should learn that some materials must be read slowly and carefully in order to grasp and retain the full import. Other materials may be "skimmed" if the purpose is to find answers to specific questions or only to get a general impression of the content. Usually specific exercises as, "Skim the page to find out where Tippie went," or, "Run your eyes very quickly over the article until you find how fast the newest jet can travel," are the most valuable methods of helping children to become aware of the importance of using different speeds for different purposes.

For the teacher who wants to determine his pupils' flexibility of reading rate, Letson suggests an informal method whereby the reader's rate in reading an easy selection is compared to his rate in reading a more difficult selection of the same length and about the same subject.[34] It would seem that such a device could be used profitably by elementary teachers to determine whether their pupils were developing into inflexible or flexible readers and to plan their reading activities according to the demonstrated needs.

Current literature reveals that there is some interest today in the use of "controlled readers." The chief purpose of these mechanical devices is to increase the reader's span of a single-eye fixation, and thus increase his speed of reading. Most studies of the effectiveness of these pacing machines have been on the secondary and college levels. There is little evidence that they are of value in increasing the reading efficiency of elementary school children. On the contrary, overemphasis on speed may disorganize the young child and decrease his reading efficiency.

To repeat, no emphasis upon speed in reading should be made in the primary grades; and in the intermediate and upper grades the emphasis should be upon flexibility of rate rather than speed alone.

Skill in using the library should be a primary objective of a comprehensive reading program. A well-equipped, adequately staffed, and well-organized school library is a "must" in the modern elementary school. It should be considered as a vital and integral part of the comprehensive reading program, and the classroom teacher and librarian should work closely together to implement the philosophy and reading objectives of the school. The library is not merely a storehouse for books; it is a vital part of the instructional program and its resources should be used to the maximum in developing reading skills, habits, and interests. The general principles operative in planning and developing an effective library program are:

[34] C. T. Letson, "Building an Informal Flexibility Test," *Education*, Vol. 80 (May, 1960), pp. 537–539.

A well-equipped school library is a "must" in the modern elementary
school.

1. The school library program reflects the philosophy of the school and en-
riches all parts of its educational program.

2. For the individual student, the library program offers valuable experiences
and instruction that start with kindergarten and, expanding in breadth and
depth, continue through the secondary school. This continuity of the library
program provides for the student a cumulative growth in library skills and in the
development of reading, listening, and viewing abilities and tastes.

3. The true concept of a school library program means instruction, service,
and activity throughout the school rather than merely within the four walls of
the library quarters. All phases of the school program are enriched by means of
library materials and services. The degree to which teachers and pupils can and
do depend on the services, materials, and staff of the library measures the extent
to which the library program is successful.

4. Every boy and girl within the school is reached by the library program
according to his individual needs.

5. Through varied types of materials, the collections of the library provide for
the many kinds of interests that its users have, for the different levels of maturity
and ability of the student population, and for the wide range of demands evoked
by the curriculum and the services of the modern school.

6. The library is a laboratory for research and study where students learn to work alone and in groups under the guidance of librarians and teachers. Thus it contributes to the growth and development of youth in independent thinking, in abilities to study effectively, and in desirable attitudes toward reading, toward other media of communication, and toward all learning and research.

7. The library program forms one facet of an over-all guidance program in the school by making important contributions through its teaching, materials, and services to the personal, social, and vocational guidance of students.

8. School library experiences serve as steppingstones to the use of other library resources in the community and to the formation of a lifetime habit of library usage, as well as to pride in the ownership of books.[35]

Another major aspect of the reading program which is the concern of all teachers is that of efficiently organizing the class for instruction. This is discussed in the following section.

ORGANIZING THE CLASS FOR INSTRUCTION

This is not a new problem. It began with the first teacher who realized that no two children are alike. It will end the day that all people are created as identical to each other as car models coming off the assembly line. Until that time, every teacher, in every grade, is faced with the question, "How can I best organize my class to provide each child with optimal conditions for learning to read?" Although no two answers are alike (teachers are as different as pupils!), in general, there are three predominant patterns used. The most common of these is grouping within the classroom.

There are many different methods for grouping children within the classroom. The traditional plan of grouping children within one classroom into two to five groups is used most widely today by teachers in the elementary school. In general, these groups are determined by the pupils' reading levels as measured on standardized tests or according to the best judgment of the teacher. There are, of course, several advantages of this plan, too well-known to merit any discussion here. There are also, however, some limitations. One of these is that, in a heterogeneously grouped class, reading levels are apt to extend over a range of ten to twelve years and the traditional three groups (or even five) do not guarantee that a pupil will be reading on his level. Another, of course, is that each pupil has various levels of reading which are not revealed on a standardized test and for which no provision is made in the traditional group pattern. A third limitation associated with this plan is the stigma attached to those reading in the "lowest" group. It has been the authors' experience, however, that this stigma is not the inevitable accompaniment of ability grouping within the classroom, but depends solely upon the type of classroom environment fostered by the teacher. Frequent admonitions to "catch up

[35] The American Association of School Librarians, *Standards for School Library Programs* (American Library Association, 1960), pp. 14–15.

with the top group" or "see how well the first group reads" will surely result in tensions and stigma, but this is caused more by poor teaching than by placing children in groups. If, however, the teacher feels seriously about the limitations of grouping his children according to reading levels, there are other methods he may use.

Some teachers have experimented with grouping in reading solely upon the basis of interests. Thus, children who have a strong interest in the same topic will function, for a time, as a reading group. This plan has some of the advantages not found in the previous one, but also has limitations in the demands it makes upon teachers to provide for the various reading abilities found in any one interest group.

A third method of intraclass grouping is on the basis of social preferences. Children are permitted to indicate the classmates with whom they want to form a reading group.

In summary, it should be stated that an effective group reading program will probably make use of all three methods at one time or another. Thus, through flexible and fluid grouping, many teachers are able to meet pupil needs and interests with a relatively high level of success.

Cross-class grouping is advocated by some teachers. There is, at present, some interest in cutting across class lines to group for reading instruction. A typical example is as follows: There are three classes on the same grade level in a school. Reading is scheduled for approximately one hour at the same time for all three classes. At the given time, children report to their assigned classrooms for reading. The teacher of each of these rooms subdivides his group into two groups and works with each during the hour session. Children then return to their classrooms. Advantages of this plan, as reported in one trial situation, were found to be:

1. Each child had a better opportunity of being in a group of children working on his level and experiencing the same difficulties as a result of having six groups instead of three or four.

2. Each teacher had more time to prepare for daily lessons since she had two groups rather than three or four.

3. The teacher did more for each individual child since she could spend almost twice as much time working directly with a group by having only two groups.[36]

Before making a final evaluation of this plan, it is well to consider the disadvantages. There are many. In the first place, the plan appears to divorce the teaching of reading from other areas of the curriculum. This is directly in opposition to the expanded concept of reading held by most modern educators and described in the previous section. What value is there in Teacher A working with a pupil in his basal reading program,

[36] I. E. Aaron, F. Goodwin, and V. Kent, "Fourth Grade Teachers Experiment with Cross-Class Grouping for Reading Instruction," *Elementary English*, Vol. 36 (May, 1959), p. 307.

if Teacher B must develop his reading competencies in all other areas? How will Teacher B in other curriculum areas provide for reading needs revealed in Teacher A's lessons? Also, how can a worthwhile "follow-up" program of related activities be developed when reading is taught in isolation from the daily, on-going experiences of the entire classroom program? Lastly, does not this plan ignore the interrelationships which are known to exist between reading and the other language skills? (*See Chapter Five.*)

A second disadvantage would seem to be the rigidity of scheduling which is necessitated by all three classes having reading at the same time.

A third disadvantage frequently mentioned is the adjustment which children must make to more than one teacher. Again, it is perfectly possible that this adjustment may be easily made by some children, but it is a point worth consideration in appraising the values of the plan.

Another disadvantage is the fact that a teacher must study almost twice as many children as he would in a self-contained classroom.

A variation of this plan cuts across grade levels as well as class lines, and groups children of perhaps the third, fourth, and fifth grades into instructional groups. This plan is based upon the fallacious reasoning that children of similar reading levels as measured on a standardized test, have identical reading proficiencies, regardless of chronological age, intelligence, and experience. Research has proved rather conclusively that this is not so. In addition, the social harm done to a mature fifth-grader by sending him to read daily with a group of third-graders should be seriously considered by all teachers to whom this plan may seem to offer a solution for their reading problems.

A third organizational pattern which has received considerable attention in recent years is the individualized reading program. Current literature is filled with discussions and descriptions of this topic which, in general, give positive support of its value. Some of the most pertinent aspects of the topic are discussed briefly in the remainder of this section.

Individualized reading is based on certain fundamental premises. Lazar gives these as follows:

Reading is a matter individual to each child.

A child should have the opportunity to proceed at his own pace.

The reading experiences should eliminate comparisons with others.

The level of the reader or reading material should be subordinate to the act and enjoyment of reading itself.

Allowing a child some freedom of choice in selection of his reading materials will develop real purpose for reading.

Instruction in reading and reading itself are constantly interwoven.[37]

[37] M. Lazar, "Individualized Reading: A Program of Seeking, Self-Selection, and Pacing," in N. Larrick, ed., *Reading in Action,* International Reading Association Conference Proceedings, Vol. 2 (1957), p. 142.

Individualized reading has certain basic key characteristics. The three basic characteristics of the individualized program are *seeking, self-selection,* and *pacing.* These mean that a child reads a book of his own choosing, at his own rate, and keeps his own records. It does *not* mean that the responsibility of the teacher is in any way lessened. Exactly the opposite is true. In the first place, the teacher may help with guiding the child's selection of a book in order that higher levels and wider interests may be realized. Secondly, the teacher holds regularly scheduled conferences with each child in order to diagnose individual needs and appraise individual progress. Thirdly, the teacher also keeps accurate records of books read, special difficulties revealed, and reading preferences noted. In such a program, the reading interests and abilities of each individual are encouraged to develop in accord with *his growth pattern* under the steady guidance of a capable teacher.

Advocates of individualized reading report many advantages. Advantages noted by Darrow and Howes are:

Individualized reading becomes an effective way to capture and build interest—an all-important basis of learning. . . . Parental satisfaction with the program (once understood) helps to build home-school relationships and co-operation. . . . Children may forge ahead in reading at own rate of speed. . . . Builds self-confidence in pupils. . . . Offers opportunity for self-direction. . . . Eliminates forced competition among groups in favor of voluntary competition among individuals. . . . Teachers better able to relate to the needs, abilities, and goals of the learner.[38]

In addition, classroom teachers who have tried the program appear to be, in general, enthusiastic about its results. Parkin indicates its gains as,

freedom of choice and the joy that accompanies it; release from the tethering gait of the group; release from the stigma of the group label; a relaxed attitude toward reading; the pleasure of making reading a live, dynamic activity; more time for reading for the purposes that reading can serve; a change of emphasis from competition with the group to competition with one's self.[39]

The same writer, also, reported that pupils revealed their enthusiasm with the program through such comments as, "because I can choose any book I want," "can read as fast as I want," and "no one knows what group I'm in because there aren't any groups."

In general, therefore, it would seem that the strong enthusiasm of educators, classroom teachers, and pupils would result in increasing growth and popularity of individualized reading. There are, however, some problems which may hinder this development.

Individualized reading presents some problems. There are, of course,

[38] H. F. Darrow and V. M. Howes, *Approaches to Individualized Reading* (New York, Appleton-Century-Crofts, Inc., 1960), pp. 25–27.
[39] P. Parkin, "An Individual Program of Reading," *Educational Leadership,* Vol. 14, (October, 1956), p. 38.

some practical problems which even the most ardent advocates readily recognize. In general these are:

1. *Limited supply of books.* This may be a serious financial problem in some systems. To be successful, individualized reading should enable the pupil to choose from a variety of books representing a wide range of interests and reading levels. If this is not possible, obviously much of the inherent value of the program is lost.

2. *Incompetent or indifferent teachers.* Not even the most persuasive "salesman" of individualized reading would attempt to sell it on the basis that it is an "easy" way to teach. On the contrary, a good program is an exceedingly difficult one to plan and administer. Experience, maturity, and ability are certainly three highly desirable assets in the teacher who attempts to put this plan into action. On the other hand, enthusiasm, willingness-to-learn, and knowledge of the support from the school administration and parents are probably just as important in determining the final outcome of the program.

3. *Large classes.* It is difficult to say at what size a class should be in order to make the program most efficient. Again, this depends on the enthusiasm and competency of the teacher. Common sense, however, would appear to indicate the impracticality of using this approach in an excessively large class.

4. *Grade level.* Opinion appears to favor the individualized approach more for upper grades than for primary grades. There is, however, some evidence that it can be used effectively in primary grades. Vite describes a successful program with first and second grades.[40]

5. *Difficulty of evaluation.* Some teachers have refused to adopt the individualized program because of lack of conclusive evidence of its superiority over the traditional group procedure. It is, of course, extremely difficult to measure objectively the advantages claimed for individualized reading. Reading achievement can, and has been, measured but interest, enthusiasm, and attitudes toward reading are less tangible and more difficult to measure. The sheer number of books which some children read, as reported by many teachers, is very impressive and may be some indication of reading growth but this may not be a very reliable measure. In general, the "wait and see" attitudes of some writers and teachers are directly attributable to the lack, at this time, of positive evidence of the superiority of the individualized program.

A combination of organizational patterns is advocated by some. Schools differ; teachers differ; and children differ. There is considerable danger in accepting any single method or pattern as *the* best. A far more sensible course is to take the strengths of *all* proposals and formulate a *best* for

[40] I. Vite, "A Primary Teacher's Experience," in A. Miel, ed., *Individualizing Reading Practices,* Practical Suggestions for Teaching, No. 14 (New York, Teachers College, Columbia University, 1958), pp. 18–43.

each situation. Many teachers have done this and combinations or modifications of the three basic patterns described appear in countless situations. Some teachers prefer to divide their classes into groups and supplement this with extensive individualized reading. Others permit several pupils to work in an individualized program while the remaining work in groups. Still others prefer to start the year in a group organization and move gradually into an individualized program. In general, this practice of combining methods or adapting them to the individual situation meets with the recommendations made by many prominent reading authorities. Typical of these are the following statements:

It seems that a defensible program in reading will combine the best features of both individualized and group instruction in reading.[41]

To find one plan of class organization to be executed effectively by all teachers with all children is as difficult as finding a word to rhyme with *orange*.[42]

DEVELOPING PERMANENT READING INTERESTS

If one were to rearrange in order of importance the aims of reading instruction given on p. 146, there are many who would place the development of favorable and lasting interests at the top of the list. In a sense, the success of any reading program can be judged on this basis alone. A teacher who gives his pupils a deep and permanent interest in reading is probably, at the same time, accomplishing all other aims of reading. How can this goal be realized in the elementary school?

Reading is related to children's needs. Children's interests in reading are, in reality, the *purposes* with which they turn to reading, or the *needs* they satisfy through their reading. Jacobs classified and defined these as:

1. *The need for recreation.* It probably should be pronounced *re-creation*. In the best sense of the word, entertainment is the reason for turning to the reading of a story or poem. Teachers cannot ignore children's purposes to be entertained. They purpose to avoid boredom, to escape from the too immediate, to be challenged and brightened, and elevated in spirit.

2. *The need for a sense of identification.* Children seek out stories and poems that give them a sense of identification. We all seek to be identified with the world, with other people, with ourselves. The young child needs to get his feet firmly planted on this earth. He needs to sense what it means to walk as a human being, independent of others, through a natural world of sky and sea and plants and animals. Through stories and poems, the young child gets another dimension of what it means to walk the earth as a member of the human race.

3. *The need for aesthetic fulfillment.* We may differ as to what we call beautiful, but we all seek beauty. Young children seem particularly receptive to the

[41] P. Witty, "Individualized Reading—A Summary and Evaluation," *Elementary English*, Vol. 36 (October, 1959), p. 410.

[42] E. A. Betts, "Developing Basic Reading Skills . . . Through Effective Class Organization," *Education*, Vol. 78 (May, 1958), p. 571.

beauty of well-written prose and poetry. They find aesthetic satisfaction in precise words, neatly-designed expressions and phrases, charmingly genuine repetition, well-chosen names. They delight in the harmony of imagery.

4. *The need for spiritual nurture.* One of the wonderful things about young children is their quest for meanings—meanings of significance and consequence. They are concerned with the ethical, the moral, the truly religious, the universal . . . The story or poem is the radiation of a human need that a child senses and feels and wants to comprehend more fully.[43]

These, then, are the basic needs of all children which may be satisfied through reading. Their specifics, in turn, are determined by many factors, the most common of which are mentioned on the following pages.

Children's reading interests are determined by many factors. Numerous studies have been made in an attempt to discover the common factors which influence children's reading interests. Briefly these can be summarized as:

1. *Age.* All studies reveal that reading interests are affected by maturity. In general, the change appears to be gradual, although more decided in children of elementary school age than high school students. Norvell summarized his findings on this point as:

It appears from the evidence presented that the degree of maturity reached exerts a major influence upon children's reading interests and that as children grow older the *rate of change* in interest gradually diminishes.[44]

2. *Sex.* Again, there appears to be common agreement that sex influences the reading choices of children. In the past, it was generally believed that sex was a negligible determinant of reading choices among elementary school children. More recent studies, however, appear to indicate that this conclusion may not be entirely valid. Taylor and Schneider report significant differences between reading interests of boys and girls of grade five through eight, with these differences more sharply differentiated as children progressed through the middle and upper grades.[45] The following recommendations of Norvell are of interest on this point.

Sex is so powerful a factor in determining children's enjoyment of reading materials that any selection considered for use in mixed classes should be checked for interest for boys and for girls, and if rated low by either group, rejected in favor of one approved by both groups.

Sex is a significant factor in children's choices in reading as early as the third grade.[46]

[43] L. Jacobs, "Developing Ongoing Interest in Reading Through Stories and Poetry," in N. Larrick, ed., *Reading in Action,* International Reading Association Conference Proceedings, Vol. 2 (1957), pp. 21–22.

[44] G. W. Norvell, *What Boys and Girls Like to Read* (Morristown, New Jersey: Silver Burdett Company, 1958), p. 33.

[45] M. Taylor and M. Schneider, "What Books Are Our Children Reading?", *Chicago Schools Journal,* Vol. 38 (January–February, 1957), pp. 155–160.

[46] G. W. Norvell, *op. cit.,* pp. 183–184.

**Peer recommendations play an important role in molding children's
reading interests.**

3. *Intelligence.* In general, it is difficult to arrive at a generalization concerning the degree to which native intelligence affects reading interests.
Huber reports a striking similarity of choices between dull, average, and
bright children.[47] Norvell supports this viewpoint with, "Superior, average,
and slow pupils usually enjoy the same kinds of reading materials." [46]
There are, however, some differences of opinion on this point and the only
safe conclusion appears to be that intelligence is not as great a determinant
of reading choices as other factors.

4. *Peer recommendations.* There is a growing awareness among teachers
that peer recommendations play a major role in molding children's reading
interests. These are, apparently, much more influential than recommendations from teachers, librarians, or parents. Books which are highly recommended by friends and classmates are, inevitably, those most eagerly
sought. In attempting to stimulate pupil reading interests, Clark observes
that, "the group status of the child telling about the book influences the

[47] M. B. Huber, *The Influence of Intelligence Upon Children's Reading Interests*
(New York, Teachers College, Columbia University, 1928).

book's success with others." [48] Such an observation may have important implications for other teachers in determining the most valuable activities and materials of their free reading programs.

5. *Individuality*. The one inescapable conclusion and the most significant fact for teachers which can be drawn from all the studies on this topic is that children's reading preferences are highly personal and individualized. A knowledge of the general determinants of reading interests is certainly helpful to the teacher in planning his class library and yearly reading program. However, the directing of that program toward the specific interests of individual children is infinitely more important. Peter's reading interests are determined to some extent by the vital statistics that he is male, ten years old, and of average intelligence. To a far greater extent, however, Peter's interests are determined by all that is, or ever was, Peter!

Children's reading interests are an integral phase of their total development. Children, like adults, are interested in reading what they know and can understand. As they mature, their experiential and interest horizons broaden in a compatible pattern. Thus, very young children are interested in stories about people, animals, and events within their framework of experience and comprehension. Gradually these interests broaden to include stories of faraway places (real and fanciful), interesting people, and tales of mystery, adventure, and excitement. Thus, on all age levels, children turn to the types and kinds of books which are compatible with their total growth at that time.

Many worthwhile activities may be used to stimulate reading interests. By far the most important aids to developing permanent interests in reading are: (1) materials, (2) time, and (3) subtlety and insight on the part of the teacher.

It was mentioned earlier in the chapter that the school library should play a vital role in the modern reading program. Unfortunately, current estimates of the number of elementary school libraries state that "at least 75 percent of the elementary schools are without school libraries." [49]

In view of these discouraging figures, it becomes imperative that the teacher provide a classroom collection of books for his pupils. How can this be done? There is just one answer. Collect them in any way you can manage! Buy some and borrow others. Persuade the parents' group to contribute some. Ask your principal to stretch his petty cash account. Encourage children to bring books from home. Exchange with other rooms and teachers. Enlist the aid of your town, county, and state libraries. The fact remains, through one way or another, teachers who believe strongly in a free reading program *do* provide books for their classrooms. What some teachers can do—others must do!

[48] R. Clark, "When Children Praise a Book," *Elementary English*, Vol. 36 (May, 1959), p. 311.
[49] American Association of School Librarians, *op. cit.*, p. 5.

Secondly, it is important that pupils be given some time to browse among books and read at their leisure. Providing books does not do much good if youngsters are only given forty-five minutes on Friday afternoon as a "free reading period." Precious minutes snatched from various parts of the day should allow the youngster time to explore the ever-unfolding wonders awaiting him at the library table or bookcase.

Thirdly, the attention of the teacher should be directed toward new techniques he can use for stimulating interest. Many teachers have found that an occasional short conversational period in which children are permitted to chat informally and share opinions about books they have read is highly desirable. Others like a class discussion or part of a "sharing period" devoted to spontaneous book reviews—"Would anyone like to tell us about a good book he has read lately?" One teacher devoted a section of his bulletin board to a chart of the "Book of the Week." Children were encouraged to write reviews of their favorite books and one was selected each week to be placed on the chart. Other teachers like to widen interests by regularly scheduled lessons in which they introduce their pupils to many new books pertaining to a central theme, such as stories about pioneers, animals, or space travel.

In general, activities which do *not* stimulate permanent reading interests are those which are artificially and extrinsically motivated. To read a book because a written report is required on Monday or to get a gold star beside one's name on the "Books We Read" chart is *not* reading with purpose, love, or deep satisfaction.

A worthwhile reading program should attempt to raise the level of interests and appreciations. With some few exceptions, any reading is better than none. This is true, not because there is any inherent value in reading "trash" but because it can be used as a stepping stone to better reading. The first important thing is, therefore, that the child read *something*. The next is that the teacher make a slow, gradual, but consistent effort to raise the appreciational level little by little. The first requirement for this task is *subtlety*. Too often, teachers, in their eagerness, attempt to move youngsters' reading tastes too abruptly from where they are to where they should be. This can be a fatal mistake to which the oft-repeated question, "Why do we have to read this stuff?" will readily testify.

In addition, in order to raise gradually the children's literary appreciations, it is necessary that the teacher himself recognize a book of high literary quality. Fortunately, the number of books for children is steadily increasing so that sheer quantity is no longer a problem. This increased quantity has, however, in some cases brought with it a problem of quality. The characteristics of worthwhile books for children listed by Jacobs are worthy of study by all teachers who place quality above quantity in choosing from the present market of juvenile literature.

WORTHWHILE BOOKS FOR CHILDREN

1. Books that present significant content that is rooted symbolically in big ideas and genuine feelings.

2. Books that use language which is precisely right for the content and appropriate to the mood and spirit of the content, whether or not it fits exactly some system of vocabulary control.

3. Books that have an integrity and beauty of their own—not a so-called beauty of contrivance and cuteness, but rather a subtle beauty of substance and style that integrally pervades the ideas and feelings being conveyed.

4. Books that find their bearing in authentically trusting children with what is relevant to the human enterprise of living and being.

5. Books that engender honest sentiment.

6. Books that extend the imagination of the reader.

7. Books that, with simplicity and grace, use language precisely and artistically.[50]

READING DISABILITIES

This section summarizes briefly the major points of agreement concerning the problem of reading retardation and its significance to elementary classroom teachers.

Retardation in reading is a problem of major concern. On the whole, there appears to be some evidence that children today are better readers than those of past years. Teaching methods and materials have improved and research has added much to our knowledge of the reading process. Nevertheless, learning to read is an extremely difficult and complex task which poses a serious problem for many children. It is difficult to gauge accurately the extent of reading retardation, chiefly because of the differences of definition and conflicting findings of many studies. Betts estimates that "About one child in four has difficulty in reading," [51] although many of these would probably not be labeled reading disabilities. Bond and Tinker summarize various studies on the extent of reading retardation and conclude, "The percentages of seriously retarded readers (one year in the lower grades and two years or more at the higher levels) range from about 10 to 25." [52] The significance of these statements lies not in the precise number but in the fact that reading retardation is prevalent enough to be the concern of every teacher.

There is lack of agreement upon terminology related to the problem. "Remedial," "corrective," "disabled," and "retarded" are terms used in-

[50] L. Jacobs, "Books for Beginning Readers: An Appraisal," *Education,* Vol. 80 (May, 1960), p. 517.
[51] E. A. Betts, "Signs of Reading Difficulties," *Education,* Vol. 77 (May, 1957), p. 566.
[52] G. L. Bond and M. A. Tinker, *Reading Difficulties: Their Diagnosis and Correction* (New York, Appleton-Century-Crofts, Inc., © 1957), p. 7.

discriminately by many teachers. Consequently, there is lack of understanding concerning the exact nature of what constitutes a reading problem. For purposes of efficient group instruction, however, the interest of the teacher should be focused upon the ratio between the child's native ability as determined by standardized nonlanguage tests *and* the level of his reading performance. For instance, a child in the sixth grade whose mental age has been determined by reputable standardized nonlanguage tests to be approximately 7.5 years and who is reading at a high second or low third-grade level should cause his teacher no grave concern. He is really doing fine! The teacher's major problem as far as this pupil is concerned is to continue to give him the same type of instruction he has been getting and to provide him with reading materials geared to his chronological maturity and social interests as well as to his reading ability. On the other hand, another child in the same grade, also reading on a low third-grade level, but whose mental age is 11.5 *is* a disabled reader. In general, the first child needs nothing more than the type of instruction he is presently receiving from a patient and understanding teacher. The second needs careful diagnosis and remedial treatment from the classroom teacher *and* the reading specialist.

The causes of reading disabilities are many and varied. The extensive literature on the causal factors of reading disability points to one incontrovertible conclusion. No single factor but, rather, a constellation of factors lie at the root of most reading problems. In most instances, therefore, diagnosis is extremely difficult for even the trained clinician and may be impossible for the classroom teacher. It is important, nevertheless, that the teacher be aware of some of the major causes of reading retardation in order to understand better the specific needs of each pupil. A brief examination of these can be made according to the most significant (1) physical, (2) educational, and (3) social and emotional factors related to reading disability.

1. Physical factors related to reading disability. The extent to which visual handicaps are related to reading disabilities has been widely investigated and was discussed briefly in connection with readiness earlier in the chapter. Many studies show a high proportion of far-sightedness among poor readers and, conversely, a higher-than-average proportion of near-sightedness among superior readers, but cause-and-effect relationships have not been clearly established. In general, authorities are extremely cautious in drawing conclusions concerning the relationship of visual difficulties to reading disabilities from the existing evidence. Robinson states,

Authorities continue to believe that there is a definite relationship between visual abilities and reading failure, although the existing research has given little support to this conclusion.[53]

[53] H. M. Robinson, *Clinical Studies in Reading II*, Supplementary Educational Monographs, No. 77 (Chicago, University of Chicago Press, January, 1953), p. 159.

Johnson's conclusion agrees:

The preponderance of evidence appears to lead to three conclusions. First, visual functioning and reading achievement are not significantly related. Second, visual difficulties may be contributing factors in reading disability. Third, detection and correction of visual difficulties may enhance comfort and efficiency in reading.[54]

As with visual difficulties, wide investigation has been made of the relationship between auditory limitations and reading disabilities. Johnson summarized research on this problem with the statement,

It would appear that there is no convincing evidence that auditory acuity and reading achievement are closely related. Poor auditory discrimination appears to be rather definitely linked to, and possibly a causative factor in, reading disability.[54]

Lateral dominance (eye, hand, and foot preference) is a third physical factor which is suspected by many to be related to reading disability. Again, there appears to be no conclusive evidence that left-sided dominance, right-sided dominance, or mixed dominance is related to success or failure in reading. Bond and Tinker conclude,

The evidence that left-handedness, mixed dominance, or lack of dominance may be involved in reading disability is equivocal. Careful analysis of data and conclusions indicates that, in certain rare clinical cases, one or another of these anomalies may contribute to reading disability as part of a pattern of hindering factors.[55]

Other physical disabilities which have been investigated include glandular of motor disorders and various types of brain injury, but the incidence of these is believed to be too small to warrant discussion here.

In summary, it can be concluded that the *exact* relationship of certain physical factors to reading achievement has yet to be determined. The complexity of the total problem and the interrelationship of multiple factors have, to date, prevented the research worker from finding "the final answer."

2. Educational factors related to reading disability. The second major category of factors related to reading retardation pertains to the failure of the school to fit its program to the specific needs of the child. In general, educational factors include *poor* instruction which, in turn, has numerous manifestations. Disregard for the importance of readiness; "lock-step" instruction in the classroom; overdependence upon one specific method or technique; and failure to "learn" children as well as "teach" them are examples of instructional weaknesses contributory to reading failures. Under educational factors, also, are included certain administrative weak-

[54] M. S. Johnson, "Factors Related to Disability in Reading," *Journal of Experimental Education*, Vol. 26 (September, 1957), pp. 5–6.
[55] G. L. Bond and M. A. Tinker, *op. cit.*, p. 101.

nesses such as (1) overly large classes; (2) inflexible grade standards; (3) overemphasis upon competitive grading systems; (4) failure to provide specialized diagnostic and remedial services; and (5) lack of home-school co-operation. All of these should be the concern of every teacher, administrator, and board member if a direct and successful campaign is to be launched upon the problem of reading retardation now existing in the schools.

3. Social and emotional factors related to reading disability. Here, again, it is difficult to determine the precise relationship between these factors and reading disability. One thing is certain. The proportion of personal maladjustments among retarded readers is greater than among achieving readers. The difficulty, however, lies in determining cause-and-effect relationships. Do emotional instabilities and social insecurities cause reading difficulties? Or do reading difficulties precipitate them? Probably both relationships are operative. Emotional disturbances may contribute to reading disability, which in turn, aggravates the emotional maladjustments. It is interesting to note in this connection that no single trait nor discernible personality pattern has emerged from the numerous studies of retarded readers. Various traits such as aggressiveness, hostility, defensiveness, and withdrawal have been found repeatedly but no convergence of pattern has been noted.

Summary

This chapter discussed the major aspects of a modern reading program geared to an expanded concept of the nature of reading. It was pointed out that the concept of reading has emerged from that of mere "word calling" to "understanding the meaning" to the generally accepted present idea of "reading as thinking."

Readiness for beginning reading was discussed according to specific types of readiness: (1) physical readiness; (2) social and emotional readiness; (3) verbal readiness; (4) mental readiness; (5) experiential readiness; and (6) attitudinal readiness. No single instrument appears to be adequate for measuring all types of readiness and predicting reading achievement. The "formal" and "informal" types of readiness programs were discussed briefly according to their major limitations and strengths.

Word recognition and identification was discussed as a foundational step in reading. All clues to word identification were illustrated with particular emphasis upon the present controversial phonics issue. It was pointed out that disagreement on this question is probably not so pronounced among modern authorities as agreement. Phonetic analysis was recognized as one of the valuable aids to word identification and suggestions were offered as to when and how to use it.

For purposes of clarity, reading comprehension was discussed on the two levels of: (1) factual or literal comprehension, and (2) interpretative comprehension. The extent of the reader's experience in relation to reading with understanding was discussed at some length. The importance of developing critical reading skills in all grades and in all curriculum areas was emphasized strongly. The study skills of: (1) locating information, (2) organizing information, and (3) adjusting the reading rate according to purpose and material, were reviewed.

Organizing the class for reading instruction was considered as one of the most pressing problems faced by all teachers. Three presently-used methods were examined: (1) intraclass grouping; (2) interclass grouping; and (3) an individualized program. The advantages and problems of the individualized approach were discussed in some detail. The conclusion was reached that the organizational pattern should be determined by each individual situation. Many authorities recommend a combination of patterns as the most desirable solution.

Children's reading interests were examined according to the major factors which determine them. Suggestions for expanding reading interests were offered.

The important area of reading disabilities was examined briefly according to the three major factors of: (1) physical handicaps, (2) educational limitations, and (3) social and emotional maladjustments. It was stressed that research has had difficulty in isolating single factors related to reading retardation because of the interdependency of multiple factors as well as the difficulty of determining cause and effect relationships.

STUDENT PROJECTS

1. Write a detailed plan of how you can use a current popular TV program or motion picture as a springboard to a worthwhile reading program in your classroom. Mention specifically the grade level, the name of the program or movie, and the books and activities you plan to use. Be sure to list the desired outcomes of this type of reading program.

2. Prepare a "book talk" through which you will introduce your class to twenty or thirty books devoted to a central theme. Prepare some illustrative materials to accompany your talk which will help to arouse children's interest in these specific books.

3. A friend has written you concerning her four-year-old daughter, who appears to be very anxious to learn to read. She asks your advice on whether she should try to teach her to read before she enters school. Answer the letter explaining to your friend the many considerations she should weigh before making a decision. Give her numerous suggestions of worthwhile experiences and activities she may substitute for the formal reading experience if she so desires.

4. Examine several new children's books according to Jacobs' criteria for worthwhile books quoted on page 181. Which ones would you recommend for your school library? Why? Which would you not recommend? Why not?

5. Jack is a boy of average intelligence in your sixth-grade class. He is reading on a fifth-grade level. His parents are college graduates but, in your visit to their home, you notice that the bookshelves in their $40,000 house are filled with knick-knacks instead of books. How will you plan to ask Jack's parents to co-operate with you in improving his reading?

6. Ed enters your sixth-grade class in November. He brings very incomplete records with him from the last school he attended in another state. As far as you can observe, he is a total nonreader. What course of action will you take? Whose help will you seek? Explain in detail.

7. Visit a kindergarten teacher who uses readiness workbooks. Ask her to tell you the major strengths and limitations of her readiness program as she sees them. Do the same with another teacher who uses an informal approach. What are your conclusions?

8. Write a lesson plan for developing an experience chart in the first grade, following a trip to a dairy farm. What related activities could follow this lesson?

9. You have been asked to write an article for your state educational association organ on *Developing Critical Reading Skills in First Grade*. Make your article of practical help to primary grade teachers by using illustrations of materials, activities, and types of questions you use in your first grade to develop these skills.

10. Ask permission to administer to an upper-grade class the informal test for determining flexibility of speed mentioned on p. 169. Tabulate your results. Suggest types of activities you would use in a follow-up program with the inflexible readers.

11. Visit a teacher who is presently using an individualized approach to reading. What are the observable strengths and problems? Talk to the teacher, principal, and several pupils about the program. Evaluate the program upon the basis of your observation *and* the reactions secured from the individuals with whom you talked.

12. Make a file of games, activities, and devices you can use to develop auditory discrimination in your readiness-for-beginning-reading program.

13. Observe a first-grade, second-grade, and third-grade reading lesson. Make notes on each teacher's use of word identification clues. Draw comparisons as to clues used most extensively on each grade level. Do you see any specific pattern emerging? What sort of pattern?

14. Secure last year's statistics on publication and circulation similar to those given at the beginning of this chapter for the year 1959. Do your figures show an increase or decrease in the quantity of reading material published since 1959? Give reasons to explain this trend.

15. Construct an informal questionnaire to determine the specific reading interests of your class of children. How will your results help you to plan your reading program for the remainder of the year?

16. A new elementary school is to be constructed in your town. In the interest of economy, the school board plans to omit a library. Prepare a talk which you will present at a school board meeting showing that the school library is a "must" in today's elementary school. Describe the type of library which would be adequate for an estimated enrollment of six hundred pupils in grades one through six.

BIBLIOGRAPHY

ARTLEY, A. Sterl, *Your Child Learns to Read* (Chicago, Scott, Foresman and Company, 1953).

BETTS, Emmett Albert, *Foundations of Reading Instruction,* rev. ed. (New York, American Book Company, 1957).

BOND, Guy L. and TINKER, Miles A., *Reading Difficulties: Their Diagnosis and Correction* (New York, Appleton-Century-Crofts, Inc., 1957).

BOND, Guy L. and WAGNER, Eva Bond, *Child Growth in Reading* (Chicago, Lyons and Carnahan, 1955).

BURTON, William H. and collaborators, *Reading in Child Development* (Indianapolis, The Bobbs-Merrill Company Inc., 1956).

CARTER, Homer L. J. and McGINNIS, Dorothy J., *Learning to Read: A Handbook for Teachers* (New York, McGraw-Hill Book Company, Inc., 1953).

CAUSEY, Oscar Samuel, *The Reading Teacher's Reader* (New York, The Ronald Press Company, 1958).

DARROW, Helen F. and HOWES, Virgil M., *Approaches to Individualized Reading* (New York, Appleton-Century-Crofts, Inc., 1960).

DAWSON, Mildred and BAMMAN, Henry A., *Fundamentals of Basic Reading Instruction* (New York, Longmans, Green & Company, 1959).

DeBOER, John J. and DALLMANN, Martha, *The Teaching of Reading* (New York, Holt, Rinehart and Winston, Inc., 1960).

DURRELL, Donald D., *Improving Reading Instruction* (New York, Harcourt, Brace & World, Inc., 1956).

EPHRON, Beulah K., *Emotional Difficulties in Reading* (New York, Julian Press, Inc., 1953).

FIGUREL, J. Allen, ed., *Reading in a Changing Society,* International Reading Association Conference Proceedings, Vol. 4 (1959).

GRAY, Lillian and REESE, Dora, *Teaching Children to Read,* 2nd ed. (New York, The Ronald Press Company, 1957).

GRAY, William S., *The Teaching of Reading and Writing: An International Survey,* UNESCO (Chicago, Scott, Foresman and Company, 1956).

GRAY, William S., *On Their Own in Reading,* rev. ed. (Chicago, Scott, Foresman and Company, 1960).

GRAY, William S. and ROGERS, Bernice, *Maturity in Reading: Its Nature and Appraisal* (Chicago, University of Chicago Press, 1956).

HARRIS, Albert J., *How to Increase Reading Ability,* 3rd ed. (New York, Longmans, Green & Company, 1956).

HESTER, Kathleen B., *Teaching Every Child to Read* (New York, Harper and Brothers, 1955).

HILDRETH, Gertrude, *Readiness for School Beginners* (New York, Harcourt, Brace & World, Inc., 1950).

HILDRETH,, Gertrude, *Teaching Reading* (New York, Holt, Rinehart and Winston, Inc., 1958).

HUNNICUTT, C. W. and IVERSON, William J., *Research in the Three R's* (New York, Harper and Brothers, 1958).

LARRICK, Nancy, ed., *Reading in Action,* International Reading Association Conference Proceedings, Volume 2 (1957).

LARRICK, Nancy, *A Parent's Guide to Children's Reading* (New York, Doubleday and Company, Inc., 1958).

McKEE, Paul, *The Teaching of Reading in the Elementary School* (Boston, Houghton Mifflin Company, 1948).

McKim, Margaret G., *Guiding Growth in Reading in the Modern Elementary School* (New York, The Macmillan Company, 1955).

Miel, Alice, ed., *Individualizing Reading Practices,* Practical Suggestions for Teaching, No. 14 (New York, Teachers College, Columbia University, 1958).

Monroe, Marion, *Growing into Reading* (Chicago, Scott, Foresman and Company, 1951).

National Education Association, Department of Elementary School Principals, *Reading for Today's Children,* 34th Yearbook, 1955.

Norvell, George W., *What Boys and Girls Like to Read* (Morristown, N.J., Silver Burdett Company, 1958).

Norvell, George W., *Reading Interests of Young People* (Boston, D. C. Heath and Company, 1950).

Russell, David H., *Children Learn to Read* (Boston, Ginn and Company, 1949).

Stone, Clarence R., *Progress in Primary Reading* (St. Louis, Mo., Webster Publishing Company, 1950).

Tooze, Ruth, *Your Children Want to Read: A Guide for Teachers and Parents* (Englewood Cliffs, N.J., Prentice-Hall, Inc., 1957).

Witty, Paul A., *Reading in Modern Education* (Boston, D. C. Heath and Company, 1949).

Yoakam, Gerald A., *Basal Reading Instruction* (New York, McGraw-Hill Book Company, Inc., 1955).

CHAPTER 7

Writing

THE SECOND OF THE THREE R's, *Ritin*, is actually the fourth channel of communication and is normally undertaken by an individual only after he has achieved initial security in listening, speaking, and reading. Actually, writing is a complex and difficult task involving numerous skills and abilities, the number and type of which are dependent upon the level of writing. The following diagram illustrates the levels of writing and the skills employed at each level.

Skills Employed at Each Level of Writing

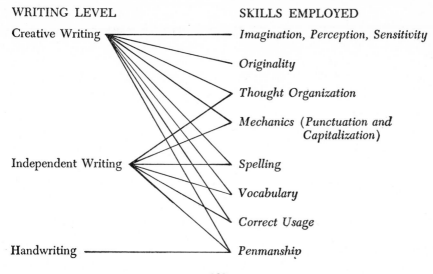

WRITING LEVEL	SKILLS EMPLOYED
Creative Writing	*Imagination, Perception, Sensitivity*
	Originality
	Thought Organization
	Mechanics (Punctuation and Capitalization)
Independent Writing	*Spelling*
	Vocabulary
	Correct Usage
Handwriting	*Penmanship*

Since handwriting represents the simplest level of writing, in that it employs the single skill of penmanship, let us examine this area before progressing to the levels of independent and creative writing.

Section 1: HANDWRITING

In the modern language arts program, handwriting is considered as a tool, not an art. The early art of "scrivening" which was introduced into the later colonial schools had, as its major objective, the perfection of style. Elaborate penmanship was a highly respected, greatly admired art, and pupils spent endless hours striving to master the flourishes and intricacies of acceptable letter forms. Generally speaking, this primary objective, the perfection of an ornate style, remained constant until twentieth-century theories of learning forced a re-evaluation of the entire language program. Today, teachers realize that handwriting is a tool for expressing one's thoughts and ideas; it is not an end in itself. An effective instructional program in handwriting, therefore, will develop the mechanical skills needed for the task, but will always be cognizant of the expression of thought as the main objective of writing. In general, this is the type of program,

(1) that provides methods, procedures, techniques; (2) that provides a combination of activities and systematic instruction; (3) that emphasizes legibility; (4) that gives children adequate time to form and fix correct writing habits; and (5) that carries over into the writing of the individual, in school and out.[1]

The over-all trend in handwriting instruction has been away from the emphasis upon handwriting as an end in itself toward the functional and utilitarian concept of handwriting as a necessary tool for the expression of thought. The concept recognizes that (1) legibility, (2) reasonable rate of speed, and (3) satisfactory style are the three criteria which should determine the quality of handwriting. To attain these, the handwriting program is carefully geared to the physical and social needs of children and is developed through a proper balance of purposeful writing opportunities and meaningful drill on specific weaknesses.

READINESS FOR HANDWRITING

Developing writing readiness is stressed in the primary grades. Although the kindergarten teacher usually has little or no responsibility for the formal teaching of penmanship, she should try to develop a consciousness of the necessity of writing and an understanding that writing is "talking written down." In her daily program she will capitalize upon many opportunities to record the stories and oral contributions of the children and develop in them an awareness of the importance and usefulness of writing

[1] A. L. McCalmont, "Current Trends in the Teaching of Handwriting," *American School Board Journal,* Vol. 135 (October, 1957), p. 66.

Writing readiness is developed in the primary grades.

as a tool of communication. For instance, before taking the class to the library for a story hour, the kindergarten teacher may say, "When we are in the library, how will anyone who comes into our classroom know where we are? How can we tell Mrs. Keating, our principal, where we are if she wants us?" Through these and similar questions the teacher tries to develop the idea of writing a message. She then manuscripts on a large card (while the children watch), "We are in the library," and asks a child to hang it on the door as they leave the room.

Various other incidents which occur during the school day will provide opportunities for the kindergarten teacher to develop an awareness of the importance of writing. One teacher, for instance, after conducting a science experiment with her children asked, "How can we ask our janitor to save this glass of water on the window sill which we are using for our experiment?" She encouraged children to word the message, "Please do not empty our glass of water." This was written on a card and a child was asked to place it near the glass. Incidents such as these are extremely helpful in developing a consciousness of the need and importance of writing.

A major part of the writing readiness program for young children is concerned also with the provision for exercises and activities preparatory for writing. Gray states that:

> In most cases where children attend nurseries, kindergartens or infant schools, preparatory training is provided through simple play activities of various types—handwork, drawing or modelling. In other cases the training provided is much more specific; for example, free motion at the blackboard, or the tracing in the sand of a word, such as one's name.[2]

Through creating an awareness of writing as an avenue of communication and through providing suitable activities for neuromuscular development the kindergarten teacher lays a foundation of readiness upon which the program in other grades will be built.

THE PRIMARY GRADE PROGRAM

Most schools teach manuscript writing in the primary grades. Manuscript writing is a modification of a vertical script which was used in Europe several centuries ago. It became fairly well established in English primary schools during the early years of the twentieth century and was introduced into New York schools in the early nineteen twenties. Since then, research has determined rather conclusively that it is the most suitable type of writing for young children, chiefly for the following reasons:

In the first place, manuscript writing is very easy for the young child to master since it uses no intricate strokes but consists entirely of circles, partial circles, and straight lines. Also, its unjoined letters are most suited to the child's muscular and visual development, as well as to his short concentration span. Secondly, there is some evidence that the use of the simple manuscript letter forms encourages writing fluency in young children. Thirdly, there is reason to believe that manuscript writing is an aid to initial reading since the letter forms the child meets in each are somewhat similar, thus avoiding unnecessary confusion. The evidence on this point has been summarized as follows:

> The evidence in the case of manuscript writing in relation to reading is about as conclusive as anything to be found in the field of educational research. There seem to be no studies of any weight which would discredit the statement *that manuscript writing is a distinct aid to young children who are learning to read print*.[3]

On the facing page is an illustration of a manuscript alphabet in capital and small letters: [4]

2 W. S. Gray, *The Teaching of Reading and Writing*, UNESCO Publication (Chicago, Scott, Foresman and Company, 1958), p. 193.

3 P. Cutright, "Script-Print and Beginning Reading and Spelling," *Elementary English Review*, Vol. 13 (April, 1936), p. 140.

4 *The Manuscript Alphabet* (Columbus, Ohio, The Zaner-Bloser Company, n. d.).

A a B b C c D d E e F f G g H h I i
J j K k L l M m N n O o P p Q q
R r S s T t U u V v W w X x Y y
Z z ————— 1 2 3 4 5 6 7 8 9 10 —————

In general, there is considerable uniformity among the numerous "systems" of manuscript writing in use at the present time, with slight differences existing only in regard to the formation of a few specific letters. Moreover, there are few, if any, set rules regarding size or spacing, for these will depend upon the materials used, the size of the paper, and the content to be written.

Systematic instruction in handwriting usually is begun in the first grade. This statement does not mean that writing is of no concern to the kindergarten teacher, for, as was stated previously, a major emphasis in today's schools is upon writing readiness. Furthermore, in some schools, certain children, depending upon their maturity, will be taught to write their names or to write labels or simple directions for use in the kindergarten room. In the first grade, however, the teacher is responsible for beginning a systematic program of handwriting instruction. Some authors specify, as a minimum requirement for writing, a sight vocabulary of two or three dozen words, but many others state only that the child should be able to read what he has written. In any case, sometime during the first month or so of school, the first-grade teacher will capitalize upon the "teachable moment" to introduce the pupils to a group writing experience. Such a lesson may be similar to the one described below.

INTRODUCTORY GROUP HANDWRITING LESSON

(GRADE 1)

OBJECTIVES

To stimulate in pupils an increasing awareness of the importance of writing as a tool of communication.

To develop initial facility in the skill of handwriting.

PROCEDURE

Teacher: We have been making many plans for our party. We have planned our program and menu very carefully, but there is one important thing we have not done. Who is coming to our party?

Children: Our mothers.

Teacher: Yes, we are inviting our mothers to our party. What would be the best way of doing this so that they will surely not forget to come?

Child: We can tell them about it when we go home.

Teacher: This is a good way but some of us may forget to ask our mothers. There is another way of asking them which may be even better. Has anyone ever received a *written* invitation to a party?

Child: Yes, I have.

Teacher: What did it say?

Child: It asked me to come to the party.

Teacher: Yes, this is the way some people ask their friends to come to a party. They *write* the invitation so they are sure no one will forget it. Do you think you can write an invitation to your mother asking her to come to our party? I will help you. (*Distributes materials*)
The first thing we should write is *Dear Mother* so that she will know it is just for her. Watch me as I write this part on the board. I'll do it very slowly so that you can do it after me. (*Teacher writes on board one letter at a time. Children copy. Individual help given when necessary. No emphasis is made on precise formation of letters, or spacing.*)

Teacher: What have we written on our papers?

Child: Dear Mother.

Teacher: All right, now what shall we say to her? What do we want her to do?

Child: Come to our party.

Teacher: Can anyone read everything we have written on our invitation?

Child: Dear Mother, Come to our party.

Teacher: Fine. Now Mother will know that we really want her and she will try not to forget to come. Have we forgotten something? How will she know who wrote the invitation?

Child: We can write our names on the invitations.

Teacher: Yes, let's write our names. If you need it, use your name card in your desk and I'll help you if you have any trouble. (*Children copy or write their names on invitations.*)

EVALUATION

Teacher: Why did we decide to write our invitations to our mothers?

Child: So we wouldn't forget to ask her to come.

Teacher: Yes, that's true. Sometimes writing is a better way of asking than speaking, isn't it? Now, what must we remember to do with our invitations?

Child: Take them home.

Teacher: Let's be sure to do that when we go home today.

Following this initial lesson, children should have daily contacts with functional writing which will concentrate on writing stories, invitations, memoranda, thank-you notes, lists, labels, and numerous others. Such functional writing experiences must be supplemented by "follow-up" practice on certain group and individual needs, although the teacher should always keep in mind that the primary emphasis is on the functional rather than the artistic aspects of writing.

As the year progresses the first-grade teacher gradually introduces the names of letters as she writes them on the board. She is careful to mention that "The next letter is *M*," or, "This word begins with a capital S which looks like this," so that children become acquainted with the names of letters and common punctuation marks.

The material used in the introductory phases of the first-grade program are usually 8″ × 11½″ unlined paper and black crayons or beginners' pencils. After children become fairly secure in the mastery of the common letter forms, they should use 1″ lined 8″ × 11½″ paper. Emphasis on keeping the letters on the lines, however, should not be stressed until they have achieved a reasonable facility with the formation of letters on unlined paper.

Usually, the first half of the second-grade program consists of a refinement and extension of the work in the first-grade program. The more difficult and uncommon letters are introduced, materials change to finer lined paper and thinner pencils, and practice is individualized according to specific difficulties and needs.

THE TRANSITION FROM MANUSCRIPT TO CURSIVE WRITING

There is considerable controversy over when and how to make the transition from manuscript to cursive writing. Just as the large majority of schools favor manuscript writing for the primary grades so do they prefer cursive or "script" writing for the intermediate and upper grades, with the transition usually made in the second, third, or fourth grades. A recent survey of 1294 school systems reports that current practice is "almost universally in favor of making the change in either Grade 2 or Grade 3 but that the trend is strongly in favor of Grade 3." [5]

Reasons given by the school personnel for preferring to make the transition in Grade 2 include,

heavy curriculum load in Grade 3, the advantage of having the change made by the teacher who teaches manuscript, the prevention of children making the change on their own and the prevention of the manuscript habit becoming too fixed . . . the eagerness of some children and parents to write in cursive.[6]

Reasons for favoring Grade 3 include,

the desirability of mastering manuscript before making the change, the attainment of sufficient maturity and muscular coordination before tackling cursive, the

[5] F. N. Freeman, "The Transition from Manuscript to Cursive Writing," *Elementary English*, Vol. 35 (October, 1958), p. 367.
[6] *Ibid.*, p. 371.

advantage of retaining manuscript as a ready instrument of written expression through Grade Three, the postponement of the change until the majority seem ready, the making of the change when it is the easier, and the postponement of the date to avoid interference with the development of reading.[6]

Even though there is not complete agreement on exactly *when* to make the transition, it is apparent that most schools *do* change the pupil from manuscript to cursive writing at the late primary or early intermediate level. This practice is not completely universal, however, for in a few schools children are taught manuscript writing throughout the entire elementary school.[7] The advantages of this plan are usually proposed as follows:

1. Manuscript writing is more legible than cursive writing.

All perception studies show that the farther hand-written letter forms depart from the vertical the less legible they become. Joining the letters, increasing the slant, elongation of the letters, and added loops all decrease legibility, because legibility is directly proportionate to the degree of similarity between machine printed type-face and hand writing style.[8]

2. Manuscript writing, contrary to popular opinion, is not "slower" than cursive writing. Research on this point is contradictory and inconclusive. One writer explains the popular, but unsubstantiated, belief that cursive writing is speedier as follows:

Psychological illustrations tend to distort impressions about speed of manuscript writing as compared with cursive style. The finished hand-written page of a good manuscript writer gives the impression of having been painstakingly hand-lettered . . . Cursive longhand while being done looks "busier" than manuscript style; and it is, because the process is more elaborate. These illustrations help to explain the impression that fluent, rapid writing is possible only in cursive longhand.[9]

3. Manuscript writing is accepted today by banks when used for legal signatures. This negates a frequently used argument for transferring to cursive writing.

4. Teaching and learning the transition from manuscript to cursive writing consumes time which might better be spent on more valuable activities.

Changing over comes at a time when the children need to concentrate on the rudiments of written expression. In view of the fact that our national and world economy demand the most efficient instruction of elementary school children in all phases of literacy, this manifest source of waste in education should be eliminated at once.[10]

[7] A. E. Hendricks, "Manuscript and Cursive Handwriting in Brookline," *Elementary School Journal*, Vol. 55 (April, 1955), p. 452.

[8] G. Hildreth, "Manuscript Writing After Sixty Years," *Elementary English*, Vol. 37 (January, 1960), p. 5.

[9] *Ibid.*, p. 8.

[10] *Ibid.*, p. 11.

5. Manuscript writing is easier for the left-handed child. "It is easier for left-handed children to write, as they have fewer problems in slant and placement of paper and can write with straight wrists." [11]

Despite these rather convincing arguments, there is little indication that the present trend is to continue manuscript throughout all the grades. Let us, therefore, consider briefly how the transition is made in most schools.

Some systems advocate a gradual transition through a means of connecting certain manuscript letters. This type of transition is illustrated below: [12]

Autumn
Sing a song of seasons
Something bright in all,
Flowers in the summer
Fires in the fall.

In other schools, the transition is made simply by providing practice on the new forms and integrating it with spelling and other functional writing experiences. On the whole, the authors have found that children are oriented to the change by observing their parents and older brothers and sisters writing in cursive style. If the change is made when children are psychologically ready and after they have achieved security in reading and manuscript writing, there is little reason why it should not be accomplished with a minimum of strain.

INDIVIDUALIZED INSTRUCTION

Group instruction in handwriting decreases as children progress through the grades. As opportunities for children to write independently are multiplied in the regular execution of their daily work, the need for a definite writing lesson decreases to some extent. Thus, the daily lesson of the primary grades may be reduced to a weekly lesson in the intermediate grades or less in the upper grades. With these older children, the group lesson in which all children practice the same letter or stroke, is kept to a minimum and is used only when a need has been revealed in their written work.

[11] A. E. Hendricks, *op. cit.,* p. 448.
[12] Reprinted by permission of The Bobbs-Merrill Company, Inc., from Stone and Smalley, *Manuscript Basic Handwriting,* Book III, p. 10. Copyright ©, 1946, by Charles Scribner's Sons.

Infinitely more desirable than the group handwriting lesson in the upper grades are *individualized practice activities*. In such situations the teacher will return to the pupils samples of their written work with certain errors noted and the correct forms presented. Spelling tests, written assignments, and any other type of work should be used as bases for individualized practice on certain specific difficulties. Children then work on these specific errors during a handwriting lesson (with the teacher working with individuals) or during any kind of independent work period.

Writing materials used in the intermediate and upper grades include adult pencils, ⅜″ lined paper, and ball-point and fountain pens of the type commonly used at home or in the business world.

Individual attention should be given to the left-handed child. The left-handed child presents something of a problem to most teachers, and research is still inconclusive on the best way to teach him. Most educators agree, however, that the child who is decidedly left-handed should not be encouraged to change to his right hand. Noting the extent of the dominance is the job of the kindergarten and first-grade teacher. If she notices that the pupil is fairly ambidextrous in most activities, she should probably encourage him to use his right hand when he begins to write. Showing him how to hold his pencil, how to sit properly, and how to place his paper on the desk will help him to write with his right hand. If, however, the child repeatedly transfers his pencil to the other hand, and uses the left hand in almost all other activities, the teacher would be wise to permit him to use his left hand without further correction. In any case, the dominance of the child is definitely established by the early school years and no attempt should be made to change it in later years.

In summary, the instructional handwriting program in the elementary school should help each pupil master a pleasing, legible, and reasonably rapid penmanship, which will begin to equip him for independent written self-expression. Other skills needed for the level of independent writing are discussed in the following section.

Section 2: INDEPENDENT WRITING

The second level of writing is independent writing which, in addition to penmanship, employs the skills of correct usage, vocabulary, spelling, mechanics of punctuation, capitalization, and thought organization. The first two of these have been discussed in Chapter Five in connection with oral language. Since their needs in oral and written language are essentially the same, they have been omitted from further discussion in this chapter. Before each of the last three is discussed separately, however, it may be well to consider a major point of agreement concerning independent writing at the present time.

Opportunities for independent writing should be numerous and should

Numerous opportunities for functional writing experiences should be provided.

duplicate life experiences. As children mature, they should be offered numerous and varied opportunities to write independently in connection with all types of school experiences. The major criterion for judging the genuine value of any school writing experience is simply the extent to which it approximates an actual life situation. The teacher should ask himself, "What writing activities do people engage in *outside* the classroom?" The answer is fairly obvious. They write letters, notes, memoranda, stories, telegrams, plays, TV scripts, diaries, minutes of meetings, poems, books, advertisements, reports, newspaper articles and countless other documents. They do *not* write letters to nonexistent friends, relatives, or business concerns; they do *not* complete sentences someone else has started; they *do not* insert words in long lists of sentences composed by another. Because these and similar exercises are completely artificial and unrealistic, they should be kept to the barest minimum. A truly vitalized language program will develop a high quality of independent writing, by capitalizing upon a legion of functional opportunities, a few of which are listed below.

1. *Letters.* It would be utterly impossible to list all the opportunities which present themselves to the elementary school program for the writing

of letters and notes. At various times children have repeated opportunities to write letters to sick classmates, to parents notifying them of important school events, or to friends and classmates who have moved out of town. They write thank-you notes or invitations to other classes in the school, the school principal, the custodians, traffic policemen, the patrol captain, the secretary, the librarian, cafeteria workers, parents, and community resource people. They write business letters requesting information, ordering supplies, or thanking firms for materials received. Letter writing in all the grades constitutes a major bulk of the independent writing experiences, and correct skills and attitudes in this area cannot be overemphasized.

2. *Booklets.* Many teachers encourage children to make individual or class booklets summarizing information they have accumulated on any unit topic. If children spend time and effort on the preparation of these materials, it is most important that they be placed in the classroom or school library where they may be read by others. The old idea of requiring each child to make a booklet which was read only by the teacher (and then only to give it a grade) is defeating the purpose of a functional writing program.

3. *Stories, Poems, Plays, TV Scripts.* These are popular channels for the encouragement of creative writing and are discussed later in the chapter.

4. *Minutes, Diaries, Logs, Records.* Any imaginative teacher may provide numerous opportunities for functional writing through these and related activities. Personal diaries, class logs of trips, or observational records of science experiments are only a few of the many opportunities afforded by the school for independent writing.

5. *Newspaper Articles.* Writing articles or stories for the class, school, or town newspaper is a functional writing opportunity for children of the intermediate and upper grades.

Growth in independent writing is achieved slowly and gradually as children progress through the grades. Strickland states that the steps through which the child achieves the ability to write independently are: (1) dictation, (2) dictation with copying, (3) writing with all the help he needs and (4) writing with increasing independence.[13] Generally speaking this means that, if kindergarten children want permission to visit the town library, they will, as a group, dictate a letter to the teacher. In the first grade, the same procedure will be followed except that children will copy the class-composed letter which the teacher writes on the chalk-board. In this case, all or some of their letters will be mailed, depending upon the suitability of the situation. In the second grade, the teacher may encourage children to dictate most of the letter which he will write on the board, but may suggest that the pupils "add a sentence or two of your own before you close the letter." In the third grade or above, the pupils will probably

13 R. Strickland, *The Language Arts in the Elementary School,* rev. ed. (Boston, D. C. Heath and Company, 1957), pp. 276–279.

write individual letters with the teacher giving group guidance when necessary and individual help on spelling and mechanical difficulties.

Although this is a very generalized and brief description, it summarizes the general procedure through which children are led from a group writing experience totally dependent upon the teacher to individualized, independent writing which utilizes all of the skills discussed in this section.

SPELLING—PAST AND PRESENT

Today's spelling program is a compromise between two extremes of the past. In years past, the emphasis placed upon spelling in the elementary school has swung from one extreme to the other. In the eighteenth and nineteenth centuries, an unlimited amount of time and effort were spent in developing spelling skills, and the "star speller" of the class was a mightily respected individual. Competition was keen, and spelling bees or contests were hot-beds of excitement as children struggled to "spell down" each other. In some districts a teacher's success was judged primarily upon the spelling ability of his pupils, and in others he was required to demonstrate his own spelling proficiency before the local board in order to qualify for a position. There was no doubt that spelling occupied a secure and venerable position in the curriculum, and many were the hours which were spent trying to turn out pupils who could spell *obduracy, connoisseur, obsequious,* or *ephemeris* without a moment of hesitation or a quiver of the voice.

All this, of course, changed greatly in the twentieth century, generally because of the revolutionary changes in educational thought and specifically because of the stress upon the "sight" methods of teaching reading. A system of reading instruction where the child was encouraged to recognize a word only by "sight," where detailed analysis of individual words was discouraged, and where emphasis was primarily upon speed and fluency, naturally worked to the disadvantage of spelling. It was in this era that capable students were graduated from high school who had severe spelling limitations and who were indifferent to their deficiencies almost to the point of boasting, "I can't spell a thing." In recent years, however, the pendulum has come to rest somewhere between these two extremes, and spelling today merits a specific instructional emphasis but only in proper balance and perspective to the other language arts and curricular areas.

THE CONTENT OF THE SPELLING PROGRAM

Careful attention should be directed toward the content of the spelling program. Many studies have been made of the words used most frequently in the writing of children and adults, in an effort to determine which words children should be taught to spell. On the whole, these studies reveal that a relatively few words comprise a large percent of the writing vocabularies of both groups. Horn, for instance, discovered that two thousand words and their repetitions make up 95.38 per cent of the words written by adults.[14] Rinsland reports similar figures for children's written vocabularies, namely that two thousand and their repetitions comprise approximately 95 per cent of the running words written by pupils in the elementary grades.[15] In addition, it has been discovered that there is a considerable amount of duplication between the words used most frequently by both groups. Fitzgerald has composed a basic list of 2650 words which make up more than 90 per cent of the words used most frequently by children and adults.[16] From these and similar studies, therefore, it has been possible to determine a basic list of two to four thousand words which can be divided into grade levels and thus constitute the core of the elementary school spelling program.

Another method of determining spelling content, used by some today, is to base the entire spelling program solely upon the words for which children have an immediate need. For instance, if a class is studying a unit on magnetism and preparing an exhibit with objects to be labeled, the words needed to be spelled will probably include *repel, magnet, north, south, pole, and attract*. These, then, become the content of the spelling program for that week, and no standardized list is used.

Without a doubt, the most functional spelling program of today's schools combines the advantages of both programs described above. In other words, most teachers prefer to use the standardized list of most frequently used words as determined by research, *supplemented by* words which arise from the on-going activities of the classroom. The number of supplementary words will, of course, depend upon the needs and abilities of the group and may vary considerably according to individual abilities within the class. This type of spelling program offers three distinct advantages: (1) all children are taught the words which they probably will use most frequently in their writing; (2) spelling is integrated with other curricular areas by using words derived from immediate classroom needs; and (3) the use of the supplemental list provides opportunity for the individualization of the spelling program according to specific needs and abilities.

THE INSTRUCTIONAL PROGRAM

The systematic program of spelling instruction usually begins in the second grade. The fact that most schools begin their directed spelling

[14] E. Horn, "The Curriculum for the Gifted: Some Principles and an Illustration," 23rd Yearbook of the National Society for the Study of Education, Part I (Bloomington, Ill., Public School Publishing Company, 1924), pp. 73–89.

[15] H. D. Rinsland, *A Basic Vocabulary of Elementary School Children* (New York, The Macmillan Company, 1945).

[16] J. A. Fitzgerald, *A Basic Life Spelling Vocabulary* (Milwaukee, Bruce Publishing Company, 1951).

programs during the second grade does not mean that many first-grade children do not acquire a fairly extensive spelling vocabulary. Usually, however, this is the result of instruction in reading and handwriting rather than the formal teaching of spelling. In a first-grade handwriting lesson, for instance, the teacher is actually developing spelling ability as he names each letter and writes it on the board for children to copy. As the year progresses and children have composed and copied several notes to "mother" and as the teacher has named each letter as he wrote it, many children will have memorized the sequence of the letters and can thus spell the word. Inventories of spelling vocabularies of children entering the second grade have revealed that a considerable number could spell as many as fifty words including, *come, go, run, jump, up, down, dear, mother, friend, school, me, an, she, he, it, and, funny,* and others.

In the second grade, however, a systematic program in spelling is usually begun. This continues throughout the remaining grades of the elementary school. Usually the formal spelling program is conducted through one of the two following plans.

Weekly spelling plans are of two basic types. Most systematic spelling programs are divided into weekly plans of study. Although there may be numerous modifications depending upon the individual situation, in general, the *test-study* plan and the *study-test* plan are the two in most common use by present-day teachers. There is, however, considerable controversy over which of these is the better plan. Research has arrived at no final answer, although the majority of evidence favors the test-study plan.[17] The advantage of this plan over the other is that it requires children to study only those words which they do not know how to spell.

The following outline of a test-study plan has been used satisfactorily in grades three through six. It combines features suggested by several authorities with others which the authors have found to be effective. It should, of course, be modified or varied by teachers according to the needs of their pupils.

TEST-STUDY PLAN

(GRADES 3–6)

Monday   Pretest on a word list of 20–30 words (depending on grade level and difficulty). Words are taken from required text or from the on-going needs of pupils, or both. Each child numbers his list of words consecutively and attempts each word the teacher dictates in the pretest. Teacher collects papers and returns them the following day with the words each child will study rewritten correctly beside the incorrect forms.

Tuesday   Children enter words for the week in individual notebooks and teacher works on study steps with individuals or small groups.

[17] J. Fitzgerald, "Research in Spelling and Handwriting," *Review of Educational Research,* Vol. 22 (April, 1952), p. 91.

Wednesday	Individual study for each child with individual help and suggestions from the teacher. Children may work in pairs or singly and may be assigned such activities as: (1) using words in sentences or original stories; (2) alphabetizing; (3) exercises involving homonyms, antonyms, or synonyms; (4) exercises involving derivations and syllabication; or (5) individual silent study.
Thursday	A short quick review on the entire word list which may take the form of a game or any interesting drill technique and/or continued individual study.
Friday	Final test. Each child numbers his paper according to the words he has studied and on which he will be tested. As the teacher reads the entire list, he writes only the words which correspond to the numbers he has on his paper. Words which are missed on Friday's test are entered in notebooks and will be studied individually and included on monthly or bimonthly review tests.

Another pattern of the test-study plan found by the authors to be satisfactory for many teachers divides the class into two or three groups with, perhaps, some pupils working individually. The weekly procedure is described below.

TEST-STUDY PLAN
(THREE GROUPS—GRADES 3–6)

Monday	Pretest each group on words for the week. Correct papers and return.
Tuesday	Teacher works on study steps with Group 1. Children in Groups 2 and 3 study individually or work in pairs according to their needs or according to assignments prepared by the teacher.
Wednesday	Teacher works with Group 2. Groups 1 and 3 work independently.
Thursday	Teacher works with Group 3. Others are engaged in purposeful independent study.
Friday	Final test for all three groups.

Gates' early study of the two plans for teaching spelling concluded that the test-study plan was preferable for upper grades but that the study-test plan may be more suitable for second grade.[18] Since that time, some studies have disputed this, but the plan is still used in most primary grades, and in some intermediate and upper grades. The following is an outline of a study-test plan as it is commonly used in the lower grades.

STUDY-TEST PLAN
(GRADE 2)

Monday	Teacher introduces approximately five new words. Number will depend on grade level, ability of group, and difficulty of words. Teacher will guide study of each word according to *study steps* described below.

[18] A. I. Gates, "An Experimental Comparison of the Study-Test and Test-Study Methods in Spelling," *Journal of Educational Psychology*, Vol. 22 (January, 1931), pp. 1–19.

Tuesday	Teacher introduces the remaining words for the week. (Approximately five.) The same procedure will be followed as was used on Monday.
Wednesday	Teacher introduces "bonus" words to children with special ability. She works individually with children needing special help.
Thursday	Supervises individual work with all children. Children may study in "pairs," may complete workbooks or written assignments, or may follow an individualized study program.
Friday	Final test on words for the week.

1. Teacher may distribute a mimeographed paragraph with spelling words omitted. Teacher will read paragraph and dictate omitted words.

2. Teacher may dictate a short paragraph including all words for the week.

3. Teacher may dictate list of words.

The "study steps" of teaching spelling are fairly well standardized.

The process of learning the spelling of a new word has been thoroughly investigated during years of research, and the essential steps of procedure are well formulated and standardized.[19]

Before considering the specific steps in the "standardized procedure" for teaching spelling, it is important to stress two points. First, this procedure is based upon the importance of presenting to the pupils the *visual, auditory*, and *kinesthetic* images of the word to be learned. The exact *order* of steps, therefore, is not as important as providing pupils with an opportunity to *see* the word, *hear* it, and, finally, to get the *feel* of writing it. Secondly, it is important that the teacher keep in mind that the over-all procedure should be modified according to the needs of the pupils. Not *all* pupils will need to go through *all* steps. Superior spellers may choose to eliminate some of the study helps while poor spellers may need to spend considerable time on each one. With these two important considerations in mind, the *general* procedure for helping children to study a word is outlined below. The word to be studied is *curtain* which has been widely misspelled on the pretest.

Step 1. The teacher writes *curtain* on an uncluttered chalk board, asks the children to examine it closely, pronounces it, asks children to pronounce it, and then develops its meaning. The meaning is discussed thoroughly with figurative meanings, such as the "iron curtain," if this is within the understanding of the age group. Every precaution should be taken to insure that the meaning is familiar to all pupils and that no one is asked to memorize the spelling of a word whose meaning is vague or unfamiliar.

Step 2. The teacher divides the word into syllables by writing each syllable separately as *cur tain*. This should not be done by disfiguring the word as *cur/tain* or by underlining syllables as <u>*cur tain*</u>, for neither presents

[19] W. Tidyman and M. Butterfield, *Teaching the Language Arts* (New York, McGraw-Hill Book Company, Inc., 1959), p. 273.

as clear a visual image as rewriting the word in separate syllables. The teacher asks the children to observe the syllabicated word and to pronounce it at the same time. He analyzes the word according to rules of syllabication (if possible) and permits a thorough discussion of their use.

Step 3. After discussion of syllables the teacher helps the group to analyze specific difficulties of the word. The *tain* of the second syllable is discussed, stressing that it is spelled differently from how it is pronounced. The initial consonant, *c*, is compared to the hard *c* in *cat*, *corn*, and *cupboard*. During this procedure the teacher is careful never to stress the negative or present incorrect spelling forms. In other words, teachers should *never* show children how *not* to spell a word.

Step 4. Children are asked to close their eyes and recall the visual image of the word in syllables. They may then open their eyes and check with the board. This can be repeated several times, if necessary.

Step 5. Children may be asked to write the word, looking at the board to check, if necessary. With very slow children the teacher may insert a step here in which they copy the word from the board and then trace it with their fingers or pencils. This step appears to be somewhat successful with retarded children but probably unnecessary for others.

Step 6. The children may rewrite the word as many times as necessary, *checking the spelling each time they write.*

Step 7. Children may write the word in a sentence.

In summary, the "study steps" of spelling are today fairly well standardized, the value of each having been determined by sound research in the field. It is, however, extremely important for the teacher to modify or vary these steps according to the needs of individual pupils.

CONTROVERSIAL ISSUES

There is some disagreement over the value of teaching spelling rules. The value of teaching spelling rules has been questioned for several years, and investigations disagree on whether or not to teach generalizations and, if so, which ones. In general, most authorities agree that most spelling rules have questionable value and that the only ones which should be taught are those which have very few exceptions. According to Horn these are,

rules for dropping final silent *e*, for changing *y* to *i*, for doubling the final consonant, for *qu*, for the capitalization of proper nouns and adjectives, for the use of a period after an abbreviation, and for the use of an apostrophe in possessives and contractions.[20]

In any case, the important thing to remember is that whenever rules are taught, children should be led to discover them through a process of inductive reasoning. For instance, the teacher may call the pupils' attention

[20] E. Horn, *Teaching Spelling*, Department of Classroom Teachers (Washington, D.C., Educational Research Association of the National Education Association, 1954), p. 21.

to numerous words to which the *ing* suffix has been added and may then lead them to state the rule covering these specific examples.

The influence of instruction in phonetics on spelling ability is not fully determined. Opinions on the relationship between knowledge of phonetic elements and the ability to spell vary widely. On the one hand, there are studies which claim that intensive word analysis, including phonetic study, has a positive relationship with spelling ability. Russell's study of spelling readiness discovered that

> A first-grade program of direct instruction in reading that includes early instruction in handwriting and phonetic analysis (with emphasis on both appearance and sound of words, syllables, and letters) produces better achievement in English spelling than a more incidental first-grade program involving little "phonics." [21]

In agreement with those who claim a relationship between the two factors is Zedler who states, "Written spelling ability and speech-sound discrimination are significantly related variables." [22]

On the other hand, there are very many reliable studies which indicate that knowledge of phonics has a limiting effect on spelling ability. In other words, we know that a majority of spelling errors are made by individuals who insist on spelling words the way they sound and not the way they are spelled. Horn, for instance, cites many examples of phonetic misspellings, typical of which is *tease* which was spelled in forty-four different ways including *tes, teas, tease, tees,* and *teez.*[23] It is probably safe to conclude, therefore, that children should be encouraged to analyze the way each sound is spelled in a word when learning that particular word, but that they should be discouraged from applying phonetic generalizations to the spelling of words.

Spelling contests and extrinsic motivating devices contribute little to the modern spelling program. There is little disagreement among educators concerning the exceedingly dubious value of these practices, although they are still fairly common in some school systems. In general, however, contests such as "spell-downs" or "spelling bees" are not advocated for the following reasons:

1. In the ordinary "bee" the children are eliminated when they misspell a word. This gives the most practice to the best spellers who need it the least.

[21] D. H. Russell, "Some Factors in Spelling Readiness," in C. W. Hunnicutt and W. J. Iverson, eds., *Research in the Three R's* (New York, Harper and Brothers, 1958), p. 295.
[22] E. Y. Zedler, "Effect of Phonic Training on Speech Sound Discrimination and Spelling Performance," *Journal of Speech and Hearing Disorders,* Vol. 21 (June, 1956), p. 249.
[23] E. Horn, "Phonetics and Spelling," *Elementary School Journal,* Vol. 57 (May, 1957), p. 430.

2. Such contests encourage feelings of tension, insecurity, and inferiority among children who know they will be defeated by the abler spellers.

3. There is no provision for differentiated levels of ability.

4. Such contests rely upon oral spelling for which there is very little need and which has very little place in the modern spelling program. Since spelling is a skill required only for writing, it is useless and pointless to have children practice oral spelling, for which they will have no need in life situations.

Of equally questionable value are the extrinsic motivating devices such as gold stars, the "jet race" showing each child's weekly test score, or the Thanksgiving turkeys and Easter bunnies pasted on the perfect papers. Such motivation is of questionable value in any area because of its stress upon artificial goals for learning. Teachers should help children to develop a *desire* to learn how to spell, not for a reward, but because of the inner satisfaction which accompanies the correct performance of a task. This is often called developing a "spelling conscience" and is discussed in the following section.

DEVELOPING A SPELLING CONSCIENCE

Innumerable theories have been advanced concerning the causes of poor spelling including such startling statements as "a person is a born speller" and "intelligent people are always poor spellers." Actually, the major causes of poor spelling are not known; but it seems to be related to such factors as: (1) limited mental ability, (2) limited reading ability, (3) hearing impairments, (4) visual defects, (5) faulty listening skills, (6) poor handwriting, (7) overemphasis on phonics, (8) poor study habits, (9) inability to judge spelling accuracy, and (10) inability to visualize words.[24]

On the other hand, none of these are as responsible for poor spelling as much as sheer *indifference* to the importance of correct spelling. In other words, the individual's personality traits and attitude toward the importance of correct spelling are probably the chief determinants in spelling success. Furness states that children who are untidy, careless of detail, impetuous, and who suffer from intellectual inertia are apt to be poorer spellers than those who are neat and precise in their work.[25] Coard's investigation of poor spelling among college students reports that most of them attributed their spelling errors to indifference, haste, laziness, and carelessness.[26] It would seem, therefore, that the elementary teacher's main task is to give pupils, not only a *consciousness* of correct spelling, but also a spelling *conscience*—or a "kind of compulsion for correct written ex-

[24] E. A. Betts, "What About Spelling?" *Education*, Vol. 76 (January, 1956), pp. 310–325.

[25] E. L. Furness, "Psychological Determinants of Spelling Success," *Education*, Vol. 79 (December, 1958), pp. 234–239.

[26] R. L. Coard, "The Mystery of Misspelling," *Elementary School Journal*, Vol. 58 (November, 1957), pp. 97–100.

pression." [27] The desire for correct spelling and the realization of its importance become, therefore, the final goals of the elementary school spelling program. It is toward the achievement of these ultimate aims that all the procedures and activities discussed in this section should be constantly directed.

Mastery of the common elements of punctuation and capitalization is another skill demanded in independent writing. It is discussed in the following section.

PUNCTUATION AND CAPITALIZATION

Punctuation and capitalization are developed in association with meaningful experience in independent writing. As is true of all skills, the teaching of punctuation and capitalization should take place during numerous language activities. In the first grade, for instance, the teacher may call attention during the reading and penmanship lesson to the capital at the beginning of the sentence and the period or question mark at the close. This is true, also, in other grades in which children are introduced to the mechanics of punctuation and capitalization during their reading, penmanship, and functional writing experiences. In the upper grades, of course, there will be need to supplement this incidental teaching with developmental and practice lessons on specific difficulties as well as on correct usage. The important thing to remember, however, is that the mechanics should be taught throughout the entire curriculum and should not be considered a separate body of content which is taught for one week or one month of the school year. Unfortunately this is not always the case, and some upper grade teachers are still teaching punctuation and capitalization as a unit by itself. A sixth-grade teacher, for instance, when recently asked what punctuation difficulties his pupils were meeting replied that he was not teaching that now but would be "on" punctuation in two weeks. What could be more ridiculous? One does not get "on" and "off" punctuation as one does a horse! Rather, one learns through daily contacts with reading and writing that mechanics are necessary to clarify meaning and learns to use them accordingly.

Writing skills are graded according to difficulty and frequency of use. Many school systems and educators have devised lists of minimal writing skills to be taught at each grade level. The following is a very brief summary of the skills which are usually taught at the primary, intermediate, and upper grade levels.

PRIMARY (GRADES 1–2)

1. Use of capital at beginning of sentence and in names of people.
2. Use of capital for pronoun, *I*.

[27] E. L. Furness, *op. cit.*, p. 237.

3. Use of period or question mark at close of sentence.
4. Use of comma after salutation and close of a letter.
5. Use of comma to separate city and state or day of the month and year.
6. Use of comma in a series.

INTERMEDIATE (GRADES 3–4)

1. Use of period in abbreviations and after single initials.
2. Use of apostrophe in simpler contractions and possessives.
3. Use of quotation marks in direct quotation.
4. Use of comma to set off direct quotation.
5. Use of exclamation mark at close of sentence.
6. Use of capitals in proper nouns as days, months, holidays, organizations, cities, states, and other geographical locations.
7. Use of capitals in important words in titles and for first word in lines of poetry.
8. Use of hyphen in syllabicating words.

UPPER (GRADES 5–6)

1. Use of comma in appositives or direct address.
2. Use of colon in salutation of business letter or in writing time.
3. Use of capital letters in outlining.
4. Use of capital letters in titles (*Mr. President*).
5. Use of capital letters in names of the Deity and the Bible.
6. Use of capital letters in adjectives indicating race or nationality (*Indian, English,* etc.).

ORGANIZATIONAL ELEMENTS OF THOUGHT

Independent writing involves old and new skills of thought organization. The reader will remember that the chief organizational difficulties discussed in connection with oral language (Chapter Five) were: expression of a complete thought, run-on sentences, rambling or digression from a central idea, failure to relate ideas in sequence, and inclusion of irrelevancies. These same difficulties will, of course, appear in the pupils' written work. In the primary and intermediate grades, therefore, primary emphasis in writing is placed upon the construction of a simple sentence. Through many reading and writing experiences the children should be led to recognize the requirements and types of simple sentences. In the upper grades the teaching of sentence structure is refined and extended to include knowledge of more complicated types of sentences although the central emphasis continues to be the importance of clear, direct, and sequential expression of thought.

In the intermediate grades, also, initial work is begun on paragraphing, again through reading and writing activities. In their reading groups, the attention of pupils may be called frequently to the construction of a paragraph. They should be shown the relationship of the sentences in the paragraph, or that "the sentences are like the branches of a tree—they all lead to the trunk, or main idea." [28] In attempting to teach paragraphing, the teacher may employ numerous activities similar to the following:

Exercise 1. Distribute a story of about one page in length. Have children divide it into two or three paragraphs according to the main ideas expressed.

Exercise 2. Have children summarize orally or in writing the main idea of a paragraph.

Exercise 3. Have children underline the most important or "key" sentence of the paragraph.

Exercise 4. Have children cross out one or more sentences which are completely irrelevant to the paragraph.

Exercise 5. Draw pupils' attention to the wording and techniques many authors use to make the transition from one paragraph to another.

In addition to teaching paragraphing, the intermediate and upper-grade teachers are also responsible for teaching simple outlining, which is a vital aid to thought organization in writing. This can be done in connection with teaching paragraphing as, for instance, asking children to list the main ideas and subpoints of several paragraphs in two-step outline form. Another method, of course, is to discuss a story or an experience and ask the class to give the main ideas in sequence. After these are listed on the board, the pupils may be asked to enumerate, in outline form, related topics under each main heading.

In summary, the three main organizational elements of independent writing which should be taught to children in the elementary grades are, in order of difficulty: the sentence, the paragraph, and the simple outline.

Needing all of the skills of "independent writing," but going a step beyond, is "creative writing," which is discussed in the following section.

Section 3: CREATIVE WRITING

The authors fully realize that their distinction between "creative" writing and "independent" writing is not a clear-cut one, for few people agree on the precise definition of "creative." To some this term refers only to the select and inspired writing of the gifted few. On the other hand, some use the term to designate any material written by the child for which he has chosen the subject and form. It is not the purpose of this brief discussion to belabor the point of "what is creative?" The authors wish only to defend their classification by recognizing a difference, intangible and nondefinitive though it may be, between writing which calls for independence (recording the minutes of a meeting or writing a business letter) and an-

[28] H. Greene and W. T. Petty, *Developing Language Skills in the Elementary School* (Boston, Allyn and Bacon, Inc., 1959), p. 315.

other type of personal writing, which is here called "creative." For purposes of clarity, therefore, "creative writing" in this discussion is interpreted to be written self-expression which is characterized by a freshness of approach, an originality of form and content, a sensitivity to mood and feeling, and an active imagination.

How does one teach this type of writing? There are many who say that one doesn't and can't. Applegate, for instance, states that the teacher can only "help children to release the creativity in them that seeks expression." [29] Let us reword the question, then. How does a teacher release and guide creative expression? The following are some of the techniques which creative teachers use to encourage creative expression in children:

Recognition of the natural creative powers of children. In many respects, children are much more creative than adults in that they do not suffer from the inhibitions and stagnated imaginations which often accompany maturity. The three-year-old who, when told by his father to wash his sandy hands in the ocean, pointed at the setting sun and said, "Look, Daddy, the sun is washing its hands in the ocean, too," was creative. The four-year-old who, when asked if he kept the secret his mother told him, opened his arms wide and replied, "I told it away," was creative. The six-year-old who entranced her first-grade classmates with the story of "Tit-Tat-Toe"— three clothespins who lived on her mother's clothesline—was creative. All of these children had the "newness" and "originality" which is the essence of creativity and which, if recognized by the teacher, can be encouraged and guided in many different ways.

Facilitation of creative writing. When the child has a desire for expression, the teacher should make it as "easy" as possible for him to put it on paper. With younger children, still unused to the mechanics of writing, this may be done by encouraging them to dictate their ideas to the teacher who will then write them. Burrows emphasizes the importance of this procedure as follows:

When freed from the physical drudgery of handwriting, pupils enjoy a sense of power which in itself spurs creativity. The rapid flashing of childlike imagination, when caught by the teacher's record, takes on a dignified form which others can see and hear. The child composer, hearing or seeing his work, senses the satisfactions of personal projection. He sees that words stand for ideas which only a short time before were an invisible part of him. Characters and events reach out beyond the confines of time and place and the pupil's new sense of personal power propels him toward further expression.[30]

As children become older they should be encouraged to do their own writing but they should not be hampered by overemphasis upon the skills

[29] M. Applegate, *Helping Children Write* (Scranton, Pa., International Textbook Company, 1949), p. 6.

[30] A. T. Burrows, *Teaching Composition: What Research Says to the Teacher* (Washington, D.C., Department of Classroom Teachers, American Educational Research Association of the National Education Association, 1959), p. 4.

of correct writing. The spontaneity and originality of children's creative thought cannot survive the ordeal of precise attention to spelling, punctuation, and other skills. *After* the first draft is completed, the child may be encouraged to "polish" it with these technical skills, but attention to spelling and punctuation should never take precedence over the creative act in this type of writing.

Motivation. There are numerous ways in which elementary school teachers may motivate creative writing in the classroom. The use of a film was found to be successful in one instance for motivating high quality writing.[31] Discussions of group and individual experiences, direct and vicarious, will often lead to creative writing. Offering children the first line of a poem or story and asking them to complete it may produce desirable results. Discussion of a possible title and story for one or two still pictures has been successfully used by many teachers. Discussions of the sounds and meanings of words can be used on any grade level to encourage creative writing.

Freedom from "assigned" topics. Creative writing comes from within; it cannot be ordered or commanded. In general, the practice of "assigning" topics and "requiring" a certain story or composition will produce very little of truly creative writing. Children may be motivated toward expressing themselves in writing but the final choice of subject must be theirs alone.

Opportunity to write. Children should not be coerced into writing by the dictates of the teacher but, on the other hand, numerous opportunities should be provided for writing throughout the day and year. Edmund, for instance, reports that the average number of stories written during a school year by a group of seventh-graders was less than four.[32] If we are to encourage creative writing, we should certainly avoid assigning the weekly story or composition but, by the same token, we should make sure that children have numerous opportunities to write and subtle but positive encouragement to do so. Furthermore, these opportunities do not have to be confined to a specific time or lesson of the day, for there should be ample opportunity for an individual to indulge in creative writing at various moments of the day. Creative writing should be the brightly colored thread which runs continuously through the often commonplace tapestry of the school day. It does not necessarily have to be confined within the time boundaries of a preplanned, scheduled "lesson."

A creative teacher. Other things being equal, the creative teacher will stimulate creativity in children. Contrast two teachers: It is a dreary, misty, foggy morning. The one begins the school day by saying, "Boys and

[31] P. Witty and W. Martin, "An Analysis of Children's Compositions Written in Response to a Film," *Elementary English,* Vol. 34 (March, 1957), pp. 158–163.
[32] N. R. Edmund, "Writing in the Intermediate Grades," *Elementary English,* Vol. 36 (November, 1959), p. 493.

girls, I know that it's not a very nice day today but we can't let the weather interfere with our work. If you work extra hard this morning, I'll ask Mr. Mathews if we can use the gym this afternoon so that the bad weather won't interfere with our play period." The other starts the day with, "Let's arrange our chairs in a cozy circle this morning. How many of you walked to school through the fog? Did some of you ride on the bus? How did the fog make you feel when you were walking or riding through it? How does it make you feel now when you look out at it? What does it remind you of? Would you like to listen and see what the fog reminded a great poet of? (*Reads Sandburg's* Fog.) Did this poem give you ideas? Would you like to write or draw your ideas about the fog?" Which teacher will meet with more success in "teaching" creative expression?

Creativity is a fragile plant. It needs someone to watch over it carefully, someone to give it an opportunity to grow, and someone to provide a climate conducive for growth. Who but a creative teacher can do this?

Summary

This chapter has discussed the fourth channel of communication, writing, under the major classifications of: handwriting, independent writing, and creative writing. It was stated that the major trend in handwriting has been, over the years, a shift away from traditional formalism with its emphasis on style toward today's functional and utilitarian concept. The handwriting program of the elementary school was presented with stress on writing readiness in the kindergarten. Manuscript writing in the first and second grades was discussed and contradictory viewpoints presented as to the need and time for the transition to cursive writing. In the upper grades, emphasis was placed upon the need for individualized instruction and functional writing opportunities. Some attention was given to the left-handed writer and his needs.

Independent writing was analyzed according to its components of correct usage, vocabulary, spelling, mechanics, and thought organization. The first two of these were omitted from this chapter because they had been discussed in Chapter Five in connection with oral language. The spelling program of the elementary school was discussed according to present-day philosophy. Included was a presentation of weekly spelling plans and the *study-steps* through which the spelling of a specific word is learned and taught. Controversial issues such as the value of spelling rules, the place of phonics in the spelling program, and the use of contests and extrinsic motivating devices were examined.

The mechanics of writing, punctuation and capitalization, were discussed and general suggestions for grade placement of these skills were offered. The major organizational elements of writing which were considered were: the complete sentence, the paragraph, and the simple outline.

The highest level of writing, creative writing, was discussed with the recognition that it was distinguished from "independent writing" through such qualities as "newness," "originality," "sensitivity," and "imagination." Factors conducive to creative writing in the classroom were examined. These included recognition of the natural creative powers of children, facilitation of creative writing, freedom from "assigned" topics, opportunity to write, and finally, a creative teacher.

Chapters Five, Six, and Seven have been devoted to a discussion of the language program with a repeated emphasis upon such key concepts as motivation, individualization, functionality, and integration. To summarize and illustrate these, a learning experience which embodies all of them is described briefly below.

AN INTEGRATED LANGUAGE EXPERIENCE
(Grade 5)

Mrs. Hansen had worked diligently since the first of the year to stimulate her fifth-graders' interest in the world of books. At first it had been hard work but, through patience and encouragement, she had finally awakened some interest in and appreciation of literature. In March, her principal asked her if she would care to be responsible for the assembly program that month. She discussed it with her pupils and they replied eagerly in the affirmative. Then the big question arose, "What shall we do for our program?" They talked about using a play in their reading books; they didn't like that idea. They talked about reading some favorite poems to the other classes; they discarded that. Finally, one of the children suggested that they write their own play! A fine idea! But who would write it? What would it be about? Finally, after much discusion they agreed that each one would find his favorite scene in a favorite book and try to write it as a play. What a job! New books were eagerly read, old books were reread, library shelves were raided as each pupil tried to decide upon his favorite scene in a favorite book.

And then the actual writing! How do you write dialogue in a play? Where do you put the quotation marks? How do you make characters "come alive" for an audience? And finally, how do you make your "favorite" also the "favorite" of the audience?

It took some time but finally each pupil had his play ready. Now, how to choose which one? Plays had to be "tried out"—which meant that readers had to read with expression and feeling. Positive critical attitudes had to be developed as the pupils analyzed objectively the appeal of this play, the practicality of that one, and the humor of another. Finally, they agreed. This one would be presented on the school stage. But that was only the beginning! Now came the "try-outs" for all the characters; the scenery committee had to be organized; the costumes had to be designed and made; invitations needed to be written; and so much, much more had to be done!

At long last, the big day arrived! The play was a success! Everyone enjoyed it! And when the last tired youngster had straggled out of the classroom, Mrs. Hansen sat at her desk and tried to list on paper the values and learnings the experience had provided her pupils. Here is what she wrote:

1. An accelerated interest in reading beyond her wildest expectations.

2. A deep appreciation for literature and an awakening feeling of "kinship" with certain favorite authors and books.

3. An unequaled and prolonged experience in "creative" writing.

4. An expanding vocabulary.

5. An opportunity to use and a resultant mastery of certain mechanics of writing (quotation marks, commas, exclamation marks, etc.).

6. A mastery of certain spelling words (of which she had kept a record).

7. A functional oral language experience with increasing awareness of the demands of correct language and speech forms.

8. Practice on organizational elements of writing (relating events in sequence, etc.).

9. A feeling of "belonging" and social cohesiveness, as the entire class worked together on a common undertaking.

10. An appreciation of the worth of each member of the group, as the contributions of the artists, writers, designers, prop men, lighting experts, musicians, and others were recognized.

11. An opportunity to partake in a truly democratic enterprise.

12. An opportunity for creative art work in designing costumes, making scenery, and preparing programs.

13. An interest in and appreciation of music, since it was chosen carefully as part of the play.

14. An integrated experience in which children had related language to art, social studies, sewing, arithmetic, music, dance, and every other area of the curriculum.

15. And, in addition, all of the specific values and learnings which are realized by individuals as they partake in a truly vitalized language program in the elementary school.

STUDENT PROJECTS

1. Send a questionnaire to several schools or school systems in your state. Try to determine: (1) in what grades they teach manuscript writing, (2) in what grades they teach cursive writing, (3) when they make the transition, and (4) the method of making the transition. Can you draw any conclusions concerning an overall pattern in your state?

2. Write a lesson plan for a group handwriting lesson in the third grade.

3. Observe a class in an elementary school. What percentage of the pupils are left-handed writers? What special provisions have been made for them?

4. Give an informal "spelling test" to a six-year-old who, as far as you know, has not received any formal instruction in spelling. List the words he has learned through his reading and handwriting experiences.

5. Try to recall your own elementary school days. How was creative writing taught? How does this compare with the modern philosophy of teaching this subject?

6. Describe an integrated language experience which would have similar values to those claimed for the one described at the close of this chapter.

7. Interview several parents and leading business men of your community. How do they feel about eliminating cursive writing from the elementary school program? Would they be in favor of teaching only manuscript writing? What do they see as the chief advantages and disadvantages of such a proposal?

8. Compare several of the leading spelling textbook series. Do they contain essentially the same words for each grade level or is there wide variation? What consistencies or discrepancies do you find concerning the over-all word lists of the series?

9. Ask permission to work individually with several elementary school pupils. Ask them to "think out loud" as they study their new spelling words. What study steps do they use? How much variation do you notice among their methods of study?

10. From a set of fifth-grade papers make a "language inventory" (see Chapter Five) of the written errors you discover. Classify these as to errors of punctuation, capitalization, organization, and spelling. Outline a remedial program you would institute to attack these errors.

11. Your fifth-grade class resists strongly any attempt on your part to encourage creative writing experiences. What are some unique motivating devices you could use to overcome this resistance?

12. Prepare a paper on the pros and cons of teaching spelling rules. Contrast the conflicting opinions and research studies in this field. Weigh carefully the evidence and present a list of recommendations to guide elementary school teachers on this subject.

13. Prepare a questionnaire on possible causes of poor spelling. Distribute it to members of your college class. Do the results agree with statements in this chapter concerning the major cause or causes of poor spelling? What causes not included in this chapter are mentioned in your college sampling?

BIBLIOGRAPHY

APPLEGATE, Mauree, *Helping Children Write* (Scranton, Pa., International Textbook Company, 1949).

BURROWS, Alvina T. et. al., *They All Want to Write* (Englewood Cliffs, N.J., Prentice-Hall, Inc., 1952).

BURROWS, Alvina T., *Teaching Composition: What Research Says to the Teacher*, Department of Classroom Teachers (Washington, D.C., American Educational Research Association of the National Education Association, 1959).

Commission on the English Curriculum of the National Council of Teachers of English, *The English Language Arts* (New York, Appleton-Century-Crofts, Inc., 1952).

Commission on the English Curriculum of the National Council of Teachers of English, *Language Arts for Today's Children* (New York, Appleton-Century-Crofts, Inc., 1954).

DAWSON, Mildred, *Language Teaching in Grades 1 and 2*, rev. ed. (New York, Harcourt, Brace & World, Inc., 1957).

DAWSON, Mildred and ZOLLINGER, Marion, *Guiding Language Learning* (New York, World Book Company, 1957).

FITZGERALD, James A., *A Basic Life Spelling Vocabulary* (Milwaukee, Bruce Publishing Company, 1951).

FITZGERALD, James A., *The Teaching of Spelling* (Milwaukee, Bruce Publishing Company, 1951).

FREEMAN, Frank N., *Teaching Handwriting: What Research Says*, Department of Classroom Teachers (Washington, D.C., American Education Research Association of the National Education Association, 1954).

GRAY, William S., *The Teaching of Reading and Writing*, UNESCO (Chicago, Scott, Foresman and Company, 1956).

GREENE, Harry and PETTY, Walter, *Developing Language Skills in the Elementary School* (Boston, Allyn and Bacon, Inc., 1959).

HATCHETT, Ethel and HUGHES, Donald, *Teaching Language Arts in the Elementary Schools* (New York, The Ronald Press Company, 1956).

HERRICK, Virgil E. and JACOBS, Leland B., eds., *Children and the Language Arts* (Englewood Cliffs, N.J., Prentice-Hall, Inc., 1955).

HILDRETH, Gertrude, *Teaching Spelling* (New York, Holt, Rinehart and Winston, Inc., 1955).

HORN, Ernest, *Teaching Spelling: What Research Says* (Washington, D.C., Department of Classroom Teachers (American Educational Research Association of the National Education Association, 1954).

HUNNICUTT, Charles W. and IVERSON, William J., eds., *Research in the Three R's* (New York, Harper and Brothers, 1958).

National Department of Elementary School Principals, *Language Arts in the Elementary School*, 20th Yearbook (Washington, D.C., National Education Association, 1941).

National Society for the Study of Education, *Teaching Language in the Elementary School*, 43rd Yearbook (Chicago, University of Chicago Press, 1944).

RINSLAND, Henry D., *A Basic Vocabulary of Elementary School Children* (New York, The Macmillan Company, 1945).

SHANE, Harold G., *Research Helps in Teaching the Language Arts* (Washington, D.C., Association for Supervision and Curriculum Development, 1955).

State of New Jersey, Department of Education, *Growth in Language from Kindergarten through High School*, School Bulletin 17. (Trenton, N.J., Department of Education, 1951).

STRICKLAND, Ruth, *The Language Arts in the Elementary School*, rev. ed. (Boston, D. C. Heath and Company, 1957).

TIDYMAN, Willard F. and BUTTERFIELD, Marguerite, *Teaching the Language Arts* (New York, McGraw-Hill Book Company, 1959).

CHAPTER 8

Foreign Languages

Mrs. SNYDER IS THE PRINCIPAL of an elementary school in an average residential community. The one thousand pupils enrolled in the kindergarten through the sixth grade represent a wide range of socio-economic backgrounds and intellectual abilities. This year, in her annual report to the superintendent of schools, Mrs. Snyder devoted considerable attention to the recently instituted program of teaching French in grades three through six, which she called "the most significant single advance made in the educational program in the past several years." She commented upon the splendid gains made by the pupils and upon the enthusiastic reception of the program by the parents. Her report ended with the statement that the faculty had voted unanimously to continue, and perhaps expand, the program the following year.

Mr. Robbins is a fellow-principal and good friend of Mrs. Snyder. His school is almost identical to hers in size and heterogeneity of pupil population. In the past year or so, Mr. Robbins has expressed himself strongly at community and professional meetings on the proposal to teach foreign language in elementary schools. His most recent objection emphasized the impracticality of adding another subject to "a curriculum already stretched to the breaking point." He concluded, "I think my teachers are doing a fine job if they succeed in teaching our youngsters to read, write, and speak acceptable English. If we can give them this foundation in their native tongue, it ought to be the job of the high school to add a second or third language."

Both of these individuals are sincere, dedicated, and professional people. They are well-liked and highly respected by their pupils, teachers, and communities. Both have equal experience and training. Both have given the subject considerable thought and study and yet their conclusions are

219

at opposite extremes. Let us look at some of the pros and cons of the question which have helped these two principals arrive at their decisions.

ARGUMENTS FAVORING "FLES"

There is a crucial need today for developing understanding and appreciation of other cultures. Probably the strongest argument for "Foreign Language in the Elementary School" (*FLES*) is that we are living in a rapidly shrinking world and schools must modify their programs to meet the demands of this world. According to Freeman,

> The most significant change in the whole basis of American education in the last 20 years is the changed role of the United States in the world . . . The picture of the monolingual, isolationist 100% American of 1937 is now acknowledged to be as out of date as the bustle or the celluloid collar.[1]

The growing need for mutual understanding and greater communication among nations is evidenced in many ways. In the first place, the jet plane now makes it possible for Americans to reach any country *in the world* in less than twenty-four hours. Secondly, the UN and many other international conferences and organizations have focused our attention upon the desirability of facilitating communication with our world neighbors. Thirdly, the improved transportation facilities and abundant economy have given impetus to foreign travel on a scale never before equaled. Some indication of this is revealed from the following figures from the United States Department of Commerce: [2]

> 1938—397,875 U.S. citizens traveled out of country.
> 1948—474,048 passports for foreign travel issued.
> 1958—1,483,915 passports for foreign travel issued.

Paralleling the increasing interest in foreign travel is the expansion of teacher and student exchange programs. According to recent figures, a total of 15,448 individuals have participated in international educational exchange and training programs sponsored by the U.S. Office of Education since 1939.[3] In addition, world fairs, international exhibits, and numerous exchanges of cultural programs among countries attest to the growing need for world communication.

There is no other single factor more important in promoting world understanding, say the advocates of *FLES*, than the teaching of a second language, for only through learning the language will an individual actually

[1] S. A. Freeman, "Expanding the Teacher's Horizons," *School and Society*, Vol. 86 (December 20, 1958), p. 451.

[2] United States Department of Commerce, *Statistical Abstract of the United States* (Washington, D.C., Bureau of the Census, 1939, 1949, 1959).

[3] T. E. Cotner, *A Summary of the Exchange and Training Programs Administered by the Division of International Education* (Washington, D.C., Department of Health, Education, and Welfare, unpublished).

experience a culture and participate in a behavioral pattern of the people.

Children learn languages very easily. This marked ability is a second strong argument used for introducing children at an early age to the study of a second or third language. There seems to be some evidence that the physiological development of the brain and the flexibility of the speech organs are most conducive to language learning before the approximate age of ten or twelve. Then too, the comparative lack of self-consciousness and inhibition among preadolescents enables them to imitate sounds with greater freedom and accuracy than is true of adolescents or adults. Thus, from the standpoint of the child's psychological as well as physiological growth there appears to be justification for introducing a multilingual program in the elementary grades.

Children enjoy learning another language. There is very little disagreement on the fact that young children like to "play" with language. Unfamiliar, alliterative, or rhythmic language has a strong appeal for the youngster's ear and tongue. He loves to explore new sounds, loves to invent new words, and his informal play is filled with adventures in this direction. Recently, for instance, a group of seven-year-olds were waiting for the school bus. One child volunteered, "I have a nickel" which brought forth the immediate response, "I have a pickle." For the next five minutes, the group explored the nonsense possibilities of "I have a mickle—a dickle—a hickle—etc." and each contribution as it rolled off the tongue was greeted with much laughter and deep appreciation. Exploring all facets of language—the unknown, the secret code, the nonsense words and syllables, "pig Latin"—affords most youngsters intense satisfaction. Advocates of *FLES* propose that the elementary teacher capitalize upon this natural interest of children to introduce them to a second language during their early school years.

The cultural lag between American and European schools should be closed. Great has been the concern of some as to whether our schools are as academically challenging or culturally broadening as those abroad. These individuals point to the fact that the child in the *lycée* or *gymnasium* begins to study a second language at an early date; that the Russian ten-year-school introduces another language in the fourth or fifth year; and that many Europeans are multilingual as contrasted with the average American who "not only has no serious command of any foreign language, he all too frequently has acquired an aversion to foreign languages." [4] A similar opinion is expressed by another writer:

We boast of being an educated nation. We *are* educated in some things . . . But when it comes to talking other people's languages and speaking other tongues, we have the reputation around the world of being illiterate. [5]

[4] M. Graves, "All the Foreign Languages," *Education*, Vol. 72 (June, 1952), p. 668.
[5] J. H. Furbay, "At Home in One World," *Education*, Vol. 72 (June, 1952), p. 653.

Public opinion supports FLES. General observation and a few studies may lead one to conclude that, in general, public opinion is in favor of teaching foreign languages in the elementary grades. In 1945 a survey of adult public opinion indicated that 71 per cent of the adults questioned were in favor of children learning a language other than their own; 17 per cent were opposed; and 12 per cent were undecided.[6]

A public opinion poll of a certain city revealed the following:

> The most important finding appears to be that almost nobody thought college was the place to start teaching either a first or a second foreign language, and most persons even considered high school too late. Of those who named a modern language, 49% said we should start teaching language in grade school, 27% said junior high school, 21% said high school, and only 3% said college.[7]

In addition to this type of evidence, there are innumerable accounts of experiments introducing foreign language in the elementary grades which apparently met with strong parental approval. Typical of these is an account of intoducing French in the fifth and sixth grades: several of the parents reacted by expressing themselves "wholly in favor of starting the study of a foreign language on the elementary level."[8]

Although public opinion is not necessarily a valid justification for making an addition to the curriculum, it is, nevertheless, an argument which is frequently used by the FLES advocates.

Additional languages provide an excellent challenge for the intellectually gifted children. A certain amount of early interest in FLES was directed toward its potentialities in enriching the curriculum for the academically advanced pupils. The Cleveland plan, inaugurated in 1922, was designed for children possessing IQ's of over 115 and a similar program was started in certain selected schools of New York City as early as 1932.[9] Some educators continue to be interested in the possibilities of modern foreign languages for this purpose. They argue that no other competency could be more vital for the children who may become the future leaders of the country than the ability to communicate effectively with others.

The school should meet the sociological needs of the community. Last, but not least, the advocates of FLES point to the fact that it may be needed to bridge the gap between the school and communities which have a high percentage of foreign-born population. Experiments with teaching French in Louisiana, Spanish in California, and German in Wisconsin were

---

[6] The American Institute of Public Opinion, Princeton, N.J., unpublished report (December, 1945).

[7] R. Mehling, "Public Opinion and the Teaching of Foreign Languages," *Modern Language Journal*, Vol. 43 (November, 1959), p. 330.

[8] A. M. Selvi, "An Experiment Introducing Modern Language Activities in the Elementary School," *Educational Administration and Supervision*, Vol. 37 (May, 1951), p. 315.

[9] F. H. Thon, "French for Bright Young Children in New York Public Schools," *French Review*, Vol. 13 (February, 1940), pp. 303–313.

designed to effect closer co-operation between the home and school and mutual appreciation between English and non-English speaking pupils.

In summary, there appear to be many sound reasons for teaching modern foreign languages in the elementary school. Before drawing any conclusions, however, let us look at the other side of the coin.

ARGUMENTS OPPOSING *FLES*

Learning other languages does not necessarily effect understanding and appreciation of other cultures. This is a rebuttal to the claim that, through languages, one will develop world understanding and positive relationships between peoples. One needs only to look at Europe, with its multilingual population, to discover that ability to speak another language does not necessarily alleviate distrust and suspicion of one's neighbors. Also, if world peace is our objective, should we not be more interested in teaching Russian, Chinese, Japanese, Arabic, Thai, Indonesian, or Korean than those languages on which we are presently concentrating our efforts?

Learning a second language may retard growth in the native tongue. This is a statement which is extremely difficult to prove or disprove through conclusive research. Opinions of leading authorities differ on the extent, if any, to which bilingualism will retard facility with the original language.[10] In the absence of conclusive research, therefore, many educators advocate delaying the teaching of a second language to young children until there is sound evidence that it will not handicap the learning of their native language.

Learning a second language in the elementary grades is, for most children, an artificial and nonfunctional experience. This argument supports the premise that young children can learn a second language easily *if* they learn it as an integrative part of their natural environment. As Hildreth points out,

Around the world, English or any other language is easily picked up by children who hear the language in constant use and have genuine incentive through their play life and contacts with natives to learn to speak it themselves . . . They assimilate the new language directly as they did the mother tongue through the link between language and behavior, e.g., in sports, games, dramatic play with native children. Unquestionably, the best place for children to learn a foreign language is an environment where they are constantly exposed to the language in normal life.[11]

Hoppock supports the need for the integration of language with the child's environment with the statement, "Unless he lives in another culture

[10] H. T. Manuel, "Bilingualism," in *Encyclopedia of Educational Research,* 3rd ed. (New York, The Macmillan Company, 1960), p. 148.

[11] G. Hildreth, "Learning a Second Language in the Elementary Grades and High School," *Modern Language Journal,* Vol. 43 (March, 1959), p. 138.

where he really needs a second language to communicate, it is doubtful if he learns it in any permanent or functional sense." [12]

These and similar statements are evidence of the skepticism with which many educators view the value of introducing children to another language in an artificial classroom situation. They claim that the typical program which exposes children to fifteen or twenty minutes per day of language instruction will have very little lasting value. There is almost a complete lack of intrinsic motivation since children do not need the additional language to satisfy their demands or to communicate with their neighbors. This argument stresses the fact that there is very little "carry-over" to out-of-school activities, and because of lack of motivation and exercise, the experience becomes a highly artificial one with little educational value or permanence.

The elementary school curriculum is already overcrowded. Serious concern is felt in many quarters today over the present tendency to stretch the elementary curriculum to an unrealistic extreme. Various pressure groups insist that the elementary school curriculum become more and more elastic, and the beleaguered teacher is literally at his wit's end trying to give his pupils a sane and balanced program. Many serious-minded educators are resisting strongly the addition of this new area, the value of which has yet to be determined.

FLES means additional expense. Not the least concern of some in these days of rising school costs is the fact that teaching a foreign language may mean an additional expense. The addition of qualified teachers and the purchase of adequate equipment for the program may be prohibitive for the economy-minded school system. This viewpoint is expressed by Bolton in the following statement:

At this time when most communities are unable to provide adequate school housing, when the enrollments are sky-rocketing, and when all the penny-pinching fails to provide money to employ enough teachers for the regular work, the addition of an expensive luxury like foreign-language teaching in the elementary grades should be ruled out immediately.[13]

THE PRESENT STATUS OF FLES

FLES is truly a postwar phenomenon on the American scene. True, one can find reports of programs begun in the late nineteenth and early twentieth centuries, some of which have been disbanded and at least one (Cleveland program) which has been continuous to the present day. In general, however, the program did not gain national recognition until

[12] A. Hoppock, "Foreign Language in the Elementary School," *NJEA Review*, Vol. 30 (November, 1956), p. 129.
[13] F. E. Bolton, "Foreign Language in the Grades? Not Worth the Cost," *NEA Journal*, Vol. 45 (October, 1956), p. 445.

1953 when the United States Office of Education sponsored the Conference on the Role of Foreign Languages in American Schools. The rapid growth of the movement since that time is evidenced by the following statement:

The teaching of foreign languages in public elementary schools has now reached the proportions of a full-fledged movement. In 1940 such instruction was given in about ten communities and probably no more than 2,000 children were involved. As recently as 1949, the movement was limited to about 40 communities. But in 1955 more than 350 cities and towns in 44 states and the District of Columbia had foreign language ventures in 1883 public elementary schools and 94 college demonstration and campus schools. A total of 271,617 children were involved. In Catholic elementary schools 156,700 other children were learning modern foreign languages.[14]

In the light of these figures, there would seem little room for doubt that the program is growing rapidly at the present time. It is not, however, growing according to a marked consistency of pattern, for there is considerable diversity among existing programs. Some of these are examined below:

Current literature indicates a wide variety among existing programs. In general, there is no strong agreement among programs on the following:

The language. Several languages are offered in school systems throughout the country. In 1955 it was reported that,

Spanish is far and away the most popular language in the elementary classes. French comes next, then German, and then Italian, Latin, Norwegian, and modern Greek. Other languages, among them Swedish and Japanese, are taught in a few communities.[15]

In addition to those mentioned above, Polish is mentioned as taught in a few schools, and at least one school is presently experimenting with teaching Russian to young children.[16] In general, opinion does not appear to favor strongly the teaching of any one specific language. On the contrary, some writers claim that almost *any* second language is acceptable, for it is not the language per se which is important but rather the development of the knowledge that a second language is important to communication and that it can be learned.[17]

In general, the factors to be considered in determining the second language are: (1) social significance or the world importance of a language, (2) national interest, (3) cultural background of the community, (4) avail-

---

[14] K. W. Mildenberger, *Some Solutions to Problems Related to the Teaching of Foreign Languages in Elementary Schools,* A Report of the Committee on Foreign Languages in the Elementary School (New York, Metropolitan School Study Council, 1956), statement found in the "Foreword."

[15] "Foreign Languages in the Elementary Schools," *School Life,* Official Journal of the United States Office of Education, Vol. 38 (June, 1956), p. 14.

[16] C. W. Snyder, "Experiment in Teaching Russian in Grade 3," *School and Society,* Vol. 86 (October 11, 1958), pp. 353–354.

[17] S. A. Freeman, *op. cit.,* pp. 451–454.

ability of qualified teachers, (5) desires of the community, and (6) school integration problems.[18]

The teacher. In general, opinion is divided as to whether the instruction should be done by: (1) the classroom teacher, (2) the foreign language specialist, or (3) both working together co-operatively. Regardless of which plan is preferred, the unavailability of qualified teachers is, at present, one of the most serious administrative problems to be met in introducing a program. Very few foreign language specialists have the necessary experience and training to teach young children. On the other hand, few classroom teachers have had intensive language study. To solve the dilemma some schools of education have begun to introduce foreign language courses in their curricula for elementary teachers. Another step toward a solution is the series of summer institutes for elementary and secondary teachers of modern foreign languages conducted under authorization of Section 611 in the National Defense Education Act. In the summer of 1959 four of the total twelve institutes dealt with the teaching of foreign languages at the grade-school level.[19] In 1960 ten of the total thirty-five institutes included teachers of elementary school foreign languages.

In summary, the question of "who will teach it" remains unanswered. At the present time, the final answer is determined by each local system according to its philosophy of classroom teacher *vs.* subject specialist, and the availability of qualified personnel.

The pupils. As has been previously stated, programs vary in this respect. In many systems, a second language is offered to *all* pupils in certain selected grades; in others it is offered on an elective basis; in others, to children who are academically and mentally advanced; and, finally, there has even been some experimentation in offering it to the mentally retarded.[20]

The grade level. Again, there is a wide divergence of practice with some programs beginning as early as the first grade.[21] However, although introducing languages in the primary grades is not uncommon, the majority of systems prefer to start it in the third, fourth, or fifth grades. Reasons usually given for these grades are that these pupils are young enough to have facility in learning language, but they are also old enough to have acquired an initial mastery of the skills of speaking, reading, and writing English.

[18] K. W. Mildenberger, *op. cit.,* Foreword, p. 12.

[19] "An Evaluation of the 1959 Summer Language Institutes," *Modern Language Journal,* Vol. 44 (February, 1960), pp. 59–63.

[20] P. Angiolillo, "French for the Feeble-Minded: An Experiment," *Modern Language Journal,* Vol. 26 (April, 1942), pp. 266–271.

[21] V. V. Villegas, "Foreign Languages from the First Grade," *American School Board Journal,* Vol. 136 (February, 1958), p. 41.

The time. A daily period of fifteen to thirty minutes is frequently recommended, although the literature contains accounts of programs of as little as twenty minutes a week to as much as fifty minutes per day. In addition, some programs specify no particular time or period for the teaching of a second language but prefer to intersperse it throughout the various activities of the day.

Administrative provisions. Here again, there are wide differences among present practices. In some systems, the subject is taught as a regular part of the daily program. In others, it is offered as an extracurricular club or as a school lunch-time activity. In still others it is offered in the home or school via television and radio.[22] Advocates of *FLES* obviously support the idea of including it as part of the regular school program for all children, but this is, by no means, a consistent practice at this time.

Generally speaking, educators who support *FLES* are agreed upon four major points:

1. *Need for articulation.* In the past, some programs have been disbanded because of the administrative difficulty of maintaining a continuity and articulation of instruction. Authorities place considerable emphasis upon the need, once the program is started, to continue it *through* the secondary school level. The casual, cafeteria-like program in which the child takes a smattering of French one year, nothing the next, and a little Spanish the following year is deplored by all serious-minded educators. If a program is to be started, those responsible should plan it carefully in order to insure continuity and articulation as the child progresses from one grade to the next.

2. *Need for integration.* This is another point on which there is agreement although this agreement is not always implemented in actual practice. The feeling is strong today, however, that the second language, if taught, should be integrated with various other curriculum areas. To teach it as an isolated entity is, obviously, no more defensible than it would be for any other subject. Study of the second language should be integrated with social studies, art, music, and other activities.

3. *The method.* Finally, there is general consistency of opinion regarding the use of the aural-oral method of teaching language. Usually in the first few years, the children are taught solely through the conversational approach with the teacher usually speaking in the second language. The pupils ask and answer questions, give and take directions, sing songs, recite poems, describe pictures, enact dramatizations, play games, manipulate puppets, and through numerous other activities learn to understand and speak the language. Depending upon the age of the pupils, the first one or two years is usually devoted exclusively to this ear and vocal training. At a later date,

[22] L. B. Jones, "Elementary Foreign Language by Television," *Teachers College Record*, Vol. 60 (October, 1958), pp. 36–40.

pupils are introduced to reading and writing the language, although there
remains throughout the entire elementary sequence, a strong emphasis
upon the aural-oral approach.

4. *The materials.* Considerable interest is presently directed toward the
use of numerous audio-visual materials and mechanical equipment to
facilitate language learning. Such materials include films, filmstrips, recordings, tapes, books, slides, and songs which are conceded to have considerable value in vitalizing and enforcing the teaching of foreign languages.
Teachers who are interested in securing these aids should find especially
helpful the comprehensive list of 1717 items with annotations concerning
their purpose and suitability for various grade levels, prepared by the
Modern Language Association.[23] Other excellent sources are the annotated
bibliographies which appear each year in the January issue of the *Modern
Language Journal* and the selective list issued by the United States Department of Health, Education, and Welfare in June, 1959.[24]

AN ALTERNATE PLAN

One cannot leave the present discussion without reference to a type of
learning experience which many elementary school children are presently
enjoying but which cannot be identified with any particular group or set
of initials. This is the unified, integrative experience found in every good
teacher's classrooom in which children are motivated to explore as many
facets of a culture or people under study as possible. In a unit on Mexico,
for instance, fourth-grade children may learn to greet each other with
"Buenos Dias" as naturally and easily as they learn to cook and eat tortillas,
weave serapes, or to make and break the wonderful piñata. In such a rich
and exciting environment, the teacher will attempt to have his pupils *experience* Mexico through every possible activity and channel of learning.
Pupils will study, read, see, hear, feel, and speak the culture; they will
dance, sing, draw, and model the arts; and through all of these media they
will greatly increase their understanding of and sensitivity to, another
people—their country, their customs, their culture, and, last but not
least, their language.

Summary

This chapter has attempted to present a fairly comprehensive view of
the conflicting philosophies and practices of teaching modern foreign

[23] Douglas W. Alden, ed., *Materials List for Use by Teachers of Modern Foreign
Languages* (The Modern Language Association of America Pursuant to a Contract
with the U.S. Office of Education, Department of Health, Education, and Welfare).
[24] Marjorie C. Johnston and Ilo Remer, eds., *References on Foreign Languages in the
Elementary School*, Circular No. 495 (Washington, D.C., Department of Health, Education, and Welfare, Office of Education, June, 1959).

languages in the elementary schools. The arguments favoring and opposing the movement were presented. The present status of FLES was evaluated and the current disparities and inconsistencies of the programs now in existence were discussed.

Finally, brief mention was made of a teaching-learning experience in which children are introduced to the language of another people in the same context and degree as they are to all other aspects of a foreign culture. Advocating this plan are many educators who consider themselves neither champions nor challengers of FLES but who, wholeheartedly, subscribe to another interpretation of the same initials—Functional Learning in the Elementary School.

STUDENT PROJECTS

1. Contact your state department of education. See if you can find any facts and figures which will enable you to draw general conclusions regarding the status of FLES in your state. What disparities in practice do you find? What consistencies?

2. Interview several elementary school teachers and principals in more than one school district. What are their opinions concerning the value of foreign language teaching for elementary school children? Now interview the same number of parents or community citizens. How do their opinions compare with those of the first group? What are your conclusions?

3. You have accepted a position in a school in which 15 per cent of the pupils are Puerto Rican. The principal says there is no "formal" FLES program in operation at the present time. What implications for your teaching will these two facts have?

4. Prepare a social studies unit for your sixth grade on the ABC countries (Argentina, Brazil, and Chile) of South America. How will you integrate a study of foreign languages in this unit? Give specific illustrations of activities and lessons.

5. The PTA president has asked the faculty of your school to present a panel discussion on the pros and cons of foreign language teaching in the elementary school. What will you say in your five-minute presentation? Substantiate the viewpoint you will take with statements or facts other than those presented in this chapter.

6. Explore the possibilities of using FLES to enrich the curriculum for the mentally gifted. What are the advantages of such a program? The disadvantages? The administrative problems?

7. At present, the Boy Scouts and Girl Scouts of America offer merit and proficiency badges for learning a foreign language. Does this fact have any significance or implication for your classroom teaching? Explain.

8. Compile a bibliography of available and inexpensive books and materials which you may use in teaching the language of your choice to your fourth grade pupils.

9. As the principal of an elementary school you are convinced of the values of FLES. Outline an action program you would take to convince teachers and parents of the values you see in it.

10. Would you advocate that a requirement for your college curriculum be at least two years of a modern foreign language? Defend your answer.

11. Interview some of your fellow college students who were raised in homes in which English was spoken as a second language or not at all. Do they feel that their bilingual backgrounds helped or hindered their learning of English? Can you find any research studies which agree with their opinions?

BIBLIOGRAPHY

ADAMS, L. S. and BOLTON, F. E., "Foreign Language in the Grades?" *NEA Journal*, Vol. 45 (October, 1956), pp. 444–445.

ANDERSSON, Theodore, "The Teaching of a Second Language in the Elementary Schools: Issues and Implications," *Education*, Vol. 75 (April, 1955), pp. 490–497.

ANDERSSON, Theodore, *The Teaching of Foreign Languages in the Elementary School* (Boston, D. C. Heath and Company, 1953).

ANGIOLILLO, Paul, "French for the Feeble-Minded, An Experiment," *Modern Language Journal*, Vol. 26 (April, 1942), pp. 266–271.

BISHOP, James W., "Observations on Teaching Elementary Pupils Spanish," *Modern Language Journal*, Vol. 25 (November, 1940), pp. 138–139.

BOEHM, Lenore, "Age and Foreign Language Training," *Modern Language Journal*, Vol. 43, (January, 1959), pp. 32–33.

BROOKS, Nelson, "The Meanings of FLES," *Teacher Education Quarterly*, Vol. 16 (Fall, 1958), pp. 27–29.

Committee on Foreign Languages in the Elementary Schools, *Some Solutions to Problems Related to the Teaching of Foreign Languages in Elementary Schools* (New York, Metropolitan School Study Council, 1956).

ELLERT, E. E. and ELLERT, L. V., "Teaching Modern Language to the Elementary School Child," *Educational Research Bulletin*, Vol. 32 (January, 1953), pp. 1–6.

FREEMAN, Stephen A., "Expanding the Teacher's Horizons," *School and Society*, Vol. 86 (December 20, 1958), pp. 451–454.

HICKS, Georgina L., "Teaching Foreign Language to Children," *Modern Language Journal*, Vol. 43 (January, 1959), pp. 29–31.

HILDRETH, Gertrude, "Learning a Second Language in the Elementary Grades and High School," *Modern Language Journal*, Vol. 43 (March, 1959), pp. 136–141.

HOBBS, Nicholas, "Child Development and Language Learning," *School and Society*, Vol. 78 (July 25, 1953), pp. 17–21.

HOPPOCK, Ann, "Foreign Language in the Elementary School," *New Jersey Education Review*, Vol. 30 (November, 1956), pp. 128–130.

JONES, Lloid B., "Elementary Foreign Language by Television," *Teachers College Record*, Vol. 60 (October, 1958), pp. 36–40.

KEESEE, Elizabeth, *Modern Foreign Languages in the Elementary School* (Washington, D.C., U.S. Department of Health, Education, and Welfare, 1960).

KIRCH, Max S., "Specialist or Classroom Teacher for FLES," *Modern Language Journal*, Vol. 42 (March, 1958), pp. 132–135.

KOLBERT, Jack, "Foreign Languages in the Self-Contained Classroom," *Modern Language Journal*, Vol. 42 (November, 1958), pp. 313–316.

LIND, Melva, "Living Languages for the Elementary Schools," *Educational Record*, Vol. 37 (April, 1956), pp. 126–136.

McGRATH, Earl James, "Foreign Language Instruction in American Schools,"
An Address (Washington, D.C., Conference on the Role of Foreign Languages
in American Schools, 1953).

MEHLING, Reuben, "Public Opinion and the Teaching of Foreign Languages,"
Modern Language Journal, Vol. 43 (November, 1959), pp. 328–331.

MILDENBERGER, K. W., "The Progress of FLES," *Education*, Vol. 75 (April,
1955), pp. 498–503.

MURDOCK, Mary W. and WRIGHT, L. O., "A Fifth Grade Spanish Club Experiment
in Oregon," *Hispania*, Vol. 24 (October, 1941), pp. 261–266.

PEI, Mario, "Languages for the Very Young," *Modern Language Journal*, Vol. 32
(May, 1948), pp. 333–336.

PINTNER, R. and ARSENIAN, S., "The Relation of Bilingualism to Verbal Intelligence
and School Adjustment," *Journal of Educational Research*, Vol. 31
(December, 1937), pp. 255–263.

REDEFER, Frederick L., "Let's Study the World," *Saturday Review*, Vol. 40
(February 16, 1957), pp. 35–37.

SELVI, A. M., "An Experiment Introducing Modern Language Activities in the
Elementary School," *Educational Administration and Supervision*, Vol. 37
(May, 1951), pp. 312–315.

SNYDER, C. W., "Experiment in Teaching Russian in Grade 3," *School and
Society*, Vol. 86 (October 11, 1958), pp. 353–354.

THON, F. H., "French for Bright Young Children in New York Public Schools,"
French Review, Vol. 13 (February, 1940), pp. 303–313, and Vol. 13 (March,
1940), pp. 390–396.

United States Office of Education, "Foreign Languages in the Elementary
Schools," *School Life*, Official Journal of the United States Office of Education,
Vol. 38 (June, 1956), pp. 14–15.

VILLEGAS, Vera V., "Foreign Languages from the First Grade," *American School
Board Journal*, Vol. 136 (February, 1958), p. 41.

CHAPTER 9

Social Studies

DURING A RECENT MEETING of an elementary school Parent-Teacher Association, a member arose and addressed the following remarks to the school principal, "What do you mean by social studies? I hear my son talking about studying social studies and I don't know what he means. Is this something that we did not have when we were in the elementary school or is it just history and geography under a new name?"

The question was an excellent one and should have produced some soul-searching on the part of the principal and faculty. We hope their answer went something like this:

"It is difficult to answer your specific question for, of course, whether social studies is a 'new' subject or simply a new name for nineteenth-century subjects depends upon each individual school, both now and when you were a youngster. Furthermore, to call them 'social' subjects does not necessarily make them so. In our school, however, social studies as taught today is much more than a mere change in terminology. The subject which our youngsters are studying today and which they refer to as *social studies* represents a change from the narrowed 'history-geography sequence' of the past in several major respects: (1) a change in what we are striving to do, (2) a change in what is taught and when, (3) a change in *how* it is taught, (4) a change in the experiences and activities through which children learn, and (5) a change in the materials and tools they use for learning."

Each of these facets of the modern social studies program is examined in detail in this chapter. First, let us look at the objectives which guide today's program.

OBJECTIVES OF THE SOCIAL STUDIES

There is widespread agreement among present statements of objectives. Innumerable attempts have been made in recent years to define the objectives of social studies and, on the whole, there is widespread agreement among them. In general, the over-all goal is recognized to be the development of a constructive relationship between the individual and his society. Today, as never before, intelligent teachers recognize the need for developing in boys and girls the responsibilities, privileges, and obligations that they have toward society. Furthermore, in this context, "society" means, not only the immediate community, but the society of all nations, for as Thralls states, "We are world citizens today whether we want to be or not." [1] It is fairly obvious that this comprehensive objective represents a change from the earlier concentration upon the acquisition of isolated facts and the memorization of content. Its achievement depends upon a three-pronged emphasis on understandings, skills, and attitudes.

Many statements of objectives emphasize three directional goals. The following are illustrative of the statements which attempt to define social studies goals in terms of specific (1) understandings, (2) habits and skills, and (3) appreciations or attitudes. McLendon offers the following fairly concise list:

1. *Understanding* of the main features of the social environment; of ways in which people cope with their environment and provide for their basic needs; of social control through government and other groups; of fundamental relationships among individuals, groups, and society; and of basic characteristics and factors in the growth of civilization.

2. *Skills* in gathering, organizing, critically analyzing, communicating and otherwise utilizing the information regarding human relationships available in oral, printed, or visual form.

3. *Attitudes* such as respect for individuals, belief that democratic processes provide rational solutions for social problems, willingness to assume civic responsibilities and work for the general welfare, and belief in self-government and upholding the law.[2]

A more comprehensive list by Samford represents a compilation of objectives as stated in several state courses of study, curriculum guides, periodical references and textbooks:

OBJECTIVES RELATED TO ACQUIRING
SOCIAL STUDIES INFORMATION

1. Knowledge of democracy and the manner in which it functions.
2. Understanding of social, economic, and political concepts, starting with the community and extending into a world setting.

[1] Z. A. Thralls, *The Teaching of Geography* (New York, Appleton-Century-Crofts, Inc., 1958), p. 11.

[2] J. C. McLendon, *Teaching the Social Studies*, "What Research says to the Teacher," Department of Classroom Teachers (Washington, D.C., American Educational Research Association, National Education Association, 1960), p. 7.

3. Information dealing with contemporary affairs.

4. Acquisition of sound economic, political, and social ideas.

5. Gaining of an adequate social studies vocabulary.

6. Comprehensive knowledge of the history and traditions of our own country.

7. Learning the basic facts of consumer education.

8. Strengthening and enriching personality.

9. Securing vocational information.

10. Deriving a suitable background for other areas in the curriculum.

11. Stressing the importance of conservation education.

OBJECTIVES RELATED TO ACQUIRING SOCIAL STUDIES SKILLS

1. Ability to make use of table of contents, index, maps, charts, graphs, dictionary, encyclopedia, atlas, world almanac, selected cartoons, globe, etc.

2. Developing powers of critical thinking and independent judgment.

3. Participation in group discussion.

4. Effective presentation of oral reports.

5. Applications of social studies information to practical situations.

6. Working in groups within the classroom.

7. Using community resources as an aid to the learning of social studies.

8. Working on committees and in projects designed to help the local community and/or larger group.

9. Enlarging opportunities for growth in reading.

10. Relying upon audio-visual aids as a means of enlarging social studies concepts.

11. Giving opportunity to learn parliamentary procedures.

12. Development of leadership.

13. Collecting data.

14. Application of the rules of effective study.

OBJECTIVES RELATED TO ACQUIRING DESIRABLE SOCIAL STUDIES ATTITUDES

1. Respect for rights and contributions of others regardless of race, color, and creed.

2. Desire to participate personally in improving various groups (home, school, community, state, etc.).

3. Appreciation of the sacrifices that have gone into the making of our social order.

4. Exaltation of high social values.

5. Gaining respect for work well done.

6. Cultivation of laudable patriotism.

7. Respect for truth (accuracy).

8. Standing for high moral and spiritual values.[3]

[3] C. D. Samford, "Can Social Studies Objectives be Accomplished with Present-Day Textbooks?" *Social Studies*, Vol. 45 (April, 1954), p. 136.

Some statements identify behavioral outcomes as social studies objectives. The following is a somewhat different approach in that it represents an attempt to identify objectives as specific behavioral characteristics which should result from an effective social studies program.

Every pupil should have an opportunity to participate in learning experiences which will enable him to achieve maximum development as an individual and as a member of society—so that to the limit of his capacity, he will be a citizen who:

Is well adjusted and lives and works in harmony with others.

Strives to achieve worthy values and ideals.

Makes satisfactory adjustments to his problems through an understanding of himself, his personality, interests, abilities, and limitations.

Maintains democratic relationships with other persons, respects the worth of each individual, and realizes that each individual with his unique background contributes to the common good.

Acts as a responsible member of his family and of the community.

Thinks critically about social problems and assumes responsibility for contributing to their solution.

Appreciates our American heritage and has the attitudes, skills, and understandings required for effective citizenship in our American democracy.

Has faith in democracy and acts in accordance with democratic principles.

Uses his knowledge of the history and geography of our country for a better understanding of the present day.

Understands the processes of American government and accepts the responsibilities of good citizenship.

Thinks critically about problems in our community, state, and nation and assumes responsibility for contributing to their solution.

Understands the need for and promotes international co-operation to improve the welfare of mankind and to attain world peace.

Uses his knowledge of geography and history for a better understanding of the world and its people.

Appreciates the contributions to world civilization by the many different peoples past and present.

Understands the interdependence of the peoples of the world.

Thinks critically about world problems and assumes responsibility for contributing to their solution.

Functions effectively in his daily economic life and makes valid economic judgments.

Maintains a sound personal financial program and purchases and uses goods and services wisely.

Makes an intelligent choice of vocation.

Understands and appreciates the contributions of the many groups of workers who produce goods and services.

Understands how the environment affects the ways in which people live.

Interests himself in and understands how our economic system operates.

Thinks critically about economic problems and assumes responsibility for contributing to their solution.[4]

It is evident from an examination of the previous statements that whatever disagreement exists among them does so only superficially in terms of organization, terminology, or comprehensiveness. All of them focus directly upon the identification of relationships, abilities, and value-patterns which characterize the "socially-minded" individual of our complex world. To achieve the stated objectives demands a careful attention to the scope, content, and sequence of the social studies program, which is discussed in the following section.

SCOPE, CONTENT, AND SEQUENCE

The scope of the social studies has expanded to include several fields of specialization. The first "social" subject to be included in the school curriculum was geography. Shortly after the Revolutionary War, the white-heat of patriotism and nationalism generated a feeling that pupils in American schools should learn about their newly-won country from textbooks written by American authors. Consequently, Morse published the first American geography text in 1789, which was followed by numerous others in this field. Even so, the subjects which today are designated as "social studies" were relatively slow to gain a firm place in the elementary school curriculum and Otto states that,

Geography did not become a subject commonly taught in elementary schools until toward 1800; by 1850, geography had found a prominent place in most elementary school programs. History, on the other hand, did not achieve status as a school subject until about 1860.[5]

Still later came civics, and these three comprised the bulk of the social studies program until, in recent years, there has been included a multitude of topics which draw from many highly specialized fields. Hanna identifies the nine disciplines which constitute the primary sources for generalizations and values in the social studies as: (1) Anthropology (cultural), (2) Economics, (3) Ethics, (4) Geography (human), (5) History, (6) Jurisprudence, (7) Political science, (8) Psychology (social), and (9) Sociology.[6]

Considerable investigation and experimentation have been directed toward determining the content of the social studies. The nine contributing sources of generalizations cited above make it obvious that the elementary

[4] Committee for the Social Studies Curriculum Study, *A Guide for Teaching Social Studies, Kgn-Grade 7* (Minneapolis, Minn., Public Schools, 1957), p. 1.

[5] H. Otto, *Social Education in Elementary Schools* (New York, Holt, Rinehart and Winston, Inc., 1956), p. 227.

[6] P. Hanna, "Generalizations and Universal Values: Their Implications for the Social Studies Program," *Social Studies in the Elementary School*, 56th Yearbook of the National Society for the Study of Education, Part II (Chicago, University of Chicago Press, 1957), p. 31.

teacher has a vast amount of content from which to draw for his teaching of the social studies. The problem, of course, is in choosing and organizing the content to fit the needs of children. In Chapter Four the authors distinguished between *natural* and *contrived* motivation. They cited several disadvantages of relying solely upon natural motivation, chief of which was the danger of a haphazard, hit-or-miss, "planless" program. The content of today's social studies, therefore, is not dependent solely upon the spontaneous interests of children (which are rarely common to an entire group). Rather it is determined in accord with a carefully studied plan which, of course, must be flexible and broad enough to meet the specific needs and challenges of a particular situation. Although various plans for determining content are now in use, in general there is a marked degree of similarity among them. This is apparent from an examination of the following plans, all of which merit the serious attention of present-day educators.

Social Functions. Many schools feel that, since social studies are concerned with the social living of man, their content should concentrate upon basic human activities and functions. These are termed *social functions* by some authors and *social processes* or *areas of living* by others. Many attempts have been made to identify these basic social functions. Michaelis states that they are:

Production	Education
Distribution	Conservation
Transportation	Aesthetic expression
Communication	Religious expression
Government	Recreation[7]

Very similar is the list of basic human activities identified by Hanna: protecting and conserving life, health, resources, and property; producing, distributing, and consuming food, clothing, shelter and other consumer goods and services; creating and producing tools and technics; transporting people and goods; communicating ideas and feelings; providing education; providing recreation; organizing and governing; expressing aesthetic and spiritual impulses.[8]

Problems and Issues. Wesley and Adams advocate using current problems and issues as a basis for determining the scope and content of the social studies program. They feel that a comparative list of current problems would include economics, civics, sociology, geography, and history and would "result in a fairly complete curriculum." They defend their theory by stating:

The use of problems insures the social value and timeliness of the materials; it motivates learning and facilitates teaching, for the problem almost automatically indicates a method. The use of problems gives assurance of a rich and

---

[7] J. U. Michaelis, *Social Studies for Children in a Democracy*, 2nd ed. (Englewood Cliffs, N.J., Prentice-Hall, Inc., 1956), p. 37.
[8] P. Hanna, *op. cit.*, p. 46.

inclusive curriculum. Whether it should be the sole, or even the major, formula is an open question, but there can be no doubt that it is a workable and helpful formula for selecting units.[9]

Life Situations. Still another approach which several authorities feel has merit is the use of persistent life situations in determining the content and sequence of the social studies. This approach, suggested by Stratemeyer et al., is based upon the idea that man faces certain persistent life situations and that a study of these might constitute the total social studies curriculum. The authors emphasize that in this plan, "the focus is upon building understandings, values, generalizations, and skills through experiences arising out of daily situations that learners actually face." [10] They claim that the everyday concerns of the learner are the starting point and that these are related to persistent life situations which they identify in a master list. The reader is referred to the original source for a comprehensive listing of these "persistent life situations."

The Report of the National Council for the Social Studies on Concepts and Values suggests the following fourteen themes as a "comprehensive definition of the scope of the social studies curriculum from the kindergarten through the fourteenth grade":

1. The intelligent uses of the forces of nature.

2. Recognition and understanding of world interdependence.

3. Recognition of the dignity and worth of the individual.

4. The use of intelligence to improve human living.

5. The vitalization of our democracy through an intelligent use of our public educational facilities.

6. The intelligent acceptance, by individuals and groups, of responsibility for achieving democratic social action.

7. Increasing the effectiveness of the family as a basic social institution.

8. The effective development of moral and spiritual values.

9. The intelligent and responsible sharing of power in order to attain justice.

10. The intelligent utilization of scarce resources to attain the widest general well-being.

11. Achievement of adequate horizons of loyalty.

12. Co-operation in the interest of peace and welfare.

13. Achieving a balance between social stability and social change.

14. Widening and deepening the ability to live more richly.[11]

[9] E. B. Wesley and M. A. Adams, *Teaching Social Studies in Elementary Schools,* rev. ed. (Boston, D. C. Heath and Company, 1952), p. 192.

[10] F. Stratemeyer, et al., *Developing a Curriculum for Modern Living,* 2nd ed. (New York, Teachers College, Columbia University, 1957), p. 140.

[11] National Council for the Social Studies, *A Guide to Contents in the Social Studies,* Report of the NCSS Committees on Concepts and Values (Washington, D.C., National Education Association, 1957).

Although all of these plans are worthy of mention, they are, by no means, the only ones in present use. Modern literature contains suggestions for using "imperative needs," "generalizations," "regions and cultures" and numerous others as bases for planning the social studies curriculum. Since space does not permit a discussion of these, the reader is referred to the bibliography at the close of the chapter for a more intensive treatment of the subject.

The problem of determining sequence is currently being re-examined. Regardless of the type of plan a school uses, it must decide upon what basis it will assign specific content to a specific grade. If, for instance, a school uses "life situations" as a basis for its social studies curriculum, it must decide what aspects of what life situations will be treated at each grade level. Or, if a school uses "social functions" as its framework, it must decide how production, distribution, and transportation will be treated with increasing complexity from grade to grade. A very popular and widespread plan for determining sequence is the "principle of widening horizons" in which a child is led from his immediate environment to more remote places and cultures. Hanna says that an individual is simultaneously a member of several communities and that this "multiple membership" justifies an expanding study of communities according to the following pattern:

Emphasis 1. Home (Kindergarten and first grade).

Emphasis 2. School (First grade).

Emphasis 3. Neighborhood (Second grade). Living in our neighborhood community—today and yesterday.

Emphasis 4. Local Community (Third grade). Living in our local community (made up of several neighborhoods) and in the surrounding area (county and/or metropolitan community) of which our local community is a part—today and yesterday.

Emphasis 5. State (Fourth grade). Living in our state community (made up of the many local communities)—today and yesterday.

Emphasis 6. Region (Fourth grade). Living in our region-of-states community (made up of several adjoining states)—today and yesterday.

Emphasis 7. Nation (Fifth grade). Living in our national community (made up of the several regional communities)—today and yesterday.

Emphasis 8. The USA and the Inter-American Community (Fifth grade). Living in our inter-American community (made up of the United States and her neighbors north and south from pole to pole)—today and yesterday.

Emphasis 9. The USA and the Atlantic Community (Sixth grade). Living in our Atlantic Community (made up of the United States and her neighbors in Europe, the Middle East, and Africa)—today and yesterday.

Emphasis 10.   The USA and the Pacific Community (Seventh grade). Living
               in our Pacific Community (made up of the United States and her
               neighbors in Asia, Australia, and Southeast Asia)—today and
               yesterday.

Emphasis 11.   United States History (Eighth grade). The chronological study
               of the United States—its origin, development, and role in a
               divided world.[12]

Generally speaking, this type of sequence is used more widely today than
any other. In actual practice, there is virtually complete agreement on emphasizing the home, school, and neighborhood community during the first
three grades, with some variation of the plan in the upper grades. In general,
this plan has dominated the elementary classrooms of the country for
several years, and it has been only recently that some doubt has been expressed as to the wisdom of "strait-jacketing" the young child's learning
experiences within the confines of his immediate environment. In general,
current questions related to this plan revolve around the following points.

1. *The validity of the "deferment" theory.* Several famous studies of
thirty or forty years ago revealed many inaccurate geographical and historical concepts held by children. Davis comments upon the influence of these
studies on the elementary curriculum as follows:

> Many of the studies concluded that since children at certain age levels did not
> understand some concepts, instruction about them should be deferred until the
> children had matured sufficiently to profit from teaching. A deferment theory
> of instruction developed, substantiated by studies of misconceptions and of the
> growth of concepts, which influenced curriculum development to a considerable
> extent. Introduction of some social studies topics, formerly taught at early grade
> levels, was postponed to later grades.[13]

Today, there is considerable question about the wisdom of deferring
content until children are older, thus creating a vacuum in the primary
grades which may not be filled with experiences which are challenging
and stimulating to youngsters. The solution, as proposed by some, might
be to prevent inaccurate concepts by meaningful teaching, not merely by
delayed teaching.

2. *Wider experiences of modern children.* Because of increased travel,
television, motion pictures, and other everyday experiences of young
children today, there is considerable reason to believe that their knowledge
extends far beyond their immediate environment. McAulay reports, for
instance, that of seventy second-graders interviewed,

> twenty-three children knew Indo-China was in a hot land and knew of the fighting
> there through TV programs, movie newsreels, or radio newscasts. Eleven children

[12] P. Hanna, "Social Studies for Today," *NEA Journal,* Vol. 45 (January, 1956),
pp. 36–38.
[13] O. L. Davis, "Children Can Learn Complex Concepts," *Educational Leadership,*
Vol. 17 (December, 1959), p. 171.

knew there was a relationship between the Geneva Conference and the fighting in Indo-China.[14]

Huck reports somewhat similar findings among first-graders, more than half of whom recognized the President of the United States and who also knew that Russia was a country. This same group of children reported their chief sources of information to be direct experiences, television, and parents. According to Huck, it was found that the school supplied slightly less than five per cent of the children's information concerning these social concepts. She concludes,

> It would appear that the immediate environment of children of today has been extended to include much of the adult world. No longer is the six-year-old child's knowledge confined to his home, his neighborhood, and community. He has gathered facts and fragments of facts from every corner of the universe.[15]

From these and other studies, there appears to be some justification for questioning the sequence of social studies content as it is now taught in many schools. The solution of the problem appears to be twofold. First, creative teachers, within the framework of their required curriculum guide, must provide pupils with the academic depth and intellectual challenge suited to their experiences. An example of this is the second-grade teacher who discovered that all the pupils in her class had traveled widely in this country and nine of them had traveled abroad. Because of the wide experiences and sophistication of these youngsters, the teacher decided to give her required unit on *Community Helpers* another dimension by concentrating on workers other than the usual stereotypes of fireman and policeman. Instead of this, the teacher explored the occupations of the children's fathers. She invited a lawyer, a bank president, an obstetrician, a sales manager, an advertising executive, and the owner of a small factory to the class. As these men discussed their work and its relationship with the community, these second-grade youngsters gained an insight into the complexity of community interdependence far beyond that offered by the usual stereotypes.

Many similar illustrations could be offered to show the inventiveness of teachers in challenging the intellectual capacities of their pupils. The following incident, for instance, occurred recently during a sharing period in the kindergarten when a pupil proudly displayed his new shoes to his classmates. Instead of dismissing the incident with a, "Thank you, Chris, for showing us your new shoes. They are very nice," the teacher challenged the pupils with such questions as, "Does anyone know what Chris's shoes are made of? Did the man who sold Chris the shoes make them? Who did?

---

[14] J. D. McAulay, "Social Studies in the Primary Grades," *Social Education,* Vol. 18 (December, 1954), p. 358.

[15] C. Huck, "Children Learn from Their Culture," *Educational Leadership,* Vol. 13 (December, 1955), pp. 174–175.

How did the store man get them? What will he do with the money Chris's mother gave him for the shoes?" These and similar questions resulted in several worthwhile lessons in which five-year-olds gained valuable knowledge and concepts.

A second solution to the problem rests upon those responsible for determining the curriculum of a school system. It is time for curriculum directors and curriculum committees to reassess their present programs in the light of current research concerning the experiences, interests, and abilities of children living in the changing world of the 1960s. As Huck states, "Certainly school should be as challenging as children's out-of-school experiences." [16]

In this section the authors have analyzed the major concerns and emphases related to the scope, content, and sequence of the social studies program. The remainder of the chapter is devoted to a discussion of the distinctive instructional emphases now receiving considerable attention from social studies educators. These are: (1) Unit Teaching, (2) Social Learning and Social Living, (3) Activities and Materials, and (4) Current Affairs and Social Studies Skills. Let us examine briefly the first of these.

UNIT TEACHING

One of the guides for curriculum planning presented in Chapter Four was the statement that *integrative experiences must be a focal part of curricular planning*. This principle has resulted in organizing certain learning experiences into a "unit," the core of which frequently, but not always, lies within the social studies. It will be remembered that a unit was defined in Chapter Four as *a teaching-learning organization which calls for the integration of curricular areas, which has certain distinctive characteristics of teaching, and which usually extends over a period of several weeks*. With this definition in mind, let us briefly examine some of the questions frequently asked by teachers concerning unit teaching.

Why is unit-planning more pertinent to the social studies than to other curricular areas? The content of the social studies lends itself readily to the integration of various other curricular areas. For instance, a comprehensive study of almost any social studies topic—from early explorers to the geography of Texas—will provide natural opportunities for the development of language skills, creative art experiences, scientific knowledges and methods, and probably certain mathematical skills as well. Thus, the social studies become the "core" of the unit, and it is through the exploration of their content that knowledges and skills are developed in other areas as well.

Must all subjects be integrated with the unit? Although the social studies

[16] *Ibid.*, p. 175.

unit, at one time or another, will probably be related to all other curricular areas, complete integration is neither possible nor desirable for the reasons given in Chapter Four.

What is the average length of a unit? In the primary grades, a unit may possibly extend only over a week or two. In most elementary grades, typical units range from four to six or eight weeks.

How do I arouse preliminary interest in the unit? In a structured social studies program, the teacher must attempt to arouse the children's interests in the forthcoming unit through a series of initiatory activities, such as displays, exhibits, demonstrations, films, filmstrips, or stories.

How do I determine my objectives for the unit? The teacher must determine his specific objectives for each unit according to the needs of his particular group of pupils. He will, therefore, be guided by the needs of his class as well as by the general objectives of the social studies in stating the specific understandings, habits and skills, and attitudes he wishes to develop through any one unit. For excellent advice concerning the stating of objectives, the reader is referred to Burton's *The Guidance of Learning Activities.*[17]

What are pupils' objectives? The objectives of the pupils are usually stated as questions and problems which are developed in the preliminary planning of the unit with the pupils. Such questions as, "What Indians lived in New Jersey?" or "How do the people of Alaska live?" might be problems voiced by children which will guide their study of the unit.

What is an acceptable form for writing a unit plan? A form similar to the following has been found by many teachers to be satisfactory for writing the unit plan.

UNIT PLAN

Approximate Time: 6–8 weeks
Grade Four
Topic: New Jersey—Long, Long Ago

Problem	Tentative Procedures and Activities	Children's References
Initial motivation.	1. State problems and sub-problems.	
Cooperative planning.	2. Discuss how to solve problems. a. Reference work. b. Field trips. c. Written and oral reports. d. Visual aids, such as films and filmstrips.	

[17] W. H. Burton, *The Guidance of Learning Activities,* 2nd ed. (New York, Appleton-Century-Crofts, Inc., 1952), pp. 417–423.

UNIT PLAN (Cont.)

Approximate Time: 6–8 weeks
Grade Four
Topic: New Jersey—Long, Long Ago

Problem	*Tentative Procedures and Activities*	*Children's References*

	e. Creative arts, such as music and drawing.
	f. Physical activities and creative dramatics.
	3. Organize methods of procedure.
	  a. Individual research.
	  b. Class discussions.
	  c. Class projects, activities, and trips.
	  d. Written and oral reports.
	  e. Committee or group work.
	  f. Class singing and drawing.	

Who were New Jersey's first settlers?	1. Class discussions on the Lenni Lenape Indians.
	2. Show filmstrip "American Indian Life."
	3. Show personal slides.
	
	4. Children make individual booklets on the Lenni Lenape Indians.
	  a. Creative stories.
	
	  b. Drawings of Indian homes, clothing and ceremonies.
	
	  c. Reference notes on Indian transportation and ways of obtaining food.
	  d. Class notes on Indians' relations with white men.
	  e. Poems about aspects of Indian culture.
	  f. Prepare vocabulary chart of Indian-originated words.
		The Story of New Jersey, pp. 5–34.
		Jersey's Story, pp. 9–14.
		An Elementary History of New Jersey, pp. 1–18.
		True Stories of New Jersey.
		Little Turtle of the Lenni Lenape, p. 67.
		American Indians, pp. 108–115.

UNIT PLAN (Cont.)

Approximate Time: 6–8 weeks
Grade Four
Topic: New Jersey—Long, Long Ago

Problem	Tentative Procedures and Activities	Children's References
How did the Lenni Lenape Indians contribute to our state's history?	1. Co-operatively develop chart on the contributions of the Lenni Lenape Indians. 2. Make posters illustrating the Indians' gifts to the white man. 3. Plant a window box or garden to grow some of the food plants the Indians gave us. 4. Individual reports on the contributions of the Lenni Lenape Indians.	
Who were the first European settlers of New Jersey?	1. Make a chart listing the early explorers and the countries from which they came. 2. Reference work on individual explorers. 3. Dramatize the first meeting of Indians and explorers. 4. Compose an original story about the first explorers or settlers. 5. Locate on an outline map of New Jersey the various settlements.	*The Story of New Jersey*, pp. 35–51. *Jersey's Story*, pp. 15–32. *An Elementary History of New Jersey*, pp. 20–31.
How did the life of the European settlers compare with the life of the Indian?	1. Discussion and comparisons of colonial and Indian life. 2. Take an imaginary trip to a colonial home. 3. View and discuss personal slides. 4. View and discuss the filmstrip, "Life in the Middle Colonies." 5. View and discuss the film, "Colonial Life in the Middle Colonies."	*Boys and Girls of Colonial Days.* *Home Life in Colonial Days.* *An Elementary History of New Jersey*, pp. 32–42. *Jersey's Story*, pp. 33–63. *The Story of New Jersey*, pp. 72–108. *New Jersey: A Story of Progress*, pp. 1–40. *A Day in a Colonial Home.*

UNIT PLAN (Cont.)

Approximate Time: 6–8 weeks
Grade Four
Topic: New Jersey—Long, Long Ago

Problem	Tentative Procedures and Activities	Children's References
		Children of the Colonies. *True Stories of New Jersey.* *America Builds Homes.*
	6. Plan a colonial menu. 7. Make a hornbook. 8. Dramatize a colonial classroom. 9. Make a mural of common scenes of colonial life. 10. Write a diary of a colonial boy or girl.	
How did the Revolutionary War affect New Jersey's history?	1. Reference work on the causes of the Revolutionary War. 2. Discussions on how the causes affected New Jersey. 3. Individual reports: oral or written, on the causes of the Revolutionary War. 4. Reference work on what happened in New Jersey during the Revolutionary War. 5. Make a historical map of New Jersey showing famous scenes of the Revolutionary War. 6. View and discuss filmstrip, "The American Revolution."	*New Jersey: A Story of Progress,* pp. 43–100. *Jersey's Story,* pp. 65–119. *An Elementary History of New Jersey,* pp. 44–92. *The Story of New Jersey,* pp. 109–129. *Twelve Days Til Trenton.* *True Stories of New Jersey.* *Your America.* *New Jersey.*
When did New Jersey become a state?	1. Discussions on New Jersey's "Coming of Age." 2. Compose a class booklet of "Jersey's Famous Leaders."	
Begin motivation for next unit, "New Jersey Today."		

How do I actually initiate the unit with my class? The following lesson illustrates the method used by the teacher to introduce the preceding unit, "New Jersey—Long, Long Ago."

INTRODUCTORY UNIT LESSON
(Grade 4)

OBJECTIVE

To encourage pupils to state questions which will form the framework of their unit on "New Jersey—Long, Long Ago."

BACKGROUND

During the previous week the teacher has tried to stimulate interest in New Jersey through:

> A display of pictures and books of the Lenni-Lenape Indians.
> A display of historical maps of New Jersey.
> A visit to the New Jersey State Museum.
> A showing of the slides, "New Jersey Long Ago."
> A showing of the film, "This is New Jersey."

PROCEDURE

Teacher: During the past week, I have noticed many of you looking at our bulletin board and several people have asked me questions about it. John, you asked me a question yesterday as we were going out on the playground. Do you remember what it was?

Child: I asked what Indians they were in the picture.

Teacher: Can anyone answer that question?

Child: I think the film said they were the Lenni Lenape Indians but I'm not sure.

Teacher: Does anyone else know?

Child: I think they're the Indians who used to live in New Jersey but I don't know their names.

Teacher: You're right, they are the Indians who lived in our state long ago. Since we're not sure of their names, suppose we try to find the answer in one of our reference books. I'll list this question on the board so we won't forget it. (*Writes "Who were the Indians who lived in New Jersey?"*)

Is there anything you would like to know about these Indians who may have lived on this actual spot many, many years ago?

Child: Did they really live right where we live now?

Teacher: Let's find out. (*Writes "Where did the Indians live in New Jersey?"*) Is there anything else you would like to know about them?

Child: That filmstrip we saw on Tuesday showed them living in log houses. I don't think that's right. I think they lived in tepees.

Teacher: I'm sure some Indians lived in tepees but apparently not all tribes. Let's add this question to our list. (*Writes "What were the homes of the New Jersey Indians like?"*) Anything else?

Child: I think it would be interesting to go exploring and see if we could find some things the Indians may have left in New Jersey.

Teacher: What kinds of things?

Child: Arrowheads and things like that.

Child: They didn't leave only *things*. They left names. My father told me
            Shabbakunk Creek is an Indian name.

Teacher: Why don't we try to make a list of things the Indians left us? I'll add
            that to our questions. Notice the word I'm going to use. (*Writes
            "What contributions did the Indians leave to us?"*)
            We've been talking a lot about the Indians of New Jersey but there
            were other early people, too. What did the man at the museum tell us?

Child: He told us a story about the early settlers of New Jersey.

Teacher: Do you remember who they were?

Child: I can't remember right now.

Teacher: Let's add that to our list. (*Writes "Who were the first colonists in New
            Jersey?"*)
            I'd like to add another question about the colonists. This is it. (*Writes
            "What was colonial life like in New Jersey?"*)

Child: Last summer my mother and father showed me lots of historic places in
            New Jersey. They took me to the route that Washington used to win
            the battles of Trenton and Princeton. We ought to talk about that,
            too. I can bring in a map showing all about George Washington and
            the war.

Teacher: What war was that?

Child: The Revolutionary War.

Teacher: Who would like to make up a good question about this part of New
            Jersey's history?

Child: What war was fought in New Jersey?

Teacher: John has already told us the answer to that. Will you tell us again,
            John? Is this right? Could we turn this question around and say this?
            (*Writes "What part did the Revolutionary War play in New Jersey's
            history?"*)

EVALUATION

Teacher: Will you look at the questions we have listed on the board? Are there
            any others you want to add? These are very large questions, and we
            will need to do a lot of work to find all of the answers. Will you think
            how we should organize our work to answer these questions, and we
            will talk some more about it tomorrow.

It should be understood that the previous lesson is a condensed version
of a thorough, animated, and well-rounded group discussion. It is important to note, moreover, that the planning was co-operative but was
consciously teacher-directed. The teacher, for instance, did not hesitate
to add a question to those suggested by the children. This is a valid democratic procedure in that it establishes the teacher as a member of the group.
By the same token, however, it should be noted that the problems the
teacher accepted from the pupils are similar, but not identical, with those
he had written previously on his unit plan. In this case, therefore, the
teacher's preplanning was flexible enough to permit modification according to the interests of the children. This is as it should be.

The following day the teacher began the discussion by calling attention to the following chart which he had posted on the bulletin board.

NEW JERSEY: LONG, LONG, AGO
Do You Know:

1. Who were the Indians who lived in New Jersey?
2. Where did the Indians live in New Jersey?
3. What were the homes of the New Jersey Indians like?
4. What contributions did the Indians leave to us?
5. Who were the first colonists in New Jersey?
6. What was colonial life like in New Jersey?
7. What part did the Revolutionary War play in New Jersey's history?

This was used as a basis for the next one or two lessons which concentrated upon planning co-operatively *how* the study was to be organized. Children discussed the pros and cons of committee work, individual reports, or team research and when they finally decided on a definite procedure, the unit was under way.

How do I culminate the unit? In the early days of unit teaching, it was fairly common to culminate each unit with an elaborate activity. Frequently, this took the form of programs for parents or assembly programs and involved numerous rehearsals, extensive preparations, and nervous exhaustion for the teacher. Fortunately, these "Hollywood" productions have decreased in popularity, and today educators place comparatively little emphasis upon the elaborate summarizing phase of the unit. Burton opposes extensive culminating activities on the grounds that, "units are not thought to terminate or culminate but to be continuous," although he readily admits that, "summary reports and exhibits may ... be made at any appropriate time." [18] Jarolimek also stresses the concept of the culminating activity only "as a summary—a procedure used to cast various aspects of the unit into relationship with one another and place a capstone on the entire project." He agrees that there is very little value to be derived from elaborate performances and states, "the trend recently has been away from elaborate exhibits and performances for the benefit of others." [19]

If the elaborate culminating activity has disappeared, what has taken

[18] *Ibid.*, p. 445.
[19] J. Jarolimek, *Social Studies in Elementary Education* (New York, The Macmillan Company, 1959), pp. 99–100.

its place? It has been succeeded by a series of summaries or evaluation sessions made at frequent intervals throughout the unit. With these and the activities which take place as part of the learning process, the actual termination of the unit may be no more than a general evaluation session in which pupils analyze the success of the unit, "clean up" unfinished business, and prepare for the next unit.

The reader should keep in mind that suggestions for developing the unit will be found throughout the following three sections. Because they are not necessarily limited to unit type teaching, however, and for purposes of emphasis, they have been discussed separately from this section.

SOCIAL LEARNING AND SOCIAL LIVING

Few of us would deny the fact that the most effective learning results from direct experience. It follows naturally that social learning may be realized only if numerous opportunities are provided for social experiences. Thus, social learning is a direct outcome of social living. Provision for social living and learning, of course, is not the complete responsibility of any particular curricular area but should permeate the entire school day. The playground, the cafeteria, the assembly program, and many others are valuable proving grounds for social experiences as are all types of curricular experiences within the classroom. As each child progresses through the school day by day, it is imperative that he be provided with numerous opportunities to function as an active, decision-making, responsible, and democratic member of a group. Through such action he should gain the social concepts, skills, and values which will enable him to relate himself constructively to his society. Specifically, these many group experiences should be designed and planned to enable pupils to:

1. *Learn techniques of co-operative thinking.* As Ellsworth points out, the school is usually the first group in which the child acts as a decision-making participant.[20] Before he enters school, he has been a member of home and community groups, both of which have been governed by adult decisions. The school should provide numerous opportunities for the child to contribute his ideas, his desires, and his opinions to a group decision. Children should have opportunity to arrive at decisions through voting and then to abide by the opinion of the majority. This does not mean that all action within the classroom should depend on majority opinion for this can be carried to a ridiculous extreme. The teacher who asks children to vote daily on whether they will play kick-ball or dodge-ball; whether they will play on the north or south playground; and who shall carry the ball to the playground, is wasting time and misinterpreting the democratic process.

[20] R. Ellsworth, "Suggested Emphases for the Elementary School Curriculum," *Social Education*, Vol. 17 (February, 1953), pp. 57–61.

(The authors remember one teacher who asked children to vote on whether or not they should all wear their coats when they went out to play!)

As a matter of fact, there are many times when simply abiding by the majority opinion is not the best solution to a disagreement. Ellsworth suggests that often it is preferable to combine the best elements from all alternatives rather than merely put the matter to a vote and expect all to resign themselves to the opinion of the majority.

2. *Appreciate the integrity of each individual.* The many social experiences provided by the elementary school should develop in each child a genuine appreciation of all individuals regardless of race, religion, nationality, or socio-economic background. As children find themselves members of various groups, such as the baseball team, the school patrol, the orchestra, the stamp club, or the art show committee, they should learn to know and to appreciate all members of the human race.

3. *Maintain a healthy balance between individuality and social adjustment.* Unfortunately, the strong emphasis placed today upon social living has been misinterpreted by some to mean that the individual should relinquish his uniqueness in favor of group conformity. Much has been written on this point, and there is little need to dwell upon it here. It should suffice to say that *mere conformity* is not the goal and never has been. Rather, the goal is to develop the maximum potential of *every* individual so that he can, in turn, make a positive and unique contribution to his society, within and beyond the classroom walls.

Social learning and social living are the responsibility of the entire school program. Nowhere, however, is there greater opportunity to implement this responsibility than in the social studies program. The following socialized procedures can be used to great advantage in the social studies and should help to achieve the three desired outcomes stated just above:

1. *Group and committee work.* Although most teachers readily admit the values of group and committee enterprises, they find it difficult to implement them in actual practice. Teachers who are dissatisfied with group work frequently claim that: (1) children waste too much time in committees and too little is actually accomplished; (2) there is usually an uneven distribution of work and responsibility; (3) it is difficult to maintain a work climate with several committees in session at once; and (4) it is impossible to evaluate the end results in terms of specific accomplishments. Unfortunately, these are all too true in classrooms where committee work is mistaken for general socialization and confusion. The remedy, however, is not to discard group work but rather to eliminate its weaknesses. Only a very carefully planned and organized program will do this.

From the time pupils enter school there should be numerous opportunities for group work in connection with all parts of the daily program. In the kindergarten, small groups may be chosen to feed the rabbit or make the applesauce. These groups increase in number and frequency as children

Committee work is an important phase of the social studies program.

mature, so that by the time they are in the intermediate grades, they have become accustomed to working in small groups. Such committees now become a vital part of the actual social studies program. These will still be, however, small, short-lived, and formed only to attack specific problems which arise in class discussions. For instance, in a class discussion on Mexico, the children were interested in a comparison of its yearly rainfall with that of their own state. A group of three children volunteered to do research on this topic and report their findings to the class. The teacher assisted this group; the report was given to the class; and the group disbanded. Similar opportunities for group work arise in every classroom, and a competent teacher will take advantage of them to develop valuable social skills.

The other type of group work, and one which is much more difficult to administer, is its use as the chief means of carrying on an entire area of study. In this case, every child is working on a committee and all committees will be meeting at once. In order to make this type of work successful, very careful planning and organization are needed. The following are specific suggestions for such planning and organization.

a. During the initial planning sessions, standards for group work should be formulated, and existing standards should be re-examined and re-evaluated. Discussion should be centered upon the specific purpose of each committee and the job of each individual in the group. The following two charts were developed through co-operative planning at the beginning of a study and were used frequently by pupils to evaluate their work.

Charts Developed through Co-operative Planning

A GOOD CHAIRMAN SHOULD	A GOOD COMMITTEE MEMBER SHOULD
Try to keep his committee on the track.	Listen to suggestions from other members.
Try to see that everyone is helping.	Co-operate with other members.
Give everyone a chance to talk.	Co-operate with the chairman.
Try not to be too "bossy."	Do his share of the work.
Help committee members if they have trouble.	Remember that there are other committees working.
Try to keep his committee from disturbing others.	Share materials with others.
Abide by majority decision.	Abide by majority decision.

b. Reference materials should be clearly designated and available. Many teachers organize a book shelf or a table with all books which are related to the problem. Some teachers carefully mark these books so that children will have no difficulty in choosing materials on their reading levels. A blue marker in the difficult references, a red one in others, and a yellow in those on a very easy reading level will help children locate books which they can really use.

The organizational chart on the next page was developed co-operatively by the teacher and the pupils and was used to guide the progress of a six-week study. Notice that it makes numerous provisions for different kinds of committees which vary in size and function.

This chart does not mean, of course, that the organization is inflexible. Naturally, it will be modified as the work develops. But it does serve to highlight the need for very careful organization on the part of the teacher and pupils in order to guarantee the success of the group work.

c. The size of committees in the elementary school should probably not exceed four or five members. Groups of this size more closely approximate the normal play and social groupings of young children and permit a higher degree of personal involvement than would be true in groups of eight or ten members.

MAIN PROBLEM: HOW DID THE INDIANS AND EARLY COLONISTS CONTRIBUTE TO NEW JERSEY'S HISTORY?

Problems I and II—*Whole Class*

References

The Story of New Jersey, pp. 5–34.
Jersey's Story, pp. 9–14.
An Elementary History of New Jersey, pp. 1–18.

Problem III—*Special Committee to Work in Library*

John H.	Andrew P.
Mary Q.	Flora S.

Problem IV—*Whole Class*

References

The Story of New Jersey, pp. 35–48.
Special Report
Hilda W.

Problem V—*Special Committee to Work in Library*

Billy G.	Peter S.
Alice P.	Sara A.
	Isabelle W.

Problem VI—*Committees*

Food	*Clothing*	*Homes*
Roland Q.	Joan S.	Dorothy D.
Bob G.	Nelson F.	Harvey B.
Tommy M.	Janet S.	Rudy B.
	Evelyn R.	Edward D.

Recreation	*Government and Leaders*
Susan P.	Georgia B.
Melody W.	Linda G.
Richard R.	Wallace D.
Tom Y.	Harold O.

Problem VII—*Whole Class*

References

New Jersey: A Story of Progress, pp. 47–85.
Special Books on Library Shelf

d. Committee work must be evaluated continually. At the close of each committee session a short evaluation may be held, with such questions as: "Which groups think they accomplished their jobs today? How many had trouble? Why? What must be corrected in order to have a better day tomorrow? What are our specific jobs for tomorrow?"

e. The teacher must make it a point to visit each committee during every work session. Unfortunately, some teachers feel that they can divide pupils into committees and then permit them to work independently for an hour or more. Nothing could be more disastrous. Committee work is a relatively new experience for even the most capable and mature elementary school children, and the wise teacher will give supervision, instruction, and guidance to each group daily.

f. The teacher should meet with each committee privately before it presents its report to the group. In this way he can check accuracy and completeness of material and can help to "polish" the finished report so that it will not be dull and boring when it is given to the rest of the class.

2. The class discussion. The importance of healthful social and emotional climates, the need for informal furniture arrangement, and the necessity of balanced participation to a successful discussion were presented in Chapter Five and will not be repeated here. In addition to these, a good social studies discussion will satisfy the following two criteria.

a. It must have direction. Usually the social studies discussion is centered upon one major problem or question. In the introduction to the lesson the teacher should be sure that this problem is clear to the children. It should be stated clearly and may frequently be written on the board so that there is no confusion regarding the direction of the discussion. If the discussion begins to wander from this main topic, the teacher can always call the attention of the class back to the written statement and thus prevent the aimless irrelevancies which often characterize the nondirectional discussion lesson.

b. Pupils must have an adequate content background in order to contribute to a discussion lesson. In addition to direction, a successful social studies discussion needs to have participants *who possess information that they can discuss.* If the children have not done any advance reading or preparation for the discussion lesson, obviously they will have very little to contribute. This is a major reason why many discussions deteriorate to the point where they are carried by only a few advanced members of the group. To summarize: In addition to all the requirements for any successful discussion, a worthwhile *social studies discussion* should have direction and advance preparation on the part of all participants.

3. Other socialized procedures. Another type of lesson used frequently in the social studies is devoted to oral reports of groups and individuals. These usually follow the committee work described earlier in this section.

Panel discussions or "Round Tables" may have some value in the upper elementary grades. These usually require a fairly high degree of skill, however, and may not be successful if they are tried with immature children. One has only to think of the adult "panel discussions" he has heard which were not discussions in any sense of the word to realize that even adults have a lot to learn about this technique.

Newer techniques such as "buzz groups" and "four-eight-groups" (divide into groups of four to discuss given topic for eight minutes) are occasionally used with success by elementary teachers.

Other socialized procedures such as games or TV quiz shows may be used as review lessons to add variety to the program. These and many more should be used by the creative teacher in order to make his social studies lessons as interesting and varied as possible.

A fairly new technique which is gaining popularity in the elementary school social studies program is role-playing. It appears to have particular merit in developing social values in young children. McCarthy reports that a comparison of the techniques of role-playing and discussion revealed that the former had several advantages:

> The role playing group had the greater number of reality oriented solutions, had more morally or socially acceptable best solutions, considered more consequences to their best solution and responded in more words than the discussion group. . . . The results of this study suggest that role playing be tried by teachers and children as a technique for exploring social values.[21]

ACTIVITIES AND MATERIALS

There is need for re-evaluation of activities in the social studies program. The traditional social studies program of fifty or more years ago was conducted almost exclusively through reading and recitation. Pupils read, listened, wrote answers, and "re-cited" back to the teacher the information he had given them earlier. Newer theories of learning and child development resulted in a reaction against this verbalistic and narrow approach in favor of an "activity curriculum" in which children "learned by doing." Unfortunately, like many other good ideas, this was misinterpreted by certain incompetent teachers who were interested only in "doing for doing's sake." In the classrooms of these teachers, children hammered, sawed, built tepees, Parthenons, and kayaks, and glued raisins and absorbent cotton on giant "product maps." Activity was synonymous with noise, bustle, and confusion.

Fortunately, most teachers today take a sounder view of the place of activity in the classroom. Michaelis lists the following activities which will "secure maximum participation on the part of each child and rich interaction with the environment."

[21] W. G. McCarthy, *A Comparison of Discussion and Role Playing As Techniques for Influencing Children's Thinking about Social Values,* Unpublished Doctoral Dissertation (Palo Alto, Calif., Stanford University, 1959).

Planning	Announcing	Block building
Discussing	Giving directions	Computing
Reading	Holding meetings	Measuring
Listening	Evaluating	Collecting
Writing	Drawing	Experimenting
Telling	Sketching	Demonstrating
Conversing	Modeling	Dramatizing
Observing	Illustrating	Pantomiming
Interviewing	Painting	Expressing
Note taking	Stenciling	rhythmically
Outlining	Sewing	Composing
Summarizing	Construction	Playing
Organizing	Soap carving	Singing
Reviewing	Processing	Sharing
Describing	Manipulating	Exhibiting [22]

In attempting to select an appropriate activity from such a list, the teacher should be guided by several criteria, among which the following are of primary importance.

1. *Is the activity worth the time it consumes?* The elementary school day is becoming more crowded each year, and teachers must weigh carefully the value of each activity included. This *does not mean* a return to the narrow program of the past. It means simply that teachers must constantly ask themselves, "From the point of view of the time spent, is this the *best way* my pupils can learn this concept?" For instance, is having children spend time making a flour paste map of western United States which, at best, will be inaccurate, as valuable as giving them a clear and accurate commercial map to study? Will the hours spent on building a Greek Parthenon from scrap lumber and broom handles result in a clearer concept of the splendor of Greek architecture than the showing of a twenty-minute film on the subject? These and similar questions must be weighed carefully before a teacher decides on the activities he will include in his program.

2. *Is the activity suited to the maturation level of the pupils?* In Chapter Four, mention was made of developing motor and intellectual skills suited to the maturation level of the individual. This point is very important in choosing the type of activity in the social studies. For instance, the primary grade teacher would be extremely unwise to ask her children to partake in activities which require a high degree of muscular co-ordination, such as constructing miniatures. Large play-houses, stores, and trains in which five- and six-year-olds can work, play, climb, or ride are much more desirable than the miniatures made from cigar boxes which appear in some classrooms. On the other hand, these and other activities which require manipulative ability, such as handling marionettes, may be very valuable for children of the intermediate or upper grades whose accessory muscles have developed.

[22] J. U. Michaelis, *op. cit.*, p. 100.

**The activity must be suited to the
maturational level of the child.**

Similarly, the activity should be suited to the level of intellectual skills developed by the group. For this reason, any worthwhile activity in, for instance, the sixth grade should require the use of problem-solving skills, critical reading skills, and map-reading skills. Too often a social studies project is merely a physical activity, such as constructing an Indian tepee in the corner of the room or making native drums out of gallon ice cream cartons and inner tubes. Unless these activities involve such skills as identifying problems, locating information, collecting data from various sources, or evaluating these sources, they probably contribute very little to an effective social studies program.

3. *Does the activity contribute directly to the development of social concepts and values?* A major use of activities is the clarification of concepts. For this reason, it is extremely important that the activity approximate somewhat the actual life situation. The miniature diorama of Holland with pipe-stem-cleaner people and plastic swans floating on mirror lakes will hardly give pupils an accurate concept of present-day Holland. Nor does the scene of Columbus at the court of Spain made in a "shadow-box" with scraps of calico and toothpick furniture create any genuine impression of the grandeur of Ferdinand's court. Such projects may certainly have value as expressive art—this is not being questioned. But will they have value as far as teaching social studies is concerned?

On the other hand, activities which closely resemble the real experience help give children clear understanding and genuine appreciation. Pottery-making, weaving, spinning, cooking and eating native foods, dramatizations, and role-playing are activities through which children will come close to the actual life experience. Most classroom activities, of course, are vicarious but, other things being equal, their value increases as they approach reality. A study of Mexico which involves making a piñata, wearing Mexican native dress, cooking and eating tortillas, learning native songs and dances, weaving serapes, and making pottery may have untold value for children as it brings them as close as possible to reality.

In addition to the criteria mentioned here, there are others which should be weighed in deciding upon appropriate social studies activities. The teacher would do well to consider carefully Drummond's statement that activities and projects are of significance and worth when they

1. have content of social importance.

2. provide opportunities for children to gain deeper and more accurate understandings of the community in which they live.

3. build sound attitudes toward people in differing groups.

4. help boys and girls develop increased understanding of democratic values and traditions.

5. provide opportunities for children to learn how to solve problems through critical thinking.

6. provide opportunities for children to develop and retain social interests.

7. help children to accept the fact that the world in which we live is changing rapidly and that change can be directed and controlled as intelligent people work together co-operatively.

8. help children to learn essential social studies skills such as interpreting maps and globes, and developing a sense of time and chronology.

9. can be provided only in a school environment which itself is desirable.[23]

The social studies program utilizes a variety of instructional resources and materials. Of all materials, the textbook is undoubtedly the one which is used most frequently by the majority of teachers. Furthermore, there are few who would question its value. Wesley and Adams, for instance, say that, "While the textbook has been misused, criticized, and denounced, it maintains an important status in American schools," [24] and Moffatt and Howell state that, "A fundamental tool found in every classroom and accessible to every pupil is the textbook." [25] Also, most authorities agree that today's textbook is more attractive, more readable, more accurate, and better illustrated than was true in the past. In other words, few would deny

[23] H. D. Drummond, "Projects and Activities in the Primary Grades," *Social Education,* Vol. 21 (February, 1957), pp. 59–62, 64.

[24] E. B. Wesley and M. A. Adams, *op. cit.,* p. 313.

[25] M. P. Moffatt and H. W. Howell, *Elementary Social Studies Instruction* (New York, Longmans, Green and Company, 1952), p. 298.

the value of the textbook and none would deprive it of a place in the classroom.

In spite of this, however, there are today several controversies which revolve around the social studies textbook. In general the most important of these are:

1. *What is the role of the textbook?* Barnes distinguishes between three distinct roles of the textbook.[26] The first of these is as an "assistant-teacher" in that it embodies all of the content and method needed to teach at a certain grade level. Since modern texts contain narrative content, questions, suggestions for pupil activities and projects as well as lesson plans for the teacher, some argue that they should really be considered as "assistant-teachers," although as Barnes points out, it often becomes a question of who is the assistant—the textbook or the teacher!

Secondly, the textbook may be used as the pupil's guide to the course of study in that it contains a complete and logical coverage of the material assigned for a particular school year.

Thirdly, the textbook is a reference book for the pupil. In many modern classrooms, the textbook is considered to be a valuable reference tool— but is *one of many such sources* and is used accordingly. This view of the textbook places full responsibility upon the teacher for planning his teaching-learning activities and places him in a true leadership role in which the textbook "follows" him—he does not "follow" the text. Acceptance of this role of the textbook brings us naturally to the next point of controversy, namely:

2. *Is a multiple-textbook approach preferable to the adoption of a single text?* The acceptance of the third role as stated above will obviously demand that this question be answered in the affirmative. This point of view is presented by Michaelis as follows:

> The use of multiple textbooks along with other reading resources is essential for several reasons. No single textbook can possibly present sufficient information to cover all questions and problems that come up in a unit of work. If concepts are to be deepened, and understandings are to be based on a solid background of information, varied sources must be used, not just a single textbook. Furthermore, because the wide range of reading ability among children in a typical class may extend over five or six grades, each child needs material on his reading level; if a single text is used you can be sure that several children are wasting time and learning little or nothing. In addition, different viewpoints can be presented and discussed when many types of reading material are used.[27]

The authors agree strongly with this viewpoint. They feel that no modern program can limp along relying solely upon a single text, regardless of its high quality and comprehensiveness. Considering the wide range of interests and reading levels in any average classroom, it would certainly

[26] F. P. Barnes, "The Textbook Dilemma," *Teachers College Record,* Vol. 55 (April, 1954), pp. 369–383.
[27] J. U. Michaelis, *op. cit.,* p. 315.

seem preferable to use multiple texts rather than to prescribe a single diet for all children. Furthermore, all textbooks should be supplemented by additional reference materials. A textbook is, by its very nature, skeletal and wide-sweeping and it *cannot* give the enrichment necessary for broad understanding and appreciation. Supplementary references such as encyclopedias, dictionaries, atlases, pamphlets, booklets, newspapers, periodicals, related fictional stories and books, biographies, autobiographies, and many more are needed to vitalize the social studies program. Obviously, many teachers are hard-pressed to know where and how to secure all of these. There are three solutions to the problem. The first is that a school staff should engage in careful and co-operative buying and sharing of books. Does the sixth-grade teacher lend the fourth-grade teacher some of his books and vice versa? Is there a central book collection from which all teachers may borrow? In addition, full utilization of all library facilities (school, local, county and state) can provide the teacher with many additional pupil references. In these, and many other ways, the teacher can broaden his program even beyond the multiple-textbook type which is advocated by the majority of educators today.

3. *Do modern social studies texts make adequate provision for the development of social concepts and values?* As was stated previously, the adequacy and accuracy of the factual content in today's texts are generally satisfactory. There is, however, some doubt as to whether social concepts and values are emphasized as much as they should be. This is, of course, difficult to determine and warrants the attention of more study than has been devoted to it in the past. In general, one might conclude from a study such as that of Samford's that textbooks are attempting to meet the modern objectives of social studies but are not succeeding as well as one might wish.[28] Manolakes, for instance, reports an investigation of the adequacy of existing textbooks in teaching one of the themes postulated by the National Committees on Concepts and Values, namely, "Recognition of the dignity and worth of the individual."[29] His findings include the following,

Concepts concerning the recognition of the dignity and worth of the individual were most frequently introduced and developed through verbalized statements of a descriptive and declarative type.

Concepts were treated in such a way as to suggest that they were a secondary or incidental consideration in the preparation of textbook materials.

Concepts were not adequately reinforced after the initial presentation.

Concepts related to the dignity and worth of the individual were often contradicted by the reliance of the authors on stereotypes in textual and illustrative materials.

[28] C. D. Samford, *op. cit.*, pp. 134–137.
[29] National Council for the Social Studies, *op. cit.*, p. 20.

Concepts related to the dignity and worth of the individual could be distorted through omissions.[30]

Some commercial materials may be used effectively in the elementary classroom. During recent years, many teachers have made increasing use of the large quantity of commercial material prepared by business concerns for use in the schools. Much of this material is attractive, usable, and relatively free from advertising emphasis. Although some teachers complain about the "junk" they receive from these business houses, most of them admit that a good deal of it has value. A common-sense attitude would be to use what one finds valuable and ignore or discard the rest.

The following is a list of some of the reference sources of free and inexpensive materials available to the elementary teacher.

Free and Inexpensive Materials for the Teaching of Social Studies in the Elementary Schools

Field Enterprises, Educational Division, *Sources of Free and Inexpensive Educational Material* (Chicago, Field Enterprises Educational Corporation, 1959).

Fowlkes, John G. and others, *Elementary Teachers Guide to Free Curriculum Materials* (Randolph, Wis., Educators Progress Service, Annual).

George Peabody College for Teachers, Division of Surveys and Field Studies, *Free and Inexpensive Learning Materials* (Nashville, George Peabody College, 1959).

Kenworthy, Leonard S. and Kenworthy, Thomas L., *Free and Inexpensive Materials on World Affairs* (Brooklyn, N.Y., Brooklyn College, 1959).

Miller, Bruce, *Sources of Free and Inexpensive Pictures for the Classroom* (Riverside, Calif., The Author, 1959).

Miller, Bruce, *Sources of Free Travel Posters and Geographic Aids* (Box 369, Riverside, Calif., 1960).

Miller, Bruce, *Sources of Free and Inexpensive Teaching Aids* (Box 369, Riverside, Calif., 1959).

Salisbury, Gordon; and Sheridan, Robert, *Catalog of Free Teaching Aids* (Box 943, Riverside, Calif., 1959).

Temple University, Curriculum Laboratory, *Something for Nothing for Your Classroom*, 3rd ed. (Philadelphia, Temple University, 1957).

Wood, Hugh B., *Sources of Free and Inexpensive Teaching Materials*, Curriculum Bulletin No. 56 (Eugene, Oregon, University of Oregon, n.d.).

An abundance of audio-visual materials should be used to vitalize the social studies program. The importance of audio-visual materials has been stressed repeatedly by the authors and there is little need to reiterate it here. The ever-increasing number of inexpensive audio-visual materials makes them available to every classroom teacher. The following brief list of some of the available catalogues should be helpful to the teacher in choosing materials suitable to his age and grade level.

[30] G. Manolakes, "Concept Development in Social Studies Textbooks," *National Elementary Principal*, Vol. 37 (May, 1958), pp. 25–27.

*Audio-Visual Materials for the Teaching of Social
Studies in the Elementary School*

BARBOUR, Harriot B. and FREEMAN, Warren S., *The Children's Record Book*
(New York, Oliver Durrell, 1947).
Children's Reading Service, Record Division *Annotated List of Phonograph
Records, Filmstrips, Rhythm Band Instruments,* Kindergarten-Senior High
School (1078 St. Johns Place, Brooklyn 13, N.Y., Children's Reading Service,
Annual).
Educational Film Guide (New York, H. W. Wilson Co., Cumulative to date).
Educators Guide to Free Films (Randolph, Wis., Educators Progress Service,
Annual).
Educators Guide to Free Filmstrips (Randolph, Wis. Educators Progress
Service, Annual).
Educators Guide to Free Tapes, Scripts and Transcriptions (Randolph, Wis.,
Educators Progress Service, Annual).
EISENBERG, Philip and KRASNO, Hecky, *A Guide to Children's Records* (New
York, Crown Publishers, 1948).
Filmstrip Guide (New York, H. W. Wilson Co., Cumulative to date).
HARTLEY, William H., *Guide to Audio Visual Materials for Elementary School
Social Studies* (Brooklyn, Rambler Press, 1950).

In summary, it would seem that there is little excuse for the barren and
sterile social studies programs one still sees in occasional classrooms. In
spite of the most limited budget, the elementary teacher has access to a
helpful supply of reading and nonreading instructional materials to enrich
his social studies program. It may take some work and some initiative to
secure some of these but the results are well worth the effort.

CURRENT AFFAIRS AND SOCIAL STUDIES SKILLS

**The teaching of current affairs is an important part of the social studies
program.** To develop an intelligent interest in and knowledge of current
affairs must be primary goals of the *entire* social studies program and
should not be confined to the fifth and sixth grades as has been frequently
true in the past. Even young children in the primary grades have some
awareness and knowledge of events on the national and international level.
There is obviously no reason why this awareness and knowledge should not
be strengthened through discussion and activities in the primary grade
classrooms. In the third and fourth grades this emphasis should be increased, and many teachers on this level devote a daily period to a discussion of current topics of widespread interest. Through such discussions in
all grades, the teaching of current events should be an integral part of the
social studies program.

To reinforce the class discussions, many teachers maintain a classroom
bulletin board on which is posted daily newspaper and magazine articles
of current interest. One teacher divided this board into four sections

labeled, *LOCAL, STATE, COUNTRY,* and *WORLD* and thus helped children to locate the scene of the event and to evaluate its significance. Another way of doing this is through a large outline map of the world on which strings are run from the clipping to the current location on the map. Still another teacher headed his bulletin board with the caption:

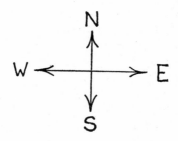

Spells News

and posted articles of widespread interest on this board. There is, of course, an endless variety of methods and devices which may be used. The important point is that consistent attention to current events and issues should be, in all grades, an integral part of the regular sequence of the social studies program.

The modern social studies program emphasizes the teaching of skills. The point was made earlier that there is a vast amount of content, drawn from many specializations, which is pertinent to the social studies program. It is obviously impossible to teach all this content; it is equally impossible to be sure that one always makes the best decision in choosing the content he *does* teach; and it is unquestionably impossible for children to retain *all* the content that is taught. It is, therefore, more important that children are taught the mastery of certain skills which they can use to locate, use, and evaluate content. One of the major trends in the social studies today, therefore, is the ever-increasing importance of the social studies skills on every grade level.

What are the social studies skills? It is, of course, impossible to make a positive classification for many of the skills discussed in other curricular areas become "social studies skills" when they are applied to the content of those disciplines. Skills of critical listening and effective speaking are probably applied to the social studies more than to any other field and are, therefore, essentially "social studies skills." The same is true of the skills of critical reading and study discussed in Chapter Six. Also, skills of writing and, most important, skills of problem-solving discussed in other chapters are very pertinent to this area and might justifiably be designated as "social studies skills." Obviously, therefore, the classification of skills in this field is a very broad one and will not be discussed here because of limited space and also because they have been treated in other chapters. In a slightly different category, however, are skills "for which the social studies have a unique responsibility for teaching but which other fields use." Within this category are commonly placed the skills of: (1) developing a sense of time and chronology and (2) developing a sense of geographic location and relationship.[31]

Both of these are fairly difficult concepts and have been traditionally delayed until the last year or so in the elementary school. Wesley and Adams, for instance, state that it is a "waste of time and effort to try to teach . . . involved concepts relating to the sphericity of the earth before Grade VI or VII." [32] In recent years, however, some writers have challenged this point of view, claiming that these concepts can be developed in young children if they are taught meaningfully. Davis, for instance, disagrees with the findings of earlier studies and states that children in the fourth, fifth, and sixth grades "significantly profited from instruction about geographic time zones." [33] It is, of course, difficult to generalize on the basis of limited research in this area, but present investigators appear to support the viewpoint expressed earlier in this chapter that children *know* and *can learn* more than we have previously thought. Most important, however, is the knowledge that these skills are cyclic in nature and must be developed over a several-year period. The three- or four-year-old, for instance, may have almost no concept of time. The present is the sole concern of this youngster, for he knows nothing of the future and cares little for the past. Gradually his sense of time deepens to give meanings to such expressions as *tonight, tomorrow,* and *last week.* Early school experiences should be geared toward helping him gain a concept of, and add to his vocabulary, such terms as *hour, minute, day, week, month,* and *season.* The calendar and the clock are indispensable teaching aids in these primary grades. Children use them to learn to tell time and also to "mark off" the passing days, record the daily weather, and in other ways to become aware of the passing of time. And as for "years," the young child's sole interest and concept are as they concern him alone. He knows that he is five years old and that his friend is six years old, but any age beyond that is difficult for him to comprehend. This was illustrated recently by a kindergartener who, in perfect seriousness, guessed his teacher's age as "around five hundred." Gradually, however, the maturity of the child permits him to relate ages and events, and to develop an initial vocabulary of time terms which have meaning for him.

A sense of chronology must also be developed over a several year period.

31 H. Carpenter, ed., *Skills in Social Studies,* 24th Yearbook (Washington, D.C., National Council for the Social Studies, 1953), p. 17.
32 E. Wesley and M. Adams, *op. cit.,* p. 307.
33 O. L. Davis, *op. cit.,* p. 173.

The teaching of current affairs is an important part of the social studies
program.

Usually the "time line" is considered one of the most valuable devices for
teaching chronology. A line drawn across the chalk board or a string across
the bulletin board upon which, at scaled intervals, pictures or notations
are posted is generally used. Other charts such as *Steps of History* or
Time Marches On can be used to give some concept of time and chronology.

The second unique social studies skill is the development of a sense of
place and location. This should be begun in the primary grades through
the use of a simplified globe and flat maps. For young children a small
(eight- or twelve-inch) globe in two colors is recommended. This can be
handled easily by them and can be used to develop such basic concepts
as: (1) the earth is round; (2) it is divided into land and water; and (3)
it makes a complete turn every twenty-four hours.

The first flat maps used in the primary grades should be those of the
child's immediate environment. Most first-grade teachers begin map study
by orienting the pupils to the school building during the early months of
the school year. A large piece of brown wrapping paper can be placed on
the floor, and teacher and pupils together can reconstruct the school plant.
To do this children will need to consider such questions as, "Where shall

A picture map of the community helps to develop map-reading skills.

The globe is an important aid in developing social studies skills.

we put the front door? Where is our room? On which side of us is Mr. Black's room? Where are the stairs? Where shall we put the lunchroom on our map?" Such a project is an excellent device for acquainting children with the school building; at the same time it introduces them to map reading.

In the second or third grades, this type of map reading can be expanded through having children make a map of their immediate community. On this they may locate their homes, the school, the stores, churches, and police station. Although scale will probably not be used as such, the teacher should try to develop elementary ideas of proportion and relationships. In these early years, also, it is important that all maps be placed correctly on the floor so that north is to the north.

As the child progresses through the grades, the more complex skills of map reading are introduced. Skills involving the ability to read the various types of scales, compute distances, and read map symbols are taught in the intermediate and upper grades. Considerable attention is given to locating places on maps and globes, beginning generally in about the third grade. From their "home-made" maps of the primary grades, children may progress to commercial maps of their state or country. These have a fascination, for children love to point out "where grandmother lives" or "where we went on our vacation." Jig-saw puzzles of United States maps are popular with intermediate grade children and have some value in acquainting them with the shape of their country and the location of the states.

In the upper grades, globes and world maps are used to develop more complex concepts of the earth and familiarity with the earth's grid system. In these grades, the children should gain a clearer understanding of the size and shape of the earth, the major water bodies and land masses, and earth-sun relationships. Vocabularies should include *continent, ocean, equator, rotation, revolution, zone, pole, axis,* and the names of the major earth divisions. In teaching the grid system it is extremely important that the teacher proceed slowly and make his teaching as meaningful as possible by using many visual aids and varied techniques. The concept of latitude, for instance, should be developed very thoroughly through a variety of methods before longitude is introduced. As a matter of fact, some educators advocate that a year elapse between teaching these two concepts in order to prevent confusion between them.

The reader will remember that Chapter Six distinguished between two levels of reading comprehension designated as "factual" and "interpretational." These two levels are as applicable to the reading of maps and globes as to words. In a recent fourth grade map reading lesson, for instance, the teacher encouraged his pupils to state certain *facts* which they arrived at from reading the map of Norway. These he listed in one column. He then went a step further and asked pupils to make *inferences* from these "map facts," which he listed in another column as follows:

GEOGRAPHIC FACTS	INFERENCES DRAWN FROM FACTS
Norway is in the northern latitudes.	Norway is cold.
Norway is covered with mountains.	Norway has short summers, long winters.
Norway is on a peninsula.	Farming is difficult.
Norway has a ragged coastline.	Norway uses the sea.
Norway's cities are located in the south.	Transportation is difficult.
	The sea is used for transportation.
	The sea affects the climate of Norway.

Through a lesson of this type, children were helped to develop the skill of "*interpreting* the map as well as the skill of *reading* it." Furthermore, as they listed their "inferences" they became aware of the necessity of checking the validity of these inferences in other sources, thus involving another major skill of critical thinking.

In summary, the teaching of the social studies skills is a previously neglected but presently emphasized feature of the social studies program. It is a broad and complex responsibility of the modern elementary teacher, but its importance to an effective social studies program cannot be overestimated.

Summary

The first part of this chapter was devoted to an examination of statements of objectives. It was stated that the major goal of the social studies is the development of a constructive relationship between the individual and society. This major aim is often defined in terms of specific understandings, skills, and attitudes or in terms of desired behavioral outcomes. Samples of both approaches were included in the discussion.

The problem of scope, content, and sequence was examined at some length. Various plans for determining content were reviewed with the conclusion that, in general, there is a definite similarity among them. The popular plan of "widening horizons" used for determining sequence was mentioned, and it was noted that this plan is presently being challenged by some on the theory that it does not take into account the wider interests and multiplied experiences of present-day youngsters.

A section on unit teaching was included to answer questions asked by many teachers and to present a sample outline of a unit plan as well as an illustrative lesson for initiating the unit.

The development of social learning through social experiences was a major emphasis of this chapter. It was stated that many group experiences should be designed to help pupils to: (1) learn techniques of co-operative thinking, (2) appreciate the integrity of each individual, and (3) maintain a healthy balance between individuality and social adjustment. Suggestions for conducting such socialized procedures as committee work, class discussions, and others were offered.

The need for re-evaluating social studies projects and activities was stressed. Criteria for evaluation were offered. The textbook, as a social studies tool, was examined at some length, and the need for supplementing its use with many other references and learning aids was strongly emphasized.

The last section was devoted to a discussion of the importance of teaching current affairs and social studies skills in all grades in the elementary school. The skills considered to be unique to the social studies were: (1) developing a sense of time and chronology and (2) developing a sense of geographic location and relationship. Suggestions for teaching these were offered.

STUDENT PROJECTS

1. Describe a typical social studies unit in any grade. Show how it includes elements from all the fields now considered to be social studies.

2. Find out what regulations your state has concerning the adoption of a social studies text. How does it compare with neighboring states?

3. Study several new or very recent social studies curriculum guides. Can you determine what "plan" has been used for specifying the scope and sequence of the content at each grade level? Do you find any strong preference for any one plan?

4. Try to visit an elementary school for an entire day. Make a list of the social studies activities you see in progress at all grade levels. Evaluate these in terms of the criteria presented in this chapter.

5. Talk with an experienced upper-grade teacher. Try to find out ˙ ᴐw he uses committee work in his social studies program. What does h the main values of committee work? What does he feel are the main p presents?

6. You are a sixth-grade teacher. Compose an objective test to appraise youɪ pupils' concepts of time and chronology. What are your conclusions?

7. Explain in detail the procedures, techniques, activities, and devices you plan to use to give your sixth-grade pupils a clear understanding of latitude; of longitude.

8. Describe how you plan to teach current affairs to your fourth-grade class this year. Will you use a separate period? How will it be conducted? What other ways will you use?

9. Write a lesson plan illustrating clearly how you would use a social studies text in the "third role" described in this chapter.

10. Criticize the assignment, "For tomorrow, read from page 162 to 170 in your social studies textbook." There are *at least* six basic reasons why such an assignment should *never* be used in an effective social studies program. Can you identify them? Can you identify still others?

11. It has been stressed that television is a main source of information for modern-day children. However, as someone has said, it is a source of misinformation as well. What implications does this statement have for your social studies teaching?

CHAPTER 10

Science is fun.
Edward Teller

INTO THESE THREE WORDS, one of the world's greatest modern scientists has telescoped the boundless natural appeal of the world of science. It is fun! Fun to wonder about things: about why the sky is blue, how fish breathe, and what makes an echo; about jet planes, atomic submarines, and rocket ships. Fun to try out things to see what will happen: will our plants grow in the dark? Will the water in the dish evaporate if we put salt in it? If and before ? What will happen to a lighted candle if we cover it with and cover answers: so *that's* why the milk bottle breaks on a standing a can collapses when we take the air out; why a compass points north; and why certain foods are good for us. Yes, figure out why things go wrong! Why didn't the mold grow before; why did the lights go out during the storm last night; did the fish die; and why didn't the eggs hatch?

This is science. Here is one area of the elementary program which should not keep the teacher awake nights worrying how to stimulate interests and curiosities, for these come built into the child at birth. Fortunately, the child has them almost intact when he appears at the kindergarten door the first day of school. Fortunately, he will still have them when he leaves the elementary school, *provided* each of his teachers considers it his definite responsibility to nurture their growth. A fairly easy task? It is and it isn't. A brief examination of the present status of science teaching in the nation's elementary schools will reveal some of the progress made and problems yet to be faced in its accomplishment.

PRESENT STATUS OF ELEMENTARY SCIENCE

Elementary science is a twentieth-century innovation. The subject which you know today as elementary science has been part of the elementary school curriculum for approximately thirty years. Its beginnings, however, are buried deep in the history of American education. A very slight start was made in the late eighteenth century when some literature for children was published which was concerned with observations and explanations of natural phenomena. It was not until a century later, however, that a few outstanding educators attempted to include elementary science as part of the school curriculum. Craig names Jackman, author of the 1904 Yearbook of the National Society for the Scientific Study of Education (later, the National Society for the Study of Education), as the father of elementary science and comments upon his being the "connecting link between the early writers of children's literature and the modern elementary science" program.[1] The interest of Jackman and others in the comprehensive aspects of elementary science, however, was totally eclipsed around the turn of the century by the popular subject, *Nature Study*, with its emphasis on formalized method, a narrowed concept of science, and sentimentalized aesthetic values. The general tendency to overemphasize this subject is revealed in the following quote from a writer of that period.

No subject in the educational world today is experiencing the undue inflation . . . that is to be seen in this one in many parts of the United States, and, as a consequence . . . we are going Nature Study mad . . . authors and publishers by the score are using the word "nature" as though it were a talisman to insure success with all things. There have appeared Nature Study Readers, Nat Study Song Books, Nature Study magazines and Nature Study articles r   is kinds.[2]

Inevitably, teachers became tired of the fetish which was mad   this subject and, as a result, it declined rapidly, leaving a void which was not filled until the late 1920s and 1930s when the present concept of elementary science gained a foothold in the elementary school curriculum. The early work of Craig and others at this time gave impetus to the movement, as did the publication of the Thirty-first Yearbook of the National Society for the Study of Education which was devoted to a discussion of a comprehensive science program from kindergarten through grade twelve.[3] From that time on, science in the elementary school grew slowly but steadily until a few years ago when international developments made it the focus of nation-wide attention and interest. Today, there is universal agreement that science should occupy a prominent and integral place in the curriculum of the elementary school.

There are certain distinguishable trends in science instruction today.

[1] G. S. Craig, "Elementary School Science in the Past Century," *The Science Teacher*, Vol. 24 (February, 1957), p. 13.

[2] H. A. Surface, "Nature Study: Is Nature Study a Fad?" *Popular Educator*, Vol. 17 (January, 1900), p. 204.

[3] National Society for the Study of Education, *A Program for Teaching Science*, 31st Yearbook, Part I (Bloomington, Ill., Public School Publishing Company, 1932).

The direction in which elementary science is presently moving is distinguished by the following trends:

1. *Science is becoming increasingly important in the entire educational program.* At the present time, there are still many elementary schools which do not have adequate science programs. Fortunately, there is reason to believe that their number is decreasing daily. The launching of the Russian satellite in 1957 succeeded in doing what many of our foremost educators had been trying to do for years; namely, to convince the lay public of the need for a dynamic and comprehensive science program in all elementary and secondary schools. As a result, much time, effort, and money have been spent, and are presently being spent, on revising old science programs or instituting new ones. True, some of these are "crash programs" which were born out of panic and are already beginning to wane. Many more, however, are well-organized, well-articulated, and well-implemented programs of sound educational value. There is every reason to hope and believe that this trend will continue and accelerate in the future.

2. *The modern elementary program emphasizes science as a way of thinking and as an investigation of problems rather than as an accumulation of facts and answers.* Zirbes comments upon the changing concept of science as being

no longer conceived as a highly organized body of collected knowledge as viewed specialists, but more or less as a study, as a way of coming to understand why s happen as they do, what man can do with natural resources, what we can live by, how we can be more intelligent about living, so that we are not de. l as often or as easily, so that we can predict, in other words, in terms of know uses and effects, and plan and act accordingly.[4]

3. *The modern elementary science program is more comprehensive than that of the past.* The antiquated science programs of the past concentrated almost solely upon the biological sciences. This was a "hang-over" from the *Nature Study* idea of 1900 and was also due to the mistaken notion that these sciences were more interesting and more easily understood by young children. Actually, there exists no research which demonstrates the validity of this theory and, on the contrary, empirical evidence indicates that interests of young children are directed toward many fields of science. As a result, such topics as magnetism, light, sound, the universe, and weather are common in most elementary grades, and some teachers experiment with such modern units as *air/space travel* or *atomic energy*.

4. *There is increasing emphasis placed upon the use of activities, resources, and materials in a vitalized science program.* Yesterday's science program, if it existed at all, was often confined to reading the textbook and perhaps examining a few stuffed specimens to which the school had fallen heir at one time or another. With this kind of science program, it was

[4] L. Zirbes, "Thoughts on the Education of Science Teachers for Today's Schools," *Science Education*, Vol. 42 (October, 1958), p. 283.

small wonder that, as research has shown, children's science interests dwindled as they progressed through the grades. Today, this type of science program is being replaced by one which uses many types of reading materials, audio-visual aids, community resources, and learning activities. Fortunately, there is a wealth of these from which the elementary teacher may choose. This richer, fuller, and vitalized program is characteristic of all elementary schools in which adequate instruction is now being offered.

5. *Science experiences are determined in accord with present-day knowledge of child growth and development.* Many research studies have been made of children's scientific interests as well as their abilities to generalize and conceptualize scientific principles. These are used in many school systems as one basis upon which the science curriculum may be constructed.

6. *There is growing awareness of the need to articulate the science program at all levels.* With the elementary school including more science in its program, there has arisen a need to articulate this work more closely with the program of the junior and senior high schools. Many forward-looking systems are now facing up to this problem by appointing vertical science committees composed of elementary and secondary teachers to plan a well-articulated, smoothly co-ordinated science program for the kindergarten through the twelfth grade.

In general, then, these are the basic, far-reaching trends which appear to characterize the modern elementary school science program. It inevitable, of course, that these trends are accompanied by some formidable problems. The most serious of these are summarized b

There are several major problems which must be overcome in order to improve the elementary science program. These may be mentioned briefly as:

1. *Teacher preparation.* Almost without exception, studies list inadequate teacher education and background as a primary drawback in improving the science program. Typical of these investigations is one by Mallinson and Sturm, who report that half of the student-teacher population which they questioned, "believed themselves inadequately prepared to teach elementary science." [5] In general, this feeling of inadequacy is caused by: (1) insufficient high school and college preparation in science, and (2) preparation which lacked the breadth of knowledge necessary for elementary science teaching. As a result, many teacher education curricula are being revised to include more science courses and a wider choice of courses in many fields of science. The preservice preparation of the elementary teacher should equip him not only with the necessary science content, but also with the ability to develop a series of exciting learning experiences

[5] G. G. Mallinson and H. E. Sturm, "The Science Backgrounds and Competencies of Students Preparing to Teach in the Elementary School," *Science Education*, Vol. 39 (December, 1955), p. 405.

which will challenge the science-oriented youngsters in our modern schools. Milgrom believes that the preparation of the elementary teacher should enable him to learn

. . . how to keep alive curiosities.
. . . how to stir new wonderment.
. . . how to arouse interests.
. . . how to whet science appetites.
. . . how to get young minds to think and reason.
. . . how to initiate investigations.
. . . how to devise intriguing experiments.
. . . how to develop problem-solving skills.
. . . how to make effective use of community resources.
. . . how to relate science to familiar elements in pupils' lives.
. . . how to preserve and nurture the inner drives that impel children to search for understanding.[6]

A number of school systems have instituted in-service programs of workshops and institutes designed to equip the teacher with the necessary background he needs. Also, the employment of a science consultant to work with elementary teachers has been a step toward the solution of this problem. Such in-service education will be necessary in increasing amounts in the future if the elementary science program is to meet the standards of superior instruction now prescribed for it.

2. *Lack of equipment and facilities.* This is a second major problem which is invariably mentioned as a handicap to effective science teaching. Piltz [7] reports the lack of physical facilities (including work and storage space, and equipment) as a major difficulty recognized by teachers as does Hubler [8] who found this to be the major problem mentioned most frequently by the teachers he surveyed and interviewed. Suggested solutions for this problem are offered in the section on materials and equipment in the latter part of the chapter.

3. *Lack of agreement on type of curriculum.* It is extremely difficult to determine a general consistency of thought regarding the type, scope, and sequence of experiences which should comprise the science program in the elementary school. Details of this topic are discussed later in the chapter.

OBJECTIVES OF ELEMENTARY SCIENCE

Many individual teachers and elementary school faculties are dissatisfied with their present science programs. They recognize the increasing im-

[6] H. Milgrom, "Implications of Research in Elementary School Science Education," *School Science and Mathematics*, Vol. 57 (November, 1957), p. 601.

[7] A. Piltz, *An Investigation of Teacher-Recognized Difficulties Encountered in the Teaching of Science in the Elementary Schools of Florida*, Unpublished Doctoral Dissertation (Gainesville, University of Florida, 1954).

[8] C. Hubler, "Teaching Materials for Elementary School Science," *Science Education*, Vol. 34 (October, 1950), pp. 218–224.

portance of science, and they wish to replace their present spotty and ineffectual program with one of value and direction. Their first problem is to formulate and define objectives which they want to serve as directional goals. How and where do they start?

First of all, it is important to realize that science objectives are closely related to the general goals of education. A re-examination of the objectives listed in Chapter Two will help the teacher to realize that all of these are directly applicable to science education. For instance, importance of the individual; consideration of unique needs and abilities of all pupils; and development of productive citizens for a democratic society are certainly goals of science teaching just as they are for all education. In addition to contributing toward these general educational goals, however, science has an additional responsibility to develop certain skills, appreciations, and understandings which can best be done within its own discipline. Today, these are fairly well-established for they have been defined repeatedly by many educators in recent years with few radical changes or differences of opinion. A fairly recent approach is interesting in that it derives the purposes of science education from: (1) the prevailing culture, (2) the nature of children, and (3) the nature of science. The following is an attempt to summarize briefly the excellent discussion of these three classifications contained in the original source:

SCIENCE PURPOSES DERIVED FROM THE CULTURE

To help children learn what they need to know from the world's storehouse of knowledge which, in recent years, has embraced more and more science.

To acquaint children with the scientific methods of investigation by which this knowledge may be acquired and tested.

To help children understand the relation of scientific knowledge to its social and technological applications.

SCIENCE PURPOSES DERIVED FROM THE NATURE OF CHILDREN

To nurture and further stimulate the curiosity of children which leads them to want to know, to explore, and to investigate.

To help children understand the principles of health, hygiene, nutrition, genetics, and energy changes in order to meet their physical and psychological needs intelligently.

To help children learn how to learn.

SCIENCE PURPOSES DERIVED FROM THE NATURE OF SCIENCE

To help children develop concepts which will enable them to know and understand their world.

To help children apply these concepts in explaining or describing new situations.

To help children test ideas in their own experience and understand the difference between this kind of validation of knowledge and the authoritarian or mystical explanations.

To help children develop attitudes consistent with the spirit of science and to appreciate the importance of these attitudes.[9]

In summary: there appears to be a high degree of consistency among the many statements of objectives for elementary science. It is interesting to note that educators have been much more successful in determining the goals of science education than they have been in reaching them or in formulating a definite program for their implementation. Some of the problems involved in this task are discussed in the following section.

TYPE, CONTENT, AND SEQUENCE OF THE ELEMENTARY SCIENCE PROGRAM

It is extremely difficult to appraise accurately the present-day science program because of wide variations which exist in opinion and present practice. Invariably studies which are made of existing programs report the lack of any consistent curriculum pattern. Bruns and Frazier, for instance, investigated the science programs of twenty-one large city systems and discovered, "no single clear-cut pattern that can be seen as typical of even a small number of these major school systems." [10] Particularly this is true of the *type* of science program now in operation. Schools vary all the way from those which have a very incidental and haphazard program to those which follow a highly structured one. In general, however, the type of program will fall into one of three categories.

There are three common types of science programs now in existence. First, there is the carefully planned and well-organized program which suggests specific content and experiences for each grade. In this type of program, science is considered as important as any other curriculum area. Time is provided for it in the daily schedule; the necessary money for adequate supplies and equipment is allocated from the school budget; and a sequential program of content is carefully assigned to each grade level. At times, science is taught as a separate subject. At other times, when it is feasible and natural, it is integrated with other curriculum areas. In any case, the program of science is well-planned, carefully structured, and equally important to all other curriculum fields.

A second type includes science only as it can be integrated with such major curriculum areas as social studies, mathematics, language arts, or health and safety. In a social studies unit, for instance, on discovery and exploration, some time is devoted to a discussion of the popular fifteenth- and sixteenth-century concepts concerning the earth and universe. The

[9] G. O. Blough, et al, "Developing Science Programs in the Elementary Schools," *Rethinking Science Education*, The National Society for the Study of Education, 59th Yearbook, Part I (Chicago, University of Chicago Press, Copyright, 1960, by the University of Chicago), pp. 112–115.

[10] R. F. Bruns and A. Frazier, "Scope and Sequence of Elementary School Science," *School Science and Mathematics*, Vol. 57 (October, 1957), p. 560.

class might also study and construct some of the crude scientific instruments which played an important part in the history of navigation. In this type of program, science is given a place in the curriculum, but it is more or less an appendage to the "more important" curriculum areas.

The third type of program considers science as an "incidental" learning, the direction of which is determined primarily by children's interests and daily experiences. A child in sharing period, for instance, shows his collection of shells which he has accumulated during a summer at the beach. The class appears to be extremely interested; other children volunteer to bring in shells; and the following few days or weeks are devoted to a study of maritime life.

The "ideal" program utilizes all three types of approaches. Obviously, all of these programs have many advantages. A well-planned sequence of science learnings is extremely worthwhile; on the other hand, science as it arises in other curricular areas or from the genuine interests of children is also valuable. Perhaps the only defensible solution is to combine all three approaches, and this is precisely what is now being done in some school systems. Mallinson's survey of recent studies devoted to this topic concludes that

> These studies seem to indicate that "ideal" programs of elementary science devolve on a continuous development of science experiences throughout the grades, and on science activities that have been planned definitely ahead of time but with the opportunities for flexibility.[11]

This flexibility, therefore, should permit the teacher to integrate science with other curricular areas *and* to take advantage of children's spontaneous interests while, at the same time, the planned program guarantees a continuity of learnings necessary for sound science education.

The content of the science program is derived from a variety of sources. The Fifty-ninth Yearbook of the National Society for the Study of Education states that the content of the most successful elementary science programs is derived from a consideration of:

> (*a*) the *child,* with his emotional, intellectual, and physical needs; (*b*) the *environment,* both natural and man-made, in which the child lives; (*c*) the *sciences,* especially biology, chemistry, physics, and astronomy; and (*d*) the *total school program,* as it relates to the needs of *society* for informed citizens, capable of participating in social living.[12]

Let us examine each of these.

It will be remembered that one of the objectives mentioned previously was the working out of a science curriculum based upon the study of child growth and development. In general, science educators have directed their

---

[11] G. G. Mallinson, "Survey of Research in Elementary School Science Education," *School Science and Mathematics,* Vol. 57 (November, 1957), p. 597.

[12] G. O. Blough, et al., *op. cit.,* p. 119.

efforts toward investigations of: (1) the interests, (2) the concepts, and (3) the attitudes of children.

The studies which have been made of children's interests show very little consistency, probably because interests are so dependent upon the environment and previous experiences of the individual. Young discovered that the universe was the major interest of fourth-, fifth-, and sixth-grade pupils, with other main interests listed as animals, the earth, growth, and weather. Some interest was also expressed in aviation and energy by certain groups. Little interest was indicated in plants or machines.[13] In a study of a similar age group, Von Qualen and Kambly reported the science interests, as revealed by choices of reading material, to be ancient animals, science and industry, transportation, general science, living animals, electricity, and magnetism.[14] While these and other studies indicate no definite constellation of interests at any specific grade level for all children, it is, nevertheless, extremely important that a school faculty or individual teachers attempt to determine pupil interests which can be used as springboards for the science program of a particular school or classroom. These should be carefully studied in planning the science program.

Other studies have been concerned with the science concepts held by children at various age levels. Of these, Navarra's intensive study of the expanding concepts of one child over a three-year period is especially revealing and significant.[15] A different type of study in this category is that done by Nelson, who investigated the concepts of light and sound held by intermediate-grade children, and concluded that "children of today may be able to understand more science than is now acknowledged." [16]

A third category of studies deals with an investigation of children's attitudes. Brown, for instance, discovered that the scientific attitudes of rural pupils were slightly superior to those of urban or suburban pupils.[17] He also reported that the gain in scientific attitude between fifth- and eighth-grade pupils was less than the gain of information about science, which if generally true has serious implications for the elementary teacher as to where he should place the emphasis in today's science program.

The few studies mentioned are indicative of the research now being directed toward the implications for science teaching of child growth and

[13] D. A. Young, *Factors Associated with the Expressed Science Interests of a Selected Group of Intermediate Grade Children,* Unpublished Doctoral Dissertation (Evanston, Ill., Northwestern University, 1956).

[14] V. D. Von Qualen and P. Kambly, "Children's Interests in Science as Indicated by Choices of Reading Materials," *School Science and Mathematics,* Vol. 45 (December, 1945), pp. 798–806.

[15] J. G. Navarra, *The Development of Scientific Concepts in a Young Child: A Case Study* (New York, Teachers College, Columbia University, 1955).

[16] P. A. Nelson, "Concepts of Light and Sound in the Intermediate Grades," *Science Education,* Vol. 44 (March, 1960), p. 144.

[17] S. B. Brown, "Science Information and Attitudes Possessed by California Elementary School Pupils," *Journal of Educational Research,* Vol. 47 (March, 1954), pp. 551–554.

development. It is true that present evidence is insufficient and inconsistent, but teachers may be hopeful that future studies will add to our knowledge of what science experiences are most suited to the elementary school pupil.

Second, the content of the science program should be drawn from the pupils' immediate environment. Nearby rivers, lakes, parks, industries, farms, dams, and all other facets of the child's environment should be "built into" the science curriculum. The paving of the school parking lot, the installation of the new oil-burner, the treasured fossil found on the class trip, or the crisis of the sour milk at lunch are all parts of the child's environment which hold promise for science learnings. Science truly surrounds the youngster. The good elementary school takes advantage of this fact.

Third, the content of the science program is drawn from many science fields. It will be remembered that this was mentioned earlier in the chapter as one of the modern trends of elementary science. It is particularly noticeable in the extent to which elementary science is now derived from the physical and earth sciences.

Last, the science content is drawn from other curriculum areas. From health, safety, social studies, language arts, arithmetic, and the creative arts comes much of the content which comprises the present-day science program.

Elementary science comprises three general areas of subject matter. The content of science for the elementary school is usually divided into the three basic areas of: (1) living things, (2) the earth and universe, and (3) matter and energy. These are, of course, subdivided and classified in varying ways according to individual school systems. Dubins classifies the content of several courses of study developed between 1940 and 1952 into five areas of content. The emphasis in rank order on these in the guides examined was:

> The Earth
> Living Things
> Man's Control of His Surroundings
> Energy
> The Heavens [18]

Other studies show differences in emphasis but not much in the organization of the basic content. This is not true, however, of the sequential pattern of content, for on this there appears to be no widespread agreement.

The sequence of science learnings meets with little agreement. One of the major problems facing curriculum workers today is the allocation of science content to specific grade levels. Some schools simply assign specific topics or units to each grade. Another plan is to treat one large topic on

[18] M. I. Dubins, "Curriculum-Makers' Emphases in Elementary School Science, 1940–1952," *Science Education,* Vol. 43 (October, 1959), p. 321.

successive grade levels, progressing from simple to complex concepts. Thus, "magnetism" may possibly be studied in every grade with the primary grades developing simple concepts of "Magnets pick up some things" to the upper grades, "Electricity can create a magnetic force which will run a motor."

A sequence of expanding concepts related to *Living Things* is illustrated in the list below, which is a condensation of the original source:

CONCEPTS SUGGESTED FOR THE KINDERGARTEN

Animals must be treated kindly.
Animals have babies.
Animals must have food.

CONCEPTS SUGGESTED FOR THE PRIMARY GRADES

Some animals sleep all winter.
Some animals migrate.
Some animals live on stored food.

CONCEPTS SUGGESTED FOR THE MIDDLE GRADES

Some animal life goes through different stages as it grows.
There are certain conditions all plants and animals need in order to live.
There are many varieties of ways animal life produces new animal life.

CONCEPTS SUGGESTED FOR GRADES SEVEN AND EIGHT

Some animals have not been able to adapt themselves to their living conditions.
There are plants and animals called parasites that depend on other living things for their existence.
Some animal life passes through stages when it does not have the physical appearance of its parent.[19]

Another method of determining sequence of content for each grade level is that illustrated in the Thirty-first Yearbook of the National Society for the Study of Education. This method is to take a science *principle* (a basic truth usually stated in a declarative sentence) and assign it or its sub-principles to an appropriate grade level. Since then, many studies have been made in an attempt to determine: (1) what principles of science are suited to the comprehension of elementary school children, and (2) at what specific grade or age level these are best understood. Robertson's list of 113 principles of science considered by experts to be suitable for elementary school science is an attempt to answer the first of these. This study has been used as a guide by many school systems in developing science curricula. Sample principles found by Robertson to be suitable are:

All matter is composed of single elements or combinations of several elements and can be analyzed by chemical processes and divided into these units.

[19] *Teaching Science* (Trenton, N.J., New Jersey State Department of Education, Division of Curriculum and Instruction, 1957), pp. 16–19.

All substances are made up of small particles called molecules, which are alike in the same substance but different in other substances.

All matter may change its state by absorbing or releasing energy.

Compression of a gas increases its pressure.

The environment acts upon living things and living things act upon the environment.

Certain energy forms travel in waves.[20]

Many other studies have been made in an attempt to determine the exact grade level for a certain principle. For instance, Oxendine attempted to determine the grade in which the principle, "Sound is produced by vibrating material" could best be taught.[21] He discovered that this principle was, in general, too difficult for the fourth-graders in his study but that the sixth-graders were ready for it. The value of such research probably lies more in the illustration of techniques rather than in conclusive findings, for it is difficult to generalize that "all children everywhere" would be ready for the same science principle at the same stage of development. This means that the responsibility for determining sequence lies ultimately with the local school system.

In summary, the problem of assigning topics, concepts, or principles to specific grades is one which plagues most people in the field. Wide variations exist; research findings are inconclusive and contradictory. Mallinson summarizes the situation as follows: "One of the major problems of elementary science concerns the grade placement of certain areas of science and certain principles associated with them."[22]

DEVELOPING SCIENTIFIC ATTITUDES

The elementary teacher has heard repeatedly that his task is to develop "scientific attitudes." Specifically, what attitudes are meant? There is, of course, no hard-and-fast classification, for the term is an omnibus one which includes such characteristics as open-mindedness, objectivity, persistence, desire for knowledge, questioning, curiosity, and creativity. It is interesting to note that some of these are the "natural attitudes" of children. Hence, one frequently hears the statement that children are "natural" scientists. This is not entirely true, however, for some of the scientific attitudes are antithetical to the nature of children. The teacher, therefore, has a two-fold task. First, he must nurture and strengthen those scientific attitudes which children (because they *are* children) already possess, and

20 M. L. Robertson, "Selection of Science Principles Suitable as Goals of Instruction in the Elementary School," *Science Education,* Vol. 19 (April, 1935), pp. 65–70.
21 H. G. Oxendine, *The Grade Placement of the Physical Science Principle, "Sound is Produced by Vibrating Material" in Relation to Mental Age,* Unpublished Doctoral Dissertation (Boston, Boston University, 1953).
22 J. B. Mallinson, "Survey of Recent Research in Elementary School Science Education," *School Science and Mathematics,* Vol. 58 (November, 1958), p. 607.

Children experience the "thrill of discovery."

secondly, he must develop slowly but carefully the scientific attitudes which will come only with maturity, widening experience, and *proper training*.

Scientific Attitudes Compatible with the Nature of Children:

1. *The "thirst for comprehension."* Without exception, scientists are distinguished by their questioning minds. They want to know for the sake of knowledge itself. This is the wonderful quality which Albert Einstein called the "thirst for comprehension." He added that most children have it; but few adults. This is sad but true! Children *do* have a natural thirst for comprehension. They *do* question. They *do* want to know. Not for the sake of the gold star, or the mark on the report card, or any of these artificial rewards. They want to know because they want to know! What happens, then, to this natural thirst for comprehension as children grow older? Unfortunately, it is frequently lost and the "unscientific" adult who seeks no new horizons of learning is the rule rather than the exception. If elementary schools set as their single task that of keeping alive the flame of inquiry which burns in every youngster, they would perform their function admirably!

2. *The sense of wonder.* This is often stated in mundane language as de-

veloping an appreciation of the earth and universe. It is more than that. It is an eternal sense of wonder and awe about all that surrounds us. Again, the "so what?" attitude of the blasé adult is characteristic of neither scientists nor children, for both of these have a deep appreciation of and respect for the order and perfection of the universe. This attitude should be nurtured carefully by the elementary school teacher. It is a fragile thing and will disappear unless effort is made to preserve it.

3. *The thrill of discovery.* The youngster knows a natural thrill of discovery similar to that known to all great scientists. It is to the scientist's thrill of discovery that the poet refers in the lines,

> Then felt I like some watcher of the skies
> When a new planet swims into his ken . . .[23]

The youngster, also, feels this thrill of discovery as he solves some of the riddles of his universe. He feels the deep satisfaction of learning answers and solving problems and this, too, should not be permitted to disappear as he grows into adulthood.

These then are the scientific attitudes "natural" to children. The following are in the opposite category:

Scientific Attitudes Antithetical to the Nature of Children:

1. *The spirit of perseverance.* In no other field can this attitude be developed more completely than in science. Many children are apt to become discouraged and lose interest when their experiments fail or their observations yield no results. The wise teacher will try to develop the spirit of perseverance and the importance of "sticking to the task" until the answer is found. Stories of great scientists and scientific discoveries are invariably those of repeated failures until success is finally realized. These can be read or told to children as one means of encouraging their interest in science and in strengthening their powers of perseverance. Many other devices, of course, should be used on all grade levels to develop in children this all-important quality.

2. *The attitude of open-mindedness.* As a rule, children do not have the experience, the wisdom, and the maturity to view a problem objectively and dispassionately. Critically evaluating and carefully weighing the facts before making final conclusions are important habits to be instilled in the early primary grades and re-emphasized on all succeeding levels.

3. *A willingness to examine all the evidence.* Children are prone to jump to conclusions. One of the teacher's jobs is to help them to see the error of drawing hasty conclusions upon a single piece of evidence or a lone experiment. Constant reminders by the teacher—"Are we sure that's true? . . . Couldn't that have been caused by something else? . . . Let's go back again to make sure"—are necessary to develop an awareness of the importance of weighing all the evidence before drawing conclusions.

[23] John Keats, Sonnet, "On First Looking Into Chapman's Homer."

But scientific attitudes are inseparable from scientific methods. The development of these are, therefore, discussed in the following section.

DEVELOPING SCIENTIFIC METHODS

It has been mentioned in other chapters that the emphasis upon a systematic and critical attack of problems permeates every facet of the curriculum. Nowhere, however, is this more true than in the field of science. *To help boys and girls develop the ability to solve problems* is a crucial job of the entire science program. What are some of the ways in which this can be done?

Children learn to solve problems by solving problems. Unfortunately, this is not as apparent as it may sound, for there are still some teachers who give lip-service to the goal of problem-solving and yet make little or no provision for it in their classrooms. Children do not learn to solve problems by being told to "read pages 117–122" in their science textbooks. Nor do they learn by answering ten questions in their workbooks. Nor do they learn by watching the teacher perform a demonstration accompanied by, "Now we will put another hole in the can," and, "Now you will see the difference caused by the pressure of the air." Nor do they learn by following the directions for an experiment prepared for them by the author of their textbook. All of these contribute in part, of course. But the fundamental way in which children will learn to solve problems is by being permitted *and* encouraged to solve problems which are important and meaningful *to them.* Furthermore, every teacher has an overabundance of "real" problems from which he may choose, provided he knows how to encourage their expression.

The classroom environment should be conducive to discovering problems. The formal, rigid classroom of yesterday with every minute accounted for and no opportunity provided for informal conversation neither permitted nor encouraged children to express problems of interest to them. This is not true in today's classrooms, where the social and emotional environment provides the time and opportunity for children to talk freely of their experiences and interests. The following examples are typical of problems which arise daily in the right type of classroom environment:

One morning a third-grade child left the room and, on his return, announced dramatically to the class, "The water in the drinking fountain tastes awful funny today." Immediately a discussion arose. "I want to go see." "Does it really taste bad?" "Why does it, Miss Brown?" "Will it make us sick?" "Maybe the water's dirty." "Maybe the pipes are rusty." "I'm not going to drink any more water." Miss Brown's informal classroom environment had permitted a problem to emerge which could be used as the basis for many valuable science learnings and attitudes.

Susan "shared" with her first-grade classmates her beautiful bouquet of zinnias which had won first place in the school flower show. One child asked, "Why don't you plant the seeds from those flowers so you'll get nice flowers again next year?" Another joined in, "If you plant the seeds from those red zinnias, will you get red zinnias or some other color?" Almost with one accord, the class suggested, "Let's try it and see." A "real" problem had been discovered.

Mr. Sakson asked Sam, one of his sixth-grade boys, to take a message to the principal's office on the first floor. Sam good-naturedly grumbled, "Aw, gee, why do we have to walk all that way to deliver a message? Can't we rig up an intercom system between our room and the office?" Another real problem!

In addition to providing an informal atmosphere and devoting an alert ear to children's comments, many teachers use more direct techniques in encouraging children to state their problems. In one classroom, the use of a "wonder box" in which children were encouraged to drop questions revealed their concern with "How does sound fade away?", "I wonder what is inside of somebody," and "I wonder about the sky." [24] Other teachers use similar techniques such as the *Ponder and Wonder* board or the class notebook perhaps entitled *Ask me Another* or simply *? ? ?* in which children are encouraged to write questions and problems as they occur to them.

Still more directed are the motivating devices which the teacher may use to stimulate children's questions about a preplanned unit of work. The "science corner," the bulletin board, and most of the motivating devices mentioned in other chapters are equally applicable to the field of science.

There are many "scientific methods." There is general agreement, today, that there is no one "scientific method." Methods of solving problems vary considerably and are dependent upon the situation, the investigator, and the problem to be solved. Some problems are solved by accidents; others by short-cuts; others by "lucky hunches." Invariably the process employed is highly flexible and individualized. This does not mean that the school has no obligation to teach children how to approach and solve problems in a systematic and orderly fashion. It does mean that the rigid, highly formalized "scientific method" has now become flexible enough to permit a variety of procedures. The following steps of problem-solving should be considered, therefore, not as "musts" which are always employed in definite sequence, but as suggested skills which children should master as they gain experience in discovering and solving problems:

SKILLS OF PROBLEM-SOLVING

1. Sensing a problem and wanting to find an answer.
2. Defining the problem clearly.

[24] B. A. Bohnhorst and P. M. Hosford, "Basing Instruction in Science on Children's Questions: Using A Wonder Box in the Third Grade," *Science Education*, Vol. 44 (March, 1960), pp. 146–149.

3. Hypothesizing as to the most likely explanations or possible solutions.

4. Planning the best way to attack the problem and collect the data.

5. Collecting all pertinent data.

6. Organizing and classifying data.

7. Drawing conclusions and making generalizations.

Encouraging children to sense problems has already been discussed. After these problems are expressed generally, the teacher's task is to help children state the problem clearly and definitively. As an example, consider the case of the "funny-tasting water" mentioned previously. It is apparent that these children sensed a problem, but only to a general extent. They were confronted with a situation they did not understand, but so far, no clear problem has been defined. It becomes the teacher's task, therefore, after the preliminary "feeling" of the problem, to encourage its definition. The conversation below illustrates the manner in which the teacher guided the children's general excitement about the ill-tasting water into the definition of an exact problem:

Teacher: We have been talking for several minutes about the water in the drinking fountain. Who can say exactly what it is that is troubling us? What are we wondering about the water?

Child: What do they put in it to make it taste funny?

Teacher: But do we *know* for sure that they put anything in the water? Is this the real question, then, that we are trying to answer? Who can tell us what it is?

Child: Do they put anything in the water?

Teacher: This is certainly one thing we want to know. Will we want to know more than this?

Child: If they *do* put something in the water, what is it for?

Teacher: This is part of it. Is there anything more?

Child: I don't know who "they" is. Is it our principal, or who is it?

Teacher: This is another part of the problem. Who can state clearly now the large problem which we are interested in answering?

From this type of direction, the children will be helped to formulate the major problem which may be worded somewhat as, "What happens to our water from the time it leaves the source until it gets to our drinking fountain?" As children examine this broad problem, they are encouraged to formulate hypotheses such as: "I think it's filtered. I don't know how they do it, but my father showed me a building called the city filtration plant." "I think they put a chemical in it because my aunt says city water doesn't taste like well water." "I think they put something in it because it tastes like the water in our swimming pool and my father puts chemicals in that." "I think there's something to put in water that's good for your teeth. I heard my mother say something about it." From these hypotheses will emerge suggestions on how and where to collect the necessary data, and the problem-solving method is well under way. Suggestions for helping children collect and record data are offered in the following section:

COLLECTING AND RECORDING DATA

Numerous activities and procedures may be used by children to collect data. Some of the most common are described on the following pages.

Experimenting

There is no other scientific procedure more valuable or more interesting to children than experimenting. This is a word which is added early to the vocabularies of five- and six-year-olds, and it is not unusual to hear, "Let's experiment to find out," enthusiastically suggested in the kindergarten and first grades. From these grades on, experimenting can be employed as a basic method of developing scientific concepts. In order for children to derive the most value from this activity, it is important that the teacher keep the following generalizations in mind:

Experiments are not "magic." The very purpose of the experiment is defeated if the teacher surrounds the situation with an aura of magic and mystery. The build-up of suspense and the dramatic flourish of discovery may captivate children's interests, but they will also defeat the purpose of the experiment. The authors have seen, for instance, situations in which children were so enthralled at the "show" that they forgot entirely the purpose behind it. Experiments should be used to show children how to gather data and test hypotheses; they should not be considered as "parlor tricks."

Children should understand the purpose of the experiment. In all cases, the purpose of the experiment should be clearly stated. During a class experiment, many teachers like to write the purpose or question on the board so that it may be referred to during and after the experiment. "We want to find out if air is inside the can," or "Does light travel in a straight line?" are examples of stated purposes which should be before the group as the experiment is performed.

Similarly, the stated purpose of a long-range experiment should be placed near the object. Over the cages of the two white rats, for instance, may be placed a sign, "We are comparing the effects of a balanced and unbalanced diet," so that, as days go by, children will not forget the original purpose of the experiment.

Children should participate in the experiment. Have you ever seen a class of active, eager youngsters forced to sit passively while the teacher had all the fun of performing the experiment? If experimenting is truly "learning by doing," then the children, not the teacher, should be "doing." As a general rule, children should suggest experiments suitable to test their hypotheses. They should then assist in planning the procedures, setting up the equipment, and conducting the experiment if they are to derive maximum value from the experience.

Under this point, it is well to emphasize the value of individual experiments in the elementary classroom. Many teachers provide a work-table or corner in their classrooms at which children may conduct individual experiments during their free time. Podendorf advocates individual experimentation and suggests that teachers will find it profitable to suggest experiments on cards which can be placed in a box with the necessary equipment. These cards should not contain the old "cook-book" type of directions, however, but should merely suggest to children ways to explore experiments. Under the category of *Air*, for instance, may be filed a card with the directions, "Plan a way to lift a tin can with a toy balloon," or "Find a way to put a match under water without getting it wet." [25] Children may then refer to these cards at their leisure, set up equipment, conduct the experiment, and analyze the results.

Children should be cautioned against drawing sweeping conclusions from one experiment. As was previously mentioned, children are prone to jump to conclusions, and the teacher should help them see that one experiment is insufficient evidence upon which to base wholesale conclusions. They should be helped to understand that their experiment produced *evidence*, but that this must be checked, rechecked, and verified from many different sources before final conclusions can be stated.

Experiments that "do not work" can also be valuable learning experiences. Many teachers become frustrated and discouraged when classroom experiments fail. But these incidents can usually be just as valuable learning experiences as the successful experiments. The wiring of the doll's house that does not work, the mold that doesn't grow, the bulbs which do not blossom, and many other "failures" can be used to good advantage in teaching children science. "We learn from our failures" is probably more true in this field than any other.

Children should learn the value of using a "control" when experimenting. Children in the elementary grades should be introduced to the necessity of using a controlled experiment to secure accurate results. A fifth-grade class, for instance, decided to investigate the extravagant claims they heard on television for various tooth pastes which would "destroy harmful bacteria." They chose four leading brands which they labeled *Brand W, Brand X, Brand Y, and Brand Z*. After much discussion, the class decided to use *two* samples of each brand in order to secure more reliable results. After this

[25] I. Podendorf, "Creativity in the Teaching of Elementary Science," *School Science and Mathematics*, Vol. 58 (April, 1958), pp. 286–289.

was decided, and the reason understood by all pupils, the teacher asked, "This will probably tell us which of the four brands is most effective in killing bacteria, but how do we know that bacteria might not be killed as well by not using *any* toothpaste at all?" The children discussed this point and then decided to use two clear samples as a control. Consequently, the experiment was set up using ten sterile nutrient agar petri dishes. After exposing all dishes to the air for an identical amount of time, the pupils poured a solution of distilled water and *Brand W* toothpaste into two of the dishes, making sure to cover the entire surface. They poured a similar solution using *Brand X* into two others; *Brand Y* into two others; and *Brand Z* into two others. In the last two dishes they poured only distilled water. They covered all the dishes and the experiment was under way. Through numerous similar experiments, these children were taught the necessity of using a "control" in order to secure reliable data.

Demonstrating

Most of the guides suggested under experimenting are equally applicable to demonstrating. Children should, for instance, understand clearly the purpose of the demonstration and should take an active part in performing it. Many volunteers should be needed to "pour some water in," "tell us when it gets hot," "hold it carefully," and "look what is happening" so that the demonstration is truly a co-operative project. The only other major point which needs to be stressed concerning demonstrations is the need for *careful planning*. Such planning should cover the following items:

1. The teacher should be thoroughly familiar with all aspects of the demonstration. This should be guaranteed by performing the demonstration, if possible, at home or in an empty classroom before showing it to the class. Last-minute preparations or make-shift substitutions of materials have produced chaos in more than one classroom when science demonstrations were performed.

2. The children should be seated so that they can *see* and *hear* everything that is going on. The importance of this is pretty obvious, but it is surprising the number of teachers who disregard it, to the dismay and frustration of their pupils!

3. Safety hazards must be foreseen and provided for in all cases. This is of extreme importance.

4. The demonstration should be discussed thoroughly and possibly repeated several times until the teacher is assured that the children have grasped the principle involved.

Observing

Have you ever observed a child observe? Have you studied him as he watches, for instance, men repairing a highway? Have you noticed the in-

Living things provide wonderful opportunities for children to observe.

tentness with which he studies every movement and his utter oblivion to everything else? Children are naturally keen observers. (Which is why, incidentally, most magicians admit that their hardest audiences are children.) Nothing escapes their sharp eyes. And through observation they learn. This can be even more true in the classroom where the teacher can mold the child's natural powers of observation into trained, scientific faculties.

All kinds of living things provide wonderful opportunities for young children to observe. The setting hen, the white rats, the hamsters, and the garter snake are fascinating to children who observe them with rapt attention. The parakeet cage, the tropical fish aquarium, and the ant colony enclosed in glass hold endless wonders for youngsters. All kinds of living animals have an appeal for children, who will spend hour upon hour observing them and, through observation, learn.

The classroom should provide other stimuli, also, to the child's powers of observation. Collections of shells, rocks, leaves, and seed pods will be handled and examined carefully by interested youngsters. So will cocoons, abandoned birds' nests, and almost anything else imaginable. In addition to observing them, of course, children should be encouraged to record their observations. Daily records of the temperature of the water in the aquarium, the growth of the seeds in the window box, or the amount of daily rainfall in the can outside the window should accompany observations of all phenomena.

One teacher provided an interesting opportunity for observing and recording data through calling the attention of his class to the large maple tree outside the classroom window. On September 15th he asked the class to observe the tree carefully and to record on paper the details of their observations. They also painted a picture to accompany their written report of that day. On the fifteenth day of each succeeding month, the class observed the same tree and recorded their observations with notes and an accompanying picture. Each month was compared with the previous one and on June 15th they summarized their observations of the yearly cycle of the tree's appearance. The experience yielded much in scientific knowledge and attitudes gained solely through careful observation and recording. Similar experiences can be developed on all grade levels and are of inestimable value in vitalizing the science program for boys and girls.

Group Discussions and Committee Activities

These are valuable methods of collecting and comparing data. The reader is referred to the preceding chapter for a complete discussion of them.

Reading

Reading serves a variety of purposes in the science program. The value of first-hand science experiences has been emphasized repeatedly in this chapter. It is important, however, to remember that reading also has a place in the science program. In the past, reading has often constituted the *sole* method of learning science in many schools. This is wrong. But it is equally wrong to assume that reading has no place in a vitalized science program. As a matter of fact, it is used constantly to serve many distinct purposes.

First, children should realize that it is neither practical nor possible to learn everything through first-hand experiences. They should early gain the habit of *immediately* referring to a science reference book as the fastest, easiest, and most accurate source of information on *certain particular problems*. On the other hand, other problems are best approached through experimentation and consultation, *followed by* reading to supplement or verify findings. Also, through reading, children should learn to check and compare data, test hypotheses, and become aware of the need to consult many sources before being satisfied with a final answer. It would indeed be a foolish teacher who did not utilize the excellent reading materials now available in the field of elementary science.

There are many sources of reading materials in science. Textbooks, magazines, "unit" booklets, reference books, pamphlets, and quantities of free and inexpensive materials are now available in abundance for the elementary classroom. The sources, uses, and values of several of these have been discussed in connection with reading and social studies in Chapters Six and Nine. Let us look briefly, therefore, only at those which have special significance for science.

Science textbooks. There are at least a dozen recent, attractive, and informative science series on the market. In general, these are vastly superior to the older science texts with their drab pictures and content poorly written for children. As improved as these books are, however, there may still be some question as to their suitability for the grade level for which they are written. Mallinson et al., for instance, report a study of recent science textbooks for grade four and above which indicates a wide range of readability levels, some of which were too advanced for the grades for which they were intended.[26] It is extremely difficult to generalize, however, on this topic, for many factors must be taken into consideration in evaluating the suitability of a textbook for any particular grade. The wide range of interests, reading levels, and special aptitudes found in any heterogeneous class will probably enable the teacher to choose some satisfactory textbooks from several series when filling his yearly book order.

The proper use of the textbook and the advantages of the multiple-text-book approach over the single-textbook approach have been discussed thoroughly in the preceding chapter and are as applicable to science as they are to social studies.

Library books. The elementary teacher should have no difficulty in choosing quantities of interesting science books for his classroom and school library. Various lists of science books recommended for elementary school pupils appear periodically and should be of considerable help to the teacher or administrator charged with buying books. The following list is meant to be merely suggestive, and no attempt has been made to include all of the excellent bibliographies now available:

Bibliography of Science Books for Elementary School Children (Sacramento 14, Calif., Department of Education, 1959).

Growing up with Science Books (62 West 45th Street, New York 36, N.Y., *Library Journal*, Annual).

KAMBLY, P. E., *Science Books for the Elementary School Library* (A composite of annual list published by *School Science and Mathematics*), Curriculum

---

[26] G. G. Mallinson, H. E. Sturm, and L. M. Mallinson, "The Reading Difficulty of Some Recent Textbooks for Science," *School Science and Mathematics*, Vol. 57 (May, 1957), pp. 364–366.

Bulletin No. 191, Vol. XV (Eugene, Oregon, University of Oregon, February 10, 1959).

MALLINSON, G. G. and MALLINSON, J. B., *A Bibliography of Reference Books for Elementary Science* (Washington, D.C., National Science Teachers Association, 1958).

Science Books for Children, Cornell Rural School Leaflet, Teachers Number, Vol. 51, No. 1 (Fall). (Annotated list of books published in 1950–1957).

Science Books for the Elementary School (Indianapolis, Ind., Department of Public Instruction, August, 1959).

Science Books for the Elementary School. 1960 Supplement (Indianapolis, Ind., Department of Public Instruction, 1960).

Science Books for the Elementary School (Little Rock, Ark., Arkansas Library Commission, March, 1958).

School Science and Mathematics, Annual list published since 1944.

The Traveling Elementary School Science Library (Washington, D.C., American Association for the Advancement of Science and the National Science Foundation, Annual).

The World of Science: Books for Boys and Girls, Bureau of Elementary Curriculum Development (Albany, N.Y., State Education Department, 1958).

Using Community Resources

It has been stressed repeatedly that children are surrounded by science on every hand. Every community is rich in this respect. A few guideposts are all that are necessary in order for the teacher to utilize these riches to their fullest.

Class excursions for young children should not go far from the school. It is neither necessary nor desirable to take young children on long, involved field trips. These are usually too expensive, too fatiguing, and their values are not equal to the time and trouble they involve. There is very little reason, for instance, why a second-grade teacher should take her class to the large city zoo a half-day's ride away. Children can wait until they are older for the school to give them this experience. Second-graders can, however, profit from a ten-minute walk around the city block or a few minutes' bus ride to the local dairy, poultry farm, or city park. The immediate environment should hold endless wonders for the primary grade youngster if the teacher knows how to use it, and the day-long excursions should be postponed until children are in the upper elementary or junior high school grades.

Field trips are not "picnics." It is extremely unfortunate that, in some systems, poorly managed field trips have caused school boards and administrators to ban them from the school program. This is not the solution. Rather, the solution is to prevent field trips from deteriorating into "junkets" with no real educational value. A few suggestions are offered in order to realize the potential of the field trip as one of the most vital learning aids available to children.

1. *A preplanning session is an absolute necessity.* Before *any* field trip is taken, the teacher and class should plan it together with extreme care and detail. "What is the purpose of our trip?" "What do we hope to see?" "What questions do we want answered?" "What things must we remember to take?" "Which people have special responsibilities?" "What are they?" "What are the rest of us to do?" "What time will we leave?" "From where?" "When will we return?" These and other questions should be discussed co-operatively *prior* to the actual excursion.

2. *Each child should take an active part in the experience.* Too often, the field trip is a deadly affair which takes all the children on a weary walk to a particular spot where they stand in a ring while the teacher displays and explains the object of their trip. The purpose thus accomplished, they all trudge back home again, a little, but probably not much, wiser. The good teacher, though, will make the trip more profitable by taking care to provide a maximum number of learning experiences. In the first place, there are many specific things to see along the way which should be called to the attention of children. (No trip should be made to see *one* thing only.) Then, too, all children are assigned definite responsibilities for gathering data. Notes must be taken, questions asked, and specimens collected. Through these procedures, the field trip is made an active and purposeful learning experience for *all* pupils.

3. *The evaluation session should immediately follow the trip.* In this discussion such questions as the following will be answered. "Did we find the answers to our questions?" "What did we learn?" "What were we not able to learn?" "How can we find this?" "Was our trip a success?" "Could we have improved it?" "How?" "Did we learn anything which we should remember on our next trip?" "How shall we remind ourselves of this before we plan our next trip?"

A school file on field trips will prevent many unforeseen problems. Many schools maintain a file on field trips, for which each teacher completes a card after taking a trip. On the card he records such information as: (1) distance from school, (2) directions for reaching, (3) hours open, (4) admission charge, if any, (5) names of persons to contact to secure permission to visit or particular information, (6) particular values to be derived, and (7) particular cautions to be observed. If each teacher consults this file *before* taking a trip, he may profit from others' experience and thus be able to make the trip that much more valuable for his pupils.

Community resources are numerous and varied. It is, of course, impossible to list all the community resources of value, for these will depend entirely upon the local environment. In general, however, elementary teachers consider the following typical of those resources which hold the greatest promise for science learnings:

"NATURAL" RESOURCES	"MAN-MADE" RESOURCES
Farms	Stores
Parks	Museums
Quarries, sand pits	Factories
Wooded areas	Construction sites
Lakes, rivers, streams	Markets
Gardens	Laboratories
Vacant lots	Filtration plants
Hatcheries	Airports
Bogs, barrens, etc.	Railroad stations
Bird sanctuaries	Weather bureaus
	Radio and TV stations
	Greenhouses
	Planetariums, observatories

Community resources may be invited into the classroom. Other valuable community resources are the people living nearby who may contribute a great deal to the science program. Very often such people as farmers, gardeners, game wardens, weather forecasters, geologists, pilots, physicists, zoo keepers (the list is endless) enjoy thoroughly the experience of talking to young children. There are really only two cautions to observe when inviting these people to the classroom: (1) They should know exactly what they are expected to do. (The age level of the children to whom they are speaking; the specific subject they are to discuss; the size of the group; and the amount of time they have.) (2) The teacher should have tried to make discreet inquiries as to their success in talking with young children. Unfortunately, the most learned scientist or most dedicated game warden is not always able to communicate with elementary school children. If possible, this should be determined in advance (again, the school file should be of help) so that their valuable time will not be wasted on a fruitless mission and so that the children will really profit from their visit.

This section has attempted to describe briefly the many procedures and activities in which children should engage as they collect the data they need to solve their problems. After these are secured, they should be organized, evaluated, and summarized. In such fashion will children learn the methods and attitudes demanded of them by our modern world of science.

The next section is devoted to a discussion of materials, facilities, and equipment for teaching science.

MATERIALS AND EQUIPMENT

It will be remembered that lack of materials and equipment was mentioned earlier in the chapter as one of the major problems reported by elementary teachers. This problem is discussed here according to: (1) What materials are recommended for the elementary science program?, (2) How can these materials be used and stored in the self-contained

The science bulletin board is part of a rich classroom environment.

classroom?, and (3) How can a school provide for the co-operative use of materials?

What materials are recommended for the elementary science program? Fortunately, the problem of materials and equipment can be solved without spending a great deal of money, for most authorities agree that elaborate and expensive material is neither necessary nor desirable in the elementary program for several reasons. In the first place, young children should feel free to handle and manipulate the material available to them.

This is impossible if the equipment is extremely delicate and expensive. In the second place, the elementary teacher does not *need* elaborate equipment to develop most of the basic scientific concepts which can be comprehended by young children. In the third place, practically speaking, the cost of equipping every elementary classroom with a wealth of science materials and equipment is prohibitive in some school systems. For these reasons, there is general agreement today that the elementary science program should depend largely upon simple, inexpensive, and homemade equipment. *This does not mean, however, that schools should feel no responsibility for purchasing some science equipment.* In the past, the emphasis upon homemade equipment may have convinced school administrators that any kind of makeshift or salvage material was good enough for the elementary science program and that no school money needed to be spent for this purpose. This is unfortunate, for elementary school children should have *some* opportunity to work occasionally with truly scientific apparatus and equipment. School money should be provided for this just as it is provided for paper, pencils, and books for other fields. The elementary teacher, therefore, has an obligation to use all of his ingenuity, resourcefulness, and creativity in providing his classroom with science materials, but he also has a right to expect his board of education to purchase essentials for science which can be secured in no other way.

There are many comprehensive lists of free and inexpensive materials which children and teacher may secure from their homes or local stores. Among the better-known ones are those compiled by Blough et al. [27] and Zim.[28] A slightly more recent one is reproduced below: [29]

HARDWARE STORE

glass friction rods	wire
hard-rubber rods	paints and varnishes
dry-cell batteries	scales
insulated copper wire	pulleys
electric push buttons	plumber's force cups
electric bells	mason's hammers
electric lamps and	thermometers (indoor and
sockets	outdoor)
glass funnels	flashlights
fruit jars	glass tubing
lamp chimneys	window glass (broken pieces
metal scraps	will do)

[27] G. O. Blough, J. Schwartz, and A. J. Huggett, *Elementary School Science and How to Teach It*, rev. ed. (New York, Holt, Rinehart and Winston, Inc., 1958), pp. 61–64.

[28] H. S. Zim, *Science for Children and Teachers*, Bulletin No. 91 (Washington, D.C. Reprinted by permission of the Association for Childhood Education International, 3615 Wisconsin Ave., N.W., 1953), Chapter 3.

[29] A. Aiello, "All You Have to Do Is Ask," *Equipment for Elementary Science*, Elementary School Science Bulletin Issue No. 51 (Washington, D.C., National Science Teachers Association, 1960), p. 3.

GROCERY STORE

starch
sugar
vinegar
salt
paraffin
ammonia

fruits
clothes pins
paper bags
corrugated cardboard
baking soda

DAIRY

bottles (various sizes)
containers
dry ice

GARDEN SUPPLY STORE

seeds and seed catalogs
flower pots
fertilizers
garden twine
spray guns

growing plants
lime
labels
trowels and other tools

DRUG STORE

mercury
thermometer (clinical)
soda
straws
canned heat
blotters
vaseline

forceps
medicine droppers
bottles
acid (HCL)
carbon tetrachloride
cigar boxes
limewater

MUSIC STORE

tuning forks or pitch pipes
instruments

TEN CENT STORE

knitting needles
tongs
glass tumblers
scissors
rubber bands
needles, tacks, and
    screws
mechanical toys
glue or paste
mouse traps
dyes
musical tops

magnifying glasses
thermometers
matches
string
candles
small mirrors
pans
balls
ink
sponges
balloons
cotton

GAS STATION

maps
inner tubes
old jacks
multiple pulleys

oil and grease
old wet cell batteries
small tools
cans

MEDICAL AND DENTAL OFFICE

thermometers
test tubes
test-tube racks
models of teeth
hand lenses

flasks
test-tube holders
rubber tubing
tongue depressors

FARM

sand
loam
hay or straw
leaves
insects

clay
humus
seeds
bird nests
rocks

FABRIC SHOP

scraps of different kinds
    of material
pins

cardboard tubes
netting
cheese cloth

ELECTRIC APPLIANCE STORE

worn-out extension cords
burned-out fuses
hot plates

worn-out electric appliances
burned-out bulbs
magnets from appliances

FIRE DEPARTMENT

samples of materials used to extinguish various kinds of fires

PET SHOP

aquariums
assorted animal life
animal cages

terrariums
ant houses

Not all equipment, of course, may be secured from local houses.[30]
Herewith a list of dealers in special supplies:

American Optical Co., Buffalo 15, N.Y.:
    microscopes, optical instruments
Bausch & Lomb Optical Co., Rochester 2, N.Y.:
    microscopes, optical instruments
Carolina Biological Supply Co., Elon College, N. Car.:
    biological materials, live and preserved specimens
Central Scientific Co., 1700 Irving Park Road, Chicago 13, Ill.:
    general scientific supplies and equipment, chemicals, apparatus
Chicago Apparatus Company, 1735–43 N. Ashland Ave., Chicago 22, Ill.
    general scientific supplies and equipment, chemicals, apparatus
Clay-Adams Co., Inc., 141 East 25th Street, New York 10, N.Y.:
    biological laboratory supplies, charts, models
Denoyer, Geppert Co., 5235 Ravenswood Avenue, Chicago 40, Ill.:
    biological supplies, models, charts

30 H. S. Zim, *op. cit.*, pp. 21–22.

Fisher Scientific Co., 711 Forbes Avenue, Pittsburgh 19, Penn.:
   general scientific supplies, equipment and apparatus, chemicals

General Biological Supply House, Inc., 8200 South Hoyne Avenue, Chicago, 20, Ill.:
   biological supplies and equipment, live and preserved specimens

Oregon Biological Supply Co., 1806 S. E. Holgate Blvd., Portland, Ore.:
   general biological supplies, live and preserved specimens

Standard Scientific Supply Corporation, 808 Broadway, New York 3, N.Y.:
   scientific instruments and apparatus

Testa Manufacturing Co., 418 South Pecan Street, Los Angeles 33, Calif.:
   microscopes

Arthur H. Thomas Co., P.O. Box 779, Philadelphia 5, Penn.:
   general scientific supplies and equipment, chemicals

Triarch Botanical Products, Ripon, Wis.:
   microscopes, slides and specimens

Ward's Natural Science Establishment, 3000 Ridge Road East, Rochester 9, N.Y.:
   minerals, rocks, biological specimens and supplies

W. M. Welch Scientific Co., 1515 Sedgwick Street, Chicago 10, Ill.:
   general scientific equipment

After science materials have been secured, problems of care and storage must be met.

Efficient care and storage of science equipment are imperative in the self-contained classroom. The self-contained classroom is usually a bustling, crowded place. Unless provision is made for the proper care and storage of science equipment, it will quickly become useless. Many teachers have solved the problem by devoting a specific area of their room to a science "center." A small library table, shelves, and storage cupboards can be built into this space or can be improvised by the clever teacher and his students. Children should, by all means, assist in planning the work and storage space and should assume responsibility for caring for the equipment. Alternating science "committees" can be charged with the responsibility of cleaning, caring for, and organizing the distribution of science equipment. Careful planning and management are the only means by which loss or breakage of science equipment can be prevented.

The school should provide for the co-operative use of materials. Every school faculty should make a definite effort to secure the maximum use from every piece of science equipment. This can be done through a co-operative plan. There is, for instance, no reason why *every* teacher in a building must have in his classroom all of the materials he will need to teach science throughout the year. A far more efficient and economical plan is to make most materials available on a school-wide basis. Some schools do this by providing:

1. *A central science closet or storeroom.* This can contain most of the equipment purchased by the school which can then be made available to all teachers on a "sign-out" basis.

2. *The portable science kit.* These may be purchased completely equipped; or some schools prefer to make their own.

3. *The science "cart."* Some schools report the use of the science cart or table on wheels which contains basic science equipment with directions for its use.[31] The entire table may be rolled into the classroom, or individual drawers may be borrowed by the teacher depending on his need. One of these carts on each floor of a school building appears to be a practical, economical, and efficient solution to the problem of equipment and material.

4. *The "skills" laboratory.* Some modern schools have been built with one room devoted to various curriculum activities and experiences.[32] Usually a major function of this room is to permit science experiences which cannot be explored in the regular classroom.

5. *The science laboratory.* The ultimate in science equipment and facilities is, of course, the science laboratory which supplements the science program of the self-contained classroom. These would serve essentially the same function as the special art room, music room, gymnasium, or school library. There is, however, little hope that science laboratories in elementary schools will become a widespread reality in the immediate future. Until that time, teachers and administrators should weigh carefully the value of the other suggestions mentioned previously as satisfactory substitutes.

IDENTIFYING AND PROVIDING FOR SCIENTIFIC APTITUDES

The stand taken today by a few elementary schools to the effect that "the science specialist" is not their concern is, in the opinion of the authors, completely indefensible. In the first place, the concern of every elementary school teacher should be to teach science *to* and *for* all children. This includes, of course, those pupils who possess special scientific talents and aptitudes. Therefore, in attempting to meet its responsibilities toward all individuals, the elementary school is compelled to take some cognizance of the fact that some children are more able in science than others and that steps must be taken to provide for this special ability. Secondly, there ap-

[31] U. Downing (recorder), "Experiments and Demonstrations in Elementary School Science," *Science Education*, Vol. 44 (March, 1960), pp. 75–76.

[32] G. E. Raab and J. Sopis, "Facilities for the Elementary School Science Program," *The Science Teacher*, Vol. 27 (February, 1960), pp. 25–28.

pears to be some evidence that specialized science interests begin at a relatively early age. Biographies of great scientists often attest to this fact, as have some recent surveys of national scholarship winners and current scientists.[33] It would seem, therefore, that the elementary school has a unique opportunity to recognize and encourage early indications of talent —in the field of science, as in every other field.

Many studies have been made of the characteristics of scientists in an effort to suggest criteria for identifying individuals with science aptitudes. In general, characteristics mentioned include "mental acuity, creative abilities, capacity for critical thinking, ability to see relationships, suspended judgment, and open-mindedness." [34] All of these, of course, are factors which are associated to some degree with general intellectual giftedness. Similarly, the following description of the science-prone pupil could be applicable to other fields or aptitudes.

> The portrait of the science-minded child is a very interesting one. He is above average in intelligence and is able to do many things well. He possesses many original ideas which are a great asset to him as well as to his classmates. He is eager to discuss his findings and to share them with his friends. He is able to often astonish his elders with knowledge and understanding on topics that interest him. Children who have special abilities in science have alert minds which can grasp fundamental principles so well that they are able to think about matters at a mature level far beyond their years.[35]

Although many attempts are presently being made, therefore, to determine the discrete abilities of the potential scientist, as far as the elementary teacher is concerned, it is safe to conclude that he has essentially the same talents, some more sharpened than others, which distinguish leaders in other fields of intellectual enterprise. When he *combines* these, however, with a deep and permanent interest in science, the teacher may feel fairly certain that he has a future scientist in his class. What should be his role in developing this potential?

In most schools of the nation, science-gifted children are enrolled in heterogeneously grouped classes. The teachers of these classes find numerous ways in which to provide challenge for these pupils. Special reading books and magazines, many of them on an adolescent or adult level, are appreciated and eagerly devoured by these youngsters. Special responsibilities for chairing science committees, collecting information, and record-

---

[33] J. M. Atkin, "Elementary School Science Programs: Appraisal and Recommendations" in W. O. Stanley, H. S. Broudy, and R. W. Burnett, eds., *Improving Science Programs in Illinois Schools,* Analysis and Recommendations of a Joint Committee on Improvement of Science Teaching (Urbana, Ill., University of Illinois, 1958), p. 39.

[34] P. L. Dressel et al., "How the Individual Learns Science" in *Rethinking Science Education,* 59th Yearbook of the National Society for the Study of Education, Part I (Chicago, University of Chicago Press, 1960), p. 50.

[35] J. G. Read and P. A. Nelson, "A View of Science Education: Review and Forecast," Boston University, *Journal of Education,* Vol. 141 (December, 1958), p. 28.

ing data may be liberally assigned. Challenging "homework" assignments, long-range projects, and reports should be used to stimulate the interests of these pupils. Within the walls of the classroom and the limits of the school day, the teacher should attempt to provide these pupils with the time, space, and materials required to pursue their special interests to the fullest.

In addition, some schools are initiating special sessions for science-minded youngsters. During or after school hours, Saturday mornings, and summers are being used for science clubs and classes open to volunteer students. Some of these are conducted solely by the school; others are the joint responsibility of the school and a community group, or the school and a civic agency, such as the town library or museum. In view of these and other practices, there appears to be very little basis for the criticism occasionally leveled at the elementary schools that they are not recognizing and developing specialized science abilities. The most effective science program is designed by elementary educators for *all* children—as it should be. However, any facet of this program can and should be intensified or expanded by the creative teacher to meet the needs and interests of the "science-gifted" individuals in his class.

Summary

The first part of the chapter was devoted to an examination of the comprehensive trends and problems characteristic of the modern elementary science program.

Trends included: (1) a steadily growing recognition of the importance of science; (2) a newer emphasis upon science as a method of investigating rather than an accumulation of subject matter; (3) a broadening of the scope of elementary science to include many fields of science; (4) an emphasis upon using a variety of resources and activities rather than a restricted few; (5) a recognition of child growth and development in planning the science program; and (6) a growing awareness of the need for articulation in developing a comprehensive elementary-secondary science program.

Major problems mentioned included: (1) lack of teacher preparation; (2) lack of adequate materials and equipment; and (3) difficulty of determining the most effective type of science program.

The three most common types of science programs now in existence were described as: (1) the carefully planned and structured program; (2) the science program integrated with other curriculum areas; and (3) the incidental program. An examination of several state guides revealed general agreement that the content of the elementary program is generally derived from the large areas of: living things; the earth and universe; and matter and energy. The difficult problem of sequence was discussed at some length and it was determined that there exists no general agreement on how to decide best the science content for each grade level.

Scientific attitudes were discussed according to those which seem to be compatible with the nature of children and those which seem to be antithetical to the nature of children. The skills of problem-solving were presented with an emphasis upon flexibility and the importance of recognizing many "scientific methods."

Procedures for collecting and recording data which were mentioned included experimenting, demonstrating, observing, group discussion and committee activities (discussed in the previous chapter), reading, and utilizing community resources.

The problem of proper equipment and materials was discussed. It was recognized that most equipment should be homemade, simple, and inexpensive. On the other hand, it was emphasized that the science-sophisticated youngsters in our modern elementary schools should have some opportunity to work with genuine and accurate scientific apparatus.

The responsibility of the elementary school toward the science-gifted individual was discussed at the close of the chapter.

STUDENT PROJECTS

1. Make a careful analysis of the yearbooks of the National Society for the Study of Education for the years 1904, 1932, 1947, and 1960. These are commonly considered to be landmarks for the development of science programs in American schools. What consistencies do you find existing over the years? What changes?

2. Secure catalogues from several teacher-education institutions in various parts of the country. Compare the number and type of science courses required for students majoring in elementary education. What are your conclusions? What recommendations would you make?

3. Describe a valuable learning experience which would combine science with each of the following curriculum areas. Choose a specific grade level for which each experience would be suitable:

1. Arithmetic   5. Health
2. Industrial Arts   6. Safety
3. Physical Education   7. Music
4. Social Studies

4. Draw up complete plans for an ideal "science center" in a modern self-contained classroom. Give specific descriptions of the exact amount of space and type of facilities you would advocate. Include the materials and equipment you would suggest as well as where they may be obtained and their cost. Make your report as complete as possible with description, illustrations, and diagrams.

5. Numerous school systems now have teacher committees working to revise their science curricula from the kindergarten through the high school. You have been asked to serve on such a committee. How will you attack the difficult problem of determining content for each grade? Examine several curriculum guides to see how it is done in other systems. What proposal will you make to your committee?

6. Write an outline of a unit on "magnetism" for first grade. State specifically the scientific concepts, attitudes, and methods you will establish as your objectives. Describe the types of learning experiences you will provide to accomplish these objectives. Mention the specific books and other learning aids you will use to make the experience as interesting and meaningful as possible.

7. Think of an elementary school with which you are familiar. Make a "field trip file" of the community resources which are within a twenty-minute ride from the school and which could be used for teaching science. Make a separate card for each resource. Include on each card the seven items of information suggested in the chapter.

8. You have a youngster in your class who, as far as you can tell, exhibits unusual interest in and aptitude for science. Describe numerous experiences you could provide for this pupil to meet his special needs. Are there any cautions you should observe?

9. You are the principal of an elementary school which has a faculty of fourteen teachers. You have just received a gift of $500 from the Parent-Teacher Association to spend on science equipment. This is the first time *any* money has been designated for this purpose. How would you involve your faculty in planning to spend this money? Give suggestions for the wisest use of it. How will you plan to provide maximum use of the equipment you purchase?

10. List several scientific principles which you think could be understood by primary grade youngsters. (Examples: (1) *Air occupies space,* (2) *Air exerts pressure.*) Suggest as many experiments and demonstrations as you can think of to help children learn each principle.

11. Choose one of the following topics: (1) the earth; (2) the universe; (3) weather; (4) aviation; (5) energy and machines; (6) magnetism and electricity; or (7) sound and light. Prepare an annotated bibliography of library books available for intermediate grade children on the topic chosen. Divide your bibliography into sections according to books for children reading on grade level; below grade level; and above grade level.

12. Your school follows no structured science curriculum but your principal has encouraged you to integrate science as much as possible with your social studies program. Among the social studies units you are required to teach in the second grade are: (1) the fireman, (2) the farmer, (3) the baker, and (4) the doctor. Describe the science experiences you would include as part of your work on each of these community helpers.

13. Compare the content of at least six of the recent science textbook series. How much consistency do you find in content? In method? In sequence? What are your conclusions?

14. Interview from twelve to twenty elementary school teachers, concerning their major problems in teaching science. Summarize your findings with specific recommendations for solutions to these problems.

BIBLIOGRAPHY

BLOUGH, Glenn O., ed., *It's Time for Better Elementary School Science* (Washington, D.C., National Science Teachers Association, 1958).
BLOUGH, Glenn O. and BLACKWOOD, Paul E., *Teaching Elementary Science* (Washington, D.C., United States Printing Office, 1953).

BLOUGH, Glenn O. and CAMPBELL, Marjorie H., *Making and Using Classroom Science Materials* (New York, Holt, Rinehart and Winston, Inc., 1954).

BLOUGH, Glenn O. and HUGGETT, Albert J., *Methods and Activities in Elementary School Science* (New York, Holt, Rinehart and Winston, Inc., 1951).

BLOUGH, Glenn O., SCHWARTZ, Julius, and HUGGETT, Albert J., *Elementary School Science and How To Teach It,* rev. ed. (New York, Holt, Rinehart and Winston, Inc., 1958).

BRANDWEIN, Paul, *The Gifted Student as Future Scientist* (New York, Harcourt, Brace & World, Inc., 1955).

BURNETT, Raymond W., *Teaching Science in the Elementary School,* rev. ed. (New York, Holt, Rinehart and Winston, Inc., 1957).

CRAIG, Gerald, *Science for the Elementary School Teacher* rev. ed. (Boston, Ginn and Company, 1958).

CRAIG, Gerald, *Science in the Elementary School: What Research Says to the Teacher,* Department of Classroom Teachers (American Educational Research Association, Washington, D.C., National Education Association, 1957).

CROXTON, W. C., *Science in the Elementary School* (New York, McGraw-Hill Book Company, 1937).

Department of Elementary School Principals, *Science for Today's Children,* 32nd Yearbook (Washington, D.C., National Education Association, 1953).

HEISS, Elwood D., OBOURN, Ellsworth S., and HOFFMAN, Charles W., *Modern Science Teaching* (New York, The Macmillan Company. 1950).

HUBLER, Clark, *Working with Children in Science* (Boston, Houghton Mifflin Co., 1957).

HULL, J. Dan and REID, Seerley, *Mathematics and Science Education in the United States Public Schools* (Washington, D.C., Department of Health, Education, and Welfare, 1958).

National Society for the Study of Education, *A Program for Teaching Science.* 31st Yearbook, Part I (Bloomington, Ill., Public School Publishing Company, 1932).

National Society for the Study of Education, *Science Education in American Schools,* 46th Yearbook, Part I (Chicago, University of Chicago Press, 1947).

National Society for the Study of Education, *Rethinking Science Education,* 59th Yearbook, Part I (Chicago, University of Chicago Press, 1960).

National Science Teachers Association, *Science Teaching Through Problem Solving* (Washington, D.C., National Science Teachers Association, 1957).

RICHARDSON, John S., ed., *School Facilities for Science Instruction,* National Science Teachers Association (Washington, D.C., National Education Association, 1954).

TANNENBAUM, Harold E., and STILLMAN, Nathan, *Science Education for Elementary School Teachers* (Boston, Allyn and Bacon, Inc., 1960).

UNDERHILL, Orra E., *Origins and Development of Elementary School Science* (Chicago, Scott, Foresman and Company, 1941).

WELLS, Harrington, *Elementary Science Education in American Public Schools* (New York, McGraw-Hill Book Company, Inc., 1951).

ZIM, Herbert S., *Science for Children and Teachers* (Washington, D.C., Association for Childhood Education International, 1953).

CHAPTER II

Arithmetic

A CURRENT POPULAR STORY concerns the report of the treasurer of a women's club which ended with the statement, "And so, at the present time, we have a deficit of $75.00." Immediately one member arose and proposed, "I make a motion that we give this $75.00 to a local charity." A counter-proposal followed, "I think we should give it to the school." Finally, a compromise was proposed by a third member who suggested, "Let's give 50 per cent to a local charity and 75 per cent to the school!"

An exaggeration? Perhaps. And yet one might not need to look too far to discover similar true-life examples of "arithmetical amnesia." Consider the society matron who can never balance her bank statement; the newly-weds who bought a refrigerator on the installment plan "because it was cheaper that way;" the housewife who ruined the biscuits when she made $\frac{1}{2}$ of a recipe which called for $3\frac{3}{4}$ cups of flour; and the history professor who wanted to pave his garage floor and discovered too late that there are 27, not 9, cubic feet in a cubic yard of wet cement!

These are *not* exaggerations. They are true incidents which are duplicated every day in life situations which demand mathematical thinking. Why? What is the difficulty? Were not these people taught arithmetic in school? The truth is, they had a minimum of approximately forty minutes per day of arithmetic instruction throughout all of their elementary school years. Are they unintelligent or slow-witted? On the contrary, they are probably above average in native intelligence. What then, is the trouble? To answer this question it is necessary to review briefly the history of arithmetic as it has been taught in the elementary schools of this country in past years.

Arithmetic is no newcomer to the American educational scene. On the contrary, it has been firmly entrenched in the elementary school curriculum since earliest days. It is true that the very earliest colonial schools were primarily concerned with reading and religion, but as early as 1800 arithmetic had become a fairly common subject in the program. True, the ordinary teacher was often, himself, not an "arithmeticker" and the catechetical and copybook method of instruction had little resemblance to present-day concepts of good teaching. Nevertheless, arithmetic was "here to stay" very early in the nineteenth century.

Unfortunately, however, when the early printed textbooks succeeded in establishing the subject as part of the school program, they also succeeded in reducing it to the level of mere abstraction, verbalism, and symbolism. As a result, arithmetic was probably taught more poorly in the colonial schools than it had been centuries before, when the abacus and counters were widely used. Nor did this condition change to any great extent in later years. Dependence upon verbalism, isolation from meaningful life situations, emphasis upon the mechanics of computation, and rote memorization were the chief characteristics of a method of teaching arithmetic which prevailed in the schools until the early decades of the twentieth century. This has been termed the "drill theory" of teaching arithmetic.

The "drill theory" stressed mastery of the mechanics of arithmetic through rote memorization and repetitive practice. As has been stated, the drill theory emphasized only the computational skills of arithmetic and completely neglected the development of meaning and understanding. Rules, formulas, generalizations, and processes were taught through the copybook and drill pad, and attempts to develop quantitative concepts, number relationships, and abilities to rationalize arithmetically were conspicuous by their absence. The following section on the multiplication of decimals taken from a popular textbook [1] of the nineteenth century illustrates the general procedure of: (1) presenting pupils with a rule to be copied and memorized and (2) providing ample opportunities to apply the rule until mastery is achieved.

MULTIPLICATION OF DECIMALS
Rule

1. Whether they be mixed numbers, or pure decimals, place the factors and multiply them as in whole numbers.
2. Point off so many figures from the product as there are decimal places in both the factors; and if there be not so many places in the product, supply the defect by prefixing cyphers to the left hand.

Examples

1. Multiply   5.236
   by   .008
                                        2. Multiply   3.024
                                           by   2.23

etc.

[1] N. Daboll, *Schoolmaster's Assistant, Improved and Enlarged, Being a Plain Practical System of Arithmetic* (Norwich, Hubbard and Marvin, 1818), pp. 80–81.

That this type of text organization and mechanical teaching had strong advocates through the early years of the twentieth century is evidenced in the following statements from teachers of that time.

The first work in arithmetic should be almost entirely mechanical. Young children commit to memory easily, but they are not greatly given to reasoning on abstract matters; so until they are very sure of themselves on whole numbers, they should not be troubled with the questions involving whys and wherefores.[2]

In some schools one-fifth, or even in extreme cases one-fourth of the entire school day is occupied with it [arithmetic]; and a large portion of this time is, in earlier grades, devoted to drill. And the major part of this time is well spent.[3]

In summary, it is safe to say that the "drill theory" with its emphasis upon complicated problems, mental gymnastics, and rote memorization dominated the teaching of arithmetic until the early twentieth century when it was challenged by a diametrically opposite philosophy of learning termed the "incidental learning theory."

The "incidental learning theory" represented the opposite extreme of the drill theory. The theory that learning is a natural result of incidental experience became popular in the 1920s and 1930s and represented a complete reaction against the well-entrenched drill method. It assumed,

that children will themselves, through "natural" behavior in situations which are only in part arithmetical, develop adequate number concepts, achieve respectable skill in the fundamental operations, discover vital uses for the arithmetic they learn, and attain real proficiency in adjusting to quantitative situations.[4]

Unfortunately, there were probably as many pedagogical sins committed under this theory as under the older drill theory, for it is no more defensible to assume that learning takes place through mere exposure to certain situations than it is to assume that it can be realized solely through repetition and practice. On the other hand, the claim of the "incidental theorists" that arithmetic, like all other areas, can best be taught as part of an integrative learning experience would be accepted as sound by most modern-day educators. In general, however, research and experience cast serious doubt upon the validity and practicality of incidental learning and today, almost unanimously, educators subscribe to the "meaning theory" in teaching arithmetic.

THE MEANING THEORY IN ARITHMETIC

In the original discussion of this theory in 1935, Brownell defined it as follows:

[2] R. S. Moore, "Object of Number Work," *American Primary Teacher*, Vol. 23 (May, 1905), pp. 336–337.
[3] "The Drill Side of Arithmetic," *Primary Education*, Vol. 22 (September, 1914), pp. 432–433.
[4] W. A. Brownell, "Psychological Considerations in the Learning and the Teaching of Arithmetic," *The Teaching of Arithmetic*, 10th Yearbook, National Council of Teachers of Mathematics (New York, Teachers College, Columbia University, 1935), p. 12.

The "meaning" theory conceives of arithmetic as a closely knit system of understandable ideas, principles, and processes. According to this theory, the test of learning is not mere mechanical facility in "figuring." The true test is an intelligent grasp upon number relations and the ability to deal with arithmetical situations with proper comprehension of their mathematical as well as their practical significance.[5]

A few years later, the same author clarified further the "meaning of meaning" by distinguishing between meaning *for* and meaning *of* arithmetic.[6] The first refers to an understanding of the social significance or the practical application of arithmetic in daily human activities. The second connotes an understanding of the basic laws, concepts, operations, and relationships which govern the science of mathematics. The fact that these two aspects of arithmetic are interrelated; that they are equally important; and that they must both be stressed in the effective arithmetic program is the paramount thesis of the modern "meaning theory."

The social aspect has contributed to two major changes in the arithmetic curriculum. One of the chief results of the emphasis upon the social significance of arithmetic has been the elimination of some of the content previously taught. Studies which have used the life needs of adults and children as bases for determining curricular content have been influential in eliminating much of the "deadwood" which had no practical value. Into this category would go such content as: (1) extensive study of Roman numerals; (2) adding or multiplying such fractions as:

$$\frac{5}{14}+\frac{1}{2}+\frac{7}{32}+\frac{3}{10} \text{ or } \frac{35}{72}\times\frac{4}{170}\times\frac{3}{18}$$

(3) memorization of multiplication facts beyond 9×9; and (4) unrealistic addition of decimals involving "ragged" right-hand columns such as $14.753 + 8.2 + 9.7645 + 14.01$.

Another result of the emphasis upon the social aspect of arithmetic has been to integrate the subject with other areas of the curriculum. Today, arithmetic is not confined to a textbook or a certain period of the day; rather it is explored functionally as the need arises in all other learning areas. In the social studies, the teacher will discover an endless number of opportunities for teaching arithmetic as he introduces his class to such skills as reading and constructing graphs, diagrams, and tables; interpreting map legends and scales; and gaining concepts of size, population, or distribution. Science will offer an equal number of opportunities to develop quantitative concepts and skills as children perform experiments, measure progress, and record data. Similar opportunities will arise daily in all other

[5] *Ibid.*, p. 19.
[6] W. A. Brownell, "The Place of Meaning in the Teaching of Arithmetic," *Elementary School Journal*, Vol. 47 (January, 1947), pp. 256–265.

"Buddy teaching" is an effective device for reinforcing arithmetical
concepts.

fields as children paint, draw, march, sing, speak or listen. Indeed it is
difficult to visualize an activity or a curricular field in which arithmetic
does not play a major role. The wise teacher will capitalize upon as many
of these activities as possible to supplement, *not replace*, the sequential
arithmetic program.

The mathematical aspect of arithmetic is receiving an ever-increasing
emphasis in the modern program. The comparatively recent emphasis on
the mathematical aspect of arithmetic is directed toward giving the pupil
the "know-why" as well as the "know-how" of the subject. This differs
sharply from the old "drill theory" when pupils were taught *how* to perform
an operation but never *why*. Consider, for example, the division of a decimal
by a decimal. There are few adults who cannot recite the rule nor perform
the operation necessary for placing the decimal point in the quotient. But
how many adults know *why* this rule works, or why they were taught to
use the caret device? This is a typical example of the mechanical computation and rote memorization which has no place in a theory of teaching which places primary emphasis upon the development of quantitative
concepts and number relationships. Furthermore, the superiority of the

meaning theory over the older school is not one of mere speculation or opinion but is amply supported by research and experience.

Recent research indicates the superiority of the meaning method over other methods. In the past decade or so, considerable research has compared the meaning theory with other methods. Such studies as those conducted by Brownell and Moser,[7] Swenson,[8] and Anderson [9] indicate the general superiority of teaching by meaning. In addition, a recent and very comprehensive study was reported by Stokes who investigated (over a fifteen-year period) 80,000 children's reactions to meanings in arithmetic. Stokes concluded that, "In summary, it appears that we have evidence that a program of meanings will improve learning in arithmetic." [10] This growing mound of reputable research has produced a general unanimity of agreement among modern educators which is revealed in the following typical statements:

There are many concepts and relationships that the child must learn in arithmetic. He must not only know their *meaning* but also *understand* when and how they operate.[11]

Here is something that every teacher should frame and place where it may be seen each morning before the school day begins: WHAT CHILDREN LEARN MEANINGFULLY STAYS WITH THEM BETTER AND IS APPLIED MORE SUCCESSFULLY THAN WHAT THEY "LEARN" BY MERE DRILL.[12]

Some evidence from research and much evidence from classroom experience substantiate the position that when meanings are acquired pupils learn with less drill, apply better, retain over a longer period of time, and pursue learning with more enthusiasm. Recognizing this, current arithmetic textbooks, courses of study, and classroom practice all place increasing emphasis on pupil understanding of the *why* of operations, the relations between various processes and to

---

[7] W. A. Brownell and H. E. Moser, *Meaningful versus Mechanical Learning: A Study in Grade III Subtraction,* Duke University Research Studies in Education, No. 8 (Durham, N. Car., Duke University Press, 1949).

[8] E. J. Swenson, "Organization and Generalization as Factors in Learning, Transfer, and Retroactive Inhibition," in *Learning Theory in School Situations,* University of Minnesota Studies in Education, No. 2 (Minneapolis, Minn., University of Minnesota Press, 1949), pp. 9–39.

[9] G. L. Anderson, "Quantitative Thinking as Developed under Connectionist and Field Theories of Learning" in *Learning Theory in School Situations,* University of Minnesota Studies in Education, No. 2 (Minneapolis, Minn., University of Minnesota Press, 1949), pp. 40–73.

[10] C. N. Stokes, "80,000 Children's Reactions to Meanings in Arithmetic," *The Arithmetic Teacher,* Vol. 6 (December, 1958), p. 286.

[11] L. J. Brueckner, *Improving the Arithmetic Program* (New York, Appleton-Century-Crofts, Inc., © 1957), p. 45.

[12] R. L. Morton, *What Research Says to the Teacher: Teaching Arithmetic,* Department of Classroom Teachers, American Educational Research Association, (Washington, D.C., National Education Association, 1953), p. 8.

the number system, and development of ability to generalize arithmetical knowledge.[13]

In general, it can be said that meaningful teaching leads to (1) greater retention over periods of time, (2) greater transfer potential, and (3) increased ability to solve new processes independently.[14]

In summary, today's "meaning theory" attempts to develop in the learner, not only the computational skills, but the understandings and applications of these skills in life situations. But this is not a simple nor easily attainable goal! On the contrary, it is an extremely complex one, the realization of which depends upon such major considerations as: (1) readiness for learning, (2) sound instructional procedures, (3) sequential program of content and skills, (4) recognition of pupil needs and abilities, and (5) use of teaching aids and materials. Each of these is discussed in the remainder of the chapter.

READINESS FOR LEARNING

Readiness is recognized as a basic prerequisite for learning in the modern arithmetic program. Today's emphasis upon meaningful learning has produced a mountain of investigation and writing concerning the exact definition and place of readiness in a developmental learning program. Although authorities differ in detail, there is no disagreement over the basic premise that a condition of readiness must be present in order for learning to take place. In general, this condition of readiness has the following characteristics:

Readiness embraces many factors. Early studies of readiness tended to identify it only with mental maturity. It was this concept of readiness which resulted in the construction of various tests which attempted to determine the mental age required to perform certain skills. Allocation of these skills to grade and age levels was made accordingly. Recent research, however, has resulted in a much more comprehensive definition of readiness, which includes such interrelated factors as "experience, intelligence, maturation, degree of understanding, and intrinsic purpose." [15] A similar definition is given by Burton who states that readiness is,

the pedagogical counterpart, so to speak, of maturation but includes social and intellectual maturity as well. For example, we say that at a certain time a child is ready to read, ready for formal arithmetic . . . His physical and neurological

---

[13] J. L. Marks, C. R. Purdy, and L. B. Kinney, *Teaching Arithmetic for Understanding* (New York, McGraw-Hill Book Company, Inc., 1958), p. 51.

[14] D. Dawson and A. K. Ruddell, "The Case for the Meaning Theory in Teaching Arithmetic," *Elementary School Journal*, Vol. 55 (March, 1955), p. 399.

[15] C. E. Bartram, "An Analysis and Synthesis of Research Relating to Selected Areas in the Teaching of Arithmetic," Doctoral Thesis (Columbus, Ohio, Ohio State University, 1956).

maturity and his experiential background are such that he could read, could do abstract arithmetic . . . if circumstances demanded these things.[16]

A state of readiness must be present at each grade level for each succeeding task. A serious mistake of some teachers has been to consider readiness as a condition necessary only for *initial* instruction in any area. Occasionally upper-grade teachers, for instance, feel that they are in no way concerned with readiness, for this is the peculiar responsibility of the kindergarten teacher who must get pupils "ready to learn." Nothing could be further from the truth. Readiness refers to no single state but rather to a series of recurring conditions. No pupil is ever "ready for arithmetic." He may, however, be ready for the introduction of a specific concept or skill which can be, depending on his total maturation, previous related learnings, and experiential background, anything from presentation of $5 + 4 = 9$ to the rationalization of the division of fractions. It is imperative, therefore, that all teachers be aware of the importance of readiness and that they become as proficient as possible in determining its state of existence at each successive level.

The determination of readiness depends on several factors. The alert teacher can frequently diagnose the extent of readiness by informally observing and listening to children. The kindergarten teacher, for instance, will discover almost immediately that her five-year-olds have entered school with a wide variety of quantitative experiences. For example, one five-year-old confided to his teacher that his father's new license plates were "just right" for his family. When the teacher asked him why, he replied, "Because they say 145 and that stands for our family. 1 is for Cindy, our dog, 4 is for my father, mother, brother, and me and 5 is for all of us put together." This youngster, through this brief statement, revealed a mature grasp of the concept of five as a total of two groups of one and four. Other reports of "having two teeth pulled," of "going to school a half day," and of "being 6 years old today" will indicate to the kindergarten teacher the quantitative experiences of her pupils, upon which she can build her program of number concepts and counting skills.

In an identical fashion, the upper-grade teacher may determine readiness through carefully observing and listening to his pupils. Conversations of intermediate- and upper-grade children are filled with references to common and decimal fractions, denominate numbers, percentages, and other arithmetical terms which will enable the teacher to diagnose the extent of the children's readiness for a systematic attack on these areas.

Another important technique for determining readiness is the careful inventory of pupils' demonstrated masteries and weaknesses. A loose-leaf notebook in which is recorded each pupil's specific errors and their probable

[16] W. H. Burton, *The Guidance of Learning Activities*, 2nd ed. (New York, Appleton-Century-Crofts, Inc., 1952), p. 192.

causes is an indispensable aid in diagnosing his "subject-matter readiness" for the next level of difficulty. A sixth-grade teacher, for instance, who wishes to introduce a group to the multiplication of decimals should be able to consult his inventory for the answers to such questions as, "Have they mastered the multiplication facts?", "The multiplication algorism of whole numbers?", "Do they understand place value?", and "Do they understand decimal notation?" Positive answers to these and similar questions should eliminate the pitiful cases of floundering experienced by some children as they are precipitated through the grades into arithmetical skills and content for which they have built no solid foundation.

A third device for determining certain aspects of readiness is the standardized test. Such tests are available on all grade levels and will measure the mastery of certain specific skills preparatory to the next level of difficulty.

Readiness involves motivation. From what has been said previously, it is obvious that readiness is dependent upon a complex hierarchy of concepts, skills, and experiences. None of these, however, is more crucial than the element of motivation. Just as a pupil must have maturity and experience necessary for a new step, so must he have an *interest* in it, and a *desire* to learn it. This stimulation of interest, need, and intellectual challenge is a major responsibility of teachers at all levels. Nothing in the past has been more detrimental to effective learning than the misconception held by some teachers that readiness was the materialization of a magical state dependent upon the learner's maturity and unrelated to what was happening in the classroom. The teacher who simply "waits for children to be ready" is an illustration of this fallacious reasoning. No teacher should merely "wait" for readiness to set in. On the contrary, he should embark upon an active program of instruction which will: (1) confront pupils with meaningful problem situations which demand new knowledges and skills, (2) introduce them to a variety of exciting learning materials and aids, and (3) challenge their "thirst for comprehension" of intellectual vistas yet unexplored.

In summary, there is no other psychological principle which plays a more important role in the program of meaningful arithmetic teaching than readiness. As such, it should be a prime concern of every conscientious and capable teacher.

INSTRUCTIONAL PROCEDURES AND PRINCIPLES

Presenting New Learnings

In presenting new learnings, today's teachers attempt to lead their pupils through *discovery and exploration* to the comprehension, formulation, and practical application of the new concept or skill. How is this accomplished? The following suggestions are presented as guides to presenting new materials which should be applicable on all grade levels. It should be remembered, however, that these are very general and should be modified by creative teachers as they adapt their instruction to the specific situation and individual pupils.

The new learning should be presented to children in a concrete and meaningful situation. To introduce pupils to the new learning in an actual social experience is generally more desirable than using a standard textbook approach. Suppose, for example, a third-grade teacher wishes to introduce "carrying in addition" to a group of children. He may confront them one day with a problem as, "We have 27 children in our class and 14 parents are coming to our program. How many chairs will we need for all of us?" To arrive at an immediate answer to this problem, several children may suggest counting. After this is accomplished, the teacher may say, "We counted to find our correct answer of 41. And that is one way of solving a problem like this. But we learned long ago to use a short method of counting. What do we call it? Let's write this problem on the board and see if we can discover how to answer it by *adding*." "Who can tell us how this problem differs from others that we have added? What is our new difficulty? Can anyone figure out how to add an example like this when the sum of the right-hand column is more than one digit?" This is an important step found to be helpful by many teachers in that it often indicates the group's readiness for the new step. "Wild" or absurd answers or evidence of a complete lack of understanding may indicate to the teacher the need for some reteaching or a slower pacing than he had originally planned. After several suggestions have been made by the children, however, the teacher will propose that the algorism be developed using concrete or semiconcrete materials.

The teacher and class co-operatively work out the algorism using visualization and manipulation of materials. The teacher may develop this step in the following manner. "Let's look at the example we have written on the board. Our first addend is 27. Who can place these markers in the place chart so that they say 27? How many markers did you put in the tens pocket? Why 2? How many in the units pocket? Why 7? Let's also put in the pockets markers to represent the second addend, 14. How many will go in the tens place? Why 1? How many in the units place? Why 4? Now let's see what we have. Count the markers in the units pocket. We have 11. What can we do with 10 of these? That's right, we can trade them for one "ten" marker. Where will we put it? So, instead of 3 tens and 11 units we now have 4 tens and 1 unit. Who will write this on the board? Is this the answer we had when we counted? Then we have discovered a way other than counting to get the answer to our problem. Let's see exactly what we did."

	tens	units
2 TENS and 7 UNITS and	11	1111111
1 TEN and 4 UNITS	1	1111

MAY BE RE–GROUPED TO FORM

	tens	units
3 TENS and 11 UNITS	111	11111111111

MAY BE RE–GROUPED TO FORM

	tens	units
4 TENS and 1 UNIT	1111	1

Varied practice is provided to reinforce meaning. After initial under-standing has been achieved, the teacher will proceed to what Burton calls the "integrative phase of skill learning," in which understanding is de-veloped through varied practice consisting of "many functional contacts and exploratory activities." [17] Such practice should be aimed at the rein-forcement of meaning and should be of sufficient length and variety to as-sure the teacher that this goal has been realized. Following the same pro-cedure as stated previously, children should be permitted to work out many problems similar to the original $27 + 14 = 41$, using a wide variety of concrete and semiconcrete materials. After a *sufficient amount of time* (may be from one to several lessons) has been devoted to this "varied practice" to guarantee that the group has a clear concept of "carrying," the teacher will encourage pupils to formulate the generalization.

Children should be encouraged to formulate and state the generaliza-tion governing the new skill. "Now that we have worked several examples correctly, who can tell us exactly what we did each time? Is there anyone who could put this in a clear sentence which will help us to remember it?" The generalization is stated in clear language, probably written on the board, and may be referred to in subsequent lessons.

Children are finally encouraged to attempt the abstraction. "Now that we have worked enough examples to understand exactly how they are done, are we ready to try some without using the markers? How many people think they could do an example using only their pencils and paper? Let's try this one. In our seed sale last week, John sold 25 boxes of seeds

[17] *Ibid.*, p. 559.

and George sold 28 boxes. Let's see how many boxes both boys sold. How will we write the problem? Let's work it out with pencil and paper. What is the answer? Let's check it by using our markers again." In a similar fashion children will be encouraged to solve other problems, returning as often as necessary to the concrete and semi-concrete stages for reaffirmation and re-clarification.

After thorough attention has been directed toward the development of understanding, the teacher will provide a sufficient amount of drill to insure proficiency.

Providing Repetitive Practice

Drill or "repetitive practice" differs from the integrative practice previously described in that its primary aim is to develop mastery, not meaning. That this phase of learning has a place in the meaning theory has been supported by reliable research over the past thirty years. Teachers should not overlook the value of practice but, rather, should place it in proper perspective to other phases of the program. Brownell offers the following suggestions for maintaining a proper balance between meaning and drill:

1. Accord to competence in computation its rightful place among the outcomes to be achieved through arithmetic;

2. Continue to teach essential arithmetical meanings, but make sure that these meanings are just that and that they contribute as they should to greater computational skill;

3. Base instruction on as complete data as are reasonably possible concerning the status of children as they progress toward meaningful habituation;

4. Hold repetitive practice to a minimum until this ultimate stage has been achieved; then provide it in sufficient amount to assure real mastery of skills, real competence in computing accurately, quickly, and confidently.[18]

The following general guidelines will help the teacher to implement these suggestions as he plans and administers practice lessons and materials:

Repetitive practice must follow, never precede, understanding. This is a basic premise which meets with agreement among modern arithmeticians and has been demonstrated thoroughly in the general teaching procedure described previously.

A variety of activities will increase the value of recurring practice. Drill exercises can, and often do, become extremely tedious, dull, and distasteful to children. To avoid this, the wise teacher should try to instill as much variety as possible into his practice sessions. This is not too difficult a task, for there are hundreds of ideas and devices at his command which will help to avoid some of the monotony and drudgery often associated with

[18] W. A. Brownell, "Meaning and Skill—Maintaining the Balance," *The Arithmetic Teacher*, Vol. 3 (October, 1956), p. 136.

drill. Flash cards, practice sheets, games, and many others may have value provided they are used with discrimination.

Practice periods should be comparatively short and should be wisely placed in the daily schedule. Equally important to variety is timing in planning practice sessions. An unreasonably long or poorly-timed drill period will result in the physical and mental fatigue which often leads to the "I-hate-arithmetic" attitude on the part of some children. To avoid this, the teacher will probably find it more valuable to limit his practice periods to ten or fifteen minutes depending on the age of his pupils. The authors have found, also, that inserting a few minutes of oral or written practice at odd intervals of the day usually pays dividends in pupil interest and attitude. Five minutes before children leave for lunch, or a few minutes between other classes, devoted to a spirited oral drill of addition facts, for instance, is wise classroom planning. The authors recall one third-grade teacher who, when drilling on the harder addition and subtraction facts, would add to her "Good morning" greeting to each child a basic fact to be answered. The sheer absurdity of the situation delighted the children, and at the same time, provided valuable practice in memorizing the facts.

Certain types of practice exercises should be paced at a reasonable speed. It must be kept in mind that the purpose of repetitive practice is proficiency. It is important, therefore, that exercises, games, and assignments designed to serve this purpose should place some premium upon the importance of speed. In other words, "flash cards" should be "flashed" and speed tests timed if efficiency is to be secured. If, for instance, a teacher "flashes" a card, $4 + 3$, at a child and then waits long enough for him to count mentally to reach the answer, the purpose of the drill is defeated. In such a case, it is much more desirable that the teacher show the answer, ask the child to repeat the entire fact, for instance, "four and three are seven," and then proceed to another fact, only to return to the one causing difficulty at a later time. It is worth repeating that this type of practice activity is designed to serve the sole purpose of fixing skills after understanding has been achieved. If, for instance, the child's answer to $3 + 9$ is 4 or some equally absurd answer, serious reteaching is probably in order. Working with the child individually, the teacher may attempt to show him the relationship between $3 + 10 = 13$ and $3 + 9 = 12$, or that $9 = 3 + 3 + 3$ and that, therefore, $3 + 9$ is equal to $3 + 3 + 3 + 3$ or four 3's or 12. Such mathematical relationships should be interpersed throughout the entire practice period, particularly if children give indication that they are merely guessing the correct response.

Before leaving this point, a word of caution is called for in order not to mislead zealous teachers into placing an undue emphasis on speed. Brisk pacing is called for *only when the practice is designed to elicit automatic response* such as in the given illustration of flash-card drill. In the large majority of written practice exercises and tests, teachers should be *extremely cautious about stressing speed.* As Morton says,

> This emphasis on speed tends to go contrary to current emphasis on teaching pupils to be thoughtful about what they do, to estimate answers in advance, and to judge after finishing whether or not their answers are sensible, all of which requires time.[19]

The purpose of the practice should be clear to, and accepted by, the pupil. As in other learning experiences, motivation is heightened in practice situations if the pupil recognizes a need for the activity as related to his own goals. If, for example, the pupil understands thoroughly that the process of "carrying" in addition is necessary in order for him to solve efficiently some of the problems which do and will confront him daily, he will recognize that practice is necessary in order for him to perfect this skill. On the other hand, if the endless rows of examples which drearily face him each day are considered only as a chore to be dispensed with as quickly as possible in order to keep the teacher happy, the resultant value will be proportionate.

Paralleling a program of sound instructional procedures is a sequential and planned arithmetic curriculum. Obvious limitations of space prevent a detailed discussion of all phases of the modern arithmetic curriculum, but the following section attempts to emphasize the major concepts, relationships, mathematical laws, and skills which comprise the content of arithmetic as it is taught from the kindergarten through the sixth grade.

A SEQUENTIAL PROGRAM OF CONTENT

There is very little serious disagreement today on the desirability of a carefully planned, carefully graduated program of mathematical content for the elementary grades. The "queen of the sciences" is, after all, structured upon an orderly and sequential progression of concepts and proficiencies which may allow for some, but not much, deviation. One may, for instance, teach certain types of column addition before teaching "adding by endings" but it is difficult to conceive how anyone could teach children to carry in multiplication before they can add. It seems almost needless to state that a planned curriculum does not ignore the interests and experiences of the pupils but is determined by: (1) a consideration of pupil interest, maturity, and purpose, and (2) an adherence to the orderly structure of the subject.

Although there is general agreement upon the need for a planned program, there is not the same degree of agreement upon the grade placement of specific topics. Several years ago, considerable interest was shown in delaying certain phases of arithmetic until the intermediate grades and beyond. Studies advocating the postponement of arithmetic were, how-

---

[19] R. L. Morton, *op. cit.,* p. 27.

ever, generally refuted and today the developmental program, which encompasses all grades of the elementary school, is generally preferred. In this type of program, various areas of content are considered as developmental strands or cyclic instructional tasks which begin with the child's first quantitative experiences in the kindergarten and increase in complexity and intensity throughout each succeeding grade. Generally speaking, these major instructional tasks are: (1) developing an understanding of numbers and the number system; (2) developing understandings and skills in the four fundamental processes; (3) developing understandings and skills in common fractions; (4) developing understandings and skills in decimal fractions; (5) developing competencies in the use of common units of measure; and (6) improving problem-solving. Each of these is considered on the following pages, not according to rigid grade placements, but as spiral-like patterns which are expanded throughout the entire elementary school.

Developing an Understanding of Numbers and the Number System

A basic concept of number is introduced in the early primary grades. From their earliest exposure to language, young children have contact with basic quantitative concepts and vocabulary. It is upon this experiential background that the kindergarten teacher builds as he initiates pupils into the systematic world of numbers and the number system. The beginning step in this induction is aimed at developing a basic understanding of the numerical symbols, *1, 2, 3, 4, 5, 6, 7, 8, 9,* and *0.* Early in his school career the pupil should realize that all numbers may be written through the use of ten symbols called numerals. He should understand that 5 is a *symbol* used to denote a group which may be *00000* or *000 00* or *00 000* or *0000 0* or *0 0000.* This concept is fundamental to all later work in arithmetic and should be developed gradually as the pupil in the primary grades is introduced to number symbols and names. The strengthening of this concept does not mean, however, that the very young child should be unnecessarily confused by such terms as *symbol, numeral, number, notation* (the writing of number symbols) and *numeration* (the expression of number names). In general, it seems advisable to delay these fine distinctions of usage until the intermediate or upper grades, although the young child should be aware of the concept, if not the precise terminology.

In addition to understanding the meaning of numbers, the five- or six-year-old should develop such related competencies as: (1) a firm sense of the one-to-one relationship of numbers; (2) the ability to count these rationally (as contrasted to rote counting, which is pure memorization); and (3) the ability to read and write the corresponding symbols and names. As familiarity with larger numbers grows, the pupil will be ex-

The concept of place value is
important.

posed to two-digit numerals which will involve a beginning understanding
of the positional notation of the Hindu-Arabic number system.

**No other concept in recent years has been more vigorously stressed in
the elementary grades than that of place value.** Children in the primary
grades are led to understand early that the *place* in which the symbol is
written determines the meaning of the number. For instance, in 5555
there are four identical symbols. However, each of these denotes a different
quantity depending upon the *place* it occupies. This basic concept is not
too difficult for young children to grasp provided it is introduced early
and expanded continually in all grades. In the primary grades children
can discover that 23 cents can be grouped as 2 dimes and 3 cents and that,
when written as *23*, the 2 represents the 2 dimes and the 3 represents the 3
cents. Similarly, by working with concrete materials they can move toward
the understanding that an abstract number, such as 67, may be expressed
as 67 units or as 6 tens and 7 units. Repeated opportunities to work with
place-value charts, boxes, or labeled cans into which coins, straws, milk-
bottle tops, pebbles, beads, or corks can be placed may be extremely
valuable on *all grade levels* and should not necessarily be confined to the
primary grades, as is frequently the case.

In developing the concept of place value, some teachers follow the practice of fastening ten "markers" into a bundle to show that 1 ten is really

the same as 10 ones. Spitzer, however, claims that this will give children an incorrect concept in that the ten markers in the tens column will indicate not 1 ten but 10 tens, whether they are fastened together or not.[20] In general, the authors agree with this viewpoint and advocate teaching children to trade the 10 unit markers for 1 ten marker exactly the way they may trade 10 cents for 1 dime. (Notice the illustration on page 320 in which this was done.)

The concept of place value will, of course, embrace an understanding of the place of zero in the number system. The following three interpretations of zero are usually introduced to children in the primary and intermediate grades and strengthened in the upper grades. As these children become increasingly competent in their use of numbers, they should understand that:

a. Zero, like all the primary numerals, serves as a placeholder.

b. Zero indicates a starting point.

c. Zero means "not any."

Children should understand the base-ten property of our number system. A base of ten simply means that, in all notation, each place is ten times greater than the place to its immediate right. This concept of *base-ten* is usually introduced in the intermediate grades and is reclarified at succeeding intervals as children become more aware of number relationships. In the intermediate and upper elementary grades, several teachers have found it worthwhile to explore the number-base concept further by providing enrichment work for advanced pupils. Such work may consist of acquainting them with the story of the discovery and history of the binary (*base-two*) system used in electronic computers or the advantages claimed for the duodecimal (*base-twelve*) system. Whereas a few years ago this work was usually reserved for the junior high school level, many teachers today find that their advanced fifth- and sixth-grade students enjoy learning about varied base systems and appreciate the challenge of constructing their own notational systems using any base they choose.

Another cyclic concept which should be developed throughout all the grades is that the Hindu-Arabic system is an additive one. As children gradually begin to understand positional notation and base-ten properties of the number system, they can also develop an understanding of its additive quality. They can be led to discover, for instance, that 582 stands for the sum of 500 + 80 + 2. This concept again is probably best demonstrated through the use of a chart or box into which markers denoting different quantities may be grouped and regrouped.

In summary, it should be repeated that firm understanding of numbers and the number system is a cyclic instructional task which is taught in

[20] H. F. Spitzer, "Some Questionable Arithmetic Practices," *The Arithmetic Teacher,* Vol. 4 (October, 1957), pp. 175–178.

successive stages of complexity in all grades from kindergarten through six. Without this basic understanding, children will find it extremely difficult to develop understandings and competencies in the four fundamental operations, which form the second developmental strand of content in all grades.

Developing Understanding and Competencies in the Four Fundamental Operations

Concentrated instruction should be devoted to the understanding and mastery of the processes of addition, subtraction, multiplication, and division. Pupils should be helped to realize that all of these processes are refinements of the basic process of counting. Addition is only an efficient method of counting and multiplication is merely a quick method of adding. Subtraction is the inverse of addition in that it is "counting backwards" and division is a short method of subtraction. It is most important that the child, as he is introduced to each of these processes, realizes their interrelationships. This major understanding is, again, developed continually through a concentrated program of instruction in all grades, the actual start of which usually occurs in the first grade with initial work in addition and subtraction.

The teaching of the basic addition facts follows naturally from the concept of rational counting and exploring relationships. Combinations of all one-digit numbers with each other and with themselves are commonly called the basic addition facts. Strictly speaking, this term is in error for they are not really "facts" but generalizations. However, the term is used so commonly that to attempt to avoid it would only be confusing. Excluding the zero, there are 81 facts ranging from $1 + 1 = 2$ to $9 + 9 = 18$. In the majority of schools, pupils have been introduced to all the addition facts by the end of the second grade. Many of the pupils have achieved a high degree of mastery of them by that time.

It should be noted here that the order of presentation of new facts does not meet with unanimous agreement among teachers. Two common orders are used. The first is often called the *add 1, add 2* organization, in which facts are introduced as follows:

$$
\begin{array}{ccccccccc}
1 & 1 & 1 & 1 & 1 & 1 & 1 & 1 & 1 \\
1 & 2 & 3 & 4 & 5 & 6 & 7 & 8 & 9 \\
\hline
\end{array}
$$

$$
\begin{array}{ccccccccc}
2 & 2 & 2 & 2 & 2 & 2 & 2 & 2 & 2 \\
1 & 2 & 3 & 4 & 5 & 6 & 7 & 8 & 9 \\
\hline
\end{array}
$$

The other approach, which is more commonly used and the one favored by the authors, is the *number family* organization. This is the type of organization in which all facts of the same "family" are developed before proceeding to another "family." In other words, following the teaching of $2 + 3 = 5$, the other facts of the five-family would be introduced: $3 + 2 = 5$, $4 + 1 = 5$ and $1 + 4 = 5$. By learning these facts in this organization, the child is introduced to the following two important principles of addition which will stand him in good stead when he meets harder work.

a. *The commutative law.* The sum remains the same despite the order of the addends, which children should be led to express in such language as, "It doesn't matter which number comes first—the answer is always the same." Example: $3 + 2 = 5$ and $2 + 3 = 5$

b. *The theory of compensation.* The sum of two addends is unchanged if one is reduced and the other is increased by the same number, which children express as, "Take one from the top number, add it to the bottom one, and the answer is the same." Example: $2 + 3 = 5$ and $1 + 4 = 5$

Harder addition follows initial mastery of the basic facts. After children have achieved mastery of a sufficient number of addition facts, they are introduced (often in the second grade) to harder computation in arithmetic. This involves simple column addition in which the new skill of adding an unseen addend to a seen one is introduced,

$$\begin{array}{cccc} 4 & 2 & 1 & 2 \\ 2 & 3 & 2 & 2 \\ 1 & 5 & 4 & 3 \\ \hline \end{array}$$

adding by endings without bridging the decade

$$\begin{array}{cccc} 4 & 4 & 4 & 4 \\ 12 & 22 & 32 & 42 \\ \hline \end{array}$$

and with bridging the decade

$$\begin{array}{ccccc} 8 & 8 & 8 & 8 & 8 \\ 17 & 27 & 37 & 47 & 57 \\ \hline \end{array}$$

Teaching *carrying* in addition should present few serious difficulties if children have been given a firm fundamental comprehension of place value. The two most common errors made by pupils are: (1) failure to carry,

$$\begin{array}{cc} 14 & \qquad 14 \\ 12 & \qquad 12 \\ 17 & \qquad 17 \\ \hline 33 & \qquad 313 \end{array}$$

and, (2) carrying the wrong digit,

$$\begin{array}{c} 14 \\ 12 \\ 17 \\ \hline 61 \end{array}$$

Since both of these errors probably stem from a failure to understand place value, a need for reteaching this concept is indicated before proceeding to more complex computations.

The subtraction concept has three interpretations. The literal meaning of "subtraction" is "to draw from under." It is a modification of the French term *substraction* which was frequently used in colonial days along with such variations as *extraction, detraction,* and *subduction.* One of the major difficulties which teachers face in introducing the subtractive concept is the fact that it has three different interpretations, namely:

a. Subtraction has a *comparative* quality.

Example: Mr. Smith has 12 cows. Mr. Jones has 4 cows. How many more cows does Mr. Smith have than Mr. Jones?

b. Subtraction has an *additive* quality.

Example: Mary is saving her money to buy a watch which costs $12. She now has $4. How much more does she need to buy the watch?

c. Subtraction has a *take-away* interpretation.

Example: John had 12 cents. He spent 4 cents for candy. How much does he have left?

Gibb has reported that children "do not as a group conceive that one basic idea appears in all applications." [21] She further reported that solutions of problems using the "take-away" interpretation were less time-consuming and involved a higher degree of correctness than in the other two interpretations. In the light of this study, it would seem advisable for teachers to be aware of the difficulty which the varying concepts of subtraction involve and to explore the possibility of confining early experiences with subtraction to the "take-away" concept.

The basic subtraction facts are usually developed concurrently with their corresponding addition facts. There appears to be justifiable evidence to support the practice of teaching corresponding subtraction and addition facts simultaneously in a "learning unit"; for instance,

$$
\begin{array}{cccc}
4 & 5 & 9 & 9 \\
5 & 4 & 4 & 5 \\
\hline
9 & 9 & 5 & 4
\end{array}
$$

In order to prevent confusion, however, it is recommended that subtraction *not be introduced* until children have mastered a substantial number of addition facts. Only then should they be introduced to the corresponding subtraction facts and, when they have been mastered, should the remaining facts be presented in the learning units described above.

[21] E. G. Gibb, "Children's Thinking in the Process of Subtraction," *Journal of Experimental Education,* Vol. 25 (September, 1956), p. 78.

Compound subtraction is introduced in the intermediate grades. Compound subtraction calls for a "regrouping" or "transformation" of the minuend or subtrahend. The terms "borrow" and "pay back" are firmly entrenched in the vocabularies of most adults although they are definitely incorrect, for actually *at no time* does one either borrow or pay back, when performing compound subtraction. To the contrary, depending upon the process used, one either "regroups" the quantity represented by the minuend or he adds an identical quantity to both the minuend and subtrahend, thereby not altering the difference. Although many of the textbooks still use the terms "borrow" and "pay back," teachers are urged to use the more accurate terminology when introducing the process to children.

The two most common methods for doing compound subtraction are the *decomposition method* and the *equal-additions method* which are illustrated as follows:

DECOMPOSITION METHOD

3_11
$4\ 2_12$
$1\ 4\ 5$
$\overline{2\ 7\ 7}$

Using ordinary numbers, you cannot take 5 ones from 2 ones. You may transfer 1 ten from 2 tens to the ones column which will make 12 ones. 5 from 12 is 7. You can't take 4 tens from 1 ten but you can transfer I hundred to the tens column which will make 11 tens. 4 from 11 is 7. 1 from 3 is 2.

EQUAL-ADDITIONS METHOD

4_12_12
$_2 1_5 4\ 5$
$\overline{2\ 7\ 7}$

Using ordinary numbers, you cannot take 5 ones from 2 ones. You may add 1 ten to the 2 ones to make 12 ones. 5 from 12 is 7. Because you added 1 ten to the minuend you must also add it to the subtrahend, which will make 5 tens in place of 4 tens. You cannot take 5 tens from 2 tens but you may add 1 hundred (10 tens), which will make 12 tens. 5 from 12 is 7. Since you added 1 hundred to the minuend you must add it to the subtrahend which makes the 1 hundred become 2 hundreds. 2 from 4 is 2.

Controversy has waged for years as to which of these is more desirable. No absolute evidence exists as to the superiority of one over the other, although at the present time the preponderance of opinion appears to favor the decomposition method for the following reasons: (1) it is unquestionably the one used most frequently in this country; (2) most authorities feel that it can be rationalized more easily and clearly than the equal-additions; and (3) research supports it slightly more than the other. Such studies as those of Brownell and Moser [22] and, more recently, Rheins and Rheins [23] favor the decomposition method over the equal-additions method, if both are taught meaningfully. On the other hand, some writers

[22] W. A. Brownell and H. E. Moser, *op. cit.*
[23] G. B. Rheins and J. J. Rheins, "A Comparison of Two Methods of Compound Subtraction," *The Arithmetic Teacher*, Vol. 2 (October, 1955), pp. 63–68.

present a strong case for the equal additions method.[24] Apparently, the only safe conclusion to be drawn at the present time is that more research is needed to prove the superiority of one over the other and, until that time, teachers should be thoroughly familiar with both and should use the one recommended by their particular school system.

Two other types of subtraction occasionally mentioned are similar to the two processes described above, but use an additive terminology and concept. The *additive-decomposition* method uses an additive terminology and a decomposition process; and the *additive-equal additions* method uses an additive terminology and an equal-additions process.

Ordinarily the concept and process of multiplication is introduced in the third grade after children have established a secure mastery of addition and subtraction. Children can be led to discover the concept of multiplication as a short method of adding, through such experiences as:

1. We have 5 members on the art committee. Each member will need 3 pieces of paper. How many pieces of paper will the committee need?

ADD	MULTIPLY
3	3
3	5
3	$\overline{15}$
3	
3	
$\overline{15}$	

2. Each member of the committee will also need 2 paint brushes. How many brushes should we order?

ADD	MULTIPLY
2	2
2	5
2	$\overline{10}$
2	
2	
$\overline{10}$	

As these and similar problems are presented, children will gradually grasp the concept that multiplication is a more efficient method of adding when all addends are the same. As this concept is repeatedly reinforced, the pupils will gradually be presented to the multiplication facts.

The eighty-one multiplication facts are presented in the intermediate grades. There are 81 basic multiplication facts which correspond to the 81 addition facts. These should be presented in meaningful context, and their relationships to each other should be examined by pupils. Most authorities advocate that they *not* be presented in the old multiplication "table" order, but on the contrary presented in random order as $2 \times 5 = 10, 4 \times 5 = 20,$

[24] J. T. Johnson, "Whither Research in Compound Subtraction?" A Second Communication to the Editor, *The Arithmetic Teacher,* Vol. 5 (February, 1958), pp. 39–42.

$6 \times 5 = 30$, etc. After children have discovered each of these generalizations, they should be encouraged to rearrange them in tabular order so they can see the relationship and progression from $1 \times 5 = 5$, $2 \times 5 = 10$, $3 \times 5 = 15$, etc. It is important to note, however, that after these tabular relationships have been understood, the facts should be rearranged in nonsequential order to be practiced and memorized.

Initial work with multiplication facts should also stress the relationship between $4 \times 5 = 20$ and $5 \times 4 = 20$, so that children may see that the commutative law (p. 328) is applicable to multiplication as in addition.

Multiplication beyond the basic facts is also introduced in the intermediate grades. Multiplying a two-digit number by a single number without carrying represents the first progression in difficulty beyond the basic facts. Such examples as 23×2, 14×2, and 21×7 should be rationalized so that children understand fully the distributive quality of multiplication, which means simply that children should recognize that 23×2 is a regrouping of $20 \times 2 + 3 \times 2$. A thorough understanding of this principle plus a firm foundation in place-value should prepare the pupil for work involving two-digit multipliers and the writing of partial products, for example,

$$
\begin{array}{r}
42 \\
14 \\
\hline
168 \\
42 \\
\hline
588
\end{array}
$$

is a short method for:

$$
\begin{array}{rrr}
42 & 42 & 168 \\
4 & 10 & 420 \\
\hline
168 & 420 & 588
\end{array}
$$

Traditionally, the introduction of division has been delayed until the third or fourth grade, although in recent years some experimentation has been done in introducing the concept as early as the first grade.[25] Faced with actual problems such as, "We have 12 pieces of colored chalk for our art committee. 4 people are on the committee. How many pieces of chalk may each person have?", many primary grade teachers will encourage their children to figure the answer through placing objects in groups and thus establishing an initial concept of division. If some incidental work of this type takes place in the primary grades, the succeeding teachers will have a foundation upon which to begin formal computation involving division.

The concept of division, as introduced in the elementary grades, includes two types of situations. Division may be defined merely as the in-

[25] D. S. Ambrosius, "Division for First-Graders?" *The Arithmetic Teacher*, Vol. 3 (February, 1956), pp. 27–28.

verse of multiplication and, as such, it has two distinct interpretations. The first of these is the *measurement concept,* which is operative in problems where one is to find the number of groups of specified size which can be obtained from a larger group. Example: "If there are 8 seats in an auditorium row, how many rows will we need for our class of 32 children?" The second interpretation of division is the partitive concept, which calls for finding the size of a given number of groups which can be obtained from a larger group. Example: "We have 32 cookies for 8 people. How many cookies may each person have?" The authors do not recommend that children should be confused by overstressing the terminology of the measurement and partitive interpretations of division, but they should grasp the concept that the process is operable in two different types of situations.

Also, because the measurement concept of division is usually easier to grasp [26] and more frequently met by young children,[27] it seems to be a sound procedure to give it the greater portion of attention in the early stages of teaching division.

A third concept of division, that of *ratio,* may be explored informally in the upper elementary grades, but formal teaching of it is usually postponed to the junior high school.

The division process is presented according to graduated levels of difficulty. The even division facts ($12 \div 3$) constitute the first level of difficulty. Just as addition and subtraction facts may be taught in "learning units" so may multiplication and division facts be taught in the same order, for instance, $5 \times 3 = 15$, $3 \times 5 = 15$, $15 \div 3 = 5$ and $15 \div 5 = 3$. Here, also the same procedure is recommended: establishing an initial mastery of several multiplication facts, then introducing the corresponding division facts, and from then on presenting them simultaneously in "learning units."

The uneven division facts ($16 \div 3$) follow the introduction of even facts and pave the way for the division algorism using a one-digit divisor. Initial instruction in such examples as $24 \div 2$ should stress two important principles of division. The first of these is the *distributive principle,* so that the child will be helped to see that $24 \div 2$ is a combination of $20 \div 2$ and $4 \div 2$. The second basic principle, which is receiving considerable attention from modern teachers, is the *short method of subtraction principle.*

The concept of division as successive subtraction is clarified in many levels of computation. From the pupil's first introduction to the computation of division, he should be helped to understand the relationship of the process to subtraction. The teacher may demonstrate the idea that in $15 \div 5$ the 5 may be obtained 3 times from 15. This concept continues with

[26] A. G. Gunderson, "Thought-Patterns of Young Children in Learning Multiplication and Division," *Elementary School Journal,* Vol. 55 (April, 1955), 453–461.

[27] E. H. Hill, "Teachers: Two Kinds of Division," *Journal of Education,* Vol. 137 (May, 1955), pp. 16–18.

algorisms using 2-figure divisors so that children have a clear comprehension of the rationale underlying the mechanics of long division. This can be illustrated as follows:

FIRST STEP

$$1+1+1+1+1+1+1+1+1+1+1 = 11$$

```
14)154
    14
   140
    14
   126
    14
   112
    14
    98
    14
    84
    14
    70
    14
    56
    14
    42
    14
    28
    14
    14
    14
     0
```

SECOND STEP

$$10+1 = 11$$

```
14)154
   140
    14
    14
```

THIRD STEP

```
    11
14)154
    14
    14
    14
```

The previous illustration is typical of the meaningful and rational approach to division which should eliminate the "long-division bugbear" which has haunted children who were taught only the mechanics of the process without understanding its rationale.

Developing Understandings and Skills in Common Fractions

The teaching of fractions extends through the entire elementary program. A third major developmental strand which runs through all the grades is the teaching of common fractions. There was a time, of course, when this task was not considered in such a light but was treated as a specific block of subject matter usually assigned to the fifth grade. As a matter of fact, one of the authors has a painful memory of "introducing" the subject to her fifth-graders one morning twenty-five years ago with the woefully incorrect statement, "Today we are going to start our study of a brand new subject in arithmetic called fractions." Today, fortunately, such appallingly poor practice has generally disappeared, and many recent curriculum guides make provision for the study of fractions at the earliest grade level.[28]

Long before children enter school, many of them have developed a vague concept and a limited vocabulary of fractions. They know, for instance, that a half a piece of candy is smaller than a whole piece, and that as more people share an apple the smaller the pieces become. It becomes the kindergarten teacher's responsibility, therefore, to refine these beginning concepts to the point of accuracy. For instance, youngsters who have made a start toward recognizing each of two pieces as a half should be helped to understand, through successive informal experiences, that a half is not merely one of two pieces but one of two equal pieces. These and related concepts can be expanded throughout the informal program of the primary grades.

This spiral-like pattern continues through the intermediate grades where children may be introduced to reading, writing, and simple computation involving fractions. Making recipe books, constructing scenery for the class play, and numerous other opportunities will present themselves in the intermediate grades for the development of skills and concepts of fractions. Morton suggests that such experiences should help pupils develop the following understandings concerning common fractions:

1. The denominator (the lower number) of a fraction tells the number of pieces into which the object was divided.

2. The numerator (the upper number) tells how many pieces we are using or talking about.

3. The larger the denominator, the smaller the pieces and the smaller the fraction if the numerator remains the same.

4. The larger the numerator, the larger the fraction if the denominator remains the same.

5. If both the numerator and the denominator of a fraction are multiplied by the same number, the value of the fraction is not changed.

6. If both the numerator and the denominator of a fraction are divided by the same number, the value of the fraction is not changed.

7. If the numerator of a fraction is less than the denominator, the value of the fraction is less than 1. The fraction is called a *proper fraction.*

8. If the numerator of a fraction is equal to the denominator, the value of the fraction is equal to 1. The fraction is called an *improper fraction.*

9. If the numerator of a fraction is greater than the denominator, the value of the fraction is greater than 1. This fraction is also called an improper fraction.[29]

[28] *Guide to the Teaching of Arithmetic: Grades One and Two* (Long Beach, Calif., Long Beach Unified School District, 1960); *Guide for Teaching Mathematics K-9,* Bulletin No. 3, Curriculum Department (Trenton, N.J., Trenton Public Schools, 1959).
[29] R. L. Morton, *Helping Children Learn Arithmetic* (Morristown, N.J., Silver Burdett Company, 1960), pp. 45–46.

Computation with fractions involves a carefully graded sequence of difficulties. The mastery of addition, subtraction, multiplication, and division of fractions is stressed in the fifth and sixth grades with the teacher giving particular attention to: (1) the previously mentioned understandings, and (2) the importance of teaching new steps according to graduated difficulty and complexity. The following example, for instance, illustrates the progression of difficulty *in a single process*—that of adding two proper fractions.

a. Adding fractions with like denominators:

$\frac{1}{3} + \frac{1}{3} = \frac{2}{3}$ (without reducing)

$\frac{1}{4} + \frac{1}{4} = \frac{2}{4} = \frac{1}{2}$ (reducing to lowest terms)

$\frac{2}{3} + \frac{2}{3} = \frac{4}{3} = 1\frac{1}{3}$ (reducing improper fraction to mixed number)

$\frac{3}{4} + \frac{3}{4} = \frac{6}{4} = 1\frac{2}{4} = 1\frac{1}{2}$ (reducing improper fraction to mixed number and lowest terms)

b. Adding fractions with unlike denominators using one seen denominator as the common denominator:

$\frac{3}{8} + \frac{1}{4} = \frac{5}{8}$ (without reducing)

$\frac{1}{2} + \frac{1}{6} = \frac{4}{6} = \frac{2}{3}$ (reducing to lowest terms)

$\frac{1}{2} + \frac{3}{4} = \frac{5}{4} = 1\frac{1}{4}$ (reducing improper fraction to mixed number)

$\frac{1}{2} + \frac{5}{6} = \frac{8}{6} = 1\frac{2}{6} = 1\frac{1}{3}$ (reducing improper fraction to mixed number and to lowest terms)

c. Adding fractions with unlike denominators using an unseen common denominator:

$\frac{1}{2} + \frac{1}{3} = \frac{5}{6}$

The preceding is illustrative only of the many difficulties met in a single process. It should be noted that in step "c" there should be no undue stress placed upon the importance of using the *least common denominator*. As a matter of fact, insistence upon the "least common denominator" has been one of the "sacred cows" in arithmetic teaching for too long. Children should understand that this device will be helpful if the answer is needed in lowest terms, otherwise the use of any denominator is defensible. When adding $\frac{1}{4}$ and $\frac{1}{6}$ many children will prefer to use a denominator of 24 rather than 12, and there is no sound reason for insisting upon the lower one.

Multiplication and division of fractions are taught in the upper grades. Both of these processes, with all the various gradations of difficulty, are usually taught in the fifth and sixth grades. Multiplication is taught, with and without cancellation, with children realizing that cancellation is a short cut which may or may not be preferred when multiplying simple fractions.

The division of common fractions has aroused considerable discussion in recent years, the details of which are too involved to consider at length in this chapter. Opinions range from advocating its postponement until the junior high school to teaching its mechanics and rationale along with multiplication. When taught, the following methods appear to be used most frequently to rationalize the process.

a. The inversion method:

$$\frac{3}{4} \div \frac{1}{2} = \frac{\frac{3}{4}}{\frac{1}{2}} = \frac{\frac{3}{4} \times \frac{2}{1}}{\frac{1}{2} \times \frac{2}{1}} = \frac{\frac{3}{4} \times \frac{2}{1}}{1} = \frac{3}{4} \times \frac{2}{1} = 1\frac{1}{2}$$

b. The common denominator method:

$$\frac{3}{4} \div \frac{1}{2} = \frac{3}{4} \div \frac{2}{4} = \frac{3 \div 2}{1} = 3 \div 2 = \frac{3}{2} = 1\frac{1}{2}$$

Each has its advantages and disadvantages and, according to a recent study, both are equally acceptable and,

Perhaps both should be taught in order that the process may be given meaning through the use of the common denominator method, and the students may then choose the method with which they work more easily.[30]

Developing Understandings and Skills in Decimal Fractions

Meaning and rationalization are stressed. Children in the early grades have had contact with decimals in problems using money, but it is in the upper grades that they begin to use decimals in other contexts. It should be stressed that the primary goal is the development of a thorough concept of decimal fractions and of their relationship to whole numbers and common fractions. The place-value chart, recommended earlier for primary grades, can be expanded to include decimal places, and is just as vital a teaching aid here as it was in the lower grades. In actual computations involving decimals, the chief instructional task is rationalizing the placing of the decimal point since, otherwise, the computation in all four processes is the same as that used with whole numbers. The placing of the decimal point in addition and subtraction involves little difficulty. In multiplication and division, however, the step must be rationalized thoroughly and completely.

Unfortunately, in the past, when multiplying or dividing decimals, pupils obediently counted the number of places in the product or inserted the caret in the dividend, without the least idea what they were doing. Today, many teachers help pupils rationalize these processes by comparing the decimal fraction with its common fraction counterpart. For instance, if the pupil can see that 4.78×1.4 is really

$$4\frac{78}{100} \times 1\frac{4}{10}$$

[30] L. Stephens and W. Dutton, "Retention of the Skill of Division of Fractions," *The Arithmetic Teacher*, Vol. 7 (January, 1960), p. 31.

and that when you multiply hundredths by tenths your answer will be thousandths, he will be able to discover for himself that a short method of doing this is to count the decimal places in the multiplicand and multiplier and fix an equal number in the product.

In division, the pupil should understand the following:

$$.4\overline{)\,.24} = \frac{24}{100} \div \frac{4}{10} = \frac{\frac{24}{100}}{\frac{4}{10}} = \frac{\frac{24}{100} \times \frac{10}{4}}{\frac{4}{10} \times \frac{10}{4}} =$$

$$\frac{\frac{24}{100} \times \frac{10}{4}}{1} = \frac{6}{10} = .6$$

Another method of rationalizing the division of decimals is to show that it is the inverse of multiplication. The child knows that the decimal places in the multiplicand and multiplier must be added to place the decimal point in the product. Therefore, he can discover that, in order to place the decimal point in the quotient, he can *subtract* the number of places in the divisor from the number in the dividend, adding zeros to the dividend if necessary.

Example:

$$\begin{array}{r} 4.5 \\ .4 \\ \hline 1.80 \end{array}$$

$$.4\overline{)\,1.80} \quad \begin{array}{r} 4.5 \\ \hline 1.80 \\ 16 \\ \hline 20 \\ 20 \end{array}$$

Subtract decimal places in divisor from decimal places in dividend to find that there should be 1 decimal place in the quotient.

This is an old method which was fairly common at one time and is still advocated by some as being arithmetically desirable.

Developing Competencies with Common Units of Measurement

The first experiences children have with measurement are very informal as they realize that something is "longer," "little," "more," "less," "jumbo," or "king-size." As early as first grade, however, pupils may be introduced to some of the common units of linear measure (*inches, feet, yards*) or liquid measure (*pints, quarts*). These experiences may often be provided through the unit activities of measuring the space needed for the class post office; filling the aquarium tank with the correct amount of water; or measuring the dimensions of the hamster cage. In general, by the time elementary school pupils leave the sixth grade they have received a fairly basic understanding of the most common units of length, time, capacity, weight, and temperature. These measurements are rarely, if ever, intro-

Children are introduced early to the common units of measure.

duced in tables although after children have learned the common units they may be arranged in a table to see relationships and comparisons.

A basic concept of measurement which can be introduced in the early elementary grades is that of approximation—that no measurement is ever "exact." Although this concept is not given particular emphasis in the primary grades, there is no reason why the child of nine or ten cannot grasp the concept that the length of his room can be measured by feet, inches, half-inches, quarter-inches, eighth-inches, etc. and that each becomes more precise, but none are absolutely exact.

The following third-grade lesson is typical of the opportunities which present themselves for the functional teaching of measurement in the elementary grades.

DEVELOPMENTAL LESSON ON LIQUID MEASUREMENT
(Grade 3)

OBJECTIVE

To introduce the concepts:
2 standard cupfuls = 1 pint
2 pints = 1 quart
4 standard cupfuls = 1 quart

PROCEDURE

Teacher: The other day, Ginny said she was worried about changing the water for the turtle. When we changed the water before, David said that we had added too much water. Is that right, David? But Beth didn't agree with him and she said that we hadn't added enough. So we really aren't sure as to how much water there should be.

I looked it up in our book about turtles last night and it said that we should have 1 quart of water for a tank our size. How much is that? Let's find out. I have several containers on the table. Who can pick out the one which contains one quart? How do we know?

Child: It says it on the outside.

Teacher: That's right. That means this container, when filled to the very top, will hold one quart of water. But I have other containers here. What is this one?

Child: A pint.

Teacher: That's right. This will hold one pint. How many of these will be needed to fill the quart container? Who can estimate how many? Let's see who is right. Will John come to the table, fill the pint container with water, and transfer it to the quart container?

Will we need another pint? Will Patricia fill the pint container again and transfer it to the quart container? Does it fill the quart to the brim? Do we have any space left over? What have we discovered?

Child: That 2 pints are the same as 1 quart.

Teacher: I'll write that on the board. (*Writes 2 pints = 1 quart*)
Now I have still another container on the table. What is this called? You have seen your mother use it in cooking.

Child: A measuring cup.

Teacher: Some people call it that and some call it a "standard cup" because it is a certain size. Let's see how many standard cupfuls are in a pint. What do you estimate the number will be?

Will Laura fill the cup with water and transfer it to the pint? Did it fill it?

Will Donald do the same thing? Did it fill it this time? What have we found out?

Child: Two cups equal 1 pint.

Teacher: Good. Let's say two *standard* cups because sometimes cups are different sizes. I'll write this on the board, also.

Teacher: Now look carefully at what we have written on the board and someone see if he can tell us something else that we have discovered today. Compare what we have said on both boards.

Child: If 2 cups equal 1 pint, and 2 pints equal 1 quart, then 4 cups will equal 1 quart.

Teacher: I wonder if that's true. Shall we prove it by actually doing it? Who will fill the cup with water again and transfer it to the quart container? (*Proceeds with 4 cupfuls*)

What else have we discovered today?

Child: That 4 cupfuls equal 1 quart.

Teacher: Very good. Let's write that on the board. Now let's look at our flannel board and make a picture list of the things we have learned today.

I will put a picture on the board. Who will come and put a picture beside it of what it equals. (*Puts pint container on board. Child puts 2 cupfuls beside it as below.*)

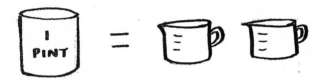

Teacher: Now I'll put another picture on the board. Who can find its equal? (*1 quart = 2 pints*)

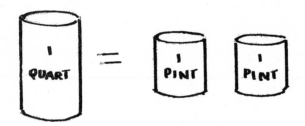

Teacher: And now a third picture. Who can complete it? (*1 quart equals 4 cupfuls*)

EVALUATION

Teacher: Let's return to our aquarium tank. How much water did we say the turtle needed?

Child: 1 quart.

Teacher: How could we put this amount into the tank?

Child: Fill the quart container and then pour it in the tank.

Teacher: What is another way we could do it?

Child: Pour two pints into the tank.

Teacher: And still another way?

Child: Pour 4 standard cupfuls into the tank.

Teacher: Good. We have discovered that we can use any of these three containers to measure one quart. Now we will be sure always to have the correct amount and we won't have to worry about having too much or too little.

Improving Problem-Solving

The following example of Sally's approach to problem-solving is, unfortunately, not as unique as it should be.

If there are a lot of numbers, I add. If there are just two numbers with lots of parts, I subtract. If there are just two numbers and one is a little harder than the other, I divide if they come out even. But if they don't, I multiply.[31]

Actually, there has been considerable investigation made concerning the difficulties which children encounter in solving verbal problems. In general, these may be classified as: (1) unfamiliarity with the situation, (2) failure to understand the vocabulary, (3) failure to analyze relationships in order to determine correct processes, and (4) computational difficulties. Adherence to the following general principles should help to eliminate many of these.

The problem should be socially significant to the learner. The emphasis upon the social aspect of arithmetic has resulted in eliminating many of the absurd and artificial problems found in the very early textbooks. Actually, the revolt against the "unreal" problem is not new as evidenced from the following statement, made in 1915:

The pedagogical fashion in problems at present is happily not that of a few years ago when pupils meditated upon unhappy snails who spent their lives ceaselessly climbing one foot and slipping back two feet on the side of a well. We have eliminated puzzles and "catch" problems. In their place we should substitute practical problems related to the child's experience either actual or imagined and to situations in which he may have a real interest.[32]

[31] E. Reinhardt, *American Education: An Introduction* (New York, Harper and Brothers, 1954), p. 235.

[32] L. M. Murphy, "Primary Plans for February," *Teachers Magazine*, Vol. 37 (February, 1915), p. 220.

Today, one finds two hopeful trends in providing pupils with socially significant and applicable problems. In the first place, textbook authors have definitely made an attempt to include problems of interest and significance. Secondly, there is evidence that teachers find it extremely worthwhile to compile a file of experience problems which they and/or their pupils compose to supplement those of the text.[33] This appears to be an excellent device for strengthening problem-solving competencies which could be utilized profitably by all teachers.

The vocabulary and form of the problem should be on the pupil's reading level. An investigation of recent arithmetic textbooks has indicated that an unfamiliar and difficult vocabulary constitutes a serious handicap to problem-solving.[34] If the teacher finds this to be generally true, he must make every attempt to develop vocabulary skills and, in extreme cases, to rewrite the problem. It should be fairly obvious that pupils cannot begin to attack the solution of a problem rationally until they understand its import clearly and completely.

Pupils should be encouraged to select the correct process or processes by seeing relationships between the given data. Notice the following problem.

Sam needs 7 pieces of wood $1\frac{3}{4}$ feet long. Can he cut them from a board $8\frac{3}{4}$ feet long? How many more pieces does he need? [35]

Unless a pupil can visualize this situation and can understand the relationship of the three numbers, he will be totally lost as to what processes to employ. In similar problems, pupils have been known to attack blindly a solution by adding the two mixed numbers or following some equally unreasonable procedure, because they had no understanding of the relationships of the data. If they could be helped to visualize 7 pieces of board, each $1\frac{3}{4}$ feet long, laid end to end beside 1 plank of board $8\frac{3}{4}$ feet long, they would have a fairly secure understanding of the steps they needed to take to answer the problem. Another device found by some teachers to be helpful in clarifying relationships is substituting small and familiar numbers in the problem. In the previous problem, for instance, children may be handicapped in seeing relationships because of their comparative unfamiliarity with mixed numbers. If the problem were to be restated as,

Sam needs 5 pieces of wood 2 feet long. Can he cut them from a board 6 feet long? How many more pieces does he need?

[33] A. F. Doherty, *A Collection and Analysis of Pupil Built Problems in Arithmetic*, Unpublished Masters Thesis (Boston, Boston University, 1952); and D. Berglund, et al., "Another Look at Problem Solving," *The Arithmetic Teacher*, Vol. 5 (December, 1958), pp. 315–316.

[34] F. C. Repp, "The Vocabularies of Five Recent Third Grade Arithmetic Textbooks," *The Arithmetic Teacher*, Vol. 7 (March, 1960), pp. 128–132.

[35] H. G. Wheat, G. Kauffman and H. R. Douglass, *Row-Peterson Arithmetic: Book Six* (Evanston, Ill., Row, Peterson and Company, 1954), p. 164.

the pupil would be better able to understand the relationships and processes needed to arrive at the solution.

**An informal approach to problem-solving is preferable to the traditional
formal approach.** Numerous studies have been made in an attempt to
compare the informal or individual approach to problem-solving with the
"formal structuring" approach (*What does the problem tell you? What
does it ask you?*). By far the large majority of these studies favor the informal approach and agree generally with the following findings and
conclusions made by Burch:

> The pupils involved in this study tended to score higher on the test which
> did not require them to go through steps of formal analysis. This finding obtained
> despite the fact that most of the subjects had had good training in using the
> formal analysis procedure. . . . Much of the time that is now devoted to teaching
> formal analysis might well be better spent in guiding pupils to think more care-
> fully about the sizes, the relationships, and the dynamics of the quantities
> described in each problem.[36]

The emphasis on the informal approach, however, should not be interpreted as meaning that no direct teaching of problem-solving is done.
It does mean that teachers should help pupils analyze problems in many
different ways instead of forcing them to answer a structured series of
questions which may prove to be a harder task than solving the problem!

**Children are encouraged to attempt a variety of solutions in solving
problems.** Today, there is considerable interest in encouraging pupils to
attempt to solve a problem using several different procedures. Such a
technique will have value: (1) in teaching the pupils that rarely is there an
"absolute" method for solving any problem, (2) in helping them to gain
an insight and understanding of numerical interrelationships, and (3) in
demonstrating that different procedures may be used to "check" the
solution.

**The practice of searching for "cue" words in problems should be dis-
couraged.** Listed among the more significant conclusions drawn by
Bartram in his analysis of certain research studies in teaching arithmetic
was that children should not be taught to search for "cue" words in problems.[37] In other words, children should not be taught that "how many
more" always tells us to subtract or "how many altogether" means to add.
Objections to using such a crutch of "cue" words include: (1) it is not
always true; (2) it is of no help in multistep problems; and (3) it encourages a mechanical attack as opposed to developing insight and comprehension of relationships.

Pupils should be encouraged to estimate answers in attacking verbal

---

[36] R. L. Burch, "Formal Analysis as a Problem-Solving Procedure," *Journal of Education,* Vol. 46 (November, 1953), p. 47 and p. 64.
[37] C. E. Bartram. *loc. cit.*

problems. The practice of estimating answers is a valid one which should be encouraged. It helps children consider the problem as a whole unit and it also gives them a check on the accuracy of their answer.

Children should be given practice in solving problems mentally. Outside the classroom walls, many of the quantitative problems one meets must be done mentally. Today there is an increased interest in sharpening pupils' abilities to work certain types of problems without benefit of pencil and paper. A practice sheet of verbal problems which contains the directions, "Try not to use pencil and paper. Think of the answer in your head and write only it on your paper," is a device which may be used in any grade in the elementary school.

In problem-solving, attention should be directed toward both the process and accuracy of answer. There seems to be no point to the controversy which arises as to whether the teacher should devote more attention to the process or the final answer when developing problem-solving abilities. Obviously, both are important. The Internal Revenue Bureau is not satisfied if one has used the correct process in figuring his income tax if his final return is incorrect! On the other hand, a correct answer is not much good if it is the result of an accident or a "lucky guess." The important consideration is, "Does the pupil understand the problem and can he do the necessary computation to arrive at a solution?" If the teacher uses this consideration as the broad base to teaching and testing problem-solving, it appears to be immaterial as to how he chooses to "mark" the pupil's finished work.

On the preceding pages, the authors have attempted to discuss briefly the six developmental strands which interweave to form the sequential program of arithmetic instruction from kindergarten through the sixth grade. The next section is devoted to techniques and methods which may be used in adapting instruction to the competencies of individual pupils.

MEETING INDIVIDUAL DIFFERENCES

For some unfathomable reason, the idea of grouping the class for arithmetic instruction does not appear to be as widespread as it is in other areas, particularly reading. This is especially hard to understand when one thinks of the structural nature of the subject and the necessity of giving each pupil a firm foundation for the next step in learning. To sweep a child along with his class simply because the majority appear ready for the next difficulty seems to be completely indefensible. The authors cannot make too strong a plea for grouping for arithmetic instruction.

A traditional method of grouping is the "permanent" (*double-track, triple-track*) organization, in which the class is divided into two or three groups with the program adapted accordingly in pacing and content. In a third grade, for instance, the teacher may introduce carrying in addition to "Peter's group" while "Linda's group" will be working on practice exercises of the basic addition facts. This is a sound teaching procedure provided that it allows for flexibility and mobility. Children should be permitted to move from one group to another when this seems desirable. Frequently a teacher will prefer to withdraw a pupil from either group to work with him individually for a certain length of time. Depending upon the heterogeneity of the class, many teachers find that this procedure appears to meet the needs of their pupils, and throughout the year they work according to a two- or three-group pattern, giving individual attention when it is needed.

Another equally sound procedure for grouping is the "flexible" pattern used by some teachers. According to this plan, the teacher may group his entire class as a unit for the "discovery-exploration" and "integrative practice" phase of a new learning. At this time the teacher will present the problem, encourage children to discover the solution, and verify the solution through repeated experiences with concrete and semiconcrete aids. After the teacher feels that general comprehension has been achieved, he will follow up with a written exercise to discover the level of mastery of the abstraction. Upon the basis of his diagnosis of these results, he will split the class into various groups and prepare assignments accordingly. Some children will have demonstrated complete mastery of the concept and process and they will be ready for deeper challenge and enrichment. Some will reveal only a need for additional practice in order to master the mechanics of the process. Some will reveal a "half-formed" concept which will indicate further need for integrative practice involving visualization and manipulation. Others may reveal a total lack of comprehension and, for these few, the teacher may find it necessary to repeat the entire "discovery-exploration" phase. Pupils will accordingly work in a small group-individual pattern until the next step is presented, at which time the teacher will again combine them into a single group.

A variation of this pattern may be used in a class in which there appears to be only a very small group who need additional attention. This "remedial" group may work daily with the class, but may have a second daily session with the teacher. Such a pattern, of course, would be equally effective if the abilities of pupils warranted a small "enrichment" group operating in the same manner.

At the present time, research does not appear to favor any one method of grouping.[38] The important point to be stressed is, therefore, that grouping *should be done*. How it is done will depend upon the size and heterogeneity of the class as well as the maturities and abilities of the pupils.

---

[38] D. Holmes and L. Harvey, "An Evaluation of Two Methods of Grouping," *Educational Research Bulletin*, Vol. 35 (November 14, 1956), pp. 213–222.

Although completely individualized instruction may be a very sound procedure in some curriculum areas, it does not appear to be equally defensible in arithmetic. In other words, to apply the basic teaching procedure described on pages 318–323 *to each individual as* he progresses to *each new level* in arithmetic would appear to be a completely inefficient and impractical procedure. This does not mean that the teacher should not attempt to utilize such sound educational devices as individualized assignments, specially prepared practice-exercises, and "buddy-teaching" (children working in pairs). It does mean that, in general, any type of *group* organization which permits considerable attention to the varying abilities of pupils is more conducive to efficient instruction and economical use of school time than a program of completely individualized instruction.

INSTRUCTIONAL AIDS AND MATERIALS

A comprehensive survey of this topic would necessitate a discussion of all textbooks, workbooks, films, filmstrips, recordings, realia, manipulative materials, charts, pictures, practice exercises, and games which should be used to vitalize the arithmetic program. Rather than attempt a task of this magnitude, the authors suggest a minimal list of aids, most of which should be in the permanent possession of every teacher from first through sixth grade. These include:

1. A collection of common measurement devices as:
   a. An oversized tackboard clock with manipulative hands.
   b. A large tackboard or plywood thermometer operable by the pupils.
   c. All common units of measure—pint, measuring cup, quart, peck, ruler, and yardstick.
   d. Set of scales.

2. A flannel board or felt board. These can be secured from commercial houses, but a very satisfactory one can be made from an old card table covered with felt or flannel. This can be used "face-up" or can be used as an easel resting on two legs with the other two legs folded.

3. A place-value pocket chart or box into which markers can be placed. In the upper grades, the chart should contain "pockets" for decimal fractions.

4. A series of charts illustrating the basic properties of numbers and the number system.

5. An abacus or counting frame.

6. A collection of small concrete manipulative objects, such as corks, pebbles, straws, cubes, sticks, beads, and play money.

7. A collection of "semiconcrete" aids such as cardboard discs, squares, and circles, which can be used for visualizing concepts of numbers and fractions.

8. A collection of practice exercises and educational games.

An arithmetic corner is important in the elementary classroom.

9. A class-made "arithmetic dictionary" into which new vocabulary words are added throughout the year.

10. An arithmetic library.

The above suggestions should enable the teacher to make a start in developing an "arithmetic laboratory" or an "arithmetic corner" in his elementary classroom. For suggestions as to additional valuable aids and their uses, the reader is referred to the following sources:

BERGER, Emil J. and JOHNSON, Donovan A., *A Guide to the Use and Procurement of Teaching Aids for Mathematics* (Washington, D.C., National Council of Teachers of Mathematics, 1959).

GROSSNICKLE, F. E., JUNGE, C. and METZNER, W., "Instructional Materials for Teaching Arithmetic," *The Teaching of Arithmetic*, 50th Yearbook of the National Society for the Study of Education, Part II (Chicago, University of Chicago Press, 1951), Chapter 9.

HESS, A. L., "A Bibliography of Mathematics Books for Elementary School Libraries," *The Arithmetic Teacher*, Vol. 4 (February, 1957), 15–20.

HUTCHESON, R., MANTOR, E., and HOLMBERG, M., "The Elementary School Mathematics Library. A Selected Bibliography," *The Arithmetic Teacher*, Vol. 3 (February, 1956), pp. 8–15.

JOHNSON, D. A., "Commercial Games for the Arithmetic Class," *The Arithmetic Teacher*, Vol. 5 (March, 1958), pp. 69–73.

THOMAS, Robert M. and SWARTOUT, Sherwin G., *Integrated Teaching Materials* (New York, Longmans, Green and Company, Inc., 1960).

URBANCEK, Joseph J., compiler, "Mathematical Teaching Aids," Supplement, *Chicago Schools Journal*, Vol. 35, Nos. 3–6, November-December, 1953; January-February, 1954.

FUTURE DEVELOPMENTS IN ARITHMETIC TEACHING

At the present time, there appears to be considerable interest in experimenting with new content and materials in the elementary school arithmetic program. In general, the heightened interest in these experimental programs may be traced to certain far-reaching sociological and scientific movements in this country and abroad. Such factors as the following have been tremendously significant in directing our attention to the re-evaluation and reappraisal of the entire field of elementary arithmetic:

1. The rapidly changing social scene with its "jet-age" statistics has outmoded many of the problem data now in use.

2. The present furor of criticism (valid or not) directed toward the schools has precipitated considerable agitation for further research and experimentation.

3. The ever-increasing technological advances have suggested a need for acquainting young children with a "new" mathematics.

4. The interest in revamping college and secondary mathematics programs has filtered down to the elementary school level.

5. Research, experience, and observation have demonstrated the limitations and weaknesses of past arithmetic programs and procedures.

6. The accelerated interest in providing sufficient challenge for the academically-gifted pupil has introduced new content into the elementary school program.

7. The "explosion of scientific knowledge" has highlighted the increasing need for trained scientists and mathematicians.

Whether one agrees on the extent to which these developments *should* influence the elementary school is, at the moment, immaterial. What is important is that they have precipitated some exciting research and experimentation which should point the way to a better educational program for our schools of the future.

Typical of the present interest in improving the elementary school program are such studies as those being conducted by the Elementary School Curriculum Committee of the National Council of Teachers of Mathematics; the School Mathematics Study Group, Conference on Elementary School Mathematics, and the University of Illinois Committee on School Arithmetic.

In addition, current literature is filled with studies reporting the introduction of new content or new materials in the elementary grades. Such recent articles as those by Parsons,[39] Lerner and Sobel,[40] and Sawyer [41] indicate an interest in introducing at an earlier level concepts and content formerly reserved for the secondary schools. Similar articles report the use of such devices as calculators,[42] computors,[43] and slide rules [44] in teaching elementary school arithmetic.

As was stated earlier, the authors, as well as many others, may not necessarily agree with all the recommendations of these and similar experimental studies. They do agree strongly, however, that research and experimentation is a healthy and exciting feature of our modern elementary school arithmetic program and, as such, it should move "with full steam ahead."

Summary

The first part of the chapter was devoted to a discussion of the three common theories of arithmetic instruction: the *drill theory*, the *incidental learning theory*, and the *meaning theory*. Because of the preponderance of evidence in its favor, the meaning theory, with its emphasis upon teaching arithmetic as a socially significant and mathematically meaningful subject, was strongly advocated. In order to teach arithmetic successfully in this manner, it is necessary for the teacher to direct his attention toward such major considerations as: (1) readiness for learning; (2) sound instructional procedures; (3) a sequential program of concepts and skills; (4) recognition of pupil needs and abilities, and (5) the use of teaching aids and materials.

Readiness for learning was defined in its broad, modern-day concept, which includes such interrelated factors as experience, intelligence, maturation, degree of understanding, and purpose. Its importance at each grade level was discussed together with suggestions for determining the extent of its presence for specific tasks.

Generalized instructional procedures and principles were divided into: (1) those which dealt with presenting new learnings, and (2) those concerned with providing repetitive practice. The latter was accorded a place in meaningful teaching, although teachers were urged to include repetitive

[39] C. Parsons, "Algebra in the Fourth Grade," *The Arithmetic Teacher*, Vol. 7 (February, 1960), pp. 77–79.

[40] N. Lerner and M. Sobel, " 'Sets' and Elementary School Mathematics," *The Arithmetic Teacher*, Vol. 5 (November, 1958), pp. 239–246.

[41] W. W. Sawyer, "Algebra in Grade Five," *The Arithmetic Teacher*, Vol. 7 (January, 1960), pp. 25–27.

[42] L. L. Beck, "A Report on the Use of Calculators," *The Arithmetic Teacher*, Vol. 7 (February, 1960), p. 103.

[43] H. F. Fehr, et al., "Using Hand-Operated Computing Machines in Learning Arithmetic," *The Arithmetic Teacher*, Vol. 3 (October, 1956), pp. 145–150.

[44] J. J. Gramlich, "Slide Rules for the Upper Elementary Grades," *The Arithmetic Teacher*, Vol. 5 (February, 1958), pp. 29–33.

practice only in proper perspective to the major emphasis of developing understanding.

The necessity for a planned and sequential program of content was emphasized. The *developmental curriculum* was discussed according to the cyclic instructional tasks designated as: (1) developing an understanding of numbers and the number system; (2) developing understandings and skills in the four fundamental processes; (3) developing understandings and skills in common fractions; (4) developing understandings and skills in decimal fractions; (5) developing competencies in the use of common units of measure; and (6) improving problem-solving abilities. Each of these was considered according to its major arithmetical concept, as well as according to the basic laws governing its operation.

Two organizational plans were discussed for adapting the content and pacing of the arithmetic program to the needs of the learners: *permanent organization* and *flexible organization*. Both were accepted as equally valuable. The teacher's choice should be determined by the size and heterogeneity of his class as well as by the maturities and abilities of the pupils.

A minimal list of teaching aids was offered and supplemented by suggestions as to where additional material could be obtained.

A few typical examples of experimentation with content and teaching tools were included in the last section of the chapter. Although not necessarily agreeing with all the recommendations of recent studies, the authors strongly supported the idea that research and experimentation are vital for the improvement of elementary school arithmetic.

STUDENT PROJECTS

1. Compare an elementary arithmetic textbook published prior to 1900 with one published in the last five years. What changes in content do you note? What similarities? What conclusions can you draw concerning grade placement of topics? Compare the verbal problems in each. What are your conclusions?

2. Observe a group of preschool youngsters in an informal play situation. List the vocabulary they use and the activities in which they engage that have quantitative significance. What conclusions can you draw concerning their experiential readiness for number work?

3. Start a file of experiential verbal problems which you could use to supplement the arithmetic textbook in an intermediate or upper grade.

4. A fellow-teacher complains to you, "I don't know what to do about Jack. One day he knows an addition fact, the next day he doesn't. I just don't know how to help him!" What advice would you give?

5. In a Parent-Teachers meeting, an irate parent asks, "I asked my son in third grade if he had begun the multiplication tables yet and he didn't even know what I meant! Don't they teach multiplication in the schools today?" What is your reply?

6. Conduct an informal survey of the method of grouping used for arithmetic instruction by several elementary school teachers. Do you find any consistent pattern?

7. Prepare a paper on *Teaching Arithmetic in the Elementary School in 1975.* Support your predictions with examples of present-day experimentation, research, and opinions of leading authorities.

8. Write a series of lesson plans you would use to introduce compound subtraction in the third grade. Show clearly how you will attempt to maintain a balance between "meaning" and "drill."

9. If you are going to do student teaching this year, make or collect the materials suggested in the minimal list on pages 347–348 which you will be able to use in your assigned grade.

10. Construct an informal inventory to measure a fourth-grade pupil's understanding of the four properties of number and of the number system mentioned in this chapter. What are your conclusions?

11. Construct a vocabulary list of arithmetical terms appearing most frequently in current elementary arithmetic textbooks on a specific elementary grade level. Administer the test to a group of children on that grade level. What do you discover?

12. Survey several recent arithmetic curriculum guides or courses of study. What consistencies do you find in the allocation of subject matter to grade levels? What inconsistencies? Are most of the guides constructed for a "developmental curriculum" or a "segmented curriculum"? Give evidence to support your answer.

13. Compose a test of ten verbal problems involving addition and subtraction for the third grade. Administer the test individually to several children and ask them to "think out loud" as they work the problems. What did you discover about their mastery of these two processes? In what areas do they need remedial teaching? How would you provide this?

14. Your principal has asked you to serve on a committee to purchase books for the school library. Prepare an annotated bibliography of "mathematics books" which you would recommend for purchase.

15. Try to get permission to ask a sixth-grade class to write a short composition on *My Favorite School Subject* or *My Least Favorite School Subject.* Is arithmetic mentioned in either of these two categories to any noticeable extent? How does it compare with other subjects? What explanation for this can you give?

BIBLIOGRAPHY

Banks, J. M., *Learning and Teaching Arithmetic* (Boston, Allyn and Bacon, Inc., 1959).

Brueckner, Leo J., *Improving the Arithmetic Program* (New York, Appleton-Century-Crofts, Inc., 1957).

Brueckner, Leo J. and Grossnickle, F. E. *Making Arithmetic Meaningful* (New York, Holt, Rinehart and Winston, Inc., 1953).

Brueckner, L. J., Grossnickle, F. E., and Reckzeh, John, *Developing Mathematical Understandings in the Upper Grades* (New York, Holt, Rinehart and Winston, Inc., 1957).

Burton, W. H., *The Guidance of Learning Activities,* 2nd ed. (New York, Appleton-Century-Crofts, Inc., 1952).

CLARK, John R. and EADS, Laura K., *Guiding Arithmetic Learning* (New York, Harcourt, Brace & World, Inc., 1954).

DYER, Henry S. et al., *Problems in Mathematical Education* (Princeton, N.J., Educational Testing Service, 1956).

GROSSNICKLE, Foster E. and BRUECKNER, Leo J., *Discovering Meanings in Arithmetic* (New York, Holt, Rinehart and Winston, Inc., 1959).

GROSSNICKLE, F. E. and METZNER, W., *Use of Visual Aids in the Teaching of Arithmetic* (Brooklyn, N.Y., Rambler Press, 1950).

HENRY, Nelson H., ed., *The Teaching of Arithmetic*, 50th Yearbook, National Society for the Study of Education. Part II (Chicago, University of Chicago, 1951).

HICKERSON, James A., *Guiding Children's Arithmetic Experiences: The Experience-Language Approach to Numbers* (Englewood Cliffs, N.J., Prentice-Hall, Inc., 1952).

HOLLISTER, George E. and GUNDERSON, Agnes G., *Teaching Arithmetic in Grades One and Two* (Boston, D. C. Heath and Company, 1954).

MARKS, J. L.; PURDY, G. R.; KINNEY, L. B., *Teaching Arithmetic for Understanding* (New York, McGraw-Hill Book Company, Inc., 1958).

McSWAIN, E. T. and COOKE, Ralph J., *Understanding and Teaching Arithmetic in the Elementary School* (New York, Holt, Rinehart and Winston, Inc., 1958).

MORTON, Robert L., *Helping Children Learn Arithmetic* (Morristown N.J., Silver Burdett Company, 1960).

MORTON, Robert L., *Teaching Children Arithmetic* (Morristown, N.J., Silver Burdett Company, 1953).

MORTON, Robert L., *What Research Says to the Teacher: Teaching Arithmetic* (Washington, D.C., National Education Association, 1953).

MUELLER, Francis J., *Arithmetic: Its Structure and Concepts* (Englewood Cliffs, N.J., Prentice-Hall, Inc., 1956).

PIAGET, Jean, *The Child's Conception of Numbers* (New York, The Humanities Press, Inc., 1952).

ROSENQUIST, Lucy L., *Young Children Learn to Use Arithmetic* (Boston, Ginn and Company, 1949).

SPENCER, Peter L. and BRYDEGAARD, M., *Building Mathematical Concepts in the Elementary School* (New York, Holt, Rinehart and Winston, Inc., 1952).

SPITZER, Herbert F., *The Teaching of Arithmetic*, 2nd ed. (Boston, Houghton Mifflin Company, 1954).

STOKES, C. Newton, *Teaching the Meanings of Arithmetic* (New York, Appleton-Century-Crofts, Inc., 1951).

Studies in Mathematics Education, *A Brief Survey of Improvement Programs for School Mathematics* (Chicago, Scott, Foresman, and Company, 1959).

SWAIN, Robert, *Understanding Arithmetic* (New York, Holt, Rinehart and Winston, Inc., 1957).

WHEAT, Harry G., *How To Teach Arithmetic* (Evanston, Ill., Row, Peterson and Company, 1956).

WILSON, Guy M. et al., *Teaching the New Arithmetic*, 2nd ed. (New York, McGraw-Hill Book Company, Inc., 1951).

CHAPTER 12

The Visual Arts and Music

IT SHOULD BE FAIRLY APPARENT to the reader by now that the authors consider the development of the individual's creative potential to be a fundamental and vital characteristic of modern-day elementary education. Because this emphasis should permeate the entire curriculum, it has been mentioned repeatedly throughout this book. For example, certain areas of creativity, such as creative dramatics or creative writing, have been specifically discussed in preceding chapters. There will not, therefore, be any attempt made in this chapter to discuss all of the various facets of the broad curriculum field usually designated as the "creative arts." Instead, the present discussion will be limited to an examination of two of these "creative arts": the visual arts and music.

Although both of these areas have been, in a very narrow sense, part of the American elementary school program for approximately one hundred years, it is only recently that they have been regarded as integral and vital parts of the curriculum for *all* pupils. Formerly they were considered as "fads or frills"; or as "busy work" for idle hands or empty heads; or as a Friday afternoon "reward" for good behavior; or as a means of putting on a "show" for parents or the community; or, in a few cases, as a type of punishment. It has really been only in the last few decades that these subjects have come of age as integral parts of the entire educative process. True, their security in the curriculum has been very recently threatened by an overemphasis upon "toughening up" the school program by those who went into orbit along with the first Russian satellite. But, on the whole, the authors fail to detect any widespread tendency to jettison these fields or even to relegate them to the extreme periphery of the educational program. Sane and informed educators apparently recognize and accept their values today just as they did prior to the recent wave of educational hysteria, to which the following resolution passed by the American Association of School Administrators readily testifies:

The American Association of School Administrators commends the president, the Executive Committee, and the staff, for selecting the creative arts as the general theme for the 1959 convention. We believe in a well-balanced school curriculum in which music, drama, painting, poetry, sculpture, architecture, and the like are included side by side with other important subjects such as mathematics, history, and science. It is important that pupils, as a part of general education, learn to appreciate, to understand, to create, and to criticize with discrimination those products of the mind, the voice, the hand, and the body which give dignity to the person and exalt the spirit of man.[1]

With this resolution in mind, let us first turn our attention to the place of the *visual arts* in the elementary curriculum.

Section 1: THE VISUAL ARTS

It was Montesquieu who said, "He who would talk with me must first define his terminology." In this section, the authors feel particularly compelled to heed this admonition because of the numerous and often confusing terms which appear in current literature. The term *visual arts* has been chosen to mean that area of the elementary school curriculum which is concerned with the production and appreciation of two-dimensional and three-dimensional art. As such, it comprises the narrower fields of specialization frequently designated as "fine arts," "crafts," and "industrial arts." Although the authors are aware of the unique objectives and specialized contributions of these narrowed areas, they feel that the overlapping which exists makes it impractical and unnecessary to discuss or teach them as separate subjects for young children. The variety of art materials and experiences offered in the elementary school can best be considered within a broad integrated curricular area, and the teacher does not need to be overly concerned about drawing fine lines of distinction between the specialized subclassifications. For purposes of clarity, therefore, the reader should keep in mind that the term "art education" used frequently in the following pages, refers to the teaching of the visual arts as defined here.

The Present-Day Concept of Art Education

The following two statements, written fifty-five years apart, reveal to some extent the change that has taken place in the philosophy of art education during the twentieth century:

The one important thing to remember is, that in all our teaching we must impress upon the minds of the young children that they are to represent the object as they see it. I find that their little minds run wild when they begin the

[1] Resolution adopted by the 1959 Convention of the American Association of School Administrators, Atlantic City, New Jersey.

study of flowers, leaves, etc. They know them so well that they are unwilling to leave their imaginations out, and the results are a mixture of trueness and un-trueness, but with careful guidance charming results can be secured.[2]

By giving every child the opportunity to choose the ideas that are most mean-ingful to him, creative expression provides for individual differences in a very real and direct way. Each child is not only permitted but also *encouraged* to select an idea that is uniquely his own and is as different from the work of others as he, himself, is different. . . . Creative expression encourages each child to develop the expression of his individuality in this way.[3]

Actually, the change in art education is more widesweeping than two brief quotations can possibly indicate. The following few pages are devoted to an examination of the basic beliefs upon which the present-day concept of art education is predicated.

Art education should be offered to all pupils. The modern concept of art education emphasizes its broad values for *all* pupils, not merely a gifted or privileged few. In the first place, the arts, probably more than any other field, foster individuality and diversity among people. It is this element of diversity as opposed to conformity, possible only in a free society, from which a democratic state derives its strength.

The great scientist, Albert Einstein, has said, "Making allowances for human imperfections, I believe that in America the most precious thing in life is possible, *the development of the individual and his creative powers.*" No field contributes more toward this development of the unique potential of *every* individual than the arts. As one of these, the visual arts should and must be offered to all pupils.

Secondly, art education has values for all pupils in that it enables them to understand the civilization of the ages through the basic medium of human communication—the arts. From the earliest primitive man, the visual arts have been used as a basis for the communication of ideas and the trans-mission of culture. As one writer asks,

If the function of education is to equip each student with an understanding of man and his works (such understanding being the foundation of intelligent thought), how is it possible to ignore his oldest and often clearest means of expressing himself to others? [4]

Thirdly, probably the most comprehensive aim of art education is to develop *art consumers*. Relatively small numbers of pupils now enrolled in our schools will develop into creative and productive artists. But *all* of them will develop into consumers of art who will be called upon daily to distinguish between good and poor taste in the clothes they wear, the

[2] C. W. Conkling, "Drawing—Nature and Color," *American Primary Teacher,* Vol. 23 (October, 1904), p. 59.

[3] B. Jefferson, *Teaching Art to Children* (Boston, Allyn and Bacon, Inc., 1959), pp. 16–17.

[4] G. S. Wright, "Aspects of Understanding in the Visual Arts," *Art Education Bul-letin,* Vol. 16 (April, 1959), p. 13.

houses they furnish, the cars they buy, and the buildings they construct. One needs only to glance around him to realize that there is a crying need to improve the aesthetic taste of the general public. What can do this better than a sound program of art education?

A fourth value of art education is its contribution toward the development of creativity. This does not mean creativity in the narrow sense of developing fine artists but rather of developing individuals who think and live creatively in many areas. Brittain summarizes the creative person as follows:

He would have rich experiences; that is, he would interact freely with his environment though his life on the surface may appear no more "romantic" than any other. He can use his experiences in new situations, is quick to see relationships, and can assemble many pertinent ideas to focus upon a problem. He is flexible in his approach to new ideas, and can easily handle numerous thoughts at once. He has an abundance of energy which he voluntarily uses to alter displeasing situations and to invent, write, paint, or otherwise produce. He has a certain sensitivity to his environment, seeing differences and similarities where others miss them. He can think abstractly and his thoughts are often unusual or novel; sometimes he seems intuitive and has insight into problems or situations. He is usually a well-adjusted and happy person.[5]

From this description of a creative person, it is apparent that art education may contribute toward creativity, not merely in the arts, but in other fields as well. If this is true, it becomes clear that art education has value for all pupils, not for the purpose of making them all creative artists, but to enable them to live rich and happy lives whether they are artists, scientists, shoemakers, teachers, clerks, doctors, or truck-drivers.

Art education contributes to the total integrative growth of the individual. When art education finally succeeded in establishing itself as a full-fledged discipline rather than as a mere appendage to other curricular areas, there was a strong feeling about the importance of "art for art's sake." Today, this emphasis has changed to "art for the child's sake." In other words, the importance of art is to be measured, not by the final product, but by its contribution to the total development of the individual. The *process*, rather than the *product*, is important. This viewpoint is accepted by most art educators today, one of whom stresses the contribution of art to the child's emotional, intellectual, physical, perceptual, social, aesthetic, and creative growth.[6] Let us examine these briefly.

Art education contributes toward the emotional growth of the individual by: (1) encouraging a high degree of self-identification, (2) providing a

[5] W. L. Brittain, "An Experiment Toward Measuring Creativity," in *Research in Art Education,* 7th Yearbook (Washington, D.C., National Art Education Association, 1956), p. 41.

[6] V. Lowenfeld, *Creative and Mental Growth,* 3rd ed. (New York, The Macmillan Company, 1957), pp. 48–59.

natural avenue for the expression of feelings and sensitivity, and (3) sensitizing pupils to the inner conflicts and emotions of others as expressed through their art. In addition, expressive art offers the individual a deep sense of fulfillment and self-satisfaction, as evidenced in the manner in which children (and adults) proudly display and carefully treasure the results of their creative efforts. Also, the therapeutic value of art for the emotionally disturbed is generally recognized today.

Intellectual growth is fostered by art education in many ways. Through art, the child learns to identify a problem, to appraise the methods and materials he may use to work toward its solution, and to evaluate, appraise, and refine his procedures. In short, the operation of all of the previously mentioned factors presently associated with creativity would appear to contribute to the individual's intellectual growth.

Concerning physical growth, Lowenfeld states,

Physical growth in the child's creative work is seen in his capacity for visual and motor co-ordination; in the way in which he guides the line, controls his body, and performs his skills.[7]

Similarly, it is evident that art education contributes to the pupil's perceptual growth by its demands upon his kinesthetic, visual, auditory, and other senses.

According to Lowenfeld, the individual cannot learn to assume the responsibility necessary to live co-operatively in society until he learns to identify himself with his own experiences. Through the creative process, he "not only discovers his own self and *his* needs but also learns to identify himself with the needs of others." [8] Thus, the creative experience leads him toward the awareness of the group and his responsibility toward it, which in turn results in his social growth. Previously mentioned, also, was the contribution art makes to the child's social growth through acquainting him with the visual arts as the most basic form of human communication.

The provision for aesthetic and creative growth is discussed throughout the entire chapter and need receive no specific discussion here. It is necessary only to summarize: a basic emphasis of the modern concept of art education is upon its intrinsic value in the development of the integrative growth pattern of each individual child.

Art education does not make an artificial distinction between expression and appreciation. Art education has long been faced with the dual task of developing creativeness and appreciation. In days gone by, however, teachers frequently thought and taught that these were separate entities. One was supposed to be an active process; the other a passive one. Frequently, the art program was overbalanced in favor of the one which had most personal appeal for the teacher. Today, no such artificial distinction

[7] *Ibid.*, p. 54.
[8] *Ibid.*, p. 56.

exists, and expression and appreciation should both be included in the majority of art experiences offered to children, particularly in the middle and upper grades. The child, for instance, who creates a picture should, at the same time, grow in his aesthetic appreciation of the harmony and form of the composition. Similarly, children who are consistently exposed to tasteful art work, ancient or modern, grow in their aesthetic understanding which, in turn, is redirected toward their own creative efforts. Thus, each area complements the other, and both are vital to a well-balanced modern program of art for children.

The visual arts are often integrated with other curricular areas. As was mentioned previously, this chapter's concentration upon the visual arts should not be interpreted to mean that they are considered apart from other areas of the elementary school curriculum. This is certainly not the case. Very often they are integrated with various other fields, particularly the language and dramatic arts. Writing and illustrating stories; preparing the script, costumes, and scenery for the class play; and making and presenting puppet shows, are ordinary activities which integrate the visual arts with other areas. Similarly, they are often integrated with the social studies and science. It should be stressed, therefore, that art education, in addition to its own intrinsic worth, has value in vitalizing and integrating many aspects of the entire elementary educational program.

As a summary to this brief discussion of the modern philosophy of art education, the reader is referred to the following *Statement of Beliefs* developed by the National Art Association.

As an Art Teacher, I Believe That

Art experiences are essential to the fullest development of all people at all levels of growth because they promote self-realization of the whole individual by integrating his imaginative, creative, intellectual, emotional and manual capacities, and social maturity and responsibility through cultivating a deepened understanding of the problems, ideals, and goals of other individuals and social groups.

Art is especially well suited to such growth because it: encourages freedom of expression, emphasizes emotional and spiritual values, integrates all human capacities, and universalizes human expression.

Art instruction should encourage: exploration and experimentation in many media, sharpened perception of aesthetic qualities, increased art knowledge and skills, and the creative experience in significant activities, and the realization that art has its roots in everyday experiences.

Art classes should be taught with full recognition that: all individuals are capable of expression in art, individuals vary markedly in motivations and capacities, and art is less a body of subject matter than a developmental activity.

Because art experiences are close to the core of individual and social development and because they pervade all phases of living, THE NATIONAL ART EDUCA-

TION ASSOCIATION believes that *all* teachers should have basic training in art.[9]

Levels and Types of Art Expression

Numerous attempts have been made to define the developmental levels of art expression. In recent years, many studies have been made in this country and Europe to define the developmental levels through which children progress in their art expression. Early European studies made a general distinction between the schematic (conceptual) and visually realistic stages. In the first of these, the child is said to draw *according to his schema or concept.* Thus, his pictures will have no perspective and no proportion. The ground or floor will be represented by a base line and the sky and earth will seldom meet on the horizon. His houses may have transparent walls through which people can be seen (frequently called, "X-ray art") *because he knows they are there.* Thus, the child draws, in this stage, *not what he sees but what he knows.* In the realistic stage, the individual makes an attempt to represent his environment as he sees it. He frequently becomes concerned about details of clothing, facial features, and in "making things look right."

Later studies attempted to refine these two broad classifications. The Cleveland studies of 1935–1942 recognized five stages as: (1) the primitive schematic stage; (2) the full or developed schematic stage; (3) the mixed stage (intermediate between the schematic and true-to-appearance); (4) the true-to-appearance stage, and (5) the perspective stage.[10] More recently, Lowenfeld has defined the developmental levels of self-expression as: (A) scribbling stages (2 to 4 years); (B) preschematic stage (4 to 7 years); (C) schematic stages (7 to 9 years); (D) the stage of dawning realism (9 to 11 years); (E) the pseudo-realistic stage (11 to 13 years); and (F) the period of decision (adolescence).[11]

A third author delimits periods of creative growth according to the stages: (A) manipulative stage (2 to 5 years); (B) presymbolic stage (5 to 7 years); (C) symbolic stage (7 to 9 years); (D) inceptive realism stage (9 to 11 years); (E) analytical realism stage (11 to 13 years); and (F) projective realism stage (13 to 15 years).[12] The reader is referred to the original sources for a complete description of each classification system.

It is apparent that, in general, art educators agree that self-expression

[9] National Art Education Association, "Statement of Beliefs" in *Art Education Organizes,* 1949 Yearbook (Washington, D.C., National Art Education Association, 1949).

[10] T. Munro, B. Lark-Horovitz, and E. Barnhart, "Children's Art Abilities: Studies at the Cleveland Museum of Art," *Journal of Experimental Education,* Vol. 11 (December, 1942), pp. 97–184.

[11] V. Lowenfeld, *op. cit.,* pp. 86–277.

[12] I. deFrancesco, *Art Education: Its Means and Ends* (New York, Harper and Brothers, 1958), pp. 571–575.

develops according to a general sequential pattern. The unique and individual growth of each child should, however, take precedence in the teacher's mind over any general classification in which the child's chronological age or some other characteristic might place him. The importance of keeping these classifications elastic and subordinate to the individual growth pattern is forcefully stated in the following:

No one would deny the importance of the psychological growth of the individual in the art process, such as the age level characteristics or the particular schema. These general characteristics were originally intended to help us understand the nature of the child. Unfortunately, in recent years, they have been misused to classify children according to age level patterns and put them into so many nice pigeonholes. . . . We are confronted with a new and dangerous stereotype: the schematic child! General characteristics should serve only to help us discover the uniqueness in individuals.[13]

Some attempts have been made to classify individuals according to "types" of art expression. More controversial than the stages of self-expression are the creative types proposed by some authorities. Lowenfeld, for instance, distinguishes between creative types: (1) visual, (2) haptic, and (3) undetermined. He describes the first two as follows:

VISUAL

The visual type, the observer, usually approaches things from their appearance. He feels as a *spectator*. One important factor in visual observation is the ability to see first the whole without an awareness of details, then to analyze this total impression into detailed or partial impressions, and finally to synthesize these parts into a new whole. The visual type first sees the general shape of a tree, then the single leaves, the twigs, the branches, the trunk, and finally everything incorporated in the synthesis of the whole tree.

HAPTIC

The main intermediary for the haptic type of individual is the *body*-self-muscular sensations, kinesthetic experiences, touch impressions, and all experiences which place the self in value relationship to the outside world. . . . The haptic type, therefore, is primarily a *subjective type*. . . . Since the haptic type uses the self as the true projector of his experiences, his pictorial representations are highly subjective; his proportions are proportions of value.[14]

Several writers have criticized these classifications and have stressed the invalidity of classifying personality types according to the production of art work. Barkan, for instance, takes exception to the classification of types in precedence to the uniqueness of the individual,[15] while Gaitskell reports research which, to date, does not support Lowenfeld's classifications but which, on the contrary, indicates that many individuals possess both visual

[13] V. D'Amico, "Coming Events Cast Shadows," *School Arts*, Vol. 58 (September, 1958), p. 11.
[14] V. Lowenfeld, *op. cit.*, pp. 265–266.
[15] M. Barkan, *A Foundation for Art Education* (New York, The Ronald Press Company, 1955), pp. 168–169.

and haptic characteristics.[16] According to Gaitskell, "A sounder and more practical viewpoint in the business of art education is to consider each child as a dynamic individual, capable of personal growth and of unique artistic output." The classroom teacher should be familiar with the stages and types of art expression proposed by certain authorities, but he should be primarily concerned with the unique growth of the individual child.

Instructional Methods and Procedures

Methods of teaching art generally fall into three categories. There are three schools of thought on the best method of teaching art: (1) *direct teaching method;* (2) *free-expression method;* and (3) *guidance method.* The first of these is the oldest in the schools and the least popular among today's art educators. It stresses the importance of art experiences which are carefully controlled and teacher-directed. Children are taught the basic art principles and how to apply them to their own efforts.

The opposite extreme of direct teaching is the free-expression method. This school of thought became popular largely through the work of Franz Cizek of Vienna whose many disciples, here and abroad, believed that the child's art work should be entirely free from the influence of the teacher. It was believed that true art was "caught not taught," and the teacher was warned constantly of the harm he might do by superimposing his standards upon the child's creative output. Needless to say, there are many outspoken criticisms today of this extreme viewpoint. D'Amico states,

> We have developed a precious attitude toward the child, often protecting him from the positive guidance to the extent that the art experience loses its vitality. This has led to a bootleg type of teaching where the conscientious teacher secretly gives the kind of help a child needs, but she fears to admit it openly because she might be branded as indoctrinary. . . . Of course, a person who does not know how to help children should let the child alone. But a person who has spent four or more years specializing in the development of children through art has a more vital contribution to make than keeping out of the child's way.[17]

Gaitskell voices essentially the same philosophy in the statement,

> One important lesson we have learned in the past is that a *teacher* is needed while art is engaging the attention of pupils in an elementary school. As mentioned previously, some teachers who were influenced by an Expressionistic type of program failed to play a sufficiently strong role as teachers of children. As a result, their art programs, although largely founded upon commendable ideas, failed through lack of suitable teaching methods. The contemporary program on the other hand, rests upon the foundation of a strong belief in the need for both teaching and a reasonably consistent pedagogy. This pedagogy is most concerned with motivation and actual teaching, and with the media and tools of expression.[18]

[16] C. D. Gaitskell, *Children and Their Art* (New York, Harcourt, Brace & World, Inc., 1958), pp. 148–152.

[17] V. D'Amico, *op. cit.*, p. 9.

[18] G. D. Gaitskell, *op. cit.*, pp. 38–39.

Working with wood is a vital phase of the visual arts program in the elementary school.

The third method, and the one to which most modern art educators subscribe, is the guidance method. This is not to be confused with the general concept of guidance, but means simply that the teacher should feel a responsibility toward helping and guiding the child's art expression toward its highest fulfillment. The secret of the success of this method lies in the *amount* and *timing* of the guidance. Neither too much nor too little is desirable; too soon is harmful and too late is useless. It is apparent, therefore, that this method relies heavily upon the judgement of the teacher and his sensitivity to each child's needs. We must have creative teachers to develop creative learners. Art teaching, today, however, is not wholly a personal matter, for there are some general principles which can be followed. These are summarized briefly below:

The "guidance" method has certain basic characteristics. The first of these is a *permissive environment*. The importance of a free and informal classroom environment to an effective art program cannot be over-estimated. Such an environment must encourage children to express themselves freely and spontaneously without fear of ridicule or censure from teachers or peers. It must encourage them to express themselves through their art with originality and individuality, free from the pressures of conformity and group standards. It must, also, contain a wide variety of materials and encourage children to experiment with all of them. Lastly, it must permit some flexibility of scheduling, for creativity does not start and stop according to a rigid timetable. It goes without saying that such an environment must operate within acceptable social and academic standards, of course, and should never be confused with the anarchic environment which a few misguided teachers excuse on the grounds that it is conducive to the creative growth of their pupils.

Secondly, *teacher-pupil rapport* is most important in guiding art expression. Cole's delightful book illustrates very vividly the overwhelming importance of the personal relationship between teacher and pupil.[19] She stresses the importance of the teacher's praise and encouragement and claims that "the teacher likes my work" is of maximum importance to the child. This does not mean that teachers should praise indiscriminately, of course, for the pupil soon learns to recognize and disregard empty approbation. It does mean, however, that the approach of the teacher should always be positive rather than negative as he comments upon Susan's use of color, George's feeling for composition, or the boldness of Tony's figures.

Providing children with *experiences* is a vital necessity of a dynamic art program. Pupils cannot create from a vacuum, and the teacher must, through a variety of devices, help children enjoy and recall experiences which can be "re-created" through their art. This can be done by encouraging children to "act out" an art assignment, such as, "You are playing your favorite game." By asking the child to go through the motions, he will help him to get the "feel" of the action which the child can then transpose to his art form. Only by deeply experiencing—by feeling, being, seeing, touching, smelling, and hearing—will the child have the rich background from which all creativity springs.

Motivating the child to express himself is another important keynote of today's art methods. Many techniques can be used to stimulate the child's desire to express himself, but the most common is probably the guided discussion or questioning by the skillful teacher. For instance, to suggest

[19] N. Cole, *The Arts in the Classroom* (New York, The John Day Company, 1940).

that pupils "draw a picture about Thanksgiving" is completely ineffectual, but a thorough discussion of experiences associated with the holiday is most valuable. "What do you do on Thanksgiving Day? Do you have guests for dinner? How many? Where do they sit at the table? Where is Mother? Do you help her in the kitchen? How do you feel when you are eating your dessert? How do you feel after dinner? What do you do?" The difference between this type of motivation and the sterile "draw a picture" type should be fairly obvious.

During the entire art lesson, the teacher should offer *assistance* and *instruction* where they are needed. Constantly circulating around the room, the teacher will give such help as, "You are 'stuck' on how to draw a baseball pitcher? Show me how he stands. How does he wind up? How does he throw the ball? How do your arms feel? Your legs? Your back? See if you can't make your picture say this." "Do you think you should draw little tiny people on such a large sheet of paper? Try to make your people big and strong so they look as though they belong on this big piece of paper." Or even such direct guidance as, "Try using stronger colors to see if you like the effect," will give the pupil the benefit of the teacher's guidance without inhibiting the pupil's originality.

In this brief discussion, emphasis has been placed upon a desirable method of art instruction which meets with fairly unanimous agreement today. There are also some negative practices concerning which there is very little difference of opinion among the leading art educators. These are discussed in the following section.

Questionable Practices in Art Education

Art contests are considered detrimental to a worthwhile art program. In general, reputable art educators are opposed to contests in which children's art products compete for prizes, medals, or ribbons. Such activities place an unwarranted emphasis upon the final product; promote conformity rather than individuality; and, in general, are diametrically opposite to the general goals and aims of modern art education. Statements condemning this practice are prevalent in current literature, and are typified by the following:

Competition in contests, usually contrived by adults, which involve tensions about winning a prize for being "best" is harmful to an art program for young children.[20]

Formal art competition I believe to be harmful. Competition in art among young children presents no single valid criteria by which one work or the work of one child can honestly be designated as an inspiration to fellow classmates.[21]

Recent extensive experimentation has proven children who are promised awards or other prizes as stimulation have the tendency to lose their own personal

[20] G. Abbihl, "Art Contests," *School Arts*, Vol. 58 (April, 1959), p. 33.
[21] F. M. Logan, "Art Contests," *School Arts*, Vol. 58 (April, 1959), p. 33.

identity in their art expression as compared to children who work under the same conditions without such rewards. Any form of reward extrinsic to the creative process, such as prizes or ribbons, is harmful to the creativeness of children because it diverts the child from his own individual experience to values not related to art expression.[22]

Coloring books and prepared patterns are generally considered harmful to creative art. In spite of the fact that coloring books and cut-out patterns have been the subject of strong criticism, they are still to be found in some classrooms. Teachers occasionally defend their use on two grounds—that they present a correct visual image to the child or that they help to develop motor control—neither of which has been substantiated through research. On the contrary, there is some evidence [23] which indicates that these devices cripple the child's creative power, although there is not unanimous agreement on this point.[24] If educators do not agree, however, on the *extent of harm* done by these devices, they *do* agree that they unquestionably fail to *foster* or *promote*, in any measure, the creative power of the individual. They are completely incompatible, for this reason, to the objectives of the modern art program and, consequently, there would seem to be no place for them in the elementary classroom.

"Gimmicks" or "tricks" have no place in a well-planned art program. Conscientious teachers, in a desperate attempt to add variety to their art programs, have occasionally been misled by the appeal of a "gimmick" or "trick" method of art production. One author describes string painting (pieces of string are dipped in paint, dropped on a paper, the paper is then folded over, and the pieces of string are pulled out, thus creating a "design") as one of these.[25] There are, of course, many others. In evaluating the worth of any of these, the teacher should keep in mind that art expression is a conscious activity in which the individual seeks to define an experience which has meaning and direction for him. Aimless doodling or purposeless playing with materials does not represent any true artistic endeavor and consequently should not appear in the classroom under the guise of "art" work.

Creative Experiences in the Visual Arts

The wealth of creative experiences which may be offered to young children is so great that it is difficult to attempt a comprehensive discus-

[22] V. Lowenfeld, "Art Contests," *School Arts*, Vol. 58 (April, 1959), p. 33.

[23] I. Russel and B. Waugaman, *A Study of the Effect of Workbook Copy Experiences on the Creative Concepts of Children*, Research Bulletin, Eastern Arts Association, Volume 3, Number 1, 1952; H. Heilman, *The Effect of Workbook Stereotypes on the Creativeness of Children*, Unpublished doctoral dissertation (Pennsylvania State University, 1954).

[24] R. A. Daniel, "Coloring Books: The Blind Spot of Art Education," *Art Education Bulletin*, Vol. 16 (September, 1959), pp. 18–20.

[25] J. Schwartz, "Short Cuts, Quickies, and Tricks in Art," *School Arts*, Vol. 59 (May, 1960), p. 47.

sion of them. Those included on the following pages are some of the more popular because they do not make extensive demands on the teacher's ability or school budget. To these, the teacher should add others as he seeks constantly to provide his pupils with a rich variety of creative experiences and tempting materials with which to express themselves.

Painting. Opaque tempera paint and water colors are the paints used most frequently in the elementary school. Of these, tempera is most desirable (particularly for young children) because it is versatile; easy to handle; allows "painting over"; and comes in rich, satisfying colors. Tempera may be purchased in dry or liquid form in a wide variety of colors. A large supply of baby food cans, frozen juice cans, or ½-pint milk cartons is desirable for mixing, thinning, and distributing the base colors.

Water-color boxes usually contain six or seven colors, although some larger boxes contain fifteen or more colors. Water-color painting is considerably more difficult than tempera painting and is usually reserved for the intermediate and upper grades.

Proper brushes for painting are very important, and it is a false economy to buy the cheapest on the market. Easel brushes with ½" or ¾" bristles and an over-all length of about 12" are recommended for elementary school use. Camel's-hair water-color brushes are usually considered more practical for young children and are less expensive than sable brushes. Camel's-hair brushes come in three qualities—goat hair, pony hair, and squirrel hair. Brushes should be thoroughly cleaned and stood upright to dry after every using. Because they are all made of animal hair, it is a good idea to store them with mothballs or flakes over the long summer vacation.

Painting and drawing activities are both individual and co-operative. Individual work is usually done at the desk, easel, or improvised easel made by covering a bulletin board or chalk board with several layers of newspaper. In individual activities, children should be discouraged from drawing outlines in pencil before painting.

Group activities are directed toward making large murals or friezes and are usually done on heavy kraft paper spread flat on the floor or bulletin board. Such group activities require careful preplanning before beginning to paint. On large group projects, outlines can be hastily sketched with chalk or a hard eraser before children actually begin to paint.

Another type of group picture is the montage, which is a large composite of whole or partial pictures by many individuals. This offers valuable experience in group planning and working and is used by some teachers to avoid the monotony of concentrating all co-operative two-dimensional art experiences wholly upon murals.

Finger painting. Finger painting is a relaxing and informal art activity which is usually thoroughly enjoyed by children. Finger paint may be purchased in a variety of colors, or it can be made by adding dry tempera to a paste of starch or flour and water. The paint is applied, in small quantities, to the slick moistened surface of the paper. Effective finger painting requires freedom of motion (using fingers, hands, or forearms) and speed in order to prevent the paper from drying. It is recommended for all grades in the elementary school and frequently children (and adults) who are inhibited in other types of art work will finger paint with freedom, rhythm, and a remarkable feeling for design.

Drawing and coloring. These are other popular art activities and are usually done with wax crayons, chalk, pastels, or charcoal. Colored chalk is probably the most satisfactory material in this classification because of its versatility and wide range of colors. Wax crayons offer many creative possibilities when used correctly, but there is a constant danger of over using them to the neglect of other media. Actually, they permit a more flexible art program than many teachers realize. In addition to their common use for drawing and coloring, they can be used for textile decoration, can be used in combination with tempera or water color paints for some interesting effects, and can be applied heavily to paper or cardboard and then scratched or etched.

Pencil and pen-and-ink drawings are not recommended as art activities for elementary school children.

Printing. Printing is a satisfying and creative experience for young children and can be done with a variety of materials. Fingers, small pieces of sponge, or wood dowels can be dipped into tempera paint and used to make designs. Potatoes, carrots, turnips, or similar materials can be used by cutting away a slice, carving a design on the exposed surface, dipping it in paint, and printing on the paper or cloth.

Linoleum-block printing demands sharp tools for cutting a clean design on the linoleum block. Very satisfactory results can be obtained with older children but, because it is a fairly difficult and demanding task, this activity is usually not recommended for children below grade five or six.

Printing is a most popular method for making designs. It is frequently used for making covers for books or school magazines, greeting cards, place mats, gift wrapping paper, table cloths, and window drapes.

Working with paper. There are numerous possibilities for using paper in the art program. All types of paper—manila, newspaper, colored construction paper, tissue paper, cellophane, aluminum foil, gift wrapping paper, cardboard, "oaktag," paper bags, and corrugated papers offer a variety of textures and designs which can be used to advantage. Scissors, paste, staplers, rulers, and cellulose tape are the only tools necessary to permit a wide use of paper. Paper can be used for paper sculpture (three-dimensional cut-paper forms) or for strip-paper work. Paper bags can be used for making masks, or for making paper-bag puppets and animals. The small scraps of paper left from these activities may be used to make designs and can also be saved to be used later in making papier-mâché.

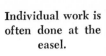

Individual work is often done at the easel.

The felt board adds variety to the art program.

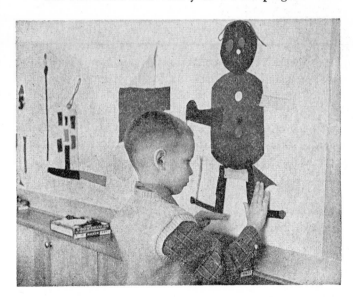

Modeling and sculpturing. A variety of media can be used for these art experiences. Papier-mâché is a popular medium and can be used for making puppet heads, and small human and animal figures. Papier-mâché can be made from torn newspapers (tissue paper is recommended by some because of its soft texture and pliability) mixed with boiling water and wallpaper or flour paste until the correct consistency is determined. It can then be molded into the desired shape and painted with tempera paint when thoroughly dry.

Clay modeling is probably the most ideal three-dimensional art activity. Modeling clay can be purchased in dry form to which water must be added, or it can be purchased ready for use. Clay offers so many advantages as an art medium that it is extremely unfortunate that it is not found in more classrooms. Teachers' lack of self-confidence and their reluctance to have pupils work with clay because of its "messy" qualities, probably account for the limited use made of it in some schools. Actually, neither of these drawbacks is insurmountable. Several well-written books are now available with detailed instructions to the teacher for working with clay; and, with careful preplanning and good classroom management, clay need not create as many housekeeping problems as most teachers imagine. Children love to experiment with clay—to roll it, pat it, squeeze it, knead it, and finally mold it into an object of strength and individuality. By all means, they should be given numerous opportunities to do so!

"Plasticene" is preferred to clay by many teachers because it presents fewer problems of storage and does not require the careful preparation of a work area that clay does. "Plasticene" may be purchased in a variety of colors and, in many ways, is a very satisfactory medium for younger children. However, it does not harden, cannot be painted, and does not, therefore, offer the permanence and completeness of expression that clay does.

Making Mosaics. Colorful and interesting mosaics can be made by gluing pebbles, seeds, cereal, bits of colored glass, or tile on plywood or cardboard. Mosaics are usually recommended for upper-grade pupils because they require perseverance, patience, and attention to detail.

Weaving. Weaving is a primitive craft which many intermediate and upper-grade children thoroughly enjoy. Looms can be purchased or made and can be strung with yarn or raffia. Children can often make attractive mats which may be used in the classroom or may be taken home as gifts. Basketry is another form of weaving to which children should be exposed in the elementary school.

Miscellaneous. Numerous other art activities are to be found in a balanced and comprehensive program. Children may make dioramas, collages, string designs, mobiles, and others to experience the thrill of discovering new materials, new methods, and new outlets for their need to create and express.

Section 2: MUSIC

The typical American child probably awoke this morning to the strains of music coming from his radio-alarm clock. There is a good chance that he continued to listen to music while he dressed and ate breakfast with other members of the family. On his way to school, he may have hummed or sung to himself as he walked along. When his school day is ended this afternoon, he will probably stop in the corner store to buy ice cream or candy and to listen to the juke-box into which his teen-age elders are busily dropping their dimes and quarters. Perhaps he will have to hurry, then, to get to his music lesson on time, and from there he will return home to "help" his father assemble the family's new stereophonic hi-fi set. Some television in the evening will probably end his day.

Music is inextricably woven into the fabric of the lives of boys and girls. They live with it, reproduce it, and respond to it during most of their waking hours. Since *some* type of music is part of the daily lives of *all* children, the basic goal of the school music program should be to make this area of living as enriching and rewarding as possible, so that the child may enjoy the many intrinsic values which music has to offer. What are these values?

Values of Music

1. Music is a source of enjoyment and pleasure. The greatest value of music lies in the fact that it is sheer enjoyment and pleasure. Mursell emphasizes this primary value of music as follows:

Music, first and foremost, is one of life's great natural pleasures. All time through and everywhere, people have enjoyed listening to it, participating in it, creating it. Why human beings enjoy music we do not fully understand. But very evidently they do. Indeed, one may go so far as to say that if human beings did not enjoy music, there would be no such thing as music in the world.[26]

Since the primary value of music lies in the enjoyment it offers, it naturally follows that enjoyment must constitute the foundational aim of the music program, and that, within the framework of the elementary curriculum, *no other aims,* such as the development of *aesthetic appreciations or technical skills, should supersede the aim of enjoyment.* From the time the child enters the kindergarten, therefore, he should be introduced to a rich program of music which will develop in him a lasting attraction to music. In order to accomplish this aim, the school must gear the musical activities to the maturity and previous experiences of the pupils. Music which is too difficult, too adult, or too strange will not develop the firm foundation of genuine enjoyment upon which all other values depend.

[26] J. L. Mursell, *Music Education Principles and Programs* (Morristown, N.J., Silver Burdett Company, 1956), pp. 37–38.

Music is a source of enjoyment and pleasure.

2. Music is an aesthetic and spiritual experience. Many people fear, and probably with some justification, that there is today an increasing emphasis placed on material gains and a decreasing interest in the aesthetic and spiritual aspects of life. If this is true, certainly there is no better medium for regaining or retaining a balance of values than through music. This thought has been expressed by one writer as follows,

Children, as well as adults, need beauty and react to it in positive terms. Children listen with rapture to a lullaby beautifully played or sung, their bodies reflecting complete absorption in the music. This capacity to respond to beauty is inborn.[27]

3. Music is a creative experience. We have pointed out earlier in this chapter that there is a creative potential in every person. Music offers a broad avenue for the release of this potential since, in many instances, no materials or tools are needed for creating other than the person's own voice. Thus, regardless of age or circumstances, man has within him a tool for creativity which he can use, and has used, in every culture and in every age, to produce music.

[27] A. V. Wilson, "Why Music Education?" *National Elementary Principal*, Vol. 39 (December, 1959), p. 7.

4. Music is a socializing experience. The social values of music are almost too numerous to mention. In the first place, music can quickly break the barriers of strangeness and shyness among individuals as evidenced by the popularity of singing as an "ice-breaker" at any social gathering. Secondly, probably never does an individual become more completely a part of a group than when he joins a chorus or orchestra where the contribution of *each* individual is absolutely necessary to the entire group. Still another social value of music was recently exemplified by a large-city concert at which a chorus from abroad entertained an appreciative American audience. At the close of the concert, the director announced that the group's last number would be a popular American folk song—sung in English—and invited the audience to participate. The entire audience arose and the hall was filled with music from the stage and floor—each group momentarily forgetting the political, geographic, cultural, and language differences which separated their countries. Thus music has the value of helping peoples of the world learn to live together in peace and friendship.

5. Music develops understandings of other cultures. Not only does music help develop social harmony, but it also aids in developing understanding of other cultures. The lovely Negro spirituals, for instance, have a story of their people to tell, as do the courageous ballads and folks songs of the early American pioneers. The songs of the Latin countries are mirrors through which we may see the folkways and customs of the people. The same is true of nations, races, and religions, for the music of a people is a reflection of its social, spiritual, and emotional values as well as of their economic and political circumstances.

6. Music has a therapeutic value. The therapeutic value of music is so universally recognized that it is almost unnecessary to discuss it here. It has been employed over the ages by men as a relief from pain, suffering, and deprivation. More recently, it has been used, with a high degree of success, with mentally ill and emotionally disturbed individuals, and one can read many accounts of these persons reacting positively to music when all other therapeutic measures were unsuccessful. It goes without saying that the therapeutic values of music have definite implications for the classroom teacher, who can employ it to calm the fears of a crying child, in cases of serious emergency, or during fire or air raid drills.

The six basic values discussed briefly here appear to merit the serious consideration of elementary teachers in planning and developing effective music programs for their pupils. In general, these values will be most fully realized in a program which is distinguished by the following characteristics:

A music program of value is an integral part of the total school experience. To be truly a functional and enriching experience for children, music cannot be confined within the limits of a weekly or biweekly period of twenty or thirty minutes. It should, rather, be a part of the total school experience and should, wherever possible, be integrated with other curricular areas. For instance, there are numerous opportunities to integrate music with social studies to the fuller enrichment and enjoyment of both areas. To illustrate: one second-grade teacher recently complained that her pupils did not like music. After some discussion, her principal asked her what songs she was teaching, and she mentioned several songs which had no timely significance for her pupils at all. But on her bulletin board were numerous pictures of trains; an airport hangar was built in the corner of the room; and it was evident that the children were deeply interested in their unit on transportation. How much more meaningful would have been their music and how much richer their social studies if they had learned some delightful children's songs about trains, planes, trucks, and buses, as part of their unit study. Similarly, music can be integrated with such areas as literature, science, art, and physical education in a way to make each area more productive and meaningful for the child.

A music program of value is designed for ALL pupils. Earlier in the chapter, considerable emphasis was placed upon the importance of the visual arts for all children and not merely for a gifted few. This philosophy meets with strong endorsement from music educators, as evidenced by the slogan of the Music Educators National Conference, "Music for Every Child—Every Child for Music." This has not always been true in the past, of course, for in many schools music was intended only for a select few, while the others were encouraged to be a "good audience." Today's emphasis upon music for *all* children, however, should not be interpreted to mean that musical experiences should be *identical* for all children. In this field, as in all others, the teacher must recognize that a wide range of individual interests and abilities exists within his class. These differences make it necessary to provide numerous different types of music experiences.

A music program of value includes a wide variety of activities. The well-balanced modern music program includes a wide variety of activities for children of all ages. In general, no effective music program can be said to be complete without full provision for (1) singing, (2) listening, (3) playing, (4) responding to the rhythm of music, and (5) creating. Each of these is discussed briefly on the following pages.

Singing

A successful singing program depends upon many factors, the most important of which are:

1. The selection of songs which have natural appeal for children. Many a music program has been ruined by the teacher insisting upon teaching songs which were not appealing nor interesting to children. Fortunately today, the many excellent series of song books now available will assist the teacher in selecting appropriate songs for his grade level. However, it should be remembered that wide variations exist among children, and the fact that a song is recommended for a certain grade is no guarantee that it will appeal to the teacher's individual class. In general, the teacher may be guided by the following criteria in selecting songs for his pupils.

Songs which have appeal for most elementary school youngsters are those which

a. Are related to their personal experiences and interests (songs about pets, seasons, holidays, familiar characters, etc.)

b. Have word content which is easily understood.

c. Are simple and easy to sing because of appropriate length, and repetition of rhythmic and tonal patterns.

d. Are placed within range of children's voices. (Keys which give primary grade voices a comfortable range "fall roughly between middle C and F on the fifth line of the staff.") [28]

e. Have a pleasing rhythm.

2. The teacher. The *attitude* of the teacher is most important to the music program, for unless he is enthusiastic about *singing* and about *teaching singing* there is little hope that his pupils will derive much benefit from the experience. Unfortunately, many teachers feel extremely insecure in teaching music, even to very young children, because of their apparent inability to carry a tune. Most writers point out that this inability, *if it exists*, is the product of inexperience and lack of training and can be overcome by the conscientious teacher who earnestly tries to do so. Moreover, as Tipton states, often the feeling of inadequacy is not justified by lack of ability but by such factors as the following:

1. Often there has been a conspicuous meagreness in the musical preparation of classroom teachers at the college level, sometimes merely amounting to a perfunctory gesture in this direction.

2. Some of these classroom teachers are among those who, almost 80 percent strong, have had no musical experience (previous to the one or two required music courses in college) since they were in the seventh grade. The result is a six-or seven-year musical "gap" in their school experience.

3. Some of them are the grown-up versions of unhappy "monotones" or "non-singers" who in primary grades were mistakenly instructed to "sit and listen" while other more fortunate children sang, and who thereafter retained this psychological "label" within themselves.

4. Some are convinced that music is an exclusive field in which only skilled musicians dare to teach. They feel themselves to be strangers or intruders, believing that they will never have anything of musical consequence to offer children.[29]

[28] *Music for Children's Living,* Bulletin Number 96 (Washington, D.C., Association for Childhood Education International 1955), p. 22.
[29] G. Tipton, "For Better Classroom Music . . . In-Service Education," *National Elementary Principal,* Vol. 39 (December, 1959), pp. 16–17.

Several suggestions are offered to the teacher who, for one reason or another, hesitates to teach singing to his pupils. First, teach the song to yourself at home (with a piano or recording if possible) until you are firmly acquainted with the melody. Secondly, if this does not work, do not hesitate to use a phonograph record to introduce the song to children. Although this is not as desirable as using your own voice, all authorities agree that it is an acceptable substitute when necessary. Ellison suggests the following procedure for using a phonograph record to teach a new song to the class,

With the same kind of introduction you might use if you were going to sing the song yourself to the class, play the record for the group. After a couple of hearings, encourage the children to sing along with the record where they can. Join in yourself.

As the children learn the song, you may want to turn down the volume of the phonograph so that the children's voices dominate. When you feel that they know the song fairly well, have them try the song without the record. Together focus on the weak spots and listen to the record again without singing. Then try the song again without the record. Gradually, over a period of time, the children learn the song. It is likely, too, that if you try this with your children a number of times, another year you might know that particular song well enough to try to present it without the record.[30]

A third procedure, used by some teachers who have neither a piano nor a record player in the classroom, is to use a very able child to sing the song to the others. The teacher might first work with this child alone (teaching him the tune by "picking it out" on the auditorium piano, for instance) and then ask him to sing it for the class, gradually encouraging others to join him.

In summary, it is important that the teacher make the strongest possible effort to provide his pupils with rich singing experiences. If, in order to do this, he must rely upon whatever "crutches" are at his disposal, he should not hesitate to do so. This is a far more defensible procedure than depriving his pupils of singing because, in his words, he can't "sing his way out of a paper bag!"

3. **The procedure.** Children first learn to sing by "ear" or by imitating the teacher. This is called teaching a song by *rote* and is the method used until pupils are introduced to the reading of music. In general, most authorities advocate the *whole method* or the "*all-join-in*" method of teaching a new rote song, which means simply that children learn it the way they learn any new song from the radio or television. That is, they listen to it sung repeatedly, gradually joining in on the parts they know, until finally they have mastered the entire song. Using this method in the classroom is far preferable to the *phrase method* in which children learn a new song phrase

    30 A. Ellison, *Music with Children* (New York, McGraw-Hill Book Company, Inc., 1959), pp. 82–83.

by phrase—an extremely artificial situation. Of course, in the "all-join-in" method there may be need for "polishing" certain phrases, but this is undertaken only after children learn and like the song in its entirety.

It should be kept in mind, that any one music lesson should rarely be devoted entirely to the teaching of a new song. Rather, a single lesson should include a wide *variety* of activities, including hearing a new song, reviewing very familiar favorite songs, "polishing" recently learned songs, and providing opportunities for solo singing. The teacher, therefore, in teaching a new song will probably want to introduce it to the pupils, sing it a few times, and go on to some other musical activity. The following day he will again sing the new song, encouraging pupils to join in where they can. This procedure will be used over a period of several days until finally the pupils have added the new song to their repertoire. The advantages of gradually familiarizing pupils with a new song in this way as compared to teaching it for complete mastery within a twenty or thirty minute lesson should be fairly obvious.

In the primary grades, most songs are sung in unison, although some teachers make a faint start toward part singing with these children. Mursell suggests that part singing may be started by the primary teacher adding a brief musical fragment, either vocally or with a simple melody instrument, to some of the unison songs of these grades.[31] These early beginnings may then be followed with rounds (popular with most children), which will pave the way to true part singing in the upper grades.

Before leaving this discussion of singing, it should be stressed again that an adequate school program should provide for the varying abilities of children. The teacher will have in his group "uncertain singers" who will need considerable experience and help in singing but who should *never* be excluded from the regular singing activities of the classroom. On the other hand, there will be several children in the group who exhibit considerable talent and interest in music, and provision should be made for these as well. School choirs and glee clubs are usually excellent activities for the more musically talented, provided: (1) their membership is entirely voluntary; (2) they are an integral part of the regular school program and are conducted during the school day; (3) they are not organized solely in the interests of giving "performances" for the school or community.

An aspect of the singing program which has not yet been mentioned is the reading of musical symbols. This is defined as "the process of reading symbols into sound."[32] According to Mursell, "the teaching of music

[31] J. L. Mursell, *op. cit.*, p. 222.
[32] R. G. Petzold, "The Perception of Music Symbols in Music Reading by Normal Children and by Children Gifted Musically," *Journal of Experimental Education*, Vol. 28 (June, 1960), p. 271.

reading is one of the chief points of dispute in music education today." [33]
The authors refer the reader to the bibliography at the end of this chapter
for an examination of this complex problem.

Listening

Of all types of musical activity, whether in or out of school, listening is the
most basic. Music is an aural art. Its distinguishing characteristic is tone. Its
constituent elements of melody, rhythm, harmony, and form enter our consciousness through the medium of musical tone perceived through the ear. Together with such factors as tempo, dynamics, and vocal or instrumental tone
color, these four basic elements constitute what there is to hear in music.[34]

There can be little question that listening is a basic musical activity
upon which other activities are dependent. One must listen to music, for
instance, in order to respond to it rhythmically. It is equally important to
listen when one is trying to learn a new song either vocally or on an instrument. Beyond these, however, listening has a value of and in itself in
developing a genuine understanding, appreciation, and enjoyment of
music. It is to this purpose of music listening that this discussion is directed.

In order to effect a successful listening program in the elementary
grades, the following general principles should be considered:

**The selection should be carefully chosen according to the interests and
maturity of the pupils.** Many teachers have made a mistake of going "too
fast—too soon" in attempting to introduce their pupils to good music.
Certain composers, such as Beethoven or Bach, may have wide appeal for
adults but not necessarily for children. This does not mean, however, that
children do not respond favorably to classical music. On the contrary,
there is some evidence to show that the opposite is true and that young
children respond more favorably to classical music than do older pupils.
Rogers, for instance, reports a study of children's preferences of four
categories of music: (1) seriously classical, (2) popular classical, (3)
dinner music, and (4) popular music. It was found that,

children increased their preferences for popular music and dinner music as they
grew older. Conversely, their preferences for seriously classical and popular classical decreased as they advanced from Grade 4 to 12.[35]

It would seem, therefore, that the teacher need have no fear that there
is not an abundance of classical or semiclassical music which will have

[33] J. L. Mursell, "Growth Process in Music Education" in *Basic Concepts in Music
Education,* 57th Yearbook of the National Society for the Study of Education (Chicago, University of Chicago Press, 1958), p. 147.

[34] W. C. Hartshorn, "Listening . . . A Basic Part of Music Education," *National
Elementary Principal,* Vol. 39 (December, 1959), p. 33.

[35] V. R. Rogers, "Children's Musical Preferences as Related to Grade Level and
Other Factors," *Elementary School Journal,* Vol. 57 (May, 1957), p. 434.

appeal for children, provided it is correctly chosen. In general, selections which will be enjoyed and appreciated by children in the elementary grades are those which:

1. *Are of an appropriate length.* Hayden suggests that the selection should be no longer than three to five minutes.[36] This appears to be somewhat debatable although certainly the selection should not be long enough to produce boredom and restlessness on the part of active young children.

2. *Are related to the interests of children.* Types of selections which will probably have appeal for children are suggested by McMillan as:

Songs and Dances of the People—folk songs, ballads, songs of many national and racial groups, songs sung by famous American balladiers, Negro spirituals.

Songs of the World of Nature—songs of the seasons, of the excitement of a storm: "sound" pictures of weather, clouds.

Songs of the World of Make-Believe—of fairyland, witches, dwarfs, ghosts.

Toys in Music—dancing dolls, wooden soldiers.[37]

3. *Tell a story.* Many authorities advocate that children's first listening experiences should be with "program music"—music which tells a story. Such selections as *Till Eulenspiegel's Merry Pranks, Invitation to the Dance,* and *Pinocchio, A Merry Overture* will have appeal for children because of the story quality.

In addition to choosing selections which will have appeal for children, the teacher should attempt to give children a purpose for listening.

A directed listening activity should include a purpose for listening. There are two general types of listening experiences which should be included in the elementary school program. The first of these is an informal or incidental program in which children are casually exposed to musical selections of quality at any time during the day. During art class or rest time, for instance, the teacher may put some soft background music on the record player. One teacher discovered that the few minutes just before lunch was a good time for children to put away the work of the morning and relax by listening to a selection on the phonograph or piano. Such listening opportunities can be provided at any time during the day and do not necessarily require a *purpose* for listening as does a directed listening activity.

The directed listening activity is devoted exclusively to the listening and appreciation of music for its own sake. In order to make this experience of value, the teacher should introduce the selection, discuss it briefly and provide children with a purpose for listening. Some aspects of a selection which might lend themselves to listening purposes are:

---

[36] R. Hayden, "Teaching Music Appreciation in the Elementary Schools," *Music Educators Journal,* Vol. 43 (February–March, 1957), pp. 56–59.

[37] L. E. McMillan, *Guiding Children's Growth Through Music* (Boston, Ginn and Company, 1959), pp. 135–145.

1. *Tonal quality and pattern.* Children may be encouraged to listen to the quality of the soprano, alto, and other tonal qualities. They may also learn to identify the tonal pattern as it returns and leaves.

2. *Identification of instruments.* Children may listen to the instrumental aspects of a selection, for instance, which instrument carries which theme.

3. *Rhythm.* Children may be helped to identify rhythm patterns, and to express these by moving their arms and bodies.

4. *Design.* The composer's use of themes and tunes, for instance, their repetition, is frequently referred to as the "design" of music and can be understood and appreciated by young children. McMillan defines this quality as, "Design in music is simply the way it is organized or planned in order to make it easy for our minds to follow, grasp, and retain it." [38]

Opportunities should be provided for both individual and group listening experiences. Many teachers arrange their room environment to provide for individual or small group listening activities. A "music corner," for instance, may contain a record player which can be played very softly for two or three children while others are busily engaged with other interests. Or, if the teacher is fortunate enough to have a set of earphones in the classroom, a child may listen to music at various times of the day without disturbing the others. Such an activity has a great deal of value for some children and has been utilized to advantage by some teachers.

Opposite from the small group or individual listening experience is the concert program which many systems have instituted in their elementary schools. Concerts performed for the entire school by visiting vocal or instrumental artists can be a very enriching experience for young children, and every attempt should be made to include several of them in the school program each year. Furthermore, a "concert series" may not necessarily entail a great deal of expense, for often there are talented individuals within the local community who would be glad to perform for little or no remuneration. Also, many schools enrich their own offerings by exchanging programs with other schools. The authors remember one elementary school, for instance, in which the annual visit from the junior high school orchestra could have been no more eagerly anticipated or appreciated if it had been the Boston Symphony!

In this section, an attempt has been made to emphasize the importance of an effective and enriching program of music listening for children in all elementary grades. It should be repeated that listening is the foundation of the music program and, as such, it should occupy an important place in the elementary school.

[38] *Ibid.*, p. 139.

Playing

It was pointed out earlier that a wide variety of musical experiences is necessary to provide music for *all* children. Children, for instance, who are limited or disinterested in vocal music may find a strong appeal in instrumental music. In general, opportunities for instrumental music are of two types: (1) the "extraclassroom" activity such as the school orchestra, band, or ensemble, and (2) class instruction. The first of these is usually the responsibility of someone other than the classroom teacher and need not, therefore, be discussed here. It is sufficient to state simply that they, like the glee club or choir, are valuable parts of the total music program and should be encouraged in all schools. The problems of securing instruments and qualified instructors are somewhat more complicated than those presented by a vocal group, but these can be, and have been, overcome by energetic faculties and principals who seek to enlist the aid of parents, community groups, and exchanges from other schools.

Within the classroom the teacher also has a responsibility for the instrumental phase of the music program. This usually begins in the primary grades with the playing of simple rhythm instruments. These can be either purchased from a commercial house or made by children. From these instruments children can graduate to the autoharp or the inexpensive flutes which are popular with intermediate grade children. These and other instruments may be played in all grades and may be used effectively as accompaniment for vocal music.

The classroom teacher's responsibility to the instrumental program also includes teaching children to recognize the various instruments and their classifications. Through the use of pictures, actual instruments, and recordings children should be taught to recognize the four major classifications (the strings, the woodwinds, the brasses, and the percussions) and the common instruments in each classification.

Responding Rhythmically

Children should be given many opportunities to respond rhythmically to music through the instruments of their choice, whether they are bells, blocks, cocoanut halves, triangles, cymbals, castanets, drums, or any of the other numerous instruments which can be purchased or made. It should be noted, however, that the use of rhythm instruments is compatible with the objectives of today's music program, *provided* that this program is directed toward encouraging the spontaneous response of children to music. It is extremely unfortunate that, in some schools, the "rhythm orchestra" has become as highly co-ordinated and perfected as an adult symphony orchestra. This is a highly artificial distortion of the original purpose and value of rhythm instruments and would appear to have little justification in a music program attuned to the needs of young children.

Frequently, the child's body is the instrument through which he can respond most eloquently to the rhythm of the music. Skipping, running, turning, hopping, and walking to music should be almost daily occurrences in most elementary classrooms, together with the creative and interpretative rhythms mentioned in the following chapter.

Creating Music

"Creative music activities are those by which children themselves bring music into being." [39]

If one accepts this broad definition, it is evident that most musical activities may be, in a sense, interpreted as creative. As one hums a tune or plays a melody on the piano, he is "creating" music although interpreting or "re-creating" might be a more accurate term. A narrower definition of "creating" is the composing of original music—words, tune, or both—and it is to this specific aspect of creativity in music that these remarks are directed.

There are three ways in which children may create original music. They may make up the words to a familiar tune; they may compose music for a familiar poem or rhyme; or they may do both.

Composing words to accompany a familiar tune is a common activity of all elementary grades. This might first take the form of composing a second or third verse to a familiar song. From this type of beginning, children may be encouraged to add words to a melody which they have heard often on the record player or piano. Discussions of the mood of the selection ("What do you think about when you hear the music?") will help to find words which can be fitted appropriately to the music.

The opposite type of creative endeavor is that in which children compose a tune for a familiar verse. This can be begun in the primary grades by adding music to some of the short poems or nonsense jingles which children enjoy so much. If the teacher feels insecure in writing the music, he can always use a tape recorder to capture the original music. Creating music may be done vocally by children or, as they experiment with their song flutes or other instruments, they may improvise a melody or tonal pattern which can be fitted to familiar words.

The third type of creative activity is that in which children compose both the words and music to a selection. This activity can be the outgrowth of numerous other projects—in the language arts, sciences, or social studies. One third-grade class, for instance, in studying their community, decided that their town should have its own song. They started out by writing a verse about the community and then composed an original tune to accompany their words. Such creative attempts may accompany any

[39] L. K. Myers. *Teaching Children Music in the Elementary School,* 2nd ed. (Englewood Cliffs, N.J., Prentice-Hall, Inc., 1956), p. 139.

activity or interest of the children and can be anything from a song about the new white rabbit in the classroom to one about their trip to the moon.

There are, of course, many conditions necessary to stimulate creative music activities. The total class environment, rich and varied experiences, the attitude and creative interests of the teacher, and flexibility of time scheduling are as important in music as they are in the other aspects of creativity discussed in other sections of this book.

Materials and Aids for Teaching Music

Fortunately, there are many resources for the teaching of music upon which the classroom teacher may rely. The following is a brief list of those which are practical and available for most elementary schools.

1. *Books.* As has been mentioned earlier, there are several excellent series of song books now on the market. These include teachers' manuals which may be particularly helpful to the inexperienced or insecure teacher. In addition, the classroom and school libraries should contain books of music. Song books, biographies of composers, stories of operas and symphonies, and others should be available to children.

2. *Recordings.* The excellent and comparatively inexpensive recordings now available should make it possible for each school to develop a record library. Most of the basal song books have accompanying recordings of selected songs which are available from the publisher, and children greatly enjoy hearing these records of songs contained in their own books. In addition, of course, the record library should contain as many other good recordings as it is possible to secure within the school budget.

3. *Record player.* The ideal situation is to have one of these in each classroom and their cost is such today that this is not prohibitive in most situations. If record players must be shared, care must be taken to purchase a type which can be handled and moved easily, for many a record player has been put out of commission in a very short time by careless handling and constant moving from one room to another. It seems also wise to caution teachers and administrators against the false economy of purchasing the most inexpensive instrument available, for even the best recording can be ruined if played upon an inadequate instrument.

4. *Piano.* A minimum of one piano in a building is a very modest requirement, and fortunately many schools are privileged today to have pianos in several classrooms, particularly those of the primary grades.

5. *Films and filmstrips.* These are available in quantity and deal with a variety of musical subjects, such as the instruments of the band, the composition of the symphony orchestra, stories of the lives of composers, and stories of the music of other peoples.

6. *Instruments.* These include the regular orchestra and band instruments. Many schools, over a period of years, have accumulated a decent

collection of these from gifts and wise expenditures of school funds. In addition, other types of instruments such as the autoharp, xylophone, orchestral bells, ukelele, and guitar make comparatively inexpensive and practical additions to the school instrumental collection. Still other instruments such as tonettes, flutophones, symphonettes, song flutes, and melody flutes are very inexpensive and can be purchased in quantity for class use. In addition, the common rhythm instruments, bells, drums, and cymbals, should be available for use by children in all grades. Lastly, instruments made by the children, for instance, drums and shakers, may be included in the orchestral collection of the elementary school.

7. *Radio and television.* These may be used to advantage in the elementary classroom, for there are several excellent programs which are now produced specifically for children. A more directed use of them, however, is presently being made in several systems in which music is taught by a music specialist once or twice a week over radio and closed TV to several classrooms within a system. These "special" music lessons are supplemented on other days by musical activities under the direction of the classroom teacher with the entire program co-ordinated through the use of a detailed manual distributed to all teachers. There are, of course, advantages and disadvantages of this plan, some of which are touched upon in Section 3 of this chapter.

A Music Check List

The following check list is presented as a summary and re-emphasis of the major features which distinguish a worthwhile program of music in today's school.

Is music regularly scheduled and taught as an integral part of the weekly classroom activities?

Is there an up-to-date music guide (developed locally or at the county or state levels) suggesting the activities and materials which can be used at each grade level throughout the school year?

Are the classroom musical activities child-centered in terms of individual development?

Do classroom musical activities consist of more than just singing songs?

Is listening to worthwhile music a major classroom musical activity?

Is emphasis placed on using and understanding the notational symbols of the musical score?

Are children becoming acquainted with the music of a growing number of major composers including American composers?

Are there provisions for whatever remedial assistance in music is needed at each grade level?

Are library reference materials about music and musicians available for student use in your school?

Is attention given to developing in each child a sensitivity to tone quality in singing, in speaking, in playing instruments, and in listening to sound-reproducing equipment such as the phonograph?

Are children with special musical interests and abilities encouraged to take part in musical activities which provide opportunities for group performance?

Have teachers recently enrolled in music workshops, summer or extension classes or other continuing activities along musical lines? [40]

The following section is devoted to a brief examination of a very pertinent problem related to the teaching of the visual arts and music in the elementary school.

Section 3: INSTRUCTIONAL PERSONNEL

Until this point, the authors have deliberately refrained from mentioning a major problem in the areas of visual arts and music: Who should be responsible for teaching them? The broad question of utilization of staff is examined in Chapter Sixteen, but the authors do not feel that a discussion of the visual arts and music can be completed without some recognition of the heated (in some places) controversy which now revolves around the question of instructional responsibility for these subjects. Should the classroom teacher be responsible for teaching them? Should a specialist be employed? If so, what should be his duties? What should be the role of the principal? Some opinion claims that the classroom teacher is not, and cannot be, qualified to teach *all* subjects, particularly those requiring highly specialized talents and knowledges. Others claim that the "specialist" does not have an opportunity to know the pupils intimately and that he, therefore, teaches subject matter divorced from the children's needs as well as from other areas of the curriculum. And so the debate goes on and on!

Keeping in mind the aims and values of the visual arts and music, it seems to be fairly obvious that the full responsibility for their attainment cannot rest solely upon *one* person. Let us, therefore, examine briefly the responsibilities of the classroom teacher, the specialist, and the principal in implementing the aims and values of the visual arts and music.

1. *The classroom teacher.* Without question, the person most responsible for the growth of his pupils in *all* areas of instruction is the classroom teacher. He must keep in mind the broad aims of education and relate them to the physical, intellectual, social, and emotional growth of each of his pupils. In order to do this, he has several advantages over any other staff member. He knows the individual strengths, limitations, and special talents of his pupils; he works with them over a longer period of time than any other individual; and he can integrate any area of the curriculum

[40] O. M. Hartsell, "Quality in Elementary School Music," *NEA Journal,* Vol. 49 (March, 1960), p. 29.

with any other where it is functionally desirable to do so. He is, and should be, the *key* figure in the instructional program. As such, he has a right to expect assistance from other qualified staff members which will make him more effective in his area of responsibility. In the case of the visual arts and music, these are the specialist and the principal.

2. *The specialist.* It would seem that not even the most ardent advocate of the self-contained classroom would deny that the specialist in art or music plays a vital role in the total educational program. His specialized talents and music training enable him to strengthen, supplement, and enrich the instructional program of the classroom teacher, but *never to replace it.* The role of the specialist as a "consultant" to assist teachers in administering and planning their programs, rather than to teach children, appears to be favored by many. Peterson, for instance, found that a majority of principals in one state preferred this plan for grades 1–3, although 53 per cent of them favored a plan in which all music was taught by the music specialist in grades 4–6.[41] In general, however, it seems safe to conclude that the wisest use of the specialist is not as a substitute for the classroom teacher, but rather as a resource person. In this role, he assumes such responsibilities as:

a. Assuming leadership in organizing and administering the art or music program.

b. Organizing workshops, meetings, institutes, and other types of in-service programs.

c. Assisting in the classroom when called upon by the classroom teacher *for a specific purpose.*

d. Demonstrating specific techniques and procedures.

e. Keeping teachers informed of newest developments in his specialized field through newsletters and bulletins.

f. Collecting, organizing, and distributing materials.

g. Organizing a library of available books and other resource aids.

3. *The principal.* The important role of the principal is stressed in the following statement which is, of course, equally applicable to the visual arts:

> The elementary school principal is in a key position to help make the music program effective in an aesthetic and functional manner. Fundamentally, he must believe in the value of music as it contributes to worthy objectives of education. He must desire to grow musically and he must be willing to vitalize the music education program. His role as a helper to classroom teachers will be most effective as he evidences genuine enthusiasm, sound and democratic organization, and as he promotes effective, purposeful communication.[42]

[41] W. J. Peterson, "Organizational Plans Favored by Administrators for Elementary School General Music," *Music Educators Journal,* Vol. 43 (January, 1957), pp. 48–51.

[42] O. B. Aftreth, "The Principal's Role in the Music Program," *The National Elementary Principal,* Vol. 39 (December, 1959), p. 26.

In this key role, the principal has several specific responsibilities such as:

a. Facilitating the work of the specialist and classroom teacher by opening and maintaining lines of communication between them.

b. Encouraging schoolwide enterprises such as concert series and art exhibits.

c. Encouraging exchange of these enterprises with other schools.

d. Purchasing and distributing facilities and materials needed by the classroom teacher and/or the consultant.

e. Co-ordinating the entire instructional program to provide as rich, balanced, and integrative educational experience as possible for all pupils.

Summary

Chapter Twelve was concerned with two of the arts now considered to be integral parts of the elementary curriculum. The *visual arts* was the term used to denote that area of the curriculum which is concerned with the production and appreciation of two-dimensional and three-dimensional art. The basic principles of the present-day art program were considered to be: (1) art education has value for *all* pupils; (2) art education contributes to the *total integrative growth* of each individual; (3) art education does not make an artificial distinction between expression and appreciation; and (4) art education should be integrated with other curricular areas.

Much study has been directed toward the classifying of art production according to maturity levels and personality types. There is no full agreement on these classifications, and many authorities emphasize that the uniqueness of the individual should take precedence over classification according to generalized types.

Methods of teaching art were listed as: (1) *direct teaching method*, (2) *free expression method*, and (3) *guidance method*. The general philosophy and advantages and disadvantages of each were examined briefly.

Certain practices in art today are considered highly questionable by reputable authorities, and their incompatibility with the objective of the elementary art program was emphasized.

A brief description of some of the numerous creative experiences which should be offered to pupils in the elementary school concluded the section on the visual arts.

Section Two was concerned with music, and its values for children in today's society. Statements of values which were considered to have most significance for planning the school music program were: (1) music is a source of enjoyment and pleasure; (2) music is an aesthetic and spiritual experience; (3) music is a creative experience; (4) music is a socializing experience; (5) music develops understandings of other cultures; and (6) music has a therapeutic value. In order to realize these values, it was stressed that the music program should comprise many varied activities, such as singing, listening, playing, responding rhythmically to music, and creating. Each of these activities was examined briefly.

The last section dealt with the problem of personnel for teaching the visual arts and music. The controversy over whether the classroom teacher or the specialist should be primarily responsible for instruction was examined briefly. It was suggested that the classroom teacher, consultant, and principal were *all* vital to a broad and enriched program.

STUDENT PROJECTS

1. Write a lesson plan for teaching an art lesson in the sixth grade. Describe exactly the motivational procedures you will use. How will you help children evaluate their work? What role will you take while children are working on their pictures?

2. In many informal art lessons discipline becomes a major problem. List specific guides which teachers in the elementary school might use in teaching art, which would help to minimize the possibility of poor classroom behavior.

3. As a first-grade teacher you ordered several rhythm instruments for your class. The principal deleted this item from his budget but suggested that you discuss the matter with him sometime in the near future. How will you defend your need for the instruments? Explain how you intend to use them to enrich the music program for your pupils. What will your answer be when your principal asks you about the values of rhythm instruments which pupils can make?

4. Describe several art activities you have seen or participated in when you were in the elementary school and which you would classify as "gimmicks or tricks." What are the differences between these and true art experiences?

5. You are an elementary school principal and a group of parents has protested against their children learning Negro spirituals and Christmas carols in school because of their racial and religious significance. Should such music be excluded from the public school program? Consider the question carefully and prepare a statement for your local newspaper explaining and defending the stand you take on this issue.

6. The first music listening lesson you taught to your sixth-grade class was a total failure. Children were bored and restless and complained bitterly about listening to "long hair" music. Explain in detail the type of listening program you plan to use in this class for the next month. What will be your objectives? What materials will you use?

7. Do you agree with the following statement? Defend your statement with reading from other authorities and, if possible, from your own experience in working with children.

The child has a marvelous ability to express himself. If properly drawn out and encouraged, he needs no help. The moment a teacher draws on the board or paints on paper, that moment is the child crippled and inhibited. That moment is he ruined for confidence in his own way of doing. Hands off! [43]

8. Send a short questionnaire to twenty-five to fifty primary grade teachers asking them if they think coloring books have harmful or detrimental effects on

[43] N. Cole, *The Arts in the Classroom* (New York, The John Day Company, 1940), p. 9.

their pupils' creative abilities. Compare their answers with present research on this topic.

9. You have recently been appointed as an elementary school principal. During October of your first year in this position, you notice many classrooms in your building which have chalk-board borders of Halloween cats, pumpkins, and witches, all obviously cut from patterns. In other classrooms you notice that similar figures are pasted on the window panes. What is your leadership role in improving the art program in this situation? Mention some specific techniques and procedures you will use when working with your faculty on this problem.

10. Investigate thoroughly the question of teaching music reading in the elementary school. What are the chief points of agreement? Of disagreement? What are your conclusions?

11. Some administrators claim that one of the chief values of music in the school is its use as a "public relations" instrument. Is this a value of music which justifies its place in the school program? What are the many factors which would be considered in answering this question?

12. Describe several worthwhile activities which will integrate the visual arts and music. Be sure to specify the grade level for each. What are the *specific* values you hope to realize through *each* experience?

13. To what extent are art and music consultants employed by communities in your state? Are they titled teachers, supervisors, or consultants? What are their duties? What certification do they need?

14. Compile a portfolio of twelve art masterpieces which you could use as the core of an art appreciation program in the fifth grade. Defend your choice of each picture according to the interests and maturity of ten- or eleven-year-old children. Be sure that you include a balance between classic and modern art as well as foreign and American artists. Describe how you will introduce your pupils to these works of art.

15. Choose a social studies unit for a specific grade level. Explain in detail how you will integrate music with the unit, being sure to include singing, listening, playing, responding rhythmically, and creating in your plan.

BIBLIOGRAPHY

ANDREWS, Frances M. and COCKERILLE, Clara E., *Your School Music Program* (Englewood Cliffs, N.J., Prentice-Hall, Inc., 1958).

BARKAN, M., *A Foundation for Art Education* (New York, The Ronald Press Company, 1955).

BROOKS, B. Marion and BROWN, Harry A., *Music Education in the Elementary School* (New York, American Book Company, 1946).

CANE, Florence, *The Artist in Each of Us.* (New York, Pantheon Books, Inc., 1951).

CARABO-CONE, Madeline and ROYT, Beatrice, *How To Help Children Learn Music* (New York, Harper and Brothers, 1955).

COLE, Natalie R., *The Arts in the Classroom* (New York, The John Day Company, 1940).

D'AMICO, Victor, *Creative Teaching in Art, rev. ed.* (Scranton, Penn., International Textbook Company, 1953).

DEFRANCESCO, Italo L., *Art Education: Its Means and Ends* (New York, Harper and Brothers, 1958).

DYKEMA, Peter W. and CUNDIFF, Hannah M., *School Music Handbook,* new ed. (Evanston, Ill., Summy-Birchard Publishing Company, 1955).

ELLISON, Alfred, *Music With Children* (New York, McGraw-Hill Book Company, 1959).

ERDT, Margaret H., *Teaching Art in the Elementary School* (New York, Holt, Rinehart and Winston, Inc., 1954).

GAITSKELL, Charles D., *Children and Their Art* (New York, Harcourt, Brace & World, Inc., 1958).

GRANT, Parks, *Music for Elementary Teachers* (New York, Appleton-Century-Crofts, Inc., 1951).

HENRY, Nelson B., ed., *Basic Concepts in Music Education,* National Society for the Study of Education, 57th Yearbook (Chicago, University of Chicago Press, 1958).

JEFFERSON, Blanche, *Teaching Art to Children* (Boston: Allyn and Bacon, Inc., 1959).

JONES, A. N., *Music Education in Action* (Boston: Allyn and Bacon, Inc., 1960).

KEILER, Manfred L., *Art in the Schoolroom,* 2nd ed. (Lincoln, Neb., University of Nebraska Press, 1955).

KINSCELLA, Hazel G. and TIERNEY, Elizabeth M., *The Child and His Music* (Lincoln, Nebraska, The University Publishing Company, 1953).

KNUDSEN, Estelle H. and CHRISTENSEN, Ethel M., *Children's Art Education* (Peoria, Ill., Chas. A. Bennett Company, Inc., 1957).

LANDIS, Mildred M., *Meaningful Art Education* (Peoria, Ill., Chas. A. Bennett Company, Inc., 1951).

LEONHARD, Charles and HOUSE, Robert W., *Foundations and Principles of Music Education* (New York, McGraw-Hill Book Company, 1959).

LINDSTROM, Miriam, *Children's Art* (Berkeley, Calif., University of California Press, 1957).

LOGAN, Frederick M., *Growth of Art in American Schools* (New York, Harper and Brothers, 1955).

LOWENFELD, Viktor, *Your Child and His Art* (New York, The Macmillan Company, 1957).

LOWENFELD, Viktor, *Creative and Mental Growth,* 3rd ed. (New York, The Macmillan Company, 1957).

McMILLAN, L. Eileen, *Guiding Children's Growth Through Music* (Boston, Ginn and Company, 1959).

MORGAN, Russell and MORGAN, Hazel, *Music Education in Action* (Chicago, Neil A. Kjos Music Company, 1954).

MUNRO, Thomas, *Art Education, Its Philosophy and Psychology* (New York, Liberal Arts Press, 1956).

MURSELL, James L., *Music Education Principles and Programs* (Morristown, N.J., Silver Burdett Company, 1956).

MURSELL, James L., *Music and the Classroom Teacher* (Morristown, N.J., Silver Burdett Company, 1951).

MYERS, Louise K., *Teaching Children Music in the Elementary School* (Englewood Cliffs, N.J., Prentice-Hall, Inc., 1956).

National Elementary Principal, *Creative Schools,* 23rd Yearbook, Department of Elementary School Principals (Washington, D.C., National Education Association, 1944).

PEARSON, Ralph M., *The New Art Education, rev. ed.* (New York, Harper and Brothers, 1953).

PIERCE, A. E., *Teaching Music in the Elementary School* (New York, Holt, Rinehart and Winston, Inc., 1959).

SHEEHY, Emma D., *There's Music in Children,* rev. ed. (New York, Holt, Rinehart and Winston, Inc., 1952).

SHEEHY, Emma D., *Children Discover Music and Dance* (New York, Holt, Rinehart and Winston, Inc., 1959).

SCHULTZ, Harold A. and SHORES, J. Harlan, *Art in the Elementary School* (Urbana, Ill., University of Illinois Press, 1948).

SNYDER, Keith D., *School Music Administration and Supervision* (Boston, Allyn and Bacon, Inc., 1959).

WILT, Miriam E., *Creativity in the Elementary School* (New York, Appleton-Century-Crofts, Inc., 1959).

WINSLOW, Leon L., *The Integrated School Art Program,* 2nd ed. (New York, McGraw-Hill Book Company, 1949).

ZIRBES, Laura, *Spurs to Creative Teaching* (New York, G. P. Putnam's Sons, 1959).

CHAPTER 13

Health, Safety, and Physical Education

ANY THIRD GRADE TEACHER who has tried to teach compound subtraction to a child suffering from a splitting headache, sick stomach, or throbbing tooth is fully aware of the importance of physical health to the total educative process. Similarly, a teacher who has attempted to interest an unhappy, insecure, group-rejected sixth-grader in the Constitutional Convention realizes that social health is a primary concern of the school program. Also, the first-grade teacher who attempts to help a six-year-old distinguish between *then* and *there* after he has been dragged to school, kicking and screaming, by his older brother does not need to be told that her pupils' emotional health must be one of her major considerations. These teachers, and all others faced with similar problems, understand and wholeheartedly agree with today's philosophy that the social, mental, and physical health of children is the broad base upon which all other aspects of the school program depend. It is this realization that has led to the steadily increasing emphasis upon the importance of an adequate school health program, which according to many authorities is one of the most significant educational developments of the twentieth century. Some of the sociological and educational factors which, over the years, have contributed to the development of the school health program are mentioned in the following section.

FACTORS INFLUENCING THE DEVELOPMENT OF THE SCHOOL HEALTH PROGRAM

There are, of course, an untold number of factors which have contributed over the past century to the steadily increasing emphasis upon school health. The most far-reaching factors are usually considered to be:

1. *Beginnings of a Public Health Movement.* The year 1850 is usually considered to mark "the beginning of public health as an organized movement in this country." [1] In this year, the publication of the *Report of the Sanitary Commission of Massachusetts* indicated an awakened awareness of the importance of health as a community responsibility, which inevitably directed attention toward the health and sanitation features of the school.

2. *Concern over the control of communicable diseases.* As the trend toward urbanization grew during the middle nineteenth century, more schools were established and an increasing number of children attended school. The detection and control of childhood contagious diseases became a major problem faced by the teachers of the day. Although the emphasis was on exclusion of the sick rather than on a preventative program, nevertheless the school began to realize faintly its responsibility toward the health of its students.

3. *The temperance movement.* In 1872, a law was passed in Ohio requiring that the harmful effects of narcotics and alchohol be taught in all schools. Other states followed in Ohio's lead, and many included other aspects of personal hygiene in their programs as well. These early laws, still widely in effect, contributed directly to the awakening need for health education for the young citizens of the country.

4. *Influence of European "physical training" programs.* Toward the latter part of the nineteenth century, when the school day and school year became longer, the need for providing children with some sort of physical activity as an antidote for long hours of inactivity became apparent. The leading educators of the day turned to Europe for a solution to the problem and found it in the organized "physical training" programs of English, German, and Swedish schools. These were adopted or modified to meet our public school needs, and the door was opened to admit the beginnings of our modern physical education program.

5. *The child study movement.* No other single factor was more important in promoting health education than the child study movement of the twentieth century. New knowledge of how children grew, developed, and learned brought into focus the emphasis upon the total child. No longer were the physical, social, emotional, and intellectual aspects considered as separate entities but rather as an integrated whole, the development of which was seriously handicapped by the neglect of any one factor.

6. *The World Wars.* Both great wars of the twentieth century revealed to the American public some startling statistics concerning the physical fitness of its youth. In the wake of each of these wars, there has come an increasing emphasis upon the need for developing educational programs which make adequate provisions for promoting the physical welfare of all children and youth.

[1] R. E. Grout, *Health Teaching in Schools,* 3rd ed. (Philadelphia, W. B. Saunders Company, 1958), pp. 9–10.

7. *The importance of safety education.* The mechanized, industrialized, swiftly-paced, highly-pressured lives which most of us live today have made safety education one of our primary national concerns. The holiday predictions of the National Safety Council and the daily accounts of accidents in the newspapers or on the radio forcefully remind us of the ever-present need for safety education in our schools.

8. *Advances in medical science.* The spectacular gains made in medical science in recent years have placed health in the forefront of national consciousness. These have, however, necessitated informing children and adults of their proper use, limitations, and advantages. Educating the public to the advantages of the Salk vaccine, for instance, as well as organizing a program for its administration have become, in many instances, a direct responsibility of the school, in connection with public health authorities.

9. *Present concern over mental health.* The fact that more than half the hospital beds in the country are filled with mental patients, and that present statistics show an increase in broken homes, divorces, crime, and juvenile delinquency is indicative of a major problem which this nation is facing at the present time. In many instances, this has caused health educators to re-examine and broaden the school health program to include all phases of personal health and well-being.

10. *Present emphasis on fitness.* In the last few years there has probably been more interest in the total problem of youth fitness evidenced by our national leaders than ever before in our history. The president's Council on Youth Fitness created by Executive Order on July 16, 1956 had as its slogan, *Youth Fitness is National Fitness* and brought to national attention the need to examine the problem carefully from every angle. Since then, many conferences on the national and state levels have been held to discuss the fitness of youth and its implications on our national welfare and progress.

It is important to note that the present concept of fitness is a very comprehensive one which embraces all aspects of the individual's health. The following definition is illustrative of the broad concept of fitness held today by many educators, one of whom states that "total fitness" includes,

such interrelated attributes as: sound organic health beyond the level of mere freedom from disease or infirmity; physical strength, co-ordination, agility, and endurance to perform duties normally required without undue fatigue; emotional stability to meet the strains of modern living; social adaptability in accord with prevailing cultural standards; and spiritual and moral traits that improve the quality of human behavior—all bound together into a sort of body, mind, and soul composite pattern.[2]

[2] C. L. Brownell, "A Profile of Fitness in Education," *Teachers College Record*, Vol. 59 (April, 1958), p. 398.

It should be apparent from the foregoing discussion that the school has a heavy responsibility for the total health of its students. Those schools which have accepted this responsibility have developed vigorous and comprehensive health programs. Such programs are *not* confined to a specific daily lesson, nor relegated to a particular area of the curriculum, nor to the responsibility of any one faculty member. On the contrary, the modern health program, *more than any other school feature*, permeates every aspect of the school. It extends into every nook and corner of the physical plant; it becomes a part of every learning experience or activity; it overflows into the home and community; and every teacher, pupil, and parent plays an active role in its successful implementation. It is obvious, therefore, that its comprehensiveness cannot be confined to a discussion in any one chapter, and, for this reason, the reader has found constant reference to the total health of the pupil throughout this entire volume. In this chapter, the discussion will be confined to *the classroom teacher's responsibility* toward the major aspects of the school health program designated as: (1) a healthful school environment, (2) an instructional program of health and safety, (3) school health services, and (4) physical education. Each of these is discussed in the remainder of the chapter.

Section 1: A HEALTHFUL SCHOOL ENVIRONMENT

Like a rare violin, each school has a unique and inimitable personality which makes it different from every other. Much of this "personality" is attributable to the general tone or environment of the building, which can be sensed by a perceptive person the minute he opens the front door. Some schools are happy schools—some are not. Some are healthful and safe places in which boys and girls grow and play and work—some are not. Some are clean, well-organized, and well-kept—some are not. Some build feelings of security, well-being, and friendship—others do not. What causes these differences? In general, they can be said to be the result of a combination of the physical, socio-emotional, and intellectual environments. The first two are a vital part of the school health program and are considered briefly in this context here.

The Physical Environment

The physical environment of the classroom is a major responsibility of the teacher. Among the most important physical aspects of the classroom which merit the daily attention of the teacher are:

1. *Lighting.* A recent estimate to the effect that lighting of 75 per cent of all the nation's classrooms is below minimum standards indicates the seriousness of this problem for all teachers.[3] In order to determine

[3] "Using the Classroom for Better Learning," *The Educational Trend* (New London, Conn., Arthur C. Croft Publications, February, 1955).

the adequacy of light in his classroom, a teacher must be familiar with the standard units of light measurement. A foot-candle is the unit used to measure the *intensity* of light and is defined as "the amount of light cast by a standard candle one foot away from the light." [4] A minimum of twenty-eight to thirty-two foot-candles of intensity is recommended for school lighting, although the exact amount varies considerably with the task to be performed. More important, however, than the intensity of the light coming from the source is the brightness of the light reflected from all surfaces within the room. This luminosity varies considerably according to the type and color of the surface upon which it falls. A white or off-white ceiling, for instance, has a reflection value of approximately 80 per cent. Light pastel walls reflect approximately 50 to 75 per cent, whereas dark walls or slate chalk boards reflect less than 10 per cent of the light cast upon them. The brightness of the reflected light is, therefore, the important factor to be considered. It is measured in units of "foot-lamberts." In other words, if thirty foot-candles of light fall on a surface which has a reflection value of 80 per cent, the resulting brightness is figured to be 80 per cent of thirty, or twenty-four foot-lamberts. Accordingly, "The foot-lambert . . . and not the foot-candle, becomes the prime factor in any consideration of eye comfort and efficiency." [5]

Insufficient light is, without question, harmful but probably more harmful is the glare of light from the reflection of shiny and glossy surfaces. This is a problem faced by many teachers in new schools as well as old, and every effort should be made to remove such sources of glare from the classroom.

Obviously, a teacher can do very little about changing or removing the light fixtures in his classroom, How, then, can he improve the lighting conditions? Actually, there are several very important steps he can take toward providing adequate lighting conditions for his pupils, such as:

a. Measure accurately the present light needs. Obviously the first step in an improvement program is to determine exactly what the needs are. Through the use of a light meter, the teacher or principal should determine the adequacy of light in the classroom. It is important to note that there is a wide variation in lighting from one side of the room to the other, and all sides and corners should be tested to appraise the entire situation.

b. Request improved lighting conditions. Very often the teacher's request is honored when the room is to be repainted or new equipment is to be purchased. If this is the case, the teacher can improve his classroom lighting by requesting that the ceiling be painted white or off-white; and the walls and trim a pleasant pastel shade. He may also suggest that the dark

[4] *Making the Best Use of the Eyes* (New York, National Society for the Prevention of Blindness, Inc., Publication 439, n. d.), p. 5.

[5] C. D. Gibson, *Eye Comfort and Efficiency* (New York, National Society for the Prevention of Blindness, Inc., Publication 465, n. d.), p. 4.

varnished wooden floors be resanded and that new blond movable furniture replace the dark stationary type.

c. Cover or resurface dark wall areas. To some extent the classroom teacher may improve the lighting conditions by covering or repainting dark wall surfaces, such as brown bulletin boards or little-used slate chalk boards, both of which are considered "light traps" in the older school buildings. Light paint, cloth, or wallpaper has been used successfully by resourceful teachers in covering these undesirable dark wall areas.

d. Cover or remove glossy surfaces. Glare is an ever-present problem and *must* be considered by the conscientious teacher. Covering glass surfaces, such as window panes in closet doors, as well as removing glass surfaces from hanging wall pictures will help to reduce the amount of glare to which children are daily exposed.

e. Regulate wisely the sources of light. There is no better light than natural daylight. The best source of daylight comes from the top of the windows, and shades or blinds should be regulated to take advantage of this fact. The most satisfactory plan, according to some, is

to place at the center of each window two buff or light gray shades of translucent material of a texture that will not crack, one shade to pull up and the other, down, with a metal bar between rollers to prevent streaks of light.[6]

However, there is no complete agreement on the best type of shade or blind, and consequently many different types are presently found in classrooms. The teacher should experiment with those of his particular situation until he discovers the best way to utilize them to the full advantage of his pupils' eye comfort.

f. Arrange furniture. The blond, movable classroom furniture of the present is decidedly superior to the older type. Desk and table tops are usually finished in natural wood or laminated plastic, which have a reflection value of approximately 40 per cent.[7] Generally, the furniture is of two types: (1) the separate table and chair, and (2) the tubular unit in which the desk and chair are connected by a metal tube. Both types allow for a variety and flexibility of furniture arrangements and should not be used in one rigid or regimented pattern. As children move their desks and chairs to accommodate a number of activities, however, care should be taken that they do not face the windows. Light may come from over the pupil's left shoulder, right shoulder, or back for most ordinary tasks. During writing tasks, the light should fall over the left shoulder to avoid the shadow of the hand on the paper. The reverse is true, of course, in the case of the left-handed child.

These are but a few of the possibilities by which a classroom teacher

[6] W. Hathaway, *Daylight in the Schoolroom* (New York, National Society for the Prevention of Blindness, Inc., Publication 459, n. d.), p. 6.

[7] C. S. Allen as told to B. Gasker, "Classroom Illumination," *NEA Journal,* Vol. 43 (October, 1954), p. 422.

may improve the lighting conditions of his classroom. The importance of proper and adequate light is a feature of the physical environment which cannot be overstressed and which *must* be the constant concern of the elementary teacher and administrator.

2. *Color.* A second aspect of the physical environment which is receiving considerable attention today is the wise use of color. Schools, factories, hospitals, and public buildings are experimenting with the effect of color on the behavior and achievement of individuals. There has been some experimentation which reports not only improved social attitudes and behavior, but also an increase in scholastic achievement by children who attended a school painted according to approved principles of color design and harmony. In general, it seems safe to assume that wise use of the basic principles of color harmony does have some positive effect upon the feelings and performances of children, as well as adults.

3. *Ventilation and Heating.* In many schools, ventilation and heating are thermostatically controlled. Such control places little responsibility upon the classroom teacher. Where this is not the case, the teacher should ask help from the principal or custodian in determining how to regulate the temperature to the maximum comfort of his pupils.

4. *Acoustics.* By wise use of his own voice, by daily scheduling to avoid outside distractions (see Chapter Five), and by careful provision for the hard-of-hearing child, the classroom teacher may, to some extent, control the acoustical features of the classroom.

5. *Sanitary and Safety Provisions.* It is obvious that a healthful environment is possible only in a clean and safe classroom. Sinks, drinking fountains, and lavatories placed in the classroom should be scrupulously clean at all times. Closets, shelves, drawers, desks, and other storage space should be periodically cleaned and able to pass inspection for fire hazards. The teacher should exercise particular caution in the storage and use of such equipment as paper cutters, scissors, knives, paints, paint brushes, bats and balls, and any mechanical equipment which accompanies the workbench found in some elementary classrooms.

Pupils should be involved in caring for the physical environment of the classroom. The maintenance of many of the physical aspects of the classroom should provide valuable learning experiences for children. Committees formed to check the presence of safety hazards, to regulate the window shades, or to control the ventilation will offer pupils the opportunity to develop social responsibilities. In addition, involving children in the care of the physical environment is a valuable means of developing many important health and safety concepts. From the kindergarten on, therefore, children should, within reason, be permitted to share those responsibilities of classroom maintenance which will result in valuable social, health, and safety learnings.

Thus far, the discussion has pertained only to the physical environment of the classroom. There are, however, other features of the school plant which merit the attention of teachers. These are now considered briefly.

The physical environment of the entire school plant should be carefully appraised. The main features of the school-wide physical environment which should be considered are:

1. *Hallways and stairs.* These should be kept clean and free from obstacles. The following practical suggestions should be of use:

Nonslip wax on the floors will prevent countless falls. Doorways situated close to stairways should have doors that open away from the stairs. All doors (if not recessed) should swing back flat against the wall. Stairways should be wide and well-lighted, with handrails on both sides and one in the center. If small children use the stairs, there should be a second rail for their use, a foot below the regular one.[8]

2. *Playground.* The playground should be carefully maintained, free from traffic hazards, and the apparatus kept in A-1 condition. Sand under the swings and bars and yellow lines around each piece of equipment are recommended.[8]

3. *School bus.* During the school year, 1959–1960, more than 170,000 public-school buses transported approximately thirteen million boys and girls to and from school.[9] The mechanical condition of the bus should be checked at regular intervals and the health and reliability of the driver considered carefully in order to safeguard the lives of these youngsters.

4. *The cafeteria.* The cafeteria should be clean, healthful, and pleasant. It should be supervised and inspected daily by the principal or a person in authority. (The use of the cafeteria as a health instructional aid is discussed later in the chapter.)

The Socio-Emotional Environment

The socio-emotional climate is equally important to healthful living. One fifth-grade teacher borrowed a line from John Masefield to use as a motto for his classroom. On the rear bulletin board, in prominent letters, read the legend, "The days that make us happy make us wise." [10] The children in that particular classroom *were* happy—and they did learn! Unfortunately, this is not true of *all* classrooms, for in some, the hostilities and fears of children create an unhealthful socio-emotional environment. In general, the two main causes of a negative type of socio-emotional climate for which the teacher is responsible are:

[8] B. Johnson and S. A. Abercrombie, "A Safe Environment for Learning," *NEA Journal,* Vol. 49 (October, 1960), p. 24.
[9] K. A. Johnson, "The Road to School-Bus Safety," *NEA Journal,* Vol. 49 (October, 1960), p. 25.
[10] John Masefield, *Biography.*

1. *Rejection.* Widespread feelings among pupils of rejection by the teacher indicate a poor emotional environment in the classroom. Furthermore, the anxiety which pupils feel concerning their relationship with the teacher is probably greater than most teachers realize. Billy, for instance, returned home from the first day of school to an anxious mother waiting to hear of his reaction to kindergarten. When asked to tell about his first day, he broke into a wide smile, breathed a sigh of relief, and said, "Well, there's lots to tell. But first of all—my teacher likes me!" The teacher who establishes a strong rapport with his pupils has done much to create a healthful socio-emotional climate in his classroom.

2. *Fear.* Many studies have been made of children's fears. On the whole, those which are most closely related to the school environment are: (*a*) fear of the authority of the teacher, (*b*) fear of failure, and (*c*) fear of competition. The teacher who insists upon unrealistic standards of discipline (absolute quiet or long periods of sitting still) or who uses sarcasm, threats, ridicule, indiscriminate punishment, or other retaliatory measures to secure control of the classroom generates tensions, hostilities, and fears among his students. So, also, does the teacher who constantly compares one child's performance with that of others or attempts to force children to higher standards with, "You are not trying"; or, "You will have to go back to the low group." In the classrooms of these teachers, temper tantrums, crying spells, endless bickering, arguing, fighting, withdrawn behavioral patterns, and epidemics of cheating or stealing are symptoms which indicate that greater attention should be directed toward the socio-emotional aspects of healthful school living.

There are, of course, many other aspects of children's social and emotional health which, because of space, cannot be discussed here. The reader is referred to other chapters, particularly Three and Fourteen, for further consideration of this topic as well as to the books included in the bibliographies at the close of these chapters.

Section 2: HEALTH AND SAFETY INSTRUCTION

An effective instructional program in health and safety is the vital core of the entire school health program. Its broad aim is "the intelligent self-direction of health behavior." [11] Included within this comprehensive goal is a hierarchy of objectives which is examined in the following statement.

Instructional Objectives

The objectives of health and safety instruction should culminate in changed behavior. To change behavior is not a simple task which can be accomplished in one fell swoop. On the contrary, it depends upon the

[11] J. K. Rash, "Philosophical Bases for Health Education," *Journal of Health-Physical Education-Recreation,* Vol. 31 (January, 1960), p. 35.

realization of numerous objectives which can be classified into the following categories.

Knowledge and Concepts. The fact that much health content taught in the past remained merely on the verbalization level has caused some teachers to belittle the importance of teaching pupils the basic facts of healthful living. This is extremely unfortunate for two reasons. In the first place, there is some evidence to support "the belief that there is a positive relationship between health knowledge and health practice, i.e., that those better informed as to the facts of health tend better to practice more healthful living." [12] Secondly, there is also evidence that children hold numerous health and safety misconceptions which are decidedly harmful and which can be corrected only through a meaningful program of instruction. Among the many harmful misconceptions held by fifth- and sixth-grade children, Dzenowagis and Irwin list the following:

1. The best doctors always promise to make people healthy.

2. The only good way to help a drowning person is to jump in the water to save him.

3. It is usually safe to go swimming alone if you know how to swim.

4. Oil, grease, and gas fires should be put out with plenty of water.[13]

The lowest (but very important) plateau of health teaching is, therefore, concerned with teaching the facts and knowledges necessary for healthy and safe living. Eventually, these should merge to form basic *concepts* which are listed by one writer as:

1. Good health is a state of complete physical, mental, social and spiritual well-being, as well as the absence of disease or infirmity.

2. Keeping oneself in good physical and mental health helps one meet more successfully the mental and emotional problems in everyday living.

3. Growth and development—physical, mental, emotional, spiritual, and social—is a continuing process throughout the life of the individual. Both are influenced by diet, exercise, rest, relaxation, recreation, and by freedom from sickness and accident.

4. Participation in vigorous play and exercise, out-of-doors when possible, helps develop fitness and is important to the development of muscular strength and co-ordination.

5. Proper application of body mechanics to activities associated with everyday living helps the individual use his body efficiently and gracefully.

6. Adjustment to life consists of changing a situation when possible, or accepting unalterable realities.

[12] R. E. Schneider, *Methods and Materials of Health Education* (Philadelphia, W. B. Saunders Company, 1958), p. 87.
[13] J. G. Dzenowagis and L. W. Irwin, "Prevalence of Certain Harmful Health and Safety Misconceptions Among Fifth- and Sixth-Grade Children," *Research Quarterly,* Vol. 25 (May, 1954), pp. 150–163.

7. Recreation is an essential part of normal life, and a wide range of interests contributes to the development of a well-rounded personality.

8. Voluntary and official health and welfare agencies are essential to the maintenance of good community health.

9. An understanding of the nature of the human being—physical, mental, emotional and social—is basic to application of the principles of healthful living.[14]

Skills and Habits. The next plateau of objectives is the development of desirable skills and habits which Starr lists as:

1. To evaluate one's health habits and make needed changes.

2. To organize time to provide for balanced living.

3. To know and use correct terms when discussing physical and mental health.

4. To recognize early signs of illness and to seek and follow professional advice.

5. To seek proper medical and dental advice.

6. To dress properly for all occasions and seasons and to exercise good taste in personal appearance and wearing apparel.

7. To carry out essential practices of cleanliness and sanitation.

8. To follow rules of safety and accident prevention at work and play.[15]

Attitudes and Values. Eventually, health teaching which has meaning and purpose should develop certain essential attitudes and values. The category of attitudes includes,

1. Readiness to accept responsibility for maintenance and improvement of the best health possible for oneself.

2. Readiness to accept consultation and care for physical, emotional or social problems.

3. Appreciation of the responsibility of each individual to make the community a safer place in which to live.

4. Respect for health laws and safety regulations which protect health and life.

5. Desire for gaining and maintaining good health and physical fitness through physical activities.

6. Understanding that relief from stresses and strains can come through participation in a wide variety of wholesome leisure time activities.[16]

In addition to developing the objectives listed thus far, the teacher should be aware of the importance of promoting essential health *values.* As Burnett points out, our modern life with its emphasis on competition, status, and materialistic gains has tended to degrade the values placed

---

[14] H. M. Starr, "Putting Health Instruction to Work for You," *The National Elementary Principal,* Vol. 39 (February, 1960), p. 15.

[15] *Ibid.*

[16] *Ibid.*

upon health and safety.[17] To develop within the student a firm and positive pattern of health values is the final plateau of objectives, from which changed behavior is the natural result.

Scope and Sequence of Content

Certain areas of health content are usually included in the elementary school curriculum. In general, there is some, but not much, difference between the classifications of content recommended by various authorities for the elementary school program. Irwin and others determined a list of 305 fundamental concepts of healthful living appropriate for elementary school instruction, which they divided into the following categories:

Healthy Living	Food and Nutrition
Growth and Development	Sleep and Rest
Safety and First Aid	Posture and Exercise
Bacteria, Viruses, and Immunity	Recreation and Play
Cleanliness	Elimination of Wastes
Infectious and Parasitic Diseases	Clothing
Heart and Circulation	Light and Air
Cancer	Vision and Hearing
Dental Health	Health Service
Mental Health	Community Health [18]

Slightly different is the list of content categories proposed by the Joint Committee on Health Problems in Education of the National Education Association and the American Medical Association.

Food and Nutrition	Communicable disease control
Exercise, rest and sleep	Homes and schools
Eyes and ears	Clothing
Mental and emotional health	Teeth
Body functioning	Safety and First Aid
Cleanliness	Community Health [19]

The following classifications and brief accompanying descriptions have been determined by the authors after an examination of numerous courses of study and textbook series, and are not dissimilar from those previously indicated.

1. *Cleanliness and Grooming.* Includes desirable habits of washing and bathing; knowledge of proper dress according to season and occasion; and care of the teeth, eyes, nose, and ears.

[17] R. W. Burnett, "Values and Health," *Journal of Health-Physical Education-Recreation,* Vol. 29 (October, 1958), pp. 17–18, 34–35.

[18] L. W. Irwin, C. D. Merrill, and W. M. Staton, "Concepts of Healthful Living of Functional Value in the General Education of Elementary School Pupils," *Research Quarterly,* Vol. 24 (December, 1953), pp. 435–441.

[19] C. C. Wilson, ed., *Health Education,* Report of the Joint Committee of the National Education Association and the American Medical Association (Washington, D.C., National Education Association, 1948), pp. 214–215.

2. *Food and Nutrition.* For years, this category included the importance of a balanced diet according to the *Basic Seven* food groups:

   a. Leafy green and yellow vegetables.
   b. Citrus fruits, tomatoes, raw cabbage.
   c. Potatoes and other vegetables and fruits.
   d. Milk, cheese, ice cream.
   e. Meat, poultry, fish, eggs, dried peas and beans.
   f. Bread, flour, cereals.
   g. Butter and fortified margarine.

Recently the United States Department of Agriculture proposed a simplified revision of the daily food plan according to the *Essential Four* groups:

   a. Bread, cereals.
   b. Meat (beef, veal, pork, lamb, poultry, fish, eggs) with dried beans, peas, and nuts as alternates.
   c. Vegetable-fruit group.
   d. Milk group.[20]

A comparison of the two groups reveals that no basic changes have been made in the thinking as to what constitutes a balanced daily diet. The latter classification, however, is simpler and easier for children to remember, and it is recommended that elementary teachers use the *Essential Four* in teaching a balanced food plan.

3. *Fresh Air, Sunshine, Play, Exercise, Recreation.* Importance of proper amount and type of play and exercise; good posture; importance of fresh air and sunshine in building healthy bodies; desirable hobbies and other recreational activities.

4. *Sleep and Rest.* Need for proper type and amount for healthful living.

5. *Control and Prevention of Disease.* Importance of cleanliness; need for proper dental and medical attention and examination; proper use of medicines and drugs; symptoms, treatment, and control of contagious diseases; the common cold.

6. *Structure and Function of the Body.* Knowledge of proper terminology, structure, and function of major parts and systems of the body.

7. *Sex Education.* Proper terminology, positive attitudes, and accurate knowledge of sex information suited to the needs and interests of young children. This has been a long-neglected area in the elementary school, but one which is becoming increasingly important. Eggert, for instance, states that forty-three of forty-five state departments replying to a survey agreed that an effective program of sex education should be the responsibility of the elementary school.[21]

[20] Agricultural Research Service, *Essentials of An Adequate Diet,* Agriculture Information Bulletin No. 160 (Washington, D.C., United States Department of Agriculture, November, 1956), p. 1.
[21] C. L. Eggert, "Critical Examination of Sex Education in the Elementary School," *Research Quarterly,* Vol. 25 (March, 1954), pp. 20–25.

8. *Community Health.* Responsibilities of public health officers and programs; community health problems, such as sewage, food inspection, and water filtration.

9. *Safety Education.* General safety needs such as traffic, home, school, water, and fire safety; specific safety needs determined by location and situation; responsibilities of safety officers and patrols; first aid.

10. *Mental, Social, and Emotional Health.* Understanding the basic needs; importance and characteristics of good health in these areas; interrelationship of these areas with physical growth and development.

The sequence of content is determined by the increasing complexity of concepts in each basic classification. Occasionally a curriculum health guide is organized according to an "alternate-year plan" in which a particular topic, such as "care of the teeth," is taught every other year. A far more common plan is to organize the content of each major classification into a graded series of concepts according to their complexity. Thus, each major division of content is taught each year with children progressing steadily from the simpler to the more complex concepts.

Still other systems use no course of study to predetermine scope and sequence of content. In these schools, the health instruction is tailored to meet the present needs of the group. The advantages and disadvantages of each plan, as well as a proper balance between them, have been discussed fully in other chapters and need not be repeated here. Let us turn our attention, therefore, to some of the recommended procedures for teaching health and safety to young children.

Instructional Procedures

Effective health teaching depends upon proper motivation. In order to take health learning beyond the verbalization level, teachers must try to insure a positive and purposeful motivation. Learning in this area *should not be motivated by fear.* Too often, the negative aspects of health—the "this will happen to you if you don't do that" approach—is used with ineffective results. Children should not be threatened or scared into health learnings. Rather, the accent should be upon the importance and satisfaction of healthful and safe living and the steps toward its achievement.

Another type of wrong motivation occasionally still used in health classes is the "sugar-coated" approach. Children learn about Mr. Carrot, who helps them to see in the dark, or Mrs. Green Leafy Vegetable, who lives in their refrigerators. Such nonsense has no place in a sound, sensible, and purposeful health program. It insults the intelligence and good sense of our modern youngsters and makes a mockery of the teaching-learning process.

As in all other areas of the curriculum, the most meaningful health learning is motivated by a desire to solve a problem. Children are very curious

The safety patrol plays a vital role in the elementary school.

about their bodies, their activities, and their environment, and daily health or safety learnings may emerge from these areas. "Why shouldn't I eat only the potato chips and dill pickles on my lunch plate?" "Why do I have to brush my teeth every morning?" "Why do people catch colds?" "What is a cold?" "Why does the school nurse wear a white uniform?" "What causes a stomach ache?" "Why did the men spray the weeds near the schoolground?" "Why must cars stop for the school bus?" These and hundreds of other similar questions are constantly on the minds and lips of elementary school youngsters. To use them as the focus for the instructional program is to employ a purposeful type of motivation from which genuine learning should result.

There are two common organizational plans for teaching health and safety. In the first of these, health and/or safety is taught as a *specific curriculum area.* In this plan, these subjects take their place in the program as regularly scheduled, identifiable curricular areas. Lessons are scheduled and textbooks or other learning aids are used as they are in other subjects.

In the second plan, health and/or safety are *not* taught per se but are integrated with other curricular areas. There is no conclusive evidence at the present time as to the superiority of one of these plans, *when both are well taught.* In general, however, many teachers feel that health and safety cannot be separated logically from other areas and that integration is, therefore, necessary and desirable. It would be extremely difficult, for instance, to draw a fine line between health and science experiences as they are taught in the elementary school. Several of the science problems mentioned in Chapter Ten, such as, "Why does the water taste funny?" and, "Which brand of toothpaste most effectively kills harmful bacteria?" are, of course, health problems as much as they are science problems. It is equally impossible to separate science and safety experiences. During last December, for instance, a sixth-grade teacher taught several lessons on electricity and electric circuits. Through several effective visual aids, he demonstrated how the Christmas tree lights, outdoor decorations, and electric trains place a heavy burden upon the electrical system. The children learned what causes a blown fuse and the safety factors involved in the situation. Was this a science or a safety lesson? The answer is obvious.

Similarly, health and safety often cannot be separated from the social studies content. The study of the community, for instance, may include numerous health and safety concepts. So, also, can a study of foreign cultures or ancient civilizations, or almost any social studies area one can name. One fifth-grade teacher, for instance, in teaching transportation placed a heavy accent upon the automobile and the importance of traffic safety. The children invited a traffic safety engineer to talk with them; they surveyed the traffic hazards of their own community; they discussed these with the local chief of police; and they talked, read, and learned about the safety equipment of the modern cars—including lights, brakes, and safety belts!

It is not necessary to detail further the possibilities of integrating health and safety with other subjects. For many reasons, an integrated approach is preferred to teaching these areas separately but, in either plan, the teaching can and should reach much higher than the verbalization plateau referred to earlier in the chapter.

All aspects of the school should serve as instructional aids in health and safety. Much valuable health and safety education can be realized through utilizing all parts of the school plant. There is, for instance, no richer source of health knowledge than the school kitchen and cafeteria. Unfortunately, there is some evidence that "the school lunchroom is not used as a laboratory for health education to the extent that is desirable." [22] This is extremely unfortunate in view of the fact that approximately one-third of the children attending school in this country eat their noon meal in the school.[23]

What are some of the ways that the school lunchroom might be utilized more effectively as a learning laboratory? There are many, for instance: (1) Taking the class to the kitchen to see the equipment and talk with the dieticians. Some questions which may be asked are: "Why do we have an electric dishwasher?" "Why don't they store the cartons of food in the kitchen instead of a storeroom?" "Who makes up the menus?" These and other questions can be used as the bases for valuable health lessons. (2) Asking the dieticians to visit the classrooms and discuss the cooking and preparing of food with the children. (3) Allowing children to participate in planning the weekly menus. (4) Embarking upon such activities as making curtains for the lunchroom, making place mats or tablecloths, making murals for the walls, or organizing clean-up campaigns. (5) Offering children the opportunity to prepare and cook certain dishes for their class as part of a social studies unit. All of these will help to make the kitchen and lunchroom a more valuable learning laboratory than it may be at the present time.

The second feature of the school program which should be used to the fullest is the school bus. This can also be made a learning laboratory by permitting children to examine the bus, talk with the driver, or receive a visit from the transportation supervisor. Also, involving children through a school bus patrol, through studying the safety considerations of the various bus routes and stops, and through many other activities will result in worthwhile learnings.

In addition to the cafeteria and school bus, the playground, gymnasium, playroom, or any other spot in the physical plant should lend itself to functional health and safety teaching in the classroom of a resourceful and creative teacher.

A third channel of meaningful teaching is through a study of seasonal or timely topics. A current neighborhood safety or health hazard—a dangerous road, lake, or abandoned well—might motivate a valuable health study. So, also, may events of seasonal interest and holiday fun, such as the hunting season, ice-skating, or swimming. In these seasonal topics, however, the teacher should be aware of the vital importance of going beyond

---

[22] C. C. Wilson and E. W. Mood, "A Survey of School Lunch Practices," *American Journal of Public Health,* Vol. 45 (February, 1955), p. 166.
[23] *Ibid.,* p. 163.

The school bus is a valuable laboratory for functional safety learnings.

the mere stating of rules of conduct which children have probably heard in every grade, over and over, and which they still do not put into practice. Along with items of seasonal interest are those of current news which can be used to advantage—such as the "cranberry scare" of 1959 or the wide publicity given to the possible dangers of the plastic bags used by cleaners.

A variety of activities and materials should vitalize the instructional program. Throughout this chapter, an emphasis has been placed upon health and safety instruction as a problem-solving, exploring, discovering, practicing, and applying experience. It cannot be stressed too strongly that all sorts of activities—in the classroom, throughout the school building, and in the community—should be utilized if the health instructional program is to be of value. Similarly, a variety of learning aids will help clinch valuable concepts and attitudes. These may be secured from numerous sources at little or no expense to the teacher. For a recent and comprehensive list of available free and inexpensive health instructional materials the reader is referred to the annotated guide developed by LeFevre and Boydston, which lists approximately one thousand appropriate health-teaching materials, classified by subject and grade level. It will be supplemented, according to these authors, by a yearly list of new materials appropriate for classroom use.[24]

Section 3: SCHOOL HEALTH SERVICES

Recent years have seen a decided expansion in the health services offered by the school. Today's services have been identified by one writer as: (1) Health appraisal: "evaluating the total health status of a child by such means as the health history; teacher, nurse, and parent observations; screening tests such as physical growth evaluation by weighing and measuring, testing visual and auditory acuity and color perception; and medical, dental, and psychological examinations"; (2) Health counseling and follow-through; (3) Emergency care; (4) Communicable disease control; and (5) Maintenance of the health of all school personnel.[25]

Obviously, there are many personnel other than the classroom teacher involved in the implementation of these services. The roles of several of these are examined in the following chapter. Our concern, at the moment, therefore, is the role of the classroom teacher and his responsibilities in the health service program. These will probably fall into the following categories:

1. *Health appraisal.* No one has a better opportunity nor graver responsibility for appraising the pupils' health than the classroom teacher. His prolonged daily contact with his pupils will enable him to note flushed faces, watery eyes, listlessness, poor appetites, and thousands of other symptoms which should be referred to the proper authority for diagnosis and treatment. As part of his appraisal role, also, the teacher may serve as sort of a health technician in assisting (or assuming full responsibility, in some schools) in weighing, measuring, or screening for vision and hearing defects.

Not only is the teacher in the front line of the actual appraisal program, but he also has the major responsibility for *educating* children concerning the appraisal services. Many classroom learning experiences, for instance, should be concerned with the health examination prior to its actually taking place. Children should be permitted to visit the nurse's office where the examination will be held and to examine the weight scale, height chart, telebinocular, doctor's stethescope, and similar appraisal devices. They should have an opportunity to talk with the nurse, physician, dentist, dental hygienist, or any other functionary with whom they will have contact. Through these, and many other procedures, the classroom teacher

[24] J. R. LeFevre and D. N. Boydston, *An Annotated Guide to Free and Inexpensive Health Instruction Materials* (Carbondale, Ill., Southern Illinois University Press, 1959).

[25] S. L. Smith, "Improving the Quality of School Health Services," *The National Elementary Principal,* Vol. 39 (February, 1960), p. 22.

should attempt to integrate the appraisal services with his instructional program.

2. *Health counseling.* The classroom teacher, in all his formal and informal contacts with children, serves continually as a health counselor. All of the health instructional program is, in a sense, health counseling. In addition, much counseling takes place during a personal interview between teacher and pupil. Guides for successful counseling are included in the discussion of guidance presented in the following chapter.

3. *Emergency care.* The teacher is frequently called upon to act in a health or safety emergency situation. It is, therefore, imperative that *every* elementary teacher have a fundamental knowledge of first aid. In addition, the teacher should be thoroughly familiar with the laws of his state and the rules of his school system concerning the application of first aid. In some states the application of *any* medication by the teacher is prohibited. For instance, the teacher may apply water and a clean bandage to the skinned knee of a youngster, but this is the extent of the aid he is allowed by law to administer.

Not only should the teacher be familiar with the legal and local definitions of his responsibilities, but he should also be aware of the importance of considering *all* aspects of the situation in administering first aid or relief from physical discomfort. A teacher, in one situation, for instance, recently became the center of an involved court case for administering toothache drops to a pupil whose family, because of religious convictions, protested strongly.

The elementary teacher is frequently called upon to administer emergency care to his pupils. The authors feel that they *cannot* overemphasize the importance of the teacher's knowing the fundamental principles of first aid as well as his legal and moral responsibilities in applying it.

4. *Co-ordination of Health Services.* In many systems, the classroom teacher is expected to assume an active role in co-ordinating the school health services. The Florida State Department of Education, for instance, recently passed a regulation requiring "that each public school designate a faculty member as School Health Co-ordinator," whose task is to serve as the chairman of the Faculty Health Committee, "giving continuous attention to school health." [26] In other systems, teachers are expected to serve on the School Health Council, the membership of which might include, depending upon the local situation, the local health officer, the principal, a physician, a dentist, the school nurse, a psychologist, a guidance worker, a nutritionist, the school custodian, the school dietician, a dental hygienist, pupils, parents, and representatives from community health offices or agencies. The function of the council is to co-ordinate and promote the schoolwide health program. Where such a council exists, it is

[26] Z. Maynard, "Florida's Grass Roots Health Approach," *Journal of Health-Physical Education-Recreation,* Vol. 29 (March, 1958), p. 25.

usually considered one of the most important aspects of the total educational program.

Section 4: PHYSICAL EDUCATION . .

Characteristics of an Effective Program

1. The physical education program is a pleasant, informal, but directed activity. For children of elementary school age, the physical education period should be a happy and informal experience. Unfortunately, in some schools, this has been interpreted to mean an unplanned, purposeless, haphazard type of program which consists of letting children run wild on the playground or in the gymnasium. Certainly children should have some time for "free play" during the school day, but this is not a valid reason for allowing the physical education program to deteriorate to the point where its sole objective is to "let children run off surplus energy."

The modern physical education program is, therefore, far from a purposeless, unplanned "break" in the school day. On the contrary, it is carefully planned and directed toward the achievement of certain definite objectives. Shepard defines these as follows:

1. The maintenance and development of organic vigor.

2. The maintenance and development of neuromuscular skills.

3. The maintenance and development of standards of behavior; the growth and development of emotional poise and control.

4. The development of interpretive judgments.

5. The development of knowledges, understandings, and appreciations relevant to the science of physical education and the activities of its program.[27]

Not only is today's physical education program directed toward the achievement of clearly stated objectives, but its content is carefully organized and graded toward the ultimate realization of these objectives. A recent study of urban systems states that seventy-nine per cent of those systems investigated reported that they had curriculum guides in physical education available to their teachers.[28]

Today's elementary school physical education program is characterized by: (1) a statement of definite objectives, (2) an organization of content into sequential levels of difficulty, and (3) an increasing attention to the proper means for evaluating the attainment of the stated objectives.

2. The physical education program is planned in accordance with the

[27] N. M. Shepard, *Foundations and Principles of Physical Education* (New York, The Ronald Press Company, 1960), p. 95.

[28] E. Schneider, *Physical Education in Urban Elementary Schools: A Study of the Status of Physical Education for Children of Elementary School Age in City School Systems* (Washington, D.C., Office of Education, Bulletin 1959, No. 15, 1959), p. 20.

developmental level of the pupils. All physical education activities are designed to serve the total needs of boys and girls on a specific developmental level. The aspects of growth and development which have meaning for physical education are defined by Miller and Whitcomb as: (1) bodily growth, (2) motor development, (3) health status, (4) socio-emotional development, and (5) intellectual development. The specific characteristics of children in each of these categories should be considered carefully in designing the physical education curriculum.[29]

3. Problems of space and equipment are carefully considered. Classrooms, all-purpose rooms, auditoriums (with removable chairs), gymnasiums, and playgrounds can be used for the physical education program. For *all* indoor activities children should be required to wear sneakers or rubber-soled shoes. If the temperature and floor surface permit, children may be permitted to go barefooted. Bare feet are decidedly preferable to socks or stockings, for the latter may cause numerous falls on slippery floors.

It is also desirable for children, in all grades, to wear some type of dress which will permit complete freedom of movement. It is not necessary, however, that a regulation uniform be required. Many schools permit children to wear their own shorts, dungarees, or coveralls.

The classroom teacher's personal equipment needs to include nothing more than a pair of low-heeled shoes with rubber soles for lessons in the gymnasium. *No teacher nor pupil* should be permitted on the gym floor with leather-soled shoes—for reasons of their own safety as well as floor maintenance.

Small equipment necessary for an adequate physical education program includes: rubber playground balls of assorted sizes, beanbags, jumping ropes, hoops, wands, wooden paddles, baseball bats and softballs, soccer balls, footballs, basketballs, volleyballs, percussion instruments (tom-toms, drums, tambourines), tenpins, and duck pins. Large portable equipment includes: jumping standards, sawhorses, volley ball nets and standards, mats, and mat covers. Various types of permanent equipment or apparatus such as slanting ladders, swings, or monkey rings may be installed in the gym or on the playground and should be utilized to advantage by the teacher.

4. Physical education activities are integrated with other aspects of the curriculum. There are two main approaches to the functional integration of physical education with other curriculum areas. On the one hand, a game, dance, or other physical education activity may be the *outcome* of a classroom unit on, for instance, Mexico. On the other hand, these activities may be used as a catalyst to *precipitate* the classroom unit. There are, of

[29] A. G. Miller and V. Whitcomb, *Physical Education in the Elementary School Curriculum* (Englewood Cliffs, N.J., Prentice-Hall, Inc., 1957), pp. 6–10.

course, many other possibilities for integrating physical education with almost all curricular areas. Singing games, rhythmics, and dance are a natural combination of movement and music, while jumping or bouncing may offer excellent opportunities for developing abilities to count by ones, twos, fives, or tens.

5. All children are given an opportunity to participate. The physical education program is designed for *all* children, and "there should be no elimination of children on the basis of inadequate performance except in extremely rare cases." [30] If children are eliminated through the natural development of a game, of course, they are forced to be inactive for a period of time, but this should be short in order to permit them to rejoin the game as soon as possible.

6. The program meets the recommended minimum standards of time allotment. A statement prepared by a joint committee of the American Association for Health, Physical Education, and Recreation and the Society of State Directors of Health, Physical Education, and Recreation recommends that children in the elementary school should have a minimum of thirty minutes of physical education daily. In the primary grades, it is desirable to divide the time into two periods of approximately fifteen or twenty minutes each.[31] In some states a minimum similar to this is required by law. Other states have no legal minimum requirement. In general, there appears to be agreement on the thirty-minute minimum daily requirement, although there is abundant evidence to indicate that many schools still do not meet it.

7. Adequate provision is made for recreation and supervised play. Considerable emphasis was placed previously upon the importance of a carefully planned, definitely directed program of physical education. This does not, however, mean that the school day should not include time for activities of a purely recreational nature. Properly spaced "recess periods," devoted to free play and hobbies are an important phase of the daily program. The classroom teacher must remember, however, that he is *always* responsible for the safety of his pupils and, under *no* circumstances, should these activities be conducted without the presence of a faculty member or his adult substitute. (In some systems, parents or part-time adult workers aid in the supervision of the play activities during recess or lunch periods.)

8. A well-balanced program includes a variety of activities. The activities included in a comprehensive elementary school program are usually classified as: (1) games and game activities, (2) movement exploration, (3) rhythms and dance, (4) self-testing activities, (5) aquatics (for the

[30] G. Andrews, J. Saurborn; E. Schneider, *Physical Education for Today's Boys and Girls* (Boston, Allyn and Bacon, Inc., 1960), p. 8.

[31] American Association for Health, Physical Education, and Recreation and Society of State Directors of Health, Physical Education and Recreation, *Physical Education: An Interpretation* (Washington, D.C., National Education Association, n. d.), p. 7.

small percentage of schools which have swimming pools), and (6) outdoor education. These are examined later in the chapter.

Present Status of Physical Education

A recent study of 523 school systems reveals interesting data concerning their physical education programs. The following findings of this study should be of interest to the classroom teacher:

79% of the school systems indicated that curriculum guides in physical education are available to the teacher.

75% indicated that classroom teachers assist in preparing the physical education guide.

Many school systems indicated that physical education is integrated with social studies, language arts, music, art, health education, mathematics and science.

Basketball, softball and touch football are the most popular sports among boys. Softball, volleyball and basketball are the most popular sports of the girls.

63 of the 523 systems sponsor camping and outdoor education programs . . . of these, 32 serve only children of the elementary school . . . 13 serve only the secondary school . . . and 18 serve both.

85% employ special teachers, consultants, or specialists in physical education.

62% of the systems provide in-service education in physical education for classroom teachers.

54% of the approximately 12,210 school buildings provide excellent or adequate gymnasiums or playrooms; 28% provide excellent or adequate dressing-room and shower facilities; less than 1% provide swimming pools.

Approximately ⅞ report that physical education facilities are used by the community in out-of-school hours during the school year.

Approximately ⅔ indicate that facilities are used by the community during school vacation periods.

Approximately ½ indicate that community facilities are used to obtain more adequate space for physical education.

Approximately ½ of the systems sponsor summer recreation programs independently or in co-operation with other community agencies.[32]

It should be kept in mind that these data were secured from urban elementary schools. It seems reasonable to conclude, however, that they are fairly representative of the general status of physical education across the country. If this is true, it is apparent that the subject, on the whole, enjoys a secure position in the elementary school program and that some systems are aware of the newer trends in this field, particularly that of school camping and outdoor education.

The remainder of the chapter is devoted to an examination of the major activities of the physical education program.

[32] E. Schneider, *op. cit.*, pp. 1–91.

The Activities Program

Games and Game Activities. These are the backbone of the elementary school physical education program, for never was a child born or bred who did not like to play games. The wise selection and organization of games can determine the difference between a rich and vital program or a sterile, time-consuming one. There are, of course, many points to be considered by the classroom teacher who attempts to select an appropriate game from among the hundreds available to him. Some of the questions he should ask himself in selecting and organizing this aspect of his program are considered below.

Is the game suited to the physical, social, and emotional level of the pupils? A game must offer a challenge to the children, but it should not be too difficult. Dodge ball, for instance, which demands accurate and well-co-ordinated throwing and catching is not suitable for primary grade youngsters. Also, a game like "The Thread Follows the Needle" is equally unsuitable for these children because of its complicated formation. Then too, some games require a high level of group co-operation, which makes them unsuitable for many elementary youngsters who are still highly individualized and self-centered. In this classification are certain team games and relays which, in general, should be delayed until children have matured to the point of identifying themselves closely with the group. Then too, the emotional maturity of pupils must be taken into consideration. As Andrews and others point out, a game like "Cat and Rat" might be too difficult for six-year-olds for many reasons, one of which is that these youngsters become so excited and enthusiastic that they simply cannot remember to hold hands and keep the circle joined.[33]

Is the game of a low competitive nature? Intense competition is to be avoided in the elementary school. Games, for instance, which place a high premium on winning and a severe penalty on losing are apt to induce such undesirable concomitants as emotional overstimulation or cheating. In general, the negative aspects of strong competition mean that most games should be of the intraclass type. Fourth-, fifth-, and sixth-grade children, however, occasionally need and enjoy the stimulus of interclass games, and for these youngsters a very informal intramural program may be organized with satisfactory results.

Does the game lend itself to the development of specific motor skills? Games are fun but this is not full justification for their place in the physical education program. On the contrary, they should be used for the development of certain motor skills suitable to the child's maturity. For this reason, the teacher is justified in devoting some time to the practice and perfection of certain skill deficiencies revealed in the game. "Corner ball," for instance, demands accurate throwing, or the game loses its point and children

[33] G. Andrews, J. Saurborn, and E. Schneider, *op. cit.,* p. 81.

do not enjoy it. A teacher may point this out to his pupils and may consequently devote a portion of the next lesson to the teaching and practicing of specific throwing skills. It should be kept in mind that these skill-practice periods emerge from a need revealed in the game, as illustrated here, and are not taught in isolation from the game program.

Are the directions easy to understand? Games with long, involved, complicated directions are not popular with elementary school youngsters. Too often, in introducing a new game, the teacher spends so much time in explaining detailed directions that the children lose all interest in the game. Preliminary directions should be kept only to the barest minimum needed to get the game started, and other directions can be added as it progresses. If the teacher follows this plan, however, he must be sure to inform the children that "other things will come up during the game which I'll explain as we go along" or children may accuse him of changing the rules as the game progresses.

All of the preliminary planning of the game, including giving directions, should take place *in the classroom*. Children should, of course, be included in the planning. "How many teams shall we have? Who are the captains? How many people on a team? What are the important points about the game we need to remember? What equipment do we need?" These, and other points should be discussed *before* the children leave the classroom for the playground or gymnasium.

Another part of the preliminary planning session should be devoted to agreeing upon certain signals between the pupils and the teacher. The teacher should be sure that pupils understand the hand signal to start the game, to stop it, and to prepare to return to the classroom. The wise use of hand signals is usually all that is necessary for most elementary game periods. Such signals help to maintain a pleasant informality and avoid the use of the harsh and shrill whistle which is usually not needed to supervise the informal games of the elementary school.

Does the game involve repetition? The point was made earlier that games are designed and selected to develop certain skills. In order to accomplish this, and because children enjoy it, the game should make adequate provision for repetition.

Does the game allow for equal participation? An elementary school child is an active and eager youngster, and he wants to be sure that he "gets his turn." In general, approximately equal participation can be insured through the proper selection and organization of the game. Careful attention to each individual, as well as balancing teams according to abilities, will help to achieve widespread participation.

Movement Exploration. This classification is exactly what its name implies and includes those activities which encourage children to experiment with, and explore the possibilities of body movement. Movement

Self-testing activities are a vital part of the physical
education program.

Folk-dancing is a worthwhile
activity in the intermediate
and upper elementary grades.

exploration is, essentially, the answer which children discover to questions or problems posed by the teacher. "How many different ways can you swing parts of your body?" will encourage children to experiment, explore, and discover that they can swing one arm—both arms—one leg—back—forward—in a circle—fast—slow—smoothly. On another problem, "Let's see what is the smallest space we can fit our bodies into" will bring forth responses of curling up tightly in a ball, or crouching in a tight stoop, or perhaps of stretching into a long, thin line. This is the exploring of movement—an aspect of the school program which is important, satisfying, and natural to the growth and development of children.

"Whenever movement takes place time is consumed, energy is released, and space is covered." [34] Thus, the basic principles of time, force, and space become the essential factors of movement. Movement explores space —direction, such as forward or backward; level—high or low; and dimension—large or small. It involves time-tempo and meter; and it necessitates force—intensity or accent. All of these are considered in posing problems of movement exploration with children.

There are two basic *types* of movement. One is *locomotor:* the movement of the body from place to place as in walking, jumping, skipping, galloping, hopping, running, sliding, and leaping. The other is *axial*, which includes activities where the individual remains in one spot but moves the parts of his body—pushing, pulling, twisting, or lifting. A third classification is, of course, a combination of both of these.

There is little doubt that movement exploration is a vital and creative aspect of the physical education program, and its educational possibilities should be investigated by the teacher who wants to provide his pupils with a wide variety of avenues for learning.

Rhythms and Dance. These involve the same factors and types of movement discussed in connection with movement exploration. They differ, however, from this activity in that they involve moving to music or to a rhythmic beat.

Creative rhythmics constitute a major portion of the physical education program of the primary grades. These youngsters have a natural creative urge, and there is no more satisfying outlet for its expression than through the movement of their bodies. Rhythms are usually done to the accompaniment of a drum, tom-tom, or piano. These are preferable to the record player because they permit more flexibility. The piano, for instance, can pick up the rhythm which a child expresses—and can follow his expressionistic interpretations which, obviously, the record player cannot do.

In general, creative rhythms are more successful when taught in a large area such as the auditorium or gymnasium. If these are not available, the

---

[34] E. L. Sehon and E. L. O'Brien, *Rhythms in Elementary Education* (New York, A. S. Barnes and Company, 1951), p. 6.

resourceful teacher can use his classroom space for this purpose, with a little wise organization and planning.

Dance includes all types: social, folk, square, tap, and creative. All of these are extremely valuable for children, although the simple folk and country dances are often preferred by many classroom teachers. Unfortunately, the value of these has often not been realized because of the unwise selection occasionally made by the teacher. It is, for instance, very important that the dance be suited to the social interests and physical abilities of children. It should not involve complicated patterns, nor should it have cultural significance which is beyond the level of understanding or interest of the immature child. Criteria for the selection of appropriate folk dances are:

1. Can the children perform the basic step used in the dance in time to the music and in all the ways necessary for its use; or will drill on the step be apt to interrupt the progress of learning the dance?

2. Can the dance be learned quickly, so that its whole configuration can be grasped by the children at one time; or is it long and involved, with successive parts which take several dance lessons to learn, so that the children's feeling of accomplishment is retarded, and everyone, including the teacher, becomes bored with the process?

3. Are the successive parts short, so that movements must be continually changed, or are they long enough so that there is time to remember what comes next?

4. Does the dance allow free, vigorous, and informal movement; or is it constrained and overprecise, employing small, controlled foot patterns, polite and formal bows and gestures, and complicated hand-foot co-ordinations?

5. If the dance has a particular literal meaning, is it understandable, childlike, and apt to hold the interest of the group performing it; or does it have more adult significance, romantic overtones, or far-fetched cultural symbolism? [35]

A second point to be considered in deriving full value from dances is that they should be taught *as part of the culture of the people.* Thus, they should be integrated strongly with the other aspects of the classroom program, particularly social studies. For instance, the trade guild dances and fisherman dances are expressions of the customs, habits, and lives of these people, and they should be taught in this context if they are to have value and meaning for young children.

Self-testing Activities. These include "the natural activities of childhood, such as running and jumping, climbing and balancing, and manipulating balls and other small objects, as well as stunts and tumbling." [36] Such activities have a natural appeal for children and are a major factor in developing co-ordination, balance, agility, and strength. It is fairly obvious

[35] R. L. Murray, *Dance in Elementary Education* (New York, Harper and Brothers, Inc., 1953), pp. 114–115.

[36] E. Halsey and L. Porter, *Physical Education for Children* (New York, Holt, Rinehart and Winston, Inc., 1958), p. 346.

that considerable care should be exercised in the selection and execution of these activities in order to achieve desired values, as well as to protect the safety of children. Several sources listed in the bibliography contain descriptions of suitable activities for each developmental level as well as suggestions for teaching them.

Outdoor Education and School Camping. Perhaps no other aspect of education has grown more rapidly in the last few years than an interest in the values of outdoor education and school camping. The snowballing of interest in this area has now reached the point where "almost half of our states have programs in school camping." [37] The First National Conference on Outdoor Education held in May, 1958 was a major milestone in this field in that it "set forth a common philosophy and identified the movement as a significant development in education." [38] This conference set forth the contributions of outdoor education as follows:

1. *To science.* Outdoor experiences can provide basic beginnings, satisfy the curiosity, and constitute a framework for this field.

2. *To conservation.* There are abundant possibilities for teaching the wise use of human and natural resources.

3. *To fitness.* Outdoor education provides significant opportunities for physical, emotional, and spiritual fitness.

4. *To education for leisure.* Skills for the intelligent use of time for leisure are important outcomes.

5. *To adult education.* There is great interest among adults and families in outdoor pursuits, to which a continuing program of outdoor education can contribute. Creative living helps to prepare people for a changing world.

Naturally, there is wide variety in the types of outdoor education programs among the school systems which have now included them in their curriculums. Some systems provide a week or two of camping experience as a part of the curriculum of the regular school year. In most cases, this experience is designed for boys and girls in the upper elementary grades. For primary grades, the day camp or daily outdoor excursion is popular in some areas. Other systems co-operate with public or private camps to provide experiences during the summer vacation for their pupils as an extension of the school program. Still others provide vital experiences in outdoor education by designing and utilizing the out-of-door environment of their schools and communities to greatest advantage. Young, for instance, describes an "outdoor education laboratory," adjoining the school building which contains "two brick fireplaces . . . grill . . . outdoor picnic tables . . . planned landscaping . . . a wildlife area . . . provisions for many

[37] *Ibid.,* p. 141.
[38] J. W. Smith, "Professional Report from the First National Conference on Outdoor Education," *Journal of Health-Physical Education-Recreation,* Vol. 29 (October, 1958), p. 10.

outdoor activities, such as casting and archery, with plenty of space left for other interests that will develop." [39]

Regardless of the type of program, there is little doubt that forward-looking educators are intensely interested in extending the educational program beyond the school building and into the out-of-doors. It will be interesting to see the gains which are made in this direction in the next decade of educational progress.

Summary

This chapter has examined the comprehensive aspect of the elementary school known as the School Health Program. Factors which led to the development of the present-day vigorous programs found in many school systems were presented. Section 1 was concerned with the classroom teacher's responsibility in providing a healthful school environment for his pupils. Aspects of the physical environment which were considered were lighting; color; ventilation and heating; acoustics; and provisions for sanitation, cleanliness, and safety. The importance of a healthy socio-emotional climate was emphasized and it was stated that the two most common causes of a negative environment for which the teacher is responsible are rejection and fear.

Section 2 was concerned with the instructional program of health and safety. The major aim was cited as "the intelligent self-direction of health behavior," which may be realized only through a hierarchy of objectives classified on levels of knowledges and concepts, skills and habits, and attitudes and values. The scope and sequence of content were examined according to ten common classifications. Suitable instructional procedures for an effective program of health and safety were suggested and contained emphasis upon the importance of proper motivation, organizational curriculum plans, and worthwhile learning activities and experiences.

Section 3 discussed the School Health Services with particular attention to the role of the classroom teacher. Responsibilities of the classroom teacher were seen as falling into the categories of: (1) Health appraisal, (2) Health counseling, (3) Emergency care, and (4) Co-ordination of Health Services.

The last section was devoted to a discussion of physical education. Eight characteristics of an effective modern program were suggested. Some of the findings of a study concerning the present status of physical education were presented to show that the subject apparently enjoys a secure position in most schools across the country. The remainder of the chapter was concerned with the physical education activities program, which was discussed according to the categories of: (1) games and game activities, (2)

---

[39] J. M. Young, "Classrooms Move Outdoors," *Journal of Health-Physical Education-Recreation,* Vol. 30 (December, 1959), p. 26.

movement exploration, (3) rhythms and dance, (4) self-testing activities, and (5) outdoor education and school camping.

STUDENT PROJECTS

1. Measure the adequacy of light in one of your college classrooms. How much difference do you find between various parts of the room? Make a detailed plan for improving the light. Take into consideration all factors such as ceilings, walls, floor, furniture, windows, shades, and others which have a bearing on the situation.

2. Talk to a lighting engineer on the advantages and disadvantages of incandescent *versus* fluorescent lighting. Which does he recommend? Do his recommendations agree with research findings and current literature on this subject?

3. What are the laws in your state concerning education as to the harmful effects of alcohol and narcotics? When were these laws passed? Talk to several elementary school teachers. How do they put the required teaching into effect?

4. Suppose you were asked to order furniture for your elementary classroom. Would you buy separate desks and chairs or tubular units? Why? Would you buy a desk and chair for each child or would you experiment with other furniture units which are now available? Investigate the new kinds of school furniture now available and make a detailed plan of how you would furnish a classroom for thirty children of a specific grade. Estimate the cost involved.

5. The staff of a new elementary school wanted to experiment and so a different type of furniture was purchased for every classroom. What factors would you consider in determining which type was the most superior? How could these be measured?

6. Talk with several elementary school principals. Do they have health councils in their schools? Who are the members? What are the functions and responsibilities of the council? What are its relationships with parents, faculty, and pupils?

7. See if you can get permission to ask a class of upper elementary grade children to write a brief composition on *Things I Worry About*. What do you discover that has implications for the socio-emotional environment of the classroom?

8. Compile a list of worthwhile activities, experiences, and teaching aids you could use to teach third-graders the four food groups of a balanced diet. In what way do your activities include the school kitchen and cafeteria as a "learning laboratory"?

9. Visit an elementary school during the lunch hour. What percentage of the children stay for lunch? How is this part of the day made into a valuable learning experience? In what ways could it be improved?

10. Do you think health and safety can be taught more functionally as identifiable "subjects" or when they are integrated with other subjects? Give several illustrations to support your answer.

11. Your principal has asked you to be faculty advisor to the school patrol. What do you plan to do which will make this organization a valuable and central part of the entire school safety program? How will you enlist the aid of parents, fellow faculty members, and the community?

12. Last fall, a teacher arrived in school one morning only to hear that four of his sixth-grade boys were in the juvenile shelter for throwing nails and glass in the street on "tic-tac" night. How should this teacher handle this incident in his classroom?

13. In your role of principal, prepare a faculty newsletter informing all faculty of the laws in your state regarding the administration of first aid. Include, also, local regulations and peculiarities which would have a bearing on this problem.

14. Talk with a school nurse, school doctor, school psychologist, and dental hygienist. How does each of these functionaries describe his role in relation to the classroom teacher?

15. What are the legal minimum time requirements in your state for physical education? How does this compare with other states?

16. Apply the eight characteristics listed in Section 4 to an elementary physical education program with which you are familiar. In what specific ways does the program meet each of the characteristics? In what specific ways does it fail to meet them?

BIBLIOGRAPHY

ANDREWS, Gladys, *Creative Rhythmic Movement for Children* (Englewood Cliffs, N.J., Prentice-Hall, Inc., 1954).

ANDREWS, Gladys, SAURBORN, Jeannette, and SCHNEIDER, Elsa, *Physical Education for Today's Boys and Girls* (Boston, Allyn and Bacon, Inc., 1960).

BROWNELL, Clifford and HAGMAN, E. Patricia, *Physical Education: Foundations and Principles* (New York, McGraw-Hill Book Company, 1951).

BUCHER, Charles A., ed., *Methods and Materials in Physical Education and Recreation* (St. Louis, Mo., The C. V. Mosby Company, 1954).

BUCHER, Charles A. and READE, Evelyn M., *Physical Education in the Modern Elementary School* (New York, The Macmillan Company, 1958).

CASSIDY, Rosalind F., *Curriculum Development in Physical Education* (New York, Harper and Brothers, 1954).

DAVIES, Evelyn A., *The Elementary School Child and His Posture Patterns* (New York, Appleton-Century-Crofts, Inc., 1958).

Department of Elementary School Principals, *Health in the Elementary School,* 29th Yearbook (Washington, D.C., National Education Association, 1950).

EVANS, Ruth, BACON, Thelma I., BACON, Mary E. and STAPLETON, Joie L., *Physical Education for Elementary Schools* (New York, McGraw-Hill Book Company, 1958).

FRASER, Ellen D., BRANSFORD, Joan B., and HASTINGS, Mamie, *The Child and Physical Education* (Englewood Cliffs, N.J., Prentice-Hall, Inc., 1956).

GROUT, Ruth E., *Health Teaching in Schools,* 3rd ed. (Philadelphia, W. B. Saunders Company, 1958).

HALSEY, Elizabeth and PORTER, Lorena, *Physical Education for Children: A Developmental Program* (New York, Holt, Rinehart and Winston, Inc., 1958).

HARNETT, Arthur L. and SHAW, John H., *Effective School Health Education* (New York, Appleton-Century-Crofts, Inc., 1959).

LARSON, Leonard and HILL, Lucille, *Physical Education in the Elementary School* (New York, Holt, Rinehart and Winston, Inc., 1957).

LASALLE, Dorothy, *Guidance of Children Through Physical Education,* 2nd ed. (New York, The Ronald Press Company, 1957).

MILLER, Arthur G. and WHITCOMB, Virginia, *Physical Education in the Elemen-*

tary School Curriculum (Englewood Cliffs, N.J., Prentice-Hall, Inc., 1957).

O'KEEFE, Pattric R. and ALDRICH, Anita, *Education Through Physical Activities,* 2nd ed. (St. Louis, Mo., The C. V. Mosby Company, 1955).

SCHNEIDER, Elsa, *Physical Education in Urban Elementary Schools* (Washington, D.C., U. S. Department of Health, Education, and Welfare, Office of Education, Bulletin 1959, No. 15, 1959).

SCHNEIDER, Robert E., *Methods and Materials of Health Education* (Philadelphia, W. B. Saunders Company, 1958).

SEHON, Elizabeth L. and O'BRIEN, Emma Lou, *Rhythms in Elementary Education* (New York, A. S. Barnes and Company, 1951).

SEHON, Elizabeth L., ANDERSON, Marian H., HODGINS, Winifred W., and VAN FOSSEN, Gladys R., *Physical Education Methods for Elementary Schools,* 2nd ed. (Philadelphia, W. B. Saunders Company, 1953).

SHEPARD, Natalie M., *Foundations and Principles of Physical Education* (New York, The Ronald Press Company, 1960).

SMITH, Helen N. and WOLVERTON, Mary E., *Health Education in the Elementary School* (New York, The Ronald Press Company, 1959).

SMITH, Julian W., ed., *Outdoor Education for American Youth* (Washington, D.C., American Association for Health, Physical Education, and Recreation, 1957).

TURNER, C. E., SELLERY, C. Morley, and SMITH, Sara, *School Health and Health Education,* 3rd ed. (St. Louis, Mo., The C. V. Mosby Company, 1957).

VANNIER, Maryhelen and FOSTER, Mildred, *Teaching Physical Education in Elementary Schools* (Philadelphia, W. B. Saunders Company, 1954).

VOLTMER, Edward F. and ESSLINGER, Arthur A., *The Organization and Administration of Physical Education,* 3rd ed. (New York, Appleton-Century-Crofts, Inc., 1958).

WILLGOOSE, Carl E., *Health Education in the Elementary School* (Philadelphia, W. B. Saunders Company, 1959).

WILSON, Charles C., *Health Education,* ed., Joint Committee on Health Problems in Education of the National Education Association and the American Medical Association (Washington, D.C., National Education Association, 1948).

WILSON, Charles C., *Healthful School Living,* ed., A Report of the Joint Committee on Health Problems in Education of the National Education Association and the American Medical Association (Washington, D.C., National Education Association, 1957).

WILSON, Charles C., ed., *School Health Services,* A Report of the Joint Committee on Health Problems in Education of the National Education Association and the American Medical Association (Washington, D.C., National Education Association, 1953).

PART IV

Increasing Awareness of
Individual Differences

CHAPTER 14

Guidance in the Elementary School

GUIDANCE IN THE ELEMENTARY SCHOOLS in this country has evolved slowly as an identified discipline; yet it has been in operation for many years. Wherever there has been creative teaching, there has been effective guidance. Although guidance itself is a multidefined term, the authors of this book consider it basically as *a service or a series of services within or without the classroom that helps to make children more receptive to instruction and to learning*. It is also a point of view held by those who are sincerely interested in helping all youth live satisfying and productive lives.

Kowitz and Kowitz define guidance as a process "to reconcile the uniqueness of the individual with the complex but necessary rules of our culture." [1] Cottingham reports that guidance may be a series of approaches as shown by the chart on the following page.[2]

Regardless of how one defines the term, guidance has assumed an increased importance in the minds of American educators since the passing of the National Defense Education Act in 1958. This expansion has paralleled considerably the increasing emphasis on child study and child growth and development. To every child are given rights and responsibilities, a self-realization being the most important. To help each boy and each girl to achieve a maximum self-realization is the *raison d'etre* of guidance.

The rapid development of guidance in the elementary schools since World War II has focused its emphasis on preventive and developmental phases. As Kowitz and Kowitz write,

[1] G. T. Kowitz and N. G. Kowitz, *Guidance in the Elementary Classroom* (New York, McGraw-Hill Book Company, 1959), p. 58.
[2] H. F. Cottingham, *Guidance in Elementary Schools* (Bloomington, Ill., McKnight & McKnight Publishing Company, 1956), p. 3.

Perhaps the most important difference in the elementary school guidance program is that it is not primarily concerned, as in later years, with redirection and re-forming, but rather with establishing desirable patterns.[3]

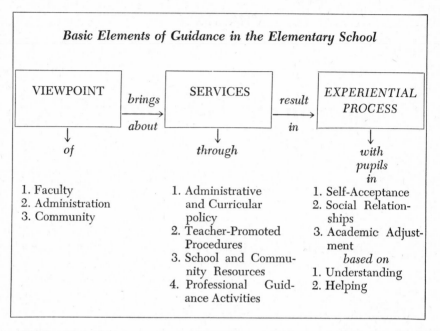

Basic Elements of Guidance in the Elementary School

VIEWPOINT	*brings about*	SERVICES	*result in*	*EXPERIENTIAL PROCESS*
↓ *of*		↓ *through*		↓ *with pupils in*
1. Faculty 2. Administration 3. Community		1. Administrative and Curricular policy 2. Teacher-Promoted Procedures 3. School and Community Resources 4. Professional Guidance Activities		1. Self-Acceptance 2. Social Relationships 3. Academic Adjustment *based on* 1. Understanding 2. Helping

While all guidance programs should be preventive in emphasis, this is particularly true at the elementary school level. As Wilson writes,

The curriculum of the elementary school has made available a rich variety of opportunities for understanding children and giving them a chance to express their interests and needs.[4]

Three specific questions that need to be examined whenever one reviews the role of guidance in the elementary school include: (1) Who are the essential personnel and what is the role of each? (2) What are the fundamental services? (3) How might a school staff evaluate the guidance services in an elementary school?

ROLES OF ESSENTIAL PERSONNEL

There is no blueprint for the best organizational pattern for the administration of guidance services in the elementary school. In some schools the principal assumes the guidance leadership role; in others it is the school psychologist; in still others it is the school social worker; in some a guidance counselor; and in others a guidance committee. Regardless of

---

[3] G. T. Kowitz and N. G. Kowitz, *op. cit.*, p. 41.

[4] F. Wilson, "Guidance in the Elementary School," *Education*, Vol. 75 (March, 1955), p. 450.

who might assume the leadership role, the team approach is a better answer in the development of guidance services. Members of such a team would include: the principal; the classroom teacher; the medical unit, including the school psychologist, the school physician, the school nurse, the school dentist, the dental hygienist; and possibly a staff member who is responsible for special education in the school. There is a need, however, for a careful defining of the responsibilities of each. Brimley, in his 1950 study of 227 schools, found a startling confusion in the minds of the staff regarding their guidance responsibilities.[5]

Guidance at all levels should look to the classroom teacher as the focal point of all services. The guidance program at the secondary level has developed with an administrative emphasis, but guidance in the elementary schools has evolved in close relationship with the activities of the classroom teacher.

Teacher education programs throughout the country are offering guidance courses to prospective teachers and to those in service, emphasizing the importance of the guidance point of view for all school personnel. What is this guidance point of view? It is a sensitivity to the needs of youth and a sincere effort to help each child achieve his maximum self-realization and to live both a satisfying and productive life. The 1955 Yearbook of the Association for Supervision and Curriculum Development describes a classroom teacher with a guidance point of view as,

one who knows: (1) that all children face a variety of adjustment problems in the normal course of growing up; (2) that it is in the resolution of these problems that all children need guidance . . . (3) that children of the same chronological age are at different levels of readiness for a given learning experience . . . (4) that a teacher must be skillful in gathering and using the data needed to determine readiness; (5) that success in school work is intimately related to the way a child conceives of himself as a human being, and to the emotional satisfaction he is achieving in his relationships with others . . . (6) that children learn many things within a given context and plans with reference to the whole constellation of possible wholesome learnings . . . and (7) that the true measure of his success is the degree to which children come to understand themselves more fully and to direct themselves more wisely.[6]

Teachers who study carefully this description of their role are generally relieved from the fear that guidance is one thing more to be added to their already busy schedule. They see it, as it is, a very functional part of effective teaching. Kaback describes the role of the teacher as, "knowing about the individual; understanding the individual; feeling with the in-

[5] R. F. W. Brimley, *The Management of Elementary Schools*, Unpublished Doctoral Dissertation (Washington, D.C., George Washington University, 1950).

[6] C. M. Low, "Setting Our Sights," *Guidance in the Curriculum*, Association for Supervision and Curriculum Development, 1955 Yearbook (Washington, D.C., National Education Association, 1955), pp. 14–22.

dividual; and accepting the individual." [7] Knowing, understanding, feeling with, and accepting are key words for all teachers.

It is the teacher's responsibility not only to instruct, but also to help each child be receptive to instruction. The specific functions of the classroom teacher in the guidance program will be elaborated upon during a major part of this chapter. Inlow writes of the teacher's role in guidance,

Assuming that elementary teachers are permitted and encouraged to accept their guidance roles, specialists in a system can then perform their basic functions more effectively—can administer to the needs of the more exaggerated problem cases and spend the major part of their time getting classroom teachers ready to help themselves. [8]

While teachers assume the major role in the guidance program in an elementary school, other pupil personnel functionaries are needed. As a result of the startling increase in student populations, the development of varied and enriched curricula, the appearance of increasingly diversified student needs, and the complexities and the frustrations of living in the twentieth century, superintendents and school boards of education are slowly but definitely, as budgets permit, adding to their pupil personnel staffs. While there are many school systems that do not have these additional functionaries on either a full-time or a part-time basis, the fact that there is an increase in the number of specialized personnel in guidance makes it advisable to discuss briefly the role of each.

The following table from a study by Rosecrance and Hayden reflects this trend. [9]

SPECIALIZED PERSONNEL

	1935		1955	
	FULL-TIME	PART-TIME	FULL-TIME	PART-TIME
Psychiatrists	5	7	4	13
Psychologists	127	17	163	5
Social Workers	15	7	269	8
Examiners	18	17	25	—
	165	48	461	26

The arrival of these additional staff members should be viewed by the classroom teacher as an occasion for relief rather than with a feeling of apprehension. Their arrival supports and assists the classroom teacher, who becomes an operational co-ordinator of the pupil personnel services for

[7] G. R. Kaback, "The Role of the Teacher in a School Guidance Program," *Education*, Vol. 75 (March, 1955), pp. 466–470.

[8] G. M. Inlow, "Guidance and Curriculum Should Get Together," *Educational Administration and Supervision*, Vol. 43 (April, 1957), p. 235.

[9] F. C. Rosecrance and V. D. Hayden, *School Guidance and Personnel Services* (Boston, Allyn and Bacon, Inc., 1960), p. 100.

his boys and girls. He employs the services of these specialists in a helpful, positive way.

Let us consider the role of each of these specialized personnel.

School Psychologist. In some elementary schools the school psychologist is part of the medical team; in others he operates independently. In either case, he should be a key resource person who can assist teachers, parents, and pupils via his professional competencies. His duties and responsibilities will naturally vary from school to school, depending on the number of other functionaries employed, the philosophy of the school, the attitudes of the faculty and the community, and basically on the competency and the personality of the school psychologist himself.

The Thayer Midcentury Conference dealing with the functions, qualifications, and training of the school psychologist identifies the following functions of this specialist:

(1) measuring and interpreting the intellectual, social, and emotional development of children; (2) identifying exceptional children and collaborating in the planning of appropriate educational and social placements and programs; (3) developing ways to facilitate the learning and adjustment of children; (4) encouraging and initiating research, and helping to utilize research findings for the solution of school problems; and (5) diagnosing educational and personal disabilities, and collaborating in the planning of re-educational programs.[10]

Part of the Thayer Conference was devoted to reports from superintendents from the entire United States, including city, rural, and county superintendents. They agreed that the primary need for psychological services is to aid teachers in preventing future emotional maladjustment in their boys and girls.

The most important role that the school psychologist should play in the elementary schools is in his work with teachers, who many times need help in their role as supportive and preventive counselors. A school psychologist who threatens a teacher with a display of his competencies or with psychological jargon soon loses his effectiveness. He should never forget that he is in the school to be of service. To teachers also goes the responsibility of helping the school psychologist identify in what areas he may be of most assistance. It must be kept in mind, however, that the role of a school psychologist is *not* one of a therapist.

A classroom teacher at the Thayer Conference summarized clearly, in the opinion of the authors of this book, what a classroom teacher wants from a school psychologist:

I want a person to help me *in* the classroom in problems where I will need help. I want one to help me with a solution to my problem rather than to give me a *diagnosis* of my problem. I want one to *help me* solve my problems *within* my classroom setting . . . rather than to take my problem *from* my classroom. I

[10] N. E. Cutts, ed., *School Psychologists at Mid-Century* (Washington, D.C., American Psychological Association, Inc., 1955), p. 30.

want one to give me advice on my relations with my fellow staff members if I need it. I want one who may give me ideas on new techniques of teaching, but not one who would do them for me . . . I want one who would be a member of the *team*.[11]

School psychologists in large school systems work with psychiatrists and psychometrists. Most psychiatrists work on a part-time basis. Psychometrists focus their attention on evaluation, testing, and research.

School Social Workers. The school social worker is identified differently in different schools. He may be called a visiting teacher, an attendance officer, or by some other designation describing his role as a liaison officer between the school and the home. Educators commonly agree regarding the need to employ someone who can work with busy classroom teachers to co-ordinate the role of the home and the community with that of the school. Hourihan describes this service as

the need to bring the methods of social work to bear in helping children whose problems in the school stem from social and emotional causes within the child, his home, or some other area of his environment.[12]

These problem areas may be identified initially by the classroom teacher with the school social worker, who would then follow through with parents and community agencies; or they may be identified by the school social worker, who would enlist the co-operation of the classroom teacher. The school social worker is in each case a trained liaison person between the school, the home, and the community. Generally the school social worker operates from a central office and is not assigned full time to any one school. In some states a statewide program has been inaugurated. The initial one was in Michigan, beginning in 1944.

Hourihan divides the responsibilities of the school social worker into four areas:

(1) *intensive cases,* involving casework interviews with the child on a regularly scheduled basis; (2) *consultative cases,* including frequent conferences with the child, the classroom teacher, and other school personnel; (3) *co-operative cases,* during which time the school social worker works co-operatively with a community agency and serves as a liaison between the agency and the school; and (4) *supportive cases,* involving conferences during which the social worker provides supportive counseling in an attempt to help the child in his school adjustment.[13]

Here again is a responsibility for the classroom teacher. He and the school social worker must understand clearly the services each can contribute to the total education of the boys and girls within a school.

Medical Staff. The size of the medical team varies from school to school.

---

[11] *Ibid.,* p. 71.
[12] J. P. Hourihan, "School Social Work Services," in F. C. Rosecrance and V. D. Hayden, *School Guidance and Personnel Services* (Boston, Allyn and Bacon, Inc., 1960), pp. 138–139.
[13] *Ibid.,* pp. 144–145.

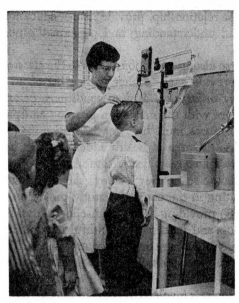

The school nurse is an important
person in the guidance program.

Its component members, however, should include the school physician, the school nurse, the school dentist, the dental hygienist, and probably the school psychologist. In most cases the school physician and the school dentist are part-time personnel who work with the school staff and whose main function is the periodic health inspection of each boy and girl. To the school nurse and the dental hygienist go the responsibilities for health education, emergency health care, and follow-up activities. The school nurse is without doubt the focal point of the medical team. The American School Health Association includes in her functions such general areas as

leadership and resource in the development of the total health program; participation in planning and policy making; serving as a consultant to school personnel, parents, and children; and serving as liaison worker with the community.[14]

The school nurse first meets the incoming child before he enters kindergarten or first grade. Her initial contact with both the youngster and the parents is usually part of the kindergarten round-up held in the spring of the year. At that time the nurse not only initiates the beginning of the child's health record, but also establishes rapport and understanding with both the parents and the child. After the child enters the school, the nurse

[14] National Committee of School Nurses, "Recommended Policies and Practices for School Nursing," American School Health Association, *Journal of School Health*, Vol. 27 (January, 1957), p. 3.

must continue her relationship, provide health education and counseling, show warmth and understanding, and perform the necessary follow-up activities.

The school nurse also has a responsibility to the classroom teacher. Each fall she should provide each teacher with a list of all pupils who have visual or auditory difficulties, cardiac conditions, or any other infirmity that might interfere with the maximum learning and participation of the child. The school nurse must help teachers identify pupils who are ill, work with them in the area of health education, and help teachers meet the needs of youth who have physical disabilities.

In some schools the school nurse enjoys such additional responsibilities as: (1) participating in the curricular study program; (2) working with cafeteria staffs; (3) providing health counseling to staff members; and (4) helping to develop and preserve a healthful environment in the school. Health councils are found in many elementary schools. These councils may include pupils, faculty, or both. The nurse serves as a consultant to these councils.

The dental hygienist is involved in periodic check-ups, health counseling, and follow-up activities. She, too, works with the classroom teacher in the area of health education.

Special Education Personnel. The personnel involved in special education in a school are concerned with at least three classifications of pupils: (1) the mentally retarded; (2) the physically handicapped; and (3) the emotionally and socially disturbed. In some schools the gifted youngster is also their responsibility. The responsibility of special education personnel is to meet the needs of these children, but also to provide as nearly normal a program as possible for them. These persons should work closely with the rest of the staff, both as a means of helping the staff keep apprised of the curricular offerings and as an opportunity to help them understand the role of special education.

Guidance Counselor. A guidance counselor is viewed by the authors of this book as a "generalist" when compared to the specialists we have described on the previous pages. Whenever a guidance counselor is assigned to an elementary school, his responsibilities include: (1) working with teachers to help them secure and utilize as much data as possible concerning each child; (2) maintaining a testing service, dependent on the amount of his psychological training and experiences; (3) co-ordinating the orientation program (as discussed later in this chapter); (4) securing and providing guidance information for teachers that may supplement or enrich classroom activities; (5) referring certain cases to the specialized personnel; (6) providing in-service education in mental health for staff members; (7) fostering sound public relations; and (8) developing a research program.

Guidance Committees. In some elementary schools the principal appoints a guidance committee consisting of classroom teachers who are interested in guidance activities, and the members of the pupil personnel staff. The responsibilities of these committees are: (1) study of existing mental health and guidance activities within the school; (2) recommendation of policies and procedures; (3) performance of evaluations and follow-up services; and (4) recommendation of research studies. Members of this committee frequently talk to community groups, PTA groups, on radio and television programs, and publish articles in the local newspaper.

In summary, school staffs must remember that, regardless of the personnel added, the chief pupil personnel functionary in the elementary school is and must be the classroom teacher. Guidance, however, can contribute significantly to the teaching-learning process. As Froehlich writes,

(1) The teacher is helped to understand the child and thus is able to devise teaching approaches which have the greatest chance of success. (2) Services are provided for the child which help him to understand and to accept his role in the school situation. (3) Parents are not only helped to understand their child but also are aided in seeing how they can support the teacher-learner relationship. (4) The resources of the community are marshalled by the guidance program when a child presents problems which cannot be adequately handled by school personnel.[15]

If the reader feels after completing this section that there are duplications in the responsibilities of the various specialized personnel, he is probably right. These duplications are eliminated at the local level through conferences. The final assignment of specific responsibilities depends on the training of the person involved, his experience, and his personality.

FUNDAMENTAL GUIDANCE SERVICES

Guidance at all levels involves five basic services: (1) collecting information about each child; (2) maximum utilization of the information collected; (3) orientation; (4) informational service; and (5) placement and follow-up. Obviously these services cannot and should not be provided by the pupil personnel staff alone. They involve the co-operation of all the school personnel.

Collecting Information

As Traxler summarizes,

Elementary school teachers do comparatively little talking about guidance services, but they probably enter into guidance activities in connection with their daily teaching more extensively than do teachers at any other level. Nevertheless, they may be expected to do an appreciably better job if they are acquainted with the uses of cumulative records, test results, anecdotal procedures,

---

[15] C. Froehlich, *Guidance Services in Schools* (New York, McGraw-Hill Book Company, 1958), p. 368.

the psychology of counseling, and other techniques of a modern guidance program.[16]

Considerable attention was given in Chapter Three to the procedures that teachers might use in the collecting of helpful information about children. Probably no other staff member in the entire school system has as equal an opportunity to collect dynamic and helpful data about boys and girls as does the elementary school teacher. He spends a minimum of five hours a day, approximately one hundred and eighty days a year, with twenty-five to thirty-five boys and girls. What a potential storehouse of information he should have to answer current and future questions!

Elementary school teachers, however, are busy people, and the collecting of these data must not be left to chance. School staffs like to have assistance, and they should be helped in every possible way in the collection of these data. Procedures for teachers to collect data (discussed in Chapter Three) include: (1) review of records; (2) observation; (3) anecdotal records; (4) informal conversations with children; (5) daily logs; (6) sharing periods; (7) rating sheets; (8) autobiographies; (9) testing; (10) sociometry; (11) health inspections; (12) home visitations; and (13) case histories, case studies, and case conferences. If classroom teachers are to understand their boys and girls, and if they are to provide meaningful learning experiences, they must use as many of these techniques as possible. Pupil personnel functionaries must help teachers collect and utilize the data available.

Utilization of Information

Too frequently school systems develop an elaborate system for collecting data, but they do very little in the maximum utilization of the information secured. Extensive folders are maintained, but little used; charts and graphs are developed; many tests are given; and staff members spend hours in research. If the data collected are not extensively used, the time, the effort, and the expense that are expended in the collection of this information are of little use.

The effective utilization of data in an elementary school involves a two-pronged approach: (1) centralization of data; and (2) counseling of a nonclinical nature by the teacher.

While the data collected in different classrooms may be used differently but effectively by different teachers, the local use of data is not enough. There should be a centralization of data if they are to have maximum value for a maximum number of people. Probably the first step is to involve the entire staff in the development or re-evaluation of a central school record system. It is possible to secure record forms from the United States Office

[16] A. E. Traxler, *Techniques of Guidance*, rev. ed. (New York, Harper and Brothers, 1957), p. 14.

of Education and from other school systems. If this is done, the authors of this book wish to express a plea that these forms be used only as guides. A superimposed record system, just as a superimposed list of objectives, can be very meaningless.

The development of a functional record system can be the basis for a dynamic in-service education program. Study groups can be set up by the faculty and administration to explore the following questions:

(1) How extensively and how effectively are the current cumulative records used? (2) Why are they not used more extensively? (3) What are the kinds of information that teachers need to know? (4) What is the best procedure for securing these data? (5) What is the responsibility of the teacher in collecting, selecting, and reporting items of information? . . . (6) How can the records be made usable and available for all teachers? [17]

No matter how effective a job is done by a school staff in the development of a functional cumulative record, provision for continuous evaluation is a "must." Warters lists some helpful guides for elementary school staffs who are working on pupils' records:

1. The development and revision of record forms for use in a particular school should be a co-operative project.
2. The faculty should start with simple records that all of its members can use so that they may progress smoothly and steadily toward use of more comprehensive records.
3. Usable items that will actually be used are the ones to be included in the record forms adopted.
4. Certain questions regarding practical details should be considered before the first supply of record forms is prepared.
5. The adoption of the cumulative record form agreed upon should be considered tentative.
6. Revision, like the development of record forms, should be a co-operative undertaking.
7. When a cumulative form has been agreed upon for tentative adoption, a bulletin of instructions should be prepared.
8. Some definite general plan should be formulated for gathering, reporting, and recording information to be contained in the cumulative records.
9. Confidential information should not be put into cumulative records.
10. All teachers should share in the work of collecting and reporting information on students. Not all, however, should record information on cumulative record forms. . . .
11. Cumulative records should be used by all faculty members; so they should be placed where all may use them easily.
12. Cumulative records should cover the entire span of the student's school career from kindergarten through college. [18]

[17] F. C. Rosecrance and V. D. Hayden, *op. cit.*, p. 55.
[18] J. Warters, *Techniques of Counseling* (New York, McGraw-Hill Book Company, 1954), pp. 252–260.

The responsibility for the maximum utilization of the data collected is not resolved, however, when a central records system is developed. School staffs must constantly be sensitive to the danger of having all "system" and little "service." Such basic questions as, *Are the data being used widely? Are the data being used constructively and positively?* must always be in the foreground of the thinking and planning of administrators, teachers, and pupil personnel functionaries in every elementary school. The degree of effectiveness of data is measured by the degree to which teachers utilize these data in their everyday teaching. Effective teaching requires the teacher to know each of his boys and girls well.

Another important phase in the effective utilization of data is the role played by classroom teachers in listening to and talking with boys and girls. Data collected about boys and girls can be helpful in counseling, but may also be limiting and inhibiting. Teachers who know their children can probably listen more sensitively to boys and girls than school functionaries who merely have a knowledge of the children from records. One caution, however: no teacher or other school functionary should inform a child of his conclusions before the boy or girl is ready to accept or to formulate these conclusions from data himself. The conclusions of the teacher are less important than the self-realization of the child.

While authorities will agree that classroom teachers cannot and should not engage in clinical counseling, they can and do participate in many individual conversations with boys and girls in their class, during which considerable counseling does take place. Willey and Andrew describe this relationship when they write,

Counseling is a mutual learning process involving two individuals in an educational environment, one who is seeking help from a professionally trained person, and the other, who by reason of his breadth of training and background, utilizes many adjustment techniques and methods in assisting the individual to orient and direct himself toward a goal leading to maximum growth and development in a social and democratic society.[19]

There follow certain basic principles that should help teachers foster maximum counseling effectiveness whenever they talk with boys and girls:

A basic principle is for the teacher to be an effective listener. Too frequently teachers find it very difficult to listen and not to feel compelled to do a major part of the talking. We have all felt the urge to tell someone our problems whenever we have been disturbed about a situation. As adults we dislike being interrupted at such a time; so does a child.

Just listening during the initial outburst, however, is not enough, for teachers must then allow the child to explore avenues of solution verbally and mentally. The child must play a major role in these explorations if this experience is to help him to resolve his problems.

[19] R. D. Willey and D. C. Andrew, *Modern Methods and Techniques in Guidance* (New York, Harper and Brothers, 1955), p. 323.

Teachers must also listen without reflecting censure, anger, or shock. The teacher should not contribute more emotion to an already filled hopper. To be a calm, patient, objective *listener* is a prerequisite for any kind of counseling. To listen with a "third ear," as described by Reik,[20] is essential in the counseling process.

Teachers, when conferring with boys and girls, must be interested in establishing rapport with each child. Rapport is a state of empathy, a comfortable feeling on the part of the child that the teacher understands him and is interested in helping him help himself.

There are many procedures for establishing rapport: a reference to a previous experience the teacher and the child have shared, a compliment, or a comment about a child's interests or hobby. The best procedure is a warm, genuinely sincere attitude toward the child. Teachers must not consider the establishment of rapport as "tricks of the trade," for such an attitude cannot help but be felt by the child. Teachers and parents will agree that children are difficult to fool. Sincerity, pleasantness, enthusiasm, and consistency of behavior go a long way toward helping teachers help youngsters.

Boys and girls should be given an opportunity to express negative feelings in a permissive and objective atmosphere. Teachers who are professionally-minded frequently become confused at this point and raise such apprehensive questions as: Suppose he criticizes another teacher? Suppose he criticizes my principal? The teacher's role, in such a case, whenever he is working through a counseling relationship, is to help the child gain a fairer picture of the teacher's colleague. One has two choices: (1) to stop the child immediately, or (2) to allow the child to finish his statement, and then to evaluate with him why he feels as he does. The latter seems preferable in the long run, for it clears the air much more readily. Repression of feelings frequently results in increased emotional disturbance.

Obviously teachers must not encourage gossip or criticism about their colleagues, and all negative remarks must be clarified in the child's thinking. Have not we all been able to see things more clearly after we have freed our mind of festering negative thoughts and feelings? The counselor should develop effectiveness in bringing

feelings consciously into the picture without taking sides and . . . to develop his function as that of a mirror which shows [the child] his real self and enables him, aided by this new perception, to reorganize himself.[21]

After rapport has been established, after negative feelings have been expressed, then the teacher must help the child evaluate these negative feelings and develop more positive ones. This has been defined by some

---

[20] T. Reik, *Listening With the Third Ear* (New York, Farrar, Straus and Company, Inc., 1948).

[21] C. Rogers, *Counseling and Psychotherapy* (Boston, Houghton Mifflin Company, 1942), p. 144.

authors as helping the child to gain insight. It is at this point that the teacher-counselor has the responsibility to furnish essential information that the boy or girl can use in evaluating his present situation and in planning for the future. Care must be taken not to force the child to intellectualize acceptance. Feelings are much more important than intellectualization at this point. Whether Peter is having difficulty in arithmetic is not nearly as vital as how he feels about this difficulty.

Children must be given an opportunity to arrive at and to try out tentative solutions to their problems. The successes and the failures of these tentative solutions should be carefully discussed and evaluated as the child becomes more and more independent.

Summaries and evaluations of the counseling sessions should be developed by the child, not by the teacher. A teacher who says, "Today we have covered the following points . . . haven't we?" has minimized some of the effectiveness of the counseling process. How much better to ask, "What do you feel that we have accomplished today? How do you feel now? Why do you think you feel the way you do?"

Tyler notes three basic factors in all effective counseling situations: acceptance, understanding, and communication.[22]

Counseling is defined as a process of helping boys and girls change their behavior patterns and develop more effective self-understanding, self-discipline, and self-decision-making. It is of interest to note here that the same basic principles of effective counseling are basic to effective teaching. Rogers summarizes these common principles as they appear in effective teaching:

Initially the leader has much to do with setting the mood or climate of the group experience by his own basic philosophy of trust in the group, which is communicated in many subtle ways.

The leader helps to elicit and clarify the purposes of the members of the class, accepting all aims.

He relies upon the student desire to implement these purposes as the motivational force behind learning.

He endeavors to organize and make easily available all resources which the students may wish to use for their own learning.

He regards himself as a flexible resource to be utilized by the group in the ways which seem most meaningful to them, in so far as he can be comfortable operating in these ways.

In responding to expressions from the group, he accepts both the intellectual content and the emotionalized attitudes, endeavoring to give each aspect the approximate degree of emphasis which it has for the individual and the group.

As the acceptant classroom climate becomes established, the leader is able to change his role and become a participant, a member of the group, expressing his views as those of one individual only.

[22] L. E. Tyler, *The Work of the Counselor* (New York, Appleton-Century-Crofts, Inc., 1953), pp. 23–58.

He remains alert to expressions indicative of deep feeling and when these are voiced, he endeavors to understand these from the speaker's point of view, and to communicate this type of understanding.

Likewise when group interaction becomes charged with emotion, he tends to maintain a neutral and understanding role, in order to give acceptance to the varied feelings which exist.

He recognizes that the extent to which he can behave in these differing fashions is limited by the genuineness of his own attitudes. To pretend an acceptant understanding of a viewpoint when he does not feel this acceptance, will not further, and will probably hinder, the dynamic progress of the class.[23]

In summary, the utilization of data collected by an elementary school staff is an extremely important phase of the elementary school guidance program. These data should be found in a functional cumulative record and should be utilized by teachers through their classroom teaching and through their informal counseling with boys and girls. Teachers must learn to develop a counseling attitude and must understand the basic principles of effective counseling, which are the basis of effective interpersonal relationships.

The authors now turn to the third service of an elementary school guidance program, orientation of boys and girls as they pass through the many transitional periods of our school program.

Orientation

One of the major responsibilities that an elementary school staff has is to help boys and girls meet positively the transitional periods through which they will pass as they grow older. As Farwell and Peters write,

If one considers a guidance program on a longitudinal basis, a firm foundation for understanding the uniqueness of each boy and girl in our schools must begin at the kindergarten level. It is folly to permit our children and youth to proceed toward maturity without a regard of their ongoing psychological, sociological, mental, and physical development.[24]

A child must be helped to enjoy such transitional stages as: (1) his moving from home, where he has experienced considerable individual attention, to school, where he becomes one of a group; (2) his transition from one grade to the next; and (3) his moving in many school systems from the comfort and security of the elementary classroom to a larger and more complex junior high school. Feelings of apprehension and of the unknown, frustrations, conflicts, and anxieties must be kept at a minimum through the co-operation of an understanding school staff working with

[23] C. Rogers, "Client-Centered Teaching," in *Client-Centered Therapy* (Boston, Houghton Mifflin Company, 1951), pp. 401–402.
[24] G. F. Farwell and H. J. Peters, "Guidance: A Longitudinal and a Differential View," *Elementary School Journal*, Vol. 57 (May, 1957), p. 442.

the other members of an orientation project. School staffs each year face the question of how this can effectively be done.

While most authorities will agree that the school cannot be all things to all people, they will advocate that each school staff evaluate and plan carefully the leadership role it will play in initiating and sponsoring a preschool orientation program. Donley reports a study of orientation programs in many communities. In this study he points out that the programs vary considerably, but that, "in most every school the Parent-Teacher Association plays a large part in the pre-school orientation program. . . . In some cases a Parent-Teacher Association Committee does most of the planning." [25]

Purposes of a preschool round-up or orientation program must be carefully identified by each elementary school staff working with parents and community groups. In Donley's study, a typical listing of activities was identified by the staff in Erie County, Ohio, as follows: (1) registering children prior to school entrance; (2) providing preschool children an opportunity to become acquainted with the teacher and the classroom situation; (3) telling parents about the organization and operation of the system; (4) informing parents regarding the instructional program; (5) explaining the requirements for physical examinations of children prior to school entrance; (6) acquainting parents with the school lunch program; and (7) extending an invitation for PTA membership.

Larger cities tend to have Child Welfare Councils which may or may not work in co-operation with the Community Co-ordinating Council. The plans for the Child Welfare Council are usually initiated by the school nurse and other representatives of the pupil personnel services who work with the Parent-Teacher Association and representatives of community social agencies.

The membership of such a council would generally include: representatives from the elementary schools, the visiting nurse association, children's hospital, baby clinics, the school health department, child study groups, and interested social agencies. The specific members vary in reference to the size, philosophy, and interest of the community.

The activities sponsored by the Child Welfare Council may include:

Physical Inspections. Boys and girls who anticipate enrollment in kindergarten or first grade the following fall are given a physical inspection during the preceding spring by either the school physician or the family doctor. Generally it is performed by the latter. At that time, the school nurse interviews each child and at least one of his parents. This enables her to establish rapport with the child and his family and to initiate a school health record for each child. This procedure makes it possible to discover

[25] M. O. Donley, Jr., "Welcome to Our Schools," *NEA Journal*, Vol. 48 (February, 1959), pp. 23–25.

data that will help identify health problems which, if not corrected early, may become negative factors in the child's adjustment to his initial contact with school and in his succeeding school career.[26]

Involvement of Parents. Also during the preceding spring, mothers are invited to attend a series of meetings with resource people. The goal of these conferences is to help parents prepare for the transition from home to school and to help parents assist their children in making this transition as positive as possible. Kindergarten and first grade teachers discuss the kinds of learning experiences that the boys and girls will have. Members of the medical team discuss the importance of maintaining and preserving mental and physical health. Resource people explain the community services available in the areas of child welfare and child guidance. Suitable films may be shown and discussed. The roles played by nursery schools and kindergartens in the total development of boys and girls are also explored with interested parents.

The importance of developing positive attitudes in these young children is strongly stressed with parents, both through group and individual conferences. Parents are cautioned about giving boys and girls the impression that school is an unpleasant place. Rather they are encouraged to stress the fact that school and learning are interesting, fun, and even exciting.

The goals of individual interviews with the parents may be summarized as follows: "(1) the initiation of the much needed practice of having parents and school personnel meet regularly; (2) the providing of an opportunity for the school staff to get an idea of each child's interest and personality pattern; and (3) the initial identification of areas in which the parents and teachers can work together." [27]

Tot-Lots. In some congested communities the Child Welfare Council introduces the idea of "tot-lots," suitable playing locations with play activities adequately supervised. Psychologists agree that

Pre-school youngsters who must play in a small space in a congested area are likely to engage in bickering and to develop hostile attitudes toward one another which may inhibit their satisfactory school adjustment.[28]

Other programs are found in schools across the country. Schools in smaller communities already have adopted many ideas from the larger cities and are developing very effective preschool orientation programs.

In Dearborn, Michigan, youngsters who are anticipating enrollment in kindergarten or first grade the following September and their mothers are invited to spend a day visiting during the preceding May. Each day during the month, a few youngsters are invited. These youngsters are then directly involved in the school activities of the morning or afternoon.[29]

[26] F. C. Rosecrance and V. D. Hayden, *op. cit.*, p. 30.
[27] *Ibid.*, p. 32.
[28] *Ibid.*, p. 31.
[29] M. O. Donley, *op. cit.*, p. 23.

In Liverpool, New York, a similar program was initiated in 1956 and developed rapidly. Here the parents participate in conferences with the classroom teachers and other staff members while their youngsters are attending a kindergarten or first grade class. An evaluation report based on the first year of the prekindergarten workshop and visitation program reflected the following benefits to the school and to the parents,

The children (120 participated) seem eager for, or at least unfearful of school; the parents (also 120) now know most of the answers and will not be telephoning anxious questions next fall; the parents know the school's open-door policy; they will be more ready for the parent-teacher conferences and will work more effectively with the teachers; and, of course, the parents now know why kindergarten is a "must" in the Liverpool schools. The PTA also showed a gain in an eager, friendly body of potential members.[30]

Another very common procedure is to give pamphlets or brochures to boys and girls and their parents. In the Monroe-Woodbury Central School in New York, a mimeographed brochure is issued for parents. It is entitled, *Your Child and Kindergarten*, and includes such sections as, "What Do We Do in Kindergarten"; "What Do We Learn in Kindergarten"; "Our Programs" (giving daily schedules week by week); "Some Suggestions to Parents"; "How Parents Can Help the Teacher"; "Clothes and Equipment Needed"; "Health Needs and Procedures"; and "Absence Regulations." [31]

In Decatur, Georgia, a first-grade class developed a leaflet entitled, *Welcome to Our School.* The leaflets were hand-lettered by the first-graders and told an illustrated story of the fun boys and girls have in school.[32]

The variety of programs developed by school systems to help boys and girls initiate their school careers smoothly are innumerable. They include publications, visitations, conferences, programs put on by kindergarten and first-grade youngsters, and the use of audio-visual aids.

One of the most elaborate programs with which the authors are familiar is one developed by the California Congress of Parents and Teachers. This includes: (1) a health examination program, including a spring canvass of communities to determine the number of preschool students and a fall check-up to verify the earlier count; (2) observation classes, led by credentialed teachers in which each mother keeps a record of her child at play and later discusses his conduct with other participating mothers and the teacher; (3) parent participation in the nursery school program; and (4) a ten-day workshop program designed to train parents and lay parent-education leaders for study discussion groups.[33]

[30] C. Hassel, "Pre-Kindergarten Workshop," *School Executive,* Vol. 76 (June, 1957), p. 57. Copyright, 1957, Buttenheim Publishing Corporation.

[31] Developed by the staff of the Monroe-Woodbury Central School, Orange County, New York.

[32] M. O. Donley, *op. cit.,* p. 24.

[33] *Ibid.,* p. 25.

The transition from one grade to the next is an important annual occasion in most children's lives. Boys and girls pass from one grade to the next regularly throughout their school careers in the traditional graded school system. To some this is a time of happy anticipation. Others look with dread toward the end of a school year during which they have become well adjusted to a classroom, to a teacher, and to a familiar routine. The classroom teachers can assume major responsibility at these periods of transition.

The teacher in the "feeding" grade can do many things. He can help each boy and each girl to develop to his maximum. Each child will then be more ready for the ensuing experiences. The teacher can emphasize the delight of the next year's experience—an interesting teacher, challenging work, a pleasant classroom, and exciting projects.

Here also is a place where two teachers can work together. Boys and girls as well as classroom teachers must see the relationship between the work of the previous year and that of the succeeding year. Projects developed by boys and girls in both the third and fourth grades working together will emphasize, for example, a relationship between the work in each of the grades. Visits to the room to which the child will be moving helps him to become familiar with the classroom and acquainted with the teacher. Parent-Teacher groups and "room mothers" working with the teacher may also co-operate in sponsoring programs and parties for the boys and girls as they plan to enter the succeeding grade.

Care, patience, and ingenuity must be exercised in reference to the boy or girl who is not promoted. While the authors of this book do not recommend automatic promotion, every resource must be utilized to be certain that retention is the best thing for the child in question. The parents, the principal, the classroom teacher and pupil personnel functionaries should be involved in each situation, and every case must have individual attention. The adults involved must be able to help the child face his experience with understanding and confidence. This problem is further discussed in Chapter Fifteen.

Another giant step in a child's educational career is his leaving the security of his elementary school sixth-grade classroom with a familiar teacher, familiar boys and girls, a familiar bulletin board, and a familiar routine. The child cannot help but view the complexities of a larger junior high school with some fear unless he is given assistance. This assistance is really three-pronged as viewed by the elementary school staff: assistance to the child, assistance to the parents, and assistance to the professional staff who will work with him at this next educational level.

Assistance to the boy and girl may again be subdivided into three areas: assistance offered by the sixth-grade teacher, visitations to the new setting, and talks with pupils who have experienced the same change a year earlier.

The sixth-grade teacher is a shelter of security for youngsters leaving elementary school. They feel comfortable in asking questions and in expressing some of their fears and apprehensions. Sixth-grade teachers must develop positive attitudes in children toward the new experience; and must help each child develop personally toward this new experience and to see clearly the relationship between his current work and that of the following year. Unfamiliar terms, such as, class advisor, shop courses, exploratory courses, departmentalization, study halls, and a guidance period should be examined and used freely. Language arts experiences might involve studying and reviewing the junior high school newspaper and yearbook and carrying through interviewing projects with junior high school boys and girls. The more familiar the new experience becomes in the minds of the boys and girls while they are still in the elementary school, the smoother will be the transition.

Many opportunities should be afforded the members of the sixth-grade class to visit the junior high school. This can be done formally on a visiting day in the spring of the year while the ninth-grade class visits the senior high school. A general meeting, class visitations, and club meetings are some of the typical activities. Also during the course of the year sixth-graders may be invited to attend athletic events, dramatic productions, and social activities.

As much opportunity as possible should be given to activities permitting junior high school students to talk with sixth-graders. In the spring of the year representatives from the junior high school staff often visit each of the "feeding" schools. It is most fitting that they bring along seventh-graders who were enrolled in that particular school the preceding year. Group discussions and individual conferences should be held covering such areas as curricular offerings, student activities, and other phases of the junior high school program. The authors have participated in some orientation meetings of this type where colored slides made by the junior high school student body were shown. Such a meeting was colorful, informative, and entertaining.

Parents should also be involved in this orientation program. Parents too should be invited to events held during the year at the junior high school. Some junior high school staffs hold a series of open house meetings during the evening hours, at which time a variety of activities occur: (1) an opening general discussion; (2) individual conferences; and (3) an opportunity for parents to view a sample of the program that their son or daughter will experience the following year. Every parent who has a son or daughter enrolling in the junior high school should be interviewed by a junior high school staff member prior to September. Brochures, handbooks, issues of the school newspaper, and other mimeographed materials should be distributed.

To help the professional staff to be ready to assist these boys and girls who need immediate attention, conferences are frequently held in the spring of the year, involving representatives from the junior high school professional staff, the sixth-grade teacher or teachers, and the principal and pupil personnel functionaries from the elementary school. These discussions usually include data regarding health problems, physical infirmities, indications of poor home conditions or juvenile delinquency, reports from social agencies who had worked with the child previously, major academic difficulties, as well as special talents. Great care must be exercised to be certain that these discussions are constructive and positive and are received with an attitude of helpfulness.

Elementary school staffs should constantly evaluate their orientation procedures and enrich their offerings. They must not minimize the importance of these transitional stages in the total development of boys and girls.

Informational Services

A fourth important area in an elementary school guidance program emphasizes informational services in each of three areas: educational planning, occupational planning, and personal-social development.

Educational information has more recently been referred to as educational planning—helping boys and girls and their parents plan an effective educational future. Classroom teachers and pupil personnel functionaries are concerned with: (1) the development of a sound educational philosophy; (2) the effective placement of boys and girls in the elementary school; (3) working with the "failing" child; (4) the providing of remedial classes and groups; (5) the identification of the bright child; (6) testing and evaluation process; and (7) the effective reporting of pupil progress both to the pupils and to their parents. (The last two of these will not be discussed in this chapter, for they are covered in Chapter Fifteen.) Let us first begin with the development of a sound educational philosophy.

One of the major responsibilities of an elementary school staff is to develop a sound educational philosophy, one that is evaluated regularly in terms of current trends and one generally accepted by the school staff. As was discussed in Chapter Two, this philosophy is co-operatively developed. New faculty joining the staff should be informed regarding this philosophy and their ideas should be requested.

Too infrequently the older boys and girls of an elementary school are invited to initiate a philosophy of education of their own. Too seldom do elementary school staffs discuss with them the educational goals and objectives of their school and the general philosophy accepted by the staff. Such a procedure would help these children see more clearly their educational program in perspective. The older boys and girls should also be encouraged to talk about their anticipated plans regarding junior high school, senior high, and even college. Such discussions can contribute to better focus, improved perspective, and a clearer meaning of their current educational experiences.

Without question, effective grade placement is basic to successful learning. Great care must be constantly taken by the school staff to be certain that each child is being challenged *in terms of his potentialities.* Work that is too easy or too difficult can produce hazardous results in a child's mental health. Whenever a new boy or girl enters an elementary school from another school, care must be exercised that the child is placed in the appropriate grade. School records, test results, and personal interviews must be examined conscientiously. Educational information gained from these sources must be utilized by the classroom teacher to help the transferred child in his educational development and planning.

The "failing" child must not be overlooked, either:

> Is it not disturbing that for years the percentage of pupils tasting failure in the first grade was the largest for all grades in our school system? Immaturity, lack of application, physical defects, timidity and shyness, behavior patterns, home training, nervous instability, lack of self control, speech defects, language difficulties, late entrance, and irregular attendance were some of the reasons given for "failure" in the first year of a child's school experience.[34]

It seems to the authors that an answer lies either in not promoting the child who is not "ready" for first grade or in adjusting the first grade curriculum to meet the individual needs and competencies of the boys and girls. Authorities seem to definitely favor the latter.[35] (Again the reader is referred to Chapter Fifteen.)

Regardless of the solution we must decrease the number of children who fail in first grade. The problem has been tackled in some schools through the development of records showing the age, mental development, social development, health, reading readiness, results of interviews with parents, and statements of teacher judgments.

The use of records; the efforts of classroom teachers; the specialized services of the school psychologist, the counselor, and the medical staff; and the involvement of the parents are all important facets of any school guidance program for "failing" children. Whether failure is caused by external factors brought to bear on the pupil or whether, as is sometimes true, the child brings failure upon himself, the total school staff must participate in a truly educative process, helping the child toward improved self-understanding, self-discipline, and self-realization.

To assist the "failing" child, the overage boy or girl, and the child who has been absent because of acute illness, remedial programs have been

---

[34] F. C. Rosecrance and V. D. Hayden, *op. cit.,* pp. 57–58.

[35] Association for Supervision and Curriculum Development, *Organizing the Elementary School for Living and Learning,* 1947 Yearbook (Washington, D.C., National Education Association, 1947), p. 42.

initiated in many elementary schools. School clinics and remedial classes are used to supplement the remedial assistance given by the classroom teachers. Boys and girls should be given remedial assistance outside the classroom only as long as it is absolutely necessary. Usually the assignment of boys and girls to remedial classes is recommended by the teacher working with the school psychologist or the guidance counselor. If a school does not have these specialized personnel, the teacher and the principal make the assignment. Some elementary schools have speech clinics, writing clinics, and arithmetic clinics. Elementary school staffs must always remember that the remedial work must be assigned with a positive, constructive emphasis, never with a negative attitude or with a disciplinary emphasis.

At the other end of the continuum the educational staff is confronted by the question: What is the elementary school doing for the brighter child? If each child were challenged in each elementary school classroom in terms of his potentialities, this problem would not exist. In our crowded classrooms, however, the more intellectually alert boy or girl is sometimes overlooked. The 1958 National Education Defense Act has directed the attention of educators toward identifying and furnishing stimulating programs for these students.

Occupational planning in the elementary school stresses the developmental emphasis. Although boys and girls seem to be far away from determining a career, authorities agree that there is a valuable role to be played by school staffs in helping children study occupational information. Each boy or girl tends to pass through periods of imagination, fantasy, and changing desires, but a study of various occupations he or she mentions frequently begins to reflect a pattern.

Also the goal of the staff in the elementary school is to help children develop a respect for the world of work. Hoppock writes,

How the teacher responds to the child's announced "decision" may help to determine whether the child will come to regard the choice of an occupation as important or unimportant, as something that he may properly discuss with his teacher or as something in which the teacher is not interested, as something that the child should investigate and think about realistically or as something just to dream about in fantasy.[36]

Hoppock further identifies eight purposes in presenting occupational information to elementary school children: "(1) to increase the child's feeling of security in the strange new world outside the home by increasing his familiarity with it . . . (2) to encourage the natural curiosity of young children . . . (3) to extend the occupational horizons of the child . . . (4) to encourage wholesome attitudes toward all useful work . . . (5) to begin developing a desirable approach to the process of occupational choice . . .

[36] R. Hoppock, *Occupational Information* (New York, McGraw-Hill Book Company, 1957), p. 343.

(6) to help students who are dropping out of school and going to work . . .
(7) to help students who face a choice between different high schools or
high school programs . . . and (8) to show children who really need money
how to get it without stealing." [37]

The modern elementary school teachers present occupational information to boys and girls in a variety of procedures: talks by parents of the
boys and girls in a given classroom; talks by men and women in the community who represent various lines of work, such as a doctor, a dentist,
a milkman, or a plumber; discussions of various occupations mentioned in
the books read by the class; field trips; the use of occupational bulletin
boards that tell the story of an occupational family; panel discussions; role-
playing; and community surveys.

Recognition of the importance of occupational information in the elementary school is gaining each year, for it reflects again the emphasis on
the importance of the developmental approach to important decisions.
It is never too early to help children begin to develop positive attitudes
about the world of work.

**Personal-social development is another important service in an ele-
mentary school guidance program.** Try as we will, there are always socially
and emotionally maladjusted youngsters in our elementary school classrooms.

All elementary school staffs are well aware of the fact that they must
provide information and experiences that will assist boys and girls to develop sound self-concepts, emotional security, and social stability. As
Detjen and Detjen write,

The successful teacher of today is an emotionally adjusted individual. She
is conscious of the influence of her own personality upon her pupils. . . . She likes
children and lets them know it. Teaching them and working and planning with
them is not a laborious task but a pleasure to her.[38]

One of the most effective procedures for assisting boys and girls in their
identification of interests and competencies is the development of a flexible,
varied, and creative student activity program. While the safety patrol
is generally the only permanently organized student service group, many
activities are generally found in our schools, representing the varying
interests.

Two very important cautions that should be noted in relation to the
development of these student activity groups are as follows: (1) all student
groups should be closely related to the learning experiences within the
classrooms; (2) school staffs must be certain that the emphasis is not
placed on a perfect performance of the band, the chorus, the orchestra, or

[37] *Ibid.*, pp. 344–346.
[38] E. W. Detjen and M. F. Detjen, *Elementary School Guidance* (New York, Mc-
Graw-Hill Book Company, 1952), p. 249.

the dramatic group, but rather on the need for boys and girls to have an opportunity to pursue some type of activity. Every effort should be made to provide an activity which will appeal to the interest of each child. Variety, flexibility, and an opportunity for boys and girls to be creative are the key words.

A truly effective student activity program will provide opportunities for: (1) the improving of the health of pupils through health councils and healthy communities; (2) the improving of the educational program through group and individual activities both within and without the classroom; and (3) the improving of the social and emotional development of boys and girls through activities appropriate for differing age and interest groups.

As Cottingham writes,

Guidance has as its purpose the aiding of pupils with problems relating to personal values, social skills, or educational decisions—needs not always met through the more formal classroom instructional devices.[39]

Placement and Follow-Up Activities

Placement and follow-up activities are always included in the guidance services in any school system, although they are more comprehensive at the secondary level. In the elementary school they include basically: (1) the accurate placement of each boy and girl both on the right grade level and the effective groupings of boys and girls within the classroom; and (2) the placement of boys and girls in varied and creative student activities. Both of these have been previously discussed in this chapter.

Follow-up activities are concerned with: (1) helping boys and girls determine goals and objectives and develop the skills of self-evaluation; (2) studying the progress boys and girls achieve as they pass through the elementary grades; (3) follow-up studies of boys and girls as they leave elementary school and face the complexities of junior high school; and (4) the follow-up studies of youth who leave school because of illness, because their families move away, or because of other reasons. Because of a lack of adequate personnel, time, and money, follow-up activities are generally not developed as adequately as they should be. As Roeber, Smith, and Erickson write: "The placement and follow-up services provide the follow-through and evaluation to all planning activities undertaken as the result of the other guidance services."[40]

Follow-up activities involve evaluation, and this brings us to the final section of this chapter.

[39] H. F. Cottingham, op. cit., p. 130.
[40] E. C. Roeber, G. E. Smith, and C. E. Erickson, Organization and Administration of Guidance Services (New York, McGraw-Hill Book Company, 1955), p. 223.

EVALUATION OF A GUIDANCE PROGRAM

It would be impossible to conclude a discussion devoted to elementary school guidance without indicating procedures to evaluate guidance services. In assuming leadership roles in the evaluation of guidance services, pupil personnel functionaries generally follow the following guides: (1) evaluation necessitates clearly defined goals and objectives; (2) evaluation must be co-operatively planned and carried out; (3) evaluation of a guidance program should reflect to what degree the services are an integral part of the total educational program; (4) provisions must be made for continual evaluation; (5) the most effective evaluation is generally performed at the point where the guidance is carried out; and (6) a variety of methods should be employed.

Froehlich has identified the following methods of evaluation that can be used by an elementary school staff:

1. External criteria: do-you-do-this? method.
2. Follow up: the what-happened-then? method.
3. Client opinion: the what-do-you-think? method.
4. Expert opinion: the "Information Please" method.
5. Specific techniques: the little-by-little method.
6. Within-group changes: the before-and-after method.
7. Between-group changes: the what's-the-difference? method.[41]

An entirely different procedure served as the basis for a follow-up study conducted by Rosecrance and Hayden covering the twenty-year period from 1935–1955. The sixty-two elementary schools studied identified three goals for a successful guidance program: (1) happier children; (2) more satisfied parents; and (3) more professionally-minded teachers:

In 1935, a survey of opinion about pupil personnel work in the sixty-two elementary schools and its results as judged subjectively were reported as follows:

HAPPIER *children as shown by:*

> *Improved school achievement:*
> > Fewer failures
> > Better grade placement
> > Greater interest in work and satisfaction in success
> > Greater mental development
> > More children remaining in school

> *Improved physical adjustment*
> *Finer attitudes:*
> > Better school citizenship
> > Greater pupil co-operation

[41] C. P. Froehlich, *Evaluating Guidance Procedures: A Review of the Literature,* Misc. 3310 (Washington, D.C., Occupational Information and Guidance Service, Office of Education, 1949), p. 21.

Much improved school spirit and morale
Greater sense of security . . .
Less juvenile delinquency . . .
Improved school discipline
Better social and personality adjustment
Wiser use of leisure time.

MORE *satisfied parents as shown by:*
Better co-operation
Greater confidence in teachers
Greater interest in school program and greater willingness to support it
Fewer complaints
More friendly attitudes
Greater appreciation of the school and its work
More parents coming to school for help

MORE *professionally-minded teachers as shown by:*

Better understanding of and greater interest in children as individuals:
Better knowledge of individual differences and needs
Development of feeling that teaching is imparting of instruction, and the guiding of young life in all its varying aspects

Better understanding of guidance and counseling

More intelligent handling of problems:
Reduction of problem and disciplinary cases
More objective point of view in study of the problem child
Causal factors sought in interpreting behavior

Happier teachers.

In 1955 a "repeat" study was made of these same schools, which showed the same factors being judged as tangible results of the pupil personnel program. Two new points, however, appeared in the later study: (1) after parents had come to understand the child that had had a problem at school, they understood their other children better; and (2) a reduced turnover in the teaching staff resulted from teachers becoming more interested in their work.[42]

If such goals were accepted and achieved by the elementary school guidance programs throughout the country, the development of guidance services in our elementary schools would be rapid. There is a considerable need, however, for continued research. Willey has identified the following areas in which immediate research is needed:

More explicit expression of philosophy underlying the endeavors of guidance workers.

The effect of in-service training on improvement of the guidance services . . .

More experimentation in action research by the school staff of a county, city, or building unit.

Development of techniques to quantify and assess the dynamics of the group process in the classroom.

More research on group guidance and group therapy . . .

[42] F. C. Rosecrance and V. D. Hayden, *op. cit.,* pp. 254–255.

The effect of existing curricula and textbooks on attitude formation and problem-solving.[43]

Evaluation and research must not be sold short. It must be at the forefront of the thinking of all elementary school staffs. The importance in research of the teacher working with the specialists in the pupil personnel field must not be minimized. Eaton recommended more use of the case study method in future research dealing with the functions of the school guidance program.[44]

Summary

In this chapter, guidance is defined as *a service or a series of services within or without the classroom that helps to make children more receptive to instruction and to learning.* Guidance may also be defined as an attitude, a process, a point of view, or as a series of approaches. Without question the classroom teacher is the most important person in the guidance program. No other person in the school understands the child as well; no one else can furnish as effectively the feelings of security needed by the child.

Other members of a pupil personnel team include: the school psychologist, the school social worker, the school physician, the nurse, the school dentist, the dental hygienist, and a staff member working in the area of special education. These specialized personnel have the responsibility of helping the teachers, the children, and the parents. Studies indicate that there is a decided increase in the number of specialized pupil personnel functionaries assigned to elementary schools throughout the country. Some of these are full-time employees assigned to specific schools; others are part-time and may work out of a central office.

Although guidance in the elementary schools of this country has evolved slowly as an identified discipline, guidance has been in operation in elementary schools for many years. Wherever there is effective teaching, one will find effective guidance.

This chapter included the following: (1) a description of the essential personnel in a pupil personnel program and the role played by each; (2) a discussion of the fundamental services in the guidance program in an elementary school; and (3) a procedure for helping an elementary staff to evaluate its program.

The services of the guidance program include: (1) the collecting of as much information as possible about each child; (2) the maximum utilization of the data collected; (3) orientation; (4) informational planning in

---

[43] R. D. Willey, *Guidance in Elementary Education,* rev. ed. (New York, Harper and Brothers, 1960), p. 401.

[44] R. E. Eaton, "Learning Theory and Guidance: Three Case Studies and Their Implications," Unpublished doctoral dissertation (Detroit, Mich., Wayne State University, 1960).

the areas of educational, occupational, and personal-social development; and (5) placement and follow-up.

The authors stressed the importance of teachers listening to each child without feelings of alarm, shock, or censure. The establishment of rapport through a genuine feeling of warmth, confidence, interest, and respect; the acceptance of negative feelings; the provision of essential information to be used by the pupil; the development of insight; the testing of hypotheses; and the gradual development of a feeling of independence are the facets of a counseling relationship. Counseling by the teacher is not clinical in nature, but it is of significant importance.

An elementary school staff must be constantly sensitive to the need children have to be helped through the transitional stages of leaving the security of their home for the school setting, passing from one grade to another, and the transition from the security of the sixth-grade classroom to the complexities of a much larger junior high school. These periods of transition may be fruitful experiences for each child, or they may be periods of anxiety, frustration, and conflict. It is the responsibility of the school staff, the Parent-Teacher Association, and other groups to help children meet positively and enjoy these stages of development.

There is no blueprint for the best organizational pattern for the administration of guidance services in an elementary school. In some schools the principal assumes the leadership role; in others the responsibility is accepted by a guidance counselor or other specialized functionary; in others a guidance committee assumes responsibility. Regardless of who assumes this leadership role, however, the teacher is and will continue to be the key figure, and the team approach is probably the most satisfactory answer.

Various procedures for the evaluation of a guidance program were identified. Three basic objectives for any program in the elementary schools include: happier children, more satisfied parents, and more professionally-minded teachers. A research study discussing these objectives was summarized. The authors concluded this chapter with a listing of research that should be done immediately by those working within the elementary school.

STUDENT PROJECTS

1. Survey the literature and list as many definitions of guidance as you can find. From these write what seems to you the best definition applicable to the elementary school program. Compare your definition with those of your colleagues. Justify your answer.

2. If the principal in an elementary school where you were teaching were to assign you to a guidance committee, and to ask you to identify the responsibilities of this committee, what would you say?

3. Visit three elementary schools in your neighborhood. Talk with the principal of each. Ask each principal his reaction to having a school psychologist and/or a school social worker assigned to his school. Summarize his reactions. If necessary, furnish him with essential information upon which he will make his decision. Do you agree with him? Why?

4. Select a young child whom you know, not a member of your immediate family. Talk with him or her about something that is of concern to the child. Employ as many of the suggestions for advising children as you can. Record any reactions of the child you observe and explain the possible reasons for these reactions or changes of feeling during the interview.

5. Suppose a board of education requested you to prepare a report justifying the need for additional guidance personnel in your elementary school? What kinds of information would you submit? What kinds of specific supporting data would you include?

6. An elementary school principal has told you that he does not believe in guidance, that he will have none of it in his school. How would you go about convincing him that effective guidance is already going on in his school?

7. You are assigned the chairmanship of a committee to evaluate the guidance services in your elementary school. What would be your suggestion for a plan of action? What kinds of data do you feel would be necessary to study?

8. A service club in town has requested you to speak at its Thursday luncheon on the title, *The Need for Guidance in the Elementary School*. Prepare a talk for this occasion.

9. Visit several classes in an elementary school and list the examples of effective guidance that result from effective teaching in the various classrooms. Compare your list with those compiled by your classmates.

10. This afternoon your principal asked you to assume the responsibility of an elementary school counselor. How would you define your new position? Be prepared to document your job analysis.

11. You are co-ordinating guidance services in an elementary school. You have been invited to speak to a Parent-Teacher Association meeting to answer the question raised by several parents, "Why do we need a lot of specialists in an elementary school?"

12. Visit an elementary school and study the cumulative record system. Answer the questions that are listed on page 439. What suggestions would you make after this survey?

13. Visit three elementary schools and list the orientation procedures in operation in each school. Talk with teachers and the three principals. List these procedures and make suggestions for an expansion of the program. How would you introduce these new procedures to the schools you visited?

14. Analyze your own professional development. What factors caused you to select the occupation that you did? How do you feel you could have been guided more effectively in terms of educational, occupational, and personal-social information? What kinds of information would you introduce into the elementary grades? Why?

15. Talk to a school psychologist, a school physician, a school nurse, and a school social worker, and do a complete job analysis of each. Indicate clearly and in detail how you believe each can be of specific service to a classroom teacher.

GUIDANCE

16. Select one of the suggested topics for immediate research. Outline the procedure you would follow if you were going to tackle the issue with an elementary school staff. You have classroom teachers, an interested elementary school principal, specialized personnel, and an interested board of education to work with. What would you do?

BIBLIOGRAPHY

Association for Supervision and Curriculum Development, *Guidance in the Curriculum*, 1955 Yearbook (Washington, D.C., National Education Association, 1955).

BARR, J. A., *The Elementary Teacher and Guidance* (New York, Holt, Rinehart and Winston, Inc., 1958).

BONNEY, Merl E., *Mental Health in Education* (Boston, Allyn and Bacon, Inc., 1960).

Board of Education, City of New York, *Guidance of Children in Elementary Schools* (New York, Board of Education, 1956).

BUHLER, C. et al., *Childhood Problems and the Teacher* (New York, Holt, Rinehart and Winston, Inc., 1952).

COTTINGHAM, Harold F., *Guidance in Elementary Schools: Principles and Practices* (Bloomington, Ill., McKnight and McKnight Publishing Company, 1956).

CUTTS, Norma E., ed., *School Psychologists at Mid-Century* (Washington, D.C., American Psychological Association, 1955).

California State Department of Education, *The School Psychologist* (Sacramento, Calif., State Department of Education, 1955).

Department of Elementary School Principals, *Guidance for Today's Children*, 33rd Yearbook (Washington, D.C., National Education Association, 1954).

DETJEN, Ervin W. and DETJEN, Mary F., *Elementary School Guidance* (New York, McGraw-Hill Book Company, 1952).

FINK, A. E., WILSON, E. E., and CONOVER, M. B., *The Field of Social Work*, 3rd ed. (New York, Holt, Rinehart and Winston, Inc., 1955).

FOSTER, Charles R., *Guidance for Today's Schools* (Boston, Ginn and Company, 1957).

FROEHLICH, C. P., *Guidance Services in Schools* (New York, McGraw-Hill Book Company, 1958).

FROEHLICH, C. P., and DARLEY, J. G., *Studying Students* (Chicago, Science Research Associates, 1952).

GORDON, Ira J., *The Teacher as a Guidance Worker* (New York, Harper and Brothers, 1956).

HAMRIN, S. A., *Initiating and Administering Guidance Services* (Bloomington, Ill., McKnight and McKnight Publishing Company, 1953).

HOPPOCK, Robert, *Occupational Information* (New York, McGraw-Hill Book Company, 1957).

HUMPHREYS, J. A., TRAXLER, A. E., and NORTH, R. D., *Guidance Services* (Chicago, Science Research Associates, 1960).

KOUGH, J. and DeHAAN, R. F., *Teachers Guidance Handbook*, Part I, *Identifying Children Who Need Help* (Chicago, Science Research Associates, 1955).

KOWITZ, Gerald T., and KOWITZ, Norman G., *Guidance in the Elementary Classroom* (New York, McGraw-Hill Book Company, 1959).

LINDGREN, H. C., *Educational Psychology in the Classroom* (New York, John Wiley and Sons, Inc., 1956).

MATHEWSON, Robert H., *Guidance Policy and Practice,* rev. ed. (New York, Harper and Brothers, 1955).

McDANIEL, Henry B., and SHAFTEL, G. A., *Guidance in the Modern School* (New York, Holt, Rinehart and Winston, Inc., 1956).

MARTINSON, R. and SMALLENBURG, H., *Guidance in Elementary Schools* (Englewood Cliffs, N.J., Prentice-Hall, Inc., 1958).

MORTENSEN, Donald G. and SCHMULLER, Allen M., *Guidance in Today's Schools* (New York, John Wiley and Sons, Inc., 1959).

MOUSTAKAS, C. E., *The Teacher and the Child* (New York, McGraw-Hill Book Company, 1956).

National Society for the Study of Education, *Mental Health in Modern Education,* 54th Yearbook, Part II (Chicago, University of Chicago Press, 1955).

OHLSEN, Merle M., *Guidance: An Introduction* (New York, Harcourt, Brace & World, Inc., 1955).

PETERS, Herman J. and FARWELL, Gail F., *Guidance: A Developmental Approach* (Chicago, Rand McNally and Company, 1959).

ROEBER, E. C., SMITH, G. E., and ERICKSON, C. E., *Organization and Administration of Guidance Services* (New York, McGraw-Hill Book Company, 1955).

ROGERS, Carl, *Counseling and Psychotherapy* (Boston, Hougton Mifflin Co., 1942).

ROGERS, Carl, *Client-Centered Therapy* (Boston, Houghton Mifflin Co., 1951).

ROSECRANCE, Francis and HAYDEN, Velma D., *School Guidance and Personnel Services* (Boston, Allyn and Bacon, Inc., 1960).

STOOPS, Emery and WAHLQUIST, Gunnar L., *Principles and Practices in Guidance* (New York, McGraw-Hill Book Company, 1958).

TRAXLER, Arthur E., *Techniques of Guidance,* rev. ed. (New York, Harper and Brothers, 1957).

TYLER, Leona, *The Work of the Counselor* (New York, Appleton-Century-Crofts, Inc., 1953).

WARTERS, Jane, *Techniques of Counseling* (New York, McGraw-Hill Book Company, 1954).

WHITE, V., *Studying the Individual Pupil* (New York, Harper and Brothers, 1958).

WILLEY, Roy D., *Guidance in Elementary Education,* rev. ed. (New York, Harper and Brothers, 1960).

WILLEY, Roy D. and ANDREW, D. C., *Modern Methods and Techniques in Guidance* (New York, Harper and Brothers, 1955).

CHAPTER 15

Evaluating, Reporting, and Classifying Pupil Progress

"MY MIND'S MADE UP. Don't confuse me with the facts." This typifies the attitude of those teachers who, in spite of all the evidence, steadfastly refuse to face the obvious and undeniable fact that *each of us is a unique being, different from all others in an infinite number of ways.* These are the unfortunate teachers who see their pupils "with eyes unseeing." In their classrooms, overweight Harry, immature Virginia, volatile Mary, moody Richard, creative Susan, patient Doris and all others conveniently blend and merge into a great commonality labeled "the third grade." Through such a simple expedient as pinning an identical label on all youngsters, these teachers can go happily, if blindly, on their way with no more serious problem than what to do with those contrary youngsters who cannot or will not wear their labels unprotestingly.

Fortunately for most of our elementary school children, such teachers are in the minority; a far greater number accept and understand fully the significance of the fact that "A century of research has provided ample documentation of individual differences in every dimension—physical, social, emotional, and intellectual." [1]

Recognition of the unassailable truth of this statement has resulted in the rapid growth of the elementary guidance movement discussed in the preceding chapter. It has also led to the recognition of some major educational problems, for which no simple nor completely satisfactory solution has yet been found. In general, these problems revolve around such questions as: (1) How can we best measure and evaluate the individual strengths and needs of each pupil? (2) How can we enlist the aid of parents in meeting these needs? (3) How can we organize our school for

[1] W. C. Olson, "Individual Differences: A Precious Asset." *Educational Leadership,* Vol. 15 (December, 1957), p. 142.

a program of instruction geared to meeting these needs and differences? Each of these questions is examined in this chapter.

Section 1: MEASUREMENT AND EVALUATION OF PUPIL PROGRESS

"Are the Professional Test Makers Determining What We Teach?" [2]

"Standardized Tests: How, When, Why?" [3]

"National Systems of Testing Are Harmful to Education." [4]

"Self-Evaluation Increases the Learning Tempo." [5]

Titles such as these, found in current literature, reflect the heated controversy which presently revolves around the broad problem of measurement and evaluation in the elementary schools. Such controversy, however, is certainly not new; there have been enthusiastic supporters as well as critical opponents of measurement and evaluation since the early days of testing. It is, however, true that, for many reasons, there is probably more interest directed toward this problem today than ever before in our history. In general, this interest is directed toward such questions as: (1) What are some clear, concise, operational definitions of terms? (2) What kinds of tests are available at the elementary school level? (3) What criteria should be used in selecting tests? (4) What are the possible strengths of a testing program? (5) What are some important limitations in the use of tests? and (6) What are some guides for the development and implementation of a functional testing program? Each of these is examined on the following pages.

Definition of Terms

Although the terms "testing," "measurement," "appraisal," and "evaluation" are frequently used interchangeably, they do represent different approaches and emphases, as seen in the following definitions.

"Testing" refers to the use of a previously determined or standardized instrument in the study of one or more pupils. Testing includes the two major categories of (1) standardized tests and (2) teacher-made tests. An emphasis on testing in its modern sense developed in this country early in the century and was generated by the increasing interest in the intel-

[2] A. E. Traxler, "Are the Professional Test Makers Determining What We Teach?" *School Review,* Vol. 66 (June, 1958), pp. 144–151.

[3] A. K. Boag, "Standardized Tests: How, When, Why?" *Instructor,* Vol. 65 (October, 1955), pp. 24, 115.

[4] F. Raubinger, "National Systems of Testing Are Harmful to Education." Speech delivered at the Conference of the American Association of School Administrators, February, 1959.

[5] L. Lindberg, "Self-Evaluation Increases the Learning Tempo." *NEA Journal,* Vol. 48 (November, 1959), pp. 21–22.

lectual differences believed to exist among all pupils. Binet and Simon are usually considered the pioneers of the testing movement because of the intelligence test they introduced in this country in 1908. Since then such outstanding educators as Scott, Orleans, Terman, Merrill, Otis, Thorndike and others have attempted to refine the skill of measuring essential characteristics of boys and girls. Since the origin of the movement, however, there have been those who caution against the overuse of tests and those who are suspicious of the ability of tests to measure the many intangibles that educators in a twentieth-century democracy believe are important. "Measurement," therefore, a term with broader implications, has become more commonly used.

Measurement involves the use of other means to secure quantitative results. Measurement refers to the use of tests as well as rating scales, sociograms, and other devices to secure for the measurer a more complete perspective of the child or children being studied. As Noll writes, "a measurement program generally is thought of as having broader and more pupil-centered objectives than a testing program." [6]

Both testing and measurement, however, still seemed limiting terms to many educators. As Willey points out,

> The modern curriculum is interested in the acquisition of concepts, attitudes, interests, and appreciation, as well as personal-social adjustment. . . . Growth in human relationships and development of independence and initiative are not measurable by standardized tests. [7]

Testing and measurement seemed also limited to those traits whose identification could be statistically treated. Hence a still broader term, evaluation or appraisal, found its way into common educational usage.

Evaluation and appraisal involve the use of as many quantitative and qualitative techniques as possible to help the classroom teacher and/or specialist gain a complete picture of each child. Tests are part of the evaluation program but they are not all of it. Test results furnish information but they do not answer all the questions. Evaluation or "appraisal," therefore, is an omnibus term which includes both objective and subjective techniques such as tests, as well as sociograms, anecdotal records, interviews, autobiographies, case histories, and many others. Since most of these, however, were discussed in Chapters Three and Fourteen, the present discussion will be confined to the "testing" aspects of evaluation and the important understandings a classroom teacher should have as he works with both standardized instruments and teacher-constructed examinations.

[6] V. H. Noll, *Introduction to Educational Measurement* (Boston, Houghton Mifflin Co., 1957), p. 12.
[7] R. D. Willey, *Guidance in Elementary Education*, rev. ed. (New York, Harper and Brothers, 1960), p. 165.

Kinds of Tests

The numerous and complex types of tests on the market today make any classification extremely difficult. It seems to the authors, however, that classroom teachers are faced with at least two basic questions: (1) What are the various forms that tests may take in terms of their purpose and function? (2) What are the basic traits of elementary school boys and girls that are commonly measured by standardized instruments?

Tests assume a variety of forms depending on their purpose and function in the educational program. Since we today seem to be concerned with both speed and accuracy, one aim of classroom teachers across the nation is to help their boys and girls learn to work both accurately and rapidly. To test these objectives, we have scaled tests, power tests, speed tests, and those that combine power and speed.

Scaled Tests. A scale or scaled test is an attempt to measure the degree of difficulty in a particular skill or understanding that a boy or girl can achieve satisfactorily. A scale is simply the arrangement of items usually in ascending difficulty, while on a scaled test the items are equally spaced according to statistical treatment and are in ascending order of difficulty.

Power Test. A power test is another term used to identify a scaled test. In a power test the items are arranged in order of increasing difficulty, and each pupil's score is determined from the last question or questions that he answers correctly.

Speed Test. As was indicated earlier, teachers are interested in helping their boys and girls to work rapidly. Speed tests have, therefore, been designed to measure the speed with which each child works. The questions on this type of test are of approximately equal difficulty, sufficiently simple so that no child should have major difficulty with them, and they represent more items than any child will be able to complete. Any carefully timed test that includes questions of increasing difficulty measures both speed and power. Children must be taught, however, that accuracy is more important than speed and that the degree of speed with which one works is directly related to the newness and the difficulty of the task.

The variety of forms into which tests may be classified also includes verbal, nonverbal, and performance tests. This classification is of particular interest to classroom teachers who work with small children or with those boys and girls who have language difficulties.

Verbal Test. Most of the standardized tests found in elementary schools are paper-and-pencil tests that are highly verbal in nature. Directions are written; questions are verbalized; and boys and girls are forced constantly to interpret the written word. This requires a verbal facility not possessed by all children.

Nonverbal Test. To meet this problem and to attempt to gain a fairer measurement of the trait evaluated, educational psychologists have designed nonverbal tests which substitute graphical forms, numbers, and/or three-dimensional objects for the written word. Directions for these tests may be written, or they may be presented to the group in pantomime by the classroom teacher or tester.

Performance Test. Performance tests are another form of nonverbal instruments. They generally involve the manipulation of physical objects or a written response to some form of activity. As in the previous type of test, the directions may be written so that they can be read by the testee, may be read by the tester, or may be presented in pantomime.

An equally common classification of tests is based on a specific function for the classroom teacher. In this category are the survey test, the diagnostic test, and the prognostic test.

Survey Test. Survey tests, as indicated by their name, are comprehensive in nature and are designed to give classroom teachers a general overview of the developmental stages found in their classes. These tests survey many types of skills, understandings, and competencies.

Prognostic Test. A prognostic test is a type of aptitude test in which the general aim is to predict a child's success in a future curricular area:

> As they usually test the background skills and abilities found to be prerequisite for success in the particular subject, prognostic tests are most common among subjects in which success can be rather well defined in terms of certain basic abilities.[8]

Diagnostic Test. A diagnostic test is usually limited to one particular area, and its function is to identify strengths and limitations in a child's level of achievement. Diagnostic tests are generally found in reading and other achievement tests. Readiness tests used with a diagnostic emphasis are found to be more functional than when they are used only with a prognostic interpretation.

Let us now look at a broader and still different kind of classification— group and individual tests, standardized instruments, and teacher-constructed examinations.

Group Test. Any test administered to a group of people may be identified as a group test. This is exemplified by the typical paper-and-pencil tests administered to a class of boys and girls in the modern elementary school. In some cases individual children are not accurately tested by these, and in many schools any kind of discrepancy or peculiarity noted in a child's reactions to a group test is followed by the administration of an individual test.

Individual Test. Individual tests are designed, as their name indicates, to be administered to individuals. The administration of most of these requires additional training and experience on the part of the tester, and

---

[8] H. A. Greene, A. N. Jorgensen, and J. R. Gerberich, *Measurement and Evaluation in the Elementary School,* 2nd ed. (New York, Longmans, Green and Company, Inc., 1953), p. 47.

their administration, scoring, and interpretation are extremely time-consuming. Two of the most commonly used are the New Revised Stanford-Binet Scale and the Wechsler Intelligence Scale for Children. These tests report the following advantages:

> The examiner is able to make judgments concerning the pupil's emotional adjustments, motivation, working habits, physical aspects, alertness, and special interests. The individual test minimizes the errors of measurement due to faulty understanding of directions, lack of interest, and fatigue. These are important factors when testing children under eight years of age.[9]

Standardized Test. A standardized test is one that has been constructed for a large number of people, has been administered to a large population, and whose scores have been translated into norms. A standardized instrument tends to be objective in nature and subject to statistical treatment.

Teacher-Constructed Test. No matter how refined and statistically sound standardized instruments might become, there will always be a need for teacher-made tests. Teacher education programs in the colleges and universities throughout the country offer courses to help future teachers and those in-service to plan, to construct, and to evaluate efficiently their own instruments. As Noll writes, "Clearly no standardized test of achievement can serve the needs and purposes of every local situation." [10] Effective and creative teachers identify many specific goals and objectives that are difficult to measure on a standardized instrument. These would include: critical thinking, interpersonal relations, appreciation, values, and attitudes. This difficulty is particularly true where small children are involved. Thorndike and Hagen stress that these objectives must be translated into "terms of pupil behavior" and must be divided into new categories, "content of the unit" and "process or activities." [11]

The classroom teacher should determine carefully the appropriate type of questions, (such as essay, true-false, multiple-choice, completion, matching) and should then phrase carefully and clearly each of the test items. Boys and girls should be given the experience of answering both discussion and objective questions during the course of the school year, for each type tends to stress different competencies as well as similar understandings and skills. The following cautions should be observed in attempting the difficult task of phrasing questions:

> 1. Keep the reading difficulty of the test items low in relation to the group who are to take the test, unless the purpose is to measure verbal and reading abilities . . .

> 2. Do not lift a statement verbatim from the textbook . . .

[9] R. D. Willey, *op. cit.,* p. 181.

[10] V. H. Noll, *op. cit.,* p. 108.

[11] R. L. Thorndike and E. Hagen, *Measurement and Evaluation in Psychology and Education* (New York, John Wiley & Sons, Inc., 1955), p. 29.

3. If an item is based on an opinion or authority, indicate whose opinion or what authority . . .

4. In planning a set of items for a test, care must be taken that one item does not provide cues to the answer of another item or items . . .

5. Avoid the use of interlocking and interdependent items (for instance, an answer to one question being dependent on the answer to a previous question) . . .

6. In a set of items, let the occurrence of correct responses follow essentially a random pattern. (Don't establish a pattern of correct responses in true-false and multiple-choice questions) . . .

7. Try to avoid ambiguity of statement and meaning . . .

8. Beware of items dealing with trivia . . .[12]

One must also be certain that essay questions are not vague, general, and too comprehensive.

To summarize, therefore, an evaluation program in each elementary school should include scaled or power tests, speed tests, verbal and non-verbal tests, performance tests that are relatively culture-free, survey tests, diagnostic tests, prognostic tests, group tests, individual scales to be used when necessary, standardized instruments, and teacher-constructed examinations. Teachers should have a part in the selection of these tests. The information discussed in this section, however, is equally important for teachers who have no part in the selection, but are involved in the implementation and the interpretation of the evaluation program.

A second manner of classifying tests in the elementary school is to categorize them according to the traits they are designed to measure: academic aptitude, special aptitudes, achievement, and personality or adjustment. Each of these should play an important role in the total evaluation program.

Academic Aptitude Test. The phrase "academic aptitude" to describe the traditional intelligence test has now replaced in many educational centers the term "intelligence," for educational psychologists have identified at least three kinds of intelligence: academic, mechanical, and social. The trait measured by the so-called intelligence test is, in reality, academic aptitude.

Academic aptitude was defined in Chapter Three as: (1) the ability to adjust to one's environment; (2) the ability to cope with materials found on an academic aptitude test; and (3) "the degree of availability of one's experiences for the solution of immediate problems and the anticipation of future ones." [13] It has always been and probably always will be difficult to design a truly effective academic aptitude test, for it is difficult to isolate such variables as reading ability, verbal facility, and items that are culturally dominated. Some attention has been directed during the past

---

[12] *Ibid.,* pp. 51–54.
[13] H. H. Goddard, "What Is Intelligence?" *Journal of Social Psychology,* Vol. 24 (August, 1946), p. 68.

few years toward developing "culturally free," or at least "culturally fair" tests. As Traxler writes:

These tests deserve careful consideration, although greater strength would be lent to the position of the proponents of culture-free tests if it could be shown that the factors making for success in higher education and in the higher level vocations were themselves culture free.[14]

Standardized academic aptitude tests are of at least four types: (1) instruments basically producing only one score, such as the Otis Quick Scoring Mental Ability Tests and the Otis Self-Administering Test of Mental Ability, that yield an intelligence quotient; (2) instruments offering at least two scores, such as the Henmon Nelson Tests of Mental Ability and the Kuhlmann-Anderson Intelligence Tests, that yield a mental age and an intelligence quotient, and the California Test of Mental Maturity that furnishes an intelligence quotient for language factors, one for nonlanguage factors, and one based on the total score; (3) instruments offering scores in multifactors, such as the Science Research Associates Tests of Primary Mental Abilities, including scores for boys and girls between the ages of five and seven in such areas as motor skills, perceptual speed, quantitative skill, verbal meaning and space, and results for youth between seven and eleven in perception, number, reasoning, verbal meaning and space; and (4) culture-free, individual, nonverbal, and/or performance tests, such as the Davis-Eells Test of General Intelligence or Problem-Solving Ability (Davis-Eells Games), IPAT Culture Free Intelligence Tests, Lorge Thorndike Intelligence Test, the New Revised Stanford-Binet Scale, and the Wechsler Intelligence Scale for Children.

These are only examples of the various types of academic aptitude tests that are available at the elementary school level; there are many more excellent tests of each type on the current market. Torgerson and Adams conclude:

Since intelligence-test results are frequently used to judge a child's capacity for academic work, the minimal requirement in mental testing is the administration of repeated group tests of verbal intelligence. Even though verbal tests are measures of scholastic aptitude rather than of general intelligence, they do provide the best single basis for predicting success in the basic skills.[15]

Special Aptitudes. As was indicated earlier, academic aptitude is only one of the many aptitudes possessed by boys and girls with which the school, the child himself, and his parents should be acquainted. These special aptitudes include art, music, and mechanical potentiality.

A standardized instrument suitable for the elementary school to identify potentiality in the area of art is the Lewerenz Tests of Fundamental Abili-

14 A. E. Traxler, *Techniques of Guidance,* rev. ed. (New York, Harper and Brothers, 1957), p. 53.
15 T. L. Torgerson and G. S. Adams, *Measurement and Evaluation for the Elementary School Teacher* (New York, Holt, Rinehart and Winston, Inc., 1954), p. 395.

ties of Visual Arts. This test was originally designed to measure the art abilities developed in public schools. Thus it actually combines both art aptitude and acquired skill. A careful study of the creative attempts of boys and girls in a classroom, however, must supplement any attempt to secure an index to the potential art ability of any child.

Probably the best-known test of this "special aptitudes" type used in the elementary school grades is the Seashore Measures of Musical Talents. This standardized instrument includes phonograph records that permit the tester to measure a child's sense of pitch, intensity, time, tonal memory, rhythm, and timbre.

Two tests that are used in some elementary schools to measure the mechanical aptitude of boys and girls are the Revised Minnesota Paper Form Board Test and the Stenquist Mechanical Aptitude Tests.

The special aptitudes discussed so far in this section are studied particularly in relation to the older boys and girls in the elementary school. Some authors would also list readiness tests as a type of aptitude test, particularly in the areas of reading and arithmetic. Authorities seem to agree, however, that the importance of these readiness tests is greater in the area of diagnostic value than in their use to predict future success in either academic area. The authors of this book have frequently stressed the need to use more than readiness tests to identify any child's readiness for future learning activities.

Achievement Test. According to Traxler, standardized achievement testing in the elementary grades can be divided into four basic types:

(1) tests in which one battery is intended to serve throughout almost the whole range of the elementary school grades, namely the Modern School Achievement Tests designed for grades two through nine and the new "multi-level" edition of the Iowa Tests of Basic Skills for grades three through nine; (2) tests consisting of consecutive or overlapping batteries for different grade levels, such as the Stanford Achievement Tests, the Metropolitan Achievement Tests, the California Achievement Tests, and the American School Achievement Tests; (3) tests having a different battery for each grade level, namely the Coordinated Scales of Attainment; and (4) tests consisting of a lower and higher battery, each covering a grade range and each divided into a number of separate booklets, such as the Iowa Every Pupil Tests of Basic Skills.[16]

It is impossible to indicate generally the best type, for each school staff must decide in terms of the purpose of the testing program, its scope, the degree of precision desired, and the planned utilization of results. Different tests are preferable in different situations.

Personality Test and Adjustment Inventory. The majority of personality tests and adjustment inventories are designed for high school and college youth, but there are some constructed for elementary school youth. They include such instruments as: the California Test of Personality designed for boys and girls in grade four and up; the Rogers Test of Personality

[16] A. E. Traxler, *op. cit.*, p. 77.

Adjustment with a separate scale for boys and girls; and the Guess Who Test. Without any question, evaluation procedures other than standardized instruments should be used in this area, including sociograms, rating scales, observations, anecdotal records, etc. The authors also wish to stress the need for caution in the development of this aspect of the testing program. Specialized personnel and effective public relations are both essential. Incorrect utilization of personality tests and adjustment inventories can result in serious difficulties.

With the multitudinous number of tests published each year, elementary school administrators and testing committees as well as classroom teachers are faced with an overwhelming question—How does one know which tests are effective?

Selection of Tests

This issue should be studied through a two-pronged approach: (1) a careful study of the sources of information about tests and (2) a familiarity with the criteria with which one judges tests.

There are some basic sources of information about standardized tests that can be most helpful. One of the most helpful of these sources is the Buros: *Mental Measurement Yearbooks,* published in 1938, 1941, 1949, 1953, and 1958. These volumes contain factual information, reviews of tests published from the date of the previous yearbook, and bibliographies. This is a very important reference book and should be owned and used by every school staff.

Other sources of information are catalogues from reputable testing companies, specimen sets of tests under consideration, textbooks dealing with testing and evaluation information, reviews found in scientific and professional journals, and the *Psychological Abstracts* and the *Education Index.*

These resources furnish a general overview to tests and test information. Those selecting, administering, and interpreting test results, however, need to be familiar with the important criteria by which one judges a test.

The essential criteria should include: validity, reliability, objectivity, administrability, scorability, comparability, economy, and utility.

Validity. Validity is without question the most important criterion in the selection of tests. It is defined as *the degree to which the instrument measures what it purports to measure.* If an instrument is designed to measure the *utilization* of facts, but it is used to measure the degree to which boys and girls can remember isolated facts, one can easily see how useless the results would be. It is possible also that a test may be highly valid in one situation but have little validity in another. A reading test, for example, could be highly valid in the determining of a child's ability to read with speed and comprehension, but not of high validity in determining the child's vocabulary. In conclusion, tests are valid only to the degree they measure the skill or understanding that they purport to measure and to the degree to which the instrument is used in the situation for which it was designed.

Reliability. Reliability, the second most important criterion, indicates the consistency of a measure or the *degree to which the instrument measures the same trait consistently.* It is of interest to note that a test may be highly reliable, but not valid. A highly valid test, however, will generally be reliable. Let us examine this idea. A test may consistently measure one trait, but the trait may not be the one that the test is purposed to measure. Such a test is reliable but not valid. A test, on the other hand, that measures with high validity what it purports to measure tends to have consistent results. It is, therefore, valid and reliable. The reliability of a test is generally indicated by a coefficient of reliability. Wrightstone, Justman, and Robbins point out that the major procedures for estimating coefficients of reliability are as follows:

(*a*) Administration of two equivalent tests and correlation of the resulting scores, (*b*) Repeated administration of the same test or testing procedures and correlation of the resulting scores, (*c*) Subdivision of a single test into two presumably equivalent halves, each scored separately, and the correlation of the resulting two scores, and (*d*) Analysis of variance among individual items and determination of the error variance from this statistic.[17]

Objectivity. A third criterion in one's selection of standardized tests is the objectivity of the test items. Objectivity is really the inclusion of only those items that two or more scorers would evaluate and would arrive at the identical scores. Personal opinion, bias, or subjective judgment should not alter in any way the resultant scores if the items are truly objective.

Administrability. With the increasing number of boys and girls in the elementary school classrooms, educators are more and more considering the ease of administration in the selection of standardized instruments. If many classroom teachers participate in the testing program, more consistency and possible comparability will result if the instruments selected do not require too close timing, if the test booklets are easy to unfold, and if the directions are basically self-explanatory.

Scorability. Unless a trained psychometric staff is available in a school system, educators must consider the importance of ease of scoring. There is no more certain way to alienate the enthusiasm of teachers toward a testing program than to ask them to burn the midnight oil scoring standardized tests. School staffs should, therefore, look for tests that (1) have scoring keys which necessitate less handling of the test materials; (2) have scoring devices, such as carbon inserts; (3) may be machine scored; and

[17] J. W. Wrightstone, J. Justman, and I. Robbins, *Evaluation in Modern Education* (New York, American Book Company, 1956), p. 47.

(4) advertise any other modern devices that minimize the important but time-consuming job of scoring.

Comparability. The availability of meaningful norms for a given test is extremely important. Educators should look for standardized instruments that have been administered to a large number of people, representing a population similar to that of the school administering the test. Are there norms for the section of the country in which the school is located? Are the norms available for urban and/or rural groups? Wrightstone, Justman, and Robbins suggest:

a. Tables or scales used to report scores should be designed to permit easy and accurate interpretation by the test user.

b. Norms should refer to clearly defined and described populations, or reference groups, such as grade, age, curriculum . . .

c. Although norms may be reported in terms of grade or age groups, it is desirable, also, to provide percentile equivalents or standard scores into which raw scores may be converted.

d. For some use of tests, local norms are more appropriate and important than national, regional, or other group norms.[18]

In a discussion of the importance of comparability should also be included the importance of comparable forms of a given test. If there is only one form of a test, its follow-up effectiveness may be somewhat limited.

Economy. Although economy is placed seventh on the list of criteria in the selection of tests, it is by no means unimportant. Every school system has just so much money to spend in the development of an effective standardized testing program; yet each staff wants to develop the best program possible. Suggestions for economy include: (1) a careful study of testing catalogues from reputable concerns, for the most expensive test is not always the best test in terms of its proposed utilization; and (2) the use of a test for which one can buy answer sheets at one, two, or four cents a copy is often preferable to one for which one must purchase the whole test booklet each time.

Utility. A careful study of the content of a given test and its purpose is extremely important in order for the school staff to determine how effectively the test meets local needs. One good test is preferable to many that only partly do the job. How significant is the contribution that this standardized instrument makes to the total evaluation program?

In summary, each of these criteria is important and should be carefully considered by every elementary school staff either in the selection of new tests or in the re-evaluation of the present evaluation program. Greene, Jorgensen, and Gerberich list eight questions that should be answered:

1. Does this particular test measure the skills, knowledges, concepts, understandings, applications, or appreciations I wish to measure?

[18] *Ibid.,* p. 53.

2. How much time does it take to give the test? Is it long enough to give a reliable and consistent measure?

3. Is it easily and accurately scored?

4. Has it been widely used elsewhere?

5. Does it furnish accurate and extensive norms for comparison and interpretation?

6. Is the interpretation of the scores simple and clear?

7. Do the results point the way to a remedial program?

8. Is the test economical in terms of time and money cost per unit of reliable information furnished by it? [19]

Strengths of a Testing Program

Warters summarizes effectively the strengths that may be attributed to a well-planned testing and evaluation program:

(1) Tests produce certain types of information more economically than some other procedures; . . . (2) objective tests properly administered and scored yield more accurate information than the more subjective techniques; . . . (3) tests provide information in meaningful terms through quantitative descriptions of data; (4) tests aid identification of students in need of special attention; and (5) tests can facilitate the study of growth or change in certain areas.[20]

One must not overlook the fact, however, that each of these previously listed strengths presumes the best utilization of test data. If educators are to accentuate the strengths of a testing program, they must constantly view it in relation to the total evaluation program. They must be guided by definite goals and objectives and must not lose sight of the fact that tests if they are of any value must contribute to the teaching-learning process in very specific ways.

Limitations of a Testing Program

On the other side of the coin are some specific limitations of an elementary school testing program. These must be viewed, however, within the proper perspective, for the degree of limitation depends on the selection, administration, scoring, and utilization of the tests selected. The effectiveness or the limitation of any tool depends on the user.

Traxler effectively summarizes some of the most significant limitations of the technique of objective measurement:

(1) There are important aspects of human behavior as well as important instructional objectives which cannot be evaluated effectively by objective tests available at the present time; (2) test results are influenced significantly by factors, such as motivation, physical condition and emotional tone, which are

[19] H. A. Greene, A. N. Jorgensen, and J. R. Gerberich, op. cit., p. 11.
[20] J. Warters, Techniques of Counseling (New York, McGraw-Hill Book Company, 1954), pp. 18–20.

often inadequately controlled in the test situation; (3) one is frequently misled by operation of unrecognized factors in testing, e.g., the reading-comprehension factor in arithmetic problem-solving tests, the rate-of-perception factor in closely timed tests, or the general-intelligence factor in achievement testing; (4) tests must be employed within the limits of the accuracy and consistency with which they measure whatever they are supposed to measure (no test is perfectly reliable, and practically all tests compromise with regard to validity) . . . ; (5) in the main, objective tests are used to describe performance in terms of comparisons with other individuals (this fact may discourage consideration of the pupil within the framework of his own individual capacities, limitations, and goals) . . . ; (6) objective testing is criticized frequently as being atomistic—that is, as approaching an understanding of the child by searching for bits or parts of behavior which are put together to produce a "whole" personality . . . ; (7) closely related to the limitation just given is that of overemphasis on objectivity . . . (Individual judgment cannot be ruled out of the appraisal process.); . . . and (8) a test score represents a sort of spot check, indicating the individual's status with regard to a particular quality or capacity at a given point in his growth cycle. (Since individuals vary with respect both to rate and to ceiling of growth, it is necessary to apply frequent comparable checks in order to obtain an adequate understanding of the individual.) [21]

Educators must not sell short, however, the importance of tests. They must not be "like the farmer who postpones buying a car 'til them blamed things is perfected." [22] Tests must be viewed in their proper relationship to the total evaluation program, and the evaluation program must be viewed in the proper relationship to the total learning process. "During 1958, about 122 million standardized tests were administered in schools, as compared with 108 million in 1957 and 100 million in 1956." [23] Elementary school administrators and teachers must develop guides for the development and improvement of an effective evaluation program.

Guides for the Development and Implementation of a Functional Testing Program

Space will not permit a detailed listing of all the considerations that should be carefully studied by elementary school staffs in their development and implementation of a functional testing program. Let us consider at this time a few of the most important ones:

1. **A testing program should be co-operatively planned.** Too frequently an administrative unit determines the tests, the dates for the administration of these tests, the deadlines for scoring, and then calmly sits back and expects the teaching staff to make functional use of the results. If a testing

[21] A. E. Traxler, et al., *Introduction to Testing and the Use of Test Results in Public Schools* (New York, Harper & Brothers, 1953), p. 11.
[22] C. C. Ross, *Measurement in Today's Schools*, 2nd ed. (Englewood Cliffs, N.J., Prentice-Hall, Inc., 1947), p. 98.
[23] A. E. Traxler, "Standardized Tests." *NEA Journal*, Vol. 48 (November, 1959), p. 18.

program is to be successful, classroom teachers must identify goals and objectives for their boys and girls, must determine the most appropriate procedures for evaluating these goals, and must clearly foresee the role of each test in the teaching-learning process. Only then will teachers be dynamically interested in an evaluation program.

2. A testing program must possess both short-term and long-term plans. Test results furnish some immediate data which are helpful to classroom teachers as they grade their boys and girls or as they report pupil progress to parents and to the children themselves. An effective evaluation program, however, should be based on more long-range goals and objectives. The evolving educational philosophy of the school system, the long-term goals and objectives, the predicted socio-economic changes in the community, changes in teaching procedures and materials, and any possible change in educational emphasis must be considered. Those selecting tests must remember that it is unwise to change tests frequently, for the data collected may not be comparable. An effective measurement and evaluation program must be carefully planned.

3. An elementary school staff should first determine what specific data they seek. A supplementary step to this would be for the staff to determine which of these data might be best gained via standardized instruments. Before any one is able to select specific tests, however, one must identify what he wishes to measure. It has been stated earlier in this chapter that validity is the most important criterion in test selection. The validity of a test is directly related to how the instrument will be used.

4. Assuming that an elementary school staff knows what data they seek, the next step is to study the various types of tests in order to determine those which will most effectively furnish the desired information. Authorities will generally agree that academic aptitude and achievement testing are the minimal. Staffs might well consider the advisability of studying and supplementing this minimal with the use of special aptitudes tests and tests of personality and adjustment. A truly effective testing program, however, should be no more comprehensive than the utilization of its results. To give a large number of tests and then to store them away in a closet because the personnel is not available to score and to interpret them is an obvious waste of both time and money.

5. Elementary school staffs should study the various criteria in the intelligent selection of tests. There is no advantage for staff members to review specimen sets or to study information about the standardized instruments themselves until they understand what basic items to check. One or more faculty meetings devoted to a study of validity, reliability, comparability, and the other criteria, might prove beneficial in the selection and in the utilization of standardized instruments in the teaching-learning process.

6. **There should be a careful study of as many sources of information about specific tests as possible.** Small study groups can be used effectively in the initiating and in the re-evaluating of testing programs. Teachers must be involved here in the study of tests that might be used and in the understanding of test manuals. Some psychometrists or principals have found it advisable to select parts of a test manual to discuss with teachers rather than to overwhelm them with the lengthy, highly statistical sections.

7. **Assuming that tests have been adequately selected for an elementary school, teachers should be educated to the intelligent utilization of test results.** There is a growing emphasis today on the importance of the testing program in the classroom as a teaching-learning device rather than the use of these standardized instruments at the administrative level.

Teachers should be helped to understand fully: (*a*) what each test measures; (*b*) what the possible limitations are; (*c*) how the data collected may be used most effectively; and (*d*) what additional data are needed in the study of each child's individual growth and development. Overemphasis on test scores, overgeneralization, or the use of test scores merely to substantiate a teacher's preconceived negative attitude toward a child can be extremely dangerous and most unfair. Test data must be used positively and in proper perspective to the total educational program of every school.

8. **Elementary school staffs must constantly re-evaluate their evaluation programs.** Evaluation programs must be evaluated constantly in terms of changing philosophies, teaching emphases and procedures, media of communication, and changes in the community. Great care must be taken that emphasis on the importance of testing does not result in teachers teaching for tests.

Tampering with the scales has never corrected a weight problem, and manipulating an academic environment before a testing session does not provide reliable information about general scholastic achievement.[24]

In summary, the use of standardized tests and teacher-made tests is only one piece in the "jig-saw puzzle" of the elementary school evaluation program, but without it the picture could never be completed. A second important facet is examined in the following section:

Section 2: REPORTING PUPIL PROGRESS TO PARENTS

Most memories of elementary school years eventually become clouded and dim, but few of us have forgotten those awesome and solemn occasions when the teacher stood before the class and announced, "You will now receive your report card for this month." If one's memory goes back to more than fifty years, he probably remembers sitting with folded hands,

[24] C. P. Ramsey, "Testing in Tomorrow's School." *Educational Leadership,* Vol. 17 (May, 1960), p. 508.

heart in his mouth, while the teacher silently distributed small cards of various colors. Great was the relief of those who received a blue card signifying "excellent scholarship and deportment" or a white card which meant "satisfactory" in both these areas. It was, however, a different story for the unfortunate who received a yellow card, for this meant "unsatisfactory" and was often an ominous warning that he might be "put back" to the previous grade. Those with shorter memories may recall similar scenes, differing only in the type of card. In some cases, the card may have contained percentage ratings; in others, alphabetical ratings; or in still others, coded check-marks. Or perhaps it contained none of these but consisted only of a written statement from the teacher. All of these types, and hundreds of variations and modifications have been, and are, found in the elementary schools across the land. The lack of agreement on any one type, however, is not due to mere whim or temperament on the part of teachers and administrators, but is, rather, the result of a conscientious and concerted effort to develop a method of reporting progress compatible with the changing philosophy and broadened objectives of modern education. The purposes, general characteristics, and types of reporting methods which most closely reach this goal are considered on the following pages.

Purposes of Reporting

The major purpose of the report is to promote effective home-school guidance of the pupil. Historically, the report card came into being when schools first realized that they had a responsibility to *inform* parents of their child's progress. To serve this function, it was necessary only to develop some type of efficient method, similar to the multicolored cards previously mentioned, which notified parents that the pupil had earned either the "approbation" or "censure" of the teacher. Today, this function has been broadened and modern methods of reporting provide information, not as an *end* in itself, but as a *means* of enabling the school and home to work co-operatively for the best interests of the child. It is apparent that this broadened purpose demands a thoughtful examination of the *type* and *amount* of information the school should provide as well as a consideration of the best *method* to be used. These are not easy decisions to make; hence, the wide variation of methods in use at the present time.

There are many supplementary purposes of reporting. In addition to the major purpose of reporting, most schools define other specific purposes they wish to achieve. Some of the most commonly mentioned are:

1. *To acquaint parents with the philosophy and objectives of the school.* Many schools feel that the report card is an excellent device for interpreting the school to the parents. One system, for instance, states that one of its purposes in reporting is

To interpret the school to parents—to reflect the fact that the school has clarified its objectives and the report cards should help parents to better understand these objectives.[25]

2. *To establish positive public relations.* The value of a report card as a public-relations instrument is recognized, and capitalized upon, by many modern elementary schools.

3. *To inform the child of his progress.* In a modern elementary classroom, the child should be consistently informed of his progress through a program of continual evaluation and guidance. As part of this continuous guidance, the scheduled report serves two important functions. In the first place, it summarizes, for the benefit of the pupil, his progress during a given period of time. Alexander mentions this as one of the justifiable purposes of reporting in that "the accumulation and summary of facts at reporting time may be very useful in the pupil's own plan for continued, improved progress." [26]

The scheduled report, however, should not only *inform* the pupil of his progress but should serve as a valuable self-evaluation technique. In many schools, through a teacher-pupil conference, the pupil is encouraged to evaluate himself in terms of what should be, or has been, recorded on the report. In other systems, the pupil occasionally writes his own report, either upon a prepared form, or as an informal letter, which is signed by him and the teacher before the parent receives it. Regardless of how it is accomplished, most teachers agree that a primary purpose of the report card is to aid the child in his self-evaluation, and that much of its value is wasted if this function is not realized.

In addition, there are many other purposes of reporting which have been defined by school systems to meet their specific needs. For example, one system lists such additional purposes as

To prevent emotional disturbance and disintegration, and reflect respect for individual personality.

To improve parent-child relationships, rather than serve as an unpleasant barrier.

To result in improvement of instructional services.[27]

It is apparent from this brief discussion, that one of the trends of modern reporting is the broadening of purposes beyond the single objective of imparting information. In order to realize these comprehensive purposes, the reporting method should be characterized by certain essential features. These are examined in the next section.

[25] U. S. Office of Education, Division of State and Local School Systems. *Reporting Pupil Progress to Parents.* Education Briefs, No. 34 (Washington, D.C., U.S. Department of Health, Education, and Welfare. Mimeographed. December, 1956), p. 7.

[26] W. M. Alexander, "Reporting to Parents—Why? What? How?" *NEA Journal,* Vol. 48 (December, 1959), p. 16.

[27] U.S. Office of Education, *op. cit.,* p. 7.

Characteristics of Effective Reporting

The reporting method provides for two-way communication between home and school. Whether it is oral or written, if the report is to achieve its major purpose, it *must* facilitate two-way communication between the home and school. Some written reports achieve this through providing a space for comments from the parents. The conference, of course, achieves it through face-to-face contact. Whatever type is used, the report must be a "two-way communication device" rather than merely a "one-way informational service."

The report card is becoming increasingly comprehensive. The earlier cards tended to be concerned primarily with the pupil's academic progress and secondarily with his conduct. Today, the reporting method attempts to convey a comprehensive picture of the child's total development. This usually includes an appraisal of his academic progress and study or work habits; his social-emotional adjustment and peer relationships; his health and safety needs and habits; his physical well-being as observed by the teacher; and any other personal aspects which are the mutual concern of the parent and teacher.

The report is concerned with the diagnosis of pupil strengths and needs. The modern report is concerned with the "why" of the child's progress as much or more than it is with the "what." It is not, for instance, sufficient to state, either through words or symbols, that "Connie is not doing well in arithmetic." Rather, the teacher should (1) diagnose *exactly* what the cause or source of Connie's difficulty appears to be and (2) report it to the parents with suggestions as to how they may help to remedy the trouble. In comparing the factual report with the analytical or diagnostic report, Ojemann and McCandless found that the latter, which was concerned with the "factors underlying behavior" was more helpful and satisfying to parents than the former. Among the advantages claimed for the analytical card were that it

   . . . stimulated an attitude of confidence in some parents toward the teacher and school

   . . . seemed to develop a friendly link between the parent and the teacher

   . . . seemed more personal and individualistic to some parents

   . . . gave parent and teacher a better background for a more intelligent interview

   . . . stimulated some parents to give more thought to their children's growth and pointed out some characteristics the parents had not fully realized.[28]

The tone of the report is positive, helpful, and constructive. If one keeps the ultimate purpose of reporting in mind, it is easily apparent that a

[28] R. H. Ojemann and R. A. McCandless, "Suggestions for a Fundamental Revision of Report Cards," *Educational Administration and Supervision*, Vol. 32 (February, 1946), p. 115.

positive and constructive report from the teacher will satisfy this goal far more than will a critical, complaining, or negative approach.

The report is concerned with definite and specific information concerning pupil growth. Many authorities warn teachers that they should express themselves in simple language and avoid "pedaguese" when reporting to parents. It has been the authors' experience that, in general, teachers need have little concern about communicating clearly *provided they have something to communicate.* In other words, a sixth-grade teacher who has definite and specific knowledge concerning each pupil's growth, strengths, and limitations will have relatively little trouble in sharing that knowledge with parents. From where does the teacher receive this information? Chapters Three and Fourteen, as well as the present chapter, have examined the numerous channels which should be utilized by the teacher in securing pertinent information concerning his pupils. All of these, in addition to an accumulative folder of the child's work in all curricular areas, should be used by the teacher in preparing an accurate summary of the child's total progress for the parents' report. If this is done, the teacher will find that he does not need to resort to the glittering generalities and vague terminology about which many parents have complained in the past and which, unfortunately, has been labeled "pedaguese" by a critical or uncomprehending public.

The development or revision of the reporting method should be a co-operative enterprise. Practically unanimous is the opinion today that the report, if it is to effect desirable home-school relationships, must be developed co-operatively by parents, teachers, administrators, pupils, and interested community groups. As a matter of fact, the reason given most frequently for the nonacceptance of a reporting method by parents is that they were not involved, from the beginning, in its development. The following steps are suggested as most likely "to guarantee broad acceptance of a plan for pupil progress":

Planning for Study
Making it possible for as many parents and teachers as possible to study and discuss together all elements which underlie the evaluation and reporting of pupil progress;
Providing a way for parents and teachers to explore and evaluate various ways of communicating.

Providing for Exchange of Views
Providing a way for all parents, teachers, and older children to express opinions about philosophy or viewpoints, content, and form of communication;
Study and summarizing these returns.

Developing a Tentative Plan
Providing a way for a widely representative group to define a plan of reporting to be used locally. Devising necessary forms and submitting them to many groups for suggestions and revision until agreements are reached;

Developing tentative forms to be tried out in schools; planning and producing materials to aid the teacher, and planning and producing materials to interpret to parents.

Trying Out the Plan

Soliciting co-operation of school personnel and parents in some local schools to experiment with the plan for a year or two.

Evaluating the Plan

Providing a way to secure parent, teacher, and child reactions and suggestions; Revising the forms to incorporate those ideas the committee agrees upon as important. Determining a calendar of gradual adoption acceptable to parents and teachers.

Planning Ahead

No reporting plan may be looked upon as the final answer. Continuous evaluation should be invited from children, staff and parents, and periodic revision scheduled frequently enough to keep the plan of communication in line with increased scientific knowledge of child development and the changing goals of education.[29]

The report is only one of several media of home-school communication. It is important for the teacher to keep in mind that the reporting method should be supplemented by numerous other home-school contacts in order for both to work together for the benefit of the child. Contacts used most frequently to supplement the regularly scheduled report are home visits, conferences, group meetings, telephone calls, notes, letters, and numerous others depending upon the situation.

The modern school is primarily concerned with the noncompetitive aspects of reporting. The marks entered upon the record card of the past usually indicated the child's standing as compared with other members of his class or with established norms for the grade. Newer philosophies of education have shown the fallacy of this procedure, and most modern reports are primarily concerned with the child's progress *as it is related to his individual ability*. It is true that this change in philosophy has caused considerable confusion among parents (and some teachers) as to the actual meaning of a mark or symbol on the pupil's card. In spite of conflicting practices and opinions, however, it is safe to state here that modern elementary schools are less concerned with reporting the pupil's progress compared with that of others, than they are in evaluating his progress in the light of his own particular strengths, limitations, and needs.

Basic Patterns of Reporting

The following are the basic ways of reporting progress to parents in use at the present time. It should be understood that most schools do not use any *one* pattern but combine features of several to devise a report suitable for their particular needs.

[29] U.S. Office of Education, *op. cit.*, pp. 5–6.

Numerical ratings. The oldest, poorest, and least popular method for reporting progress is the numerical system determined by a hundred-point percentile scale. The limitations and disadvantages of this method are too numerous to be examined in detail here. It should be sufficient to state that, not only does the system contain none of the characteristics of effective reporting previously defined, but it is a completely misleading and futile attempt at accurate evaluation. What, for instance, does a 93 per cent in reading mean? 93 per cent of what? And how is it possible to arrive at such a precise rating of an area as broad and complex as reading? For these reasons, and many others, numerical ratings are used by only a very few elementary schools at the present time.

Alphabetical ratings. The obvious and overwhelming limitations of numerical ratings led most schools to discard them several decades ago in favor of alphabetical ratings (A, B, C, D, E, F). Each of these letters is usually defined in terms of a judgment such as "excellent," "very good," "average," or in terms of numerical equivalents such as A = 91–100; B = 81–90; etc. The letter grades unquestionably permit more flexibility than the numerical ratings but they also present some major problems and limitations. One of the most important of these revolves around the previously mentioned issue of whether the letter should represent the child's achievement in relation to grade norms or whether it should represent his achievement in relation to his own ability. In many cases, as educational philosophy advanced, schools shifted the base of the letter mark from the former to the latter without the understanding or agreement of the parents. The result has usually been hopeless confusion and a complete failure to convey accurately or adequately the meaning intended. In an attempt at clarity, some schools resorted to a dual mark such as B/4 (your child is reading very well on a fourth-grade level) or B/F (your child is working up to his ability but he is still failing!) Other schools abandoned the familiar letters entirely in favor of such categories as O, S, U (Outstanding, Satisfactory, Unsatisfactory) or something similar. Finally, the impasse reached by many schools in attempting to solve this dilemma, together with the fact that the letter grades did not meet other criteria of effective reporting, led them to abandon all letter grades in favor of the check-list card.

Check-lists. Many schools have, and are, attempting to use a check-list on which the pupil's achievement in specific items is indicated by the teacher through the use of S or U, or by the presence or absence of a checkmark. These check-lists obviously avoid some of the problems posed by numerical and alphabetical ratings but, at the same time, present others of their own. Frequently, teachers attempt to give such a comprehensive picture of the child's progress through the check-list that it becomes much too cumbersome and complicated to serve its purpose effectively. Then too, parents have frequently objected to the check-list on the grounds that the S or U does not really give them an accurate indication of their child's progress. Finally, many educators realized that the broader purposes of reporting demanded more than mere manipulation of symbols and many abandoned the symbols entirely for one of the following types of reporting:

Narrative reports. Dissatisfaction with the limitations imposed by the use of any or all symbols led many school systems to abandon all of them several years ago in favor of a pure narrative report. This method uses only a written statement from the teacher to inform the parent of his child's progress. Like the child of the nursery rhyme, this type "when it is good it is very, very good and when it is bad it is horrid!" Advantages of a worthwhile narrative report are mainly: (1) it eliminates the competitive aspects of all marks regardless of what symbols are used; (2) it is more informative and comprehensive than any other type of written report and (3) it is more diagnostic and analytical in that it can report specific strengths and limitations as well as concrete suggestions for parental action.

Unfortunately, the narrative card has often deteriorated, in the hands of lazy or incompetent teachers, to a routine series of nonanalytical statements such as "John is doing good work in arithmetic" or "Susan is improving in spelling." Or, even worse, the narratives have been so completely vague and general that the parents received no help or information at all. At the present time, among those systems which use printed reports, few rely solely upon the narrative statements (except in the primary grades) although most of them use cards which make some sort of provision for a written statement from the teacher.

Parent-teacher conferences. Many forward-looking educators, after establishing the characteristics of effective reporting, wisely decided that a completely satisfactory and adequate report card had never been developed and probably never would be. Thus, the scheduled parent-teacher conference was adopted by many and, on the whole, appears to meet with widespread approval today. Certain recent studies [30] have concluded that, in general, the conference technique is an effective method of reporting pupil progress. And a recent national survey of current practice reports that:

In addition to the practice over many years of using a report card to acquaint parents with a child's progress in school, individual conferences with all parents now appear to be widely adopted. The importance placed on face-to-face con-

[30] B. Haake, *The Effectiveness of the Individual Parent-Teacher Conference Method for Reporting Pupil Progress in Elementary Schools*, Ed. D. Thesis (New York, New York University, 1958). J. P. Robitaille, *An Analysis of the Effect of Parent-Teacher and Parent-Teacher-Pupil Conferences on the Problems of Intermediate Grade Pupils*, Ed. D. Thesis (Storrs, Conn., University of Connecticut, 1959).

ferences as a way of communicating stands out in this survey of methods of reporting pupil progress.[31]

It is important to keep in mind that, although the conference is generally considered to be a superior method of reporting it can, if it is not done correctly, be as ineffective as any other method—perhaps even more so. In general, the value of the conference depends upon the following major considerations:

1. *Careful attention to the mechanics of scheduling.* Problems involving the scheduling of time, place, transportation, and other details, are admittedly difficult, but they are not insurmountable. They must, however, be given careful attention or the conference method is doomed to failure. Moreover, there is no single acceptable plan for administering these details, for much will depend on the local situation. Some schools, for instance, close several afternoons each rating period to permit the scheduling of conferences. In others, substitutes are hired to cover classes while the teachers are in conference. Some conferences are kept to a fifteen-minute interval with a teacher holding as many as eight or ten in an afternoon. In other situations, the conference is approximately thirty minutes and in still others it is "as long as necessary." In general, most educators appear to favor a twenty- to thirty-minute conference, held during the day or alternately on afternoons one marking period and evenings the next. Obviously, most of these decisions should be made in the light of the individual situation, and it should suffice here to repeat that no school should allow the mechanical details to determine the success or failure of the conference method of reporting.

2. *Thorough planning of the content and direction of the conference.* The amount of careful planning which precedes the actual conference is the real key to its success. In many schools, the teachers prepare a careful check-list of items which they want to discuss with the parent. In others they prepare a short written summary of their discussion points *which the parent takes with him when the conference is adjourned.* Regardless of the device which is used, extreme care should be taken that the teacher has (1) planned the content and direction of the conference, (2) identified specific items to discuss with parents, and (3) selected examples of children's work to be shown to parents to illustrate some of the points discussed. One word of warning, however. Often, the teacher plans so carefully what *he* wishes to discuss that he neglects to provide opportunities for the parent to respond and participate. This is extremely unfortunate, and it should be kept in mind that a good conference is not a monologue. On the other hand, in every successful conference the teacher *should* and *must* assume the leadership role in determining its content and guiding its direction.

[31] U.S. Office of Education, *op. cit.*, p. 16.

3. *Inclusion of all vital personnel.* The majority of parent-teacher conferences are today held between teachers and mothers, although many schools are moving in the direction of including other concerned persons. One of the disadvantages of this form of reporting has often been that the father receives only "second-hand" information concerning his child's progress. To avoid this, some schools are scheduling alternate evening conferences or making some other arrangements (providing car-pools and baby-sitters!) so that it is possible for both parents to attend the conference.

The most vitally concerned individual is, of course, the *child* and many schools have broadened their parent-teacher conferences to become parent-teacher-child conferences. The advantages of the triangular conference are many, not the least of which are these: (1) such conferences are an excellent device for promoting self-evaluation on the part of pupils and (2) the child may, when discussing his progress, throw some light upon the situation which will be very revealing and helpful to both parent and teacher. Obviously, it is ridiculous to adhere to any rigid pattern of either dual or triangular conferencing. The sensible approach appears to dictate that the pupil should attend when it is to his advantage to do so, and should not be included when this is not so.

Other interested personnel who may be invited to attend conferences, when it is desirable for them to do so, include chiefly the school nurse, school psychologist, building principal, or guidance worker.

4. *A continuous program of education and evaluation.* It cannot be stressed too strongly that successful conferencing depends upon a *continual* program of parent, teacher, pupil, and community education and evaluation. This can take several forms. Some schools hold a series of group meetings each year to reacquaint parents with the philosophy and procedures of the conference method. Others prepare a handbook, distributed annually, to parents and teachers. Still others ask parents, at the close of each conference, to complete a short evaluation form on the strengths and limitations of the conference as they see them. Also, the evaluations of older pupils are sought and studied by schools who are constantly seeking to improve their conference reporting. Regardless of the methods used, it must be clearly understood that the constant turnover of parents and teachers in any school system makes a continual and consistent program of education and evaluation necessary to a successful conferencing program.

In summary, it should be repeated that conferencing is not a panacea for all the ills of reporting, but it is a highly effective method when used correctly. Evidently, the problems it presents are far outweighed by its values, according to the following summary of a recent survey:

It seems of particular significance that in no system where scheduled conferences have been introduced have they been discontinued, despite the difficulties often encountered in arranging for them. Both parents and teachers have found this means of exchanging information exceedingly valuable and the focus is how to improve the plans for them.[32]

Before leaving this discussion, it may be well to repeat the statement made earlier, namely that *few schools rely solely on any one basic pattern* of reporting progress to parents. Combinations of all types and degrees exist and there is wide variation in practice, even within a single school system, or, occasionally, within a single school. The search goes on and on—for the final and foolproof solution to the problems of reporting has yet to be found.

Section 3: CLASSIFYING PUPILS FOR INSTRUCTION

Although there were sporadic attempts at systematically classifying children for instruction from approximately 1820 on, the opening of the Quincy Grammar School in Boston in 1848 is usually considered to be the beginning of the graded school pattern in this country. The growing numbers of school-age children, the increasing trend toward urbanization, the influence of foreign educational systems, and the growing emphasis upon "efficiency" in business and industry all contributed to the idea of classifying pupils according to grade standards for more efficient instruction. This idea was generally considered to be an improvement over the practice of assigning children of widely assorted ages and abilities to a single room, and one enthusiastic advocate of the graded plan optimistically predicted that it would set the "educational pattern for the next fifty years." The fact that today, more than *one hundred* years later, most elementary schools of the country are organized essentially along this pattern shows that the prediction was actually a gross understatement. If the organizational plan has remained virtually unchanged, however, our educational philosophy and objectives have not. Thus, modern educators are faced with the very serious dilemma of trying to fit a modern educational philosophy into an administrative pattern of the mid-nineteenth century. This "trying to fit a square peg into a round hole" is essentially the cause of the many problems of classification which teachers and administrators face today. In general, these can be considered in two broad categories, namely: (1) How do we classify several groups of children on each horizontal grade level? and (2) How do we determine the basis for moving a child vertically from one grade to the next? Each of these is considered in the remainder of this chapter.

It should be kept in mind that the following discussion does not pertain to children who are extreme social, physical, emotional, or mental deviates and who, according to qualified judgment, cannot profit from the instructional program of a "regular" elementary school classroom. For these chil-

[32] *Ibid.*

dren, special educational facilities must be provided which are not considered in our present discussion.

Bases for Grouping

The problem may be stated very simply. A school has seventy-five third-grade pupils to classify into three groups. All of these youngsters vary considerably in native intelligence, special aptitudes, emotional stability, social maturity, scholastic achievement, physical size and growth, and other aspects too numerous to mention. Which of these should be used as a basis for dividing the total group into class sections?

In general, there are two major schools of thought regarding the problem. The first of these believes that primary consideration should be given to achieving *academic homogeneity* within each group. The second places major emphasis upon the *social balance* of each group. Each of these is considered below:

Grouping upon the basis of intellectual development is commonly called "ability grouping." Several years ago, when educators began to realize fully the wide range of intellectual abilities which existed among school children, they devised several plans to provide for it. One of these was "ability grouping" (also occasionally, but inaccurately, called "homogeneous grouping"). From its inception, the plan was the center of considerable study and controversy. In general, the majority of reliable investigation has shown that ability grouping has more limitations than strengths *in the elementary school.* One of its major weaknesses is that the desired academic homogeneity is really a will-of-the-wisp which can never be achieved because of widely varying abilities within each individual. Early studies such as those of Keliher and Burr showed rather conclusively that, in spite of the most careful screening, wide ranges still existed within each class and overlapping between classes was unavoidable. These studies concluded that

. . . the writer questions the desirability of homogeneity as it is striven for in any general sense, and contends that the specific nature of abilities makes such a general homogeneity impossible of natural achievement. If it is unnatural, then the attempt to achieve it will have unnatural results.[33]

The conclusion that can be drawn here is that groups in these field situations, as they are taught at the present time, are not homogeneous and there is no way of forming homogeneous groups except with respect to one subject at a time, and even then the groups will not be entirely homogenous in the different phases of that one subject.[34]

[33] A. V. Keliher, *A Critical Study of Homogeneous Grouping* (New York, Bureau of Publications. Teachers College, Columbia University, 1931), p. 91.
[34] M. Y. Burr, *A Study of Homogeneous Grouping* (New York, Bureau of Publications, Teachers College, Columbia University, 1931), p. 41.

Another concern of those opposed to ability grouping is its negative effects upon the social development and adjustment of children. Not all studies have revealed a correlation between poor social attitudes and ability grouping, but enough have done so to warrant the serious attention of the teacher. Mann's recent study, for instance, revealed the negative effects of ability grouping upon the self-concepts of fifth-grade children. She reports that twenty-five of thirty children in a "high" group, when asked why they thought they were placed in that group, gave positive responses in terms of ability or achievement such as "I'm smart," "I work hard," or "We're smarter." Fourteen of eighteen children placed in the lowest of four ability groups gave as their reasons for this placement such negative responses as "I am not so smart," "I don't think so good," "Most of us are lazy," or "I'm too dumb." Mann concludes:

Because of the negative attitudes such as those revealed by the "low" group in this study, ability grouping was abandoned in the thirties. Are we going to repeat the same mistakes in the sixties? [35]

The undemocratic implication of "segregating" children according to intellectual ability is another basis for much opposition to this plan. Many people argue that the strength of a democracy lies in the diverse talents and abilities of all of its citizens and that these must be represented in any class group formed upon democratic principles. An interesting aspect of this point is presented by Bettelheim who argues that segregation on the basis of the intellect will inevitably result in general, if not absolute, segregation of color and/or social class. He states that this is true, not because one group is innately superior to the other, but because of the background and experience which it has in its favor. He claims that those who advocate ability grouping wish "to replace the white-color elite with an even more securely established and more up-to-date elite—the white-collar elite." [36]

There are, of course, many other arguments opposing ability grouping as well as some favoring it, and no attempt is made here to present a complete summary of all aspects of the problem. It is, however, fairly safe to conclude that, although there is some evidence of renewed interest in this basis of grouping, at present the preponderance of research and opinion does not favor it for children of elementary school age.

Varied bases are used to achieve a desirable social balance in each classroom. In most elementary schools, class groups are formed which enable each child to become a worthy, respected, contributing, and achieving member, regardless of his intellectual prowess. In order to accomplish this purpose, varying bases are used, namely:

1. *Chronological age.* Many schools maintain that the highest degree

[35] M. Mann, "What Does Ability Grouping Do to the Self-Concept?" *Childhood Education,* Vol. 36 (April, 1960), p. 360.
[36] B. Bettelheim, "Segregation: New Style," *School Review,* Vol. 66 (Autumn, 1958), p. 264.

of social balance can be attained by grouping children upon the basis of chronological age. Ketcham defends this method in the following statement:

Since chronological age is the only common predictable characteristic about a given group of children and since it is the basis on which they are admitted to school, it is the best basis for grouping *most* children.[37]

2. *Social maturity.* Since the calendrical age is not always an accurate indication of social maturity, many educators prefer the latter as a basis for grouping. Shane reports "an apparent trend favoring 'social maturity' grouping" among thirty-five outstanding school systems scattered throughout the country. He states that:

Eighteen percent of the schools indicated that the estimated social adjustment or maturity of children was their main criterion for assigning them to particular unit classrooms within a given grade level.[38]

3. *Sociometric choices.* In recent years, some schools have followed a plan of grouping according to sociometric choices of pupils. One report of such a plan is described as follows:

Sociometric choices were used as the basis for assigning seventh and eighth grade pupils to classes. Each pupil was asked before school was out in June to name three people with whom he would like to be in next year's class. He was then asked to name anyone with whom he would not like to be. The pupil was told that he would be with at least one of his three choices if at all possible.

Classes were organized around the selected leaders. It was often necessary to place several leaders and their supporters in one class. The supporters for the leaders were pupils who indicated mutual choices with the leader.

The leaders and their followers formed the nucleus of the class around whom those with few rejections were placed. The highly rejected were placed with their first choices if they had not been rejected by that choice. They were placed in the group where they would meet the least hostility.

Often small groups had formed to further a common interest or for protection; these groups were left together.[39]

This method is well accepted by a number of "outstanding" school systems according to Shane who says, "a substantial number of good schools apparently are attempting to use the judgment of teachers and various sociometric devices in order to bring together children who seem likely to work well together as a group."[40]

4. *"Chance" grouping.* Some educators feel that the most realistic social order of a group may be attained best through pure "chance." Advocates of

[37] W. A. Ketcham, "How Should We Look at Levels—From Child Growth and Development," *Childhood Education,* Vol. 32 (December, 1955), p. 159.

[38] H. G. Shane, "Grouping Practices Seem to Favor Composite Plan," *Nation's Schools,* Vol. 49 (May, 1952), pp. 72–73.

[39] "Sociometric Grouping," *California Journal of Elementary Education,* Vol. 27 (November, 1958), pp. 102–103.

[40] H. G. Shane, *op. cit.,* p. 73.

this basis form class groups by "pulling names out of a hat," by alphabetical order, or by any other chance device which will insure a wide heterogeneity of abilities and needs within any single class.

It is apparent that, regardless of which base is used, primary emphasis upon the social cohesiveness of the group will result in a wide range of academic abilities and achievements. If all of these abilities are challenged by a program characterized by: (1) flexible intraclass grouping for innumerable purposes and activities; (2) the use of a wide variety of instructional tools and materials; (3) the recognition of differentiated goals and needs; and (4) the continual diagnosis of individual strengths and limitations, there will be no need for concern that the more advanced will be "held back" by the slower pupils. Nor need there be anxiety lest the intellectually superior be "bored" by a program geared only to the average. As Cook aptly states:

> If the educational procedure of a class is such that the bright pupil is bored and unstimulated, we may be certain that the pupils of medium ability and of low ability are equally bored. A teacher who understands modern methods of instruction, working with a class of limited size and with adequate instructional material —especially books, books, and more books—makes a class exciting for the bright, the dull, and the average.[41]

The second problem of pupil classification is concerned with the method of advancing pupils from one grade level to the next. This is discussed in the following section:

Theories of Promotion

Schools throughout the country are today operating upon one of four promotional theories in assigning children each year to specific grade levels. These are known by a variety of names, but for purposes of our discussion, we will refer to them as: (1) The Grade-Standard Theory; (2) The Automatic Promotion Theory; (3) The Guidance Promotion Theory; and (4) The Theory of Continuous Progress. Each of these is examined here.

The Grade-Standard Theory. The traditional graded school was, and is, organized on the theory that children must meet certain definite standards of academic achievement in order to be promoted to the next grade level. It was assumed that adherence to these standards would insure reasonable scholastic conformity at each grade level. Children who met the adult-imposed standards were rewarded by being permitted to proceed to the next grade while those who failed to meet them were forced to repeat the grade until they did. It is a matter of record that strict enforcement of this theory resulted in children repeating the same grade as often as nine times! Today, this theory is attacked strongly on two basic points; namely, that (1) it is wholly incompatible with our modern philosophy of educa-

[41] W. W. Cook, "The Gifted and the Retarded in Historical Perspective," *Phi Delta Kappan*, Vol. 39 (March, 1958), p. 251.

tion and (2) research has shown that it has none of the advantages claimed for it. Concerning the first of these, Burton says,

Failing a pupil under this standard is as absurd as to tell a child on his ninth birthday that he cannot be nine because he has not grown so tall or so heavy as the other children in the neighborhood. No one would think of making a child "repeat" his ninth year of life but schools constantly require pupils to "repeat" a grade in which the pupil has *already done as well as his ability and strength permit him to do.*[42]

Concerning the second point, the majority of evidence substantiates the following statements:

1. *Adherence to rigid grade standards does not reduce the range of academic performance within a certain grade.* Concerning this point, Heffernan's summary of research states:

On the whole, the results of nonpromotion are shown to be not greater mastery of subject matter, but less; not greater homogeneity of mental ability in the grades, but greater diversity.[43]

2. *Adherence to rigid grade standards does not result in greater academic achievement on the part of those not promoted.* Among the many statements which substantiate this claim are the following:

Failure, in the form of nonpromotion, as a device to ensure greater mastery of elementary school subject matter does not appear justifiable in the light of findings of this investigation. From the results reported, it would seem that slow learning children who are required to repeat a grade and slow learning children who are promoted, ultimately perform at about the same level when this performance is measured in the same higher grade, in spite of the fact that the failed pupils have each spent an added year in attaining this higher grade.[44]

. . . the results of this study suggest that in a school system where a relatively rigid system of grade placement of both pupils and content exists, low-achievers in the language arts are likely to do as well when they are promoted as when they are nonpromoted.[45]

It may be concluded that nonpromotion of pupils in elementary schools in order to assure mastery of subject matter does not often accomplish its objectives. Children do not appear to learn more by repeating a grade but experience less growth in subject matter achievement than they do when promoted.[46]

[42] W. H. Burton, *The Guidance of Learning Activities,* 2nd ed. (New York, Appleton-Century-Crofts, Inc., 1952), pp. 624–625.
[43] H. Heffernan and others, "What Research Says About Nonpromotion," *California Journal of Elementary Education,* Vol. 21 (August, 1952), p. 24.
[44] W. H. Coffield and P. Blommers, "Effects of Nonpromotion on Educational Achievement in the Elementary School," *Journal of Educational Psychology,* Vol. 47 (April, 1956), p. 249.
[45] W. H. Worth and J. H. Shores, "Does Nonpromotion Improve Achievement in the Language Arts?" *Elementary English,* Vol. 37 (January, 1960), p. 52.
[46] C. M. Saunders, *Promotion or Failure for the Elementary School Pupil?* (New York, Bureau of Publications, Teachers College, Columbia University, 1941), p. 29.

3. *Nonpromotion has negative effects upon the social development of children.* Sandin's study of this question concludes:

The total findings in this study combine to show that the slow-progress children in general were less favorably adjusted socially in their class groups than were their classmates. Moreover, they exhibited behavior and attitudes which left much to be desired and which indicated that for most of them school life was not a happy one.[47]

And Goodlad says:

The total body of evidence suggests the closer affiliation of undesirable social and personal adjustment characteristics with nonpromotion than with promotion.[48]

4. *Failure usually has been found to have a devastating effect upon the personal development of children.* To many adults, failure is a stimulus which leads to renewed effort and eventual success. This is *not* true of children who, for the most part, are seriously and often permanently damaged by failure for which they are not responsible.

Failure may be a usual and necessary part of adult life, and adults may develop a number of ways to cope with it, but the continuous and disastrous failures that accompany some children throughout their school careers, with no acceptable escape from the situation, may have serious effects on the child's personality.[49]

Many other statements and studies, similar to those quoted above, convinced most elementary educators of the negative effects of adhering closely to grade standards in determining promotion. The result has been a steady decline in the percentage of retention over the years. Much of this decline, however, is explained by adoption of the following theory:

The Automatic Promotion Theory. The harmful effects of nonpromotion induced many educators to adhere to a 100 per cent promotion policy, occasionally called "social" promotion. Adoption of this theory was "an easy way out" for many uninformed teachers and administrators. It placated the parents and relieved the teachers of the responsibility of making decisions based upon the careful diagnosis and thorough knowledge of each pupil's needs and capacities. The fact that it recognized *no* distinction among pupils but rather herded them all together in one solid mass movement throughout the entire six or seven years of the elementary school apparently bothered these uncritical teachers and administrators not a bit. Fortunately, this theory is, today, as uncommon as the grade-

[47] A. A. Sandin, *Social and Emotional Adjustments of Regularly Promoted and Nonpromoted Pupils* (New York, Bureau of Publications, Teachers College, Columbia University, 1944), p. 135.

[48] J. I. Goodlad, "Some Effects of Promotion and Nonpromotion upon the Social and Personal Adjustment of Children," *Journal of Experimental Education,* Vol. 22 (June, 1954), p. 325.

[49] "Pupil Failure and Nonpromotion," *NEA Research Bulletin,* Vol. 37 (February, 1959), p. 16.

standard theory for both have been generally replaced by a third promotional theory.

The Guidance-Promotion Theory. Sometimes called the "organismic" theory of promotion, this method demands that an individual decision be made for *each* pupil upon the basis of *total growth*. In many cases, the decision will be made that, regardless of his academic standing, the pupil will profit from advancing to the next grade level with his classmates. On rare occasions a pupil, whose social maturity, physical development, emotional stability, and intellectual ability are accelerated beyond his calendrical age may progress faster than the average one-year-in-a-grade rate. On other fairly rare occasions a child may profit from spending a second year in one grade. When this is the case, however, the child should be considered as neither "repeating" nor "failing." A second year in the same grade should not be a mere repetition of the preceding year for *any* pupil. Different experiences, new texts, and varied activities *must* be offered to the retained pupil in order that he profit from his second year. Then too, the concept of "failure" should not be permitted to enter the picture. The child *failed* nothing. Rather, he is assigned to the same grade level for a second year because, in the opinion of all concerned—including the parent, teacher, principal, psychologist, and usually the child himself—he will profit most from this placement.

This theory of promotion can, and does, work to the advantage of all concerned when implemented properly. Unfortunately, it has some limitations, one of which is the difficult task of educating parents, laymen, (and some pupils) to its fundamental value. It is often extremely difficult, as many teachers and administrators know, to convince a heartbroken parent or tearful child that he will profit more by staying in the same grade another year than by proceeding to the next higher level. Although this theory, therefore, is usually considered to be the most valid for determining the rate of pupil progress in the traditionally graded school, its limitations have led some educators to investigate a more experimental approach to the problem, described below.

The Theory of Continuous Progress. In recent years, some educators have concluded that the traditional organization of the graded school does not, and cannot, permit the pupil to make steady and unbroken progress according to his own varied abilities. Thus, some interest has been directed toward nongrading the elementary school. This is a fairly recent educational innovation according to Goodlad and Anderson who state, "As late as 1949 the nongraded school concept was virtually a professional secret." [50]

The nongraded school is, in brief, an attempt to dissolve completely the traditional grade barriers, thus permitting a child to continue at his own rate through a large "block" of the elementary school. In most cases, this

[50] J. I. Goodlad and R. H. Anderson, *The Nongraded Elementary School* (New York, Harcourt, Brace & World, Inc., 1959), p. 56.

"block" is formed on the primary level and consists of what was formerly the kindergarten, first, second, and perhaps third grade. A pupil, depending upon his ability and maturity, might complete this primary unit in three years, four years, five years, or three and one-half years. He is then advanced to the fourth grade or, in completely nongraded schools, to the intermediate or upper unit which might consist of what was formerly the fourth, fifth, and sixth grades. At no time is he "promoted," "failed," or held to rigid grade standards.

It is easily apparent, even from this capsule description, that the plan offers some outstanding advantages as well as some serious problems. These have been summarized as follows:

MAJOR ORGANIZATIONAL ADVANTAGES OF THE NONGRADED SCHOOL

1. The nongraded school provides a single, unbroken learning continuum through which pupils progress. No longer are the school years divided into several parts of equal length, each with its own content and own requirements to be met. There are no predetermined barriers.

2. The nongraded school encourages continuous, individual pupil progress. Bright children do not mark time at grade barriers, waiting for their slower classmates to catch up. Slow children do not struggle in frustrated desperation to reach barriers that lie beyond their capabilities. Such artificial but nonetheless consequential hurdles have been removed.

3. The nongraded school encourages flexibility in pupil grouping. Billy is placed in a group not out of respect for artificial grade standards but out of respect for Billy. He is placed in the setting thought to be best suited to his abilities, attainments, and general maturity. He is moved when it becomes apparent that another setting would be even better suited to Billy's needs and abilities.

PROBLEMS ARISING OUT OF THE CREATION OF NONGRADED SCHOOLS

1. High among these problems is the difficulty of aligning graded and nongraded units or schools. For example, where there is only a primary nongraded unit, it must be related effectively to the grades above. Where the entire elementary school is graded, it must be related effectively to the graded junior or senior high school.

2. Another significant problem grows out of the fact that elementary school curriculum guides are generally organized around a series of topics that follow one another in a graded sequence. Changing to a nongraded structure does not automatically change the organization of either the course of studies or the curriculum of a specific school. Unless changes are made, the curricular pattern and school structure will be incompatible.

3. . . . with nongraded structure, emphasis is given to the fact that children's attainments spread out far and wide over what were formerly several grade levels. The teacher comes to see not only that the spread from top to bottom in

the whole group is tremendous but also that there is considerable spread from subject to subject in a single child's achievements. . . . The problem of setting up classroom arrangements wherein pupils and subject matter are brought together in meaningful relationship appears staggering [to the teacher].[51]

At the present time, it is impossible to gauge the success or validity of the nongraded school because of the wide variation which exists among those systems which have tried it. Some have instituted only the primary nongraded unit, the operation of which differs radically from system to system. Some have experimented with a completely nongraded organization throughout the entire elementary school. Some have tried the new plan and have already returned to the traditional graded structure. Some are now in the process of changing over to the nongraded plan.

In conclusion, there seems to be little disagreement among educators that the elementary school should be geared toward the concept of continuous progress rather than toward the older grade barrier idea. Whether the nongraded school, in its present form, is the best implementation of this concept is a question which only continued investigation and experimentation will answer.

Summary

The present chapter was concerned with the wide range of individual differences which exist among all elementary school children and their implications upon the evaluation, reporting, and classifying of pupil progress. The first section defined the terms "testing," "measurement," "evaluation" and "appraisal." It was stated that evaluation is a comprehensive term which includes the use of such instruments as sociograms, case studies, autobiographies, anecdotal records, and many others as well as standardized and teacher-made tests. Since most of these were discussed fully in Chapters Three and Fourteen, this section was limited to the basic understandings a classroom teacher should possess concerning a sound and modern elementary school testing program.

The types of tests, when classified according to *function* included scale, power, and speed tests; verbal, nonverbal, and performance tests; survey, diagnostic, and prognostic tests; group and individual tests; and the standardized and teacher-made tests. Classified according to the *trait* measured, there are academic aptitude tests, achievement tests, special aptitude tests, and personality tests and adjustment inventories.

The careful selection of tests was emphasized as a very important responsibility of every elementary school staff. Criteria for the selection of tests were examined and included validity, reliability, objectivity, administrability, scorability, comparability, economy and utility.

The strengths and limitations of a modern testing program were dis-

[51] *Ibid.*, pp. 212–213.

cussed and eight guidelines for the development and implementation of a successful program were offered.

The second section dealt with the purposes and patterns of reporting pupil progress to parents. The major purpose was considered to be *the promotion of effective home-school guidance of the pupil.* It was suggested that certain definite features characterize reporting methods which accomplish this purpose. The basic patterns of reporting in use at the present time were examined as to their advantages and disadvantages. Those considered were numerical ratings, alphabetical ratings, check-lists, narrative reports, and parent-teacher conferences. It was concluded that the parent-teacher conference most nearly meets the broad purposes of modern reporting although certain cautions must be observed in order that its potential value be realized. These were examined at the close of the section.

The last section was concerned with the methods of classifying children for instruction. The first consideration was directed toward grouping of children on a single horizontal grade level. Two basic schools of thought on this problem were examined, namely: (1) grouping according to academic homogeneity and (2) grouping according to social balance. It was concluded that the majority of reputable evidence is definitely in favor of the latter for elementary school pupils.

The Grade-Standard Theory, the Automatic Promotion Theory, the Guidance Promotion Theory, and the Theory of Continuous Progress were examined as to their compatibility with present-day educational philosophy and goals. It was concluded that the theory of continuous progress meets with almost unanimous approval among modern elementary educators, although the ideal school organization for implementing it has probably not yet been developed.

STUDENT PROJECTS

1. Visit an elementary school and learn what its total testing program is. Visit several classrooms and talk to elementary teachers to learn how the test results are used. List these and other ways you believe that the results could be effectively utilized.

2. You are the chairman of the program committee of the Parent-Teacher Association. You have been asked to devote one meeting to the topic of reporting pupil progress to parents. Write the script of a short skit which could be used to show, in a novel manner, the changes in purpose and pattern which have occurred in this area in the past fifty years.

3. Select a curricular area, such as reading, arithmetic, social studies, etc. Study carefully the tests that are available in this area as reviewed in Buros' *Fifth Mental Measurement Yearbook.* Select two of the tests listed and defend your selection, including a discussion of the criteria listed on pages 470–473 of this book.

4. Which base or bases mentioned in this chapter would you use to group according to social balance? Prepare a convincing paper to support your position.

5. You are a principal of an elementary school and have requested funds for the purchase of additional tests for your school. You already have one academic aptitude test and one reading test. Prepare a presentation for the board of education justifying your request. Indicate clearly what tests you desire.

6. Visit several classes in an elementary school and list as many evaluative procedures other than testing as you can that you observe in the classroom. Show why these procedures are needed. List carefully instructional outcomes that you observed that could not be measured by standardized instruments.

7. The "continuing teacher plan," sometimes called "teacher cycling" is claimed by some to be superior to the traditional one-teacher-per-grade organization. Investigate this plan thoroughly and prepare a report on its advantages and disadvantages. Do you have any first-hand knowledge of this plan in action? If so, ask the teachers engaged in it for their opinions. Include these in your report.

8. Prepare a test for one of your college classes following the steps that are presented in this chapter to help teachers to prepare better teacher-constructed examinations. Ask three members of your class to evaluate your test.

9. Talk with several elementary school principals and, if possible, a school superintendent. Are they in favor of the nongraded school in its present form? What do they see as its major advantages and weaknesses? What do they predict for the future as far as the over-all organization of the elementary school is concerned. Do you agree?

10. Collect the report cards from several school systems in your state. What consistencies do you note? What differences? What purposes of reporting do these cards appear to reflect? Write a complete evaluation of the methods used, according to the criteria stated in this chapter.

11. Study textbooks, testing catalogues, the *Fifth Mental Measurement Yearbook,* and other sources of information and select two examples of each of the kinds of tests defined in this chapter on pages 464–470. Show how you would use each of the types in a teaching-learning process.

12. Comment upon the following statement. What implications does it hold for present-day elementary education? What responsibilities for the elementary school teacher does it imply?

It is an over-simplification to conclude . . . that researchers are *against* and philosophers are *for* ability grouping. Yet, the strongest arguments against grouping are based on research, while the strongest arguments for it are based on a kind of intuition.[52]

13. Write an editorial defending or criticizing the development of a nation-wide or statewide testing program. Document each of your statements carefully.

14. Interview a superintendent, a principal, a classroom teacher, and a parent to determine what each one believes to be the two most important goals of a testing program. Compare your answers with those gained by other members of your class who participated in the same assignment.

15. You have been asked to serve on a panel to discuss the topic "The Place of Competition in the Elementary School." What opinion will you express? Is there a place for competition in the elementary school? Of what type? How will you react to the statement that the elementary school child should experience both competition and failure in order to prepare him for "real life?"

[52] "The Thorny Garden of Ability Grouping," *Overview,* Vol. 1 (June 1960), p. 38.

BIBLIOGRAPHY

ANASTASI, A., *Psychological Testing* (New York, The Macmillan Company, 1954).

BEAN, K. L., *Construction of Educational and Personnel Tests* (New York, McGraw-Hill Book Company, 1953).

BRADFIELD, J. M. and MOREDOCK, H. S., *Measurement and Evaluation in Education* (New York, The Macmillan Company, 1957).

BUROS, O. K., *Fifth Mental Measurement Yearbook* (Highland Park, N.J., Gryphon Press, 1958).

BURTON, W. H., *The Guidance of Learning Activities*, 2nd ed. (New York, Appleton-Century-Crofts, Inc., 1952).

D'EVELYN, K. E., *Individual Parent-Teacher Conferences* (New York, Bureau of Publications, Teachers College, Columbia University, 1945).

ELSBREE, W. S., *Pupil Progress in the Elementary School* No. 5 (New York, Bureau of Publications, Teachers College, Columbia University, 1949).

GOODLAD, J. I. and ANDERSON, R. H., *The Nongraded Elementary School* (New York, Harcourt, Brace & World, Inc., 1959).

GREENE, H. A., JORGENSEN, A., and GERBERICH, J. R., *Measurement and Evaluation in the Elementary School*, 2nd ed. (New York, Longmans, Green and Company, 1953).

HESTON, J. G., *Learning About Tests* (Chicago, Science Research Associates, 1955).

HOPPOCK, Anne S., *All Children Have Gifts*, Bulletin 100 (Washington, D.C., Association for Childhood Education International, 1958).

LINDQUIST, E. F., *Educational Measurement* (Washington, D.C., American Council on Education, 1951).

NOLL, Victor H., *Introduction to Educational Measurement* (Boston, Houghton Mifflin Company, 1957).

ODELL, C. W., *How To Improve Classroom Testing* (Dubuque, Iowa, William C. Brown Company, 1953).

REMMERS, H. H., and GAGE, N. L., *Educational Measurement and Evaluation*, rev. ed. (New York, Harper and Brothers, 1955).

ROSS, C. C. and STANLEY, J. C., *Measurement in Today's Schools*, rev. ed. (Englewood Cliffs, N.J., Prentice-Hall Inc., 1954).

ROTHNEY, J. W. M., *Evaluation and Reporting Pupil Progress. What Research Says to the Teacher*, Department of Classroom Teachers (Washington, D.C., American Educational Research Association, National Education Association, 1955).

SHANE, H. G. and McSWAIN, E. T., *Evaluation and the Elementary Curriculum*, rev. ed. (New York, Holt, Rinehart and Winston, Inc., 1958).

STRANG, Ruth, *Reporting to Parents* (New York, Bureau of Publications, Teachers College, Columbia University, 1952).

TORGERSON, T. L. and ADAMS, G. S., *Measurement and Evaluation for the Elementary School Teacher* (New York, Holt, Rinehart and Winston, Inc., 1954).

THORNDIKE, R. L. and HAGEN, E., *Measurement and Evaluation in Psychology and Education* (New York, John Wiley and Sons, 1955).

TRAVERS, R. M. W., *Educational Measurement* (New York, The Macmillan Company, 1955).

TRAXLER, A. E. *et. al.*, *Introduction to Testing and The Use of Test Results in Public Schools* (New York, Harper and Brothers, 1953).

TRAXLER, A. E., *Techniques of Guidance,* rev. ed. (New York, Harper and Brothers, 1957).

WARTERS, Jane, *Techniques of Counseling* (New York, McGraw-Hill Book Company, 1954).

WILLEY, R. D., *Guidance in Elementary Education,* rev. ed. (New York, Harper and Brothers, 1960).

WRIGHTSTONE, J. W., *Class Organization for Instruction. What Research Says to the Teacher,* Department of Classroom Teachers (Washington, D.C., American Educational Research Association, National Education Association, 1957).

WRIGHTSTONE, J. W., *What Tests Can Tell Us About Children* (Chicago, Science Research Associates, 1954).

WRIGHTSTONE, J. W., JUSTMAN, J., and ROBBINS, I., *Evaluation in Modern Education* (New York, American Book Company, 1956).

PART V

Projecting Trends of the Future

CHAPTER 16

Elementary Education: Present and Future

And in today already walks tomorrow.

SAMUEL COLERIDGE

THREE CENTURIES OF PROGRESS, marked by struggles, compromises, and achievements have contributed to the development of the modern American elementary school. It is, perhaps more than any other institution, a monument to the aspirations, dreams, and visions of a people dedicated to the democratic belief. Its existence and worth are based upon a single idea—that *all* of the children of *all* of the people should be offered an educational opportunity which will enable each to develop to the limits of his potential. This is not an easy task; on the contrary, it is one of breathtaking magnitude and complexity. The extent to which it is presently accomplished varies in as many degrees as there are individual schools. Without doubt, some elementary schools today are doing a magnificent job. Unfortunately, others are falling far short of their goals. But even if all our schools were as good as our best ones, we could still not afford to rest upon past achievements, for complacency is a luxury which none can afford today. What we are presently not doing—we must be prepared to do tomorrow. What we are presently doing well—we must learn to do better in the future. The challenges which lie ahead are many and varied. They must be faced intelligently and courageously by every elementary educator who daily "walks with tomorrow" as he guides youngsters whose feet may someday touch other planets and who will realistically cope with the world of the twenty-first century. In the following section, the major challenges presented by our dynamic and changing society to the elementary school of today and tomorrow are examined.

503

CHALLENGES OF THE FUTURE

The challenge of rapid change. Prior to the present century, society's mandate to its schools, in most instances, was to prepare the coming generation to take its place in the culture *as it then existed.* The basic task of preparing children for life in a fairly static society was one which motivated all educational programs—from those of primitive cultures to those of the mid-nineteenth century. Today, of course, the task is quite different. The school must prepare the child, not for a static culture, but for a society changing at an incredible rate in all areas of human enterprise. The advances made on all fronts—transportation, communication, medical skills and knowledge, industrialization, automation, use of power, and others too numerous to mention mean that the elementary school youngster will live in a world strange to his father and unknown to his grandfather. Furthermore, according to expert opinion, there is no reason to suppose that the rate of change will level off in the forseeable future. On the contrary, changes are expected to accelerate with unbelievable rapidity as new discoveries are made and new fields of knowledge are probed and conquered. To know how to equip boys and girls for life in this exciting and dynamic society is one of the major problems facing the elementary school teacher at the present moment.

The challenge of a rapidly increasing population. The much discussed "population explosion" is one of the gravest crises facing all countries of the world today. Some indication of today's rapid growth as compared with that of the past is given by Vogt who states that "sophisticated speculation" places the total population of the world at the beginning of the Christian era at about 200,000,000 people—less than the United States alone will have in 1975! He continues with the following statements.

Sixteen centuries later, about the time of the founding of the new world colony of New Amsterdam, this world population had little more than doubled.

By the time of the American Revolution, world population had grown nearly 75 per cent more; and a hundred years ago, it had added about another 75 per cent.

In the past hundred years it has jumped a startling 150 per cent to almost three billion, or fifteen times what it was in the time of Christ; and if it continues to grow at the current accelerating rate, it will increase more than six-fold in a little over a hundred years.[1]

The same author paints another vivid picture of these essential facts when he states that the worldwide population is mushrooming at the rate of "100 more people a minute, 6,000 the hour, 140,000 the day, 50,000,000 the year! . . . and by the time our children are middle-aged, there may be twice as many of them—perhaps increasing even faster." [2]

[1] W. Vogt, *People! Challenge to Survival* (New York, William Sloane Associates, 1960), pp. 42–43.
[2] *Ibid.*, p. 234.

To what extent has this tremendous increase been felt in the United States? Figures from the 1960 census show that our population is increasing at the rate of 18.5 per cent per decade. This means that, since 1950, we have added 28 million Americans, net—the equivalent of nearly three New Englands.[3] During these ten years, the total enrollment in public elementary and secondary schools has shown an *annual* average increase of over one million pupils.[4] This increase will accelerate during the 1960s because it was not until 1954 that the birth rate topped four million, which it has remained each year since then. This means that in September, 1960, we felt, for the first time, the full impact of over four million births six years previous, *in the first grade only*. Each succeeding year, this large group will move through the schools, *followed by an even larger group*.[5]

It is obvious that this tremendous increase in population presents a multifaceted challenge to the elementary school of the 1960s. The most immediate and serious, of course, is the crucial shortage of qualified teachers which, according to a reliable figure, was 135,000 [6] in 1960 and will be larger in the years to come. In addition, a grave shortage of standard classrooms and adequate facilities; a multiplication of administrative problems; and an increase of social and emotional problems of children caused by overcrowded home conditions, contribute to the magnitude and complexity of the problem now facing the elementary school.

The challenge of expanding frontiers of knowledge. The unbelievably rapid extension of scientific knowledge is one of the most significant and exciting developments of the modern age. A chemistry professor, for instance, recently stated that he is now teaching to his freshman classes knowledge which did not exist when he was in graduate school! This, of course, is equally true in all the fields of science. In medicine, for instance, surgical operations which were impossible a few short years ago, are now performed with complete success. In astronomy, newly developed radio telescopes have discovered many new galaxies beyond the range of even the most powerful optical telescopes, and scientists are now studying radio signals in an attempt to discover signs of communication from outer space. One could go on and on, of course, with similar examples, for in every field the scientist is steadily and successfully storming the barriers of ignorance. He is conquering the secrets which have remained hidden since the world began and, at this moment, according to some, he stands at the threshold of creating life itself! To attempt to understand, select, synthesize, interpret, and teach the implications of this knowledge to the

[3] "A Boom in People—And a Shift in Power," *U.S. News and World Report*, Vol. 49, Part II (November 28, 1960), p. 64.

[4] *Teacher Supply and Demand in Public Schools, 1960*. Research Report 1960-R7. Research Division. National Education Association. (Washington, D.C.: National Education Association, April, 1960), p. 13.

[5] *Ibid.*, p. 13.

[6] *Ibid.*, p. 15.

growing youngster is an awesome task confronting the elementary teacher of the future.

The challenge of a troubled world scene. Contributing greatly to today's feeling of uncertainty about the future is the rapidly-changing and troubled world scene. Conflicting political ideologies, world-wide economic problems, the struggle for technological supremacy, the uncertain future of the United Nations, and the rapid creation of many new and independent nations are only a few of the world-wide developments which should be of vital interest to all Americans. The days of isolation, apathy, or ignorance of world events are gone. The days ahead will demand an intelligent, alert, and informed citizenry which recognizes and fulfils its responsibilities toward all nations of the world. According to the President's Commission on National Goals:

> A basic goal for each American is to achieve a sense of responsibility as broad as his world-wide concerns and as compelling as the dangers and opportunities he confronts.[7]

The challenge to education implied in this statement is crystal-clear. It must be met by *every* classroom teacher as he prepares his pupils for responsible citizenship in the United States and world of the future.

The challenge of increasing leisure. One of the problems facing our modern culture is the wise and constructive use of an ever-increasing amount of leisure time. The average man today works fewer hours per week or year than at any other time in history, and there seems to be every indication that the impending three- or four-day week will soon become a reality for many. The average woman has been freed from many of the chores of running a house and rearing a family by the invention of everything from the automatic washer to frozen food. An abundant economy has made most of the major labor-saving devices available to the large majority of the population. The result is that most individuals find themselves in the position of having more leisure time on their hands than ever before. How shall this time be spent? Shall it be spent passively in watching television, motion pictures, and games played by others? Shall it be used to escape the tensions and fears which otherwise cannot be faced? Shall it be wasted on worthless pursuits which leave behind them nothing but emptiness and frustration? Or shall it be spent in doing, learning, creating, reading, appreciating, making, meditating, exploring, and contributing toward a richer and fuller life? This is the challenge which our present-day culture imposes upon the individual—and upon the teacher who must guide that individual toward maturity and fulfillment.

The challenge of conflicting social values. Several of the previously mentioned challenges are interrelated with a sixth—perhaps the gravest challenge—that of the conflicting value-systems now operating within our

---

[7] *Goals for Americans,* the Report of the President's Commission on National Goals (Englewood Cliffs, N.J., Prentice-Hall, Inc., 1960), p. 23.

present culture. The sources of this conflict are many and varied—and range from the "hidden persuaders" of the advertising world to the preoccupation of our mass communication and entertainment media with immorality, violence, and crime. The emphasis upon the materialistic as opposed to the spiritual; the stress upon the "easy" life instead of the "good" life; the concern with riches of the pocket rather than those of the heart, mind, and soul; the search for status rather than self-realization; the pressures of conformity rather than creativity; and acceptance based on superficial considerations rather than upon the dignity and worth of the individual are only some of the conflicting values which have contributed to the rising incidence of broken homes, mental illness, crime, juvenile delinquency, and other signs of social unrest and deterioration. To guide and mold the value-judgments of its youngsters is, therefore, probably the most serious challenge facing the elementary school at the present time.

In summary, the six major challenges presented to education in the 1960s can be said to involve both *quality* and *quantity*. Simply stated, we must offer *more* children a *better* education than we have ever achieved in the past. To meet this dual challenge, educators today are exploring and investigating new media, new ideas, and new procedures. Some of the major areas of inquiry and exploration are examined in the remainder of the chapter.

AREAS OF EXPLORATION

The far-sweeping challenge of *quality* and *quantity* involves the need for the intelligent exploration of the following areas.

The utilization and expansion of our present knowledge of the learner and the learning process. It has been stated repeatedly in previous chapters that the child-study movement of the twentieth century has been one of the primary forces in molding the modern educational program. Knowledge of the interests, needs, skills, capacities, and characteristics of the child at each level of development *must* precede the planning or implementation of his educational program. Much of this knowledge is now available and, if the quality of education is to improve, must be understood and used by every classroom teacher. We cannot afford to be like the old farmer who resisted the wares of the high-pressured farm equipment salesman by saying, "I ain't farmin' now nearly as well as I know how." Only when the gap is closed between "what we know" and "what we do" will education shift from second to high gear as it seeks to accomplish its stated objectives.

A second responsibility involves the crucial need for more investigation, more research, and more experimentation in order to expand the frontiers of knowledge in this area. For, although we have learned much about learning and the learner, there is still much which we do not know. Someone recently said, for instance, that if we were to chart our present knowledge of the learning process, it might compare to a map of the known world in about the year 1300 A.D. One of the most crucial tasks, therefore, facing educators today is the need to explore and search for new knowledge of the learner and learning which, in turn, can be transmitted into effective classroom practice.

The careful appraisal of our present curricular offerings. The curriculum is the instrument designed by the school to achieve its educational objectives and goals. World-wide social and technological developments, new discoveries of knowledge, insights into the nature of learning and the learner, events of national and world significance, and many other societal forces demand that the curriculum of the elementary school have certain essential characteristics, namely:

1. It must represent a fluid and dynamic approach to learning. The days of the static and rigid curriculum are gone. The extensive courses of study, which were laboriously developed and faithfully followed until the next "curriculum revision" fifteen years later, have been discarded. In their place, has come a philosophy which conceives of education as an ever-changing, ever-evolving process. This does not mean, however, that the trend is toward the "planless program" for, as mentioned in other chapters, actually it is moving in the opposite direction. Present indications are, therefore, that the curriculum of the immediate future *will* be planned in most areas, but it will allow for needed flexibility and it will also be continually appraised and modified to meet the demands of the particular situation and time.

2. It must include a wide diversity of experiences in order to challenge the talents of each individual. There is no doubt that concern for *each* student will be a major consideration in developing a comprehensive program to meet the needs of the future. The lock-step program which prescribed an identical set of experiences for "the third grade" is no longer adequate. In its place, must be substituted a wide variety of learning experiences which will make provision for the wide range of talents and needs which exist in *every* group.

3. There is increasing emphasis upon the longitudinal approach to curriculum development. The lack of curricular articulation between the various grades of the elementary school as well as between the elementary school and secondary school is a matter of concern to many teachers today. The emphasis upon developing a "set of threads or organizing elements" of both behavior and content, running vertically through the curriculum around which learning activities can be organized,[8] appears to be on the horizon of educational advancement.

As far as the *content* of the curriculum is concerned, educators are presently exploring the *balance* needed to attain the comprehensive goals

[8] J. I. Goodlad and R. H. Anderson, *The Nongraded Elementary School* (New York, Harcourt, Brace & World, Inc., 1959), p. 80.

of education. It is fairly obvious that the recent emphasis on science will continue. Present indications are, however, that this emphasis will not be secured through sacrificing other curricular areas or through distorting the balance of a well-rounded program. Paralleling the increasing emphasis on science, of course, is the keen interest in experimentation in arithmetic, discussed briefly in Chapter Eleven. Present indications appear to portend some exciting new developments in both these areas but, it is important to re-emphasize, these will probably not be made at the expense of other values.

Another curriculum area, presently the center of much exploration and study, is social studies. Two of the most probable future emphases in this area appear to be (1) the improvement of human relations and social values, and (2) the education of children concerning all countries and peoples of the world. Concerning the latter point, Kenworthy points out that most of our education concerning other peoples has heretofore been Europe-centered and comments: "It is woefully inadequate for boys and girls who are going to live in an international community in which Europe is but one important part.[9] A more "world-centered" approach appears to be a certainty in the social studies program of the future.

Several previous chapters have been devoted to the present and probable future emphases in the communication arts and there appears to be little need to repeat them here. Similarly, the uncertain future of foreign languages in the elementary school was examined in Chapter Eight and need not be restated here.

In summary, the present elementary curriculum has evolved from a steadily increasing interest in and concern for the physical, social, intellectual, and spiritual development of the individual and his interaction with society. It is inconceivable that the curriculum of the future elementary school would move in any direction other than toward the more successful realization of this goal.

The utilization of varied resources and aids to learning. The elementary school has come a long way since the days of the slate and hornbook. Today, the wise use of a variety of instructional tools is recognized as a basic requisite to effective learning. To this end, the modern teacher uses books, maps, filmstrips, films, globes, flannel boards, manipulative devices and hundreds of other learning aids. In addition, certain other devices are presently capturing the attention of educators although, at this time, there is heated controversy and wide disagreement as to their possible use and value. The two upon which most disagreement is centered today are the teaching machine and television.

The Teaching Machine. Sometimes termed "auto-instruction," "self-instructional devices," or "automatic tutors," the teaching machine was

[9] L. S. Kenworthy, "Education for the Community of 1985," *Educational Leadership*, Vol. 17 (May, 1960), p. 471.

originally developed by Pressey in 1926. Although it was generally considered, at that time, to be a testing instrument, Pressey claimed that the machine could be used to teach as well. Very little interest was evidenced in its possibilities however, and it was not until the 1950s that it again came to public attention. This time it was received with considerably more interest and there are, at present, numerous experiments in progress to test its effectiveness.

There are several models of auto-instructional devices now available for use in first grade through college. The range includes

no machine at all—for example, merely a set of cards in a cardboard or plastic case, or a mimeographed sheet; a write-in (constructed response) machine; a machine using slides and tape; a multiple-choice machine; a film machine; and a machine using a combination of microfilm and motion pictures; and a set of machines electronically tied in with a television broadcast.[10]

Regardless of the type, however, all machines are based upon essentially the same principles and have approximately the same basic characteristics, namely:

1. The question or problem is presented to the student either by a card or printed sheet seen through a window or from a film projected on a reading screen.

2. Some provision is made for the operator to record his answer. In some machines he indicates his selection from a number of alternative answers presented. In other machines he writes out an answer he has constructed.

3. As soon as his answer has been recorded, a student may obtain an immediate check on its accuracy. Some machines check the answer automatically. Others expose the correct answer for the student to evaluate his own work.

4. The sequence in which the items are presented is usually controlled by the machine.

5. The timing of the questions and answers is usually under the control of the student. Since these machines are designed for individual use, each student may proceed at his own pace.[11]

In summary, the machine is designed for *individual use*. It presents a question to the pupil to which he must either write the correct answer or choose from several offered; it notifies him immediately if his answer is correct; and it permits him to proceed to the next level of difficulty if he is correct; and it does not permit him to proceed until each level of difficulty is mastered. Questions or items are aimed, of necessity, toward factual and skill learnings rather than toward personal-social-moral trait learnings.

In all discussions of this topic, it is pointed out that the machine per se is not the important factor, for it obviously cannot "teach." All it can do is

[10] J. D. Finn, "Teaching Machines: Auto-Instructional Devices for the Teacher," *NEA Journal*, Vol. 49 (November, 1960), p. 42.

[11] J. W. Blyth, "Teaching Machines and Human Beings," *The Educational Record*, Vol. 41 (April, 1960), p. 116.

to transmit the series of questions or items which have been composed by teachers and which constitute the "program" or "heart of the auto-instructional concept." [12] Careful programming is an exceedingly difficult and complex task which involves such problems as: (1) defining exactly the concept or behavior desired; (2) determining the number of items necessary to elicit the desired response; (3) deciding upon the correct gradation of difficulty of all items; (4) properly spacing the items so only a tiny step of difficulty is taken each time, and (5) deciding upon how much and what type of "prompting" is desirable. Since the machine is designed to "teach" and not "test," the last-mentioned problem is of utmost importance for most of the questions should give "cues" to the correct answer just as the teacher often does in phrasing his questions during a discussion. Smith states,

> The prompt is a technique for causing emission of a response which might not normally be made . . . each question acts as a signpost at a fork, leading (the student) along a specific path of reasoning.[13]

It is apparent that careful programming is a determining factor in the success or failure of auto-instruction. As some indication of the complexity of the task, Skinner states, "At five or six frames per word, four grades of spelling may require 20,000 or 25,000 frames, and three or four grades of arithmetic, as many again." [14]

It is important in any discussion of auto-instruction to point out that the *sole issue involved* is "Can this medium contribute in any measure to a meaningful educational experience?" *The issue is definitely not* "Can the machine replace the teacher?" On this there seems to be general agreement for even the most ardent advocates of automation realize that its possibilities are limited and that it may be a tool, but certainly not a replacement, for the classroom teacher. To think otherwise would indicate a hopelessly foggy concept of what is involved in creative teaching. The machine asks questions and informs the student of the correctness of his response. Any teacher who thinks that this constitutes teaching *deserves* to be replaced by a machine.

Television. The very word is often enough to start the debate raging, for there is probably no more controversial topic in education today than the place of television in the classroom. Some educators see it as a grave threat to the individualization of instruction and the interpersonal teacher-pupil relationship which is the foundation of the American concept of teaching. These educators express fear that television will (1) tempt many school boards to sacrifice *quality* of instruction for the economy of

[12] J. D. Finn, *op. cit.*, p. 41.
[13] D. E. P. Smith, "Speculations: Characteristics of Successful Programs and Programmers" in E. Galanter, *Automatic Teaching: The State of the Art* (New York, John Wiley and Sons, Inc., 1959), p. 96.
[14] B. F. Skinner, "Teaching Machines," *Science*, Vol. 128 (October 24, 1958), p. 972.

teaching large masses of pupils simultaneously, (2) equate learning with mere passive reception, and (3) make teaching a rigid, artificial, and superficial process. On the other hand, there are those who claim that TV is "one of the best hopes this country has for solving some of its most pressing educational problems." [15] Advantages claimed for it include: (1) it *does* help to solve the problem of educating the ever-rising school population; (2) it raises the quality of instruction by using only superior teachers; (3) it has untold possibilities for broadening and enriching the curriculum; and (4) it is of value in raising and varying the educational offerings of the very small school or rural system.

Regardless of whether one views TV as a salvation or menace, it is undeniably true that it is gaining increasing attention throughout the country. From its feeble beginnings in the early 1950s, classroom television has now grown until, according to a recent figure, 569 school districts of the nation's 45,000 "make regular use of televised instruction." [16] Probably the most firmly established and well-known of these systems, at present, is the famous Hagerstown, Maryland, project where "special TV instruction, prepared and produced by the school's own teaching staff, is sent by cable to 16,500 children in 37 different buildings." [17] According to a poll of the teachers in this system, nine to one voted that they thought television improved the quality of education, and the reaction of parents and pupils appeared to be equally favorable.[18]

Today, experiments of all types and kinds are in progress, including beaming telecasts to several schools from a circling plane. The investigation and research continue on all fronts as educators try earnestly to capitalize upon the advantages and eliminate the dangers of "electronic education."

In summary, it should be repeated that the only intelligent course open to teachers is to investigate with objective interest any tool, device, aid, or machine which may help them to do a *better* job in teaching boys and girls. This is not to say that any equipment shall or can *replace* the teacher for, as stated previously, this is *not* the issue. As Montagu says, "The best equipment with which the teacher can provide the child is himself—the teacher's own being." [19]

The current proposals for utilization of staff. Current literature contains many proposals for the utilization of staff other than the common "one teacher per class" pattern. In general, these proposals concern (1) team

[15] J. L. Burns, "The Promise of Classroom Television," *National Parent-Teacher*, Vol. 55 (November, 1960), p. 11.

[16] F. M. Hechinger, "Teaching with TV," *The New York Times* (May 1, 1960).

[17] J. L. Burns, *op. cit.*, p. 9.

[18] *Ibid.*, p. 10.

[19] M. F. A. Montagu, *The Direction of Human Development* (New York, Harper and Brothers, 1955), p. 303.

teaching, (2) the use of nonprofessional personnel, and (3) departmental-ization. Each of these is examined briefly below:

Team teaching. Various communities have experimented with team teaching for various reasons. Some, undoubtedly, are genuinely seeking newer and better methods of classroom instruction. Some are attracted by the novelty of the idea, while others are desperately trying to meet an acute teacher shortage. It is not, however, the authors' intention here to evaluate motives but simply to present briefly the different forms which team-teaching has taken in school systems throughout the country.

1. *The team-leader type* involves the selection of one, two, or three master teachers who are assigned the responsibility of planning, imple-menting, and evaluating the "teams." In most cases, these individuals are relieved of one-third or one-half of their classroom teaching, and in some instances they are not responsible for any direct teaching. Their respon-sibilities are chiefly administrative and co-ordinative and include

the identification of pupil needs and readiness . . . the assignment of pupils to groups . . . directing the continual re-examination and development of the cur-riculum . . . and . . . the training and supervision of junior and less experienced personnel on the team.[20]

2. *The associate type* has no team-leader but is comprised only of two or more teachers who work together with a larger number of boys and girls than is normally found in a regular classroom. Both, or all, members of the team assume equal responsibility for planning, implementing, and evalua-ting the instructional program.

3. *The master teacher—beginning teacher type* is not particularly new, for one of the authors worked in a team-teaching situation of this type more than fifteen years ago. Its chief purpose and advantage is that,

Sharing the responsibility for instructing a group of youngsters permits the less experienced members of the team to mature under the direction of ac-complished professionals.[21]

4. *The co-ordinated-team type* is, according to many, not really team teaching at all. It refers to the practice of combining two or more classes in the lunchroom, auditorium, or gymnasium for the specific purpose of teaching a music lesson, teaching a physical education lesson, showing a film, or something similar.

It appears to be impossible, at this time, to evaluate conclusively the worth of team teaching or to predict its future. It can only be concluded that the merits of any proposal involving the proper utilization of teaching talent should be evaluated in terms of its effect upon the pupils. Thus far,

[20] R. H. Anderson, E. A. Hagstrom, W. M. Robinson, "Team Teaching in an Ele-mentary School," *The School Review,* Vol. 68 (Spring, 1960), p. 77.
[21] L. L. Cunningham, "Team Teaching: Where Do We Stand?" Midwest Adminis-tration Center, *Administrator's Notebook,* Vol. 8, Number 8 (Chicago, University of Chicago Press, April, 1960), p. 3.

the evidence which is available indicates that "little or no difference was found in the achievement of the youngsters taught by teaching teams when compared with youngsters taught in the traditional manner." [22]

The use of nonprofessional personnel. The emphasis upon "freeing the teacher for teaching" has led to the employment of nonprofessional personnel by some school systems. These individuals are usually designated as "teacher aides," "school assistants," "instructional secretaries," "paraprofessionals," or "lay readers." [23] The duties which they are presently assuming in schools where they are employed include: arranging materials for classes, reading and story-telling, managing the milk fund and other collections, housekeeping chores, arranging bulletin-board displays, keeping attendance and other class records, helping supervise playground and cafeteria, administering first aid, helping with wraps, supervising bus loading, helping on excursion trips, processing books and supplies, scoring objective tests, correcting papers, setting up and operating audio-visual aids, typing and cutting stencils for class use, helping in library, and supervising study halls.[24]

The following generalizations have been drawn by a recent survey of school systems which presently employ nonprofessional personnel:

1. The inauguration of a teacher-aide program requires a realistic appraisal of the work to be done in a modern school system—a process which should awaken taxpayers to the fact that overworked teachers have long subsidized vital parts of the school program for which the community should assume financial responsibility.

2. Some of the reports lift a curtain on the grim conditions under which teachers and children are working in many schools. For example, in one school system a single teacher may be responsible for as many as 99 kindergartners a day.

3. Teacher-aides are being employed, not to promote the establishment of larger classes, but to preserve the effectiveness of qualified teachers where large classes are unavoidable. As one reporter put it: "The aide program has done what we wanted it to do—helped a teacher to be more effective with a large group. However, all teachers involved are agreed that they would rather have 30 children and no aides than 40 children with an aide."

4. Elementary schools seem to offer more situations where noninstructional assistance can be used than do secondary schools . . .

5. Not all teachers can work effectively with aides; some seem unable to adapt their classroom procedures to include the help to which they are so unaccustomed.

6. It is important that aides understand the over-all policies of the school system and any conditions or regulations applying to the particular schools in which they serve.

7. Paid aides are preferred to volunteer workers.[25]

[22] *Ibid.*, p. 3.
[23] Educational Research Service Circular No. 5, *Teacher-Aides: Current Practices and Experiments,* American Association of School Administrators (Washington, D.C., Research Division, National Education Association, July, 1960), p. 1.
[24] *Ibid.*, p. 3.
[25] *Ibid.*, p. 4.

Departmentalization. Invariably, the issue of effective utilization of staff involves a discussion of the departmentalization of instruction *vs.* the self-contained classroom. This is not a new issue, of course, for departmentalization has been practiced in various elementary schools throughout the country for more than thirty years, and in some extremes, has even been introduced into the kindergarten. Today's "generalization *vs.* specialization" controversy has, however, reintroduced the issue in many educational circles and has given wide publicity to such departmentalized programs as the "Dual Progress Plan." In general, however, the majority of reputable opinion strongly supports the many advantages of the self-contained classroom for the elementary school as against "fragmenting the child" [26] by departmentalized instruction. This does not mean, of course, that the elementary school should not utilize the services of the "specialists," as discussed in Chapter Twelve. It simply means that one teacher should have the opportunity and responsibility for working, over a prolonged period of time, with a single small group of children in order to understand and guide them most effectively. We may have learned how to split an atom, but we have not yet learned how to split a young child among six or seven teachers a day with anything but harmful results.

The reader is reminded that this discussion pertains to the elementary school and not to secondary education, where a consideration of factors other than those examined here is important.

The extension of elementary education. Another area of exploration in which many people are currently interested is the extension of the elementary school program. In some discussions, this interest is directed toward extending the elementary school to include prekindergarten programs for three- and four-year-olds. Many experimental schools now offer such a program, and there is every reason to expect that the scope of the future elementary school may well be broadened to include the "before-five" program.

Other proposals for extending the educational program are concerned with the concept of the all-year school, which continues to receive increasing attention in some systems. The various experiments in year-round education which have been, and are being, attempted throughout the country differ widely in purpose and organization. In general, the four basic organizational patterns involving a longer school year are the following:

1. *The Four-Quarter Plan.* This plan provides for a "48 week, four-quarter, staggered-vacation school year which allows students to attend three of the four quarters." [27] It represents an attempt to utilize facilities

26 E. R. Snyder, *The Self-Contained Classroom*, Association for Supervision and Curriculum Development (Washington, D.C., National Education Association, 1960).

27 *Year-Round School*, American Association of School Administrators (Washington, D.C., National Education Association, 1960), p. 4.

and staff more *economically* than the traditional school year. Ogden states that "the motivating factor is essentially financial" and adds:

> The program is not intended to enrich the students' experience or accelerate progress in school. Its single objective is to house more students in a fewer number of classrooms.[28]

The plan is not new. It has been tried sporadically in various communities since the early 1900s. Most systems, however, which have tried the idea have abandoned it after a few years because of the problems it created. Some of these, according to one system which abandoned the plan in 1938, were:

> The scheduling of classes became such an intricate task that weeks were required for the planning of just one quarter. The sports schedules of both schools became hopelessly tangled; graduation took place four times a year, instead of only once or twice; and custodial staffs complained bitterly that necessary repairs —usually made in the summertime—were impossible under the "year-round" set-up. Worst of all, perhaps, was the new system's effect on the teachers. Morale was shaken badly; professional development, usually a summertime affair, since most universities and colleges offer special courses for educators in July and August, came to an abrupt halt and resignations rose." [29]

In summary, the four-quarter plan appears to offer little educational value or advancement. The consensus of opinion appears to agree with that of one superintendent who states, "I am convinced that the advantages of organizing our schools on an all-year basis are more than offset by the disadvantages." [30]

The Forty-Eight Week School Year. This is a proposal to lengthen the school year to approximately forty-eight weeks with thirty days' vacation for all pupils and teachers. It is frequently discussed but so far has not been adopted by any system according to the following statement:

> At the present time, compulsory all-year schooling is not known to be in operation anywhere in the country. It is generally believed that the advantages of the plan do not outweigh its disadvantages although the plan is destined for further experimentation.[31]

The Voluntary Summer Program. It seems fairly obvious that an enrichment program, offered on a voluntary basis, can offer many educational opportunities and advantages to children of widely varying abilities and needs. It can, for instance, offer remedial service for children who need individualized or small group instruction. On the other hand, it can offer an excellent enrichment opportunity for gifted children in all areas. The

[28] C. L. Ogden, "The Four Quarter Plan . . . How Practical an Idea?" *American School Board Journal*, Vol. 133 (July, 1956), p. 20.

[29] H. Berman, "Do Our Schools Need More Time?" *American School Board Journal*, Vol. 135 (November, 1957), p. 36.

[30] V. D. MacPherson, "Keeping Schools Open All Year," *Nation's Schools*, Vol. 56 (September, 1955), p. 54.

[31] American Association of School Administrators, *op. cit.*, p. 12.

favorable reaction with which most educators view this plan is indicated in the following statement:

More school systems each year seem to be moving in the direction of extending the school program into the summer months in one form or another. The summer remedial, avocational, recreational, enrichment type of program answers a great many of the needs of school systems, for it lends itself to maximum flexibility and adaptation to local needs and provides for many enrichment activities which cannot reasonably be included in the regular school session.[32]

The "Professional" Summer Program. Some systems are presently operating a summer program designed primarily for the in-service education of the faculty. In such programs, teachers attend workshops, serve on curriculum committees or evaluation committees, or prepare special materials or teaching aids needed during the regular school year. One description of a program of this general type states that it is designed to "develop growth in instructional competence" and that its specific aims are to achieve:

(1) time to prepare for the school year ahead, (2) increased knowledge and competence in school subjects and teaching technics, and (3) personal growth through self-participation in special activities.[33]

It is easily apparent that the last two patterns mentioned are motivated by an attempt to strengthen and enrich the quality of the educational experience. As such, they appear to hold some promise for a bright educational future. The merits of both plans, as well as their combinations and modifications, have been summarized as follows.

1. The needs of children, both directly and indirectly, are provided for.
2. The professional growth of teachers is accelerated.
3. Teaching becomes a full-time profession.
4. Teachers begin the regular school year with a greater sense of security.
5. Curriculum revision can take place in a relaxed atmosphere.
6. Greater time can be devoted to the selection of textbooks and other teaching materials.
7. System-wide workshops and committees provide teachers with an opportunity to understand other teachers and their problems.
8. Teachers have an opportunity to become better acquainted with students and parents.
9. Teachers have a greater opportunity to become an integral part of the community.
10. Teachers' salaries more nearly approach a professional level.
11. Opportunity is provided for adequate orientation of new teachers.
12. Opportunity is provided for teachers to learn about the community and to become better acquainted with the philosophy and services of the school system.

[32] *Ibid.*, p. 13.
[33] M. A. Wenger, "Glencoe's Summer Program Has Two Aims: Competence and Enrichment," *Nation's Schools,* Vol. 64 (October, 1959), p. 60.

13. As teachers participate in workshops, orientation programs, examination and discussion of students' records, and the many other activities of the summer-school program, they become better able to guide and direct children during the regular school year.

14. Opportunity is provided for system-wide, vertical curriculum meetings which contribute to an understanding of the total curriculum by all teachers.

15. All resources, human and material, are used to the maximum.[34]

The preparation of elementary school teachers. Elementary school teaching is an extremely taxing and challenging task. It requires superior personnel who, in general, possess characteristics similar to those described in the following:

They must be broadly educated, as well as especially versed in child development and the principles and materials of learning. And with it all they must be sympathetic to the needs of children, emotionally constituted to deal with them positively, and flexible enough to adjust to the changing needs and stages of child development and the emerging directions of the society. They must be observant and professionally disciplined enough to evaluate and keep effective records of the achievements and progress of each child, and they must possess the professional motivation to make teaching a lifetime career.[35]

What are the major emphases in teacher education which should receive increasing attention in the development of these superior teachers? In general, they seem to be the following:

1. *The identification of specific competencies needed for effective teaching.* The first step in a teacher education program is the identification of certain specific qualities which the teacher should possess. Many studies have been made of this problem, and the evidence oppears to indicate that such competencies *can* be specifically identified and *should* be used as a basis for determining the content and nature of the teacher education program.

2. *The recruitment of promising individuals.* Recruitment of capable students for teaching must be done early by the elementary teacher, secondary teacher, principal, and guidance counselor. At the same time, attack on problems of improved salaries, improved certification requirements and others will increase the status of the profession which, in itself, will constitute a strong factor in recruiting from among the most able of our high school students.

3. *The improvement and extension of the undergraduate teacher education program.* There are many interrelated issues which must be resolved as educators attempt to improve the quality of preparation of the elementary school teacher. Major questions on which there is no consistency or agreement at present include: "What shall be the place of general education in the program?" "What percent of the total program shall be devoted

---

[34] American Association of School Administrators, *op. cit.,* pp. 17–18.
[35] Educational Policies Commission, *Contemporary Issues in Elementary Education* (Washington, D.C., National Education Association, 1960), pp. 24–25.

to this area?" "How much, and what type, of specialization is desirable for the elementary teacher?" "What percent of the program should be devoted to professional education?" "What type of professional laboratory experiences are most desirable for the prospective teacher?" "How should the sequence of professional laboratory experiences be organized?" and "How can the 'theory' and 'practice' of professional education be more closely integrated?"

There are, however, a few "trends" on which there seems to be rather widespread agreement. One of these is the inclusion of an internship as part of the preservice preparation of teachers. The acute need for a prolonged period of apprenticeship as part of the undergraduate program is stated in the following:

All teachers need an apprenticeship as part of their preparation. As doctors became professional when moved to the bedside, so teachers must extend the comparable experience to assure a better than even chance of success. It is a strange twist of logic that spokesmen across the country look for break-throughs by gimmicks when the need for additional instructional apprenticeship screeches everywhere.[36]

It is important to note, however, that this internship will not be merely a superstructure built upon a previous period of course work. It will be closely integrated with the entire sequence of professional work which will attempt to integrate theory and practice through the provision for numerous and varied contacts with children in many situations.

The second generally recognized trend is the need for a five- or even six-year program of preservice preparation. Some universities have already taken this step and now require five years for the teaching certificate. Others are in the process of adopting it and, according to the consensus of opinion, it seems reasonably safe to predict that, within a comparatively short time, the five-year program will be required for all elementary teachers.

4. *The continued emphasis upon the in-service education of teachers.* Regardless of the length or quality of the preservice program, a dynamic in-service program will be needed to raise the level of teaching competency. Workshops, institutes, summer programs, reimbursement for professional travel and study, and others are indicative of the current recognition of the importance of in-service growth of teachers, and there is every reason to expect this emphasis to accelerate in the future.

5. *The "tightening up" of certification requirements for all teachers.* The emphasis upon raising the certification requirements for teaching is revealed in the following recommendation of the newly created National Commission on Teacher Education and Professional Standards.

[36] L. Vander Werf, "A Single Profession for All Teachers," *School and Society*, Vol. 88 (September 24, 1960), p. 321.

520 THE ELEMENTARY SCHOOL

That there be one standard license to teach, endorsed by area of specialization and obtained on the basis of graduation from an accredited program, satisfactory passing of a comprehensive examination of background information, institutional recommendation of fitness to begin to teach, and satisfactory performance during one year of full-time responsible teaching. Fulfilling requirements for this license will require six years generally.[37]

The last major exploratory area currently occupying the attention of educators is the improvement of facilities, examined below:

The improvement of school buildings and facilities. New school buildings are being erected continually to replace those which have outworn their usefulness as well as to accommodate the ever-increasing numbers of children. Although these schools for the future vary widely according to the financial, geographic, and social factors of the community, in general they have two basic common characteristics.

First and foremost, the elementary school *is built to implement the comprehensive goals of a present-day philosophy of education.* It is a functional and efficient building in which growing youngsters can work and play. As a general rule, it is a one-story structure, built to house no more than one thousand pupils. Its classrooms are much larger than those of earlier schools, thus permitting a wide variety of activities and the use of many materials. Occasionally, the walls of the classroom are portable, thereby making possible a flexible educational program in which children may participate in varied sized groups for certain activities. In, or adjacent to, the well-equipped classroom are a sink, drinking fountain, lavatory, work corner, science laboratory, library nook, and "creative corner." Wise planning and utilization of space makes possible the storage of a wide variety of equipment and materials. The furniture, also, reflects the changing educational program for, in many rooms, it consists of varied-size tables, chairs and work units, which are far different from the "one desk and chair per pupil" arrangement of the traditional classroom. In addition, provision is made in each room for the use of television, films, filmstrips, tape recorders, and numerous other instructional aids. In some rooms may also be found a "communications booth" similar to the foreign language laboratory of the secondary school or college.

School-wide facilities for all children include the cafeteria, gymnasium, well-equipped playground, guidance center, auditorium, and "tutoring" or "skills" laboratory which can be used for all kinds of creative activities as well as for giving individual or small-group help to children of varying academic needs.

The second basic characteristic of many modern schools is that they have been built as "community-centered" schools. For this reason, special facilities for parking, heating, lighting, cooking, entertaining, etc. have

[37] M. Lindsey, Director, *New Horizons.* National Commission on Teacher Education and Professional Standards (Washington, D.C., National Education Association, 1960), p. 3.

been considered so that the school may truly function as a vital center for community activities and interests.

Summary

The modern American elementary school stands today as a monument to the democratic ideals of its country. Its future is uncertain for, at no time in its history, has it been faced with more pressures, unresolved issues, and problems than those which now confront it. On the other hand, at no time in its history has it had the advantage of such a sound foundation of reliable research, widespread public interest, and wise leadership which it has today. In order to capitalize upon these assets, the elementary teacher must be fully aware of the challenges which will face him in the next decade. These have been identified in this chapter as (1) the challenge of rapid change; (2) the challenge of a rapidly increasing population; (3) the challenge of expanding frontiers of knowledge; (4) the challenge of a troubled world scene; (5) the challenge of increasing leisure; and (6) the challenge of conflicting social values.

In an effort to meet these challenges, elementary education is presently exploring many new ideas and proposed solutions. The areas which merit the exploration and investigation of present-day teachers were identified in this chapter as: (1) the utilization and expansion of our present knowledge of the learner and the learning process; (2) the careful appraisal of our present curricular offerings; (3) the utilization of varied resources and aids to learning; (4) the current proposals for utilization of staff; (5) the extension of elementary education; (6) the preparation of elementary school teachers; and (7) the improvement of school buildings and facilities. Some of these appear to hold promise for the future. Others may not. But all must be explored *completely* and *objectively* by those who assume the responsibility for guiding boys and girls toward the world of the future.

STUDENT PROJECTS

1. Prepare a fifteen-minute talk for a Parent-Teachers meeting on any one of the six challenges examined in this chapter and its implications upon the elementary school of the future.

2. Current discussions of the elementary school curriculum often revolve around the issue of centralization of control *vs.* local autonomy. In this connection, a National Curriculum Commission is frequently proposed. Investigate the literature on this topic and prepare a paper on the pros and cons of the proposal.

3. Talk with several elementary school principals. Ask their opinions concerning "trends" in elementary education designed to meet the dual challenge of *quality* and *quantity*. Do you find any consistency of opinion?

4. Question several present and prospective elementary teachers concerning the four basic patterns of the "all-year school." Which do they think has most promise for the future? To which are they most opposed? Why?

5. Investigate the present national status of kindergarten education. In how many states is it compulsory? In how many is it made available through public funds? What needs will have to be met before elementary education will extend *beyond* this level to include the three- and four-year olds?

6. Try to visit a school system which is experimenting, or has experimented, with nonprofessional personnel in the schools. What are the duties of these individuals? What do teachers and administrators see as the major advantages and disadvantages of the plan?

7. Design a "classroom of tomorrow," including all of the facilities you think it should have. Include in your report diagrams, illustrations, and descriptions explaining and justifying your ideas.

8. Interview several parents concerning the two proposals mentioned in this chapter for *extending* elementary education. Are they in favor of either or both? What are their reasons? See if you can secure enough consistency of opinion to predict a "trend" in this area.

9. Talk with several members of the Education Department of your college. What are the basic issues and problems involved, in their opinion, in the proposed five-year preservice program for teachers?

10. Schools are presently investigating the possibilities of open-circuit and closed-circuit television. Investigate the literature concerning both of these and compare the advantages and disadvantages of both.

11. Prepare a carefully considered talk for a service club such as the Lions, Rotary, Kiwanis, or Zonta on the possible future of the teaching machine in education. Document your discussion with evidence from the current research in this field.

12. Elementary education has been accused by different sources of neglecting the retarded, the average, and the gifted! For which of these groups do you think this criticism is most justified? What will the future hold for the education of this group in your opinion?

13. Do you feel that the present keen interest of the public toward the schools will work to the eventual harm or benefit of the schools? Cite specific instances to justify your answer.

14. Describe in detail a well-rounded yearly program of in-service education which would help to close the gap between educational research and classroom practice which now exists in many systems.

BIBLIOGRAPHY

———, "Curriculum Planning and Development," *Review of Educational Research*, Vol. 30 (June, 1960), pp. 185–274.

Educational Conference, 1959, *Curriculum Planning to Meet Tomorrow's Needs* (Washington, D.C., American Council on Education, 1960).

———, "The Schools of the Future—1985," *Educational Leadership*, Volume 17 (May, 1960).

American Association of School Administrators, *Year-Round School* (Washington, D.C., National Education Association, 1960).

ANDREWS, Leonard O. and PALMER, R. R., "The Education of the Elementary School Teacher," *The Education of Teachers: New Perspectives*. Official Report of the Second Bowling Green Conference, Bowling Green State University, June 24–28 (Washington, D.C., National Commission on Teacher Education and Professional Standards, National Education Association, 1958).

COTTRELL, Donald P., ed., *Teacher Education for a Free People* (Oneonta, New York, American Association for Colleges for Teacher Education, 1956).

CUNNINGHAM, Luvern, "Team Teaching: Where Do We Stand?" Midwest Administration Center, *Administrator's Notebook*, Volume 8, Number 8 (Chicago, University of Chicago, April, 1960).

Educational Policies Commission, *Contemporary Issues in Elementary Education* (Washington, D.C., National Education Association and the American Association of School Administrators, 1960).

Educational Research Service Circular No. 5, *Teacher-Aides: Current Practices and Experiments* (Washington, D.C., American Association of School Administrators and Research Division of the National Education Association, July, 1960).

GALANTER, Eugene, ed., *Automatic Teaching. The State of the Art* (New York, John Wiley and Sons, Inc., 1959).

GOODLAD, John I. and ANDERSON, Robert H., *The Nongraded Elementary School* (New York, Harcourt, Brace & World, Inc., 1959).

HILL, H. H., *Major Concerns in Teacher Education*, 1959 Yearbook (Oneonta, New York, American Association for Colleges for Teacher Education, 1959).

LIEBERMAN, Myron, *The Future of Public Education* (Chicago, University of Chicago Press, 1960).

LINDSEY, Margaret, Director, *New Horizons*. National Commission on Teacher Education and Professional Standards (Washington, D.C., National Education Association, 1960).

LINDSEY, Margaret *et. al.*, *Improving Laboratory Experiences in Teaching Education* (New York, Teachers College, Columbia University, 1959).

MIEL, A., *Trends in Curriculum, Teaching, and Guidance* (Washington, D.C., White House Conference on Children and Youth, 1960).

MORSE, Arthur D., *Schools for Tomorrow, Today*. A Report on Educational Experiments Prepared for the New York State Education Department (New York, Doubleday and Company, 1960).

National Commission on Teacher Education and Professional Standards, *Education of Teachers: Curriculum Programs* (Washington, D.C., National Education Association, 1959).

National Education Association, Research Division, *Studies of the Utilization of Staff, Buildings, and Audio-Visual Aids in the Public Schools* (Washington, D.C., National Education Association, 1959).

————, *Teacher Supply and Demand in Public Schools*, Research Report 1960–R7 (Washington, D.C., National Education Association, April, 1960).

SAYERS, Ephraim V. and MADDEN, Ward, *Education and the Democratic Faith* (New York, Appleton-Century-Crofts, Inc., 1959).

SNYDER, Edith R., ed., *The Self-Contained Classroom*, Association for Supervision and Curriculum Development (Washington, D.C., National Education Association, 1960).

STILES, L. J. et al., *Teacher Education in the United States* (New York, The Ronald Press Company, 1960).

THAYER, V. T., *The Role of the School in American Society* (New York, Dodd, Mead and Company, 1960).

INDEX

Singing, 374–378; factors for successful program of, 374–378; part, 377; procedures for teaching, 376–378; unison, 377

Single-textbook approach, in science, 295; in social studies, 260–261

Sizemore, R. A., 156

Skills, basic, 15–16, 33; critical reading, 161–166; health, 402; intellectual, 90–91, 257–258; motor, 89–90, 257, 416–417; study, 166–171; writing, 189, 209–210

"Skills" laboratory, 304

Skills, social studies, 263–269; classification of, 264–265; geographic location and relationship, 265–269; importance of, 264; objectives, 233, 234; time and chronology, 265–267

Skimming, 168–169

Skinner, B. F., 511

Smith, B. O., 76

Smith, G. E., 34, 453

Smith, M. K., 119

Smith-Hughes Act, 18

Sobel, M., 350

Social adjustment, balance with individuality, 251

Social aspect, of arithmetic, 313–314

Social concepts, provision for in social studies textbooks, 261–262

Social functions, as bases for social studies, 237, 239

Social intelligence, development of, 36–38

Social learning and living, 250–256

Social maturity, as basis for grouping, 489

Social processes, as bases for social studies, 237

Social promotion, 492–493

Social readiness, for reading, 149

Social studies, 232–272, 509; activities and materials, 256–263; current affairs, 263–264; disciplines of, 236; objectives of, 233–236; scope, content, and sequence of, 236–242; skills of, 263–269; social learning and social living, 250–256; unit teaching, 242–250

Society for Research in Child Development, 58

Society's concept of the child, 45–46; as a miniature adult, 45–46; innate depravity of the child, 45; pawns of labor, 46; training children for the state, 45

Sociometric choices, as basis for grouping, 489

Sociometry, 64–65

Songs of appeal to children, 375

Southern colonies, 5

Sparks, P. E., 156

Specialist, foreign language, 226; music and art, 386

Speech, 116–137; articulatory disorders, 123–124; choral speaking, 133–134; content of program, 117–120; conversational skills, 120–121; developmental lesson, 129–132; discussion skills, 121–122; dramatization, 134–137; errors of language usage, 124–126; foreign speech, 124; goals of modern program, 117; imitation of, 126–127; incidental activities, 127–128; individual teaching, 127; infantile speech, 124; instructional program, 126–133; introduction into curriculum, 117; motivation of, 128–129; opportunities for expression, 120–122; participation index, 121–122; types of problems, 122–124; vocal disorders, 123

Speed, in arithmetic drill, 322–323; in reading, 168–169, 201

Spelling, 201–209, 213; causes of poor spelling, 208; content of program, 201–202; controversial issues, 206–208; developing a spelling conscience, 208–209; extremes of past programs, 201; plans for instruction, 203–205; "study steps," 205–206; systematic instruction in, 202–206

Spelling bees, 201, 207–208

Spencer, H., 9

Spitzer, H. F., 326

Stages of language growth, 104–105

Stanley, W. O., 76

Starr, H. M., 402

State supervision, battle for, 8

Statement of Beliefs, of National Art Association, 359–360

Stevens, Thaddeus, 7

Stimulus-response bond theory, 80

Stokes, C. N., 315

"Story" method of teaching reading, 155

Stratemeyer, F., 238

Strickland, R., 200

Structural analysis of words, 154–155

Stuart, H. C., 58

Student exchange programs, 220

Study skills, 166–171; adjusting the rate of reading, 168–169; locating information, 167; organizing information, 167–168; using the library, 169–171

Study steps in spelling, 205–206

Study-test plan, of spelling, 204–205

Stunts, in physical education, 420–421

Sturm, H. E., 276